ON THE EDGE

ON THE EDGE

The Life and Times of Francis Coppola

Michael Goodwin
and
Naomi Wise

William Morrow and Company, Inc.
New York

To Joseph Goodwin and John Burks, storytellers

To Charles Mingus, who taught us about art and work

To the good teachers at Hunter College High School
(you know who you are)

Library of Congress Cataloging-in-Publication Data

Goodwin, Michael, 1941–
    On the edge: the life and times of Francis Coppola / Michael
  Goodwin and Naomi Wise.
        p.   cm.
      Bibliography: p.
      Includes index.
      ISBN 0-688-04767-X
      1. Coppola, Francis Ford, 1939–   . 2. Motion picture producers
  and directors—United States—Biography. I. Wise, Naomi.
  II. Title.
  PN1998.3.C67G66   1989
  791.43'0233'092—dc20
  [B]   89-12238
                                                            CIP

Printed in the United States of America

First Edition

1 2 3 4 5 6 7 8 9 10

BOOK DESIGN BY NICOLA MAZZELLA

Contents

Introduction

Still the Guy Who Shot
The Godfather

> *Francis believes you only have a chance to do something terrific, both artistically and commercially, if you're on the edge of disaster.*
> —FRED ROOS, longtime associate

IN MANY WAYS Francis Ford Coppola is more interesting than his films. His work—which is, at its best, immensely impressive—speaks for itself, and it raises two major questions: What happened to Coppola? And why do we all care so much?

Coppola has directed sixteen and one-third motion pictures in all and written, produced, coproduced, codirected, cowritten, conceived, and/or distributed many more. His lifework to date includes three and a half masterworks (*The Godfather, The Conversation, Godfather II,* and the first half of *Apocalypse Now*) and two very good, very eccentric films (*Rumble Fish* and "Rip Van Winkle"—a short, charming TV episode he did for *Faerie Tale Theater* in 1985). Two of his movies (*The Godfather,* which he directed, and *American Graffiti,* which he produced) have proven extraordinarily popular and amazingly profitable. But his work also includes expensive flops, pretentious failures, and forgettable jobs for hire. There are many directors (Martin Scorsese, Stanley Kubrick, and Richard Lester, to name three current practitioners) whose careers are more consistent, whose artistry is more certain, and whose best films may be better than Coppola's.

No matter. Coppola is *inherently* fascinating—as an artist, as a patron of artists, as a scientist, as a dreamer, as a utopian, as a builder, as a destroyer, as a megalomaniac, as a victim (and masterly exploiter) of the media, as a bigger-than-life hero of a classic success story, as a tragic martyr to his own failures, as his own worst enemy. Above all, he is fascinating because he is a paradox, an artist who may have murdered his own muse.

No one who has anything to do with the movie business is impartial about Coppola. We cannot claim to be, either. In 1975 Michael Goodwin was senior editor and film critic for a small San Francisco entertainment magazine called *City* when Coppola took it over. During the year that followed, Coppola and Goodwin were in frequent contact. They spoke about films, filmmaking, journalism, food, wine, and the state of the universe. Goodwin was invited to view rough cuts of *The Conversation* and *Godfather II,* make suggestions, and generally share Coppola's filmmaking adventure. He enjoyed the relationship immensely; Coppola was charming, open, and full of great stories. Goodwin interviewed him several times, for articles that appeared in the magazine; Coppola later told others he thought those interviews had been the best, and most accurate, that had ever appeared. Around this time Naomi Wise, who was writing for *City,* met Coppola on a number of occasions, too. At the end of a year, Coppola fired the entire staff, Goodwin included.

Some years later, when Coppola was shooting *The Outsiders,* Goodwin sent a message asking if he would be willing to cooperate with a book-length biography. After several days a message came back via the film's press officer. "Francis asked me to tell you," she said, "that he holds you in the highest regard, but he doesn't want a book written about him at this time. He's been approached many times, and his response has always been that since he hasn't yet succeeded in doing what he wants to do, a biography would be premature."

All attempts to explore the parameters of Coppola's refusal were met with increasingly hostile replies from Coppola staffers; the great man himself could not be reached. He refused to talk with us and told his friends and associates to do the same, leaving us no choice, in many cases, but to fall back on the often unreliable press coverage he hates. Furthermore, since his enemies are not reluctant to speak for attribution, silencing his friends seems singularly self-destructive. But what else is new?

There's no denying it would have been good to have had fuller access to Coppola's current associates. Nonetheless, many of his older friends, who still remember him as a brash, self-confident young man, did talk with us. Significantly, those who became close to him during or after *Apocalypse Now* were far more reluctant to be interviewed. The *Apocalypse* shoot was a watershed for Coppola. It changed him utterly, driving him to a nervous breakdown from which some feel he never fully recovered. He became less idealistic, less generous, more volatile and vulnerable, and far more self-centered and self-protective. His judgment seemed to grow clouded, his vendetta against the press began, and he ceased, for the most part, to make successful films. He developed a siege mentality, encouraged in part by the most protective of his inner circle of employees. The friends he made before *Apocalypse*, and afterward, were very different.

The Cruelty of the Close-up

No one is sure anymore exactly when the first filmmaker made the first close-up (a shot of a face that filled the screen). It was probably sometime between 1895 and 1900.

One thing that *is* known is that audiences reacted with horror.

Since pioneer filmmakers' only dramatic model was the stage, the first film actors were always photographed at full length on the screen, as if the camera were sitting in the fifth row of a theater. When some unnamed genius decided to violate the safe theatrical distance and push the camera close enough to see every pore in the actor's face, every blemish, every flaw and wrinkle and bag, the audience was deeply shocked. It wasn't *natural* to get that close to someone—unless you were kissing him or her, in which case your eyes were probably closed anyway.

We've grown accustomed to close-ups in the ninety years or so since they were invented, but those early film audiences

were right: Close-ups *are* unnatural and inherently unflatter-
ing. Even the most beautiful movie star looks dreadful in close-
up, unless he or she spends hours being made up, and the
lights are set just so, and the camera shoots from the most flattering angle, and the focus is soft.

An honest biography is a close-up from which there is no
cutaway. Flaws loom unbearably large. The lies and self-
deceptions and betrayals and failures and cowardices to which
all humans are privy sometimes seem overwhelming.

We have tried to minimize other distortions. Whether we
mean to or not, all of us are more comfortable when we've
found a way to turn life into well-shaped fiction—a good story,
with a moral and a theme. By the time a real incident has made
its way to these pages, it's often been "improved" and mythol-
ogized (sometimes by Coppola himself). We have done the best
we can to counteract this process, both by cross-checking facts
whenever possible and by maintaining a healthy skepticism
whenever a story has seemed too perfect. But all too often we've
been forced to rely on accounts we don't entirely trust. Join us
in resisting the tendency to reduce the chaos and complexity
of Coppola's life, and his manifold achievements, to a joke, a
tragedy, a melodrama, or a puzzle with a neat solution.

Thanks

We owe gratitude in great measure to many friends who
helped us along the way. We are particularly indebted to Dave
Blake, Scott Eyman, Greil Marcus, Joe Medjuck, and Peter
Moore for their invaluable help with the manuscript. We also
owe our deepest thanks to many witnesses, storytellers, journalists, and film workers who generously contributed their time,
memories, insights, and contacts, including those who, at their
own request, are not named here. Those we can acknowledge
publicly include Steven Bach, Carroll Ballard, Paul Bartel, Scott
Bartlett, Bill Bonham, John Burks, Bill Campbell, Jon Davison, Rudi Fehr, Ernie Fosselius, Allen Garfield, Wally Gentleman, Sam Hagerty-Hammond, Jack Hill, J. Hoberman, Eric
Holzinger, Leland Katz, Dave Kehr, John Mayer, Todd Mc-
Carthy, Bob McClurg, John Meyer, Dick Miller, Walter Murch,

Joel Oliansky, Charlie Pickel, Francine Price, Al Ruddy, Hank Schloss, Mal Sharpe, Steven Silberstein, M.D., Morgan Upton, Steve Wax, and Frank Zuniga.

A special thank-you goes to the dedicated and knowledgeable staff of the Margaret Herrick Library of the Academy of Motion Picture Arts and Sciences, who helped us thread our way through approximately one thousand English-language articles that have been written about Coppola over the past twenty-two years. We are also obliged to the Directors Guild of America, the Pacific Film Archive Library, the San Francisco State University Library, the San Francisco Public Library Arts Collection, the UCLA Library, and Larry Edmond's Book Store in Hollywood for assistance in locating additional research materials.

And we are deeply grateful for the faith and steadfastness of our editor, Douglas Stumpf.

Chapter One

Secret Microphones (1939–1956)

I know more about every aspect of filmmaking, from photography to music—including writing and acting—than any other filmmaker in the world, and that's not a boast.
—FRANCIS FORD COPPOLA (1976)

FRANCIS COPPOLA SAT in an auditorium in the basement of New York's Museum of Modern Art on a Tuesday afternoon in 1956. The seats were thin and hard, and every few minutes the whole place shook as a subway train rumbled underneath. A man played piano at the left of the screen. The seventeen-year-old kid didn't care about any of that. He had been to the movies plenty of times before—pirate movies, musicals, science-fiction thrillers—and in fancier theaters, but he had never seen anything like this.

A mob of people in tattered, old-fashioned clothing ran across the movie screen in dreamlike silence. Then the image on-screen cut to a low-angle shot of a woman standing on a high pedestal at the foot of some giant statue, making an impassioned speech to the crowd; a ladder crossed the frame in a diagonal line above her. The composition reminded the kid of some of the paintings just outside the auditorium. The next shot showed exactly the same scene, but from farther away, and now he could see that it was a statue of a Russian czar.

Several other figures, carrying ropes, climbed up to join the
woman; this was shown in three fast shots: a low angle, a closer
low angle, and a big close-up. The way the shots fitted together was interesting.

The next image was a close two-shot of men tying a rope
around the statue's head. Then, suddenly, in a quick flurry of
rapid-fire shots, Francis could see that groups of men and
women had attached lots of ropes to the statue. The rhythms
of the shots and their rapid alternation of angle, distance, and
composition made Coppola realize that something important
was about to happen on the screen.

The image of the statue and the swinging ropes was replaced by a short, high-angle shot of a sea of soldiers—thousands of them—raising their guns. The next shot was at ground
level, rolling sideways through the sea of soldiers. Then the
screen cut away from the soldiers to show fifty or sixty sickles,
raised against a white sky. Back to the soldiers. Back to the
sickles. Soldiers. Sickles. Whatever it was was going to happen
right now.

In medium shot the ropes came taut, and the giant statue
began to topple. This was it! But then, unbelievably, just before the statue hit the ground, the screen cut back a few seconds in time, and the ropes came taut and the giant statue began
to topple again. And once more the screen cut back, and the
ropes came taut and the giant statue began to topple a third
time. Finally the action was allowed to finish. The statue of
the czar hit the ground with a crash.

Francis Ford Coppola sat transfixed as Sergei Eisenstein's
Ten Days That Shook the World unreeled before his eyes. He
had just seen the entire Russian Revolution in twenty-five shots.
He felt shaken. It might have been the E train, but it might
also have been his entire future rumbling into a new, revolutionary configuration.

"On Monday I was in the theater," he remembered. "On
Tuesday I wanted to be a filmmaker."

He would get his wish. And wish he hadn't.

Francis Ford Coppola was born on April 7, 1939, in Detroit, Michigan. His middle name is usually ascribed to the fact
that this event occurred at the Henry Ford Hospital, but it may
just as well have been inspired by the *Ford Sunday Evening*

Hour, a radio program on which his musician father, Carmine Coppola, had a job.

His mother, Italia, came from a theatrical background, too; in fact, she had played a small part in an early film by the famous Italian director Vittorio de Sica. Her father, Francesco Pennino, had been a musician, a playwright, and a popular songwriter in Italy. He came to American as Enrico Caruso's pianist and had arranged for the first Italian films to be imported into America. During the silent pictures era Paramount Pictures offered him a job writing the orchestral scores that accompanied road-show silents in the biggest houses. Pennino refused. He didn't want his children in Hollywood.

Francis's father, Carmine, had grown up in New York City, a talented child of Neapolitan heritage. *His* father was a machinist, not a musician. One night, according to a favorite family story, the nine-year-old Carmine was playing in the machine shop when several shady characters came in. Carmine's father locked the door, and the men produced a number of machine guns, which Carmine's father proceeded to lubricate so they would work smoothly the next time they were needed to kill somebody. Meanwhile, Carmine looked at the gunmen, and the gunmen looked back.

"Who's he?" they asked.

"It's all right," answered Carmine's father. "That's my son. Don't worry. He is studying the flute."

Then, while Carmine's father oiled the guns, Carmine played the hoodlums a tune. When they left, they gave Carmine's father $100 (/$1,200)* so the boy could continue his musical studies.

When Carmine received a scholarship to the Juilliard School in 1928, his artistic career seemed assured. After graduating, he went to work as a concert flutist with several top-line orchestras. Then, in the late thirties, he moved his family (which now consisted of his wife, Italia, and one son, August) to Detroit in order to take a job as first flutist, arranger, and assistant

---

*Any book about life in Hollywood has to deal with the fact of inflation. For instance, while the $400,000 budget of Buster Keaton's 1927 feature *Steamboat Bill, Jr.* seems amazingly low compared to the multimillion-dollar budgets of modern features, one has to remember that in 1927 $400,000 bought as many ham sandwiches as $2.7 million buys today. To keep things in perspective, we will, where appropriate, follow dollar figures with their 1989 equivalent, in parenthesis, preceded by a slash. Hence Buster's *Steamboat* budget would appear as $400,000 (/$2.7 million).

orchestra conductor for the radio show called the *Ford Sunday Evening Hour*, a program of "good music" that had been going out over the CBS national network every Sunday night since 1934.

The Coppolas were still living in Detroit when Francis was born in 1939; his brother, August, was five years older. In 1942, when Francis was three, Carmine was hired as first flutist by Toscanini's NBC Symphony Orchestra. He quit the *Ford Sunday Evening Hour*, and the family moved back to New York City, where a third child, Talia, was born in 1946. Carmine stayed with Toscanini for nearly ten years, until 1951, but despite his success as a classical musician, Carmine Coppola was not content. He didn't want to spend his life playing other people's music; he wanted to conduct, and to write his own. On one occasion he was so miserable he went running out into the backyard and, in front of the children, threatened to push his hand into a power lawn mower to end his career as a flutist. He was restrained.

Toward the end of his stay with the NBC Symphony Orchestra Carmine came home in triumph to tell the family that Toscanini had finally agreed to let him conduct. Francis went to Radio City Music Hall for the great night. He sat through a long concert, conducted by Toscanini, waiting for Carmine to take the baton. Finally, when the concert was over, and everybody was walking out, his father got to conduct the exit music.

Despite his father's frustrations, Francis's earliest years, during the mid-1940s, when Carmine had a steady job, were probably his happiest. There were some memorable disasters, however. One day Carmine heard about an innovative automobile designed by Preston Tucker, and he was so impressed he not only invested $5,000—a large portion of the family's cash savings—in Tucker's company, but even ordered one of the cars himself. When Carmine took Francis to a car show to see Tucker's prototype, the boy was deeply impressed. "I thought it was really beautiful," he said later. "I remember the day. I remember the buttons on the car. And I kept asking my father when our Tucker was going to come. And then he told me, little by little, that it was never going to come because all the other auto companies thought it was too good and they put him out of business. I thought that was an injustice, something new and interesting and productive being destroyed by something progressive [sic] and dark and shadowy."

Preston Tucker became a hero to Francis. Carmine told
him what a great man Tucker was, and sometimes Francis must
have imagined himself actually *being* Tucker: a flashy, glad-
handing showman who went out and sold exciting new ideas
and got people to believe in him.

"I was in a wonderful kindergarten in a neighborhood by
the beach," Francis recalled, "and my memory of being five
years old is really wonderful—it's still the best five or six years
of my life." He was, by his own admission, an exotic kid with
very few friends, but he enjoyed a warm family life and the
company of his big brother. "August was my idol. Just took me
everywhere and taught me everything. You know, when he went
out with the other guys, because he was the leader of the gang
and he was tremendously handsome, still is. . . . He could
easily have shaken me, said, 'I don't want to take him.' "

August was a precocious child. Francis remembered his
reading André Gide and Jean-Paul Sartre at nine, and telling
his wide-eyed younger brother anecdotes about James Joyce.
Everything Augie tried seemed to come easily to him. Talia
thought of him as a sort of Renaissance prince. Of course, it
couldn't *all* have been hero worship; deep down, Francis must
have been a bit jealous of August for being smarter, more
handsome, more popular. Many years later Francis told a reporter, "Augie was 'the smart one,' Talia was 'the pretty one,'
and I was 'the affectionate one.' " To make matters worse, Carmine and Italia acted as if their second son were also second
best. "When I was young," Coppola recalled some years later,
"no one ever liked anything I ever wrote. . . . In my family,
that's what the issue was. My father had talent and my brother
had talent. I didn't and my sister didn't and my mother didn't—
no one else did."

The Coppolas praised August constantly for straight-A
grades that, they felt, set a standard for their younger children.
Even many years later, after Francis had won six Oscars, Italia
was capable of saying, "If it wasn't for Augie, Francis would
be nothing. If Francis had been my first son, the family wouldn't
be this famous today. . . . Augie is brilliant. I thank God he
was the first."

It's easy to see what a powerful effect growing up in such
a competitive household might have on a sensitive child. Fran-

cis must have longed for the approval his parents showered on Augie, and on some level he seems to have made a lifelong connection equating happiness with imitating his artistic older brother, the brilliant and gifted intellectual.

In fact Augie *did* inspire Francis. "[H]e was like the star in the family and I did most of what I did to imitate him. . . . My whole beginning in writing started in copying him, thinking that if I did those things, then I could be like him."

In 1951 Carmine left Toscanini to try his luck as a freelancer, and his career began to lose momentum. First he got a job arranging for the Rockettes' Radio City Music Hall stage shows. Then he worked on an Anna Maria Alberghetti musical for Paramount, *The Stars Are Singing* (released in 1953), and conducted the orchestra for David Merrick's touring stage shows. There was little financial security for the Coppolas as they moved back and forth across the country with Carmine looking for work. It wasn't a happy time for any of them. Francis once observed, "Our lives centered on what we all felt was the tragedy of [Carmine's] career."

At his mother's insistence, Francis always ended his prayers by saying, "Let Daddy get his big break." However, while working after school at a Western Union office in 1954 he sent his father a fake telegram from the head of Paramount's Music Department: "Dear Mr. Coppola, you've been made the composer of *Jet Star*, please come to Hollywood immediately." Carmine was overjoyed, yelling, "It's my break! It's my break!" When Francis told his father the telegram was a fake, Carmine was heartbroken.

Francis never knew where the family stood. "One minute we had a little bit of money, the next my father was saying he couldn't afford the mortgage. It was tempestuous." It was also the start of a complex, ambivalent attitude toward money—and his father—and, in fact, his entire family. In 1974, talking ostensibly about *Godfather II*, he told a reporter, "Everyone has something unresolved about his family. With his father, his mother, his sister. Maybe he makes more money than his father, or less. The family is a subject everyone cares about."

His younger sister, Talia, felt that the whole family's life was centered on keeping their demanding paterfamilias happy. Francis once described Carmine as "a frustrated man who hated anybody who was successful."

Like all children, Francis must have daydreamed about what he'd be like when he grew up. He might grow up to be like Augie, the artist, but then, too, he might be just like his father, the beloved artistic failure, the powerful man who stood at the center of everyone's lives. If he was going to be like Carmine, he would do *anything* to be a success. But at the same time, since he loved Carmine, he wouldn't want to hurt him by being *more* successful than he was; he wouldn't want Carmine hating him for his success. Thinking about Carmine and success must have been terribly confusing.

In any case, there was never any doubt about what constituted the proof of artistic success. Francis once noted, "Ever since I was a little kid, I was raised to be successful and rich. If you were raised as I was, everything you do is to make your family proud of you." And Italia remembers the nine-year-old Francis writing her a letter which said, "Dear Mommy, I want to be rich and famous. I'm so discouraged, I don't think it will come true."

Still, if Carmine and Italia were hungry for the kids to be successful, they knew better than to aim them at careers in the arts; Carmine's long, hard struggle as a musician, and his foundering career, were painful object lessons on the dangers of such a course. But the seductive show biz influences were there just the same, along with a dreamy sense that somehow everything would always turn out OK. "A lot of what I'm like," said Francis, "is from the fact that I was the audience of the most remarkable family. My mother, who was a kind of childlike woman, pushed a lot of magic. I believed in Santa Claus until I was nine or ten."

Carmine and Italia's attempts to steer their younger son away from a theatrical career suffered an unexpected setback in 1948, when Francis came down with polio. He was only nine. He spent almost a full year in bed on 212th Street in the Woodside area of Queens, paralyzed in his left leg, left arm, left side, and entire back. It's a painful subject he's mostly managed to avoid, but once he said, "When the fever hits, it hurts. And then you can't move your legs."

Once, his mother put him into the bathtub and then went to answer the phone. Left alone, with his paralyzed muscles unable to stop him, Francis slid deeper and deeper into the tub, struggling to keep his head above the water. When Italia

returned, she pulled him out, but a few minutes later she was
laughing about it. "Ha! If I hadn't of come back you woulda
drowned!" she shouted in relief.

Carmine's job in a TV orchestra enabled him to bring home
a television set, still an exciting and expensive new invention
and far from commonplace in middle-class homes. "My greatest pleasure during that year was to watch Horn & Hardart's
Children's Hour every Sunday morning," Coppola said. "I loved
little children very much then, as I do now, and I dreamed of
being involved with them someday in theatrical activities. I
had a Jerry Mahoney puppet that I could make talk and sing,
and I had a tape recorder, a record player, and other equipment that I could use to make up shows with. I am sure that
from those shows came the idea of my own studio." Carmine
had an 8 mm movie camera and a tape recorder, which Francis
began using to make sync-sound movies—movies in which he
always played the hero. It's unlikely that they were art films;
Francis hadn't seen any. "I went to the movies like everyone
else," he remembered, "but in those days movies were just
movies. We just went on Saturdays to see a Dracula picture."

He was still terribly lonely, and although he charged his
little friends admission, the shows were mainly ways to get
other kids to come and play with him. Shy and socially inept,
he thought of himself as "funny-looking, not good in school,
nearsighted, and I didn't know any girls." Even his mother
told him he was funny-looking—especially compared with the
handsome Augie.

It was the first appearance of a persona that would become
one of the most important creative facets of Coppola's adult
life: Francis the storyteller, the polio kid, the entertainer, putting on shows that reflected a sensitivity that sprang directly
from his isolation. "The popular kid is out having a good time,"
he said once. "He doesn't sit around thinking about who he is
or how he feels. But the kid who is ugly, sick, miserable or
schlumpy sits around heartbroken and thinks. He's like an oys-
ter growing a pearl of feelings which becomes the basis of an
art."

By the fall of 1952, when Francis was thirteen, he'd recovered the use of his legs and entered high school. One high
school after another. It wasn't his fault. The family was back
on the road as Carmine looked for work; that made it impossi-

ble for Francis to settle down scholastically. "I never went to any school longer than a few months," he remembered. "I went to twenty-four schools before college, so I never really took in any of them."

Finally, in the mid-1950s, the family settled down in Great Neck, Long Island, in a pleasant house with a yard and a basement. Carmine installed track lighting, which at the time was a very new invention, and Italia installed a profusion of comfortable furniture. "There were eight million chairs in the living room," a friend recalled. "It was impossible to enter that room without feeling an immediate desire to sit down."

Francis's major interest at the time was science. Carmine was determined that August should grow up to be a doctor and Francis an engineer.

Secret microphones were one of his passions. "When I was a kid about thirteen or fourteen," he later said, "there was a tremendous sense of power in putting microphones around to hear other people. There was a sense of being important and superior because I could tap a phone and no one knew. I even had a plan to put microphones in the radiators of all the rooms in the house so that I could tune in on what I was going to get for Christmas."

Francis knew how to make all kinds of explosives, and using master controls hidden in the garage, he set off orchestrated barrages of pyrotechnics in the backyard. But the explosions themselves weren't really the point. "It wasn't that you could blow something up," he said, "but that you could push a button and it would blow up. That was the part I liked. I liked remote control. When I got into college [theater] you could push a button and a whole bunch of sets would go up and a whole bunch of sets would come down. That was the part I always loved, the idea of remote control."

Describing Harry Caul in *The Conversation*, Coppola noted, "Somewhere along the way he must have been one of those kids who's sort of a weirdo in high school. You know, the kind of technical freak who's president of the radio club. When I was a kid I was one of those guys like I was just describing. In fact, my nickname was 'Science.' You know, 'Hey, Science, come over here and tell him about induction coils.' And I was president of the radio club. I became attracted to the theater because it fulfilled the two poles of my life: one was stories, and the other was science. I was just as much attracted to the theater because of its technical aspects—lights, dimmers, sets, etc."

Francis decided he wanted to be a nuclear physicist when he grew up. He even scraped together the exorbitant sum of $50 to buy an atomic energy lab made by A. C. Gilbert, with a Geiger counter and a cloud chamber with a radioactive needle. When he got it home, his sister broke off the radioactive needle, but he kept the toy for many years. In fact, he claimed he still had it as late as 1981. You never know when you're going to need an atomic energy lab.

When the nerdy Francis tried to make friends with the beautiful sons and daughters of the rich Long Island families that surrounded him, they rejected him. He was jealous of the glamour kids, but in the meantime he shifted his popularity campaign to the "rocks"—the ducktailed sons of the people who *worked* for the rich kids' families. He was big for his age, sturdily built, and tall enough to look intimidating. "Most of the kids who act tough are just bluffs anyway," he said, "and I'd get them into headlocks until they cried." He even joined a gang called the Bay Rats.

It was the youth gang era of *The Blackboard Jungle*, of hoods and debs and turf wars in the slums and suburbs alike. Coppola's high school was so tough that a willingness to fight wasn't always enough to carry the day. The fifteen-year-old Coppola was beaten up and shaken down for quarters. He retreated into a fantasy world in which he was the leader of a secret paramilitary army of brainy kids who would fight gang wars with high-tech weaponry. He dreamed up an entire arsenal of weapons, but the scheme backfired when Carmine discovered Francis's space age ordnance files and sent him off to the New York Military Academy at Cornwall-on-Hudson, on a tuba scholarship.

He spent one and a half years at the military academy—his longest stay at any single high school—and he hated every day of it. There were no girls, and on top of that his inner pendulum was swinging temporarily away from science and toward literature, a sissy subject that was not exactly stressed in military school. He made pocket money by writing love letters for other students. He'd prop a picture of a fellow cadet's girl friend on his desk, stare at it until inspiration struck, and fire off a long, passionate letter, for a dollar a page.

By this time Francis's big brother, Augie, was an A student at UCLA. When Francis discovered that he was going to be stuck in Cornwall-on-Hudson right through the summer, he did what any red-blooded kid would have done: He ran away to spend the summer with his brother. It was a taste of paradise. "[August] lived in some little dinky house in Westwood, and we had three other guys living there, and there were a couple of girls living there and it was this wonderful summer . . . all this intellectual stuff, reading books. That's when I started to write, to be included in that crowd that I was five years too young for."

During his senior year at New York Military, Coppola took another tentative step toward a show biz career: He wrote the book and lyrics for a class musical. But when another student rewrote them over his bitter objections, he became angry and ran away for the last time. He made his way back to Great Neck, and, since his folks were gone (Carmine was on the road conducting the orchestra for *Kismet*), he enrolled himself at Great Neck High School, from which he was graduated in the spring of 1956.

Chapter Two

Big Man on Campus
(1956–1960)

COPPOLA ENROLLED AT Hofstra College that fall. He was only seventeen, but he'd been awarded a drama scholarship by Dr. Bernard Beckerman, head of the drama department. He showed up for his first day driving a Nash Metropolitan.

It was a talented student body. Among his schoolmates were James Caan, Robert Spiotta (who became president of Zoetrope Studios twenty-seven years later), Ronald Colby (who became a producer at Zoetrope), Lainie Kazan, née Levine (Maggie in *One from the Heart*), singer Steve Lawrence, and Joel Oliansky, who went on to write Emmy-winning TV scripts for *The Senator* and *The Law*, and the screenplay for *Bird* (Clint Eastwood's film about bebop alto man Charlie Parker) and to write and direct *The Competition*.

Coppola hadn't been on campus more than four months when he founded the Hofstra Cinema Workshop by the simple expedient of pronouncing himself president and waiting for people to sign up. It was a radical move. In those days everyone went to the movies, but cultured people seldom talked about them; toney conversational subjects were art, classical music, and literature. Critic Andrew Sarris was just beginning to convince people that it was OK to take commercial Hollywood movies seriously.

Coppola arranged to screen 16 mm prints of some Eisenstein films at Hofstra and drew the posters himself, making a point of listing the cameraman's name. There were also three films he wanted to *make: The Scarlet Letter, Portrait of the Artist as a Young Man,* and a slightly mysterious one about "an incident that happened in this country in 1948," that was probably a biography of Preston Tucker.

He tried his hand at a simple film first. With his pal Joel Oliansky, he set to work writing a screenplay and raising $300 to shoot it. The boys shot a few sound tests in the gymnasium, but their enthusiasm waned when they couldn't figure out how to synchronize the picture and the sound. "We didn't have a Moviola," noted Coppola. "Didn't know what a Moviola was."*

On another occasion Oliansky agreed to stage a low-rent production of *Julius Caesar* for an experimental TV station at a local high school, with Coppola playing Casca. When they arrived at the makeshift TV studio, Oliansky realized there was exactly one microphone.

"What are we gonna do?" he asked. "I've got these people scattered at various points of the landscape here in their black turtleneck sweaters. . . ."

"Why don't you just, uh, pass the microphone back and forth?" suggested the teacher in charge.

"I don't think that will do," said Oliansky, rolling his eyes.

With half an hour to airtime, and the entire student body watching, Coppola wandered away, a distant look on his face. When he came back several minutes later, he'd figured out a way to rig a mike boom by Scotch-taping the microphone to a fishing pole.

"Francis was very valuable," said Oliansky. "From the beginning he was interested in the machinery of it all. I was self-protectively *not* interested."

Still a freshman, Coppola became music-drama editor of the student magazine, *The Word* (edited, conveniently enough, by Oliansky, who was a year ahead of him). That same year he wrote a short story for the magazine called "Candide—or Pessimism," by "François-Marie Arouet de Coppola." Coppola's enterprising spirit made such a powerful impression on campus litterateurs that Oliansky devoted a full installment of his *Hofstra Chronicle* column, "High Dudgeon," to a profile of Coppola; it was Coppola's first ink. Oliansky predicted that he

---

*It's a clumsy (and moderately treacherous) editing machine that runs work print and sound track simultaneously, allowing you to synchronize and edit image and sound.

had an enormous future, that he'd either go all the way or burn himself out, no middle ground. He also wrote that Coppola had "owlish good looks," a phrase that so delighted the seventeen-year-old Coppola that he took to quoting it frequently.

Thirty-two years later Oliansky hadn't changed his mind all that much. "He's the same guy he always was," he noted. "He was always a little pretentious, he was always what he is today. I think that's what I love about him."

As a freshman Coppola performed small roles in *Once in a Lifetime, Best Foot Forward,* and *As You Like It.* As a sophomore he and James Caan were on the lighting crew for *Hamlet;* Coppola headed the same crew for *Blood Wedding* and directed construction on *Light Up the Sky.* For *Of Thee I Sing* he not only directed construction but collaborated on updated dialogue and lyrics, and essayed a bad Ezio Pinza imitation playing the French Ambassador. He was also a member of the stage crew for *Picnic.*

It was rare, at that time, for students to direct major Hofstra productions, but somehow Coppola managed to talk his way into directing a production of Eugene O'Neill's *The Rope.* It is a difficult play under the best of circumstances: pretentious, melodramatic, and technically demanding. At one point the roof of the set has to collapse and gold coins have to fall out, and Coppola devised a complicated lighting scheme that made it even tougher.

"He must have had eighty-seven light cues," remembered Oliansky, who was rehearsing his own, simpler play in the next room, "and he stayed up night after night with his crew working on this impossible set."

Actually, Oliansky was finding it hard to work with all the noise coming from Coppola's room. Coppola would yell at the cast, the cast would scream back, nobody thought he knew what he was doing, and he was in despair. Finally Oliansky couldn't take it any more and took his pal aside.

"Francis," he pleaded, "don't give orders, try making *suggestions,* just say, 'Try this.' "

So for the next few days, instead of hearing Coppola screaming orders, Oliansky heard him bellowing, "Try this! Try this!"

Rope was clearly heading for disaster, and everybody knew it. The actors told their friends that Coppola didn't know what he was doing; none of the technical elements were working; the crew went around complaining about their inept director.

Both plays, Oliansky's and Coppola's, were set to premiere the same night. Oliansky's hit the boards first, and everyone loved it. He was pleased, but at the same time he was worried about his pal, whose troubled production was to follow.

Then the curtain rose on *The Rope*, and everything people said wouldn't work *worked:* The roof collapsed just as it was supposed to, the gold coins fell perfectly, light cues clicked, performances were fabulous, and a special flute score recorded by Carmine underscored the emotional elements beautifully. It was a triumph, a smash, a knockout.

Drama department chairman Dr. Beckerman considered *The Rope* the best student-directed show he had ever seen. It won the Dan H. Lawrence Award for outstanding direction.

Coppola had been complaining about girls, or more precisely their lack in his life, for months. "Well," Oliansky had told him, "if you ever want to get laid, I think directing may be your only opportunity. It's the only thing that ever gets *me* any. Not because women will sleep with you to get parts, but because there's a certain authority that attaches to you. . . ."

A few weeks after the triumph of *The Rope,* Coppola pulled Oliansky aside and declared, with a grin, "You know what you said about girls and directing? Well, you're absolutely right!"

On that note of triumph, Coppola went off to summer camp, where he had a job as a counselor. It was a terrific summer; he loved working with the younger kids, and to add to his pleasure he was working on the final production details for *Inertia,* a show he'd be producing and directing in the fall semester.

Inertia was to be the first play at Hofstra directed, written, and produced entirely by students. Coppola wrote the book and lyrics, based on H. G. Wells's "The Man Who Could Work Miracles," and Steve Lawrence composed the music. It was designed around a brand-new theatrical toy that had just arrived at Hofstra—an Izenauer Pre-Set Winch System, which allowed you to program complicated set changes: Push a button and a whole bunch of sets would rise into the flies while another bunch descended. Coppola was enchanted.

Unfortunately, while he was still at camp a number of technical problems arose with the untested equipment, so he asked Oliansky to try to simplify the book. Oliansky was amused by the challenge and turned Coppola's pretentious superproduction into a one-set musical. With 125 pages of script and nine songs, it was still no picnic, especially considering there was no budget and time for only three rehearsals with the student orchestra.

Nonetheless, *Inertia* was a big success—perhaps, Oliansky suggests, because nobody knew what to expect. Between *The Rope* and *Inertia*, Coppola went, in a matter of months, from being a nobody to being a campus superstar. He was elected president of *both* student drama clubs: Green Wig (the official drama society) and the Kaleidoscopians (the musical comedy club). He promptly merged both clubs into a single, new organization and declared that instead of just having meetings, they were going to put on a play every Wednesday. A lot of students began coming to see the shows. Consequently, Coppola was able to get a hefty $30,000 (/$125,000) budget from the university.

He told several people that he'd read a biography of Lenin and was patterning his life after him. Many students and faculty members were outraged; Coppola already had a reputation as a loudmouth, but this was seriously uncouth. Still, he seems to have learned little from the brouhaha; only a few years later he made a similar (and similarly controversial) remark about patterning his life on Hitler.

In his senior year he wrote book and lyrics for, and produced (but did not direct), *A Delicate Touch*, an original musical comedy, set in Paris, about a school for pickpockets, based on a scene from the 1946 Ginger Rogers comedy *Heartbeat*. Flush with his success from *Inertia*, he made this a true super production, with a huge budget, expensive orchestrations, a profusion of sets, and full implementation of the Izenauer Pre-Set Winch System (which was finally working). He even insisted on hiring a thirty-piece professional orchestra. "I did the wheeling and dealing to pay them," Coppola said. "When the overture started it looked like it was going to be a Broadway show, but then it went progressively downhill."

Oliansky remembered *A Delicate Touch* as being "the most elaborate musical the world ever saw. It had eight hundred scenes, ninety-two songs, a cast of millions, orchestrations out the gazoo . . . and of course, it was a catastrophe. My fondest memory of it was the entire front façade collapsing toward the audience, and [some kid in] Bermuda shorts, riding out on a ninety-foot batten, reaching out and grabbing it and pulling it back just in the nick of time."

Coppola redeemed his theatrical reputation later in the semester by directing a highly praised production of *A Streetcar Named Desire,* in which business major Bob Spiotta played Stanley Kowalski and Coppola's girlfriend Emmy played Stella. By midway through the rehearsal period, Emmy had become Spiotta's girl instead.

Coppola had not abandoned film entirely. During his junior year he sold his car and used the money to buy a 16 mm camera and make a movie—or at least a piece of one. It concerned a mother who goes to spend a day in the country with her children. After a pleasant time she falls asleep; when she wakes up, her children are gone. "The idea was that everything that had seemed so beautiful before now becomes ugly to her because it represents a possible danger to the missing children," Coppola said. "I wanted to experiment with . . . looking at the same thing two ways. I shot part of it but never finished it. I just didn't have the technical expertise."

Coppola was graduated from Hofstra in 1959 with a B.A. in theater arts, and he promptly enrolled in UCLA's Film School as a master's candidate. His family was not entirely pleased. Uncles would get him in corners, ask if he was really serious about going to school to learn about movies, start telling him how he'd never break in, and urge him to reconsider engineering.

His uncles were right. The notion of going to school to break into the movie business was unheard of at the time. From the earliest days of the film industry, a wishful filmmaker had started out by getting a menial job at a studio—in the mailroom, perhaps, or the prop department—and gradually working up to a job as montage editor, script reader, or assistant director. For fifty years young filmmakers had learned how to make films by making them. The very idea of a film school was laughable. Moreover, the craft unions were virtually closed to anyone not a relative of someone already in the business.

Even so, with the end of the studio system, a new approach was clearly needed, and although, as yet, no one from a university cinema program had made much of an impact on the industry, film school seemed to be an idea whose time was coming. As it happens, Coppola was to be one of the very first film school graduates to break into the business, opening a door through which a mob of talented film-mad youngsters followed.

In any case, if you wanted to study professional filmmaking in 1960, there were only three serious choices: New York University (NYU), the University of California at Los Angeles (UCLA), and the University of Southern California (USC). They all were quite different. NYU was far from Hollywood and tended to turn out documentarists and technicians for New York's TV industry. USC aimed at preparing its students for jobs in the film industry. UCLA (whose film program was actually part of its theater arts department) was relatively arty.

USC and UCLA were rivals, and the no-nonsense types at USC tended to be contemptuous of the aesthetes at UCLA. "UCLA trained people for making protests on film," said John Milius, a graduate of USC. "They were concerned with taking drugs and making experimental films. USC trained people for Hollywood. We were very much concerned with making the Hollywood film, not to make a lot of money but as artists."

Walter Murch, a classmate of Milius's, concurred: "We felt UCLA was just producing drug-induced frenzies of a totally uninteresting personal nature," he said, "and they felt we were soulless technoids producing overblown technical exercises."

Of course, Augie had gone to UCLA, but considering Coppola's theatrical history at Hofstra and his artistic inclinations, Francis probably would have ended up there anyway.

When Coppola arrived in the summer of 1960, he was broke, and he got a job. Two jobs, actually: one in the NBC mailroom, and the other as a busboy at a restaurant he and Augie favored, Kelbo's. Even so, he couldn't afford his own place, so he got himself a roommate, too. One night the roommate, who didn't know Coppola very well, asked him what he was going to do with his life. Coppola gave him a *look*. "I'm going to be a film director," he said.

At first it seemed that UCLA might not have been the best choice of film school. The students, Coppola felt, were negative and defeatist, and only two student films were made per semester. The film program was set up in little wooden bungalows, completely cut off from the main UCLA campus, so the film students seldom crossed paths with the regular UCLA undergraduates. In comparison with his Hofstra theater experiences, Coppola found it depressing and lonely; there was none of the *La Bohème* camaraderie he'd imagined in his high school fantasies about going to film school—"working on films and drinking wine at night, and there are beautiful girls who are working on the film and you're all in it together." In fact, as he remembered it, he barely had two friends—and neither of them was a beautiful girl.

Actually he had at least four friends, and they were among the most talented students at the school. Steve Burum, a quiet, reserved young man, was the best cinematographer at UCLA. Dennis Jakob was an off-balance version of Augie, an eccentric hipster-intellectual with a passion for existentialism, Bertolt Brecht, Friedrich Nietzsche, and Alfred Jarry. Coppola was especially excited to meet Bart Patton, who (as a child) had played Scampy the Clown, with a light bulb nose, on *Super Circus*, a popular TV show syndicated out of Chicago. Coppola remembered watching him with pleasure when he was recovering from polio, and the two immediately became fast friends. And then there was Jack Hill.

Hill was considerably older than Coppola—a talented twenty-eight-year-old musician who had originally enrolled in UCLA's music department. However, since Hill's father worked in the movie business (he designed the Sleeping Beauty Castle at Disneyland), it was probably inevitable that Jack would drift from scoring other students' films to writing them and finally to directing them. Hill went on to become one of the most interesting of the mid-seventies exploitation filmmakers, with a series of strikingly personal psychosexual melodramas that were shot through with outrageous comedy. He discovered Pam Grier and wrote and directed her first (and best) films, including *The Big Doll House, The Big Bird Cage, Coffy*, and *Foxy Brown*. He also wrote the now-legendary ad catch line for (someone else's) unremarkable biker movie, *Naked Angels:* "Mad Dogs from Hell, Hunting Down Their Prey with a Quarter Ton of Hot Steel Throbbing Between Their Legs!"

Coppola's first film at UCLA was a short psychological horror film called *The Two Christophers*, about a boy who finds that another boy has the same name he does and who wants to kill the name usurper.

The following semester, nearly the entire Coppola coterie—Jakob, Hill, and Coppola himself—got to direct longer films. Coppola's was a black comedy called *The Terrible Ayamonn Mourneen,* later called *Ayamonn the Terrible,* a pun on Eisenstein's *Ivan the Terrible.* It was shot partly by Frank Zuniga (later a director at Disney) and partly by Steve Burum (later to film *Rumble Fish,* among other Coppola features), who gave it a strikingly noirish look, much like *They Live by Night.* Carroll Ballard, Coppola's chief rival as the most talented film student at UCLA, was a grip.

In light of Coppola's subsequent life and career, *Ayamonn Mourneen* is a very interesting film. A curmudgeonly, possessed/obsessed Irish sculptor by the name of Ayamonn Mourneen has only one artistic subject: himself. His ultimate triumph will be to sculpt a twelve-foot head of himself. He works at it for four days, without eating or sleeping, until the monument is complete. It's magnificent. Then, exhausted, he collapses into sleep and has a horrible nightmare in which the head starts to yell at him—just as he yells at everyone else. In the dream Ayamonn chops off the statue's mouth. Then he wakes up and discovers he can no longer talk. But he's nice to everyone forever after.

Coppola wanted *Ayamonn Mourneen* to have a slick, professional, Hollywood look, and he did his best to see that it got it, despite an eight-day schedule and having to shoot the interiors in a studio the size of a two-car garage. After six days he'd fallen so far behind that he went to his faculty adviser, Dick Hawkins, to plead for four more days. Hawkins said no.

Coppola refused to take no for an answer. He dogged Hawkins's footsteps, following him around, pleading with him. "How can you leave me with half a picture?" he demanded.

When Hawkins refused to reconsider, Coppola did an amazing thing. In the midst of a heated discussion he fell to the floor, clutching his stomach, and went into convulsions.

Hawkins turned white. "OK, Francis," he said, "OK, OK, OK. You can have your extra days."

Zuniga wanted to take Coppola to the hospital, but as soon as the crew got him some air, he recovered. "I'm sure he was just hyperventilating," said Zuniga, "but it was real. He was hyper to begin with, and then he'd get so emotionally caught up in what he wanted that he was unable to handle it."

For an image in the dream sequence, in which the head yells at the sculptor, Coppola ran the camera backward, turned a fan on the head, and had a small crew of students throw earth and leaves at the statue. "As soon as the stuff went into the fan," reported Carroll Ballard, "everything would disappear, and you couldn't see anything, and ten seconds later twenty-five coughing people would emerge from all the orifices of that building." But the shot worked. When the film was reversed in the projector, it looked as if everything in the room was spewing in a hurricane torrent from the statue's mouth.

Cut-rate special effects were only the beginning. Coppola's abilities as a hustler were already irresistible. For instance, he wanted a fancy crane shot of the egotistical Ayamonn passing Michelangelo's "David" and muttering that it's rotten art. The statue wasn't a problem; there was a good copy in Forest Lawn Cemetery. But Forest Lawn never allowed commercial filmmaking.

Coppola called the mortuary. "Look," he said, "it's just a little student film, we'll have a skeleton crew with a hand-held camera, no heavy equipment to wreck the grass. . . ." The cemetery boss said OK. Next, Coppola called the Chapman Company, manufacturer of the biggest, finest, most expensive camera crane in the world. "Listen," he said, "if you loan me one of your cranes I can get you a beautiful photograph of one of your beautiful cranes next to Michelangelo's 'David.' . . ."

So off he went to Forest Lawn, only now he had a sixty-man, professional-size crew, and a gigantic Chapman crane. The cemetery staffers nearly dropped dead, but before they could stop him he got his shot.

Coppola rapidly began to get a reputation at UCLA, and he started to enjoy himself. He was becoming a star, nearly monopolizing the facilities and equipment. "He gave me the impression that he had enormous privileges of some sort bestowed upon him, and arrived with everything on his side," Ballard remembered. "He had the whole film school at his beck and call." The other students may have secretly resented him, but they all leaped at the chance to work with him—or for him.

There were several good courses at UCLA. Coppola's directing teacher was Dorothy Arzner, a onetime film editor who had been Hollywood's only woman director of the thirties. Her reputed lesbianism curtailed her career, but Arzner has since become a cult heroine for her strong, highly individualized women characters, like the daredevil airplane pilot played by Katharine Hepburn in *Christopher Strong*. Arzner was impressed by Coppola's script for *The Two Christophers*, and she encouraged him. She also saved him from starvation by bringing boxes of cookies to class for him. Coppola was particularly grateful to her for standing up for him when the other instructors doubted his talent. "That was the first time in my life anyone had said something encouraging," he stated at the Directors Guild of America Tribute to Arzner in 1974, to which he made a classically theatrical entrance, holding the Golden Globe award he'd just won for producing *American Graffiti*.

It was a nice thing for him to say about Arzner, but it caused considerable hilarity among the UCLA faculty members in the audience. "If there was *anything* he never was, it was a poor, frightened, innocent young fellow," remembered Hank Schloss, Coppola's editing teacher at UCLA. "He was the darling of the department; all the faculty hovered over him. I don't know why he persists in that because I never heard of Francis being turned down by the faculty for anything."

Chapter Three

Playgirls, Ax Murderers, Mad Dogs From Hell (1961–1962)

COPPOLA WAS BROKE. In fact, he had been broke as long as he could remember. He had been forced to give up his summer jobs so he'd have time for class and production workshops, and he was subsisting on $10 a week that his father sent him for expenses, at a time when the lowest-paid mailroom flunky earned at least $40 a week. He had to find a way to pay for his tuition, and he was desperate to make a film. Finally, he decided to try and solve both problems at the same time, earning his filmmaking tuition in a radically new way—by filmmaking. "Nudie" filmmaking.

Russ Meyer's *The Immoral Mr. Teas* had recently come out, and had made a lot of money in the "nudie cutie" suburban art theater market. It was relatively innocent, but nonetheless it was something of a shocker at the time—and commercially historic. Coppola figured he could do better. Some of his classmates considered making nudies the worst kind of sellout, but Coppola didn't think there was anything wrong with it. "It was the only scene I could find that actually gave you a chance to fool around with a camera and cut a film," he said. Coppola later never made any secret about having shot nudies, but he always insisted that they were very mild, describing them as "inane comedies in which you saw a couple of boobs once in a while."

As Coppola told it, it wasn't even his idea. A group of interested investors approached him and asked him to write something like *Mr. Teas.* His backers liked the script he wrote and offered to buy it—but for someone else to direct. Coppola balked; directing it was the only reason he'd written the silly thing in the first place. He shopped the script around, raised $3,000 from a friend, and in 1961 the twenty-two-year-old Coppola shot his first commercial film: a short called *The Peeper.*

"It was a cute little premise about a man who discovers that they are shooting pin-ups near his house," he remembered. "The whole film dealt with his attempts to see what was going on. Every method he used would backfire. He would haul a gigantic telescope up to his room—twelve feet long—and he would focus it, but all he would see would be a belly-button. Then he would do something else, and *that* would backfire."

Coppola built a set in an abandoned department store in Venice, spent several days interviewing nude models provided by the producers, and shot as quickly as possible. "I had so little money," he recalled, "that I had no place to sleep except on our sets. It was rather depressing to shoot these wild bedroom scenes and then have to sleep in the same bed at night." (He had moved in with a girl in Topanga Canyon, but apparently they had had a temporary falling-out.)

The Peeper was a little too arty for the nudie marketplace; Coppola couldn't get anyone to distribute it. Finally he made contact with some people who had made a terrible nudie western about a cowboy who gets kicked in the head and sees all the cows as naked women. Coppola talked them into letting him write and direct new footage so he could combine *The Peeper* with the topless oater. The combined result was released in 1961 as *The Wide Open Spaces.*

Coppola raised another $3,000 to pay for the new material and hired classmates Jack Hill and Frank Zuniga to help out with camera and editing. His financing seems to have been of the "creative" variety—i.e., he may have sold the film twice, raising the second $3,000 without telling his first backer. In any case, Hill remembered Coppola's friend, the source of the original $3,000, storming into the editing room one night in a screaming rage and nearly getting into a fistfight with Coppola.

Another time Zuniga recalled Coppola's begging one of the backers for more money. "He was pleading with the man, saying, 'I need more money, I need more money, we just can't do it with this kind of money,' and the guy is saying, 'No, absolutely no, you told me fifteen thousand dollars.' And all of a sudden I see Francis on the ground again, and he's holding on to his stomach, and this poor man is saying, 'OK, Francis, you can have the money,' and I thought, My God, this guy's got a technique down that's really incredible!"

Coppola's next nudie cutie was *The Playgirls and the Bellboy*. It started life as a long, boring black-and-white German melodrama that included one sequence with a group of nude dancers. Coppola added about forty minutes of nude sequences in color and 3-D. His pal Al Locatelli designed the sets, and Hill stayed on as cameraman. Hill's pay was a $25 exposure meter; Coppola couldn't have gotten much more.

Coppola shot three nudies in all. Eventually they were cut together and released under the title *Come On Out*.

Variety didn't get around to reviewing any of Coppola's nudies until 1982, when Kino International released yet another reedited combination of the original footage as *Tonight for Sure*. The review noted:

> [*Tonight* is] chock full of nudity . . . and at least two of the half-dozen or so women on view are real lookers, a circumstance considered unusual in this disreputable field. There's no below-the-belt frontal nudity, and film would undoubtedly earn an R rating if submitted for classification today.
>
> Storyline is ridiculous. Two definitive dirty old men who fashion themselves as moral crusaders slip into a Hollywood burlesque house to plot the cessation of the lewd, indecent behavior transpiring therein. In the meantime, they relate how they've each arrived at their righteous beliefs. The older one, leader of the local League Against Nudity, has made a career of spying on undraped women through telescopes. His companion, a grizzled miner, relates the awful tale of his cowpoke buddy Jamie, who, after hitting his head on a rock, has the misfortune of seeing naked ladies wherever he goes. Two yarns are cut in with stripteases being performed at the club, which results in very few minutes passing without another look at some skin.

With the money from the nudies, Coppola was able to take
a small step up in the world: He bought an Italian motor-
scooter.

Meanwhile, UCLA Film School continued apace, but now
that Coppola had gotten a taste of commercial filmmaking, he
longed for more. While continuing his studies at UCLA, he
contrived to enroll in one of the most extraordinary film schools
in the world, the Roger Corman Institute for Advanced Exploitation Filmmaking.

There never was such a school, of course, at least not by
that name. What there was was Roger Corman, "King of the
B's," a brilliant thirty-five-year-old filmmaker specializing in
cheap genre films called exploitation pictures, designed to sell
on their sensationalism and topicality, not on their stars or production values. Corman had graduated from Stanford, studied
modern English literature at Oxford, and begun directing in
1955 with a series of ultra-low-budget features that brought in
phenomenal profits. He had *War of the Satellites* on drive-in
screens three months after Sputnik went up. He made nine
full-length features in 1957 alone, often working on schedules
of five to ten days and budgets of $50,000 (/$210,000).

The films he made in the fifties and early sixties are leg-
ends now—*Attack of the Crab Monster, Machine Gun Kelly,
Teenage Caveman, The Little Shop of Horrors.* Corman claims
that every one of his first twenty-seven pictures made a profit,
some for him, but most of it for his distributor, American International Pictures (AIP), which was owned by Jim Nicholson
and Sam Arkoff. Corman moved into the sixties with the stylish (and highly profitable) Edgar Allan Poe series, starting with
House of Usher and ending with two of the best American horror pictures ever filmed: *The Masque of the Red Death* and
The Tomb of Ligeia, lensed by Nicolas Roeg.

Corman's films have been shown at New York's Museum
of Modern Art, the Cinémathèque Français, the National Film
Theater in London, and virtually every major film festival in
the world. He's responsible for pioneering a series of profitable genres that include biker films, drug movies, women-in-
jeopardy pictures (a genre that reached its apotheosis, according to Corman, in the TV series *Charlie's Angels*), car-crash
movies, and the like.

Corman's speed, style, economy, and sense of the marketplace make him of keen interest, but in addition, thanks to his policy of hiring promising young filmmakers and teaching them the ropes, his no-nonsense techniques and penny-pinching production methods have become immensely influential. Director Jonathan Kaplan tells a story about making *The Student Teachers* for Corman in 1973. "The script called for wall-to-wall kids. But when I got to the set there were only ten extras. So I called Roger, and he said, 'Jon, I once shot the war between Greece and Italy with five men and a bush. Surely you can shoot a high school corridor.' That's real movie magic, and Roger teaches you how to do it."

The honor roll of assistants who started their Hollywood film careers with Corman includes Allan Arkush, Paul Bartel, Peter Bogdanovich, Joe Dante, Jon Davison, Jonathan Demme, Monte Hellman, Jack Nicholson, and Martin Scorsese, to name only a few. But Coppola was the first.

At some point in 1961 Corman asked Dorothy Arzner if she had any talented students who needed work; she recommended Coppola and Hill. Corman liked Coppola's *Ayamonn* script. Moreover, the fact that Coppola had made those nudies pleased Corman immensely; it proved that the kid understood how to work fast and cheap and wouldn't waste Corman's time putting down his product. Coppola went to work for Corman. Hill ended up doing some camera work, writing, and editing, too.

It was an important moment for both Corman and Coppola. Corman eventually got his biggest-time "graduate," a commercially successful, artistically unassailable filmmaker of whom he could be proud. As for Coppola, he began to learn the all-important tricks of professional filmmaking—advanced techniques that Peter Bogdanovich once described (with refreshing honesty) as lying, stealing, cheating, shooting cheap, and getting away with it. Film schools don't teach these essential subjects; Corman specialized in them.

Coppola's jealous UCLA comrades had given him a fairly bad time for selling out to the nudie producers, but this time he really got trashed. "I was a copout because I was willing to compromise, and I still am," he recalled in 1970. ". . . I got to make my movie, and my friends at UCLA, who were equally talented, did not get the chance to make theirs."

In fact, as Coppola well knew, the job with Corman was a

step up the exploitation film ladder from the nudie racket. Corman had bought a cheap package of Russian science-fiction pictures from Mosfilm, but in order to play them off, he had to keep audiences from finding out they were Russian. He was contractually obligated to put the words "A Mosfilm Production" on the screen, but with typical genius he contrived to print the line so low in the frame that the 1.85 aperture plate in the projector hid it below the screen.

Coppola's first assignment was to make up a whole new story for one of these Russian retreads with the idealistic title of *The Heavens Call (Nebo Zovet)*. To start with, Coppola had to write a script and supervise dubbing it over the original sound track. In order to get the job, he assured Corman he spoke fluent Russian—a bald-faced lie.

Fortunately it turned out that Coppola didn't need any Russian; he just looked at the scenes and made up whatever he thought the characters might be saying. It was probably just as well. Corman had no use for idealistic science-fiction films; drive-in audiences wanted sex and violence, and it was Coppola's job to provide them.

"In one scene," said Coppola, "a Russian astronaut sees a figure of a Golden Astronaut—presumably a symbol of Hope—standing on a crag holding a golden flare. It was really lovely. Roger said, 'We've got to put two monsters up on the crag.' Roger wanted one monster to be a male sex symbol and the other to be a female sex symbol. Obviously, one had to devour the other. We said, 'This is too much, you can't just . . .' But we could, and we did—matting in sex and violence where the Russians had the Golden Astronaut of Hope."

Coppola shot some new footage, demonstrating typical resourcefulness in the process. For instance, he needed a shot of two mobs of people enthusiastically waving the flags of two warring futuristic countries, and of course, Corman refused to pay for extras. Coppola and Hill promised some starving student $5 to make the two sets of flags, and then they drove to the Pasadena Rose Parade in a Volkswagen with a sunroof. People were lined up, waiting for the parade to start. Coppola jumped out of the Volkswagen with his hands full of flags. "We're making a UCLA student film," he announced, handing them out. "When I signal, wave the flag and cheer." Then he jumped back in the car, Hill grabbed the camera, Coppola signaled, everybody waved a flag, and Coppola got his crowd shot, for free.

Coppola worked on the Russian retread for nearly six months, receiving a grand total of $250, but he had no complaints. Corman gave him a little office and a couple of cutting rooms, and he must have felt as if he'd gotten started at last.

He was so anxious to impress Corman that he'd deliberately work all night, so when Corman arrived in the morning, he'd be sure to find him slumped over the Moviola. It worked, too. The boss was pleased with his new assistant and the refurbished Russian science-fiction film, which he released as *Battle Beyond the Sun.*

The fact that it was almost unwatchable didn't trouble Corman a bit. His top-of-the-line exploitation films had to deliver a reasonable amount of excitement for the drive-in crowds, but he also needed cheap, marginally acceptable products to fill out drive-in double bills. *Battle*'s special effects were low-rent, but there were enough of them to keep audiences from setting fire to the concession stand, and the new dialogue Coppola had concocted turned an unreleasable film into a marketable commodity for peanuts.

Even so, *Battle* is probably one of the worst films Corman ever released—and that covers a lot of territory. It starts with a silly, long-winded precredit narration ("The future of mankind is being decided behind closed doors . . .") delivered over a series of close-up shots of model spaceships, many of which appear to be cheap plastic hobby-shop items tricked out with a few flashing lights. The models go up and down on visible wires. Then we are shown Erector set wheels wobbling around a thin shaft ("The wheel was one of man's first inventions . . ."), after which the titles finally begin.

The actors listed in the credits (Edd Perry, Andy Stewart) are all imaginary, since Coppola had to invent American-sounding names to disguise the Russian origin of the cast. Some of the production credits are imaginary, too. Coppola seems to have been less pleased with the film than Corman, or maybe the sellout chorus at UCLA was getting to him; in any case, credit for the screenplay goes to Nicholas Colbert and Edwin Palmer; the director is listed as Thomas Colchart. Coppola did sign the film, but only as associate producer (Francis Ford

Coppola). Jack Hill is listed as production assistant, and special music is by Carmen *(sic)* Coppola.

Coppola's jerry-built plot revolves around a race to Mars between two antagonistic future alliances, North Hemis and South Hemis. Both sets of astronauts are forced to make an emergency landing on an asteroid. There they battle space monsters while waiting for a fuel rocket to arrive so they can go home. Everything ends happily.

The dialogue isn't bad, exactly; it's just terminally pointless. What can you do with a scene in which astronauts chat while reading meters?

"Temperature reading?" says Astronaut Number One.

"Point 934, rising," says Astronaut Number Two.

"That checks," says Astronaut Number One.

The bargain-basement rubber monsters Coppola (and his friend Al Locatelli) provided to spice up the sequence on the asteroid are the best things in the movie—or the funniest, anyway. One is a Vagina Monster—a potato-shaped creature with wobbling tentacles and a big, toothed slit in the middle of its chest. The other is a Penis Monster, a snaky character waving a big eyeball in front. "Al Locatelli and I made the monsters out of foam rubber and cooked them in the oven in my apartment," Coppola recalled. "They spilled all over the rugs, and I got kicked out of the place."

When Corman got a look at Francis's Freudian monsters, he was aghast. "Francis, you know we can't put this in a picture," he remonstrated.

"Nobody will ever know," Coppola insisted. "The only reason it seems raw to you is you know the origin of what it's all about."

As it happens, Coppola was right. "We never had any complaints about it," Corman said. "Nobody protested, no censorship problems whatsoever. And the film turned out to be fairly successful."

Corman began calling Coppola whenever he wanted cheap labor. He usually paid him $400 (/$1600) a week—fabulous money for a grad student. "He had me doing everything: I did a little bit of editing, a little bit of writing, I was on a sound stage. . . . I did some second-unit photography; on Roger's films, everyone got to do everything," Coppola remembered. "It was really like an intensive course in the mechanics of putting a film together."

Coppola wrote several more Russian-to-English conversions, taking a credit as "Alfred Posco" for reworking a ten-year-old picture called *Sadko* (retitled as *The Magic Voyage of Sinbad*). He was dialogue director, and assistant-to-everybody, on two of the popular Edgar Allan Poe horror pictures Corman was releasing through AIP, *Tower of London*, starring Vincent Price, and *The Premature Burial*, with Ray Milland.

Meanwhile, UCLA was offering a $2,000 prize for the best original student script, in a contest endowed by movie mogul Sam Goldwyn. Coppola considered that vast amount of money, contemplated the competition, and confidently announced to Jack Hill, "I'm gonna win the Goldwyn award." In a single night, working in a frenzy, he wrote *Pilma, Pilma*, an expansion of his short *The Two Christophers*. (At least that's the story he's always told; it's hard to imagine *typing* an entire script in one night.) The story is about a boy who, in a frenzy of sibling rivalry, decides to kill his big brother. Coppola turned it in and forgot about it.

Several months later Corman drew Coppola aside. He had assembled a group of friends to go to Europe on a trip that would be part work, part vacation. He wanted to shoot a film called *The Young Racers*, one that would follow the Grand Prix racing circuit and incorporate the actual races into the story. Corman needed a sound man and asked Coppola if he could recommend anyone. Coppola replied that *he* was a terrific sound man, and Corman gave him the job. Coppola, who knew next to nothing about recording sound, rushed home, found a book of instructions for the Perfectone sound recorder, and started reading: "Push button A. . . ."

Unfortunately there was a bit more to it than pushing button A. When the first rushes were screened, the noise of the camera was clearly audible over the dialogue, and cameraman Floyd Crosby pointed the finger of scorn at the film school sound man. Coppola pointed right back at Crosby. "Yes," he said, "but it's the cameraman, it's not my fault. It's your fault."

"Obviously," Corman recalled, "the sound man is supposed to blanket out the camera noise; you can't truly blame that on the cameraman. But it showed me that Francis was thinking fast, even if not correctly, at that early date."

The storytelling scenes of *The Young Racers* were actually shot in five days (not a record for Corman, but getting close), and in addition to Coppola, the crew included Robert Towne

(who later wrote *Shampoo, Chinatown,* and major scenes for
The Godfather, and wrote and directed *Tequila Sunrise*) and
Israeli producer-director Menachem Golan (who was to become half owner of Cannon Films), all together on location in
Ireland, where filmmaking could be done on the cheap. Although Coppola had been officially hired as a sound man, he
ended up as second-unit director, shooting most of the racing
footage.

"Francis had *guts,*" remembered actor Bill Campbell. "He
picks up the goddamn hand-held camera, he gets out on the
racetrack, and he's shooting pictures of these damn racing
drivers driving past him within six feet!" All the while he was
on the lookout for his main chance, and when there was $20,000
left over after *Racers* was in the can, he saw it shining.

When Corman mentioned that he had a title he liked,
"Dementia," Coppola told him a story he knew his boss couldn't
refuse. "Roger always makes pictures that are like other pictures," Coppola noted, and *Psycho* was a big hit at the time, so
he dreamed up a low-budget horror film "with a lot of people
getting killed with axes and so forth," designed to cash in on
Hitchcock's successful thriller.

He sold the picture to Corman on the basis of one scene,
and a fabulous scene it was. "The time is late at night. The
place is Dublin. A woman comes out of a castle. She is carrying a bag. She stops, opens the bag, and takes out five dolls.
She ties string around the necks of the dolls, then attaches the
strings to a weight. Then the woman takes off all her clothes
and dives into a pond. She places the weight on the bottom of
the pond, and the dolls start to float up toward the surface. The
woman starts to turn in the water, and there she finds the perfectly preserved body of a seven-year-old girl with her hair
floating in the current. The woman rushes to the surface and
screams the words, 'Axed to death!' Roger said, 'You've got a
picture, kid.'"

Coppola later admitted that he didn't have the slightest
idea what the woman was doing in the pond, or what happened next, or even what the scene was about.

Corman liked the scene, but what he liked even more was
the fact that Coppola swore he could make the film for exactly
$20,000 (/$78,000)—the same $20,000 that happened to be left
over from *The Young Racers.* Corman agreed, on the condition
that Coppola make it in Ireland and in fewer than ten shooting

days. Then he flew back to America, leaving Coppola a secretary who was supposed to cosign all the checks. As soon as Corman left, Coppola (who was learning the business faster and better than Corman suspected) had the secretary sign a check for the entire amount and deposited it in another account. Then he sat down and wrote the screenplay directly on mimeo stencils. It took him three nights.

The closer Coppola got to actually shooting *Dementia*, the less certain he became that he could actually bring it in for $20,000. So when English producer Raymond Stross (who later made *The Fox*) became interested in the film, Coppola happily sold him the British rights for an additional $20,000. As a fringe benefit, he got to use the Ardmore Studio in Dublin (of which Stross was part owner) for free. When Corman heard about the new investor, he tried to withdraw the original $20,000, but since it had been moved to another bank account, he couldn't touch it.

A bunch of UCLA pals (and sister Talia) paid their own way to Dublin in order to help and/or hang out. One of the newcomers was twenty-six-year-old Eleanor Neil, a cute, shy, soft-spoken ash blonde from California with delicate features and fine Irish skin. Neil was a successful artist, with a studio and assistants, who made tapestries that sold for big bucks. She had been going out with John Vicario, whom Coppola had hired to be camera operator. Ostensibly, she came to hang around with her boyfriend, but at Bart Patton's suggestion Coppola hired her to help Al Locatelli with the art direction; her final screen credit reads "Set Director."

When she met Coppola, it was love at first sight. He found her extremely attractive, and the attraction was mutual. The fact that she was a fine artist made her all the more appealing. "She was a class item," remembered actor Bill Campbell. "She was a super human being, her tolerance level was superb, and she loved Francis dearly. Even back then, Francis was always a wee bit . . . gregarious, a little bit wild. And she was able to handle that; it was completely opposed to her particular personality. Maybe that was one of the things that attracted her."

Francis and Eleanor grew deeply involved; some people thought the love affair came at an awkward time for the film, since Coppola seemed to be devoting at least as much energy to his new girl friend as to *Dementia*.

Coppola has said that *Dementia* was the only film he ever

enjoyed working on. He installed cast and crew in two rural manor houses rented by Bart Patton and Mary (*Twist Around the Clock*) Mitchell, the two most presentable cast members. Everyone was thrilled to be in Europe, to be working, to have a little money. "We were young and making a feature film," remembered Coppola. "I think that kind of enthusiasm has a lot to do with the fact that when you're young your standards are low. If you shoot something that looks like a real movie, that puts you into euphoria."

Dementia starred Patrick Magee, Luana (*The Pit and the Pendulum*) Anders, several members of the prestigious Abbey Players (whom Coppola sweet-talked into taking small roles), some Irish actors who had worked on *The Young Racers*, and Bill Campbell. Campbell, who had starred in *The Young Racers*, was a well-established actor and was initially reluctant to do Coppola's low-budget quickie; the only reason he'd agreed to appear in *Racers* was that his brother Robert (now a famous mystery novelist and the author of such books as *Alice in La-La Land*) had written it. Coppola implored him endlessly. "I'm gonna be famous some day," he promised Campbell. "I promise I'll make it up to you. If anything great happens in my life, I'll make sure that I pay you back. I won't forget the favor you did me." Finally Campbell figured what the hell, and said yes.

Like most first films of later-to-be-famous filmmakers, some of the details have grown fuzzy. In one version of the folktale it took Coppola and his nine-man crew exactly seven days to shoot *Dementia*, most of it in a motel room. In an alternate account (one that sounds more believable), Coppola spent nine days at Ardmore and two weeks in the countryside. Aside from frantic telegrams ("Dailies look great. More sex and violence. Love, Roger"), Corman left Coppola pretty much alone; it would have been difficult for him to do otherwise from eight thousand miles away.

When *Dementia* was done shooting, Coppola left for Yugoslavia, taking Eleanor with him. Corman had invested some money in a Yugoslav whodunit called *Operation Titian* (starring Bill Campbell, among others), and Coppola was supposed to be script supervisor and story editor, making sure that it would be playable (dubbed, of course) in the American market. Francis and Eleanor spent eight weeks in Dubrovnik, and it was a glorious, passionate vacation; but once again, Coppola seems to have paid much closer attention to Eleanor than his filmmaking duties. When Corman got the picture, it was unreleasable. The story goes that Coppola told him, "Well, that's what you get for fifty grand. Now if you give me twenty thousand more, I'll get it done for you." Corman declined. The best footage was cannibalized for several Corman pictures, including *Blood Bath* and *Track of the Vampire*.

Coppola returned to Los Angeles to discover that *Pilma, Pilma*, his quickie script of the year before, had won the 1962 Sam Goldwyn Award. In addition to taking the $2,000 cash prize, Coppola sold it one week later for $5,000. "All that money for one night of passionate writing," he marveled. His schoolmates were furious; it seemed that for this flamboyant character, *everything* turned to gold. Carroll Ballard had been thrilled to win second prize in the contest, until he discovered who'd come out number one. Shortly thereafter Coppola left UCLA. He still owed a thesis film, but he was working on that.

The honeymoon with Corman was over, especially after a traumatic screening of the first rough cut of *Dementia*. Coppola had put together an hour of material (including some last-minute inserts he had gotten Jack Hill to shoot for him) to show the boss, and Corman brought *his* mentor, AIP's Sam Arkoff, presumably so he could show off his hot new protégé. To Corman's horror and embarrassment, the plot was virtually incomprehensible; all the transitions and connecting material were missing. On top of that most of the night footage was impenetrably murky.

Corman was furious; he took his pencil, broke it over his knee, and stormed out of the screening room. Coppola stalked out after him, and they got into a screaming argument. To Hill's amazement, Coppola's powers of persuasion carried the day; he convinced Corman that the picture was wonderful, that it would be a great success. All it needed was a little additional material to fix it up.

Coppola wrote several new sequences, including a new opening. He shot scenes in a boat rowing on a lake in Griffith Park and did underwater shots in Hill's father's swimming pool. But now that Coppola was back in Hollywood, and within easy reach, he and Corman began to have increasingly serious disagreements over the editing of *Dementia*. Corman insisted on dubbing the dialogue (despite Coppola's anguished objections) and adding voice-over narration to explain scenes he found confusing. Furthermore, Corman thought the film needed more violence to be truly commercial, and when Coppola balked, he got Hill to write a couple of scenes, which Coppola sulkily directed. Eventually Corman hired Hill to write and shoot several more scenes entirely without Coppola's involvement.

"Roger wanted some more violence," said Coppola, "another ax murder at least—which he got, though not from me."

"At that time Francis had a way of starting something and then going on to something else," Hill commented, "mostly because he had a better opportunity. Often he'd leave the projects with extremely difficult problems that other people would have to solve."

In any case, *Dementia 13* (the "13" was added because there was already a film called *Dementia,* and someone at Corman's office hoped that adding a "13" might help get bookings on the thirteenth of every month) is an uneven film—not surprising, considering Corman's interference. But if it's less than a triumph, it's far from a disgrace. Set mostly in a gloomy Irish castle, it focuses on a sinister family (a slightly dotty mother and her two sons) obsessed with the mysterious death of a young girl, Kathleen. When two nice young women marry into the family, several brutal ax murders set the pot of repressed emotions boiling. Even this early in his career, Francis was beginning to touch on the issues of brothers, and families—although the *Dementia* clan makes the Corleones look like angels.

A very young-looking Patrick Magee, playing a sardonic doctor-detective with perceptible relish, is by far the best thing in the film. He does the best he can with several sections of awful dialogue, and when he gets lines like "Drink's the only road to survival in *this* climate" or when he's stalking the mad ax murderer, chanting, "Little fishie in the brook, daddy's got you on a *hook*!" he's marvelous.

There's generally too much screen time spent on people wandering around the castle corridors, looking for they-know-not-what (a familiar element in Corman films, which were always coming in short, needing padding), and *Dementia* owes far more to the Corman-Poe potboilers (with their haunted castles and sinister parents) then to *Psycho*. Still, thanks to clever directorial touches by Coppola, several scenes are unexpectedly powerful. There's a great scene when one of the young women surprises her fiancé (a sculptor, wearing welding goggles as he wields a cutting torch), and he erupts into furious anger at being interrupted. The scene jumps into frightening high tension when he pulls off his goggles and stares at her for a *very* long moment before he recognizes her.

The opening sequence, with a man and a woman arguing in a rowboat on a midnight-black lake, is also very striking. Coppola stages it over distorted rockabilly music from the man's tape player, and when the man dies of a heart attack, the woman dumps his body overboard and throws the tape after him. The scene ends with a shot of the tape player sinking through black water, still gurgling rock and roll. And the primal scene, the one with the underwater dolls that sold Corman on the film, is quite strong, although Coppola changed the ending. Instead of screaming, "Axed to death!," the woman *is* axed to death as she emerges from the water.

Albert Locatelli is listed as art director, and there's a credit line reading "Second Unit Written and Directed by Jack Hill." The next-to-last credit reads "Produced by Roger Corman" and the last one reads "Written and Directed by Francis Coppola." No "Ford" this time.

What with one thing and another, Coppola felt that Corman had betrayed him. Corman was disappointed with his protégé's decidedly noncommercial feature. Nonetheless, when he asked Coppola to go up to Big Sur to shoot some footage with Jack Nicholson for a picture called *The Terror*, Coppola went.

The Terror was already well on its way to becoming an underground legend, less for its excellence than for its labyrinthine, incomprehensible plot. In fact, Peter Bogdanovich (who used clips from *The Terror* in *his* Corman film, *Targets*) warned Nicholson that if the picture was ever rereleased, it might destroy his career.

There were good reasons for the plot problems. Corman had been about to finish *The Raven*, a marvelous horror comedy starring Peter Lorre and Boris Karloff. It was Friday afternoon, and Daniel Haller's Gothic castle set was scheduled to be taken apart. But when Corman realized that the stage would stand vacant for a whole weekend and that as long as he got the sets torn down by 9:00 A.M. Monday, he could use the stage for free, his eyes got a familiar gleam. He'd pay Boris Karloff to work Saturday and Sunday and shoot some key interior scenes in the castle; then he could shoot exteriors, inserts, and surrounding material at his leisure. If he moved fast, he could get a *really* cheap Boris Karloff picture.

It was the kind of audacious scheme that often brought out the best in Corman and his associates. He called up Leo Gordon, a heavyset character actor who was one of his occasional screenwriters, and told him to write some spooky castle scenes for Karloff; don't worry about continuity or plot, Corman told him, just write something fast. Gordon pulled a few unfinished scripts from his trunk, scavenged the most lurid horror sequences, and rushed them over to Corman. Nobody slept that weekend, but by 9:00 A.M. Monday, when the sets came down, Corman had a marvelous collection of weird scenes in which Karloff and a very young Jack Nicholson (trying halfheartedly to do Errol Flynn, dressed in Marlon Brando's leftover *Napoleon* costume) wandered around the castle set, uttering atmospheric dialogue that made no sense whatsoever. None of the actors knew what was happening; it must have been immensely funny.

The laughter stopped as soon as Corman discovered there was no way to make the scenes fit together into any kind of coherent plot. Several editors tried and failed. Corman realized he'd need to shoot a *lot* of new material to make sense out of what he already had. One such attempt was set in a big water tank, where various characters pretended to kill each other with Styrofoam rocks; Dennis Jakob doubled Karloff. It didn't help. Before *The Terror* was done, sequences were directed by Corman, Coppola, and Monte Hellman, each one attempting to make sense out of the growing tangle of dialogue, motivation, and conflict left by the previous directors.

In the end the only solution they could devise was to turn the butler (played by Corman standby Dick Miller) into the villain and shoot a scene where he delivers a complicated speech in which all the dangling plot elements are tied into an unlikely knot.

But that stage of desperation was still months away when Corman sent Coppola to Big Sur, hoping a few days of shooting would untangle the plot. Along with cast and crew, Coppola brought his girl friend and his sister.

The Coppola group stayed almost two weeks. The locals

came out to watch, and Coppola signed them on at $10 a day.

Nicholson hated the movie, and Miller was not crazy about Coppola. "He was young then," Miller recalled, "and he was very arrogant. He tried to come out as self-assured, but there's a difference. He seemed to be very full of himself."

Miller found Eleanor a bit prudish. "I would tell these jokes," he said, "and she was the only one who said, 'Well, I don't think that's very funny.' They were good dirty jokes. And *he* got a little upset. I said, 'Come on, this is a joke, what is it, you're up here living in sin and you're talking to me about telling dirty jokes?'"

On one occasion, Miller remembered, Coppola got into an argument with one of the supporting actors and started ranting about his education. "I've got a degree in cinema," he yelled, implying that the actor couldn't be right because Coppola had a better diploma.

Miller couldn't stand it anymore. "Bullshit!" he yelled. "I've got a Ph.D.!" After that there was no love lost between Miller and Coppola.

Miller didn't notice any particular directorial genius coming from the film school whiz kid, but he thought Coppola did well considering the problems. "It was formula," Miller noted. "I'm not gonna say he was brilliant or he was incompetent. I mean, nobody knew what the picture was about. So there was no advantage to being the director or not being the director. Everybody was in the same boat; *nobody* knew what was happening."

Coppola tried his best to deliver some high-class footage. He stole a sequence from *The Thief of Bagdad* in which Sandra Knight leans over a stream, looks in, and sees Nicholson's reflection. For another scene he sent Nicholson out into the crashing surf and kept waving him farther and farther from shore. Nicholson, wearing a heavy dress uniform and boots, nearly drowned.

But Nicholson got revenge. Coppola had spent hours setting up a shot in which Nicholson would come around a turn in a mountain trail, and as he approached the camera, clouds of butterflies would rise. Crew members had spent most of the day catching butterflies. Finally, Coppola started the camera, yelled "Action!," crew members released the butterflies, the butterflies filled the frame, and Nicholson appeared around the bend, doing what can only be described as an outrageous fag act. As the last of the butterflies fluttered away and Coppola muffled a scream, Nicholson just grinned foolishly. "Gee," he said, "I didn't know that was a take."

Coppola ended up shooting an enormous amount of film, none of which helped the plot at all. Meanwhile, he was brooding unhappily about the way Corman had messed up *Dementia,* and when he came back from Big Sur with the new scenes in the can, he told his boss he was quitting.

At the same time he became aware that his draft board was taking an unhealthy interest in him. He had already done military school; basic training held no appeal. But he was twenty-two, unmarried, out of school—prime cannon fodder. Fortunately an easy solution was at hand. He and Eleanor Neil were still very much in love, and the subject of marriage had begun to come up. Now all the circumstances argued against putting it off. A week after he quit *The Terror,* he and Eleanor Neil were married.

Chapter Four

Seven Arts:
Working in the Script Mine
(1963–1966)

COPPOLA WASN'T UNEMPLOYED very long. He'd already turned down a feeler from Universal Pictures; as he told his friends, he was afraid if he went to work there, he'd end up doing television stuff. Fortunately producer Ray Stark, who had made *The World of Susie Wong* and was then working at a relatively new outfit called Seven Arts, was impressed by Coppola's Goldwyn screenwriting award and offered him a contract for $375 (/$1,500) a week to speed-write a script for *Reflections in a Golden Eye*.

Before he went for the final interview at Seven Arts, Coppola stopped off at Bart Patton's house so Patton's mother, Belle, could make sure he looked OK. She decided that he looked just a bit young, so she powdered his hair to add a few years and sent him on his way. Apparently the makeup job was a success; Coppola got the assignment.

Now his fellow film students at UCLA were really jealous. The day he signed with Seven Arts, someone hung a big sign on the bulletin board that said, SELLOUT. Evidently, it hurt more than Coppola would ever admit. Even years later he would, with surprising bitterness, occasionally identify himself as "the famous sellout from UCLA."

Coppola couldn't have picked a better time to sign up; Seven Arts was on a roll. It was a packaging entity that bought properties, turned them into first-draft scripts, got commitments from stars and directors, and then sold the packages to major studios, which would assume financial responsibility for producing the movies. Between 1957 and 1965 Seven Arts put together twenty-four such film packages, making so much money (and developing such a good line of credit) that its owners began to think about getting into distribution themselves.

In 1963 Seven Arts had just paid Carson McCullers $50,000 for the screen rights to *Reflections,* a story of suppressed homosexual passion set in an army base. No one had been able to get a decent screenplay out of it, and the option was running out. Writing at top speed, Coppola finished the script in six weeks, and much to his surprise, everyone loved it. "The reaction was such a load of baloney," Coppola said. "Everyone read it and said, 'Fantastic, who's this genius? It must be Dalton Trumbo writing under another name.' They gave me all that junk. Everything is either one hundred per cent or nothing."

John Huston, who was set to direct, said he liked the script, too, but he was unable to shoot the film immediately. (Some years later, when he did finally make *Reflections,* Huston used another script.)

In any event, Seven Arts raised Coppola's salary to $500 (/$1,900) a week. He and Eleanor moved into an A-frame house in Mandeville Canyon. Coppola's seventeen-year-old sister, Talia, moved in with them, and Coppola did something he'd been thinking about for months: He bought a Jaguar.

He also called his Hofstra pal Joel Oliansky, who was doing well back on the East Coast, working on a novel and writing industrial shows for the New York World's Fair. "I'm signed up with Ray Stark here at Seven Arts," Coppola said. "I'm a staff writer! They've got a huge deal with Paramount, and they need scripts. Would you be interested in such a thing?"

Oliansky was interested. Coppola met him at the airport, lent him his credit card so he could rent a car, and got him an office on the same floor as his own at Seven Arts. He also showed Oliansky the ropes. "Ray Stark doesn't read a lot of things," he'd say, "so make sure Phil Feldman [producer, business manager, and vice-president of Seven Arts] reads your stuff." And after everyone went home, just for fun, he would take Oliansky down to the third floor, which was locked but which Coppola had a secret way of opening, and they would read confidential memos on the executives' desks. They never learned much of import.

"Francis used to stare at me," Oliansky remembered, "and smile, and say, 'You're gonna be *so* rich. Do you realize writers are starting to make gross deals?' And I'd think, 'What the hell is he talking about?' "

Coppola's next assignment was working with producer Fred Coe on a screen adaptation of Tennessee Williams's short play *This Property Is Condemned*. (Coincidentally, Coppola had directed it at Hofstra.) The package included Elizabeth Taylor, who liked Williams's original so much she had talked her husband, Richard Burton, into directing the screen version.

The assignment ended badly. Elizabeth Taylor had wanted Montgomery Clift for her leading man, and when the studio said no, she quit, taking Burton with her. Natalie Wood was brought in to replace her, a young Robert Redford eventually got the male lead, and three or four different directors (including Richard Rush and Sidney Pollack) were hired, and fired, one after another. "I had left the project by then," Coppola said, "and fourteen other writers came in. The final script wasn't really very close to what we had done, not that ours was that much better."

Next up, Coppola wrote an original comedy for Seven Arts called *My Last Duchess*, which was eventually shot by Ken Hughes under the title *Drop Dead, Darling*. Coppola later confessed he had overwritten it badly; Hughes threw away most of Coppola's script and expanded the prologue into a complete movie. Coppola received no screen credit.

He wrote *The Fifth Coin*, which got as far as the assignment of stars (George Segal, Nancy Kwan) and a director (Alexander Mackendrick) before it was shelved. He also penned an adaptation of Oliansky's novel *Shame, Shame on the Johnson Boys*, a satire on folk singers, hoping to direct it himself, but nobody wanted it.

Coppola became what he described as a "clutch writer" for Seven Arts, "a trouble-shooter, salvaging movies that were teetering on the brink of catastrophe" and averaging three scripts a year. After one year the twenty-four-year-old was making $1,000 (/$3,800) a week. It was big money, and he managed to save nearly $20,000. But the only reason Coppola wanted big money in the first place was to make movies, and $20,000 was chicken feed. "I was really frustrated," he said, "because I could buy a Ferrari, or I could buy a sailboat, but I couldn't make a film. So I decided I was gonna risk it all on the stock market and either have $100,000 and make a film, or have nothing."

Like his father before him, Coppola decided to invest his money in new technology. He bought stock in a wonderful toy called a Scopitone that had been introduced in the 1940s and was currently enjoying a brief vogue. It was a cine-jukebox, designed for bars, that showed three-minute musical films on a small built-in screen. Coppola loved the machine; but it never caught on, and when the company went under, he lost every cent.

With his nest egg gone, Coppola fell back on grinding out scripts for Seven Arts, including *The Disenchanted* and *The Fifth Country.* "I wrote about ten scripts in two and a half years," he said later, "so they'd like me and say, 'OK, let the kid make a film.' " Instead, they assigned his scripts to other directors.

His output during this period was prolific, and it paid well enough for Francis and Ellie to start a family. Their first child, a son, Gian-Carlo Coppola (nicknamed Gio), was born in 1963.

Meanwhile, in September of that same year, another child of Coppola's, *Dementia 13,* was released by Corman in Los Angeles. Coppola claims it got very good reviews, and that he made money on it, but neither of these claims can be documented. For all intents and purposes, *Dementia* dropped from sight as completely as if it had never been made.

Early in 1965, after Coppola had been slaving for two years in the Seven Arts script mine, Stark offered him a reward: a "vacation" trip to Paris to help a writer who was working with French director René Clément on Seven Arts' *Is Paris Burning?* Stark told Coppola that the writer was ill—dying, in fact. If "the pencil fell out of his hand," Coppola was supposed to pick it up. He could even take Eleanor and Gio.

What Coppola *really* wanted was to direct, but Ray Stark's answer was the same as always: "Kid, don't worry, your turn will come. You're twenty-two, [or twenty-three or twenty-four], you're making a thousand a week, you've got a house, a kid, two cars, what more do you want?" At one point it made Coppola so furious he wrote a screenplay for Stark about a guy who wants to direct a movie so badly he goes crazy. It didn't make any difference.

Coppola was beginning to wonder how much longer he could put up with Ray Stark and the grind at Seven Arts. His feelings can be inferred from a joke he started telling: "I found out how to run a production company," he would grin at his pals. "First you need a creator, a visionary, a guy who selects the scripts and makes the movies. Then you need a money man, a lawyer, somebody who understands banking, investments, distribution. And then you need an asshole."

In any case, the twenty-five-year-old Coppola spent the first months of 1965 in Paris, working closely with fifty-two-year-old René Clément. Clément was a sensitive, individualistic filmmaker who had been making pictures since 1936. In 1952 his *Forbidden Games,* which underscored the horrors of war by depicting their effect on children, had brought him to the attention of film audiences around the world.

For Coppola, working with Clément should have been fun, but the vacation quickly turned into a nightmare. An unwieldy team of French screenwriters had been hired at the insistence of government bureaucrats as a nationalistic gesture, but that was only part of the problem. The essence of the novel's plot was the battle between the Communists and the Gaullists for control of Paris when the Germans moved out, but according to Coppola, the French writers and producers were insisting that everyone in France was a hero and there were no French Communists, but even if there *were* French Communists, they were very nice, and big pals with the Gaullists.

Coppola tried to quit. Then Seven Arts sent Gore Vidal to Paris to help, and the older, more experienced writer convinced Coppola to stick it out a little longer. "It was a junior-senior relationship," said Coppola. "Vidal is a very bright guy, and he had it all figured out. He knew it was all a lot of baloney, and he would say, 'Francis, yes,'—with that cigarette holder and all—'Go back and figure out a scene for such and such, and I'll work on it.' He took it all very casually. He knew what he was talking about."

By the time the script was done, Coppola hated it with a passion. But because of a Writers Guild technicality, Coppola and Vidal were the only writers on the project who could get screen credit, which, by then, they desperately did not want.

Coppola blamed producer Paul Graetz for some of the problems; Clément had no power and backed down whenever Graetz disagreed with him. "For some stupid reason, Clément's contract didn't give him a say over the script," Coppola recalled, "and for some equally stupid reason, Graetz wanted to keep it that way. So to circumvent this, Clément's ideas were presented as mine at story conferences, and of course I didn't mind since Clément's ideas were invariably the best." Coppola learned the lesson well: A director could protect himself only if he had full control over the script.

Coppola made up for the frustrations of his day job by working on a secret project at night—a script that would become his first personal picture, *You're a Big Boy Now*. He put in some very private jokes. When the young protagonist of *Big Boy* talks back to his mother, for instance, Coppola had her turn to her husband and say, "Are you going to let him talk to your wife like that?" It was one of Italia's favorite lines. Coppola was proud of the script, and he was sufficiently paranoid (i.e., professional) to take out some insurance.

To make sure that his employers, Seven Arts, would not claim ownership of a script he was writing on his own time, Coppola scraped up $1,000 and took out an option (against $10,000, to be paid when filming started) on a book by British novelist David Benedictus with a vaguely similar story line. Coppola's script focuses on a nineteen-year-old kid who lives in New York and works in the stacks of the New York Public Library; Benedictus's book is about a nineteen-year-old kid who works in a shoe store. But there were so many similarities Coppola felt he and Benedictus were writing about the same thing, and this way, even if Seven Arts disputed the ownership of the script, Coppola could point to his exclusive ownership of the property on which the script was based.

It was a big gamble for a young man with very little money. "No one's willing to do that any more," Coppola observed in 1968, with considerable truth. "I would have done anything. That's the difference. . . . The secret of all my getting things off the ground is that I've always taken big chances with personal investments."

As long as he was already in Europe, Coppola wanted to film *Big Boy* on the Continent, but according to him, Seven Arts wasn't interested in a $20,000 movie shot in black and white with a hand-held camera and unknown actors. The company made him come home.

Coppola was so demoralized and negative about the *Paris* misadventure that he quit Seven Arts (and was fired at the same time). He was totally broke. He'd lost all his money on the Scopitone deal, he owed the bank $10,000, and he and Eleanor had just had another son, Roman. He was so depressed by his financial problems and the professional trap in which he seemed to have gotten himself caught that he decided to move to Denmark. He actually went so far as to fly there to check out the lay of the land. Then, as if things weren't bad enough, Seven Arts executives appropriated his script of *You're a Big Boy Now*, claiming (as he'd suspected they would) that since he'd written it on their time, they had a right to keep it. "I had nothing," he recalled. "I had *nothing*. Not even a friend. I had lost all my friends because I was such a success."

Coppola was rescued by veteran producer Frank Mc-Carthy, who was developing a big-budget film for Twentieth Century-Fox based on the life of General George Patton. McCarthy had bought the rights to Ladislas Farago's hot-selling biography of the general and hired the well-known writer Calder Willingham to adapt it for the screen. Now he needed a screenwriter, preferably one with a military background, to compose the actual script. Coppola was at pains to point out that he had actually gone to military school. ("What they didn't know," he noted later, "was that my only military background was playing tuba in a military academy band.") The $50,000 (/$186,000) deal was signed in May and duly reported in the *Hollywood Reporter*, an entertainment trade daily; it was an unusually high fee for a near-fledgling screenwriter. Aside from Oliansky's column in the *Hofstra Chronicle*, the *Hollywood Reporter* story marks the first time anyone in the news media thought Coppola was worth writing about.

"It's ridiculous," he noted not long afterward. "I was five when World War II ended. But since *Is Paris Burning?* I've become a Second World War specialist." Then, with sharp bitterness left over from his French experiences, he added, "But lots of things are ridiculous. People hire you because you might bring with you 'fresh ideas,' and then they make you do what they've always done. Producers are stupid and insecure!" Still, Coppola recognized a big break when he saw one. He put the $50,000 in the bank, moved into an office at Twentieth Century-Fox complete with a motherly secretary, and set right to work on his shiny portable typewriter. It was to take him six months.

In fact, he had barely heard of General George Patton. When McCarthy had first approached him on the screenplay, Coppola thought Patton was a Civil War general. But as he became more familiar with Patton, Coppola began to think of the general as a medieval knight living in the wrong century. "He's a fascinating character. He wrote poetry and was either an illuminated latter-day Don Quixote or a paranoiac causing useless death because of a point of honor."

Coppola never quite resolved that "either/or," which many critics later held against him, but several years later he talked about the script with Stephen Farber and set the critics straight:

> I read all about Patton, and I said, wait a minute, this guy was obviously nuts. If they want to make a film glorifying him as a great American hero, it will be laughed at. And if I write a film that condemns him it won't be made at all. So I came up with what I thought was a brilliant solution, to make him a man out of his time, a pathetic hero, a Don Quixote figure. . . . I thought I would have the best of two approaches. The people who wanted to see him as a bad guy could say, "He was crazy, he loved war." The people who wanted to see him as a hero could say, "We need a man like that now." And that's exactly the effect the movie had, which is why it was so successful.
>
> I was more interested in techniques. I was playing with a presentational style—the idea that you have a character just stand in front of the audience for five minutes, and the audience would know more about him just by looking at him than if you went into his past and told about his family life. That's why the best part of that film, in my opinion, is the opening scene. It was the best scene in my script, too.

Coppola's Patton was more brilliant than corporate-style generals like Dwight D. Eisenhower and Omar Bradley, but his brilliance could emerge only when the less talented (but more highly placed) generals gave him permission. Patton was simultaneously in total command and not in command at all. Critic Michael Ventura, writing some years afterward, considered Patton Coppola's most complete self-portrait.

As 1965 ended, there was still no director set, but Coppola and the executives at Twentieth Century-Fox were talking about John Huston.

The year 1966 would be a big one for Coppola in many ways, but especially in the media. On January 2 the Calendar Section of the Los Angeles *Times* ran a short, admiring profile by Axel Madsen titled "Coppola Breaks the Age Barrier." It was the first piece about Coppola in a general-interest publication.

Several days after Madsen's article came out, the *Hollywood Reporter* confirmed that the *Patton* screenplay was indeed done and added, "Hollywood scuttlebutt is already so enthusiastic that six top male stars have asked to read the script."

The script was even better than that. Four years later it would save Coppola's career.

Chapter Five

A Big Boy Now (1966)

COPPOLA RETURNED TO the bloody battle to direct his first mainstream film, *You're a Big Boy Now*. "I really had to hustle to get that film made," he recalled. "I buffaloed the whole thing through. Nobody wanted me to direct a film."

Coppola allied himself with producer Phil Feldman, who was then in the process of extricating himself from his four-year job as business manager and vice-president at Seven Arts. The company was in the process of merging with Warners, and Feldman decided it was time to go independent. He was an interesting character. A graduate of Harvard Law School, he'd been part of the team that broke the Japanese code during the war. He had gone on to get a job as a lawyer with the powerful Famous Artists talent agency, and from there he had moved directly to Seven Arts. Some people considered him unnecessarily abrasive, since he often ended up being the guy who had to tell people they were fired, but he got on fine with Coppola.

Feldman announced a program of six films, with Coppola's picture at the top of the list. He also soothed everyone's hurt feelings and worked out a deal with Ray Stark to resolve the dispute over who owned the script: Coppola would receive no writer's pay for *Big Boy*, but Stark would pay him a nice bonus when the film went into release. It was a giant break for Coppola, and he owed it to Feldman, whose faith gave him his real start at last. Now all they had to do was get the movie shot.

Coppola went into his Preston Tucker hustler mode. "I don't ask anybody if I can make a movie," Coppola noted a few years later. "I present them with the fact that I am *going* to make a movie, and if they're wise they'll get in on it. In this world of motion pictures, very few can resist getting in on something that looks like it's going. [Feldman and I] were shelling out our own money and using credit cards and what have you. We said we were already making it, that it was almost too late to get in. So Warner Brothers-Seven Arts said, 'Well, we might as well make this movie.'"

Convincing Warner-Seven to come up with the tiny $250,000 (/$902,000) budget had been hard enough. Finding actors proved even harder. Part of the problem was that the central character was nineteen years old, and there were very few young actors who were sufficiently well known to be bankable. Coppola decided to cast relative unknowns in the central roles and surround them with an ensemble of better-known performers, so that even if none of the actors was a big star, the overall impact of the package would suggest stars.

For the leads, he chose Peter Kastner and Karen Black. Of the two, Kastner was the more experienced, since he had actually made a film—a well-received Canadian study of tortured adolescence called *Nobody Waved Goodbye*. Karen Black was an Actors' Studio graduate whose only credit was a Broadway chiller called *The Playroom*. It folded after a month, but her performance had been singled out for special praise by the New York Critics Circle.

Now that Coppola had his unknowns, he needed to sign better-known performers to surround them. "He used to call me up in London from Hollywood in the middle of the night," remembered author David Benedictus, "and say, 'We've been offered Warren Beatty and Natalie Wood and an eight-million-dollar budget, but I knew you wouldn't be interested so I turned it down.' I'd groan and turn over and go back to sleep."

Fortunately, shyness was not one of Coppola's problems. Without the benefit of an introduction (or even courtesy calls to their agents), he phoned Rip Torn, Michael Dunn, and Julie Harris and talked them into looking at the script. That script was his secret weapon. "Many actors, if you show them a script that excites them, they might recognize that it represents something new and go along with you," noted Coppola. The gamble paid off. Every one of his cold-phone-call candidates accepted a supporting role, and W-7 agreed to raise the budget to $1.5 million (/$5.4 million). Later Coppola insisted the film cost only $800,000 in all.

He also sent a copy of the script to Geraldine Page. "I get scripts daily," she said, "but this one made me laugh. *Really* laugh. I had never met this young man, but I trusted him implicitly. . . . The boy is marvelous, really marvelous."

Elizabeth Hartman, who at the time was mainly cast in tremulous, mousy roles, agreed. "This perfect stranger called me up and said he wanted me for this sadistic, *sexy* woman who destroys men with one glance. I nearly cried. I said, 'Have you ever *seen* me? Do you know what I look like?' "

Now Coppola had the actors and the money, but he was discovering that actually shooting the film made preproduction look like a picnic. For one thing, he needed to film key sequences in the main branch of the New York Public Library; but the library had had unhappy experiences with filmmakers in the past, and officials on the library board felt that Coppola's movie would interrupt daily routine. The refused permission.

Desperate, Coppola and Feldman managed to get to Mayor John Lindsay and reminded him of his pledge to cut the red tape that made it so hard for film and TV shows to work on city locations. As it happens, the mayor's office was at that moment preparing an order designed to simplify the permit process, and Lindsay agreed to overrule the library veto.

Coppola rehearsed for three weeks on an empty stage before shooting began, using two scripts—the shooting script (which no actors were permitted to read before the cameras rolled, so their performances wouldn't get stale) and a second, rehearsal script, with extra dialogue. He had intentionally cast against type; now he wanted to give the actors a chance to feel out their characters via improvisation. He observed:

> The entire system of rehearsing actors for films is totally inadequate. In the theater, the actor has sufficient rehearsal time to evolve a role, to get it to a final performance level. But in film, the actor is called upon to hit his performance level for a given scene almost immediately, without having had sufficient time to develop his role. When the film actor *does* have the op-

portunity to rehearse, as he does with Sidney Lumet, he rehearses the film scene by scene, never as a whole. . . . One of the problems in film acting is getting a visualization of the film in its entirely.

Coppola's extended improvisations often had nothing to do with the story of the film; they were intended to let the actors explore their relationships with one another. He had the cast speak dialogue for scenes which, in the film, would be entirely visual and wordless. After a week and a half Coppola brought in a live audience and had the cast play the rehearsal script straight. Now, for the first time, Coppola began to get a sense of what his film was going to be like.

"It taught me a lot," he noted. "How to make shortcuts, how to turn fat characters into thin ones, how to shoot three and four scenes at a time, how to handle the actors." What's more, since the dialogue in the rehearsal script was completely different from the shooting script, the actors could begin filming with their characterizations fully evolved and without sacrificing the freshness that comes from working with new material.

Even with the nudies and *Dementia* behind him, and all his careful preparation, the first day of shooting was tougher than he'd expected. With nine actors and forty crew members looking to him to tell them what to do, Coppola was so nervous he had no idea where the camera went or how to match the action from one shot to the next. Coppola asked the crew to leave the set for half an hour while he figured everything out.

It was easier working outside, on location, where Coppola's familiarity with the new camera equipment and film stock gave him enough leverage with the experienced and skeptical crew to shift the balance of power in his favor. They shot at night, without lights, using Eastman's new high-speed 5251 color film, which let Coppola ride around in the back of a convertible, simply pointing the camera wherever he wanted it. "We were warned that the footage would come out black," he remembered, "but all of it developed beautifully. The old-line technicians baby the film. They work under the theory that you are supposed to create an artificial environment and then control it. But you can never create an artificial environment as beautiful as natural life." (He changed his mind rather drastically on this point, but *One from the Heart* was years away.)

"We shot one scene in a department store. Peter Kastner steals a Gutenberg Bible and is chased into May's department store by fourteen people and a dog with a wooden leg. I wanted to see what would happen when this madness hit May's at 11 in the morning with no one outside the film having the slightest idea what was going on. . . . It was terrific. It started a riot. Little old ladies were having heart attacks. One guy grabbed Peter and started a fight with him—which Peter won. Some kids started ripping Peter's clothes off of him. My only regret is that we didn't have thirty cameras to get everything down on film." Unfortunately, as Coppola himself admitted, the scene was more exciting in real life than in the finished movie.

Roger Corman had taught his protégé how to shoot films in five days. *Big Boy* took twenty-nine days, a short schedule by Hollywood standards, but a long one by Corman's. Coppola felt bad about taking so long (the original shooting schedule had only been fourteen days) and blamed it on the technicians, "who were trying to put us in a box with the way things had always been done before." Coppola's was a typically New Wave complaint. All around the world, light portable equipment was making a new kind of filmmaking possible, but many old-time technicians found it hard to get used to.

In any case, *Big Boy* was shot all over New York, jumping from location to location. "We'd grab three shots in the public library," said Coppola; "then we'd zip across town to grab a couple more; and even though those shots might only appear for a couple of seconds it's just as much work to set them up as if you'd had 40 minutes of straight dialogue. To some of the guys on the crew it was a nightmare, they just couldn't understand what I wanted. Time and again they would arrive with trucks packed tight with all manner of equipment. 'What's all this for?' I'd ask. 'Who needs all this stuff?' "

Coppola was paid only $8,000 (/$29,000) for writing and directing *Big Boy*, and he claimed he turned down a $75,000 writing assignment to do it, but he never said what it was. In any case, he owned 10 percent of the film, so he would get a piece of any profits it made. In fact, he would have done it for nothing. It was his shot. "*You're a Big Boy Now* is a very flashy film in many ways," he allowed four years later. "I would like to be more subtle. But flashy films do attract attention, and whether it is good or bad, my picture succeeded on that score."

Shortly after *This Property Is Condemned* opened to universally savage reviews, the Sunday *New York Times* Entertainment Section printed the biggest, flashiest, nicest feature Coppola had ever received: "Offering the Moon to a Guy in Jeans," by Rex Reed. Structured as a behind-the-camera feature on the filming of *You're a Big Boy Now*, Reed's profile described Coppola (wearing a red T-shirt with the word "Underplay" across the front) as "the Orson Welles of the hand-held camera." It's hard to imagine how Reed arrived at such a remarkable comparison on the basis of three nudies and the silly *Dementia 13*, but it was eminently quotable and set the laudatory tone for an exciting feature full of good quotes and revealing details. It was probably the single most important media break Coppola would ever get.

Coppola came off at his best in Reed's story—charming, articulate, alternately modest and confident. "I can't get used to coming to work every day and watching all these people making more money than my father made in his lifetime, and they're all waiting for me to tell them what to do," he said.

Coppola talked a lot about money in Reed's story, but at the same time he made it clear that he hated big-bucks film-making and would be happier making low-budget art movies in black and white. It was a theme he'd trot out for journalists again and again. "My idea of making a movie is you take four guys and you go out and grab a movie," he insisted. "But there's so much money involved around here that I go around all day depressed. There might be five ways of knocking a chair over, but when you got people like [Julie] Harris and [Geraldine] Page waiting for you, you got no time to experiment. . . . With all these big stars and all these producers with dollar signs in their eyes, I don't know what I'm doing anymore."

And then, for his socko final paragraph, Rex Reed let Coppola set the tone for a career in which the contradictions between big money and film art would provide a constant tension. "Yes, I do know what I'm doing," said Coppola. "I'm turning out the most expensive underground movie ever made."

Is Paris Burning? opened to dreadful pans, and it was probably just as well that Coppola had his hands full editing *Big Boy*. By December 2 *Big Boy* was finished. Presumably

Coppola was pleased with it since he submitted it to UCLA as
his thesis film.

As the title suggests, *You're a Big Boy Now* is the story of
a young man coming of age. Bernard Chanticleer (Peter Kastner) is a bright, personable nineteen-year-old who works in
the stacks of the New York Public Library. He's a terrible klutz,
he's terrified of girls, and to make matters worse, he's stuck
with the most monstrous set of parents (Rip Torn and Geraldine Page) ever set upon God's good earth.

The plot begins when Bernard moves into his own room
in Miss Thing's (Julie Harris's) boardinghouse. Shortly thereafter he meets Amy (Karen Black), an attractive young woman
who works in the library, but he rejects her advances because
he's fallen hopelessly in love with an off-Broadway actress,
Barbara Darling (Elizabeth Hartman). He moves in with Darling, but she proves to be a sadistic bitch, and eventually he
leaves her, confronts his parents, declares his independence,
and ends up with Amy.

The film is well staged by Coppola and very nicely shot
by director of photography (DP) Andrew Laszlo, a talented
cinematographer who went on to become Walter Hill's DP and
shoot (among many others) his stunning *The Warriors*. *Big Boy*
suffers most from an overly precious, heavy-handed style in
the writing and direction, which causes most of the characters
(especially Bernard's parents and Barbara Darling) to become
caricature monsters. There are also too many sequences in which
the characters run aimlessly through the streets of Manhattan,
accompanied by easy-listening rock from John Sebastian and
the Lovin' Spoonful, who also pop up on screen at the oddest
times.

Even so, the visual excitement (running around, etc.) is
one of the film's strongest suits. *Big Boy* tells its story with
images and a sharply observant camera. The best scenes in the
film are those in which Bernard roams the funky streets of
Broadway and Times Square, with Coppola's camera right behind him—documentary sequences that capture a vivid portrait of New York City in the mid-sixties: novelty stores, porno
grind houses, dime-a-dance halls, Merit Farm minimarkets, sex
magazine stores, the Playland pinball arcade, the Automat.

You're a Big Boy Now is an uneven film, with many of the
usual weaknesses of first films by ambitious filmmakers. But in

many ways it's an impressive effort, and it put Coppola on the map as a serious director, as he'd hoped it would.

Less than two years after *You're a Big Boy Now* was finished, he told Joseph Gelmis that he "really hated it. I went through all of this energy [but] by the time I got to make it, I didn't know whether I wanted to make it any more. Because one of the great pities was that I had written it before Dick Lester's *The Knack* came out, and yet everyone said it was a copy. It was definitely influenced by *A Hard Day's Night*. But it was all there already before I even saw *Hard Day's Night*. One of the troubles of the film business is that you're always sort of forced to do things three years later."

Even if, as Coppola has said, the Lesterian style of *Big Boy* was a cliché by the time it came out, he was still proud of the fact that it was the first youth film to use a rock score—after *A Hard Day's Night*. "I wanted to make a film that had the energy of a musical comedy," he noted. "I always thought of *You're a Big Boy Now* as a musical film."

Chapter Six

Two Beards in Missitucky
(1967)

YOU'RE A BIG BOY NOW had its first public screening in December 1966, and Charles Champlin, the respected film critic for the Los Angeles *Times*, devoted most of his review to interviewing the twenty-seven-year-old bearded boy wonder who'd actually made a commercial feature film for his master's thesis.

"There's a fantastic field in the under-a-million-dollar film," the young director told Champlin. "If you're willing to concede on one known personality, and if you make it in color, which is ridiculously easy to do, you know you'll get your money back from TV even if your film falls on its face.

"I want to make films in Denver, Hartford, Seattle, places nobody ever makes films," Coppola went on prophetically. "Give me $400,000 and six guys who love to make films and I'll do it."

Finally Champlin burst into a bemused rave about the movie itself. "It is one of those rare American things, what the Europeans call an *auteur* film," wrote Champlin.

Initially the film opened only in Los Angeles, but Champlin's rave alerted the national press. One month later *Time* magazine hit the street with a review headlined "Growing Up Absurd." It was a mixed review that criticized *Big Boy*'s "custard-pie plot" and "fallen archness" at the same time it praised "some of the wackiest free-association camerawork since Richard Lester made the Beatles work *A Hard Day's Night*." *Time*'s anonymous reviewer should get full points for making a keen prediction. Noting Coppola's vast, undisciplined energy, he (or she) added, "In his first big-league effort, Coppola flashes more than enough talent to suggest that he will make a major movie."

On February 1, 1967, Army Archerd devoted his *Daily Variety* column, "Just for Variety," entirely to Francis Ford Coppola. The hook for Archerd's column was that Coppola had signed a new deal with Seven Arts, and an extraordinarily good one. Coppola would write three films: *The Conversation, The Rain People,* and *The Scarlet Letter.* Best of all, he would get to direct one film, on which he would get an (unspecified) piece of the adjusted gross. This was most unusual; generally, percentage deals (especially for young, relatively powerless filmmakers) are for cuts of the net profit, not the gross, because net profits are calculated by studio accountants using a highly creative bookkeeping system in which huge box-office ticket sales are often swallowed by all sorts of mysterious expenses.*

---

*Unfortunately it is necessary, at some point, to discuss movie money, and this is probably as good a point as any.

Just as Eskimos have twenty words for different kinds of snow (denoting how important snow is in their world), filmmakers have almost as many words for different kinds of money. A quick lexicon of movie money goes like this:

NEGATIVE COST

This is what it costs to make one print of the film including shooting, editing, mixing the sound, and all postproduction.

RELEASE COST

This figure represents the "total cost of making and releasing a film," from preproduction through theatrical release. It is calculated by adding the "negative cost" to the "distribution costs" (making prints, advertising, and, in many cases, about 15 percent of the negative cost to cover studio overhead). Distribution costs are usually calculated as a flat figure, rather than a percentage of the negative cost, because, except for very cheap and very expensive films, distribution costs tend to be about the same regardless of negative cost. On a big film the distribution costs these days are usually around $10 million—most of which goes for TV ads. (Do not confuse distribution costs with distribution fee—a percentage of the income, usually 30 percent, that the distributor deducts before passing any money to the studio, or individuals, that "own" the picture.)

BREAK-EVEN POINT

Hence, to estimate the "break-even point" for a big film, add $10 million (the distribution cost) to the negative cost. This is how much money the distributor must receive to cover its investment. Money received after the break-even point should be called "net profit," but calculation of the sum that gets split up as "net profit points" has become so complicated that many distributors use another term to describe money received after break-even: "in-house profits." In this book, we'll use the more familiar (but less precise) term: "net profit."

GROSSES

Technically, grosses are "all the money taken in at the box office" (less state and federal taxes charged by the theater),

Coppola bragged to Archerd that he'd been offered thirty films as a result of *Big Boy*. He said: "Few of our current filmmakers start from scratch with their own pictures, like, say, a Fellini or a Bergman. You know it's *their* film. That's why I'm only doing originals—if I don't have the guts to do it now I

but

Daily Variety's grosses reflect only "domestic gross"—that is, box-office income from the United States and Canada. "Foreign income" may amount to as much again. It's important, when you read charts and listings of gross income, to determine whether they are reporting domestic or worldwide grosses.

RENTALS

In any case, box-office grosses are not what the distributor gets, nor are they what a director's "percentage of the gross" is based on.

After a theater owner pays federal and state taxes on the box-office gross and deducts a contractually determined amount to cover his basic operating expenses (the "house nut"), he divides what's left into two piles, keeps one, and sends the rest to the distributor. The portion the theater owner sends to the distributor is what filmmakers call "rentals." The percentages vary, depending on how long a film has played. Initially the distributor may receive as much as 90 percent of the take, but that percentage falls off fast. A decent rule of thumb is that by the time a film has played off, "domestic rentals" will probably amount to between 40 and 60 percent of domestic gross.

The relationship between foreign gross and rentals is so complicated that no one has ever tried to establish a rule of thumb. In most cases, "foreign income" is reported as just that, income (not grosses, not rentals). These things vary widely, but it's a safe assumption that on a big film foreign income (to the distributor) will be roughly equal to domestic rentals. But remember, the foreign and domestic distribution rights are often sold to two different outfits, and in any case there are often additional expenses for foreign release.

This means that as a *very* crude rule of thumb, and if the same distributor handles foreign and domestic release, "total worldwide rentals"—i.e., all the money that comes to the distributor from theatrical ticket sales—on a big film will be roughly equal to the domestic gross.

WHEN YOU GET A CUT OF THE GROSS, WHAT DOES THAT MEAN?

A "percentage of the gross" never means a simple percentage of the box-office take. The distributor never sees the box-office take and cannot distribute a percentage of it. When filmmakers speak of a percentage of the gross, it almost always means a percentage of a sum of money called "adjusted gross" which includes worldwide theatrical rentals, plus income from TV sales, cable TV sales, and around 25 percent of the home video sale, minus (occasionally) a 15 percent fee for studio overhead. Furthermore, if you get an up front salary, your cut of the adjusted gross probably doesn't start until the up front salary (really an advance against the percentage) has been earned back.

WHEN YOU GET A CUT OF THE NET, WHAT DOES THAT MEAN?

Generally, unless the film is a giant smash like *Star Wars* and makes so much money that the distributor can't conceal it, a cut of the net means you get nothing. For purposes of calculating net profits to be paid to participants, studios figure distribution costs, which are actually fixed, as a percentage of the rental income; the more money that comes in, the more they deduct for distribution costs. On top of that, people who get cuts of the adjusted gross are paid off first, and those amounts are deducted from the total before "profits" are calculated.

might never have the guts to do it ever. . . . My objective is to make intelligently budgeted pictures. I'm a practical person. I know you can't make pictures that aren't commercial." Archerd let Coppola's reference to Federico Fellini and Ingmar Bergman pass without comment, but it's worth noting that even at this early point in his career Coppola was not shy about classing himself with two of the best-known art filmmakers in the world. (Great filmmakers like John Ford, Howard Hawks, and Alfred Hitchcock denied being artists, whether they truly believed it or not; Coppola has always *insisted* on it.)

On March 21 *You're a Big Boy Now* opened in New York. *Newsweek* ran a rave, plus a short profile that must have made Coppola dance around the house. "Not since Welles was a boy wonder or Kubrick a kid," reviewer Joseph Morgenstern began, "has any young American made a film as original, spunky or just plain funny as this one."

Having said that, Morgenstern hedged his bet ("No masterpiece," he cautioned) before continuing his paean. *"Big Boy* will wow the Presley crowd at rural drive-ins, charm the eyes off those snakes on foreign film-festival juries, pack them in at cosmopolitan art houses, make it acceptable and even fashionable for stars to play small character roles, open the way for other young directors to break into the commercial film world, and provide adults with what they had hoped to get from Hadacol. For kids it will be a national anthem."

Morgenstern noted that Coppola came from a long line of system buckers whose family name is Artist, but at the same time he added that Coppola was getting more offers for work than he could possibly handle and that he wanted to be fat, rich, own a boat, teach film, and endow a children's orchestra. The tension between the beatnik artist and the movie mogul was fast becoming a permanent part of Coppola's media image.

Morgenstern's profile also included a provocative quote that was to haunt Coppola for many years. How did Coppola, a rule breaker and system bucker, get Hollywood to put up $1 million? asked Morgenstern. "I pattern my life on Hitler," said Coppola. "He didn't just take over the country. He worked his way into the existing fabric first. I got to make this film out of strength, not because people liked me."

Howard Thompson's *New York Times* write-up was among the most negative of the major reviews, while Richard Schickel, reviewing the film in *Life*, was little short of vicious. "The difficulty with *You're a Big Boy Now*," wrote Schickel, "is that everyone was so busy turning each other on that no one remembered to ask Mr. Coppola if, in fact, he actually had a personal statement to make or a personal style in which to make it. He does not. . . . It makes one very tired, as self-admiring brattiness always does."

Daily Variety indicates that *You're a Big Boy Now* ran for exactly one week at the Fine Arts in Los Angeles, grossing $5,000. This is not a terrific sum of money; the same week, for instance, *Fahrenheit 451*, another art film, grossed $18,000. It may have done better in Europe, but it bombed in New York, and in 1969, Coppola told an interviewer that it had lost $1 million. When asked how a picture costing $800,000 could lose $1 million, Coppola replied, "You have to figure the studio overheads, plus the advertising and the print and distribution charges. The rough average is about four times the original budget of the picture. But don't let's get into this . . . it's a very tricky and sore area."

Nonetheless, Coppola's thesis committee at UCLA considered *You're a Big Boy Now* adequate proof that he had learned how to make movies, and on March 17 he was awarded a Master of Fine Arts from the theater arts department. Five days later *Daily Variety* reported that he had been signed to direct *Finian's Rainbow* for Warner-Seven. It sounds simple enough, but in Hollywood, where the politics surrounding any big picture assignment are usually nine-tenths beneath the surface, there is much more to any deal than meets the casual eye.

The merger between Warners and Seven Arts, which had been going on for some time, was just now falling into final shape. As a result, longtime studio head Jack L. Warner was cleaning out his desk, and the power was shifting. *Finian* was to be the last film ever made under his name at the company he founded. According to *Variety*'s inside sources, *Finian*'s producer Joseph Landon was set on having Coppola as director, but Warner (who preferred the equally young, equally small-time William Friedkin) considered Coppola too inexperienced—until he was advised that Seven Arts was very high on the forthcoming *You're a Big Boy Now*. *Variety* speculated that Coppola's new assignment might be the first sign of Seven Arts' influence on the older company, and an early clue to the new direction.

In any case, if he had been offered thirty different pictures, as he told Archerd, it's hard to see why Coppola let himself get drawn into *Finian*—a problematic project, as he well knew. He already had his three-picture deal at Seven Arts; he could write an original screenplay of his own choosing, and get paid for writing it, and provided it came within an $800,000 (/$2.8 million) budget, he could produce and direct it, too. It was, from Coppola's point of view, "the best deal in the world."

Furthermore, he was already well advanced on a screenplay for *The Conversation* when he met Landon, who was just starting production on *Finian*. Landon asked Coppola to read the script, which Coppola hated. Then Landon played his ace in the hole: He made Coppola listen to the songs by composer Burton Lane and lyricist E. Y. Harburg. Coppola was familiar with them; hearing them again was a delicious experience. "It must be one of the best scores ever written for an American musical," said Coppola. "And that's how I was persuaded—by the God damn thought of doing all those wonderful musical numbers."

Carmine Coppola was, at that very moment, conducting a road-show production of *Half a Sixpence*. Francis lost no time tracking him down and offering him a job working on orchestrations for the film. Carmine was delighted, and with the prospect of a well-paying Hollywood job, he and Italia moved to California. It was their last move for a long time.

Family loyalty aside, Coppola should have known better than to get involved with *Finian's Rainbow;* it was a Trojan warhorse. When it opened on Broadway in 1947, it charmed progressive audiences with integrationist racial politics and a score loaded with songs that became instant standards: "If This Isn't Love," "Look to the Rainbow," and (the big hit) "Old Devil Moon." But times had changed.

The show was a whimsical fantasy set in a vaguely Appalachian never-never land called Missitucky (a locale roughly as realistic as Shakespeare's Forest of Arden), in which black folks and white folks live in perfect racial harmony. Trouble starts when a white racist senator ("Billboard" Hawkins, obviously modeled on the reactionary Senator Theodore Bilbo of Mississippi, a favorite left-wing target) shows up. However, when Hawkins is magically transformed into a black man, he sees the errors of his ways. Meanwhile, the main character, a charming Irishman named Finian, gets involved with a leprechaun and a pot of gold, while his daughter gets involved with a charming young hustler.

It sounds clumsy in the retelling (and in the perspective of forty years of racial struggle), but it was a daring social parable in 1947, and a hit, too. Why hadn't it been filmed sooner?

Politics, of course. In retrospect, *Finian*'s utopian parable seems perfectly innocent, far less Communist than populist, but it came out during the postwar red scare, and the Senate Permanent Investigations Subcommittee was finding reds under every bed. The subsequent anti-Communist blacklist hit Hollywood filmmakers so hard that no one (aside from John and Faith Hubley, who tried, unsuccessfully, to make an animated version) was willing to risk drawing Joe McCarthy's fire by bringing *Finian* to the screen.

The show languished for twenty years while boycotts, Martin Luther King, CORE, SNCC, freedom rides, and Malcolm X made it clear that more than magic would be needed to break the chains of slavery. By 1967, when the McCarthyist watchdog had become an elderly, disreputable hound with a bad smell and very few teeth, it was finally safe to bring *Finian* to the screen, but it had become hopelessly dated. The songs were still thrilling, but the book was embarrassing.

Coppola could see the pitfalls. "Essentially it was a white man's patronizing statement about civil rights," he observed, "and today it's mild and weak and inadequate." Still, he thought he could beat it. He had always loved musical theater, and he thought *Finian* was a lovely old show. If he could do it right, if he could find the balance, he could make it timeless, like *Snow White*.

The problems started when he discovered, to his horror, that Warners had rewritten the story to make the main character a San Francisco hippie. He hastily restored the screenplay (without credit) to bring it closer to the original.

Nor did Warner-Seven want to spend a lot of money. At that time musicals commonly cost $10 million (/$40 million), but the projected budget for *Finian* was only $3.5 million (/$12.3 million). Warner-Seven knew that Coppola would work comparatively cheaply, but they hired him mainly because they hoped he would bring in the picture on a shoestring budget. Maybe even zip it up like *You're a Big Boy Now*.

Fred Astaire was set to play Finian. That was fine, but the

female lead, Finian's daughter, was still uncast. Following the Beatles and *A Hard Day's Night*, young America had gone mad for English pop, so the studio decided to drag in some trendy Brits to play the Irish-Americans of the mythic South. The studio wanted Petula Clark, a veteran British pop star with a mannered singing style and a hit record ("Downtown"), who was under contract to Warners' record division. Coppola (whose taste in pop music has never been very hip) liked her, and she got the part. Worse yet, Canadian lounge singer-TV star Don Francks and British pop singer Tommy Steele were painfully miscast as, respectively, Petula's boy friend, the young hustler, and Og, the leprechaun.

Coppola gave it his best shot. He rehearsed for three and a half weeks and shot the film in twelve—not an unduly abbreviated shooting schedule, except, perhaps, for Astaire, who was accustomed to longer dance rehearsals. Nor, Coppola remembers, was it a luxury production. To say the least. He wanted to shoot in Kentucky, but the studio refused. Except for eight days on location, he made the entire picture on the Warners' back lot. "Apparently, the studio had spent a heap of money building a forest set for *Camelot* which they wanted to get some more use out of," he recalled.

What with the Warner Brothers–Seven Arts merger, and Jack Warner's leaving after forty-five years, things would have been a bit jagged at Warners even if *Finian* had been going well. The lot was virtually deserted; *Finian* was the only visible activity.

Except for this strange kid hanging around, wearing black chino pants, a white T-shirt, and white sneakers. He was a twenty-two-year-old USC film student named George Lucas, and he was, in his own way, just as famous as Coppola—at least on the student filmmaking circuit. Just a few months earlier, Lucas's student short *THX 1138:4EB (Electronic Labyrinth)* had won first prize in the third National Student Film Festival; everybody who was anybody knew his name. Now he had won a Warner Brothers scholarship competition that entitled him to come to the studio for six months and work in whatever department he wished.

Lucas had dreamed of working in Warners' animation department, home of Bugs Bunny, Daffy Duck, and Wile E. Coyote (created by legendary animators Tex Avery, Bob Clampett,

Friz Freleng, and Chuck Jones). By the time he got there, though, the animation department was long shut down, along with most of the rest of the studio. The only action on the lot was *Finian's Rainbow.*

"I was working on the show, and there was this skinny kid watching for the second day in a row," Coppola remembered. "You always feel uncomfortable when there's a stranger watching you, so I went up to him and asked who he was. We started a conversation, and a friendship." Lucas knew who Coppola was—the twenty-seven-year-old filmmaker was already a legend in the student filmmaking community as the first film school graduate to go big time—and Lucas asked Coppola if he could work with him.

Coppola liked Lucas immediately. "We were the only people on the production under forty or fifty," Lucas remembered. "We both had been to film school, and we both had beards." Coppola was obviously grateful for the chance to discuss nuts-and-bolts filmmaking problems with someone as bright as Lucas, but for some reason he preferred to keep their relationship informal. After two weeks Lucas was ready to walk; as long as he was stuck at a studio without an animation department, he thought he would try to scrounge up some odd ends of film and shoot a movie. Coppola was furious. "What do you mean, you're leaving? Aren't I entertaining enough? Have you learned everything you're going to learn watching me direct?"

Finally, when it became clear that Lucas was determined to move on, Coppola offered him a job as his administrative assistant. He started out taking Polaroids but soon ended up as an adviser in the editing room. He was paid only $3,000 for six months' work, but there was a bonus. Coppola promised him a job on a film he was planning to start as soon as he was rid of *Finian,* something called *The Rain People,* based on a story Coppola had written in 1960 about three housewives who leave their husbands and go off across country in a station wagon. The film would define itself, he explained, during the actual shooting. He also offered to help with a script Lucas was writing for a feature-length adaptation of his prizewinning student short *THX 1138:4EB.*

Despite their mutual interests, the two men couldn't have been more different. Perhaps that's why they became friends.

"In every way we're opposites," Lucas observed, "two halves of a whole. Coppola's very impulsive and Italian and flamboyant and sort of extravagant. I'm extremely conservative and plodding. He was constantly jumping off cliffs and I was always shouting, 'Don't do it, you'll get yourself killed!' He would jump anyway, and for a while nothing too bad would happen. I used to be called the seventy-year-old kid."

There was another big difference, too—one that would take a few years to kick in, but would loom larger as time passed. While Lucas got his art film out of his system with *THX*, and went on to become a master commercial storyteller, Coppola would grow increasingly obsessed with art, often at the expense of the storytelling that had been his strongest suit.

By the end of the second week *Finian* was in real trouble. Coppola's hurried preparations were proving insufficient. Most musicals take a year to plan and six months to shoot; Coppola was working at breakneck speed to get something in the can in twelve weeks. As with *Big Boy*, he was in too much of a rush to match action. He would shoot a scene eight times, and it would be different each time. When the editor tried to combine the pieces of film into a scene, nothing fitted together.

Instead of suspending production while he figured out what to do, he decided to fake it, to shoot the film like a Roger Corman cheapie, making it up as he went along. He started by firing Astaire's longtime choreographer, the legendary (and marvelously named) Hermes Pan, who'd staged most of the numbers for such Astaire classics as *Top Hat* and *Swing Time*. He might just as well have shot himself in the foot. Coppola described Pan as "a disaster." That probably means that Pan disagreed with him or insisted that the camera serve the choreography, not vice versa, or asked for more rehearsal time for the numbers. Pan kept his credit on the film, but he was put off the set, and it's unlikely that his departure made Astaire very happy; the veteran hoofer has rarely seemed so ill at ease as he does in *Finian*.

In any case, lacking a choreographer, Coppola had to stage the numbers himself, and this, as it turned out, was not a great idea. He had concepts for all the numbers, but no dance steps, no "combinations."

His dance numbers were very much like Scopitone films: primitive music videos. "I said, 'Grandish.' I'll shoot it on a hill and have Petula Clark hanging white bed sheets," Coppola recalled. "And 'If This Isn't Love' will be done with children's games. And 'On That Great Come and Get It Day' they're going to throw away all their old furniture in piles." But for the most part the dances were shot with no planning, no set choreography. "I know," Coppola would say, "we'll put a camera here. Fred, you go over there and you do a thing. Then let's get two girls to block in this space. . . ."

The lead dancer, Barbara Hancock (who played a mute dancer named Susan the Silent), burned her feet on a metal stage and was laid up for a week. Sets for the next scene still weren't ready. Coppola couldn't wait; there was simply no margin in the schedule. In desperation, he played the music from two of the big production numbers and told his uninjured cast members to "move to the music" while he directed them from behind the camera, as if *Finian* had been a silent movie. At another point Coppola broke with the first rule of musical filmmaking by hastily redesigning a dance number to fit the camera tracks that were already laid. Pan would have told him that you're supposed to do it the other way around. Maybe he did tell him.

It's hard to imagine a more self-destructive move than firing your choreographer in the middle of a musical. It made such a fatal impact on *Finian* that even Coppola had to admit it. "The choreography was abysmal, let's be honest," he said later.

Having put the film in deep jeopardy, Coppola tried a daring gamble to pull it out: He'd substitute montage for choreography. Thus the production number for "If This Isn't Love," starts with Woody (Don Francks) singing on the hood of a moving truck. At the point where Vincente Minnelli would have broken into dancing, Coppola goes into a series of fast cuts: Woody jumping in a sack race; Woody playing leapfrog; Woody and Sharon (Petula Clark) having a custard-pie fight, playing tug-of-war, and so on.

It's an imaginative idea, but unfortunately it doesn't work, one of the main reasons being that Coppola's fast cutting works against the internal rhythms of the song. Furthermore, as the film continues, and number after number plays out without any dancing, the frenetic montages become maddening. At several points, when Astaire throws in a couple of actual dance turns, you feel like cheering.

Coppola was determined to bring *Finian* in on budget, and he succeeded. Perhaps because he had shot hurriedly, without time to shoot extra angles and close-ups, the editing went quickly, too; there were very few options. He had expert help from veteran cutter Rudi Fehr, who began editing film in the 1920s and had been working at Warners since 1936. And he hired his old UCLA film school rival Carroll Ballard (who later directed *The Black Stallion*) to create the images for a snazzy title sequence and a pretty ending.

One sunny day Coppola and Ballard went out sailing, and although Coppola didn't feel like talking about *Finian's Rainbow*, his disgust with the system was at its maximum. Both filmmakers were desperate to do riskier, more personal pictures than Hollywood would tolerate—but how? Then Ballard seized on a historical precedent.

"Remember how Caesar became Caesar," he counseled. "He left Rome. He went to Gaul and returned to Rome to cross the Rubicon with a powerful army." Maybe, if they wanted to change Hollywood, the best way to do it might be to *leave* Hollywood. Coppola listened, and it made sense; but for the time being he just couldn't see how to do it.

Then, just when Coppola thought *Finian* had done the worst it could do to him, there was one last ugly surprise. For some reason, everyone at Warner-Seven thought Coppola's cheapie musical was going to be a giant hit; the studio executives loved it, and they decided to send it up against road-show blockbusters like *Funny Girl* and *Camelot*. To do that, they blew the 35 mm original up to 70 mm, going from a normal-screen ratio to a wide-screen ratio, and *that* meant they had to crop the top and bottom of the screen—and that meant you couldn't see Fred Astaire's feet when he danced. It was the final insult. Coppola was so upset thinking the abortion might actually be a success that he went home and told Eleanor, "God, why should I become rich and famous because of *this?*" He later added, "They were counting their millions. With all that money at stake, nobody knows *anything.*"

Actually, it's hard to say who was fooling whom, because *Finian* is a pathetically easy call. Despite a few charming scenes (including one in which a young black scientist, Howard, gets shuffling lessons from Senator Billboard's aide), there are so many problems with script, style, singing, and performances that even a studio executive couldn't miss them. For instance, in the middle of the film's most romantic number, "Old Devil Moon," Coppola pulls his camera up into a high-angle crane shot that turns Woody and Sharon into bugs pinned to a museum card. It's exactly the same shot that Hitchcock uses to make audiences squirm, and it destroys the number instantly. As he was to do again and again in musical numbers over the years to come (and with invariably disastrous results), Coppola made the camera, instead of the singers and dancers, the star.

Astaire is wasted throughout. Even in his big number, "When the Idle Poor Become the Idle Rich," instead of letting him dance, Coppola devotes most of Astaire's screen time to having him climb ladders and piles of boxes instead. The only real dancing in the film comes from Susan the Silent, a mute girl who indulges in endless leaping and posing, like a child who's taking second-year ballet and wants to show off.

Finian's Rainbow was a box-office disaster, which came as no surprise to Coppola. "It was an absurd idea to take a $3.5 million musical and send it out to compete with fucking *Funny Girl*, where they had rehearsed the musical numbers for two months!" he complained. But for the brief time before it went into release, Warner-Seven Arts execs still figured they had a musical mastermind, and they offered Coppola $400,000 to direct *Mame*. This time Coppola knew enough to say no.

"I was brought in to direct a project that had already been cast and structured," he remembered years later. "I was also working in a big studio, in a methodology I didn't understand very well. I'd express some doubts about the way things were going, and the people around me would say, 'It's going great!' We had no sour notes on *Finian's Rainbow*. Everyone kept saying how terrific everything was all the time. They were sincere, their motives were pure. But today I try to work with people who won't hesitate to say, 'We're making a mistake.' "

Coppola now turned his main energies to the film he'd told Lucas about, the one he'd started writing before he got sucked into *Finian*—the film he hoped would allow him to escape from the straitjacket of commercial, Hollywood filmmaking: *The Rain People*.

Chapter Seven
We Are the Rain People
(1968–1969)

COPPOLA WAS DETERMINED to shoot *Rain People* like a student film with a tiny crew, just enough people to load the camera and tape the sound.

He had actually started in late 1967, when on his own money he took Lucas, Bart Patton, James Caan, a small group of filmmaking buddies, and a hand-held Bell and Howell movie camera back to Hofstra to shoot a couple of football sequences to use as flashbacks. This footage would serve as a sort of screen test to prove to Warner-Seven Arts how great his wacky movie was going to be. Lucas worked as assistant cameraman, art director, production manager, and sound recordist, thereby displacing three (if not four) union technicians. Although W-7 liked the footage, union reaction was predictable; Coppola was in deep trouble even before he started.

Instead of going to the New York union, which was reputed to be tough, Coppola cut an unorthodox deal with IATSE (International Alliance of Theatrical Stage Employees and Moving Picture Machine Operators of the United States and Canada).

The kind of deal that Coppola wanted seems both straightforward and reasonable from the point of view of the filmmaker—you assemble a small crew, and you make your film wherever you want—but it went against every hard-won union agreement. State lines are technically uncrossable for union film workers. When a California crew comes to shoot location

scenes in New York City, for instance, the New York local requires the producer to hire New York technicians to "cover"
them. At first it seemed as if the union would be willing to
bend the rules for him, but then negotiations broke down. "They
are a little upset about it," Coppola admitted. "They think I'm
sort of a rat, I guess. They're starting to pull stuff like, 'Well,
he put a towel over the rug, a prop man should do that.' You
can't make a movie with that sort of thing going on. It's starting
to be 22 guys waiting around on expensive salaries for me to
have an experience."

Nevertheless, he pushed ahead. He convinced Shirley
Knight to play the lead and talked Warner-Seven into committing $750,000 (/$2.5 million), a very small sum. In early April
Coppola took his small crew back to Hofstra's Long Island
campus to pick up a few more location shots. There, Richard
Koszarski approached him to tape an interview for WVHC-FM,
the college radio station. Coppola talked about union problems
and his early career, including the now-infamous Hitler quote.

"Sometimes you pull shocking images out of the wood-
work to make a point," he explained, "and the point I was
trying to make was that all the young film students I knew who
wanted to make films sat up in the hills and talked about it,
and I went out into the Establishment, and was very sharply
criticized by my friends as being a total sell-out. My allusion
to Hitler was simply that he wasn't a revolutionary who came
down from the hills. He wormed his way into the government,
became a part of it, and then used that to take it over. The way
to come to power is to make a place in the Establishment and
then challenge and double-cross the Establishment."

Coppola's seventeen-man crew was the kind of double cross
he meant, as he lost no time in pointing out. "[The union is]
at my door every day," he complained. They called me down
and exerted pressure on Warner-Seven Arts for sponsoring me.
I said, 'Fine, but I'm going to make the movie anyway. I'm
taking a crew across the country for five months and how can
I take a [large] crew like that for a picture that's a personal
statement? Maybe if this was Cary Grant, or a big commercial
movie, you could spend five million dollars. But my movie just
isn't that kind of movie.' "

Part of the reason Coppola could get away with such a
small crew for his film was that he was using state-of-the-art

equipment—cameras and editing machines that French New Wave directors had been using for a decade but that the Hollywood establishment was just beginning to hear about. Coppola had spent $80,000 of his *Finian* money to buy it, but it would be worth it; *The Rain People* gave him a chance to show Hollywood what could be done with the new filmmaking technology.

Accompanying the production was an editing room on wheels, built around a new German editing table called a Steenbeck. Coppola called it "the editing machine of the future." It was steady and sophisticated, had excellent sound, and had actually been available for some time, but there probably wasn't a single one in all of Hollywood, where the clumsier (but more familiar) Moviola was still the editing machine of choice.

When Coppola couldn't buy what he wanted, he had it designed. Some of the custom equipment was unexpectedly complicated; when a new blimp (a silencing device for the camera) designed by Carroll Ballard was delivered to the location, it took Coppola three days to figure out how to work it.

Still, figuring out how to run the equipment was one thing; deciding what to *do* with it was something else. Coppola knew how the story would start: A pregnant woman, played by Shirley Knight, leaves her husband and starts driving. Beyond that, Coppola planned to let the film take its own direction; he would write the script while they filmed.

"It's about an automobile trip," he said, "and our entire unit will take that trip. We have very few vehicles, very few people, and everything we need to make a movie is mobile and goes with us. We'll be gone for three or four months. We start on Long Island, but literally we don't know where we're going to go. We might make a right turn, we might make a left."

As summer 1968 turned to fall, Coppola and his company (now grown to twenty) took to the road in a caravan of seven vehicles equipped with two-way radios. The collective included a number of longtime Coppola associates and some newcomers who were about to *become* longtime associates: George Lucas, Hofstra buddy James Caan (known, at the time, primarily for his performances in two Howard Hawks films, *El Dorado* and *Red Line 7000*), Robert Duvall (mainly known for his small role as Boo Radley in *To Kill a Mockingbird*), editors Barry Malkin and Richard Marks, and Mona Skager (an elegant, hard-looking woman who remained with Coppola for many years). They spent four months on the road, sleeping four to a room in cheap motels. Nobody saw much money. Coppola passed out "unofficial certificates redeemable for original certificates good for one percent of the film's net profits" but, of course, there never were any profits. Profits might have spoiled the fun.

Actress Shirley Knight was the only celebrity in the caravan, and the reason Warner-Seven Arts was risking $750,000. In 1960, at age twenty-three, she had been nominated for Best Supporting Actress for her second film role, in *The Dark at the Top of the Stairs;* she had been nominated again, two years later, for *Sweet Bird of Youth.* More recently she'd had strong character-roles in *The Group* and *Petulia,* and the female lead in *Dutchman,* a British screen adaptation of a tense racial allegory by LeRoi Jones (now known as Imamu Amiri Baraka). Although he didn't know her, Coppola had always wanted to work with Knight. "I thought she was very good," he said. "She seemed like an American actress who had some substance."

Coppola had more or less forgotten about "Echoes," his unfinished story about the three housewives who go off together in a station wagon, when he ran into Knight at a film festival. She was putting in a personal appearance to help publicize *Dutchman,* and she was crying. "Someone had been rude to her, or something," Coppola remembered. "I went up to her and said, 'Don't cry, I'll write you a movie,' and she said, 'You will? That's sweet.' And I did. . . . Most of my life has been influenced by romantic preconceptions. The idea of writing a film for an actress and making it together, like [Michelangelo] Antonioni and Monica Vitti, really appealed to me."

At the same time he introduced a minor character who had not been in the original story, a brain-damaged football player to be played by James Caan. Much later, during the editing of *The Rain People,* when Coppola became displeased with Knight's performance, he started to throw more weight to Caan. "That is definitely the flaw of the film," Coppola noted some years later. "I should have stuck with her. I chickened out."

If *The Rain People*'s production style was utopian, it fell somewhat short of idyllic. Coppola had decreed that things would move more smoothly (and more cheaply) if the expedition excluded wives and girl friends, but as director, he considered himself exempt from the prohibition; Eleanor and the kids accompanied him on the road. In addition, Lucas remembers being stuck in a cheap motel room in Blue Ball, Pennsylvania,* with no phone, no TV, and no restaurant while Coppola spent the weekend in New York. "Francis was saying all this 'all-for-one' stuff, and then he goes off and screws around in New York," recalled Lucas. "He felt he had a right to do that, and I told him it wasn't fair. We got into a big fight over it."

To make matters worse, Coppola began to have tremendous arguments with his headstrong star. She didn't trust him, he complained. She was "acting"; she was looking out for herself. Coppola said:

> She preferred the theater. I came along and promised this wonderful, idealistic kind of filmmaking. When we started to work, she realized that it had some realities to it as well, and perhaps she started to feel that this was just another Hollywood movie. . . . Maybe I was angry at her, I don't know. The character, as I had written it, had a lot of the schizophrenia that comes out in the film, but there was also a tremendously compassionate side. The whole basis of the character was that she was a mother, a mother figure. And I didn't feel that I was getting that from Shirley. I would get the high-strung, nervous intensity. I don't know how much I liked that character I saw, whereas I liked the character I had written.

Just like the character she was playing, Knight was pregnant. The roadside diner food made her queasy, and she disliked the cramped travel. She was also increasingly uncomfortable with the direction the film was taking. For one thing, she hated doing semi-nude sex scenes and hadn't expected there would be so *many* of them. Coppola had assured her she didn't have to worry about taking her clothes off, but

---

*This memorably monickered locale may be a figment of Lucas's fertile imagination.

now, as the concept of the film changed from day to day, all bets were off.

"If he had done everything he had said he was going to do, it would have been a marvelous film," she declared. Instead, to her dismay, when some of his original plans proved too difficult to execute, he simply abandoned them and filled in the gaps with more and more *plot,* in which dramatic fireworks substituted for the psychological subtlety he'd promised. "The human reactions and relationships just go out the window," she complained.

Worst of all, Knight seemed to be the lone dissenter amid an abjectly worshipful Coppola clique. She was one of the first (but far from the last) of Coppola's collaborators to discover the difficulty of being a no-person among the yes-men. "Coppola kept around him a lot of people who continually told him that he was an absolute genius," she related after the shoot. "I guess I was a constant reminder to him that this wasn't really so."

For the others, though, the cross-country adventure was mostly fun. "There are those of us who still talk about the cookouts in the back of the sound truck," Caan recalled many years later. The film grew under their eyes; scenes were shot across eighteen states, sent back to New York City for processing, and returned within three days so they could be edited en route. Oddly enough, despite the cross-country ramble, Coppola didn't shoot many exteriors; most of the scenes were shot inside motels and cars.

At one point the material started to pile up so fast they called a five-week halt and dug in at the Lakeway Lodge in Ogallala, Nebraska, so editor Barry Malkin (a childhood buddy from Queens) could assemble a string-out—a fast-and-dirty preliminary edit. Lucas prevailed on Coppola to hire his talented fiancée, Marcia Griffin, as a temporary assistant editor, neatly sidestepping the prohibition against wives and girl friends.

It was as close to a vacation as any of them got, and everyone (Coppola included) was feeling good. This was the way to make movies, all right. The city fathers of Ogallala were so tickled to have real live filmmakers in town that they offered to turn an abandoned grain warehouse into a sound stage. Coppola declined, but it reminded him of his conversation on the sailboat with Carroll Ballard. You don't have to make movies in Hollywood, he thought, you can make them *anywhere.* Hofstra. Ogallala. Even . . . San Francisco. San Francisco? Why *not* San Francisco? "We started fantasizing about the notion of going to San Francisco," Coppola remembered, "to be free to produce films as we had done on *Rain People*. It was a beautiful place to live, and had an artistic, bohemian tradition."

Meanwhile, Coppola scrounged up $12,000 for Lucas to shoot a 16 mm cinéma vérité documentary on the production. There were undoubtedly moments when Coppola regretted the decision, such as the time Lucas turned up, camera in hand, tape recorder over his shoulder, to record happily a tense confrontation between Coppola and Shirley Knight. (Ultimately Lucas decided to be discreet and not use the footage.)

Nonetheless, the documentary (eventually titled *filmmaker: a diary by george lucas*) kept shooting, and it's anything but a puff piece. It reveals Coppola at his most manic: shouting at Warners executives over the long-distance phone, shaving his beard so he wouldn't look like a hippie during a swing through the Southwest, desperately rewriting the script to include found events like a parade in Chattanooga, and moaning, "I'm tired of being the anchor when I see my world crumbling."

For all its jagged edges, *The Rain People* was an immensely important experiment. The improvisatory approach to filmmaking clearly filled Coppola with excitement. It was art, at last.

He felt he had found his style, his métier. *This* was how he would make movies. And when the caravan swung through San Francisco on its last leg into Los Angeles, Coppola looked at Lucas and said, "This is great. Let's move."

In early August the *Hollywood Reporter* printed a short item on Coppola headlined FRANCIS COPPOLA TO MAKE ONLY OWN STORIES IN FUTURE. In it Coppola reported that *The Rain People* had cost $740,000 and had taken 105 days to shoot (including, apparently, the layover time in Nebraska). Two weeks later he signed with Creative Management Associates, one of the most prestigious talent agencies in Hollywood. Shortly thereafter he announced that his next movie would be *Heaven Can Wait*, a remake of *Here Comes Mr. Jordan*, starring Bill Cosby. He also declared that he was leaving Hollywood; henceforward he would work in San Francisco, making personal, noncommercial films.

On October 9, only hours before the world premiere of

Finian's Rainbow, Coppola sat down with Joseph Gelmis in
New York City to do a career interview that covered a great
deal of ground. Coppola seemed to be nervous and under great
emotional stress, as well he might have been. *Finian's* turkey
was about to lay an egg.

He made no excuses, at least not for *Finian,* but his mood
had darkened astonishingly since the *Rain People* shoot. He
said:

> It's come to the point where I just want to get out
> altogether. . . . I'm fed up. It takes too much out of
> you. You don't get enough for it, in whatever com-
> modity you're dealing in. I think a lot of people are
> jealous of me. My contemporaries say, 'Well, there he
> is, 28, 29 years old, he's got a lot of money and he's
> making movies.' . . . They just think I'm living this
> golden life, and they don't realize that I am really
> straining and endeavoring to find some honest bal-
> ance with myself. . . .
>
> I'm thinking of pulling out and making other kinds
> of films. Cheaper films. Films I can make in 16
> mm. . . . It's not just opening night jitters. I've been
> thinking about this for six months. I'm tired. I never
> knew that so many people wished you failure. I didn't
> realize.

At the same time Coppola remained enthusiastic about
producing Lucas's science-fiction film, and cited it as his most
immediate commitment. It would be filmed, he said, in Japan
in the spring of 1969. "George is going to direct it in his own
way," Coppola promised. "It's all based on my strength now.
If *Finian* is a flop it's going to hurt George more than anybody.
I'm giving him my strength. I'm saying, 'If you want me, you've
got to give George Lucas his break.' Well, if suddenly they
don't want me, then George has got a problem."

The next morning the *Finian* reviews hit the street, and
they were not good news. Renata Adler, writing for *The New
York Times,* loathed it. The *New Yorker's* Pauline Kael didn't
like the film much more, but she was far more sympathetic.
"Coppola has done pretty well, or probably as well as could
be done short of rethinking the whole thing," she wrote. "Trying

for freshness and speed and an ethereal *Midsummer Night's Dream* atmosphere, he makes a pastiche of visual styles and lyrical effects out of what was already a pastiche. Obviously, he can't make anything good out of it; the best he can hope for is to keep the show moving, and he manages to do that."

The unsigned review in *Time* was less charitable (and much funnier). Headlined "Instant Old Age," it began by noting that "The American Negro has endured Little Rock and Selma; he will survive Missitucky," and went on to poke fun at "a lot of galvanic twitching that goes on in the name of choreography. Even so, the movie might have survived were it not for the ham-handed direction of Francis Ford Coppola, 29."

The best review *Finian* got was from the government of South Africa, which banned it as a threat to apartheid.

As 1968 turned into 1969, *Finian* died quietly at the box office. Coppola returned (with considerable relief, one imagines) to editing *The Rain People* with Barry Malkin. He screened rough cuts of *Rain* for small groups of friends; one preview audience even included Henry Miller and Michelangelo Antonioni. "Miller seemed to really dig it," Coppola said, "and Antonioni told me he liked it very much. But I'm on guard— nobody tells the truth at these things."

An important newcomer joined the Rain Persons during the sound edit. Walter Murch, a tall, gentle-mannered man with a deep voice, a walrus moustache, and a BMW motorcycle, was an old USC buddy of Lucas's. Just out of school, he was cutting TV ads at a Los Angeles commercial company partly owned by cinematographer Haskell Wexler. One morning he got a call from Lucas, asking him if he'd like to edit the sound for Coppola's movie.

"Francis met me," recalled Murch, "apparently liked me, and said, 'Here's the film, cut the sound.' He probably had heard enough from George, and that was enough for him." They had just one screening of the film together before Murch set to work.

Murch was installed in a little house in Benedict Canyon, in the Hollywood Hills, all by himself, with the film, a Nagra, a Moviola, and a transfer machine; he proceeded to try to make sense of it all. "I was frightened that it would be found out that somebody nonunion was cutting the sound," he remembered, "and I'd lose this chance to work on a feature. As a result, there are no library sound effects in the film at all, because I was afraid to go to the library. It probably was good in the long run, because it forced me into thinking up techniques and ways of doing things that I had to pull out of myself, rather than asking somebody who'd done it fifty times, 'What is the way to do this?' "

Murch was both nervous and thrilled to be left totally on his own. "Francis had a tendency to hire people and give them a great deal of freedom to do what they were doing and authority over their own domain," he said. "So in a sense you feel an upwelling of responsibility for *him*. 'He's given me so much freedom; therefore, I must take great care that this will all work out best.' It's paradoxical. By his giving so much freedom and authority to you, you feel much more beholden to him."

In August 1969 *Rain People* opened in New York City, nearly one year after Coppola and crew had shot it. Although it has its problems, it was easily the best (and most promising) film Coppola had made to date. As it opens, the main character, twenty-six-year-old Natalie (Shirley Knight), decides to leave her husband, a nice Italian-American guy with whom she has a good relationship. She's discovered she's pregnant, and is uncertain about the direction of her life as a married woman. She takes the car and heads off in no particular direction. Along the way she picks up Kilgannon, a brain-damaged ex-football player (James Caan). She plays at seducing him, but after a while she grows bored, finds him a job at a small roadside zoo, and tries to leave him behind. When Kilgannon gets in trouble for releasing all the animals, she returns to pay his fine. Upset with Kilgannon for making her feel guilty, Natalie takes up with Gordon, a caustic state trooper (Robert Duvall), but Kilgannon gets in a fight with Gordon and Gordon shoots him. Natalie decides to return to her husband.

Despite pretentious photography and too many wordless flashbacks (to fill in exposition and in lieu of interior dialogue), the premise of *The Rain People* is both intriguing and timely, especially so long before feminism became a familiar subject in the mass media. Coppola's graceful dialogue (one of the strongest elements in the film) captures this premise perfectly. When Natalie (Knight) calls her husband to explain (to herself as much as to him) why she's run away, she says, "I used to wake up in the morning and it was my day. Now it belongs to you."

Had Coppola's story been as strong as his dialogue, *The Rain People* might have been a masterwork; unfortunately his attempt to write the script as he went along didn't work; the climax of the film is both gratuitously violent and unbelievable, and the ending (in which Natalie returns to her husband) undercuts the entire film.

Nor does the improvised story line allow Coppola to maintain a tight focus on the central issue: a woman fighting for her soul. Instead, the heroine turns into a villainess of sorts. Natalie seems intensely neurotic (often speaking of herself in the third person: "Yes, she's married"), selfish, insensitive, and sadistic (at one point she orders the retarded jock to kneel to her; later she makes him watch while she puts on makeup for a date with another man, taunting him nastily). By the end of the film, when she first takes up with the brutal policeman, and then goes tamely back to her husband, we've stopped caring about her.

Nonetheless, given the dimensions of the artistic challenge the twenty-nine-year-old Coppola set for himself, *The Rain People* is more to be praised than blamed. Less childish and show-offy than *You're a Big Boy Now*, it remains a serious film about real people in a real America.

The film was not as widely reviewed as *Finian's Rainbow*. *The New York Times* assigned its second-string critic, Roger Greenspun, who (quite properly) ignored the specifics of *how* the film had been made to focus on what ended up on the screen. He liked the performances ("intelligent actors who do their roles proud") and added that Coppola "has made a relentlessly good-looking, accurate-feeling movie without the patronizing paranoia toward the American heartland and its natives that is so much in fashion these days." (He was referring, no doubt, to the tremendously popular *Easy Rider*, which had also just opened.) At the same time, Greenspun hated the ending, which he characterized as a "cowardly retreat," and "the worst thing in the movie."

Newsweek's Joseph Morgenstern, who had written one of the few sympathetic reviews of *Finian*, decided to abandon Coppola's sinking ship. His review, titled "Cryin' in the Rain," took Coppola to task for an overly literary, unfocused script.

"Where's the complexity," he complained, "the vitality, the tumbling unpredictability of life? There's no good reason why Coppola should keep hitting us over the head, to the point of mass brain damage, with his hero's innocence and his heroine's neurosis."

Like the *Times*, the *Village Voice* let its second-stringer, Molly Haskell, mop up *Rain People*. She looked at the film every bit as seriously as Coppola, perhaps a bit more seriously, and did not like what she saw. "Coppola, one of the most technically proficient of the new directors, proves himself, once again, a master of the visual cliché."

Still, Coppola had every right to be proud of the film. He was undoubtedly even prouder of the last credit at the end of the film: "Produced by American Zoetrope, San Francisco."

Chapter Eight

Utopia Lost:
American Zoetrope
(1969–1970)

WHILE HE PREPARED the final cut of *The Rain People,* Coppola was also laying the groundwork for his San Francisco studio, a utopian facility to be called American Zoetrope. It was named after a nineteenth-century movie toy invented by William George Horner, a spinning, slotted cylinder that showed simple, hand-drawn animation, but Coppola liked to point out that the name really came from the Greek words for "life" and "movement." Initially Lucas and Coppola had just wanted a little studio where they could mix and edit their films, but soon Coppola was speaking of American Zoetrope in more grandiose terms as a *filmmakers'* facility, an energy center where the newest technology could be put to work in the service of art.

Coppola and Lucas had started looking for a northern California base as early as July 1968. Among other things, Coppola wanted a nice place to raise his kids, and he found the "political and cultural ferment" in the Bay Area stimulating.

Late in 1968 Coppola, Lucas, and *Rain* producer Ron Colby made a fact-finding expedition to Denmark to look at a state-of-the-art facility called Lanterna Films. Ever since *Big Boy* Coppola had been talking about high-tech equipment as the key to a new kind of filmmaking. He fell instantly in lust with the expensive editing and mixing equipment at Lanterna; he wanted it, all of it. Burning for hardware, on the way home he stopped off at the Photokina film trade show in Cologne, Germany, and spent $80,000 he didn't have on an impulse purchase: a complete high tech sound-mixing system.

Coppola still had some funds, but even when he sold his house in Los Angeles, he didn't have enough to pay for the fully professional state-of-the-art facility he wanted. Warner-Seven had just gone through another corporate take-over. The new owner was a conglomerate called Kinney (best known for its parking lots), the head of production was talent agent Ted Ashley, and most of Coppola's friends and associates were gone. None of the new executives had any movie experience; Coppola must have felt that his seven years with W-7 gave him far greater seniority than the corporate newcomers had. Nonetheless, in a desperate bid for cash, Coppola decided to pitch them a package of low-budget script ideas.

He proposed to develop seven films, none of which would cost more than $1 million (/$3.2 million) to shoot. One was *The Conversation*, which, it was rumored, would star Marlon Brando, cost a mere $400,000 (/$1.3 million), and take only four weeks to shoot; another was George Lucas's high-prestige science-fiction feature, *THX 1138*, which Coppola would personally produce, oversee, and deliver. When Ashley seemed hesitant, Coppola impulsively threw in a film that Lucas and John Milius were working on, called *Apocalypse Now*. In fact, Coppola had no right to pitch *Apocalypse*. He wasn't involved with it in any creative way; Lucas had merely mentioned it to him once. But it seemed like a good idea at the time, and Lucas was pleased that Francis had managed to sell it for him.

At this point the W-7 execs were still high on *Finian*, and for all they knew *The Rain People* was about to become the new *Easy Rider*. They agreed to put up $3.5 million, but they may have suspected that *Finian*, *Rain*, *THX*, and *The Conversation* would die at the box office because their commitment was less than ironclad and Coppola's position was less than ideal. W-7 held all the high cards. The money it was giving Coppola was not an option, not an advance, not even an investment. It was a loan; if W-7 decided to pull out, Coppola would actually owe the company all the money it had put up.

Coppola was confident he was making the right move. "All I want from Hollywood is their money," he said. "I will be 30 years old this year, and I view that as a turning point. I want to get down to business. I'm already involved with several political theater groups [in San Francisco], and I've come to the conclusion that I'm not a hired-hand director. For good or bad, whether they are awful or terrific, I want to make movies I give a damn about. And that means the script must come from me."

In June 1969 Coppola, Lucas, Colby, and *Rain* production associate Mona Skager returned to the Bay Area with W-7's $3.5 million to find a home for American Zoetrope. With the help of John Korty, a filmmaker who lived in Marin County, they located three Marin County sites that seemed right, but their bids were unsuccessful. Time was running short; the sound equipment was due to arrive from Germany any day, and there was nowhere to put it.

Finally everyone except Lucas (whose heart was set on Marin) agreed that a large San Francisco Victorian house might make more sense than a suburban Marin County facility. They never found a Victorian, but the die was now cast in favor of San Francisco. Late in June Coppola bought a warehouse at 827 Folsom Street, in an industrial area to the south of Market Street that Jack London used to call "south o' the slot." Fashionable eclectic-modern interiors designed by Eleanor quickly transformed the warehouse; journalist Gerald Nachman described it as "a collision of Creative Playthings and Paraphernalia—red, white and blue brick walls, bubbly chairs, blowups of famous old directors and zebra-stripe slashes of color."

Incorporation papers were filed on November 14, 1969. Coppola was president (and sole shareholder); Lucas was vice-president; Skager was secretary-treasurer; Korty was first tenant. They installed Christopher Pearce as general manager. Producer Bart Patton and editor Bob Dalva (later director of *Return of the Black Stallion*) were involved as well, and Coppola's old film school friend Dennis Jakob soon appeared, too.

Lucas and Coppola found themselves at odds. Lucas had hoped for a small operation; Coppola's heart was set on a major facility, complete with an airport and a fleet of helicopters. Lucas suggested naming it Transamerican Sprocket Works; Coppola thought that sounded too much like a rock group and held out for American Zoetrope, on the theory that the initial *A* would put them at the top of the New York Stock Exchange board when (not if) the company went public.

Even while they were uncrating the German editing equipment and setting up shop, Lucas was calling all his old film school pals—John Milius, Walter Murch, Gloria Katz, Willard Huyck, et al.—urging them to come north and join the adventure. Meanwhile, Coppola and his family bought a house on Webster Street, in ritzy Pacific Heights.

Warner-Seven was happy. Coppola was happy. Every day letters and phone calls were going back and forth between Coppola and Stanley Kubrick, Mike Nichols, and John Schlesinger, all of whom wanted to get involved with American Zoetrope, or so Coppola said.

One evening Coppola was making dinner, filling a pot with water at the conference room sink, when the phone rang; he left the water running while he took the call. It was Orson Welles, who wanted to discuss shooting a 16 mm feature at Zoetrope! Coppola was so excited, and so scared of putting Welles on hold, that he let the water run while the call went on and on, totally flooding the conference room.

Coppola was in terrific spirits. An associate from that time remembered one evening when a secretary went to the refrigerator, looking to make a sandwich, and asked Coppola, "Got any bread?" Running on autopilot, he reached in his pockets, started pulling out cash, and graciously tried to hand it to her.

On another occasion Coppola took a crowd of filmmakers out to dinner and, when he couldn't find a parking place, pulled into a red zone.

"Francis, you're not above the law!" one of his pals warned.

"Yes, I am," Coppola replied blithely. "I *am* above the law." (When they returned after dinner, Coppola's car had been towed away.)

San Francisco Mayor Joseph Alioto threw a giant press party, an orgy of self-congratulation to celebrate the opening of American Zoetrope; conveniently ignoring New York City, he called it San Francisco's debut as "the nation's second-biggest motion picture center." Introducing Coppola, he boasted that the filmmaker had spent $500,000 on the physical plant, which was already providing facilities for cinematographer Haskell Wexler (who was working on the Maysles brothers' *Gimme Shelter*, a documentary about the Rolling Stones' disastrous concert at nearby Altamont) and writer-director John Korty (who was finishing up *Riverrun*). Finally Coppola took center stage. "In San Francisco," he declared, "movie makers have total control and total freedom. The difference is that in

Los Angeles you talk about deals, and here you talk about film."
Asked to describe the kind of films he'd be making in San
Francisco, Coppola replied, "Personal, original, rather hip."

The first thing Coppola did was install a pool table and a
large, gleaming espresso machine in the main reception area.
The second thing he did was publish a catalog, an amazing,
handmade document featuring Art Nouveau graphics, text boxes
with optimistic aphorisms like "FILM IS LIFE—GEORGE [sic]
MÉLIÈS," "PRESENCE" and "BEWARE OF IMITATORS,"
and a section on studio services headlined THE DEPARTMENT
OF HYPERBOLIC MARVELS. The copywriting was archly Victorian: "Our studio services are but the FINEST, second to none
and in every way SUPERIOR."

If you read between the hippie babble, American Zoetrope really did have some interesting toys. Arriflex 35 mm
cameras, Eclair 35 mm and 16 mm cameras, a Super-8 mm
camera rigged with a sync-pulse generator for shooting sync
sound, Nagra portable sound recorders, lights and sound blimps
(mostly left over from *The Rain People*)—all were available
for rent.

There were also soundproofed editing rooms equipped with
advanced Keller (KEM) and Steenbeck editing machines for
16 mm and 35 mm. In fact, Coppola had the only three-screen
KEM in California. Much like Marshall McLuhan, who insisted that the medium was the message, Coppola was convinced that the equipment was the aesthetic, and despite
resistance from many film editors, he continued to champion
the new editing machines. "You go to a Hollywood editor," he
said, "and he'll say, 'Aw, you can't cut film on that.' It's true,
you can't cut on a Steenbeck the way you cut on a Moviola,
but if you adapt yourself you can do it faster. It's like taking a
guy who flies a biplane and showing him the controls of a 707.
He's going to say, 'Aw, I can't fly this.' I think much of the
problem in American film technology is that everyone's too fast
to say 'It's no good,' without realizing that with new technologies will come new techniques."

Zoetrope's advanced Keller sound system could record, play
back, mix, and transfer sound from any one of seven strips of
film to any other, and run that sound in sync with any image
from 70 mm down to Super-8 and video. (It was so advanced,
in fact, that no one in America could repair it; all the instruc-

tions were in German, and when it broke down, a repairman had to come from Hamburg. Chris Pearce joked that the machine ought to come with a built-in telex circuit to Germany.) There were rooms for art, wardrobe, props, transfer, and coating, a kitchen, and a refrigerated facility for storing film. There was even a Dodge van nicknamed HAL after the crazed computer in *2001*. The editing rooms were available from $175 per month; editing machines went for $240 per month and up.

Not everyone was impressed. A few visiting production experts noted that Zoetrope's facilities were terrific only so long as you wanted to shoot like Coppola: on location and using available light. Nobody at Zoetrope cared two beans what the experts said. The Zoetropers had seen the future, and it was them; no soreheads were going to spoil it.

"A lot of the things I talked about years ago are beginning to happen," Coppola bragged. "I'm sitting here with the means of making films at intelligent costs. I've also got good relationships with some of the more talented young filmmakers around, because I was the one who stuck out his neck to give them the chance. . . . I believe in a couple of years we'll be far bigger and more important than any two major Hollywood studios put together."

One of his business schemes involved signing all the young Zoetrope filmmakers to long-term contracts; he had been thinking that Roger Corman, his old exploitation movie boss, had missed a great chance by not doing it. "Francis saw Zoetrope as a sort of alternative *Easy Rider* studio where he could get a lot of young talent for nothing," said Lucas, "make these movies, hope that one of them would be a hit, and eventually build a studio that way."

Word about Zoetrope spread fast, partly through enthusiastic articles in the small film magazines. Coppola was deluged with thousands of proposals, but they just seemed to fan the flames of his enthusiasm. He hired Jess Ritter, who had written a magazine article about a police riot during the violent People's Park confrontations in Berkeley, to turn the article into a screenplay, *Santa Rita*; then he hired UCLA film school grad Steve Wax to direct it. He funded another director on the basis of a twelve-minute film school short.

One night, no doubt feeling a bit like an anthropologist observing the mores of some exotic tribe, Coppola ventured into the notorious Saturday midnight show at the Palace Theater in North Beach. He had never seen anything like it, nor had many others outside San Francisco.

Midnight at the Palace was a combination of the hippies' (especially gay hippies') last stand and a kiddie matinee with the matron asleep. You bought your ticket at a minaret-shaped box-office kiosk, from an exotic young woman named Koelle, who was clothed and made up like the world's sexiest *Arabian Nights* houri. Then you entered the giant ornate theater to find onstage the Cockettes—a chorus line of bearded, gauzily clad transvestites—singing raucously and dancing a chaotic, comical cancan that displayed everything they weren't wearing under their dresses.

There were movies, too—old cartoons, avant-garde shorts, classics, and camp—but the movies were beside the point. The audience was there not to see but to be seen. People greeted friends in yells and shrieks, threw popcorn, talked back to the screen, and wandered around the auditorium to show off their crazy new outfits. (Years later, in cities all over the country, midnight screenings of *The Rocky Horror Picture Show* took on a bit of the Palace ambience.)

But on this particular Saturday night Coppola was astonished when, an hour into the show, the rambunctious audience suddenly sat down and went mute, utterly hypnotized by a hallucinatory, abstract short film called *Moon*, made by a local filmmaker named Scott Bartlett. Coppola was impressed; any filmmaker who could make that audience shut up and watch the movie ought to be at Zoetrope.

He mentioned his adventure to Lucas, and it turned out that Lucas and Bartlett were old acquaintances. A few days later Coppola summoned Bartlett to Zoetrope and promised him that he could use the equipment to finish off another short film in progress, *Serpent*, if he'd make a feature film for Zoetrope at the same time. Between them Coppola and Bartlett settled on the idea of a rock opera (all dialogue would be sung) to be called *Atlantis Rising*. Bartlett envisioned it as a version of the Adam and Eve story set on a planet populated wholly by androids whose faces consisted of TV sets.

Coppola also invited his old exploitation filmmaking pal Al Locatelli to move up and join the family. (Locatelli had helped cook the rubber monsters for *Battle Beyond the Sun*.)

Now he assumed a role of major importance at Zoetrope: the
Poet. When people showed up whom nobody wanted around,
but who needed to be treated politely, it was the Poet's job to
get rid of them. He would take them on a tour of the building,
speaking in deep, philosophical terms about the future of the
company, and subtly, inexorably, lead them downstairs, toward
the exit. "It was," remembered Steve Wax, "like P. T. Barnum
with his sign that said, THIS WAY TO THE EGRESS. Locatelli
would get them to the back door and usher them out, and they'd
find themselves standing there in the alley, and then they'd
go away."

The project that Coppola decided should be first out of the
gate was THX. Starting a film, however, requires an extremely
complicated concatenation of personnel and systems, all ready
to roll at the same precisely coordinated moment. According
to Lucas, just as everything was poised, the money failed to
materialize. Coppola flew down to Hollywood, rode onto the
W-7 lot on a motorcycle (a suggestive choice of transportation,
considering the success of Easy Rider), and burst into the office, shouting, "What's going on here? We're ready to shoot!
Where's our go-ahead? Here's the script, here's the cast. . . .
What kind of organization are you guys running? Where's our
money? You wanna be with us or don't you?"

The execs said, "Well, a-a-a-ah . . ." but coughed up no
dough.

Several days later, Coppola sent W-7 a telegram: "PUT
UP OR SHUT UP!" This time they put up, and THX started
shooting.

Suddenly there seemed to be money for the rest of Zoetrope, too. There were plans to make documentaries, government films, features, cartoons, educational films, even a TV show
by John Korty called The People, based on a series of science-
fiction stories by Zenna Henderson. Coppola had several features in development as well. There was The Conversation, of
course; there was Vesuvio, a love story set among Big Sur's
bohemians in the early 1960s, which Carroll Ballard was writing. And there was Apocalypse Now, "a story about today's
Vietnam and the psychedelic soldier," written by John Milius,
to be directed by George Lucas. Lucas planned it as a hard-
hitting, ultrarealistic cheapie, to be shot in 16 mm with lots of
documentary and newsreel footage of Vietnam intercut with

the story, to keep the budget low and the tone factual.

Meanwhile, after years of production delays, Coppola's *Patton* script, which he had written four years earlier, was about to go into release, under Franklin J. Schaffner's direction. The fact that George C. Scott had been cast in the lead was fortunate for Coppola in several respects, mainly because the actor insisted on discarding a number of subsequent rewrites to resurrect Coppola's original screenplay. (For technical reasons, Coppola shared screenplay credit with Edmund H. North, one of the rewriters).

On the other hand, it appears that Scott was less than totally enchanted with Coppola's script. In fact, according to journalist Carole Kass, who went on location in Spain with the film, Scott hated the role. "It's an unactable part," he stated. "It's an inadequate script. [Patton] was misunderstood contemporaneously, and he's misunderstood here—and I'm ashamed of being a part of it." Scott added, "I'm doing the best I can to load the part with pyrotechnics, with smoke screens, with every dirty sneak actor's trick to bring out what I want to bring out, but I'm thoroughly disgusted with the entire part."

Patton opened in New York on February 5, 1970, and although the reviews were cool (the consensus was that George C. Scott was magnificent in spite of a muddled screenplay), audience reaction was everything Twentieth Century-Fox could have wished.

Pauline Kael found it dishonest, dangerous, and reprehensible. "I think *Patton* strings us along and holds out on us," she wrote in the *New Yorker*. "Every issue that is raised is left unresolved. The Patton shown here appears to be deliberately planned as a Rorschach test. I suspect that just for the reason that people can see in it what they already believe, a lot of them are going to think *Patton* is a great movie."

Kael was exactly right. *Patton* took off like a twelve-inch artillery shell; among other fans was President Richard Nixon, who declared it his favorite movie and showed it over and over for pals and cronies at the White House, including the night before he authorized the invasion of Cambodia. (Perhaps he identified with its ruthless hero.) While Coppola, Lucas, and the Zoetrope crew were carving out an artistic empire in Northern California, *Patton* was selling tickets. And selling.

And selling. By the end of 1970 it had brought in $21 million (/$63 million) in domestic rentals, representing about $42 million in total worldwide income for Twentieth Century-Fox. It was the number three money-maker for the year; only *Airport* and *M*A*S*H* were bigger. Coppola was golden. Not only was he striking a blow for film art with Zoetrope, but for the first time he had his name on a box-office blockbuster as well.

Art and money—who could ask for anything more? It was the golden age.

It didn't last long.

At Zoetrope Coppola was horrified to discover that unauthorized people were borrowing equipment and not returning it. "The first year of operation we lost almost $40,000 worth of equipment," he said. "Company cars were taken and cracked up. It was tremendously irresponsible. I spent that whole time and all the money I had, plus all the money I could borrow, to set this company up. And it got stolen and picked away."

Worse, as early as March 1970 it was clear that *The Rain People,* Coppola's personal art film, wasn't going to make any money. *Finian,* which had now had nearly eighteen months to do business, had amassed domestic rentals of only $5.1 million.

And worst of all, there were beginning to be worried phone calls from Hollywood about the *THX* dailies. Initially, or so Coppola claimed, his deal with Warner-Seven had been a legendary love match. Low-budget youth pictures like *Easy Rider* were making lots of money, and Coppola (who was presumably in the right place at the right time to deliver more) was able to negotiate from a position of power. "I call them up and tell them I want to do a love story about a thirty-year-old caught between generations," Coppola explained, "and they say OK. Then I send a script to [Ashley's assistant] John Calley, but only as a courtesy. I realize I'll only have this freedom until I turn in a loser."

But now it was looking more and more as if *THX* might be that loser. The screenplay (by Lucas and Walter Murch) was difficult and unconventional, dealing with a bleached-out, emotionless future technocracy. The shaven-headed lovers in the film were almost sexless, and the leading actors (then-unknown Robert Duvall and still-unknown Maggie McOmie) were uncharismatic, to say the least.

Another problem was that Coppola and Lucas had decided to shoot in Techniscope, an inexpensive wide-screen process that uses standard 35 mm film and a specially modified camera to produce a wide-screen aspect ratio while cutting film and processing costs in half. However, it requires careful lighting and exposures to avoid a grainy image.

Lucas and his tiny production crew (small enough to fit comfortably into a Volkswagen bus) were pushing the Techniscope process to the limit. They used a giant light-hungry 1,000 mm telephoto lens and shot with available light in a variety of tricky locations, including unfinished BART subway tunnels under San Francisco Bay and the underground parking garage at the San Francisco airport. Word began to filter back from Hollywood that W-7 executives were extremely unhappy with the technical quality of the dailies.

Coppola was paying Lucas only a measly $15,000 (/$45,000) to write and direct; Lucas couldn't even afford to join the Directors Guild. But he didn't really mind; he was only twenty-five, and he was making a feature, on his own terms. What did bother Lucas was the presence of a hard-nosed line producer, Lawrence Sturhahn, hired by Coppola (at W-7's insistence) to make sure Lucas stayed under budget and on schedule. Whether it was Sturhahn's Hollywood expertise or Lucas's desire to be rid of him, something worked; the feature-length version of *THX* was shot in only ten weeks, exactly the same time needed for the original USC short. Lucas seldom had time for second takes; in fact, he occasionally filmed (and used) rehearsals.

Despite Warner-Seven's cool reaction to the *THX* dailies, Coppola was still optimistic, or at least he tried to give that impression. He had always told Zoetrope filmmakers that they could fine-tune their films as long as they thought necessary, and he refused to pressure the *THX* team. Nonetheless, he knew that the execs wanted to see the film as soon as possible, and he thought it would be prudent to show them a cut quickly.

By June, George and Marcia Griffin Lucas (who were married by now) and Walter Murch (working on a Steenbeck, of course) had finished a first cut. Lucas and Coppola had won part of their gamble: they had made *THX* for $800,000 (/$2.4 million), roughly half the cost than if they had made it in Hollywood. It remained to be seen if anyone would pay to see it. "I think George is a brilliant kid," said Coppola, "and will shortly be much more famous than I am." Little did he know.

The night before he was supposed to bring the rough cut of *THX 1138* down to Hollywood, Coppola dropped by Zoetrope, where Murch was finishing the temporary sound mix. Murch showed Coppola a reel, and waited nervously for his reaction. "Well," Coppola said, "it's either a masterpiece or masturbation." Nonetheless, he took the film cans and flew south to the land of money.

By now most of W-7's front money was gone, eaten up by Zoetrope's equipment, decor, and espresso machine. The only way to get more was to turn some scripts into movies. To this end Coppola had scheduled meetings with all the main W-7 production heads, and to help his pitch, he put together a "Black Box" for each executive: a large black binder containing seven scripts, including *Apocalypse Now, The Conversation, Santa Rita,* and *Atlantis Rising.*

The screening of *THX* came first, and it was a disaster. The executives loathed what they considered the grim, cold, depressing art movie that Lucas and Coppola had made with $800,000 of their money. "Warners totally dumped on it," Coppola noted. "They said it didn't have any appeal. They could have helped it a lot if they'd wanted to, but by then they were too mad at us."

The executives were now prepared to hate anything else Coppola had up his sleeve. It was not the best time to show them the Black Boxes, but Coppola had no choice.

He passed the binders around, handed out cigars, put on his Preston Tucker hat, and went into a wildly enthusiastic song and dance, telling the old pros that Zoetrope had *the secret to the future of film.* The W-7 execs were not convinced. "I think they just felt oversold and wanted to nip this overly enthusiastic person in the bud," Scott Bartlett speculated. They had some interest in *The Conversation* and, to a lesser extent, *Santa Rita,* but they weren't prepared to put down any money just yet. One script that W-7 absolutely didn't want was *Atlantis Rising,* the rock opera peopled by walking TV sets.

The day Coppola returned to Zoetrope came to be known as Black Thursday. He had gone down with high hopes. When he came back, the dream was shattered. Murch and Lucas continued to edit *THX* for nine more months (the final three overseen by W-7 producer Fred Weintraub), and it was eventually released in 1971, but it earned only a disappointing $1 million in rentals.

"There was a change in the whole industry," noted John Korty. "I can't believe that it all had to do with *THX*. *Easy Rider* was the freshest thing on everyone's mind. Then *Airport* came along, management policies shifted, and the ground beneath Zoetrope started shaking." By the time Lucas and Coppola turned in *THX*, W-7 was watching the youth market evaporate before its eyes. W-7 had lost money on several low-budget films, it saw other studios jettisoning similar projects, *The Rain People* had died a horrible box-office death, and a nationwide recession was cutting into receipts across the board.

The W-7 production heads had always seen Zoetrope as an old warehouse with a lot of hippies running around in it. Now they decided they despised all the films Zoetrope had in development; they withdrew support for *Apocalypse*, which was to have been Lucas's next film (although they kept the rights to the script); they rejected the work of Gloria Katz and Willard Huyck, who were about to write *American Graffiti*; and worst of all, they demanded that Coppola return every cent of the money they had given him. "Warner Brothers not only pulled the rug out from Francis," recalled Murch, "they tried to sell it back to him."

It was a cataclysm. Coppola was thirty, he was broke, and he didn't have a single successful picture to his credit as a director. Behind his back people were whispering, "Don't hire this guy, he's crazy." Coppola must have felt as if he were finished; he fled to Europe in despair.

Scott Bartlett got his walking papers, but he got them in slow motion. "There was no official notification," he recalled, "except . . . a kind of coolness came over everything. Francis was busy with other people, other things. I could still bill the lab expenses for working on my short to Zoetrope, though, until, I believe it was probably Mona Skager who said, 'I hope you're done, because we can't pay for this anymore, we don't have any money left.' "

Korty headed back to Stinson Beach when his Zoetrope rent soared from $200 to $1,000 a month. Haskell Wexler took his business elsewhere. Carroll Ballard broke off writing *Vesuvio* and went off to make a living doing children's films and *Sesame Street* episodes. Al Locatelli went north, as the art director for Robert Altman's *McCabe and Mrs. Miller.* Mike Nichols and Stanley Kubrick stopped returning Coppola's calls. Coppola had to tell Orson Welles that Zoetrope would be unable to do the film they had been discussing. There were staff cutbacks. Bills piled up. It wasn't long until, as Nachman put it, "Zoetrope was down to one miniskirted secretary, and instant coffee instead of espresso."

It produced a momentous change in Coppola's orientation and in many ways a heartbreaking one. He had come to San Francisco like a young general and had assumed the leadership of a prodigiously talented army of young filmmakers, all of them eager to smash Hollywood's hidebound hold on commercial moviemaking. Now he'd abandoned his troops, disbanded his professional family, given up his idealistic dream of communal success. He would succeed or fail on his own; the others would have to fend for themselves.

"We really could have done a lot more than we ended up doing," Carroll Ballard reflected many years later. "We were all so individually ambitious, we couldn't hold it together. . . . I'm regretful, I'm *sad,* that it didn't work out better. We all ended up making a few films, that's true, but I think as filmmakers we all had a lot more potential than *any* of us since realized—*far* more than any of us came close to fulfilling."

Not that Coppola was about to economize on his high-rolling style. Late in 1970, when money was still painfully tight, he sent out invitations to a reception at the San Francisco Film Festival. They were printed on expensive paper with the Zoetrope logo embossed. The invitation sent to George and Marcia Lucas bore a personal note from Francis: "This letter cost $3 to print, type, and send to you." The Lucases were slightly disgusted by the extravagance and even more by the vulgar reference to the cost.

Even though Chris Pearce was still talking, as late as October 1971, about Zoetrope as "a way and means of giving the young filmmaker that extra push that may help him break into the film industry," the emphasis was definitely shifting toward bigger-budget professional filmmaking, primarily by Coppola himself.

Robert Dalva notes that "American Zoetrope was never a collective. It was entirely dependent on Francis's success." Still, some Zoetrope employees and ex-employees felt abused, exploited and depressed. Librarian Deborah Fine (who would end up at Lucasfilms) told Dale Pollock, "The feeling from working for Francis is tough shit if you don't think you're getting paid enough, or if you don't think your working conditions are good enough. There's a million people out there that would kiss the ground to work for him for nothing."

Between making commercials and renting postproduction facilities to filmmakers like Sidney Poitier and Michael Ritchie, American Zoetrope remained a viable postproduction facility for many years, until Coppola shifted his main filmmaking activities back to Los Angeles in 1979. At one point it even entered a partnership with Coppola's brother, Augie (then a professor at Long Beach State University), in a company called Tri-Media Educational Systems. It was really a think tank, ostensibly formed to put together proposals for educational films, but its greatest achievement was undoubtedly the design and installation of a "touchie-feelie" dome at a San Francisco science museum called the Exploratorium. People would enter the dome in total darkness and feel their way around, having tactile adventures; for private parties, clothing was optional. At another point Coppola looked into buying a UHF television station in order to make and broadcast experimental programs.

But in the dark days of 1970, with W-7's financial pullout throwing Zoetrope's survival into serious question, all that was far in the future. Coppola was almost $500,000 in debt. "It looked as if we would never make another movie again," said Lucas.

Coppola had written *Patton* four years earlier, and the script had died, been rewritten, been forgotten—but now, the film was selling so many tickets that, suddenly, despite the Zoetrope debacle, Coppola was getting offers to direct Hollywood films because of the success of *Patton*. Unfortunately they were all garbage.

One of these projects was a bargain-basement ($2 million) action film for Paramount based on a best-selling Mafia potboiler by Mario Puzo, *The Godfather*. The film had been mentioned in the trades as early as March 11, 1970 (long before Coppola became involved), when Army Archerd interviewed Bob Evans and stated that "it will be made for a low price, since the best seller was owned from its inception. It will also be made sans names."

"The title role"—Evans laughed—"should look like Carlo Ponti."

Coppola hated it. It was neither artistic nor intellectual, and he turned it down several times. The gig wouldn't even pay enough to get him out of debt. Lucas happened to be in Coppola's office the day Peter Bart, Paramount's resident intellectual (he was a former Hollywood correspondent for *The New York Times*), called to plead with him one more time. Coppola put his hand over the phone, Lucas recalled, and said, "George, what should I do? Should I make this gangster movie or shouldn't I?"

Lucas replied, "Francis, we need the money. And what have you got to lose?"

It was (to use a phrase that Coppola, and *The Godfather*, would place irrevocably in American popular usage) an offer he couldn't refuse.

"OK," Coppola told Bart, "I'm in."

Chapter Nine

Birth of a Godfather
(1970–1972)

HOLLYWOOD FILMMAKERS LIKE D. W. Griffith and Cecil B. De Mille had been making "big" movies for years, but Frank Yablans may well have invented the modern blockbuster—the splashy, big-budget action movie that took over America in the 1980s (and is often mistakenly credited to Steven Spielberg). Yablans developed the blockbuster formula when he was Paramount's head of production in the early 1970s. "Emotion," he would say, "a structured story, jeopardy, romance and action," and a budget of about $6 million (/$18 million). "We want one big picture a year," he noted. "The rest are budgeted to minimize risk." Once the dramatic elements were in place, Yablans (who had been Paramount's sales chief before he was its president and had never lost his marketing savvy) was prepared to spend a bundle on advertising, set high ticket prices, and open the film simultaneously in thousands of theaters across the country. It became a familiar combination in the 1980s, but at the time it was radical.

Paramount had been grooming *The Godfather* long before its vice-president Peter Bart made the phone call to Coppola, but not as a blockbuster. When Yablans (in New York) and Robert Evans (his opposite number in Hollywood, a former-actor-turned-garment-executive-turned-producer, whose credits included *Rosemary's Baby* and *Love Story*) read the first hundred pages of Mario Puzo's novel in manuscript, they promptly installed the novelist in an office at Paramount with a stocked refrigerator and a secretary and paid him a piddling $35,000 to finish the book. Puzo eventually received a total of $80,000 (/$225,000) for film rights to the novel, plus 2½ percent of the net profits for collaborating with Coppola on the script.

It was a minor development deal in Hollywood terms, but it paid off very nicely for Paramount. With the (unintended) help of the Italian-American Civil Rights League, whose loud protests drew media attention to the novel, Puzo's potboiler became an instant best seller, selling one million hardcover copies and twelve million paperbacks before the movie opened. Long before then, however, Paramount had put production wheels in motion for a low-budget film based on *The Godfather*; it was originally set for a Christmas 1971 release.

Time was short even for a quickie, and Evans had no time to lose. His first move was to hire thirty-seven-year-old Albert Ruddy as line producer. Ruddy, a tall, rangy man in the James Coburn mode, was a reliable small-timer whose TV series *Hogan's Heroes* had maintained consistently high ratings for many years. He had also produced four small theatrical features for the "youth market," including *Little Fauss and Big Halsy*, all of which came in under budget and ahead of schedule, even if they flopped at the box office. Ruddy *needed* a film like *The Godfather* to boost him into the big time. "This isn't my kind of film," he said. "This one's just to put us on top in the industry, and to get backing for the kind of films we want to do."

Now Evans and Ruddy needed a director, ideally a hungry director who would work cheap, who knew how to shoot fast and inexpensively, and who wouldn't argue with Paramount's decisions and priorities. They offered the project to Peter Yates, who had made *Bullitt*. When he turned it down, they offered it to Costa-Gavras, who had made *Z*. When he turned it down, a friend at MGM mentioned Coppola to Al Ruddy.

Ruddy knew about Coppola. Several years earlier he had told Joel Oliansky, "Coppola, oh, yeah, let me tell you something about Coppola. Coppola'd make a great producer, you know, he's a hustler, he's got all this talk and cha-cha-cha, but he's no director." But now everyone realized that Coppola might be a perfect candidate. Not only was he on the rebound from several failures (and therefore likely to be tractable), but he even had an Italian name.

Ruddy arranged a meeting so Coppola could meet Evans,

Bart, and Stanley Jaffe, Paramount's thirty-year-old president, whose main production credit was as executive producer of *Goodbye Columbus*. Ruddy picked up Coppola forty-five minutes early and drove him to Paramount. Then they sat in the car and ran lines. Ruddy knew that staying on budget was . . . well, it was paramount.

"Look, Francis," he pleaded, "Paramount has just lost seven billion on four or five movies that went completely out of control. They had *Catch 22*, that started at eight million and went to twenty-four, twenty-five. They had *Paint Your Wagon*, which started at nine and went to twenty-six. They had *The Molly Maguires*, they had *Darling Lili*, they had *Those Jaunty Young Men in Their Godamn Flying Machines*.* They want to do this movie at a price, and that price is two million. Remember, Francis, we're gonna do it on a low budget. Now what are you gonna say when they ask you about the budget?"

When Coppola had his lines down pat, Ruddy took him inside. The Paramount execs were all smiles and handshakes. They sat Coppola down.

"I'm waiting for him to regurgitate these lines," Ruddy remembered, "but all of a sudden he goes into this diatribe about his theory of making movies, that, I swear to God, everyone's mouth was hanging—his domino theory, I mean, it was one of the most brilliant sales jobs I have ever heard in my life. Don't ask me what the hell he said, I don't think anyone understood. I'm not even sure there *was* a definitive line to what Francis was trying to sell. He is a *spectacular* salesman. He's very funny, very flamboyant. He did a twenty- or twenty-five-minute speech; he jumped up on the desk; I mean, he bowled everybody over. And that's how Francis got the movie."

Evans may have remembered the brief flashbacks of people dancing at Natalie's Italian wedding in *The Rain People*— the warmest scenes in the film. "When I hired Francis for *The Godfather*," he commented, "everybody thought I was nuts. He'd only made three movies [four, actually] and they'd all been failures, but I had faith in him. He knew the way these men ate their food, kissed each other, talked. He knew the grit."

Coppola later confessed he felt nervous around Evans,

---

*Ruddy was referring to *Those Daring Young Men in Their Jaunty Jalopies*, a 1969 flop (spinoff of the 1965 hit *Those Magnificent Men in Their Flying Machines*).

who'd started out life as a child star and was Hollywood to the
max, right down to his perfect tan. He got on better with the
slow-talking Ruddy, a well-educated lapsed architect. "Ruddy
is a nice guy," he said, "but more of a wheeler-dealer than I
am." Ruddy may have reminded him of his old boss, Roger
Corman.

Coppola's bargaining position wasn't strong, but with the
help of entertainment attorney Norman Garey, he cut a reasonably good deal for himself. He settled for a minimal $150,000
(/$452,000) for writing and directing the picture, but Para-
mount agreed to pay him 7½ percent of the net profits on top
of that. If the film went over really big, he might bring home
$1 million—enough to take care of his wife and kids for a long
time, enough for him to relax, pay off the money he owed on
Zoetrope, and make the kind of movies he wanted to make.

George Lucas expected Coppola to devote at least some of
that $150,000 to pulling Zoetrope out of the red; after all, that's
why he had taken the assignment in the first place. But Coppola had other ideas, as Lucas remembered with wonderment:
"So what does he do in the face of total disaster? He goes out
and buys a mansion. That really sums it up for him."

It was a gorgeous twenty-eight-room turn-of-the-century
Queen Anne row house, high on Pacific Heights, with turrets,
stained glass windows, a majestic stairway leading to the door,
and a spectacular view of the bay, the Golden Gate Bridge,
and the hills of Marin County. There was a heated Moorish-
style pool in the backyard, a huge kitchen (in which Coppola
promptly installed the world's biggest, shiniest espresso machine), and a ballroom in the basement, which quickly became
a luxurious 35 mm screening room with plush sofas, a Moog
synthesizer, and a harpsichord. And a Scopitone right outside
the door, as a reminder of how far he had come since he lost
all his Seven Arts screenwriting pay on the company. He also
installed a life-size video screen at the foot of his bed. Eleanor
took over the extensive refurnishing, filling the place with avant-
garde furniture and modern art, including a large portrait of
Mao by Andy Warhol.

Steve Wax was still hard at work at Zoetrope, revising the
script for *Santa Rosa,* which had survived the W-7 debacle.
But Coppola's relationship with Wax was growing troubled.
Although they were fond of each other, they'd begun to drift

apart when Wax committed a primal sin: He took Coppola at his word when he suggested that Wax try to unionize the directors, writers, and editors at Zoetrope. Coppola envisioned a vague, guildlike association of artists, a gentlemanly alternative to the combative unions (like IATSE) that he disliked so intensely. Wax named his federation the Film Workers' Union and organized some meetings. At first everything was swell. But when the union turned radical and became a militant chapter of NABET (the National Association of Broadcast Employees and Technicians), the honeymoon was over. When Wax's union began to jeopardize Coppola's already tense relationship with W-7, Wax and the other union militants found themselves being gradually, but inexorably, edged out of Zoetrope. Months later, when Coppola was well into the shoot of *The Godfather,* Wax brought charges of unfair labor practices (union busting) against Zoetrope and won. Coppola had to come up with about $10,000 in back salaries and legal fees.

Meantime, when the trades got wind of the *Godfather* deal, they paid far more attention to the Warners-Zoetrope divorce than to the unimportant low-budget gangster picture Coppola was starting. On October 1, 1970, four months after "Black Thursday," *Daily Variety* ran a short item headlined COPPOLA DIRECTS GODFATHER "ON LEAVE" FROM WARNERS-SEVEN. A companion piece appeared several days later. It noted that Ruddy would not be using Zoetrope facilities for *The Godfather.* Evans and Yablans were concerned with keeping the budget as low as possible—ideally, under $2 million—and at first Ruddy sided with them. Although much of the charm of Puzo's novel came from its period New York City ambience, Ruddy had recently written an article explaining why it was generally too expensive to shoot in New York; now he and the Paramount executives came up with a plan to set the film in the present day and move the action to St. Louis to save the cost of re-creating the period New York settings—and to avoid the New York mob.

Coppola was outraged and raised such a *kvetch* that the dispute broke into the trades as "a major difference of opinion." Although he had been hired partly because he was considered tractable, Coppola improved his position as *Patton* continued to do great business. After several months Ruddy gave in, went back to Evans, and insisted that if they were going to make the film at all, they'd have to find the money to shoot in New York City and in period. "The mob," Ruddy told Evans (and *Variety*) "just do not shoot each other any more."

Considering that Joseph Colombo, Jr., head of the Italian-American Civil Rights League (and an alleged mob boss) managed to get himself shot a few days after the film wrapped, this statement is arguable. Nonetheless, Evans and Yablans agreed to come up with another $1 million to cover the New York period shoot. It was far from the last budgetary fire fight; later, when Coppola insisted on filming in Sicily, they nearly fired him, but in the end they gave in on that one, too. Coppola was to remark later that *The Godfather* owed its success to the battles he fought before the first foot of film went through the camera.

The daily confrontations were a new way of working for Coppola. He had had things pretty much his own way at Warner-Seven, but the Paramount brass expected him to follow orders. Coppola wanted their money, but he didn't want their advice on how to make a movie, especially a cheap gangster flick like *The Godfather*.

There's a famous experiment, so famous that it may be apocryphal. A class of art students is given an assignment: Paint anything you want—any size, any style—and bring it in next week. The students have a great time, and their paintings are called Group One. The next assignment is to paint a bowl of fruit, using only red and yellow oils, using strict perspective, using flat brushstrokes, using an eighteen-inch-square canvas, etc., etc. The students complain bitterly; how can they express themselves with so many restrictions? Nonetheless, they do the paintings, which are called Group Two.

At this point the paintings are mixed up and hung on the walls of a gallery, and a group of art critics is asked to rate them. The critics are given no information about how the paintings were done, but with astonishing consistency they agree that the pictures in Group Two, the ones completed under heavy restrictions, are overwhelmingly superior to the free-style paintings of Group One.

Sometimes artists have problems integrating an unlimited universe of possibilities; they seem to do better working in a context where some decisions have already been made. Up to this point in his career Coppola had worked as a director under very few restrictions. Artistically his films were mediocre; commercially they were washouts. Now, for the first time, he had to make a film under strict restraint.

Depending on your point of view, Puzo's book is either high-class junk or low-grade literature. Puzo had set out, quite consciously, to write the biggest best seller in history. He was tired of being a starving writer of obscure, well-respected novels; he wanted to make some money. He wasn't the first writer to try, but he was one of the few to succeed. Puzo did an immense amount of research, which paid off handsomely with fascinating details of Mafia history, daily operations, and family life that were utterly convincing. In addition, writing in Paramount's office, Puzo had built in a number of highly cinematic action sequences. Many of his characters were complex and well developed, and he told his story with grace and confidence. However, in his determination to make the book commercial, he had also included a number of blatant best-seller elements that cheapened it, including a complicated subplot involving Sonny's oversized genitals. (Coppola disposed of this entire story with one lightning-quick gesture by Sonny's wife at Connie's wedding party.)

Coppola's adaptation is brilliant. He started by tearing the pages from Puzo's novel, pasting them down in a stage director's notebook, and summarizing the action with handwritten notes on each page. As a result, his screenplay is extremely faithful to the book; all the key elements come directly from the novel.

Coppola tried to drop as many of the lurid elements as he could, but there were certain events he knew he had to keep. "I hated that whole Hollywood sequence," he said at one point, "but I had to do it because I had to cut off that stupid horse's head. I had to do this, I had to do that, and by the time I did what I had to do, I had already used up the movie. So I never had time to make some of the points I wanted to make."

Coppola still gave much greater depth to the relationship between the Corleone brothers and to Michael Corleone's failed expectations of freedom, and he made explicit the role of women (who were strictly excluded from the family business) as guardians of the home. Especially, he found screen time to emphasize the ethnic family details and Catholic ceremonies that meant so much to him. "I feel that a great deal of my background as an Italian-American, with very strong memories about family rituals, the weddings, the funerals, went into the picture," he said.

Because he painted the mobsters as human beings, not monsters, many people later accused Coppola of romanticizing the Mafia. But the sympathetic portrayal was a highly cinematic element. Critics have observed that when people read novels, they tend to identify with the writer, while film viewers seem to identify with the characters, no matter how nasty they are. We might call this the Hitchcock effect, after the filmmaker who used it to such wicked advantage.

Coppola underscored the Hitchcock effect with ethnic details and a Shakespearean sympathy for his bad guys. "Villains are people, aren't they?" he asked. "They believe that they're doing something which by their moral code is good."

Puzo had few illusions about the book. "The Mafia is certainly romanticized," he admitted. "They are much worse guys than that." Even Coppola argued that the script deviated severely from the truth in "the mythic aspects of the Godfather, the great father who is honorable and will not do business in drugs. The character was a synthesis of [real-life mobsters] Vito Genovese and Joseph Profaci, but Genovese ordered his soldiers not to deal in drugs, while he did just that on the side; Profaci was dishonorable at a lot of levels. The film Godfather would never double-cross anyone, but the real godfathers double-crossed people over and over. But remember, it wasn't a documentary about Mafia chief Vito Genovese. It was Marlon Brando with Kleenex in his mouth. And the fact may be that people *like* Marlon and Jimmy [Caan] and Al [Pacino] too much."

In any case, Coppola understood that Puzo's seemingly realistic novel wasn't really about gangsters at all; it was a fairy story, an allegory, a romance about a great king with three sons. "It could have been the Kennedys," he said at one point, "the whole idea of a family living in a compound—that was all based on Hyannisport." Puzo must have agreed because as the script went back and forth between Coppola and Puzo, with each man rewriting and correcting, the elements of kingly power and succession grew stronger. The men never worked together; Puzo suggested they try it, but Coppola didn't want to. Puzo wrote the first draft. Then, while Coppola worked on one half, Puzo worked on the other. Finally they exchanged halves and started over.

At the same time preliminary discussions with Marlon Brando, a contender for the leading role, were pushing Coppola toward a more radical, socially conscious interpretation of the book. Asked about Brando's politics, Coppola once observed, "If you sit down with him and you're talking about girls, two minutes later he'll have changed the subject to ecology, or Indians, or his algae farm." Brando saw Puzo's tale of warring Mafia families as an allegory of corporate America. "The tactics the Don used aren't much different from those General Motors used against Ralph Nader," he insisted, and to some extent Coppola (whose politics were, at the time, vaguely leftist) agreed.

"For me," he said, "the Mafia was just a metaphor for America. It is transplanted from Europe; it is a capitalistic, profit-seeking body; it believes that anything it does to protect and sustain itself and its family is morally good."

On another occasion Coppola observed that in at least one important way America was inferior to the Mafia. "Both the Mafia and America feel they are benevolent organizations," he said. "Both have their hands stained with blood from what it is necessary to do to protect their power and interests. Both are totally capitalistic phenomena. But I feel that America does not take care of its people. We look to our country as our protector, and it's fooling us, it's lying to us. The reason the book was so popular was that people love to read about an organization that's really going to take care of us."

While Puzo and Coppola polished the script, 1970 turned into 1971, with a million details left to settle. Eleanor was pregnant again, the Pacific Heights mansion, in the middle of renovation, was a shambles, and all too soon Coppola would have to fly to New York City and start his gangster movie. Before he could leave, though, there was one painful, long-delayed decision to take: He "mothballed" American Zoetrope, cutting the staff drastically. Many Zoetrope staffers, who had been working on emergency wages until the studio got back on its feet again, were stunned to discover that their loyalty would not be returned. Coppola had problems of his own. Big problems.

Hostilities with Paramount were building up to a series of

pitched battles that might have been called the Casting Wars. Coppola knew that casting would make or break *The God-father,* and he was determined to use the best actors he could; but the studio kept jiggling his elbow. Evans was nervous about Coppola's giving his old friend James Caan the plum part of Sonny, the Godfather's oldest son. There were whispers about nepotism when Coppola's sister, Talia Shire, was hired to play Connie despite her rotten screen test—even though Evans had cast Shire while Coppola was in Europe, for the express purpose (said Coppola) of making him uncomfortable.

"He was real angry that I accepted without asking him first," said Shire. "He was asking for real interesting casting, and people make trades; you don't want a sister there who may suddenly fall on her face. I understand the situation. At the same time, just because you're a genius doesn't mean that you're completely developed emotionally."

Paramount was insisting on a big WASP star like Robert Redford, Warren Beatty, Jack Nicholson, or Ryan O'Neal for the key role of Michael, the Don's youngest son. Coppola knew the part belonged to off-Broadway actor Al Pacino. Pacino was actually of Sicilian descent and a member of the prestigious Actors' Studio as well. Paramount made Coppola call him back for three separate (increasingly degrading) screen tests.

The problem was that Pacino was intensely nervous, too short, looked too Italian, forgot his lines, and made up terrible dialogue to cover up. Even Puzo, who had originally backed Coppola, changed his mind. By now Coppola knew he was in danger of losing his job, but he refused to give an inch. Finally Pacino got the part, but only because Paramount knew it'd lose six months if it fired its director, and the book was becoming such a giant best seller it wanted the film out before people lost interest.

Casting movies is very unpleasant; the director sits in a room day after day, meeting another anxious candidate every five minutes. And of course, the actors feel insulted by having to wait around. So Coppola decided he would throw a casting party. He would invite fifty actors and actresses who were being considered for parts, and he would walk around and talk with each of them, and it would be a nice party. "So I did it," he said, "and all the actors were there, and I started having a very strange feeling that if I didn't see everyone, the person I hadn't seen would go home and be really depressed. I started to get the impression that I was a rich guy who had hired all these actors to be at my party because if I gave a party no one would come."

It was around that point that Bill Campbell, who had reluctantly agreed to star in Coppola's first picture, *Dementia 13*, ten years earlier, started calling. Coppola had promised Campbell that "if anything great happens in my life, I will make sure I pay you back." Campbell figured it was time. "Here's where you pay me back, pal," he thought. He was primarily interested in a shot at the role of the *consigliere*, Hagen, eventually played by Robert Duvall, but he would have happily settled for twenty weeks of work playing a gangster, wearing a slouch hat, and muttering, "OK, boss," when required. But despite a series of desperate attempts to get through, Coppola wasn't accepting any calls from Bill Campbell.

There was a hotter battle over choosing the actor to play sixty-five-year-old Vito Corleone, the Godfather. Initially, under pressure to keep the budget low, Coppola videotaped "every old Italian actor in existence," but he concluded that if an Italian actor had gotten to be seventy years old without becoming famous on his own, he wouldn't have the air of authority they needed. Finally, Coppola and Ruddy decided that age and ethnic origin didn't matter; what they needed to do was hire the best actor in the world.

They seriously considered Sir Laurence Olivier, but their first choice was forty-seven-year-old Marlon Brando. As it happens, Coppola had already made contact with Brando in connection with another project, *The Conversation*—a brief contact that had been cordial, even though Brando turned down the part and Coppola had been devastated. It wasn't until Coppola began working with Puzo that he discovered the novelist had actually had Brando in mind when he wrote the character.

Unfortunately Brando had become something of a crank; his reputation for unpredictable behavior had made him extremely unpopular in Hollywood; his last three pictures (*Candy*, *The Night of the Following Day*, and the fascinating *Burn*) had gone wildly over budget, reportedly because of hassles and arguments between Brando and his directors. Brando simply noted, "The good directors that I've worked with will say I'm a good guy. The other fellows will say I'm a bad guy." The

Paramount execs considered him unacceptable for the lead of their low-budget gangster movie. As far as they were concerned, his career was over.

Brando read the book in three days and decided that he liked the part; in fact, he thought it was "delicious." On the other hand, some months later, when asked what made up his mind, he joked, "I think it was mainly $250,000 plus a percentage." Evans and Yablans were still bitterly opposed to him, and when Ruddy and Coppola tried to win them over, they got, as Ruddy describes it, "an absolutely violent response." Evans yelled at them for being fools; he'd rather quit Paramount, he said, than hire Brando. It was a standoff. Ruddy and Coppola actually called Olivier, but he was ailing.

With time running out, Coppola refused to submit any new casting ideas, and an emergency meeting was set up between Coppola, Ruddy, Evans, and Jaffe. There were hot and cold running lawyers; it was a big-deal meeting. Halfway through, Coppola made yet another impassioned pitch for Brando, and Jaffe decided he'd had enough. "As President of Paramount Pictures," he replied, "I assure you that Marlon Brando will never appear in this motion picture, and furthermore, as President of the company, I will no longer allow you to discuss it."

Coppola begged for just five more minutes to plead his case. When Jaffe nodded, he stood up as if he were a lawyer pleading for someone's life and lined out every logical argument he could think of, one after another, for why Brando was the only actor who could play the part. He reminded Evans and Jaffe that "the mystique Brando had as an actor amongst other actors would inspire precisely the right kind of awe that the character of the Don needed," he jumped around the room, sang, and danced; even Ruddy was speechless. For his big finish, Coppola fired up a gambit he hadn't used since UCLA; he hyperventilated, clutched his stomach, and collapsed onto the floor.

Like everyone else the director had ever used it on, Jaffe was stunned by Coppola's convincing convulsions; he let himself be swayed. But he set three conditions, conditions he was sure Coppola could never fulfill. One, Brando could take no salary, just a percentage. Two, Brando had to guarantee, with his own money, that the film would not go over budget because of him. And three, Brando would have to take a screen test. This last condition was Jaffe's *pièce de résistance* because, as everyone knew, Brando never took screen tests.

Coppola and Brando were still getting acquainted, and Coppola was uneasy ("scared shitless" was how he described it) about coming right out and asking the great actor to do a test. In desperation, he told Brando that he'd like to "explore" the role with him.

"Wonderful," said Brando.

"Let's videotape it," said Coppola.

"Fine!" said Brando.

Coppola got a video recorder from some friends and showed up at Brando's house the next morning with Bart Patton (who was to serve as videotaper) and an Italian barber he'd picked for the role of Bonasera, the undertaker in the film. Coppola told *Playboy*'s William Murray:

> I'd dressed him [Bonasera] in a black suit and asked him to memorize the speech at the beginning of the movie where Bonasera asks the Godfather for a favor. But I kept him outside.
>
> Brando met us in his living room, wearing a Japanese kimono, hair tied back in a ponytail. I just started videotaping him. He began to slide into character. He took some shoe polish and put it in his hair. His speech changed: "You t'ink I need a mustache?" I was anxious to make an intelligent comment, so I said, "Oh yeah, my uncle Louis has a mustache." He dabbed on a phony mustache and, as I videotaped him, he reached for some Kleenex. "I want to be like a bulldog," he mumbled, and stuffed wads of it into his mouth. He kept talking to himself, mumbling, and finally said, "I just wanna improvise." I told my guys to keep quiet; I'd heard that noise bothers him. He always wears earplugs when he's working.
>
> Then, without warning, I ushered in my barber friend, who went up to Brando and launched right into his speech. Brando didn't know what was going on for a moment, but he listened and then just started doing the scene. It was my shot. The thing worked, I had it down on tape. I'd watched 47-year-old Marlon Brando turn into this aging Mafia chieftain.

Between Brando's impromptu makeup job and his Methodical assumption of Don Corleone's face, Evans and Jaffe were totally taken in. When they saw the videotape for the first time, they were unaware that it was Brando. "He looks Italian," Evans said to Ruddy, "but who is he?" When they found out, their last objections crumbled. Brando had the role.

Evans was in New York, keeping an eye on the last stages of preproduction; he made the announcement about Brando early in February 1971. Production, he added, would start in March.

Diane Keaton, who'd aced all her screen tests, was signed on as Michael's New England Protestant wife, Kay, and with Robert Duvall set as Hagen, the family's *consigliere,* and John Cazale as Fredo, the middle Corleone brother, Coppola's cast was complete. It wasn't an expensive cast. The actors' salaries made up only 25 percent of the film's budget, whereas it's not unheard of for big-budget pictures to pay 50 percent of their budget to their stars. And despite Brando's joke about $250,000, no one got more than $50,000 up front—although Brando was guaranteed "expense money" of $1,000 a week and a complicated percentage of the adjusted gross that was to pay him an additional $1.5 million (/$4.3 million) within months of the film's release.

The circus grew crazier day by day. Shortly after Evans's announcement half a dozen Italian actors with picket signs appeared opposite Paramount's Bronson Street gate in Hollywood. MEXICANS FOR MEXICAN ROLES, read one sign, ITALIANS FOR ITALIAN ROLES. Another read MORE ADVANTAGES FOR ITALIAN ACTORS, with the acronymic MAFIA picked out in dark letters. "All along they said they were going to cast unknown Italian actors, right?" asked Vincent Barbi. "And who do they cast? Marlon Brando, James Caan, Robert Duvall. They really built up our hopes. Some of us had three, four interviews."

"It's getting tougher all the time for us Italian heavies to get work," added another actor. "If I go for an interview to work on *FBI* they say I can't work because the Anti-Defamation League says it casts aspersions on Italian-Americans."

Meanwhile, the Italian-American Civil Rights League (IACRL) was turning out to be more troublesome than anticipated. Its loud and ludicrous insistence that the Mafia was a fictional creation of Mario Puzo had helped put the novel on the best-seller list and keep it there, but now Ruddy had received a hundred letters from various U.S. senators and representatives, even a presidential candidate, favoring the League's position. To make matters worse, the League staged a rally (emceed by Frank Sinatra) that packed Madison Square Garden, raised $600,000 to stop the film, and threatened to create labor disruptions on the shoot. Evans held a hard line in public, but Paramount was getting very nervous. "No one," Evans declared, "is going to stop us from making *The Godfather*. I know the situation is rough. We'll have our own protection for the locations in New York, Las Vegas and Sicily."

Ruddy thought it might be smarter to negotiate. In mid-March he met with the IACRL's Anthony Colombo (son of the soon-to-be-assassinated Joseph Colombo) and sixty of his loyal buddies. While the very fact that the League's threats were ominously enforceable tended to undermine its position that there was no such thing as the Mafia, Ruddy wisely decided against pointing this out; instead, he agreed that neither the word "Mafia" nor the phrase "Cosa Nostra" would appear in the film. Ruddy later insisted that only three script cuts were involved, and he added that Coppola's script had never used the word "Mafia" anyway. Fortunately for Coppola, the IACRL had no problem with "wop," "greaser," "dago," "guinea," "Family," or "Five Families."

In addition, to show his respect, Ruddy had to promise to attend a $125-a-plate testimonial dinner in honor of Anthony Colombo's dear old granddad, Joe, Sr.; to hire League members as bit players and extras; and to donate the film's New York opening night gate to the league's hospital fund.

It wasn't the League's first victory. A year earlier it had convinced Attorney General John Mitchell to forbid the Justice Department to use words like "Mafia" and "Cosa Nostra," at least in public. Nonetheless, the meeting with Ruddy made the front page of *The New York Times* and the editorial page three days later. The *Times* editorialist was most upset.

YES, MR. RUDDY, THERE IS A . . . was the headline, and the text echoed State Senator John J. Marchi in describing Ruddy's accommodation of the league as "a monstrous insult" to millions of Italian-Americans and a "hypocritical, craven act." The League would do better, it concluded, were it to oppose the Mafia instead of "trying to render it invisible by making it unmentionable." It was terrific publicity, and Paramount's commitment to the project strengthened. In response to Coppola's insistent demands for more money, the execs decided to increase the film's budget to $6.2 million (/$18 million). *The Godfather,* Paramount's low-budget gangster movie, had become Yablans's blockbuster for 1972.

With Brando's encouragement, Coppola used theater games to help his actors slip into character even before the shoot began. At one point he invited Brando, Caan, Pacino, and the rest of the family to have dinner with him at an Italian restaurant, and he had the tables arranged like a large family dining room. "It was the first time they had all met," Coppola explained, "and all I did was have them improvise for two or three hours, over a meal, that they were a family. It was very, very valuable." When they started filming, Coppola continued to give the actors skits and charades to help them deepen their characterizations and to reduce the tedium during inevitable technical delays.

On March 29, 1971, the cameras rolled. Within days Jaffe stepped down as president of Paramount and Yablans (the company's sales chief) moved up to replace him.

In the middle of April, two weeks into the shoot, the Academy Awards presentation was held . . . and *Patton* won no fewer than seven Oscars, including Best Picture of 1970, Best Director, Best Actor, and (how sweet it was) Best Screenplay. Coppola had won an Academy Award!

It was a fabulous sweep. George C. Scott, muttering darkly about "Oscar politics and studio hustling," had made it clear in advance that even if he won, he would not accept his award. His boycott drew even more attention to the film; Coppola accepted *his* Oscar and flew back east to face a waking nightmare.

The pressure was on. Coppola later remembered the *Godfather* shoot with dull horror. "Directing any large movie is like running in front of a moving locomotive," he said. "If you stop, if you trip, if you make a mistake, you get killed. And *Godfather* was worse than most." Coppola had asked for an eighty-day shooting schedule, but Bob Evans would give him only fifty-three. Then Paramount thought the rushes were dull. Worst of all, the film was growing bigger than its young director; there were recurring rumors that the execs wanted Coppola off the film. He couldn't sleep at night; when he did slip off, he had nightmares in which Elia Kazan walked onto the set, came up to him, and said, "Uh, sorry, Francis, but I've been asked to . . ."

The nightmares about Kazan had a basis in reality. Three weeks into the film, when Brando showed up for his first day's work (the meeting in the olive oil company office), things had gone very badly. Brando wanted to improvise, but Coppola was feeling time-pressured and pushed Brando into shooting the scene anyway; the dailies were so disappointing that Evans actually tried to reach Kazan, on the theory that he was the only director who could get a good performance out of Brando.

Fortunately, before Coppola heard about the Kazan option, he went in on his own and reshot the scene, and this time the rushes were much better. Shortly thereafter he met briefly with Charles Bludhorn, the head of Gulf + Western (Paramount's parent corporation), who assured him that he would not be thrown off the picture, but once Coppola found out about the phone calls to Kazan, the nightmares never stopped.

Soon afterward Ruddy remembers getting a phone call from Bludhorn, asking, "Does this movie have any subtitles on it, or what, 'cause nobody can understand a word Brando is saying!"

"Well," said Ruddy, "you will, over a period of time."

Several weeks later Coppola returned the favor. When Paramount got wind of Ruddy's agreement to hand over the opening night gate to the League, the executives were livid. Not only did Paramount cancel Ruddy's deal with the League, but several Gulf + Western execs became seriously concerned that organized crime might be moving in on the studio. Getting wind of their feelings, a nervous Coppola told Ruddy, "You know, Al, I've never worked with a producer who got another job after he worked with me." Ruddy assured Coppola that this time the jinx would be broken. Nonetheless, Paramount was so worried that it shut down the production—a cataclysmic and costly occurrence on any film shoot—and called in Coppola to talk with him about firing Ruddy. "You guys are making a big mistake," he told them. "The only guy that can produce this thing is Al Ruddy."

Ruddy was also instrumental in introducing Coppola to two men who became lifelong members of his filmmaking family. Gray Frederickson, an assistant producer working with Ruddy,

went on to take a major creative role in every Coppola picture
through *The Outsiders.* More important yet was Dean Tavoularis, who had been shuttling back and forth between Europe
and America, working on a number of interesting films, including *Petulia, Candy,* and *Zabriskie Point.* Ruddy hired him as
production designer; he was to become one of Coppola's three
or four most trusted, and most constant, professional comrades.

Coppola was working hard. Constant retakes were driving
his cast and crew crazy, and now Paramount's editor was insisting to the execs that the footage was impossible to cut properly; he claimed there wasn't enough coverage (alternate angles,
close-ups, etc.) to build effective scenes. Coppola told his allies on the set that the editor wanted to direct the film himself
and was actively conspiring with the assistant director to get
Coppola fired; Coppola fired the mutinous editors instead.

Even Al Ruddy was working behind his back to dump him,
or so he thought. Or perhaps . . . yes, Ruddy and cinematographer Gordon Willis were working together to get him canned.
Evans, who was sure his director was having a nervous breakdown, was on the phone from Hollywood several times a day,
complaining about costs and trying to enforce harsh econo-
mies. Coppola was angry and depressed. His mood made it
even harder to work. Sometimes he felt like quitting just to get
it over with, but he was caught between an artistic rock and
an economic hard place. He had bought his way out of the
Warner-Seven deal by promising to pay $600,000. It was a big
gamble, since he was only guaranteed $150,000 for directing
The Godfather; if he walked out and lost his percentage, he'd
never have a chance to pay W-7 back, and it'd foreclose on
Zoetrope. "Many times I got a message from my agent," he
remembered, "saying, 'Don't quit, let them fire you,' because
if they fired me I would get the money, and if I quit I would
lose it all and Warners would foreclose."

The pressure was so intense he couldn't concentrate on
critical script revisions; he needed help with several key scenes,
and finally, four or five weeks into the shoot, he called in Robert Towne (an old Roger Corman alumnus, who later wrote the
screenplays for *Chinatown* and *Shampoo*).

"The main problem was that there was no final scene between Michael Corleone and his father," recalled Towne.
"Coppola kept saying, 'I want a scene where they say they
love each other.' I couldn't write a scene with two people say-

ing they love each other. It had to be about something, an action. So that scene in the garden between Al Pacino and Marlon Brando is what I ended up doing—a scene about the transfer of power."

The crew thought *Godfather* was going to be the biggest disaster of all time. Word that the crew considered Talia Shire's performance amateurish reached the ears of the Paramount execs; that didn't make things any easier for Coppola. Worse yet, the crew considered Coppola's performance amateurish and made no secret about it. He remembered being in a bathroom stall, with the door shut, when a couple of crew members came in, talking about how badly the film was going and what an incompetent asshole the director was. Coppola lifted up his feet so they wouldn't recognize his shoes.

He also had big problems with cinematographer Gordon Willis, who walked off the set at least once in protest at Coppola's incompetence. When Coppola insisted on doing the shot without him, the camera operators just stared at him as if he'd gone mad. He started screaming, Al Ruddy tried to calm him down, and finally Coppola stalked off the set. A few seconds later a sound like a distant gunshot was heard across the sound stage. Coppola had just kicked down his office door.

"I agreed with Gordy on how both *Godfathers* should look—no zoom shots, and grainy, like old period photographs. But he hates and misuses actors," Coppola later opined. "He wants them to hit marks, I said no. They're not mechanics, they're artists. Gordy acted like a football player stuck with a bunch of fag actors. I was their protector."

On top of that, the presence of his sister, Talia, on the set was driving him crazy. At one point he started yelling, "Tallie's too pretty for the part. I'm going to fire her! A guy who's going to marry into a Mafia family has to have a fat little dumpy Italian girl with an ugly face. Tallie is wrong. She's got to go!" When his mother, Italia, begged him to keep her on, he relented, but not before loudly ordering the makeup department, "Put my sister's hair up, make her less beautiful."

One day an assistant producer found Robert Duvall pacing and muttering, "Tense, very tense. They're not all like this. It must come from the top. Pressure, money, bigness does it. Very tense atmosphere." According to Duvall, Paramount hired a standby director to follow Coppola around in case he screwed up. Thanks to Ruddy's deal with the IACRL, a number of mafiosi were wandering around the set, too, playing bit parts and extra roles, and making people nervous. Coppola has always denied the mob's presence, although both Duvall and Caan have spoken about it. "Al Ruddy was out having dinner with a lot of them," he said, "but I wouldn't participate in any way whatsoever with them."

It wasn't all agony. At first, to save money, Coppola slept on the sofa at James Caan's apartment. Later he rented a two-room apartment of his own and brought his family east; the boys slept in one bedroom, with Francis and Eleanor (who was, by now, very pregnant and very miserable) in the other. He put Eleanor, Roman, and Gian-Carlo in the baptism scene. There were frequent spaghetti dinners with lots of wine, and people gathered around the table. George Lucas even came east to help film material for a montage of gang warfare. When Eleanor gave birth to Sofia, their third child, during the shooting, Francis videotaped the birth. Eleanor may not have been entirely happy about her birth pangs being turned into show biz and was even less happy giving birth so far from home.

Already interest in *The Godfather* was phenomenal. When Coppola brought his crew to Wall Street at nine one morning, fifteen thousand people stopped to watch; traffic gridlocked instantaneously, and the scene ended up on the CBS-TV news. A *New York Times* editorial called it "the biggest show in town." There was even a kid with a 16 mm camera, an ex-whiz kid student filmmaker whom Coppola didn't have the heart to send away; the result was a short documentary, *The Godfather Comes to Sixth Avenue.*

Brando worked for only six weeks, but after the rocky start they were the best weeks for Coppola. For one thing, Brando swore he'd quit the film in a second if Paramount fired Coppola. That must have meant a lot to Coppola, if only as a gesture of solidarity. And despite his reputation as a pain in the neck, Brando was a pleasure to work with. "With some actors," said Coppola, "you have only to ask. I would literally tell Brando to be 'more sad,' and watch the extra lines appear on his forehead." He was also quite cooperative. At one point, when rain delayed a critical scene in Staten Island, Brando agreed to return for an extra appearance and ended up working a week for free, saving the production $40,000.

Coppola would make "suggestions" by leaving around props to which Brando could gravitate. Improvisation bought one of the most effective scenes in the film. They were trying to figure out how to stage the Don's death scene, how to give it some resonance in the middle of the sequence where he's playing with his grandson. Finally, in desperation, Brando took an orange peel, cut it so it looked like big fangs, and stuck it in his mouth. "Here's how *I* play with kids," he said. Coppola loved it immediately: The Godfather would die as a monster.

The actors went to some pains to show they were unawed by the awesome Marlon Brando. Pacino played it moody and intense; Duvall sat behind him and mocked him when he talked politics; Caan tried to make him laugh and mooned him from off camera. Brando responded by mooning Caan and the others back, just before the cameras rolled, and playing practical jokes.

Even so, Brando's legendary status spooked some of the minor players. Lenny Montana, a nonprofessional actor, played Luca Brasi, the Mafia heavy who gets his hand pinned to a bar with a knife; but before that he had to do a scene in which he thanks the Godfather for inviting him to the wedding, and he was so awed by Brando that he couldn't remember his lines. After twelve abortive takes Coppola gave up and wrote another scene in which Brasi rehearses his speech to the Godfather over and over again. With that as a setup, Coppola was able to use one of the bad takes. It was a brilliant solution, especially considering how well the scene plays in the film. Some years later Coppola noted, quite rightly, that true directorial genius lies more in improvised solutions to unexpected problems than in flawless preparation.

Despite the improv exercises, the other lead actors employed more traditional techniques to bring their characters alive. Pacino was still very edgy. Coppola took him on a guided tour of the set, explaining what all the equipment did, until the actor relaxed. Pacino said he "thought a lot about music—and of an image. I saw Michael as though there were a circle of light and heat around him, shining on his face, that he was always trying to get out of."

James Caan's approach was even simpler; he "hung around with a lot of guys in Brooklyn who weren't exactly bankers." And he became so friendly with one of the on-set mafiosi that he later sat through the guy's trial for bribery and extortion in case he was needed as a character witness. Robert Duvall remembered two Italian cronies he had slipped into a rehearsal of *A View from the Bridge;* they had said that Arthur Miller reminded them of "a man who had made it in the rackets," and Duvall based his *consigliere* on that notion of Miller.

In June, having completed no fewer than 102 New York City locations, but with the Sicilian shoot still ahead, Coppola returned to San Francisco and edited what footage there was, using his own people to assemble a rough cut, thereby sidestepping the editors from Paramount.

Coppola then took his crew to Sicily to complete principal photography. Meanwhile, Yablans was rethinking his release strategy. Coppola had been falling a day behind schedule every week, but even if he hadn't been late, sticking to the original plan—a Christmas release—would have required a very fast, very dirty edit. Yablans was beginning to realize just how good a film Coppola was making and to suspect how successful it might be. He decided a reasonable delay to ensure a strong edit was justified. GODFATHER NOT ON CHRISTMAS TREE, was *Weekly Variety*'s page one headline, under which Yablans raved about the rushes and promised an opening between March and June 1972.

By the time he wrapped principal photography in September, Coppola was sick, tired, and disgusted. An assistant director remembered a conversation with him on the last day of shooting. There are three rules of filmmaking, said Coppola bitterly: Arrive with a completed script, only work with people you trust, and shoot the film so it will be impossible for the studio to change it. "I have failed," he admitted, "on all three." He returned to San Francisco in October 1971 with five hundred thousand feet of *Godfather* footage—more than ninety hours. The movie was now scheduled for an Easter 1972 release.

Coppola is the first to admit that his rough cuts always look terrible, and *The Godfather* was no exception. He had hired Walter Murch (who had done the sound edit for *The Rain People* and would subsequently edit *The Conversation*) to supervise the sound edit on *The Godfather,* and he was there when they screened the first rough cut. Coppola was so upset that Murch had to tell him a story just to calm him down—a story about a talking horse.

"There is a thief," said Murch, "and he gets caught for the third time. The king says, 'Kill him.'

"The thief says, 'But, Your Highness, I have the most incredible talent. I can teach a horse to talk. If you spare me and give me three months in the royal stable, I will bring you a horse that talks. You can kill me then as easily as you can now, and if I succeed you will be the only king with a talking horse.'

"The king says, 'All right, take him to the stables for three months.'

"As they're taking him away, his friend comes up. 'You're crazy,' he says. 'You can't teach a horse to talk.'

"The thief says, 'Yes, but in three months the king may die, or in three months *I* may die, or in three months the horse may die. Or in three months the horse may talk.' "

As they returned to the editing table, Coppola and Murch kept reminding each other, "The horse may talk."

Technically Paramount (i.e., Robert Evans) retained final-cut privileges; if there were any disagreements over how the film was to be edited, Coppola would lose. But according to Ruddy, Evans was "never arbitrary. He gave in in a lot of areas, and the picture is better because of him."

Nearly all of Coppola's cuts ran about three hours. He had been warned that if his final cut was longer than two and a half hours, Paramount would take the film away from him and shorten it itself, presumably with a meat ax. At one point he did try a short version, based on the original script, which ended with Kay's lighting candles in church. (This scene was restored in the television *Godfather Saga* years later.) Evans looked at this cut and called it "a two and a half hour trailer." The other executives couldn't help agreeing. Fortunately, once Evans saw how good the footage was, he was instrumental in fighting for a longer version, one that would end with Michael's henchmen shutting the door on Kay, and the audience. As late as 1975 Coppola admitted, "As soon as Evans saw the film, he decided it would be a major hit. He was the guy who fought for the length."

As the years passed, the issues grew more confused and more contentious. Evans claimed that his editing suggestions saved the movie from disaster. "It was in such big trouble after Coppola finished shooting it, I spent months—working 18 hours a day—re-editing the picture to get it in shape for release." He even blamed the breakup of his marriage to Ali MacGraw on *The Godfather;* he was so busy working on it he never had time to visit her while she was on location with Steve Mc-Queen. Coppola's response was to deny it all. In any case, Evans's name did not appear in the *Godfather* credits, and he never stopped brooding about it.

One name that did appear was Carmine Coppola. Early on, at a point when Francis was dead set against doing *The Godfather,* his father had urged him to reconsider. "I told him to make the film, make some money," Carmine recalled, "and then he could do what he wanted." Now Francis returned the favor. Nino Rota had already been hired to compose the main theme, so Francis got his father an assignment to write additional music; most of the music in the Italian wedding scene was his. *The Godfather* was Carmine's first major screen credit. Francis had finally made up for the rotten telegram.

With the picture locked down at last, the final step was mixing the sound track. Ruddy remembers the first day with mixed emotions. The lights went out in the projection room, and the old undertaker's voice (accompanied by black footage on the screen) came over the speakers, talking to Brando. The first line was supposed to be "I believe-a in America, America. . . ." But what Ruddy heard was, "I believe-a in the Mafia, the Mafia. . . ." Ruddy, who had promised the short-tempered IACRL that the M word would not be heard in *The Godfather,* felt himself breaking out in a cold sweat. "Francis!" he cried in alarm, and then he realized that Coppola was laughing so hard he'd fallen out of his chair.

By mid-January 1972 studio accountants discovered that Coppola had spent $1 million they hadn't known about; Yablans was still quoting the shooting costs at $6 million, but the actual total was edging closer to $7 million (/$20 million). Still, with the growing excitement about the film Paramount had bought for its money, no one was too upset.

Yablans announced an unprecedented distribution arrangement. Operating from a position of extraordinary strength, he had arranged for two competing theater chains, Loew's and National General, to share *The Godfather* during its premiere. Initially two theaters in Los Angeles and five exclusive houses in New York City would show the film. At least 340 prints would be struck, a huge amount for the time, so the film could go wide as soon as the premiere showcasing had established it. "The idea is to make an event out of the openings," Yablans noted.

With the world premiere set for March 14, 1972, at the Loew's State I in New York City (a benefit for the Boys' Club) Yablans revealed that Brando would actually attend; although he was in Europe, shooting Bernardo Bertolucci's *Last Tango in Paris,* his contract for that film included a clause allowing a full week off to help promote the *Godfather* premiere. By February, even before the film had been shown to a single audience, Paramount was already preparing a sequel (working title: "The Son of Don Corleone") to start shooting in July; Puzo was reportedly in Italy, working on the screenplay.

The film went before an audience for the first time in late February. It was a group of five hundred exhibitors at a New York trade convention, and they hated it. According to Coppola, they made faces. " 'It's not *Love Story,*' they said. " 'It's too dark, it's too long.' "

One of the exhibitors wasn't an exhibitor at all; he was a spy. Ivor Davis, a reporter for the London *Express,* managed to sneak into the screening, and his report was rushed into print by the New York *Post* two weeks before the opening. "Brando's greatest film," he raved, and "beautifully directed." He also found it bloody and violent, comparing it with Sam Peckinpah's *The Wild Bunch.*

Over the years Coppola has been alternately amused and horrified by the violence in the film. At one point he swore he would never again make a violent film. At another, he explained that there's very little actual violence in the film, "it's just that the violence happens to characters you like." And once he noted his theory that "people are more upset by the death of animals than they are by the death of human beings. I heard so many complaints about this horse's head, and yet there were 30 people killed in the film. People would say to me, 'But you really killed the horse to get the horse's head.' And I said, 'Not I. The horse was killed by the dog food company to feed all your cute little poodles.' " (Further horse-head trivia: it came packed in dry ice, and when the shot was in the can, they gave the head to the SPCA.)

Excitement was building. Articles were appearing everywhere: *Rolling Stone, Wall Street Journal,* and the European edition of the *Herald Tribune.*

The Godfather opened on Saturday, March 11, 1972, followed by not one but two official parties: the $100-a-ticket Boys' Club Party at 21, and the real party (for the filmmakers) at the St. Regis Roof. Execs shuttled back and forth between the parties in a fleet of limos.

What the opening nighters saw was a remarkable combination of art and exploitation. The photography was murky at times, but Coppola used the darkness of the Don's office (and the evil deeds that were planned therein) to contrast with sun-drenched exterior sequences like Connie's wedding. And although the pacing was occasionally slow, he usually used the change of pace to set the stage for a dazzling action scene or a terrifying murder.

The opening and closing sequences are particularly elegant. The first words we hear (over a dramatic black screen) are Bonasera, the undertaker, declaring, "I believe in America," establishing one of the main themes of the film (the Mafia as an alternative to America). When Bonasera appears at last, it's in a giant close-up; Coppola lets the shot run, pulling back very slowly while Bonasera tells his story, pleading with the Godfather for the justice that America has denied him. The long, slow zoom back establishes extraordinary dramatic tension and draws attention to Bonasera's storytelling—and the act of storytelling that lies at the center of Puzo's book and Coppola's film. By the time Brando's back edges into the corner of the shot, Coppola has the audience in his pocket.

The ending, an ironic montage that cuts back and forth between a church (where a child is being christened and a pious Michael is becoming its godfather) and a series of brutal murders, is probably the single most admired sequence in the film. Audiences enjoyed the opportunity to stretch their imaginative muscles a bit, they appreciated getting credit for the intelligence to understand the sequence, and they loved Coppola's homicidal choreography.

For beneath its arty photography and thematic complexity, most of the film is devoted to first-class storytelling, studded with a series of extravagantly violent scenes. Faced with the necessity of maintaining audience impact through a long series of murders, beatings, and generalized violence, Coppola decided to give each new sequence a special "gag."

The scene in which Hollywood producer Woltz finds a horse's head in his bed is staged like a Corman horror film, with blood everywhere. The execution of Paulie, the Don's treasonous bodyguard, takes place off camera; all we hear are three shots, followed by Clemenza's stupendously funny line, "Leave the gun, take the cannoli"; the violent fight between

Connie and her husband is presented as a series of tense mov-
ing-camera shots that follow her from room to room, ending in
a hysterical orgy of smashing crockery; a Family member is
trapped in a revolving door and shot; muscleman Luca Brasi
has his hand nailed to a bar with a knife and is garroted from
behind; Connie's traitorous husband is beaten under a gorgeous contrail of spray from an open hydrant; later he is choked
to death in a car and kicks out the front window as he dies; a
casino boss on a massage table puts on his glasses and looks
up, there's a shot, and a lens cracks as the bullet goes into
his eye.

Although some of the murders (like the revolving door and
the cannoli hit) are very funny, Coppola's denials of excessive
violence in the film don't stand up. There are many perfectly
dispensable close-ups of bullets going into bodies; consistent
emphasis on the agonized faces of the victims; more blood than
anyone needs to get across the idea that a character is dead.

Nonetheless, Coppola had made a nearly perfect movie.

The reviews were a press agent's dream.

The night before the premiere (for New Yorkers who bought
the Sunday *New York Times* on Saturday night), Vincent Canby
was in print with a semireview, semifeature on the front page
of the Arts and Leisure section. Headlined BRAVO, BRANDO'S
GODFATHER, it stopped short of a full-scale critique, but phrases
like "slam-bang sentimental gangster melodrama," "immensely moving," "great storytelling," and "the year's first really
satisfying big American film" made no secret of Canby's opinion. "Nothing in Coppola's previous work," he added, "pre-
pares the way for this new film."

Canby was quite right. For the first time in his career,
Coppola had integrated all the facets of his creative personality, drawn from the four overwhelming influences of his youth.
His Carmine side had encouraged him to take the assignment,
make the gangster movie, go for the money. His Tucker side
kicked in with the high-powered salesmanship he needed to
get the job, the script, and the cast he wanted. His Augie self
drove him to infuse the pulp saga with complex characterizations, artful images, and European complexity. And Francis,
the storyteller, the most sensitive part of him, which had been
born watching TV and yearning to tell stories, gave the film its
narrative power and emotional depth.

Newsweek had been in print for several days with a feature headlined THE GODFATHER: TRIUMPH FOR BRANDO. It heaped praise on Brando, the script, the music, the settings, the supporting actors, and Francis Coppola.

When Canby came out with his official *New York Times* review on March 16, it was a panegyric. Coppola, wrote Canby, "has made one of the most brutal and moving chronicles of American life ever designed within the limits of popular entertainment."

Of all the encomiums, Pauline Kael's was the sweetest to Coppola's ears, establishing him at last as an Artist of the Cinema. "[Coppola] has made a movie with the spaciousness and strength that popular novels such as Dickens' used to have," she wrote. "The abundance is from the book, [but] the quality of feeling is Coppola's. The direction is tenaciously intelligent. It's amazing how encompassing the view seems to be— what a sense you get of a broad historical perspective. Like Renoir, Coppola lets the spectator roam around in the images, lets the movie breathe, and this is extremely difficult in a period film. And yet, full as it is, *The Godfather* goes by evenly, so we don't feel rushed or restless; there's classic grandeur to the narrative flow. *The Godfather* is popular melodrama, but it expresses a new tragic realism."

Good as they were, the reviews were beside the point. Hours before the theater doors were opened, unprecedented ticket lines stretched around the block, despite the unheard-of admission price of $4 (/$11). Up to then even the most expensive movie theaters had never dared charge more than $3.

The next day the lines were even longer. In a classic example of New York City cottage industry, penniless Times Square vagrants discovered they could get in line, wait until they got close to the front, and sell their places for $20 and up. To accommodate the crowds, the State I ran the first screening of the day at 9:00 A.M. (inevitably sold out) and the last at midnight (it sold out, too).

A month later, with the picture running in 372 theaters across the country, the lines were longer yet, and the cottage industry had gone nationwide. Money was pouring in from *Godfather* games, *Godfather* sound track albums, 1.5 million paperback reprints of the *Godfather* novel. The Wall Street price for one share of Gulf + Western Industries common stock jumped from $38 to $44; G + W was now worth $97 million more than before the picture opened. Old Brando hits and flops were being revived to packed houses. Newspapers were running *Godfather* editorials, and not all of them were favorable. Nicholas Gage, writing for the Sunday *New York Times*, noted: "The only interruptions to the scenes of carnage are scenes of eating and family festivities." He also reported attending a screening at which people murmured with satisfaction at every killing; one patron, he wrote, sighed, "Beautiful!" at a particularly bloody execution.

Hollywood was euphoric; there *was* a way to drag people away from their TVs after all. The country was *Godfather*-crazy. "The picture is nothing less than an annuity," said Yablans.

Soon the world was *Godfather*-crazy, too.

The American Mafia liked the film, too—so much, in fact, that it paid it the ultimate compliment: imitation. According to insiders, several obsolete customs (like kissing the hands of powerful Family members) were revived in the wake of the film.

By 1975 *The Godfather* had made more money than any film in the history of motion pictures: $285 million (/$620 million) in estimated international income, including the fees from several top-dollar TV broadcasts. As early as January 1973 domestic rentals were already $81.5 million, surpassing the previous all-time box-office champ, *Gone With the Wind* ($77 million).

This impressive factoid has been reprinted so many times that it's generally taken at face value. It is true, but several points need to be made to put it in proper perspective. First, tickets for *The Godfather* cost $4; in 1939, and during *Gone With the Wind*'s many reissues, tickets were much cheaper. But even then the figures are misleading; if you correct for inflation (calculating the rentals in 1988 dollars), the scorecard looks like this:

Gone With the Wind:	$649 million
The Godfather:	$285 million

It's no contest. As a matter of fact, the only fair way to compare the two pictures would be in terms of the number of tickets sold, and those figures are not available.

Nonetheless, $285 million is still, indubitably, $285 million. The horse had talked . . . and talked . . . and talked.

Chapter Ten

Artistic Credentials:
The Conversation
(1972–1973)

THE ASTOUNDING SUCCESS of *The Godfather* didn't seem to produce any noticeable effect on its director, at least none that his intimates could notice. "Psychologically he seems to be different than that," Walter Murch commented. "In a sense he reverses the order of things. You would think that some normal person would make the successful film and *then* buy the expensive mansion on Broadway, and you could say, 'Ah, this is the effect that fame is having.' Francis does it the other way around. He was *always* that person."

Coppola might have disagreed. Fifteen years later he confessed, "The success of *The Godfather* went to my head like a rush of perfume. I thought I couldn't do anything wrong."

In any case, he was only thirty-three years old, and with *The Godfather* continuing to sell tickets like mad, he was well on his way to his first million dollars. The two years that followed were extraordinarily productive for Coppola. Even before *The Godfather* opened, he had several projects in the pipeline. For better or worse, he was committed to the sequel, now called *Godfather II*. He was also in preproduction on *The Conversation*, a cerebral thriller he'd been playing with since 1967, one that he hoped would reestablish his artistic credentials after his well-publicized flirtation with the crass gangster movie. If he did two *Godfather*s in a row, he feared, he'd be typecast for life. In addition, before the two years were gone, he would produce a third film (for George Lucas), write a fourth (for Robert Evans), and form a utopian filmmaking company with two other young superstar directors. Nor was that all.

Coppola had begun to miss the stage. He was known primarily as a filmmaker, but his vision of an artistic utopia in the Bay Area was bigger than that. At last, he had the financial freedom to follow through on a plan he'd had in the back of his mind for some time. He wanted to become a full citizen in San Francisco's creative community.

Even before he completed editing *The Godfather,* early in 1972, he had agreed to direct *Private Lives,* a brisk Noel Coward comedy, for San Francisco's American Conservatory Theater. Time was short; the play was set to open on February 22, leaving only one month for rehearsal, and Coppola leaped into action. "I was very, very lucky it turned out all right," he admitted later. "Dress rehearsal was a disaster!" Nonetheless, the play opened to good local reviews, even though the critics made hardly any mention of Coppola at all. If he'd had the time, he might have been disappointed.

But he didn't, and he wasn't. Within days of the *Private Lives* opening in February, the San Francisco Opera announced that as part of its gala fiftieth anniversary season, Coppola would direct the American premiere of Gottfried von Einem's avant-garde opera *The Visit of the Old Lady.*

Based on *The Visit,* an allegorical tragicomedy by Friedrich Dürrenmatt, the opera revolves around a rich woman who returns to her hometown to buy the murder of an old lover. Coppola was so taken with the idea ("out of my youthful desire to do everything"), he didn't even ask for any money, and this time he had a more comfortable lead time; the opera wasn't scheduled to open until late in the year.

Furthermore, at the New York premiere of *The Godfather* in early March, Evans had asked him for a special favor. Jack Clayton, who had made *Room at the Top,* was set to direct F. Scott Fitzgerald's *The Great Gatsby* for Paramount. All the wheels were ready to roll, but Evans wasn't happy with Truman Capote's script. Could Coppola possibly manage to whip out one of his patented last-minute, high-speed, clutch-writing screen adaptations? Knocking out a complete feature script in a month is pushing it, but for Coppola and the *Godfather* team, anything seemed possible.

Since *Gatsby* (unlike *The Godfather*) was planned as a

monster from the very beginning, it seemed to make sense to reassemble the already legendary *Godfather* team. Presumably, if Evans and Yablans could have gotten Brando, they would have found a part for him; since they couldn't they hired Robert Redford to play Gatsby and Mia Farrow to play Daisy. Initially Evans had cast his wife, Ali MacGraw, as Daisy, but when she left him for Steve McQueen he decided she wasn't right for the part after all.

To the studio executives, Truman Capote's screenplay, complete with dream sequences and flashbacks, seemed too hard to follow; they wanted a straight adaptation of the novel, and Coppola took the job. "Adapting a famous novel like that is a very delicate matter," he noted. "You're forced to use the story, the characters, the dialogue." For the film to work, Coppola knew he would have to create a screen equivalent for the music of Fitzgerald's prose.

Coppola took the assignment seriously. For five weeks he spent each morning tapping away at a portable typewriter at a table at the Café Trieste in North Beach. Using the same technique that had worked so well for *The Godfather,* he pasted Fitzgerald's pages into a large director's notebook and summarized the action underneath. Afternoons he dictated dialogue sequences to a secretary.

He found himself particularly drawn to the visual elements in the novel, like the mysterious green light that flickered at the end of Daisy's dock. Perhaps it was this that inspired him to write an unusually poetic opening, studded with visual clues to foreshadow the drama: the yellow car, the house, Gatsby's room, pictures of Daisy, a Hopalong Cassidy notebook with a child's handwriting, and so on.

For the big scene between Gatsby and Daisy, a scene that Fitzgerald never wrote, Coppola decided against a romantic flashback. Instead, Coppola wrote a lengthy dialogue sequence, seven or eight minutes long, set in Gatsby's bedroom. He borrowed a lot of the dialogue from Fitzgerald's short stories and wrote the rest himself "in a Fitzgerald way of thinking. It was a kind of acting tour de force between two actors in a room, nothing else. A very austere scene with people who had been lovers, not touching each other but just talking."

Finally, for the ending of the film, he designed a scene in which Gatsby's father (whose name is Gatz) arrives, revealing

Gatsby's low-class origins. Gatz packs up his son's things; he finds the Hopalong Cassidy notebook; he finds the picture of Daisy. "Who's this girl?" he asks, ending the movie by returning to the images that started it.

Ironically these three scenes (which were the elements of which Coppola was the proudest) all were lost or changed beyond recognition by director Jack Clayton. When filming was delayed for a year, Clayton spent the time "fidgeting" (Coppola's word) with the script. Coppola loathed the final film so much he wore shabby corduroys to the black-tie opening night party.

But all that was still in the future. By the end of March 1972 Coppola had finished what Evans called "a brilliant adaptation." He took a deep breath and rushed into five days of intensely concentrated work prepping *The Visit of the Old Lady.* Then, without a break, he plunged immediately into rewrites on the script for *The Conversation.*

Coppola credits veteran director Irvin Kershner with the germ of the idea; in 1966, he recalled, he was chatting with Kershner, who remarked that while most people thought the safest way not to be bugged was to walk in a crowd, he'd heard that there were now microphones with gunsights on them, so powerful and selective they could pick individual voices right out of a crowd.

Immediately a shot came to Coppola: Two people would walk through a crowd, talking, but every time someone stepped between them and the camera, their sound track conversation would be interrupted. (This scene never appeared in the final film; a similar scene, in which the conversation is intermittently distorted, took its place.)

By 1969 Coppola had a finished draft, and he told Army Archerd it would be his very next project; it would star Marlon Brando, cost $400,000, and take exactly four weeks to shoot. (How he expected to pay Brando and come in under $400,000 is anyone's guess.)

Still, he had never told anyone but his closest associates what the film would be about. Now, with preproduction actually starting, he began to pull off the wraps. In May 1972 (one month before the Watergate burglary and nine months before it would become front-page news), Coppola told *The New York Times,* "The movie will say something significant about the nightmarish situation that has developed in our society, a system that employs all the sophisticated electronic tools that are available to intrude upon our private lives."

In addition to Kershner, the prime sources for *The Conversation* seem to have been Hermann Hesse's *Steppenwolf* (which Coppola was reading at the time), Antonioni's *Blow-Up*, and an article in *Life* magazine about bugging expert Bernard Spindell. Coppola had never realized there were bugging experts, as distinct from run-of-the-mill hard-boiled detectives. It stirred childhood memories of the network of microphones he'd thought of installing in his Long Island home to find out what he'd be getting for Christmas.

"I was fascinated to learn that bugging was a *profession*," he said, "not just some private cop going out and eavesdropping with primitive equipment." He pored over catalogs of the latest electronic surveillance hardware, and when he couldn't find an item he needed for a story point, he'd make it up. "I'd [write] a scene where somebody would do something, and experts like Hal Lipset would say, 'Oh, I heard about that,' and I'd have totally made it up."

To Coppola's sorrow, Brando wasn't interested in starring in the picture, so he cast Gene Hackman in the lead, with two relative unknowns, Frederic Forrest and Cindy Williams, in supporting roles. Thanks to his Academy Award-winning performance in *The French Connection*, Hackman was now a star, but he and Coppola had cut their deal long before either one of them became famous. Coppola had been impressed with Hackman's earlier work (*Bonnie and Clyde; Downhill Racer*) and shortly after he opened *The Rain People* (which Hackman admired), Coppola proposed that they do *The Conversation* together. *The French Connection* had just been released, but Coppola hadn't seen it, and *The Godfather* was still far in the future. Still, Hackman had agreed.

"Hackman is ideal for the part because he's so ordinary, so unexceptional in appearance," said Coppola. ". . . It's important to show that [the character] absolves himself of all responsibility; that he's the instrument of other people. He's just a *businessman*."

Exchanging Hackman for Brando wasn't the only change. The budget was now $1.1 million (/$3.1 million), up considerably from the $400,000 Coppola had asked for from Seven Arts, but still quite low for a commercial feature. And the shooting schedule was lengthened considerably. Best of all, with a reasonable amount of money to spend and no studio bosses second-guessing him, Coppola could assemble most of the cast and crew he wanted.

To begin with, he brought in Walter Murch to do sound and to edit the picture. Although this would be Murch's first film editing job, he was a likely choice; with *The Conversation*'s built-in focus on sound bugging, secret microphones, and surreptitious tape recording, many of its key scenes had been designed to work through special sound sequences that Murch would create. Coppola also hired Dean Tavoularis as production designer; he had worked with him on *The Godfather.*

For coproducer, Coppola signed Fred Roos, a soft-spoken introvert with dead-white skin, pale eyes, and prematurely graying hair, who was known primarily as one of the industry's top casting directors. A newcomer to the filmmaking family, he swiftly became one of Coppola's most trusted associates. Coppola also signed on top-rated cinematographer Haskell Wexler. Wexler had made his directorial debut in 1969 with *Medium Cool,* a well-received political feature; immediately thereafter he had rented facilities at Zoetrope, where he worked on several projects before moving on.

Once Coppola actually got down to work on the script, he found himself in deeper water than he'd anticipated. Harry Caul, his conflicted detective hero, was so introverted he bored even Coppola; the director was afraid that audiences would find it just as hard to care about Caul as he did. So he did what many writers do when their well runs dry: He drew on his unhappy childhood. "In the scene where he's in the park, and tells all that stuff about his childhood and the polio—those are things that actually happened to me," he admitted in an interview with fellow filmmaker Brian De Palma for *Filmmakers Newsletter.* Later in the same interview Coppola revealed as much about himself as Harry Caul when he added, "I think his roots are roots of guilt. Ever since he was a little kid, everything that has happened he has in some way been responsible for. . . . He must have been one of those kids who's sort of a weirdo in high school. You know, the kind of technical freak who's president of the radio club. . . . When I was a kid I was one of those guys like I was just describing. . . ."

Now he had the premise and the character, but he still needed a story—and time was growing short. He realized early that backers (and audiences) would want something more than a character study: They would want a thriller, even if it was an avant-garde thriller.

Finally, thinking of *Godfather,* perhaps, with its tale of a king and his three sons, Coppola tried to rethink his movie as a kind of political romance about a powerful man with a young, beautiful, unfaithful wife; Robert Duvall (in an uncredited cameo) would be the king, Cindy Williams would be the young queen, and Frederic Forrest would be a courtier who was sleeping with her. Coppola connected Caul with these characters by having him record a conversation in which the king seems to be planning to murder the lovers, forcing the surveillance man to decide whether or not to intervene.

Coppola never found a strong story; what he found instead, with the help of Walter Murch, was a structuralist concept. "Somewhere along the line," he said shortly after the film opened, "I got the idea of using repetition, of exposing new levels of information not through exposition but by repetition. And not like *Rashomon,* where you present it in different ways each time—let them be the exact lines but have new meanings *in context.*"

In any case, even with Hackman on board, Coppola knew *The Conversation* was too grim, too cerebral, too arty for a mass audience. "It's going to be an unusual film," he admitted. "It won't make the money *Godfather* is making, but no one expects that. That was a fluke, although *Godfather II* may do equally well because of the curiosity." One senses some relief in Coppola's insistence on the film's lack of commercial potential. After the unexpected success of the cheap gangster film, he was anxious to reestablish his reputation as a serious, original filmmaker. It was a personal test, a dare to himself to see if he could make it work.

Even while he focused his full creative energies on the script of *The Conversation,* he was also helping George Lucas with a low-budget musical about cars, teenagers, and rock 'n' roll to be called *American Graffiti.* Letting his name be used as executive producer to facilitate financing had started out as a small favor to Lucas, but the film was eating up a lot more time and energy than Coppola had planned.

Lucas had been working on the project since 1971. When he pitched his original five-page treatment, all the studio executives turned it down. For one thing, they were worried about the expense of acquiring rights to the classic rock 'n' roll tunes Lucas insisted were critical to the success of the film. Finally, he scored a low-end development deal from United Artists' president David Picker. UA would put up $10,000 to pay for writing a complete screenplay; if Picker liked it, there would be more money for rewrites. Lucas hired his friend Gary Kurtz to be producer and arranged for a script to be written, but it turned out badly, and UA passed on it. Even when Lucas's friends Bill Huyck and Gloria Katz joined in to rewrite the script, it made no difference; UA wouldn't buy it.

Finally, in desperation, Lucas brought the rewrite back to Universal, where a young executive named Ned Tanen had scored a moderate success with one ambitious, low-budget film (*Diary of a Mad Housewife*) and then flopped badly with another (*Two Lane Blacktop*). Tanen was interested, but his bosses at Universal were unhappy about the poor box-office results of the latter picture, and they set several hard conditions. They would put up only $750,000, little more than a subsistence budget; they would give Lucas only twenty-eight days to shoot; and they would not agree to Gary Kurtz as producer. They showed Lucas a list of producers they considered acceptable, and there was only one name on the list that Lucas even considered: Francis Ford Coppola.

Relations between Coppola and Lucas had been cool since the *THX* debacle; Lucas later told his biographer, Dale Pollock, that he was annoyed that "Coppola never let him forget who was the senior partner in the relationship." Furthermore, Coppola was in the middle of his own creative marathon, and on top of that, he was annoyed with Lucas for not coming to him first with *Graffiti*. (Shades of Don Corleone.) Nonetheless, he did like the script, and he realized that he was Lucas's only chance. He agreed to sign on as executive producer to keep Universal happy, but he made it clear that with his own creative commitments pressing urgently he would not be spending much time on the set. Kurtz would have to handle day-to-day production responsibilities.

Lucas thought that was swell, until Coppola decided that the name of the picture ought to be changed from *American*

Graffiti to *Rock Around the Block.* Lucas finally talked him out of *that,* and eventually he forgave Coppola, especially when the costs of the music rights began to rise toward the $90,000 studio limit, and Universal panicked. Coppola agreed to make up any cost overruns out of his own pocket to keep the studio from pulling the plug. He and Fred Roos (who was producing *The Conversation*) supervised casting for Lucas. Roos rounded up a soon-to-be-legendary cast of near unknowns, including Richard Dreyfuss, Ron Howard, Cindy Williams, Harrison Ford, Charlie Martin Smith, and Paul Le Mat. As a gesture of appreciation Lucas arranged for the local movie theater in *Graffiti* to be showing Coppola's *Dementia 13.*

Coppola and Lucas cut a complicated deal. Since there was virtually no front money, they each agreed to take 20 percent of the net profits, if there ever were any. Lucas would give some of his profit points to Huyck, Katz, the actors, and his lawyer, Tom Pollock. Coppola, in turn, would give some of his points to Gary Kurtz to compensate him for being demoted from producer to coproducer. According to Lucas, Coppola was never happy about having to pay Kurtz, and there were bad feelings later on both sides when Lucas insisted that Coppola was holding back points. Even so, when all the disputed points were given out, Coppola still retained 13 percent of the profits—a cut that eventually made him $3 million (/$5.7 million). (Years later he insisted that he'd wanted to finance *Graffiti* entirely by himself but let himself be talked out of it by his friends and his father. "That movie could have brought me over $20 million," he noted. "I lost the chance to earn enough money to set up my own studio." After *Graffiti* Coppola swore he'd finance all his films himself.)

When the first rushes of *Graffiti* proved too dark, Coppola arranged for Haskell Wexler (who was set to shoot *The Conversation*) to come on as Lucas's "visual consultant" (i.e., head cameraman) for a percentage of the profits—in lieu of a salary that Lucas had no money to pay. Lucas later insisted on Coppola's putting up half of Wexler's percentage points; Coppola was not pleased with this arrangement.

Nor was that all Coppola was up to. Some months earlier he had gotten involved with a very small, local magazine called *City* that published entertainment listings, service features, and short interviews with local musicians, artists, filmmakers, and dancers. Perennially poverty-stricken, *City* couldn't afford slick paper, expensive graphics, or high-priced writers; it looked like an underground newspaper with a cover and staples. It had been around for several years; whenever the money ran out, the publisher and editor would hit the phones in hopes of finding angels. At some point they found Coppola, who liked the idea of a magazine that celebrated the local arts scene. He kicked in a few thousand dollars, and when that ran out, he came up with a few thousand more.

In so doing, he became one of the biggest investors, and when the publisher met with him in 1972 to ask for yet more money, he agreed to buy in for a total of $15,000, but only on the condition that if the magazine couldn't get into the black by itself, he would take control. Why Coppola wanted control of a magazine is another question; maybe because it was there. Secretly many of the *City* staffers thought it would be cool if Coppola took over. For one thing, they liked his movies. For another, he was the most charming millionaire any of them had ever met. (He was also the only millionaire they had ever met.) Coppola was the door to the big time, or so they hoped.

The idea of artistic control of his own movies had been on Coppola's mind for many years, but now, thanks to *Godfather*'s great success, he had the power to do something about it. Eventually he wanted his own studio, but for the moment he would settle for being an independent distributor. After a series of discussions with Peter Bogdanovich (whose two most recent films, *The Last Picture Show* and *What's Up, Doc?*, had been big box-office hits) and William (*French Connection*) Friedkin, he completed a deal with Paramount setting up the Directors Company.

Yablans (who always claimed that it was he who first approached Coppola) made the announcement in August 1972. Paramount would put up $31 million, which the Directors Company (i.e., Coppola, Bogdanovich, and Friedkin) would use to produce twelve pictures over a six-year period. None of the films would cost more than $3 million (/$8.4 million). "This is a familial relationship," Yablans declared. "We're all in our early thirties, and we don't have a great hierarchy." And he added (with great inaccuracy), "They've gone through their growth period, indulging their esoteric tastes. Coppola isn't interested any more in filming a pomegranate growing in the desert. They're all very commercial now."

Very few of the grandiose predictions made for the Directors Company ever came true. Friedkin was busy with *The Exorcist,* and between one thing and another he never got around to making a movie for the Directors Company at all. Bogdanovich made two (*Paper Moon* and *Daisy Miller*). Coppola contributed one (*The Conversation*), and that was all she wrote.

This time, though, Coppola was far more careful pinning down the financial details than he had been on the Warners-Zoetrope deal, and as a result, he made money instead of losing it. "Part of my desire to get involved with [Friedkin and Bogdanovich] is revenge," he admitted, "for lots of vindictive, Mafia-like reasons—because I'm so mad at Warner Brothers. Billy Friedkin, Peter Bogdanovich and I are old friends, and we've all had a super-success this year. We could really take over the business, and then spend the rest of [our lives] making little movies that don't have to make money." And he added, "I now am as successful as I ever want to be, and I'm pretty rich, so I've got to change all my motivations."

And yet a strange, paranoid note continued showing up in Coppola's interviews. "I really have had it with publicity," he told Stephen Farber, "because what happens is lots of people you don't even know dislike you, for no reason. Perhaps because of jealousy."

There was now less than a month until the premiere of *The Visit*—time to get the opera into serious rehearsals. Writer John Rockwell, who observed the final, hectic week before the opening, when nearly everything seemed to be going wrong, reported that Coppola seemed unable to work under less than quasi-hysterical conditions. He watched in horror while Coppola negotiated a series of desperate, last-minute changes. For instance, Coppola spent days working out subtle business for individual chorus members, much like the close-ups in the *Godfather*'s wedding scene; it wasn't until the first run-through that he realized only the first five rows would be able to see it.

The Godfather had made Coppola a celebrity, and when *The Visit* opened, a flood of critics descended on San Francisco to see what the whiz kid would do with a serious artistic project. By and large, the reviews were tepid, but Coppola was full of enthusiasm. Perhaps he'd do an intimate production of *La Bohème* next, or a spectacular *Turandot* set in Communist China with lots of red flags. Or a vaudeville musical with music by his father. "I'm open to anything," he said, "now that I don't have to work for money any more."

But now there were only two weeks left before the first day of shooting on *The Conversation,* and the script was still not set to Coppola's satisfaction. He plunged into sudden-death rewrites.

On November 26, 1972, right on schedule, the cameras rolled on principal photography for *The Conversation,* and from the first day of shooting it was clear there were major problems. After the *Godfather* shoot Coppola had sworn that never again would he start filming without a completed script, an oath he was to honor more in the breach than the observance. Certainly the script for *The Conversation* was something of a puzzle. Many of the scenes Coppola had written were technically very difficult to shoot; the master setup in San Francisco's Union Square required no fewer than four camera crews and six cameras, working simultaneously, plus an army of sound technicians with shotgun microphones stuck in unlikely locations, including the roof of the City of Paris department store (now Neiman-Marcus). So much for keeping his crews small.

To get the "spy-eye" effect he needed, Coppola pointed out the actors to the cameramen and told them, "Try and find them and keep them in focus." Then he had the actors walk through the action again and again, surrounded not by extras but by real passersby who (if they weren't watching closely) had no idea there was a movie being shot. It took weeks. Some of the sound men were so creatively camouflaged they were busted by policemen with guns, who thought they might be snipers trying to kill Coppola. "Half our crew was in all those shots," he admitted. "It was John Cassavetes time: cameras photographing cameras."

The actors never knew if the cameras were rolling or not. Not even the camera crews were sure. At one point a cameraman walked up to Hackman (who had been doing an interview with a reporter) and asked, "Were you acting then, or what? Is she in the movie? 'Cause we've been shooting it."

Hackman had arrived on set looking young and handsome, exactly the wrong look for the eccentric character of Harry Caul. Coppola started by forcing Hackman to cut his hair so he'd look bald, and little by little he used makeup and psychology to transform him into (in Coppola's description) a nudnik.* "It really got on his nerves," Coppola remembered. "He hated looking like that."

He may also have hated the part, not because it was badly written but because the character was such a downer. "It's a depressing and difficult part to play," Hackman admitted, "because it's so low key. The minute you start having any fun with it, you know you're out of character."

In the end Hackman even made Coppola uncomfortable. In order to give his cast and crew a break at lunchtime, Coppola had set up a volleyball net, but Hackman never played. One day Coppola leaned close to actor Allen Garfield, a newcomer to the professional family. "Hackman's a real asshole, isn't he?" asked Coppola.

"What?" asked Garfield.

"He's a real asshole," Coppola insisted. "Marlon wouldn't be like this, Marlon likes to play, Marlon likes to have fun when we're not shooting. . . ."

Garfield couldn't figure what Coppola expected him to say. Was Coppola kidding or what? Finally he replied, "What are you talking about? This guy's a great actor."

"I know he's a great actor," said Coppola, "but he doesn't play volleyball, he doesn't talk, he just goes off by himself."

"Maybe he's just totally into being Harry Caul," suggested Garfield.

Coppola thought about that for a few seconds. "But still," he said, "he could be more playful, he still could show some fun. . . ."

All sorts of little disasters added to the general sense of chaos. When neighbors complained about the fog machines, and TV station KGO sent a camera crew to investigate, Coppola got mad. "Stop taking pictures," he reportedly said, "you're making me look bad." When the TV crew refused to quit, there was some pushing and shoving, and eventually KGO cameraman Harold Joseph filed a $300,000 damage suit against Coppola, charging unlawful assault. The light in Union Square proved so changeable and uncertain that the camera crews despaired of matching any of the footage well enough so it could be cut together. Coppola seemed edgy, and Hackman found

---

*Coppola's Yiddish was inexpert. He meant "schlemiel."

himself wondering if this was how things had gone during the filming of *The Godfather*, with so much improvisation, so little preparation.

But these were minor annoyances compared to the main problem: ace cinematographer Haskell Wexler. Wexler and Coppola were friends, with deep respect for each other's technical abilities, but both were artists with their own visions of how to make a film. And it became increasingly clear that those visions were different. Wexler didn't like certain locations that Coppola lusted for; they would be impossible to light, he insisted, impossible to shoot. And while Coppola was happy with neither the rushes nor the slow pace of the shoot, he was reluctant to push an important artist like Wexler.

They fussed and hassled, and finally it dawned on Coppola that Wexler was forcing him to make the film differently from the way he wanted to. Reluctantly he decided to fire him and shut down the shoot for ten days.

Coppola couldn't bring himself to fire Wexler face-to-face; he sent word to him after the film shut down. Even then, apparently, Coppola couldn't bear to tell Wexler the real reason he'd been canned. Instead, he concocted an elaborate fable about needing an excuse to give the studio for suspending the production while he wrestled with the script problems.

When Wexler read Coppola's more accurate account of the affair in the pages of *Variety*, he was so deeply hurt he wrote a letter to the paper telling his side of the story and implying that Coppola was lying to somebody. Wexler and Coppola never worked together again.

During the break, Coppola did fine-tune the script a little more and then brought in *Rain* person Bill Butler to take over the cameras. The switch slowed him down and cost him money: Within days of starting, the budget had jumped from $1.1 million to $1.6 and then to $1.9 million. Finally Coppola had to extend the shooting schedule from forty to fifty-six days. Nor did any of this solve the script problems; it just cleared some time for Coppola to wrestle with them.

For therapy, he took to running two reels of Bertolucci's *The Conformist* every day for inspiration. "He's obviously together enough that he can do absolutely anything that delights him," he thought. "Why can't I? What's happening to me?"

Had Coppola's life turned into a living hell? Not exactly.

As 1972 turned into 1973, there was still plenty for him to feel good about. *Variety* had just moved *The Godfather* to the top of its all-time top-rentals list; Coppola's little gangster movie was now, officially, the biggest money-making motion picture in history. Moreover, late in January, *Godfather* was honored with no fewer than five Golden Globe awards from the Foreign Press Association of America: Best Performance by an Actor (Brando, of course); Best Score; Best Screenplay; Best Direction; Best Picture of 1972. While none of this came as a total surprise, it certainly raised Coppola's spirits.

A few days later, on a Sunday morning in January 1973, Coppola and his cast took a break from *The Conversation* to join Lucas in putting *American Graffiti* in front of an audience for the first time. It was a morning destined to go down in movie legend. The preview audience at San Francisco's eight-hundred-seat Northpoint Theater, recruited via handouts on the street, was crazy about the film. Lucas was deeply relieved; he and Gary Kurtz had been wondering whether the nostalgia craze might have already crested, leaving their film high and dry.

Coppola was walking happily up the aisle with cheers still ringing in his ears when he encountered Ned Tanen, also shuffling toward the lobby. Coppola smiled and asked innocently how Tanen liked it. To Coppola's utter amazement, Tanen responded with a flood of angry accusations. He hated the film; he didn't think it worked at all. "You boys let me down," he snapped. "I went to bat for you, and you let me down. We'll have to see if we can release it. Why don't you come back to Universal and we'll talk about it. . . ."

"You'll see if you can *release* it?" Coppola bellowed. "I don't have time to fly to L.A. just to appease your mind! You were just in this theater for the last two hours, didn't you just see and hear what we all just saw and heard?"

Lucas, who was listening to this exchange, went into shock; his moment of triumph was turning into an all too familiar nightmare. This was *THX* all over again. But Coppola had learned a few things about power politics since the bad Zoetrope days, and he rose to the occasion like a champ. "You shouldn't even be talking to *me*," he yelled in fury at Ned Tanen, "you should be turning to your right, you should be getting down on your knees and thanking George for saving your job! This kid has killed himself to make this movie for you. And he brought it in on time and on schedule. The least you can do is thank him for doing that!"

Tanen tried to cool things out, but Coppola was just getting started. As he threw verbal punches, a crowd of Northern California filmmakers gathered, watching with thinly veiled delight as Coppola took Hollywood to task, screaming out all the anger and frustration every one of them had felt, time and time again, dealing with the studios. As his final, knockout, punch, Coppola reached for an imaginary checkbook and offered to buy the film back from UA if Tanen hated it so much. "This movie is going to be a hit!" he shouted. "This audience loved this movie. I saw it with my own eyes! I'll write a check right now. I think it's a great film, and I want it back!"

Tanen denies that Coppola ever made such an offer, but a number of ringsiders remember it. In any case, after a series of passionate negotiating sessions, Coppola managed to limit the damage to four and a half minutes of cuts, and talked Universal out of rerecording all the rock 'n' roll classics with a cheap pickup band to be called (what else?) the Universalaires. The film went on to make legendary amounts of money for everyone; by 1979 it had earned nearly $56 million (/$90 million) in domestic rentals alone, which means worldwide rentals in the neighborhood of $112 million (/$180 million), on an investment of $750,000.

Unfortunately, financial and artistic disputes had a dire effect on the relationship between Coppola and Lucas, each of whom thought that the other had put money before friendship. It isn't surprising; the emotional riptides that accompany the making of any film often cause bad feelings between the participants. But neither Lucas nor Coppola tried very hard to make up afterward. Lucas was still too upset over the "rape" of his film, and Coppola was in the middle of *The Conversation.*

Still, if Coppola was starting to feel depressed and pressured again, one night in February changed all that. On February 13, 1973, *The Godfather* was nominated for no fewer than eleven Oscars: Best Film, Best Actor, Best Director, Best Screenplay, Best Editing, Best Costume Design, Best Sound, Best Score (with Carmine Coppola enjoying the sole nomination; Nino Rota had been disqualified for having plagiarized his own earlier work), plus three Supporting Performances

(Caan, Duvall, Pacino). Then, a month later, Coppola received the honor he probably treasured the most when the Directors Guild of America gave him its citation for Most Outstanding Directorial Achievement of 1972, for *The Godfather*.

Shortly thereafter, in March 1973, the last shot of *The Conversation* went into the can. Two more weeks of shooting had been scheduled to tie up the loose ends of the plot, but Coppola decided to stop dead. The story would just have to resolve itself in the edit. As it happened, only one insert had to be shot. The film ended up costing $1.9 million (/$5 million). On March 19, within days of the completion of principal photography, the first stories about high-level government involvement with the Watergate break-in hit the front page. Suddenly Coppola's personal movie was red-hot news, and the writer-director began to look like a psychic as well.

Psychic or not, he was exhausted—until he discovered, to his horror, that between editing *The Godfather,* writing *Gatsby*, directing *Private Lives* and *The Visit*, and rewriting and directing *The Conversation* he had forgotten *Godfather II*. He had exactly three months to write the script, and despite Puzo's work on the screenplay, Coppola didn't have a hint what the film was supposed to be about. He was a millionaire, but exhaustion was a luxury he couldn't afford.

"I was in a desperate situation," he remembered. "I'd go upstairs and write and write and write, write on the blackboard, until somehow I finished the script three days before we were gonna start." He looked back with longing on the clutch writing of *The Great Gatsby*, when he'd had the luxury of working in a North Beach coffeehouse amid a crowd of admirers. Now, shut up in his office, he had nobody to stop and chat with.

Little wonder that when a reporter asked him how things were going, Coppola moaned, "I don't have any fun any more, I'm depressed all the time." He smiled when he said it, playing the cheerfully overworked artist, but deep down he probably wondered if it was really all that funny. He was operating in a daze, operating on instinct. He never had time for his wife and children any more, and he began to talk about finishing all the work and leading a normal life.

Still, he found time to fly down to Hollywood for the Academy Awards presentation in April. By now, with all the honors that had been heaped on the film, he was expecting a *Godfather* landslide. Anyway, only once in the history of the Academy had the winner of the DGA directing award not won the Oscar for Best Direction as well; that one, at least, was in the bag.

But it wasn't. Nothing was in the bag. When all the Oscars were given out, and all the speeches made, only three awards had gone to *The Godfather:* Best Picture; Best Screenplay; Best Performance by an Actor. (*Cabaret* won seven.) Brando wouldn't even take his Oscar; never one to let a political opportunity pass, he sent a young woman who called herself Sacheen Littlefeather (her real name was Maria Cruz) to refuse it for him and to complain about the way Indians were treated in American movies. (Littlefeather was an acquaintance of Coppola's; in fact, he had helped her make contact with Brando by providing the actor's address.) Coppola still had every reason to be proud—after all, Best Picture and Best Screenplay Oscars were hardly chopped liver—but years later he was still brooding about losing Best Director to Bob Fosse, who won for *Cabaret*.

After the miserable Academy Awards Coppola returned to sweating out the script for *Godfather II*, leaving Walter Murch to work on editing *The Conversation*.

Murch found himself running up against script problems that Coppola had never solved. The ending of the film had always been a bit vague. In fact, the original draft was a pure character study; it didn't even have a murder at the end. Before they started editing, Coppola and Murch had settled on a tentative story line, but when Murch followed it, nobody liked the ending. The trick lay in finding a way to balance the thriller elements and the character study so that each supported the other. Coppola looked at all the rough cuts and agreed there was a problem, but nobody could think of a solution.

Finally, with *Godfather II* nearing its start date, Coppola put *The Conversation* on the back burner; his involvement was reduced to coming back occasionally to San Francisco to look at the latest version. Murch continued taking *The Conversation* apart and putting it back together again, hoping somehow to find the elusive balance that would bring the story into focus. In the process he invented some new plot connections and rediscovered others that had been overlooked from earlier versions of the script. With the help of several brilliant sound montages, the new structure seemed to hold together, and when he put it on the screen for Coppola, it worked.

Coppola has always been generous about crediting Murch's contributions. "A lot of [the film] is due to his ability," he noted. "The picture was edited primarily by Walter Murch, assisted by Richard Chew. Walter was much more than your average editor—he was really a full collaborator on the project. Walter is an author of [*The Conversation*]."

One of Murch's ideas caused a great critical controversy when the film was released. As originally conceived by Coppola, the film would unfold through repeated reinterpretations of a short piece of taped conversation in which Frederic Forrest and Cindy Williams are heard saying, "He'd *kill* us if he got the chance." Coppola has stated many times that "It is the same exact footage of the couple talking that is repeated. In other words, I haven't done a *Rashomon* where I have slightly changed the three-minute scene so that it works better for one meaning than another."

Technically, this is true—since the *footage* is identical. However, while Murch was editing the sound, he came across an interesting bit of tape. One day, at Coppola's suggestion, he'd taken Forrest and Williams out into a small park near the location to record some "wild" takes of various key lines of dialogue, just in case. Now, listening back to the session, Murch discovered an alternate reading of the line in which Forrest changed the emphasis from "He'd *kill* us if he got the chance" to "He'd kill *us* if he got the chance."

Murch realized that using both readings—first the innocuous one and then the sinister one (as Caul suddenly realizes that Forrest and Williams are *planning* a murder)—would bring the audience inside Caul's mind. It was an unusual idea, almost a cheat, so he played the alternate take for Coppola, who liked it. It was the only way either of them could think of to clinch the idea that the detective has finally caught on to the truth. "It's tricky, but we were desperate men." Murch laughed. "I am eighty-five percent sure that it was the right thing to do."

The finished film is an impeccably grim, intriguingly paranoid fantasy, extremely European in tone and style. Every performance is sharply focused, and the script moves with economical grace toward what seems an increasingly inevitable conclusion. The film is artful without slipping across the line into artiness; it's serious without being pretentious.

The Conversation isn't much fun, but it is tremendously effective. Along with Richard Lester's *Petulia* and Alfred Hitchcock's *Vertigo, The Conversation* is a key member of the essential trilogy of great, sad films about San Francisco.

Interestingly, *The Conversation* works most effectively as music. Coppola and Murch use sound, and David Shire's fine music track, with great creativity to provide emotional cues to help the audience empathize with the guarded main character. A slow, sad, bluesy piano theme works marvelously to establish the main tone of the film. The repeated use of "When the Red Red Robin Comes Bob-Bob-Bobbin' Along" provides ironic counterpoint. Disturbing electronic compositions make the intrusion of the ominous, unspeakable, ultimately unknowable surveillance that pins Harry Caul like a helpless insect horribly immediate and personal. In some respects *The Conversation* is a musical.

On August 1, 1973, *American Graffiti* opened at a small theater in Los Angeles. One week later, some Universal exec noticed that Lucas's film had quietly set a house record: $35,000 in ticket sales in a very small theater. With no publicity.

Universal opened it in New York a few days later, with a full-page ad in *Variety* bragging about the L.A. grosses. Within hours of the opening, word was out; long ticket lines formed immediately, and house records were shattered. Now the executives began paying attention as they opened the film around the country, and early in September they took out a two-page ad in *Variety,* boasting that in nine cities across the country, their $750,000 wonder was outgrossing multimillion-dollar box-office champ *Airport.* Within days, it was bringing in $170,000 a week, making it the second-biggest picture in Universal's history. Insiders knew that Lucas deserved most of the credit, but to the general public (and much of the press), it was Coppola who had done it again.

Between his percentages of *The Godfather* and *American Graffiti,* Coppola's cash flow was little short of astonishing. In fact, he found himself with more cash than was healthy, at least in respect to taxes. So in odd hours when he wasn't working on the script of *Godfather II,* he started buying things. He already had a mansion and a rural retreat in Mill Valley, so he bought a historic eight-story triangular office building at the edge of Chinatown called Columbus Tower (to which he moved the administrative offices of American Zoetrope), half interest in a turbojet, full ownership of *City* magazine, and two new cars (a Cortez mobile home, which he used for "meditating in the hills," and a two-seat Honda coupe). He also bought a building that housed the three-hundred-seat Little Fox Theater and installed *City* magazine in the offices above the auditorium.

He acquired the requisite Mercedes-Benz limo as well, but he didn't buy it. During a casual conversation with Robert Evans about what they'd do if *The Godfather* went through the roof, Evans had promised to buy Coppola "a limo like the Pope drives." When the film hit the top of the charts, Evans conveniently forgot his promise. Under Coppola's persistent prodding, he finally delivered the limo, but in truth it was a bit of an embarrassment to Coppola, which he tried to offset by driving the Honda as much as possible.

Rumors, and several mistaken articles in the trades, reported that Coppola had also bought the historic Château Marmont Hotel in Hollywood so he'd have somewhere nice to stay when he went south to cut deals, but there was never any truth to it. It only *seemed* as if Coppola was buying up everything in sight.

people. I *never*. Wanted. To see. *Any*. Of those people again. And I don't mean Francis or Pacino or Brando."

With Ruddy out of the picture, Coppola would now write, direct, and produce; the title was officially announced as *The Godfather, Part II*, the start date was rolled back six months to January 1973, and the opening was set for Easter 1974.

In August 1972, Paramount revealed that the precise opening date for *The Godfather, Part II* would be March 24, 1974, two years to the day from *The Godfather*'s now-legendary premiere. The film was even advance-booked into the same five theaters in New York City. To some extent, this gambit was a publicity ploy, a way to remind the audience of a tie-in with an earlier film it had liked. But Hollywood is a superstitious place, and with millions of dollars at stake what harm could it do to rub the rabbit's foot one more time?

Coppola had mixed feelings about the project. "I used to joke that the only way I'd do it was if they'd let me film *Abbott and Costello Meet the Godfather*," he laughed. But he relented, partly because this time Paramount gave him complete control over the production and partly because he'd begun to dream of double-billing Parts I and II as a seven-hour, two-part epic.

"I was fascinated by the idea of a movie that would work freely in time, that would go both forward and backward in time," he said. "I felt that *Godfather* had never been finished; morally, I believed that the Family would be destroyed, and it would be like a kind of Götterdämmerung. I thought it would be interesting to juxtapose the decline of the Family with the ascension of the Family; to show that as the young Vito Corleone is building this thing out of America, his son is presiding over its destruction."

On top of which, there was the money—so much money that even Coppola was a bit embarrassed. The deal was rather complicated, but in addition to his fee for writing and directing (really an advance), Coppola's share of the film's income amounted to about 13 percent of the adjusted gross. In short, if the film sold any tickets at all, Coppola would go from being a rich artist to a plutocrat. "The way I set up the deal for *Godfather II*, it promises to make me so much money that I'll be able to finance my own work," he commented. "The fundamental use of wealth is to subsidize work."

Chapter Eleven

The Son of Don Corleone (1973–1974)

ONE OF THE reasons so many bad movies get made from good books is that a feature film simply can't cover as much plot as a novel; in terms of action, even a two-and-one-half-hour film is closer to a short story or a novelette than a full-length novel. Coppola and Puzo had solved this problem by leaving out giant blocks of the novel's plot from *The Godfather*, but Paramount (which owned the *whole* book) hated to waste the leftovers. As early as February 1972, at a point when *The Godfather* was being screened for preview audiences for the very first time, Paramount had been preparing the sequel. Mario Puzo was already working on the screenplay in Italy (this time he pulled down a better price: $175,000 [/$490,000]), and the film was planned for a start date in July 1972. Presumably the entire winning team would play again.

Less than three months later, however, it was announced that producer Al Ruddy was off the team. He had been point man in dealing with the Italian-American Civil Rights League, the FBI, the New York Police Department, and the mob, and he was sick and tired of it. "I just wanted to get out of all that crap," he said, "because I knew I had skated by. We were very fortunate getting through without any problems. Then there was an article in the fiftieth anniversary issue of *Reader's Digest* about how the production had outhustled the mob, and it caused an enormous amount of anxiety on my part. A lot of it was true, and I got a lot of very irate phone calls from certain

Coppola tried to convince himself that *this* big-budget gangster movie could be just as much a personal film as *The Conversation*. In fact, the story line he was developing was full of intimate elements with special resonance for him. The period sequences would show young Don Corleone as an Italian immigrant in New York, reflecting the experiences of Coppola's own family. The stage play in the scene where the young Vito Corleone first meets Fanucci, the Black Hand extortionist, was actually *Senza Mamma* by Francesco Pennino, Coppola's grandfather. Furthermore, the script reveals many of Coppola's personal concerns, especially that of keeping his home intact in the face of sudden wealth and his new status as a minimogul. The Corleone family of the 1950's was vastly rich and powerful, but beset by Byzantine intrigues, marital discord, fraternal rivalry, and internal decay under the leadership of a man who felt—and *was*—inferior to his own father. It's easy to imagine that Coppola might have been facing similar conflicts. Eleanor Coppola later wrote, "I remember the anxiety he felt and the struggle he had with the script of *Godfather II*, and it seems, in retrospect, at that time he was himself dealing with the same themes in his own life—money, power, and family."

As Coppola shaped the material, it fell into two distinct story lines, one that would follow the young Vito Corleone and the other devoted to his son Michael. Both stories would end with their main characters at the same age, exacting vengeance for an earlier treachery, but with major differences in their methods and targets. Vito would return, in honor, to the Sicilian village of his boyhood and personally disembowel the village strong man who'd murdered his family twenty years earlier. Michael would send professional killers to murder his rival and his traitorous brother.

Coppola devised a visual scheme to keep the two story lines separate and underline his thematic design. Vito's scenes would be shot in warm, nostalgic gold and sepia tones to reveal him as a Lower East Side Robin Hood. In contrast, Michael's scenes would be filmed in a cool, bright, modern style, with the character growing colder, harder, and more ruthless with every scene.

The biggest problem Coppola had with the script was that he didn't know if he could write in a role for Brando. Coppola, and most of the studio brass, badly wanted Brando to be in

Part II, but there was an open feud between Brando and Frank Yablans, head of Paramount. After Brando's pro-Indian protest at the Oscar ceremonies in April 1973, Yablans had bad-mouthed him all over town. Now Brando was demanding major bucks to star in the sequel, and given his fight with Yablans, he was in no mood to make concessions.

Meanwhile, the start date, September 23, 1973, drew ever closer. Location shooting was scheduled for Lake Tahoe, Las Vegas, Miami, Santo Domingo, New York, Trieste, and Sicily. Interiors would be shot in Hollywood. Finally, in August (just as *Godfather* opened in Mindanao, in the Philippine back-country), Paramount made the announcement everyone had been waiting for. Brando was out; according to the studio, he was working on "an Indian-themed picture." Robert De Niro, a relative unknown, who was then before the cameras in Martin Scorsese's *Mean Streets,* would play the young Don Corleone.

De Niro was an Actors' Studio alumnus, trained by Stella Adler and Lee Strasberg; he had appeared in several off-Broadway stage productions before making his movie debut in Brian De Palma's low-budget comedy *Greetings* (1968). Subsequently he'd appeared in several cheapies of varying quality (including De Palma's *Hi, Mom!* and Roger Corman's *Bloody Mama*), but it was his superb performance as a dying baseball player in *Bang the Drum Slowly* (1973) that attracted wide-spread attention. De Niro was not yet a star, but he was hot.

Coppola had been working on the screenplay intermittently for nearly a year and intensively for three months. Now he had to make extensive revisions to delete Brando's scenes. Although Mario Puzo was officially his co-screenwriter, Puzo's contractual responsibilities had been completed when he delivered the film's first-draft screenplay to Paramount. Coppola was stuck with the revision and restructuring.

Al Pacino was set to reprise his role as Michael Corleone from the day the sequel was conceived. Pacino had been paid only $25,000 (/$72,000) for his work in *The Godfather;* his salary for Part II would be $500,000 (/$1.3 million). In the meantime, he'd been given a plum part as a nonconformist undercover cop in Sidney Lumet's *Serpico.* That film was still in the editing room, but word of mouth on Pacino's performance was ecstatic. Now, with Brando out of the picture, Coppola needed Pacino all the more to provide continuity with the earlier film.

Unfortunately, when Pacino finally got to read the script (just a week before shooting started), he hated it. Indeed, Coppola shared many of his reservations. Coppola's quandary was similar to the one he'd faced in *The Conversation:* How could he evoke audience sympathy for a central character who showed virtually no emotion? Coppola rewrote all Michael's scenes in a mere three days. Photocopies of the script were completed just one hour before filming started.

The script continued to change even during the filming. Just as in *The Conversation*, Coppola had deferred many important narrative decisions until editing; big blocks of storytelling were put in place in the last weeks before the film's release. Although he continued to regard himself, above all, as a screenwriter, once again Coppola found himself working with an incomplete screenplay, hoping that luck, improvisation, and editing would save him.

Fortunately, Coppola was able to rehire most of the actors from Part I, and even many of the same extras. The one exception was Richard Castellano, who had played Clemenza in *The Godfather;* he was now demanding not only a huge increase in salary but the right to rewrite his own dialogue and a part for his girl friend. Coppola deleted Clemenza's scenes and signed writer-actor Michael Gazzo (author of *A Hatful of Rain*) for a new role, the amiable turncoat Frankie Pentangeli.

For the character of Hyman Roth, a Jewish mobster (based on Meyer Lansky) who offers to cut Michael in even as he plots to rub him out, Coppola pulled off a stunning casting coup. He signed septuagenarian Lee Strasberg, the legendary head of the Actors' Studio, to make his movie debut. Doubtless, it was Al Pacino who suggested Strasberg, his mentor, for the role. Nonetheless, Strasberg hadn't acted onstage in twenty years, and he had never condescended to perform on film. Pacino and Coppola knew that convincing him to accept the role would be tricky. Pacino arranged for Strasberg and Coppola to meet socially. Both the filmmaker and the acting guru understood that the one taboo topic was *Godfather II:* they chatted about classical music instead. A few days later Paramount contacted Strasberg and offered him the paltry sum of $10,000 to appear in the film; he finally received $58,000.

Neither Strasberg nor Coppola was fully pleased with Roth's scenes as written, but Strasberg agreed to try them anyway; if they didn't work in the rushes, Coppola would rewrite them. As it turned out, he never had to. Strasberg's masterly performance made the role utterly vivid exactly as written. "For me it was a lark," said Strasberg. "In no way did I try to give a sense of the theatrical elements of the Mafia. I tried to create a face of not showing emotion, the sense of a man for whom all things were business."

Because of all the last-minute rewrites, location filming began at Lake Tahoe, high in the Sierras, on October 1, 1973, seven days late. The sets for Michael Corleone's family compound were constructed at the lavish Fleur de Lac estate, built by millionaire Henry Kaiser in 1934. There's no substitute for the look of authenticity that a filmmaker gains by shooting on location, but unless the weather cooperates and everything works perfectly, it can be a risky process. Within weeks the shoot was running badly over budget and seriously behind schedule.

Tahoe is only four hours' drive from San Francisco, but at its high altitude summer ends abruptly about a week after Labor Day; the first snow usually arrives by mid-October. By the time shooting began, the weather was already frigid. For the "summer" scene of the mammoth alfresco party celebrating Michael's son's first communion, the cast, dressed in lightweight resort wear, plunged into heavy overcoats as soon as their scenes were done; the extras (mainly wealthy vacationers with weekend homes on the Tahoe shore) wore thermal underwear under their summer clothing; Coppola kept a hand warmer in his pocket.

Once this set piece was completed, the hordes of extras went back to their retirement homes and vacation spreads, but the principal actors were stuck. Everyone, cast and crew, actually lived in the stone bungalows of the set, and as winter fell many felt as isolated from the rest of the world as the Corleone family itself. In fact, they were isolated; the Kaiser estate, a fortress protected by fierce dogs and armed human guards, is accessible only by boat, seaplane, or helicopter. For all but the best-paid personnel, even a quick trip into town was prohibitively costly and complicated once the early Sierra winter set in.

Conditions were not untypical of any long shoot on a remote location, but some people began to suspect that somehow the isolation was part of a sinister plan, allowing Coppola to maintain control over everyone on the set. In the script Michael Corleone keeps his family imprisoned in the compound for their own safety. There were times when the group at Tahoe felt equally imprisoned, equally bored.

Furthermore, Pacino was something of a pain in the neck. "Lumet shot *Serpico* in eighteen *days!*" he kept reminding Coppola as the location shoot went on, and on, and on. (He was exaggerating; the *Serpico* shoot took slightly more than five weeks.) Nor was he entirely happy with Coppola's direction. "I go up to Francis, I've got a problem I want to talk to him about," he complained to a reporter. "So what does he do? He tells me *his* problems. What do I want to hear *his* problems for? He's the *director!*"

Coppola attributed the actor's tension to sheer nervousness. "Pacino is very insecure away from live theater," he observed. Happily, when *Serpico* was released in December 1973, two months into the *Godfather II* shoot, Pacino's rave reviews seemed to calm him down.

Eleanor and the three children had joined Francis on location, but they were no happier than anyone else. Ellie was growing tired of dragging herself around behind her husband, leaving her friends, her home (which she'd just started redecorating again), and her art and photography work behind to camp uncomfortably in improvised arrangements. "I was crying all the time," she remembered, adding that they spent what seemed like six months crammed all together into a small bungalow on the Tahoe set. It was actually only six weeks.

The tension began to affect Coppola, too. Throughout the making of Part II, reporters clustered around him, and his mood, as reflected in their stories, seemed to swing day by day, hour by hour, alternating between vibrant creativity and grim exhaustion. He found himself riding an emotional roller coaster. In moments of elation he gave interviews freely and reveled in his status as a wealthy, successful director; in periods of depression he wondered if he'd sold himself down the river again, only for bigger bucks this time, and he badmouthed the film as "formula schlock." At his worst he refused to talk to reporters at all, and agonized over his fame and its potential impact on his family.

Inevitably the film itself began to reflect the tensions developing in Coppola's own household. When asked, sometime later, why Kay doesn't leave Michael much earlier in the film, Coppola confessed, "Think of how many husbands have kept their wives and held their families together by promising that things would change just as soon as they became vice presidents, or had $100,000 in the bank, or closed the big deal. I've strung my own wife along for 13 years by telling her that as soon as I was done with this or that project, I'd stop working so hard and we'd live a more normal life. I mean, that's the classic way husbands lie."

Four years later Eleanor wrote, "It has taken until now for me to accept that the man I love, my husband, the father of my children, can lie, betray, and be cruel to people he loves."

In mid-November the company finally, and joyfully, left Tahoe behind. They moved on to a brief shoot in Las Vegas, filming for several days at the Tropicana Hotel's casino from 4:00 A.M. to noon, when most gamblers were asleep. Next stop was Hollywood, where, for five weeks, Coppola scrambled to shoot most of the interior sequences, at top speed, on Paramount sound stages.

On January 2, 1974, the company headed for the Caribbean, but fantasies of happy days in the sun proved illusory. If the Tahoe portion of the shoot had been tough, the Caribbean portion was murder. In Santo Domingo (standing in for both Miami and sunny Cuba) it rained incessantly. Then, late in February, after getting thoroughly drenched in a tropical storm, an exhausted Al Pacino came down with pneumonia. Doctors told him he had better stop working for a month, so after seven weeks in Santo Domingo, Coppola shut down the location shoot.

Several events brightened Coppola's mood. Universal Pictures announced that 1973 had been the best year in the company's history, largely thanks to the fact that *American Graffiti* had earned $21.3 million (/$56 million). That same month *Graffiti* won the Golden Globe award as the Best Picture of 1973. Coppola made a quick trip to Hollywood to pick up the award. "In a way, it's the best one I have," he told *Variety*.

While he waited for Pacino to recover, Coppola headed for New York to shoot De Niro's portion of the film. Fortunately Dean Tavoularis and his giant production crew were already waiting, with a street they'd just finished antiquing in time for Coppola's arrival. Tavoularis had transformed Sixth Street between Avenues A and B into Little Italy, Manhattan, circa 1918, with pushcarts, dogs, goats, chickens, horses, ancient cars, even 1918 Italian newspapers. There were strict rules for the extras: no tweezed eyebrows, no dyed hair, no nose jobs.

In Manhattan, as in the tropics, it rained incessantly, and the picture, which was already two months overdue, fell even farther behind schedule. Every day on set cost $80,000 (/$211,000).

No doubt, Coppola took comfort from the fact that *Graffiti* had just been nominated for no fewer than five Oscars (Best Film, Best Director, Best Supporting Actress [Candy Clark], Best Screenplay, and Best Editing), but his reserves of optimism and energy were badly depleted.

Although he was becoming increasingly press-wary, Coppola allowed Eve Babitz, a glamorous reporter who professed "an abject belief in his greatness" (and was also a high school pal of Fred Roos's) to visit the set. On a rainy spring afternoon in Manhattan, in the middle of an interview, he cried out to her, "Take me away from all this! Take me to some little apartment where I can write all day and dawdle around in the kitchen and when you come home from work I'd make you a nice dinner."

On the 117th day of filming, in March 1974, Coppola was so exhausted that when *Daily Variety*'s Richard Albarino asked him what was next for him, the only thing he could think of to say was "Retirement."

Increasingly, now, his fantasies seemed to be running to a beatnik paradise in Northern California. He would hold a little acting class in his theater in San Francisco, writing and rewriting scenes before trying them out before an audience. Eventually, perhaps, he'd use them in low-budget movies. Maybe he'd open a little outdoor café in North Beach and spend his days drinking espresso, immersed in witty conversation with intelligent friends, surrounded by beautiful women.

Of course, he was already surrounded by beautiful women. Even Eleanor couldn't help noticing. The "fresh crop of adoring young protégées waiting in the wings," as she observed later, started during *Godfather II*. Although Coppola told reporters that he was simply too busy to pay attention to other women, the success of *The Godfather* had made him a magnet for female celebrity hounds. He was young, famous, rich, and powerful, and as Henry Kissinger once noted, power is the ultimate aphrodisiac.

On March 27, an event took place which Coppola had been looking forward to with the kind of enthusiasm usually reserved for a tax audit. *Gatsby* opened in New York City. "It's frivolous without being much fun," said Vincent Canby in *The New York Times.* "It nearly flattens the fable to pulp," observed Charles Michener of *Newsweek.* "I'm here to tell you it *is* that bad," noted Molly Haskell in the *Village Voice.* Still, Robert Redford was so popular that it opened well anyway, and within weeks it had become the third-highest-grossing film in the country.

On April 2, 1974, the Oscar ceremonies came and went, and *Graffiti* was left empty-handed. *The Sting* took everything. "My name is anathema to an Oscar," Coppola lamented.

Five days later, April 7, 1974, was Coppola's thirty-fifth birthday. To celebrate, he bought himself a Model A Ford, which had been meticulously restored for a shot in *Godfather II.* However, he didn't get a very nice birthday present from the New York critics. Just as he was heading for Italy to complete the final segments of the *Godfather II* shoot, *The Conversation,* the art film he was counting on to point the direction for his post-*Godfather* career, opened in New York City to merely mixed reviews. Critics praised the film's artistry but found Harry Caul too cold and peculiar a protagonist to garner the kind of audience sympathy that would build suspense.

Nora Sayre (rather than lead critic Vincent Canby) got the assignment for *The New York Times.* She praised Gene Hackman's performance but found the film itself "extremely grim, a brilliant idea for a movie, and much of it works. But some of the action drags—perhaps because the style is so muted, so deliberately dry and cool, that suspense is partially muffled."

A week later *Time*'s Jay Cocks was more positive. "*The Conversation* is a film of enormous enterprise and tension. More than anything, it is a film about moral paralysis." Cocks thought that the film worked "as a subtle psychological thriller to which Coppola has given a musical construction."

Pauline Kael was equally appreciative. "This is a screenplay of the first quality, written with the eerie foresight of a real writer," she declared in the *New Yorker.* "It is very simply directed. Nothing gets in the way of the intended double meanings of the script."

Andrew Sarris wrote no fewer than three full-length essays in the *Village Voice* grappling with *The Conversation*. All were gentle pans, but when a critic gives a film three columns in a row, that's praise in itself (or evidence of deep confusion). "It is not a bad film," Sarris stated, but went on to observe that it fails as a "dramatic spectacle." He pointed out the switched inflections on the crucial tape, criticized the film's lack of "emotional wallop," and declared it "the least successful of Coppola's trinity of very personal projects." (He preferred *You're a Big Boy Now*.)

Meanwhile, Coppola and company kept shooting on locations in Trieste (where a giant dockside fish market stood in for the turn-of-the-century immigration facilities at Ellis Island) and in Sicily. Spending a few days in Rome, he arranged a meeting with Federico Fellini, the great Italian director. When Fellini, who was nearly bankrupt, commented enviously on Coppola's financial success, Coppola (smarting, perhaps, from the Oscar snub and poor box-office performance by *The Conversation*) snapped back that being rich wasn't all that great. Fellini gave him a look of pure disbelief.

Actually Coppola had thought of something worthwhile to do with his extra money. He still felt bad about a Zoetrope project that Black Thursday had aborted: Carroll Ballard's *Vesuvio*. In all the years since, Coppola's one-time UCLA rival had still not made a feature film. "Why should Carroll Ballard, whom I consider the most gifted director I have ever become involved with, have to wait five years, hat in hand, for someone to decide to let him direct?" Coppola asked rhetorically. And he picked up the telephone.

Back in Venice, California, it was the middle of the night. Ballard's phone rang, and to his sleepy disbelief he heard Coppola's voice. "I want to produce a picture," said Coppola, barely audible over the transatlantic line hiss, "and I want you to do it, so let's find a story and make a movie!"

"Great!" muttered Ballard, and went back to sleep.

Coppola's phone call could not have come at a better time; Ballard was ripe for some kind of break. Since shooting scenery to go under the *Finian's Rainbow* titles he had been working primarily as a cinematographer. Ballard had given himself an ironic nickname: Lone Dog. He had contributed a distinctive cinematic look to other people's films and had directed a series of exquisite nature shorts, TV commercials, and award-winning children's films. He'd even received an Oscar nomination for *Harvest*, a film he'd made for the U.S. Information Agency but despised as government propaganda.

After Coppola's call he got busy right away. "I put together all the stories I was interested in," Ballard remembered, "that I thought would make interesting movies. I compiled a big list and went to see Fred Roos. He didn't like any of them." Ballard's big break was put on hold.

Toward the end of May, eight months into the seemingly endless *Godfather II* shoot, Coppola took a few days off and headed up the coast from Italy to the Cannes Film Festival. *The Conversation*, which was foundering at number seventeen on *Variety*'s U.S. box-office chart, would be screened—in competition. Paramount execs, angry because *Godfather II* was running so far behind schedule, took revenge by refusing to pay the air fare for Coppola and his entourage. Frank Yablans even made a halfhearted attempt to get the picture pulled from competition, probably because he didn't want to draw attention away from *Gatsby*. So it must have been sweet, indeed, for Coppola when *The Conversation* took the Golden Palm for Best Picture. Coppola even began to hope (in vain, as it turned out) that the award would bring the film a greater audience in the United States.

"People just don't want to go see it," Coppola said. "I think they want comedy and good feelings; it's a survival thing, and I think it's good. *The Conversation*, although it had some sense of social responsibility, made people feel crummy." Around the same time he told another reporter, "I'm not going to make films that make you depressed any more. I want to do a picture that makes you feel good without being phony."

However, in an interview with *Film Comment*, he admitted he felt hurt by the film's reception. "A review of *The Conversation* describes the two characters as skimpily drawn," he noted angrily. "Here I am deliberately trying to *not* unveil their characters in a conventional way. I'm trying to give you an impression of their characters. The only film on those two characters is the same dumb conversation. I'm just showing you the same moment over and over. I'm using repetition instead of exposition. The second I do it, someone says it's skimpy."

On June 19 *Variety* carried a front-page headline: GOD II COMPLETES 8 MONTHS OF PHOTOGRAPHY. At last Coppola could go home.

When he was back in San Francisco, his emotional roller coaster roared into an upgrade. The shoot, which he'd found so agonizing, began to seem almost pleasant in retrospect. In fact, he told several reporters that it had been a very enjoyable movie to make. He felt especially pleased with the script, forgetting for the moment that it was *still* not quite finished. "When people go to see a movie, 80 percent of the effect it has on them was preconceived and precalculated by the writer," he said. "A good script has pre-imagined exactly what the movie is going to do on a story level, on an emotional level, on all these various levels. So, to me, that's the primary act of creation. The writer's the guy who started with nothing and dreamed this all up."

What frightened him was that if the film failed, he'd lose creative control over future projects. "I have a lot of theories, and I want to put them into practice while I'm still young enough to have an idea in my head. That's why I'm so scared of somehow blowing this opportunity I have. I could easily blow it; I could lose a bunch of money, and in four years be directing something, and then I'll be 40, and before I know it it'll be gone."

Coppola faced an awesome task: cutting the reels and reels of *Godfather II* down to something like a normal movie. And he still hadn't decided on the ending. Overeating to allay the tension of the nine-month shoot, he'd ballooned to 239 pounds—hefty for a man of five feet eleven inches. To diet, he fasted every Monday (a day nobody wanted to be around him). But on Sunday nights he'd go into the kitchen of Tomasso's restaurant (around the corner from his new office building in North Beach) and cook pizza or veal marengo for his pals. And to distract himself from the need to cut footage, he devoted himself to learning how to cut sashimi (Japanese-style raw fish fillets). Very likely his teacher in this enterprise was his new friend Alice Waters, who had recently opened a little Berkeley restaurant called Chez Panisse.

Coppola had met Waters through her boyfriend, Tom

Luddy, director and head programmer of the Pacific Film Archive at the UC Berkeley Art Museum. Luddy, who was immensely knowledgeable about film history and had extensive personal contracts with filmmakers around the world, was to prove an invaluable resource for Coppola in years to come, as both his cultural attaché and as a purveyor of fresh talent.

Just as he was starting to edit, Coppola had a brainstorm, or maybe it was just a way to put off the hard work of editing. The American bicentennial would be coming up in two years. July 4, 1976, would be the perfect day to release *Apocalypse Now*, the Vietnam War film he and Lucas had been talking about since 1968.

Apocalypse was still little more than a mordantly funny draft of a script by John Milius. The plan, such as it was, called for Coppola to produce and George Lucas to direct. Coppola approached Lucas and suggested that he start work on the film immediately, but Coppola offered Lucas only the same minuscule directing fee they'd agreed on six years earlier: $25,000, plus 10 percent of the profits.

That might have been fine for a hungry first-time filmmaker in 1968, but by now Lucas was an established director. Not only did he have the immensely successful *American Graffiti* to his credit, but he had just completed the first-draft screenplay for a science-fiction adventure he was calling *Star Wars*, for which he would eventually get $150,000 plus 40 percent of the net profits. (It would make him even richer than Coppola.) Coppola was unimpressed with Lucas's script. He may even have hinted that *Star Wars* wasn't worth finishing when *Apocalypse* was waiting. Lucas told Coppola to take a hike. "If you want to make it," Lucas snapped, "go make it."

Instead Coppola shelved *Apocalypse* and got down to work on editing *Godfather II*.

It wasn't long before Coppola realized that *City* needed his attention again, too. Aside from the regular infusions of money, he had become increasingly embarrassed with the magazine's underground appearance, especially in the face of criticism from big-time New York publishing pros like Clay Felker. If *City* was ever to look and read like Felker's *New York*, something had to be done.

At the suggestion of several members of the editorial staff, he hired John Burks, a former managing editor of *Rolling Stone*, who had put together the prizewinning coverage of the disastrous Rolling Stones concert at Altamont. Burks, in turn, brought in Don McCartney as *City*'s art director.

Burks's initial meeting with Coppola was a bit disturbing. For one thing, he had assumed he'd be able to pay professional rates for articles. "Here's Francis Coppola," he recalled, "so you figure, like all the chumps out there, there's plenty of money to pay writers. When I told Francis we could get better writers if we paid better, he said, 'Why would they want more money?' He figured magazine writers were like the people he knew, they'd have multi-thousand-dollar projects, and in the downtime in between they'd be dying to write more stuff, and he'd do them a favor and let them write for *City*. His idea of a magazine writer was a screenwriter between jobs."

Worse yet, while Coppola knew that he hated the magazine, he was extremely vague about how he wanted to change it. "He wanted it to be tough," said Burks, "he wanted it to be elegant, he wanted it to be a whole lot of contradictory stuff. I sized him up as sort of a charming bullshitter; I mean, he was talking through his hat."

Burks spent his first week or two soliciting story ideas from the best writers in San Francisco, everyone from Herb Gold to Lawrence Ferlinghetti. "These ideas came from people who wrote about business, " he said, "from people who were dealing with pop culture, from investigative reporters. They were the best stories that the best writers in the Bay Area could think of."

Burks brought Coppola a list of seventy-five stories, and then he sat, astonished, while Coppola shot down every one. " 'Who'd want to read this?' he'd say, or 'None of my friends are interested in that,' or 'Who cares about some small-time operation like this?' Maybe he liked two or three, like an interview with Herb Caen."

Burks tried to give Coppola the benefit of the doubt. "I thought, well, he's the publisher, and apparently he's working out of some mystical vision. It was stardust time."

He went back to his writers and compiled a shorter list of slightly less hot stories. The only one Coppola liked from *this* list was an investigative piece about the rising tolls on the Golden Gate Bridge. "I finally figured out why he liked it," said Burks. "At first I thought it was 'cause he had a taste for exposés, let's dig into this. But that wasn't it. He and his pals drove back and forth between Marin and San Francisco, and it pissed him off that they were going to have to pay another quarter."

Burks decided that the best way to get strong stories into *City* was not to tell Coppola about them until it was too late. He settled down to work. Under his aegis, *City* maintained its eight-by-eleven format, but McCartney gave the design air and class, while Burks's writers brought the text greater breadth and wit. After a while a small amount of extra money from Coppola allowed the magazine to move up to slick paper and full-color covers. Burks also managed to raise writers' rates a bit, and when circulation started to grow along with the budget, Coppola was pleased.

He got into the habit of showing up late on deadline nights. Burks remembered that staffers would be in their undershirts, hammering away at 3:00 A.M. to get the pages to the printer the next morning, "and suddenly the spotlights are on, the music comes up, the joint is filled with glitter, and here's Francis with a bunch of Hollywood pals and their wives and girl friends. They'd all be in their furs, and Francis would come in with glasses and a couple of bottles of expensive wine, and he'd be introducing us to these fucking starlets, and we'd be totally bewildered."

Coppola was particularly fond of showing off the computerized typesetting machine, with its flashing lights and digital readouts, much to the horror of editors and designers alike. He'd swish typesetter Nancy Kuzma out of the chair, sit down, and try to show his friends how the machine worked; on one occasion he managed to destroy several pages of copy.

Other times he'd send over four or five courses from whatever restaurant he happened to be eating in, along with expensive bottles of wine. "We'd have preferred to have brought them back and traded them in for the dough," said Burks.

There would be other production nights when Coppola would show up alone; sitting around, feet up on a desk, he'd chat, make suggestions, and share the excitement and the tension of putting out the magazine. With his beard and rumpled clothing, he fit right in with the staff. It was *much* more fun than editing *Godfather II*.

Coppola wanted to run a long photo essay based on a project of Eleanor's. She had been photographing people's closets. She'd get all sorts of people, from workers to artists, to stand in front of their closets with the most interesting thing in it. Coppola wanted to run a hundred photos; Burks thought it was an interesting idea (although at much shorter length), and he went to the Coppolas' house several times to talk about it. But there was a problem.

"I'd go over to dinner," he remembered, "and Eleanor would be there, and this would happen *every time:* No sooner would she get into anything, like what she was up to, like the closet project, than Francis would change the subject, yank the rug out from under her, every single time. You'd get to thinking of her as being the downtrodden of the earth. It might have even gotten to her, the stuff she was taking from Francis, because occasionally I'd meet her alone, and she always seemed apologetic about her stuff, you know, 'I know this is not very interesting, but . . .' "

For all of Coppola's complaints about the money he was losing on *City*, the magazine was still a nickel-and-dime operation compared with his filmmaking business. By the end of July 1974 the original *Godfather* had grossed about $285 million worldwide. Now Frank Yablans and NBC-TV cut a deal for the first television broadcast of the film; the fee would be an astonishing $10 million (/$23.7 million) for a two-night showing in November; Coppola's cut of the pie was about $510,000 (/$1.2 million). Coppola himself (now as much of a draw as his movie) would be the on-camera host.

The price was so high that even with twenty-eight minutes of commercials at $225,000 per minute, NBC hadn't a prayer of making its money back, but since the show was scheduled for ratings sweep week, NBC would make its profit with higher ad rates for the rest of the year. Paramount, too, had more at stake than front money. *Godfather II* was now slated to open on December 17, 1974. The television screening of Part I, less than a month before the premiere of Part II, would provide priceless publicity.

For Coppola, publishing a magazine, hosting a major TV special, and editing *Godfather II* was still a relatively light schedule. Maybe he could think of something *else* to do to keep himself from getting bored. On August 21 a *Variety* article reported that he had borrowed $180,000 to buy seventy-two thousand shares, 10 percent of the stock, in Donald Rugoff's New York-based Cinema V, a major chain of art houses. Not only would Coppola ally himself with this exhibition chain, but he would also provide movies for its theaters, wholly sidestepping normal Hollywood distribution channels.

It was a complicated deal. Rugoff, involved in an antitrust lawsuit against Cinerama's William Foreman (who owned 25 percent of Cinema V), needed an ally on the board of directors. He agreed to cosign Coppola's loan, taking responsibility for repayment if Coppola should default. He even agreed to buy back his shares if Coppola later decided to pull out. Fred Roos bought in as well for five hundred shares.

Even Coppola's friends, who had noted his prodigious energy before, were impressed with his one-Renaissance-man show, playing distributor, producer, writer, director, PR man, cook, magazine publisher, and TV host all at the same time. "He reminded me of somebody like Balzac," said Walter Murch, "who, in addition to writing however many novels he wrote and drinking forty cups of coffee a day, owned a publishing house and a printing press, and in the middle of all that somebody asked Balzac, 'Do you consider yourself a writer?' and he said, 'No, I'm not a writer.' Obviously, that's what he was, but to himself he was in a whirlpool of creativity. I remember Francis saying something similar: 'Yes, I make movies, but there is *more* than movies. . . .' He was, as Balzac was, somebody on whom fate smiled, and he wanted to test the limits of that smile, because if fate smiles on you, and you stop, you're betraying something."

At least three projects were planned for release via Cinema V within eighteen months. These included *Apocalypse Now*, perhaps with John Milius directing; *Tucker*, the picture Coppola had been talking about since his Hofstra days; and *The Black Stallion*, to be written by Walter Murch and Carroll Ballard, and directed by the latter on a very low $1.2 million (/$2.8 million) budget.

Coppola had spent some of his *Godfather* money buying up the rights to all thirty of Walter Farley's *Black Stallion* books in hopes of turning out sequels and perhaps a television series. Even before the first film was scripted, he'd received overseas sales offers in excess of $200,000.

After Fred Roos had rejected all of Ballard's ideas, Roos

and Coppola decided that *The Black Stallion* might be just the right property for him: It had nature, animals, and a child hero. Ballard was eager to direct a feature and delighted at the prospect of collaborating with Murch on the screenplay, but he was deeply unhappy with the property. It had a preachy quality that disgusted him. "I hated it," he remembered. "Thought it was *Leave It to Beaver.* It was not the kind of movie I wanted to make. But Francis had this notion that maybe that was a commercial project."

Ballard swallowed his distaste and went up to San Francisco for a meeting with Coppola and Murch, but when Coppola asked him what he thought of the story, Ballard couldn't restrain himself. "Well, it's kind of rinky-dink," he said.

Coppola was livid. "Aah, 'rinky-dink?' " he answered. "Why don't we just forget the whole thing, get outa here, forget the whole thing!"

And Ballard interjected, "Oh, wait a minute! Maybe we'll find some way to deal with it."

The script quarrels didn't end there. Ballard wanted the story to be about a little girl, given the special love that "horsey" girl children have for equines, as well as the mythic-erotic resonances of a fragile young girl taming a wild stallion. Unfortunately the hero of Farley's book was a little boy. Even the fiercely independent Ballard could see why Coppola insisted that the child in the movie version remain male. So Murch and the reluctant Lone Dog set to work writing a movie about a boy and a horse.

Meanwhile, William Friedkin exited the Directors Company after a long series of squabbles with Peter Bogdanovich. The company effectively dissolved. Friedkin blamed Paramount's Frank Yablans for its demise, and Coppola agreed that Paramount had been increasingly unpleasant.

By October 1974 Coppola and Fred Roos were firmly established on Cinema V's board of directors and had even persuaded Donald Rugoff, the company president, to change the company's name to Cinema 7. Seven was Coppola's lucky number. Simultaneously, Coppola (who was growing increasingly uncomfortable with the utopian, communal pretensions he'd originally encouraged at American Zoetrope) founded a new entity, the Coppola Company, that would be distinctly his own. Eventually, he thought, there might be a merger between the Coppola Company, which would finance and produce his films, and Cinema 7, which would exhibit them.

Despite the distractions, Coppola and his crew continued to edit *Godfather II*, and by now had reduced the footage to a five-hour rough cut. Exhibitors had already guaranteed $28 million in rentals and had actually *paid* $26 million in advance—the largest amount of front money ever paid for a film. Coppola's cut was about $3.4 million.

By November the film was down to three hours and twenty minutes. It was no easier to edit than *The Conversation,* since whole portions of the plot had been changed since shooting finished, and other portions had to be pared away to save running time.

Late in November, as scheduled, the television premiere of the original *Godfather* came and went. Ninety million viewers watched it (38 percent of all the people with their TVs turned on), placing it in the all-time number four slot (behind *Airport, Love Story,* and *The Poseidon Adventure*) in the movies-on-TV record book. Nonetheless, NBC executives were slightly disappointed; they had hoped for a world record.

As the premiere of *Godfather II* drew ever closer, editing went on. And on. "No one seems nervous," wrote Jon Carroll in *New York,* when the film, still unfinished, was mere weeks from its opening. "Doesn't Coppola always bring his pictures in at the very last minute, the surgeon delivering the baby like a parcel, on the dead run, double-parked?"

As journalists tracked him down for prerelease interviews, Coppola alternated almost hour by hour between buoyant optimism and paralyzing pessimism. "Imagine having millions and millions of people all over the world sit in a room and totally surrender their brains to you for two hours," he exulted one day, in a moment of grandiosity. "What would General Motors pay to have that?" But other days he was terrified that he'd lose it all, or that someone would read about his wealth and kidnap his children.

And then, sometimes, his confidence would return with a vengeance. "I could make five failures," he declared one day, "five pictures nobody liked, and I'd still be the guy who directed *The Godfather.*"

Mood swings aside, there were very concrete reasons for Coppola to be worried about *Godfather II.* Dark rumors spread through Hollywood that audiences would get lost in the twists of the two alternating plots. George Lucas viewed a preliminary assembly, and told Coppola he was in big trouble. "You have two movies," said Lucas. "Throw one away. It doesn't work." But Coppola had a hunch that what everyone thought was the weakness of the movie was really its strength. He refused to give up, but he was getting worried. "If the audience doesn't walk out crying," he declared, "*I'm* going to cry."

Somewhere along the way the premiere had been moved forward from December 17 to December 12. With just two weeks to go, Coppola took a group of friends, relatives, coworkers, and employees down to San Diego for a sneak preview. As the film unreeled and the audience fidgeted, Coppola became increasingly horrified. The last hour was cold and confused. Some scenes would have to be dropped, others lengthened. He'd have to give up on the idea of an intermission. There were weeks of work to do in the short days remaining.

Cutting a film can be heartbreaking. It's easy to cut bad stuff, but then you have to cut good stuff to make the other good stuff work better. Coppola had long since reached the point of having to cut some of his most wonderful sequences. Ultimately *Godfather II* was shortened by no less than 40 percent from Coppola's first rough cut. "My heart was really in the Little Italy sequences," Coppola noted sadly. "I had great scenes in the script that we couldn't include in the movie. There was one where Enrico Caruso showed up in the neighborhood and sang 'Over There' to get guys to enlist for World War I."

Furthermore, despite Coppola's plans, it had become clear that Parts I and II could not simply be shown, one after the other, to create the seamless, unified epic he'd first envisioned. He would have to reedit the footage from scratch, for what eventually would become *The Godfather Saga*. The only bright side was that this would enable him to restore some of his lost footage.

Godfather II had cost $13 million (/$31 million), more than double the original $6 million budgeted, but out of the chaos and crises and catastrophes Coppola pulled off a magnificent film.

The movie opens in Sicily, with a traditional funeral procession. During the next few minutes the local strong man murders little Vito's entire family. Vito flees to America, where he's found to have smallpox and is quarantined for several months at Ellis Island. This sequence must have been close to the filmmaker's heart, remembering his own childhood bout with disease and the long months of isolation.

While Vito sits patiently in a straight-backed chair at Ellis Island, looking out a high, barred window, Coppola dissolves from 1901 to 1958 and Michael's elaborate outdoor party for his son's first communion. On the Tahoe shore we meet the surviving members of the Family: hapless brother Fredo (John Cazale), unable to control his besotted blond virago of a wife; dissolute sister Connie (Talia Shire); stern, stoic Mama; Kay (Diane Keaton) and the children, shuffled off into the background; and old Family friend Frankie Pentangeli (Michael Gazzo), drunkenly discontented. Michael's paid-for senator insults the entire Italian race.

We return to the young Vito, now a father (Robert De Niro), using his wits and charm to make ends meet in the Little Italy of 1917, getting into crime, and rising to power in his neighborhood. Meanwhile, in the 1958 story, Michael faces a volley of machine-gun fire in his Tahoe bedroom; someone on the inside has betrayed him. He desperately attempts to retain his power and protect his life in the face of attacks from mobster Hyman Roth (Lee Strasberg) and a Senate committee on organized crime.

Back in the 1930s, Vito returns to his birthplace in the Sicilian town of Corleone and takes his revenge by killing the strong man. By the end of the modern story Michael has dominated his pet senator, reconquered his wayward sister, sent his wife into exile, kept the children, and arranged for the murders of all his betrayers, including his brother Fredo. Coppola leaves us with a grim image of Michael, sitting alone in his walled Tahoe compound. His life is in order, but his future is as bleak and empty as his heart.

The film is audacious, intricate, and moving, although it gave many first-time viewers some difficulty as a result of the complex interweaving of the two story lines. A few awkward bits of editing added to the confusion.

Vito's segments are immediately absorbing, nostalgically lyrical, and often funny. De Niro gives Vito a sweet rakishness, but there's a dangerous edge to his scenes as well. Michael's segments are far more chilling, although some are equally funny (in a more intellectual mode).

In the vivid Cuban sequence we discover that under the Batista dictatorship the country was a mobsters' playground. As Michael and Hyman Roth, high on a balcony above Havana, discuss an alliance to rule the country as a kingdom of crime, Roth slices a birthday cake in the shape of a map of Cuba and hands out the pieces to his allies. A few minutes later, Fidel Castro's forces approach the capital. It's a perfect example of how good a screenwriter-director Coppola could be; using a wordless visual, he makes it graphically clear why the country needed a revolution.

Fittingly, since Michael does his dirty work by proxy there's far less physical violence than in the first film; in fact, the greatest ferocity is psychological. In the scene where Kay tells Michael she's aborted his baby, Michael beats her and then banishes her, but the icy edge to his rage makes it a calculating show of power that's far more disturbing than a simple explosion of anger.

This coolness in the central character, and the sheer complexity of the interwoven plots, give the film a cerebral tone and a remote grandeur reminiscent of Greek tragedy. Here, however, the role of the tragic hero is divided between a father and a son. The man who gains the stature of a king doesn't suffer the tragic fall himself; instead, his son, who inherits the kingdom, pays the price. Michael Corleone is the ultimate second-generation American in a country where anything can be bought, except class.

Coppola helped his actors deliver extraordinarily convincing performances. Robert De Niro instantly attained star status, Michael Gazzo made a memorably earthy Pentangeli, and Lee Strasberg turned his role as Hyman Roth into a tour de force of subtlety and wit. Among the carryovers from Part I, Al Pacino, Robert Duvall, Talia Shire, and especially John Cazale found new depths in their characters.

Despite the dire early rumors, by the time the film went into release advance word was very high. The press treated Coppola like a prince of filmdom. In an awestruck cover article titled "Godfather of the Movies," *Newsweek*'s Maureen Orth (to whom Coppola had given a long interview during the editing) wrote, "The hottest creative personality in movies is

director-producer-writer Francis Ford Coppola. At 35, the multi-
talented Coppola is the key figure in a movie business that,
surprisingly, is 'going Hollywood'—returning to the dream-
land of studio sets, big stars, big spectacles and big money."

Even the incoming president of Warner-Seven, John Calley, was figuratively batting his eyelashes at W-7's prodigal son.
"Francis exudes an aura of boyishness, " he told Orth, "but
he's one of the most sophisticated production people around.
He has that very rare mastery of both high- and low-budget
filmmaking."

The film opened on December 12, 1974, but despite the
publicity, the word of mouth, and Coppola's high hopes, the
initial reviews were devastating.

Vincent Canby's *New York Times* review was a pitiless
pan: "The only remarkable thing about Francis Ford Coppola's *The Godfather, Part II*," he wrote, "is the insistent manner in which it recalls how much better his original film was.
. . . It's a Frankenstein's monster stitched together from leftover parts. It talks. It moves in fits and starts, but it has no
mind of its own."

Paul D. Zimmerman's generally negative write-up appeared in *Newsweek* the following week. "We grow restless
watching the predictable played out at a crawl and impatient
for some liberating energy or sudden surprise that will free
Pacino from the rut of repeated responses. This extended, highly
personal coda makes one hungry for the relatively uncompli-
cated entertainment values of the original."

Once again, the *Village Voice* tarried before its review. Finally, on April 19, 1975, Molly Haskell's headline read THE
CORLEONE SAGA SAGS. "Brando's absence hangs over the new
picture as his presence hung over the previous one," she wrote.
"The characters are not only not mythic—they are not even
very interesting. The actual dialogue could be contained on
the back of a grocery list. The artiness of Coppola's aesthetic
ultimately becomes an ethic."

If these reviews saddened Coppola, Pauline Kael's must
have cheered him immensely. Her *New Yorker* rave was the
kind of review any filmmaker would kill for:

> The daring of Part II is that it enlarges the scope
> and deepens the meaning of the first film; *The God-*

father was the greatest gangster picture ever made, and had metaphorical overtones that took it far beyond the gangster genre. In Part II, the wider themes are no longer merely implied. The second film shows the consequences of the actions in the first; it's all one movie, in two great big pieces, and it comes together in your head while you watch. . . . Coppola can go on to give us a more interior view of the characters at the same time that he shows their spreading social influence, an epic vision of the corruption of America.

She concluded: "Coppola is the inheritor of the traditions of the novel, the theater, and—especially—opera and movies. The sensibility at work in this film is that of a major artist. We're not used to it: how many screen artists get the chance to work in the epic form, and who has been able to seize the power to compose a modern American epic?"

Michael Goodwin, *City* magazine's film critic, had borrowed a technique from *Village Voice* music critic Robert Christgau: that of giving letter grades like a schoolmarm. He gave *The Godfather, Part II* a B+, finding it "complex, ambitious, and wholly-admirable," but also "a choppy, cerebral work that never seems to come together, either dramatically or thematically." (He now thinks he underrated the film badly.) Goodwin started his review by addressing the ethics of reviewing a film made by his publisher, and quoted an amiable conversation with Coppola in which the filmmaker had joked, "I don't *need* you, I've got Pauline Kael."

The following week a full-page ad for *Godfather II* appeared in *City* magazine. It consisted of a reprint, in its entirety, of Pauline Kael's *New Yorker* review.

Months later Coppola was still smarting. "Oh, they're full of baloney," was his view of the reviewers. "There isn't a critic out there who knows what he's talking about. There's a lot of extortion and blackmail practiced by critics. A lot of them force the filmmaker to participate in certain things that accrue to the critic's advantage under the implied threat of a bad review. It's corrupt right down to the bottom."

When the interviewer asked him to be more specific, Coppola declined. Weren't there *any* critics he admired? "Pauline Kael. When she writes about a film, she does it in depth. When

I make a bad picture, I expect her to blast me higher than a kite and I'll be grateful for that." He also named Jay Cocks, Steven Farber, Bruce Williamson, and (surprisingly) Stanley Kauffmann, who had blasted both *Godfathers*.

On December 20, 1974, a mere eight days after *Godfather II* opened, *The Conversation* was chosen as the Best Film of 1974 by the Committee on Exceptional Films of the National Board of Review. Coppola won Best Director honors, and Gene Hackman was chosen Best Actor. For Coppola, the award for his commercial flop must have seemed small consolation for the critical snubs awarded *Godfather II*.

Despite the critics' reservations, however, vast numbers of people wanted to see more of the Corleones. *Godfather II* opened big and grew bigger. In its first five days it did 74 percent of the business of the original *Godfather*. After a week in New York City it went into 160 theaters nationwide. For Christmas, it went into 437 theaters in a shortened version that ran only 180 minutes (down 20 minutes from Coppola's original cut). Some of the foreign versions were even shorter. In Chile, Augusto Pinochet's right-wing dictatorship slashed it to an incomprehensible 167 minutes by removing the entire Cuban sequence as well as the death of Hyman Roth. The junta didn't care for Coppola's hint that Fidel's revolution might have been justified.

On Christmas Eve 1974, Coppola stopped in at the office party of *City* magazine and personally gave each member of the staff a beribboned straw basket containing a box of imported spaghetti, a can of Italian tomatoes, a string of Italian sausages, a bottle of Sicilian wine, and Coppola's impressionistic, typed recipe for spaghetti sauce with sausage—the same recipe that Clemenza teaches Michael in *The Godfather*. (See Epilogue for a copy.) Everyone considered it a charming Christmas gift—although less charming, perhaps, than a bonus check.

The next day Coppola got a charming Christmas present of his own. *Godfather II* reached number one on *Variety's* charts of top-grossing films of the week. And a few days after that, when *both Godfather II* and *The Conversation* were honored on *Time's* ten best list for 1974, Coppola's artistic misgivings about his latest "formula schlock" movie began to abate as well.

Soon afterward, alluding to F. Scott Fitzgerald's statement

that "the lives of American writers have no second acts," Coppola told a *Penthouse* interviewer, "I view finishing *The Godfather, Part II* as the starting of a second act—in that I've lived out all my hopeless childhood fantasies." From now on, Coppola promised, he would live more contemplatively and less frantically. He was already rich, famous, and powerful enough to fulfill the dreams of any sickly, unpopular boy or any pair of demanding parents. He was on top of the world.

Chapter Twelve

The Medici Prince
(1975–1976)

THE YEAR 1975 started out as the year of awards. On January 14 *Godfather II* received no fewer than six nominations for the Golden Globe awards of the Hollywood Foreign Press Association: Best Film, Best Director, Best Screenplay, Best Actor (Pacino), Best Musical Score (Nino Rota and Carmine Coppola), and Best Film Newcomer (Lee Strasberg). Furthermore, *The Conversation* garnered four nominations as well: Best Film, Best Director, Best Screenplay, and Best Actor (Hackman). The only sour note was that *Chinatown* got *seven* nominations.

Coppola was finally in a position to spend a few months in his version of relaxation. As if he didn't have enough influence over Bay Area media with a theater, a magazine, and a filmmaking operation, he decided it would be fun to own a radio station, too. He mortgaged some of his future *Godfather II* profits and bought KMPX-FM, a local station that had been the first free-form rock radio station during the sixties; it had been sold several times since, turning to more commercial formats and losing listeners at every turn.

"All my life, all I really wanted was to be a living member of *La Bohème*," he explained to staffers at *City*. "That's the life I've always wanted to be part of, and since it doesn't exist, I have set out on the totally naive, and maybe impossible, job of creating it." But Coppola was hardly a starving artist in a garret; he was a *patron* of artists.

While he'd been working on *Godfather II*, his chic right-hand woman, Mona Skager, had been running the show at *City*, but the editors disliked her and resented taking orders from her. Now Coppola decided to take a firmer hand. He officially took on the job of publisher in January 1975 and started showing up at the magazine's offices more frequently than ever.

When the Oscar nominations were announced, on February 16, Coppola was amazed to find himself in the delightful but equivocal position of competing against himself. Both *The Conversation* and *Godfather II* had been nominated for Best Picture. In addition, *The Conversation* had been nominated for Best Original Screenplay and Best Sound, while *Godfather II* took eleven nominations in all: Best Screenplay Adaptation (Coppola and Puzo), Best Actor (Pacino), Best Supporting Actress (Talia Shire), no fewer than *three* Best Supporting Actors (De Niro, Strasberg, and Gazzo), Best Musical Score (Nino Rota and Carmine Coppola), and Best Costumes.

Coppola was even more delighted by the Directors Guild nominations: He was the first director ever to be nominated for two pictures in the same DGA competition. Early in March, he won for *Godfather II*, beating Bob Fosse (who'd been nominated for *Lenny*) and Sidney Lumet (for *Serpico*). Not everyone was pleased. *Variety*'s story noted that many of the New York-based guild members liked Lumet much better personally. "There was an embarrassingly long quiet period before a scattered round of applause started," *Variety* reported.

Joel Oliansky, his old pal from Hofstra and Seven Arts, won an award that night, too, for a TV drama called *The Law*, with Judd Hirsch. As Oliansky went up to get his gold statue, he heard Italia Coppola, sitting at Coppola's table, screaming, "Yaay, Hofstra! Yaay, Hofstra!" He was immensely tickled.

There was a party afterward at the Palladium, and Coppola and Oliansky found each other in the crowd. Oliansky and his wife, Pat, were in the process of divorcing, but he had taken her to the ceremony anyway. Coppola, who knew nothing of this, threw a happy bear hug around his old pal. "How's Pat?" he asked.

"Well," said Oliansky, "she's over there, but we're not . . . together."

Coppola waved Pat over, put one arm around her, put the other around Oliansky, and hugged them both. "A funny look came over his face," Oliansky remembered, "as if to say, 'Don't split up, don't make me think about it. . . .' "

As the Oscar ceremonies drew nearer, Francis discovered that he'd developed a burning hunger for the Academy's Best Director award, a yearning that was only intensified by the bitter memory of losing it for the first *Godfather*. He was also worried that having two films in contention might somehow split the "Coppola" vote, leaving *Chinatown* to make a clean sweep. A few days before the ceremonies Coppola talked up *Godfather II* with a writer from the *Hollywood Reporter*. "Part II is a much better film, a much more serious film, a much more ambitious film, a much riskier film than the other," he said, "to do what it attempted to do, and not just pander to an audience. . . . That was a very risky way to make a mass audience movie. It wasn't *The Towering Inferno* by any means."

With three family members up for Oscars (Francis, Carmine, and Talia Shire), the whole Coppola clan grew edgy. But Oscar night, 1975, turned into the Coppola Show. *Godfather II* took six awards: Best Picture, Best Director, Best Screenplay, Best Supporting Actor (De Niro), Best Art Direction, and Best Score. Coppola was so elated he didn't know what to do. "I never expected Best Picture," he said. "I felt *Godfather II* was too demanding, too complex. But when it won, I felt the members were telling me they appreciated the fact that we'd tried to make a film with integrity."

Carmine's award came up first on the program. In his joyous acceptance speech, he said, "If it wasn't for Francis Coppola, I wouldn't be here tonight. However, it if wasn't for me, *he* wouldn't be here." He was so excited that on the way back to his seat, unseen by the television audience, he dropped his statuette, shattering it.

Talia Shire, who'd already won an award from the New York Film Critics for Best Supporting Actress, fully expected to win an Oscar as well. She was crestfallen to lose (on a "sentimental" vote for Ingrid Bergman's cameo role in *Murder on the Orient Express*), but neither Francis nor Carmine even noticed her distress.

After his second trip to the stage Francis whispered to Italia that he'd thank *her* if he got another award, but when he took his third Oscar, he merely murmured, "I had something I was going to say, but I don't remember what it was. But thanks for giving my dad an Oscar."

Italia was now furious with both her husband and her son. "Francis was jumping up in the air saying, 'This was the best night in our lives.' Well, Tallie lost that night, and she said, 'I'm a girl, so you forgot about me.' Then Carmine gave his speech about how if it wasn't for him Francis wouldn't be here. I said to him afterward, 'Gee, Carmine, you did a great job. I hope the labor pains weren't too bad.' " It didn't help when, the day after the ceremony, a friend sent her a telegram asking: "Is Carmine Coppola a widower?"

Coppola had thought he was at the pinnacle of fame after *Godfather*. Now he was finding out what true stardom was like. Suddenly, it seemed he really *was* the Godfather to every Coppola on the planet. Letters poured in from Coppolas and Penninos all over the world, claiming to be related, asking for everything from autographs to jobs. Even *real* relatives became impossible. Talia, especially, got fed up with the lionization of her brother: "All of a sudden there are a lot of relatives—aunts and uncles and cousins—all too willing to kiss Francis's ass and trade on his status."

Just a few months earlier Coppola had said, "I've never been involved with 'yes people.' My closest friends always criticize." It had never really been true, as Hermes Pan and Shirley Knight could testify, but now, after the *Godfather II* Oscars, fewer and fewer of his associates were comfortable telling him he might be off base or out of line, even when it was obvious that he was. The yes people gathered.

The Paramount execs came up with an exceptionally dumb idea. They'd make . . . *Godfather III*, starring teen idol John Travolta as the son of Michael Corleone. Coppola threw up his hands. "I'm bored to death with gangsters!" he swore. He was willing to recut both *Godfather*s into a single epic-length film, but otherwise, his Mafia chronicles were *finis*.

As soon as the Oscars were over, Coppola left the press in the dust and fled with Ellie for two weeks of relaxation and anonymity in Rio. Writer William Murray, who had begun trying to contact him for a *Playboy* interview almost as soon as *Godfather II* was released, discovered that getting to see Francis Ford Coppola was as difficult as "setting up a tête-à-tête with the Godfather himself." It took him weeks to make the date.

"This is my last interview," were Coppola's first words into Murray's tape recorder. (Shades of Nixon.) "Enough is enough."

Moments later he leaped into the heated Moorish pool in the backyard and let out a loud series of moans for five minutes straight. Wouldn't his neighbors complain about the noise? asked the journalist. "It's my pool, I'll moan if I like," he said, sipping a cup of homemade espresso as he dunked. "Y'know, I *like* this," he added. "It's my idea of real decadence." Wearing a billowing caftan, he returned to the living room, put on a record of carnival music he'd brought back from Brazil, and sambaed around the room, either forgetting about the reporter completely or putting on a show for him.

Murray's story was a paean to success, unquestioning and unskeptical. By now *The Godfather* had grossed $285 million (/$620 million) worldwide, and Coppola, he wrote, was "the one person in the movie industry more in demand than Clint Eastwood." As for Coppola, he confessed that the more awards he received, the less secure he felt. "The artist's worst fear is that he'll be exposed as a sham," he said. "I've heard it from actors, directors, everyone. . . . Deep down, we're all living with the notion that our success is beyond our ability."

Coppola promised once again, as he had in so many earlier interviews, that he'd stick to his base in San Francisco. Too many of the bright people he knew in Hollywood had changed, he said. Instead of talking about art, all they talked about was deals. "They've become the very people they were criticizing three years ago. Like Michael, they've become their fathers. It could happen to me. One of the reasons I live here and not in Los Angeles is that I'm trying to keep my bearings."

However, when Los Angeles-based reporter Eve Babitz visited Coppola, she couldn't help noticing his princely role as they walked around North Beach together. "I don't buy *everything*," he told her. "I just buy what I need."

Among the things he needed, apparently, was *City,* but Babitz was only one of his out-of-town friends who continued to criticize the magazine. At an employee picnic one afternoon, she amazed several key editors by drawing them aside to deliver a scathing attack on what she felt was the magazine's sophomoric 1960s sensibility. Everyone knew the real source of the criticism. For Coppola, *City* was as bad as Zoetrope; he resented its disrespect toward the wealth and power that financed it.

When he had bought in for $15,000 in 1973, the magazine

had boasted a mere eleven thousand circulation. Under Burks's editorship, circulation had grown to twenty-five thousand, but the magazine was still losing money. Nobody really knew what the true figures were, but Burks was told that when he'd been hired, the magazine had been about $50,000 in the hole. Now, Coppola claimed, the loss had grown to almost $150,000. This is not a gigantic sum in the context of start-up publications, but Coppola didn't *like* the magazine.

He had originally come to San Francisco precisely because of its bohemian atmosphere, but he had grown disaffected with what he considered the corny values of the 1960s. The very *thought* of hippies made him angry, maybe because of the permanently "borrowed" equipment at Zoetrope. *City,* he thought, was still purveying those same corny values to the young and hip—the very San Franciscans who gave the city that special spirit Coppola claimed to admire so much.

Articles focused on blues as well as opera, on investigative journalism as well as trendy food and fashion. As a national recession brought a leap in local unemployment, a *City* article sardonically offered its middle-class readers a "users'-guide" to the ins and outs of the welfare system. Coppola was vaguely dissatisfied with these and similar features, but then two cover stories came out that drove him into a blind fury: "Ready for the Rapist" and the "Jug Wine Tasting."

The rapist came first. The women's movement was starting to make an impact, and it became apparent that many more rapes were taking place than were being reported—one reason being the awful treatment rape victims received from the police. Writer Robin Green wrote a strong two-part story for *City.* Part One dealt with the options open to women who had been raped. Part Two was about avoiding rape, by making yourself as invulnerable as possible: what to carry, what sort of clothes to wear, how to walk, and so on.

McCartney came up with a terrific cover. "We shot a picture of one of our ad saleswomen," Burks remembered, "and she's ready to walk down the street. She's got Mace, she's got an umbrella, she's got a whistle, and she doesn't look nutty. She looks great; she looks like a San Francisco woman. There are arrows pointing to the different things she's doing to make herself ready, and the cover line says, 'Ready for the Rapist.'

"It was a powerful story—and Francis hated it. He *hated*

it. One of the things he told me he hated about it was that it gave a hostile view toward men. He seemed to feel that the only women who have to worry about this— 'We're not interested in reaching these people,' he said, as if high-class women rode in taxis and didn't get raped. I'm sure he'd deny he ever said it."

But the article that pushed Coppola over the edge was the jug-wine tasting. "That was probably our downfall," said Burks. "It was a wonderful way to go out."

The article, which was subsequently imitated in virtually every magazine in California, was designed to find the best of the inexpensive jug wines. It took the form of a classic "blind" tasting, with one big difference: Instead of wine snobs, the tasters were people the readers could relate to, people who were serious about good wine but who drank jug wine sometimes. Many of the tasters were *City* staffers; all were irreverent, and at least half of them got happily pixilated during the tasting. McCartney designed another marvelous image for the cover: a young socialite dressed in a top hat, T-shirt, and tuxedo, with a wine jug on his shoulder, taking a swig.

The jug wine issue sold out completely in the first week. But it's doubtful Coppola would have cared. He called Burks on the phone the morning the issue came out, in a blind fury.

"He wanted to know what were we doing, how did this image ever make it onto the cover," Burks recalled. "You can either see in that how dislocated we were from Coppola's vision or how dislocated he was from his readers' sense of what they needed, 'cause it sold off the newsstand! People loved it. But from Francis's viewpoint, it was like—you let in the bums. That's not what he said, but that's what he meant. These were not *people*; these were not people that he and his friends would want to relate to. They just happened to be the core group of people putting out the magazine, whose sense of how to reach the readers was right on the money with that issue, as the sales proved. But Francis was embarrassed. He said, 'This is an embarrassment,' and something about hippies, and how much he hated hippies, and don't *ever* let this happen again!" The implication was that the next time *City* ran such a low-class story, all the editors would be out of a job.

Burks and McCartney, seeing the writing on the wall, decided to move on. Other editors stuck it out, hoping that Coppola would understand that this was a *San Francisco* magazine, aimed at a San Francisco readership that was very different from readers in New York or Los Angeles.

Everyone was miserable, including Coppola. "It was my Vietnam," he moaned a few months later. "Every month I put more into it. The stakes were getting so high that I felt I either had to get in or get out."

On May 1, 1975, Coppola got in—and threw everybody else out. His memo read:

> Dear City Magazine staff member,
>
> I realize that there have been many rumors regarding the future of the magazine and that the last month has been a difficult time for you. I have always tried to get information to you as soon as I myself had it, and that is why I am writing to you now.
>
> As you know, I did not create the magazine, but merely have tried to slowly change or influence it over the months. I realize that this was an impossible task, and that when things are set up wrong from the beginning, they haunt you for years afterward. Therefore I have decided to start all over again; fresh, from the beginning. Effective June 1st of this year, *all* employment relationships with City Publishing are terminated. However, in the week of May 12, all present staff members will be given priority in the interviews for the creation of a new magazine. . . . I am very grateful for the energy and devotion you have given to the magazine, and I am sorry that I was unable to get the magazine on its feet without such a traumatic change.

A few days later Coppola and his new art director walked into the magazine office, where a generally dispirited staff was trying to get out its final issue. In full view and hearing of the indignant editors, Coppola and his new hiree proceeded to discuss their exciting plans for redecoration of the dingy office. As soon as Coppola left, the entire staff trooped en masse to a local restaurant, ate as much as they could, and charged it to Francis Coppola.

Publication was suspended for a month while Coppola

restaffed the magazine and redecorated the office. Despite the
promise about priority, only three staffers out of twenty-five
survived the cut. The new edition would be anything but low-
rent. For *City*'s new editor in chief, Coppola hired Michael
Parrish, the editor of the staid monthly *San Francisco* (prompt-
ing the nickname "*City* of Parrish," after the now-defunct City
of Paris department store). Michael Salisbury, from *West* (in
Los Angeles), was hired at a princely salary to be art director.
Coppola, Parrish, and consulting editor Rosalie Muller Wright
toured the country, consulting with publishers and editors, including *New York*'s Clay Felker and *Ms*'s Gloria Steinem.

To cheer himself up in the midst of the ongoing magazine
crisis, Coppola bought himself a present: He located and pur-
chased a beautiful dark red Tucker automobile. It reminded
him that he still meant to make a movie about Preston Tucker.

But for now he was caught up in rewriting Milius's script
for *Apocalypse Now*. The original plan had been for George
Lucas to film this script in 16 mm, using a cast of unknowns
and integrating the fictional material with old news footage to
keep costs down to about $1.5 million (/$3.6 million). In 1974,
when Lucas declined to direct, Coppola offered the job to Milius for the same measly salary Lucas had turned down: $25,000
and 10 percent of the profits. By now Milius was becoming
successful in his own right, and he had several projects coming
up. He spurned the paltry offer, dubbing Coppola "the Bay
Area Mussolini." Finally he agreed to rewrite the script but
insisted that Coppola would have to direct himself.

Eventually Coppola ended up reshaping Milius's rewrite
to accommodate his own artistic vision. "When I read the first
draft of *Apocalypse*, I really thought in many ways it was the
perfect film story, the metaphor of a journey up a river to find
a guy," he said. "It's based on Joseph Conrad's *Heart of Darkness*. In fact, my script is based on it to an even greater extent.
The original script was profoundly interesting, and made a really
interesting and unusual statement about the war that was not
political in a very short or myopic sense, but in a big sense
was really political."

When asked why Lucas was no longer a part of the project,
Coppola replied that he was "too busy." Lucas, however, didn't
see it that way. In fact, he was furious at Coppola. Sure, he'd
turned down Coppola's insultingly low-rent offer to direct, but

he was the one who had suggested to Milius that he frame his Vietnam stories as a boat ride up a river (the very device that caught Coppola's eye), *he* was the one who'd made the original development deal with Columbia Pictures, *he* was the one who'd first sent Gary Kurtz to scout locations in the Philippines. Once he finished *Star Wars*, he explained, he envisioned *Apocalypse* as "the next logical step in his career." He just wanted more dough and more respect.

In fact, much of the tension between Coppola and Lucas revolved around the question of how Coppola had gained ownership of the property in the first place. Originally Lucas had owned the rights, which had gone to the company (American Zoetrope) in which he and Coppola were artistic partners. When Warner-Seven Arts bailed out of Zoetrope (after seeing the rough cut of *THX*), the only Zoetrope projects it kept were *The Conversation* and *Apocalypse*. Later, when Coppola paid back the money he owed, he became sole owner of both scripts.

In 1973, as he was finishing *American Graffiti*, Lucas had reminded Coppola about *Apocalypse*. Coppola said he'd be glad to produce the movie, but for 25 percent of the profits—twice as much as Lucas, who'd have to split his 25 percent with Milius. Lucas, who was still angry about the financial arrangements on *Graffiti*, thought the offer totally unfair. "I couldn't possibly have made the movie under those conditions," he recalled. Worse, he'd begun to worry that if he made another film under Coppola's aegis, Coppola's ego would somehow turn it into another Coppola movie, either by interfering in the shoot or at least by taking the credit later. He later described his feeling that for Coppola, "people disappear when they walk out of the room. He finds it incredible that people do things he doesn't want them to do, since he's controlling it all and they're all here for *him*."

Ultimately Coppola repaid Lucas for refusing the offer. In *Apocalypse Now* Harrison Ford has a cameo role, playing a creepy, intellectual military officer. His name tag reads "Colonel G. Lucas."

In any case, *Apocalypse* was Coppola's baby now, and a very risky baby it was. The only major war film about Vietnam made to date had been John Wayne's jingoistic *The Green Berets*, which, in the face of universal pans, had done hot but brief business. Although there had been plenty of "crazed Viet vets" rampage movies (and plenty more to come, culminating in *Rambo*), the war itself was not a popular subject. In fact, it had become a sort of Hollywood taboo, and distributors warned Coppola against it. However, as Fred Roos commented, "Francis believes you only have a chance to do something terrific, both artistically and commercially, if you're on the edge of disaster."

"It's best described as a macabre comedy," Coppola said. Even though it had only been six months since he'd publicly sworn off cinematic violence (in his *Playboy* interview), he now declared that *Apocalypse* would be "frightening, horrible—with even more violence than *The Godfather*." It was tentatively budgeted at $10 million (/$21.7 million), which he expected to provide entirely on his own, via advance sales of the foreign distribution rights. On May 29, 1975, *Variety* ran the first official story: John Milius was rewriting the *Apocalypse* script for Coppola to direct.

Milius is a fascinating character: part wild man, part ultra-patriot, part fanatic militarist, and all storyteller. He'd written a surprisingly charming screenplay for a biopic of Evel Knievel, a nice, conventional action script for Robert Redford's *Jeremiah Johnson*, and a surreal tragicomedy for director John Huston's oddball *Life and Times of Judge Roy Bean*. In 1973 he made his debut as a director with *Dillinger* (produced by Roger Corman, natch) from his own script. Now he was in pre-production for the film that would be his masterwork, *The Wind and the Lion*, to be shot in 1975.

He'd originally written *Apocalypse* between 1967 and 1969, based on harrowing stories he'd heard from returning soldiers. Despite his public praise of Milius, Coppola had been displeased with the original screenplay, which centered on two men: Kurtz, a Special Services officer who had gone native and disappeared into the backcountry of Vietnam, and Willard, a young soldier sent to kill him. "It took a comic-strip Vietnam War and moved it through a series of events that were also comic strip; a political comic strip," Coppola told writer Greil Marcus. The original version ended with Kurtz converting Willard and the two of them firing at the American helicopters that are coming to get them.

Subsequently Milius rewrote the script, and Coppola rewrote the rewrite. Although he was just getting started, Coppola decided to submit the rough draft to the Pentagon public affairs section as a first step toward obtaining Army cooperation. The Pentagon forwarded it to the Army, recommending that it work with Coppola to make sure the film "will be an honest presentation" of the government viewpoint on the war. Army officials took one look at the screenplay and turned livid.

Army memos excerpted in *Film Comment* tell the tale. It was "simply a series of some of the worst things, real and imagined, that happened or could have happened during the Vietnam War." There were "objectionable episodes" which presented the Army "in an unrealistic and unacceptable bad light," including scenes of U.S. officers scalping "gooks," surfing in the midst of combat, procuring sexual favors for enlisted men, and smoking grass with the grunts. The Army particularly objected to "the sick humor or satirical philosophy of the film." Furthermore, it couldn't stand the basic plot, specifically finding Kurtz's operations (and Willard's mission to "terminate" him) "as a parody on the sickness and brutality of war." The Army refused to raise a finger to cooperate with the filming unless Coppola agreed to rewrite the script. Coppola rejected the very idea. It was a total standoff.

Coppola decided to go ahead anyway. He wanted to get to work on the long-deferred *Tucker,* but decided to get *Apocalypse* out of the way first because he thought he could finish it quickly.

Coppola made many changes in the Milius script, moving it back toward the original structure of *Heart of Darkness.* Milius had started the film with Kurtz, but Coppola followed Conrad's novella and withheld any vision of Kurtz until the end. Milius's ending had a power-mad Kurtz converting Willard to his side by sheer power of machismo. Coppola preferred to have Kurtz ramble quietly and madly, an intelligent man who recognizes his own insanity. Milius disliked the rewrite. Lucas was equally displeased at the change from a low-budget docudrama to a big-budget literary movie. But why should Coppola care? He was Hollywood's Golden Boy. On June 6 UCLA even named him Alumnus of the Year. He must have been amused, remembering how his jealous schoolmates had scorned him for getting involved in making movies for profit.

The first issue of the redesigned *City* hit the newsstands on July 6, 1975. Michael Salisbury, who had designed *Rolling*

Stone, remade *City* in an uppity version of *Rolling Stone*'s image, changing the format from an eight-by-eleven-inch bound magazine to an eleven-by-thirteen-inch stapled tabloid, with double the number of pages and higher-quality paper.

The first issue did well, with contents calculated to appeal to both the old readership and the upscale audience Coppola was aiming for. It included a mocking exposé of the San Francisco Vice Squad's penchant for nabbing pensioners playing penny ante poker, and a letter from fugitive LSD guru Timothy Leary describing his life with the Black Panthers. "I want it to have an emotional feeling about it, not to be another copy of *New York* magazine, which most city magazines are," Coppola told a reporter. "I want it to be warm and personal, but still with teeth."

Editing and production costs on *City* had gone way up, but nobody knew exactly how much. Still, Coppola loved the magazine's look. He also loved playing publisher; it was like making a movie every week, but without the long delay before you found out whether the audience liked it. In the lead editorial of the first issue of the new *City,* he promised to bring in guest editors on a regular basis (he envisioned conductor Seiji Ozawa, rock star Sly Stone, Patty Hearst's ex-boyfriend Stephen Weed, and "an Italian fisherman" in this role).

His fame drew national attention to the magazine, and he gleefully revealed to *Time* his long-cherished plan: He wanted to hold the magazine's closing nights at the Little Fox Theater as public events, a sort of weekly Magazine Crisis Show. Editors would do their work onstage, with galley proofs flashing on a screen behind them. The off-the-street audience would vote on headlines and layout and offer comments on the stories, which would be published as a special page of the magazine.

The tone of Coppola's editorial, his comments to the national press, and a high-priced ad campaign designed to promote the new magazine antagonized some San Franciscans. Herb Caen, the leading columnist for the San Francisco *Chronicle,* and the ultimate SF arbiter, sniffed: "Why would Francis Ford Coppola hire a Los Angeles advertising agency to persuade us Bay Areans to buy his *City* magazine? I suppose it should also be recorded that Coppola's new toy is being designed by Mike Salisbury—also of L.A.—but leave us not be provincial. I'm not sure yet, but I think I preferred the OLD *City* Magazine." Caen wasn't the only one.

The pricey ad campaign, which increased the magazine's budget to a whopping $180,000 per month, focused solely on Coppola, not the magazine. Signboards on top of taxicabs, and posters splashed on the sides of buses, carried giant close-ups of Coppola, urging the public to pay $9.95 for a subscription. "ISN'T IT WORTH THAT MUCH," he asked in the ads, "TO SEE ME FALL ON MY FACE?" A month into the campaign some wag at the San Francisco *Chronicle* inserted a blurb for a screening of *Dementia 13* into the TV listings: "The movie is primarily of interest to film historians, and to those who wouldn't mind seeing Coppola fall on his face but don't feel like shelling out $9.95 for the privilege."

Finally, though, it was the campaign that fell on its face. Coppola had anticipated the ads would increase circulation from twenty-five thousand to a hundred thousand, but circulation rose only to thirty-three thousand. Furthermore, in one month Coppola managed to spend nearly as much money on ads alone as he'd lost on the entire magazine for the full previous two years. While some people subscribed, many of the original readers defected. The magazine's new look was very 1970s, but San Francisco seemed to prefer content over style. Coppola couldn't buy readers.

Coppola was unhappy again. He wanted, he said, a stronger editorial stance and after two issues he summarily fired editor Michael Parrish and seven of the fifteen new staff members. He'd spoken to Warren Hinckle about being the first guest editor; now he hired him permanently. Hinckle's first editorial action was to end the guest editor policy forever.

Hinckle had been the editor of the counterculture's favorite slick magazine, *Ramparts*, which gave birth (via the strike weekly *Sunday Ramparts*) to *Rolling Stone*. He was flashy, but he had little sense of financial reality. After spending *Ramparts* into bankruptcy, he founded another muckraking magazine, *Scanlan's*, which went bankrupt, too, in no time flat. "I know the guy's nutty," Coppola muttered to his friends, "but what can I do?"

The first *City* of Hinckle was the top seller in *City*'s history, thanks largely to the cover. Over a photo of a cute, pouting, lingerie-clad sexpot trying in vain to get picked up in a

bar, Hinckle ran a headline reading WHY WOMEN CAN'T GET
LAID IN S.F. Susan Berman's article subsequently drew a storm
of acerbic letters to the editor, pointing out that her choice of
bedmates was confined exclusively to doctors, lawyers, and
corporate chiefs. Other articles included a feature on foot massage, a critique of Jack London's machismo, a CIA pilot's
confessions, a warning about the dangers of anal sex, and an
attack from the left on Tom Hayden, who was then planning
to run for U.S. senator. (Hinckle had moved to the right since
his days at *Ramparts*.)

By now Coppola's *City* losses amounted to $500,000, but
after the success of the "getting laid" issue he committed an
additional million. Hoping to bring in some full-page ads,
Coppola decided to ballyhoo his magazine in L.A. In an interview in the plush Hollywood Polo Lounge, he boasted to
Charles Champlin of the Los Angeles *Times:* "A newspaper
determines the level of cultural life in its city, and neither paper up there was meeting the needs of the city." Coppola was
proud of something else, too: He'd just received a $4,000 check
for *The Conversation*, which had finally slipped into the black.

Shortly after Coppola hired Hinckle, Hinckle followed
Coppola's suggestion and signed on Manny Farber, a highly
respected "serious" film critic, formerly of *Time, Artforum*, and
the *Nation*. "If I'm going to have any film of mine panned in
my own magazine," Coppola told the San Francisco *Chronicle*,
"it's going to be by someone with the right credentials."

Coppola's obsession with the magazine amazed and distressed the staff at the Coppola Company, but nobody dared
challenge him. "We have to defer to his instincts," said Fred
Roos. "He's been right so often." Between *City*, KMPX, the
Little Fox Theater, and *Apocalypse*, he really was spending
money faster than he could make it, but he seemed to be enjoying himself for once. "I'll be broke and back to zero in a
few years," he told Roos, "so I might as well have fun."

Nor was the magazine using up *all* his time, or all his
money. In mid-July, Coppola and NBC closed an innovative
deal: For a reported $15 million (/$32.7 million), NBC bought
the rights to both *Godfathers*, including all the footage that
Coppola had been forced to cut out; Coppola would reassemble the footage chronologically into a nine-hour, multipart TV
mini-series.

And of course, there were other projects on the burner. Every morning from seven to ten, he worked on revising the *Apocalypse* script; as it drew nearer to completion, he sometimes began writing as early as five and continued until noon. He returned to his habit of doing some of his writing in a North Beach coffeehouse, a creative artist typing away with an audience of friendly kibitzers.

That still left afternoons and evenings free for fun. He announced a plan to stage *The Threepenny Opera* at the Little Fox, with Diane Keaton in the cast; perhaps he would also film it in 16 mm. He planned to audition radio drama versions of scripts in progress (including one of *Apocalypse Now*) on his new radio station. "A guy who could knock me out with a radio drama could also write me a movie," Coppola explained enthusiastically.

Furthermore, Coppola had become one of San Francisco's most fabulous hosts. At informal gatherings he would often do the cooking himself; at formal parties he'd supervise in the kitchen, making sure that every plate was exquisitely arranged. His friend Tom Luddy frequently had famous visiting directors from Europe in tow; Coppola was delighted to throw "welcome to San Francisco" parties for each of them.

At the Broadway mansion, the famous mingled with the wannabes; struggling Bay Area talent hobnobbed with international stars, and though nobody discussed deals (at least where Coppola could hear them), many hoped to be discovered.

Ambitious artists, ready to do anything to enter the inner circle of party regulars, handed their hearts to Coppola. A TV commercial producer who hoped for a movie job spent so much time attending to Coppola's social life that his secretary quit in disgust, telling her friends she'd gotten sick of listening to her boss spending all day on the phone rounding up bright, attractive female guests for Coppola's parties.

It was the height of the 1970s' sexual revolution, and the mansion's multiple hidey-holes indoors (and the heated Moorish pool in the backyard) seemed to encourage guests to leave their inhibitions on the doorstep.

Up to a certain point in the evening Ellie Coppola would shyly greet each arrival, but then she'd simply disappear into some quieter recess of the house. Friends said that she had truly become Kay Corleone to Coppola's Michael, purposely isolated from his business and deliberately blind to the party atmosphere at the mansion. Years later she herself came to share this view.

With his growing media empire and social prominence, Coppola drew gossip that he meant to run for office in San Francisco. "I don't need more power," he responded. "The most powerful man on earth is a film director. When he makes a picture, he is a god over millions of dollars and hundreds of people."

In any case, Coppola's love affair with San Francisco was beginning to sour a little. It was a great place to live, but people didn't take him seriously enough. "I didn't feel welcome there," he recalled soon after. "It's not that they turned their back on me, they made fun of me. This is the only place in America where *American Graffiti* got a bad review, in the San Francisco *Chronicle*. They didn't understand the work."

Coppola may have expected that so small a city would yield its heart to him as swiftly as a banana republic surrendering to the U.S. Marines. What he never seemed to understand was that San Francisco can be terribly snobbish; certain outsiders are never accepted. There are no real celebrities except Herb Caen and those mentioned favorably in his column—and Caen obviously didn't like Coppola. No matter how many theaters, magazines, and radio stations Coppola bought, he was still being frozen out of the city's power structure. Ever since his days at Hofstra, he was accustomed to being a big man on campus; San Francisco must have made him feel like a high school social dud again.

Few San Franciscans guessed that Coppola was in the process of quietly pulling out of the city. First he bought a Napa Valley estate to use as a country retreat, a spacious vineyard in prime wine country near the town of Rutherford, a ninety-minute drive northeast of San Francisco. The 170-acre spread included a large lily pond with a little island in the center, flowering trees, sculptured hedges, manicured vineyards, giant oaks, and redwood forests. There was also a three-story gabled Georgian manor with a deep porch on three sides, set a quiet half mile from the two-lane highway running through the valley. When Coppola moved his precious Wurlitzer jukebox full of old Caruso seventy-eights from the mansion to the vineyard, everyone knew he regarded the country estate as his home.

At the same time he moved to reestablish his base in Hollywood, buying and refurbishing offices at the Goldwyn Studio to house not only the *Apocalypse* production but *The Black Stallion* as well. Soon Fred Roos was stationed there full time, and Coppola commuted down frequently. Late in the summer of 1975 he announced, "Except for my post-production work, I've never tried to make San Francisco a film center. All of the talent is in L.A. and the key people of my film company are in L.A."

Coppola was moving rapidly toward shooting *Apocalypse*. On September 3, 1975, the *Variety* headline read MILIUS REHEATS HIS "APOCALYPSE"; COPPOLA TO MAKE "MOST VIOLENT MOVIE EVER."

Variety noted that the film would be shot in Australia and Malaysia and would have Steve McQueen as Willard and Gene Hackman as Kilgore, the surfing general. Gray Frederickson (from Al Ruddy's *Godfather* production team) and Fred Roos would coproduce. Actually, aside from the cinematographer and the coproducers, almost nothing was set—not the locations and certainly not the cast. Coppola had made a deal with famed Italian cinematographer Vittorio Storaro (who'd shot *The Conformist*, *Last Tango in Paris*, and *1900* for Coppola's idol, Bertolucci); however, as yet not a single star had accepted a role in the film.

As for shooting in Australia, when Fred Roos and Dean Tavoularis went down under for the opening of *Godfather II*, they had found the Aussies friendly and the scenery terrific; now they urged Coppola to shoot *Apocalypse* in tropical Queensland. Although Coppola hadn't visited Australia when *Variety* announced the location plans, he liked the idea of shooting jungle footage in an Anglo-Saxon country free from the greed and corruption he'd suffered in Santo Domingo. When he finally arrived, however, he found local attitudes distinctly chilly. The Australian film community still remembered very clearly how Americans had taken over their film industry in the 1940's and shut out the locals.

At first Coppola was full of enthusiasm. "It will make $100 million," he exulted. "*Apocalypse* has, in a sense, already done over $30 million. It can't lose."

The very size turned off the Aussies. "We don't know that we want a great big American film in Australia," a union official responded. "What's in it for us?" Despite Coppola's reassurances that his company wouldn't be exploitative, that he'd use large numbers of Australian technicians and actors, the mere suggestion awakened nationalistic ire among local film personnel, who were in the midst of creating a film renaissance all their own, headed by filmmakers like Gillian Armstrong, Bruce Beresford, Phillip Noyce, and Peter Weir.

After several days of hostile meetings Coppola returned to the States. He was in a foul mood and promptly turned down the latest rewrite of *The Black Stallion*.

A few weeks later, Coppola announced that he'd be shooting *Apocalypse* in the Philippines. In this location the question wasn't whether he could get permission to shoot; President Ferdinand Marcos was always delighted to extend his fullest cooperation to any Yankee filmmaker who paid the proper fees. The question was how much money Marcos would demand to put the nation's army and air force at Coppola's disposal so he could stage scenes of bombing jungle villages.

Coppola was also welcomed in Cuba, where *The Godfather* was immensely popular. He traveled to Havana on a filmmakers' exchange program with leftist producer Bert (*Hearts and Minds*) Schneider and actress Candice Bergen, and met, of course, with Fidel Castro. Coppola's account of their conversation is amusing:

"I read *Jaws*," said Castro. "It's not a very good book, but I think the movie must be good because it's a Marxist picture."

"Oh?" said Coppola.

"Yes, it shows that businessmen are ready to sell out the safety of citizens rather than close down against the invasion of sharks."

Coppola probably didn't love *Jaws* as much; it had just displaced *The Godfather* as the biggest and fastest-grossing film in history. Nonetheless, when he got home, Coppola wrote a letter to Castro. It read, "Dear Fidel, I love you. We are similar. I am heavy and so are you, no, I am fat. We have the same initials. We both have beards. We both have power and want to use it for good purposes. . . ." But he never mailed it.

Returning home, Coppola changed his plans for *Apocalypse* again. Originally he'd intended to finance the film entirely on his own; he didn't want to repeat the mistake he'd made on *American Graffiti*. He had already invested about $1 million of his own money on preproduction, and along with $7 million in advance for foreign distribution rights, he thought he'd have enough to fund the film. Unfortunately the foreign distributors were now insisting that Coppola couldn't use their money for up front production costs unless he signed major stars for all the leading roles.

Brando said he was willing to play Kurtz, but Steve Mc-Queen wanted $3 million (/$6.4 million) to play Willard. It would have been the largest salary ever paid to an actor in the history of the motion picture industry. Coppola complained but finally agreed to come up with the money—at which point McQueen said he'd take that much for the shorter role of Kurtz, not for Willard. His son was about to graduate from high school, he explained, and he didn't want to leave his family for a long shoot in the Philippines. Then Brando changed his mind and edged out of the deal.

With all these millions of dollars flying around, James Caan, who was only a mid-level star, now demanded a whopping $2 million (/$4.3 million). Then, in the middle of negotiations, he backed out; his wife was pregnant, and he didn't want to go to the Philippines. Al Pacino wasn't interested at any price; he feared for his health in the jungle. Robert Redford was on a long vacation. Jack Nicholson didn't have time to play Willard and didn't want to play Kurtz. Suddenly nobody big enough for the distributors would work for a price Coppola could afford. He was a victim of his own success.

Coppola blasted Steve McQueen for demanding $3 million for three weeks' work, and lambasted the movie industry for giving in to these unbelievable salaries. "Whose fault is it that there are only six stars in the world today?" he grumbled. "We should go back to the old studio system. As a director, I personally would never aspire to make more than $1 million out front, and I thought that was about right for actors too." It made him so furious he threw all his Oscars out the window. They broke, and Ellie and the kids picked up the pieces.

Martin Sheen was both willing and affordable, but he was stuck on another shoot in Italy and, in any case, wasn't famous enough to suit the foreign investors. In despair, Coppola called Dean Tavoularis, who was already in the Philippines, supervising construction of the sets. "Who needs stars?" Coppola yelled over the phone. "Don't be depressed, I'll make this film, I'll cast a lot of unknowns, young Al Pacinos, and sign them on with me as a repertory company, a studio in San Francisco. They'll take acting classes and do theater, too, for five years.

We'll use them to build a talent pool. The studios don't encourage or build talent. Anyway, it'll be a better movie. The
war was fought by children. Redford and McQueen are too old."
(In the end Coppola had to give back about a quarter of the
foreign distributors' money because of his failure to find a major star to play Willard.)

With the foreign distributors growing antsy, Coppola had
to give up the idea of financing the film himself. He sold part
of his exclusive ownership of *Apocalypse* to United Artists. In
return for the American distribution rights, and assuming he
could round up some stars, it agreed to put up $7 million (as
an advance against profits) to match the foreign distributors' $7
million. A tentative release date was set for April 7, 1977, Coppola's thirty-eighth birthday. The budget was still just above
moderate at $12 million (/$26 million). Coppola retained control over the film and assumed financial responsibility for any
budget overruns.

City was now on the skids for real. On December 21 an
article in the financial section of the Los Angeles *Times* reported that circulation was stuck at thirty thousand and that
the magazine was run "with a rather cavalier attitude toward
budgets."

The first days of 1976 brought other unpleasant news. After
its hot start *Godfather II*'s box-office business was falling off.
It had merely made $28.9 million in domestic rentals, placing
it behind *Jaws, Towering Inferno, Benji,* and *Young Frankenstein* as only the fifth most profitable film of 1975. Furthermore, after earning $131 million (/$186 million) in worldwide
rentals, *The Godfather,* too, had dropped to second slot behind
Jaws, which had earned $132 million in worldwide rentals after
less than a year in release.

On January 26 Coppola gave his wife an odd gift: *City.*
He didn't have time to deal with it, so he asked her to take
over, prune the staff, cut expenses, concentrate on cheaper local stories, and, above all, reduce Warren Hinckle's weekly
$45,000 losses to $15,000. "I'd hate to see it die, but I'm holding Warren accountable," Ellie said. "No more overtime. You
can't pull a magazine out of your sleeve on Friday night."

On February 12 Eleanor announced a painful decision. The
final issue would be February 18. Circulation had dropped
precipitously, and by now the magazine had lost at least $1.5
million (some said $3 million), nearly all but the first $150,000

since Coppola fired the first staff. "But finances were said to be secondary to Coppola's disappointment in its content under editor Warren G. Hinckle," wrote *Variety*. "Final break came over issue containing article about North Beach topless, which Coppola felt was beneath standards he was seeking. Advertisers had complained *City* lacked identity and was a mishmash of politics, entertainment and sex."

Herb Caen's postmortem read: "Francis Ford Coppola, who suggested last July that it might be worth a subscription to his *City* magazine 'just to see me fall on my face,' officially fell on his face yesterday. . . . After making the tough decision Sunday, Francis flew off to Manila to continue wc on *Apocalypse Now* . . . leaving Editor Warren Hinckle with the thankless job of telling the staff that it's all over. 'However,' philosophized Hinckle, 'I'm used to it—I've had three magazines shot out from under me.' " (That was one way of looking at it.)

Coppola refused to take any responsibility. His eulogy for the dead magazine consisted of one short, bitter statement. "There isn't enough local talent in San Francisco to keep a magazine like that going," he snapped.

His rotten mood lasted for weeks, but he had more immediate problems in mind. *Apocalypse* was ready to roll, but nobody would act in it.

Somebody, at least, saw the humor in the situation. A young actor named Robert Reiser took out a full-page ad in the trade newspapers, showing him standing in front of a beat-up VW wearing faded jeans and army boots. "Dear Francis Ford Coppola," read the copy, "I read about your difficulties. We artists must stick together. I'll take the 16-week role and work for double-scale. Your friend, Robert Reiser. P.S.: This Beverly Hills life is getting boring." Coppola's Los Angeles office actually interviewed the guy, but nothing came of it.

With the casting still largely unresolved, Coppola flew to the Philippines to supervise final details. He thought he could round up actors by telephone and telex, but the location was unnerving. He was used to the Hollywood jungle, with its reptilian studio execs; this jungle had genuine, nonmetaphorical poisonous snakes, plus dangerous animals and armed guerrillas lurking in the back country, not to mention horrible insects and mud slides and typhoons.

"I don't fear death," he told a reporter, perhaps trying to

reassure himself. "I haven't met my date with myself to make a movie from my heart. I've got my name in the paper and a big house, but those are my parents' dreams." Anyway, *Apocalypse* was just something to finish off quickly, to satisfy his distributors, before he could settle down to write a script for *Tucker,* the film which would be from the heart.

From the time he'd first encountered John Milius's script, through seven years of slowly edging up to directing it himself, Coppola had never taken *Apocalypse* entirely seriously. Suddenly he found himself seven thousand miles from home, in a real jungle, with a real movie to make. Mercifully (for who among us would want to know?) he didn't realize that he was living the best moment of his life, the highest peak of his fame, power, and success. A long downhill slide was about to begin. *Apocalypse* was at hand.

Chapter Thirteen
Stranded in the Jungle
(1976–1977)

IT CAN'T BE repeated too often that it's nearly impossible to make a movie. *Any* movie. A bad movie, a sloppy movie, a simple movie. So many unmanageable factors must come together: money, weather, time, creative energies, the phases of the moon. The odds against making a difficult movie, then, or an ambitious one, or (God forbid) a great one approach the astronomical.

Yet Coppola, who surely knew this better than anyone, approached the making of *Apocalypse*, which was clearly an ambitious and extremely difficult picture, with a surprising lack of terror. At least at first. Perhaps his overconfidence is understandable. Everyone, even his peers and co-workers, said he was a genius. "He is the most decorated member of our unit," wisecracked John Milius. "When Francis walks into a room, you hear and see nothing but clanking, shining Oscars."

In fact, in the eyes of the world Coppola was more than a genius; he was an auteur. It's a word (and a concept) that's been misunderstood from the start. Truffaut, Godard, and the rest of the French critics who popularized it intended it to denote a director who consistently puts a personal stamp on what is usually a collective medium, but it was immediately distorted in general usage to denote a director who could not make a bad film.

Coppola told William Murray:

There are a handful of directors today who have total authority and deserve it. And then there are a lot of other directors who really ought to be working with strong producers and strong writers, but they all think they're Stanley Kubrick. The *auteur* theory is fine, but to exercise it you have to qualify, and the only way you can qualify is by having *earned* the right to have control, by having turned out a series of really incredibly good films. . . . I don't feel that one or two hits, or one or two beautiful films entitle anyone to that much control. A lot of very promising directors have been destroyed by it.

Coppola seemed to have bought into his own *auteurité*. Perhaps it was unavoidable in the face of the universal praise and his inner uncertainties.

Coppola's U.S. distributor and co-investor, United Artists, had itself been founded by four artists (Mary Pickford, Douglas Fairbanks, Charlie Chaplin, and director D. W. Griffith) who wanted control over their own pictures; even fifty years later its executives maintained a conscious pride in the company's beginnings. If UA was willing to let a major artist like Coppola have total control, how could he do less than seize it? Coppola was ready to gamble everything he owned on his genius. He took off for the Philippines with two producers who were his own employees and a script even he found unsatisfactory, leaving his co-investors seven thousand miles away.

Slowly, subtly, inexorably, the film drove him out of his mind. "I turned into a Kurtz of sorts," he admitted later. "I was a nice Kurtz, but I could do anything that I wanted. There's a line in the film . . . where Brando looks at Willard and says, 'Have you ever considered real freedom? Freedom from the opinion of others, even from the opinion of yourself?' That's what happened to me; because I raised everything financially, I had no boss."

The madness started gradually. When Coppola left for the Philippines on March 1, 1976, to start shooting battle sequences and special effects scenes, he still needed to find stars for his film. While he shepherded hordes of extras through the crowd scenes, he continued trying to cast the leads by telephone and telex.

Dean Tavoularis had already set up two main locations, one at faraway Baler, the other at faraway Iba. Neither of them proved particularly paradisiacal. For one thing, they had a wide selection of poisonous snakes, everything from muscular little cobras to rangy six-footers so exotic nobody knew what they were called in English. There were kitten-size cockroaches, spiders that would fang you as soon as breathe, and mosquitoes that were studying to be vampires. There were also industrial-strength bacteria, such as those famed for causing cholera, typhus, and dysentery.

In exchange for an unnamed (but presumably exorbitant) sum, President Marcos had agreed to let Coppola use the American-made aircraft of the Philippine Air Force. Dick White, the flying ace who supervised the air sequences, noted, "With my helicopters, the boats, and the high morale of the well-trained extras we had, there were three or four countries in the world we could have taken easily."

Marcos also supplied security specialists to guard the special effects explosives and M-16 rifles. He even insisted on providing a full-time military bodyguard for Coppola (who didn't especially want one) to make sure nobody stole *him*. Marcos's generosity had its little drawbacks, though. A few days after filming started, smack in the middle of a critical aerial rehearsal, all the Hueys suddenly disappeared. It turned out they'd headed south to kill guerrillas.

On March 1 Coppola's family and retinue arrived: Ellie, Gio (age twelve), Roman (age ten), Sofia (age four), nephew Marc Coppola (Augie's eldest son, a young adult who would work as a production assistant), a housekeeper, a baby sitter, and a projectionist. They settled into a large rented house in Manila's ritzy Dasmariñas section. Workmen were already building a swimming pool in the backyard for them; Tavoularis had furnished the interior to Ellie's specifications, with lots of rattan and velvet that she intended to take home to the Napa Valley country house.

By March 9 Coppola had finally cast the film; he notified the actors by taking out a full-page ad in *Variety*, using the trade paper as a sort of public bulletin board. "Since this is the first notification of our choices," the ad read, "the above casting is subject to the final negotiation of deals." Many of the chosen were highly surprised, to say the least. Marlon Brando would be Kurtz, Harvey Keitel (star of *Mean Streets*) would play Willard, and Robert Duvall (no surprise) would play the surfboarding general named Kilgore. A fourteen-year-old actor named Larry Fishburne would play a soldier named *Clean*. ("I was supposed to be an eighteen-year-old kid," Fishburne remembered. "By the time we finished shooting and the film was cut, I *was* eighteen.")

Although it wasn't mentioned in the *Variety* ad, Coppola was preparing to sign Keitel, Sam Bottoms, Frederic Forrest, and Albert Hall, and Fishburne to long-term contracts. Once *Apocalypse* was finished, Coppola said, these actors would form the core of a long-term repertory theater company from which he would cast such upcoming film projects as *The Brotherhood of the Grape* (scripted by Robert Towne), *Black Stallion*, *Hammett* (a mystery about the mystery writer, based on a novel by San Francisco writer Joe Gores), and *My Country Tis of Thee*, to be written and directed by *Jaws* screenwriter Carl Gottlieb.

Coppola's revival of long-term actors' contracts raised some eyebrows in the film industry. The practice, which originated with the Hollywood studios of the 1930s and 1940s, had fallen into disrepute, partly because of its uncomfortable similarity to slavery. Actors were paid regular salaries by the studios that "owned" them, in return for which they were expected to act in films over which they had no say whatsoever. In addition, they could be lent out (whether they wanted to be or not) to other studios; if they'd become more popular since signing their original contracts, their owners often demanded big bonuses from the borrowers, but any money over and above the actors' regular salaries went to their owners. Finally, contract players were paid for only forty weeks' work and were forbidden to work on independent projects during their enforced twelve-week vacations.

He planned to sign the actors to seven-year contracts, he explained, paying them for fifty weeks a year rather than the hated forty weeks of old. He'd encourage them to take outside roles and promised he would let them keep a large share of their loan-out bonuses, about 50 percent—undeniably large compared with the zero percent the old studios allowed.

Variety hinted that Coppola's motive might lie in his anger at being spurned for *Apocalypse* by Al Pacino and James

Caan after *The Godfather* had made them stars. This time around, if any of his actors went big-time, he'd have them under contract; they'd be powerless to raise their prices or refuse roles.

Coppola now had sets and actors to perform in them. He began shooting at Baler, six hours from Manila over bad dirt roads, or half an hour by plane (when you could get a plane). It was a tiny town with a dingy little hotel and no electricity other than the volts furnished by the company's own generator; the lack of refrigeration made food poisoning endemic on the set. What he didn't have was a finished script. Something would come to him.

If Coppola wasn't sure about the story, neither was anyone else. Special effects chief Joe Lombardi thought, "This whole movie is special effects." Dean Tavoularis guessed, "This movie's about how wrong it was for Americans to go against their nature." Brando's stand-in, Vietnam vet Pete Cooper, later said the message was "that the military people were not second-class citizens and idiots. They were good hometown boys, but the war changed them."

Meantime, Coppola gave himself a birthday party in the jungle. He had a six-by-eight-foot cake flown in from home, plus a load of gourmet snack food. Everyone was impressed, in a weird sort of way. "Wow, this is the most decadence I've ever seen," an American extra murmured.

Coppola wasn't the only gourmet on the set. Cinematographer Vittorio Storaro and his Italian crew brought canned tomatoes, olive oil, and pasta from Italy; they even taught the local bakery in Baler how to make Italian bread. When they ran out of the food they'd brought with them, they arranged for a $700 care package from Rome. Unfortunately the grocery bill was somewhat inflated by shipping and customs charges of $8,000.

Coppola had to limit his own enjoyment of the pasta. He was on a strict diet and managed to lose thirty-five pounds in his first month in Asia. His dieting may have contributed to his increasing grumpiness on and off the set. However, he solaced himself with espresso from the two espresso machines he'd shipped over—a big one for the Manila house and a little stove-top model for the locations.

Eleanor was already keeping a written diary, and at her husband's urging, she also began shooting a documentary about the making of *Apocalypse*, although at first she didn't even know how to load a movie camera. Within days she lost all her camera gear in a fire started by a special effects explosion, which proved to be the film's first big physical disaster. The paint shop and the prop storage shed exploded in flames. When the conflagration was put out, the stunt men discovered that their custom-made asbestos safety suits had melted in the heat, and they had to return to L.A. to replace them. The damage cost about $50,000, including replacements for Ellie's documentary gear.

To try to make up for the rising costs, prop man Doug Madison found a connection for an unlimited supply of corpses; they were less costly than dummies. Coppola claimed to have vetoed the corpses, but Eleanor and Tavoularis both noted ravenous rats and infernal stink at the "corpse"-strewn temple set, and Eleanor's diary indicates the corpses may have been real. Nor were the stiffs the only unusual props. There were sacks full of handsome, hefty Burmese pythons. (Burmese pythons almost always play the scary snakes in jungle movies because they're impressively large but rather sweet-natured—for snakes.)

Harvey Keitel was a bone-deep city boy, and he hated the jungle. He also hated the snakes, and the heat, and the bugs. In fact, he was beginning to hate the movie and its director— especially when, on the first day of shooting, he was accidentally abandoned on a raft in the middle of the river. "Hello," he called into his walkie-talkie. There was no answer. "Hello, this is Harvey Keitel," he radioed again. Still no answer. He called again, fighting panic. No one responded; the panic won. "You wouldn't do this to Marlon Brando," he chanted over and over.

Keitel was annoyed with Brando for other reasons. Coppola was talking about delaying the completion of the shoot until the middle of summer to accommodate Brando's schedule, whereas Keitel wanted to get away as fast as possible. In any case, he was set to play the lead in another film in early fall. Finally he asked to have a meeting with Coppola to iron out the schedule.

Instead of holding the meeting, Coppola found a different solution to Keitel's problem. On April 16, Good Friday, Coppola looked at a preliminary assembly of the first week's rushes and decided to fire Keitel. He told no one but Ellie. He shaved his beard to keep the press from recognizing him and quietly flew to Los Angeles for the Easter holidays. The crew went off to Hong Kong.

Three days later a *Variety* headline read COPPOLA LOSES HIS BEARD, 38 POUNDS, AND STAR KEITEL. Coppola had still not told Keitel; instead he sent a letter to Keitel's agent, Harry Ufland, telling him that his client was out of the picture. "I had to call Harvey in the Philippines and tell him," Ufland said. "They didn't have the decency to call him. His reaction was a mixture of shock and fury—here he is stuck in the jungle. He said it confirmed his feeling that Francis could not be taken at his word."

Coppola's conscience was only slightly troubled. "Firing my lead actor, that was bad," he later confessed. "It's a terrible thing to do; sure, it jeopardizes the production, but it can also ruin an actor's career, to be fired like that. But I just pulled the plunger—I did that a lot on this movie. Still do it," he added. "That's another form of saying you're going to really try to get it right."

Fortunately Keitel had never gotten around to signing a contract, and at this point he declined. As *Variety* noted with deadpan irony, "The situation raised doubts in Keitel's mind about the desirability of being under long-term contract with Coppola."

The same day that Keitel got the sack, Martin Sheen (who was shooting *The Cassandra Crossing* in Rome) got an urgent call from his agent. He was to fly immediately to Los Angeles and meet Coppola in the VIP lounge of the airport. Without a moment's hesitation, Sheen caught a plane. By the time he got through U.S. Customs, however, only fifteen minutes were left for the meeting with Coppola before the director's plane left for Manila. There wasn't much time for talk. Coppola handed Sheen a copy of the script. Sheen, eager to work with Coppola, said he'd love to do it. Coppola took off.

But Coppola wasn't putting all his cards on the table. Back in the Philippines, he made one last try for his real first choice, Jack Nicholson, but Nicholson was still not interested. Perhaps he remembered Coppola's nearly drowning him on *The Terror*. Only then did Coppola tell Sheen that he had the part. A few days later, with *The Cassandra Crossing* in the can, Sheen arrived in the Philippines to start his new role as Willard.

The shoot was already slipping behind schedule, not just because of the jungle, the effects explosion, or Keitel's firing, but because of the changeable weather and the difficulty of shooting so many special effects. This was the most technically complicated picture Coppola had ever attempted. It scared him.

For one thing, he had to change his normal mode of shooting. He preferred to use just one camera, shooting take after take to get an actor's best performance. Here, though, he often needed to use six cameras to cover his forty helicopters, and some shots simply couldn't be retaken at all once the special effects had wrecked the scenery.

Coppola took flying lessons to distract himself from his growing terror. It was even worse when he considered that the expensive juggernaut was rolling toward a chasm over which only he could build a bridge—by writing an ending he still couldn't conceive.

Coppola knew that the movie centered on a mysterious madman, Kurtz, who'd established absolute authority over a native tribe deep in the jungle, and on Willard, a Green Beret sent by the government to murder him. But what was each of these characters really like? What would happen when they met? The answers to these questions were still vague in his mind.

Ellie was more worried about him than the script. "Francis is really in a state of anxiety and fear that the script has some good supporting characters and some good scenes, but Willard and Kurtz are not resolved and here he is in the middle of this giant production," she wrote. "Now he is struggling with the themes of Willard's journey into self and Kurtz's truths that are in a way themes he has not resolved within himself." She couldn't help noticing that Coppola was identifying not with Willard, the seeker, but with Kurtz, the monster. "There is the exhilaration of power in the face of losing everything."

Coppola was aware, if only late at night, as he was slipping into dreams, that he was taking on some Kurtz-like qualities himself, but he still thought he was a "nice Kurtz." Not everyone agreed. "It was hell for a while at the beginning of the movie," crew member Gary Fettis said. "Artistically, Coppola didn't know what he was going for, and he was a pretty hard guy to be around. The crew didn't know he didn't know. But when you'd see him typing away in his houseboat in the mornings, you suspected as much. It created a sense of chaos."

Film critics Stephen Farber and Marc Green put it less diplomatically. "Megalomania had always been a part of his boisterous personality," they wrote. "But it had previously been held in check. Now, however, he began swaggering like a blowhard general."

On top of that, Marcos and his air force were proving a mixed blessing. They were charging Coppola a fortune in helicopter rentals, but at the same time the generals seemed to regard the movie as a free pilot training program. They sent a different set of novice airmen every day, so the previous day's flying rehearsals were useless; thousands of dollars' worth of shots were ruined. To make matters worse, Philippine Air Force generals got into the habit of showing up, amid a retinue of ladies in sundresses, to sit in directors' chairs, watch the show, and generally get in the way.

The elaborate special effects often went wrong, spoiling the shot, destroying the extras' costumes, and necessitating further delays. When lightweight Hueys were used for heavy lifting, they sometimes dropped and smashed expensive equipment and props.

Even when everything went right, the special effects were terribly costly. In one spectacular napalm stunt, twelve hundred gallons of expensive gasoline went up in less than two minutes. Later, for sequences at the Do Lung Bridge and the Kurtz compound, thousands of cans of colored smoke (at $25 each) and white phosphorous explosives, called "willy petes" (at $100 each) were set off. Special effects chief Joe Lombardi was sure that *Apocalypse* ended up with the highest special effects budget of any film ever made.

Robert Duvall had no suspicion of any of this when he arrived in mid-May, tan and fit, ready to shoot the surfing sequence. He learned fast. On the very first day a Filipino officer made off with the $15,000 he was supposed to use to pay his pilots; naturally the pilots refused to work, and for the rest of the shoot they came up with new demands for money daily. Then, when Lombardi set off the explosives, they killed all the fish on the reef, and Duvall and company had to get out of the water pronto before the sharks lurking outside the reef moved in for dinner.

Ultimately Duvall's six-minute helicopter battle, choreographed to Wagner's "Ride of the Valkyries," proved to be one of the most difficult sequences in the film; it took seven and a half weeks to shoot.

Martin Sheen was having a tough time, too. Within his first

weeks on the set he cut his face four stitches' worth in a special effects sequence, fainted from the heat, and had his new
camera ruined when the boat taking him to lunch tipped over.
The production put him up in a squalid room with leaky screens;
mosquitoes chewed on him all night, and whenever it rained,
his bed got dripping wet.

Sheen (a liberal activist who had nearly become a priest
in his youth) was deeply disturbed by the raw poverty all around
him, especially the sickly kids. Partway through the shoot he
decided to donate a portion of his salary to fund an aid program for Philippine children; his first month's contribution
bought toothbrushes for five thousand kids. (He has quietly
continued to make monthly donations ever since.)

Shortly after Sheen showed up, a tiger arrived by plane
from Los Angeles to play a cameo role. Unfortunately its crate
was too large to fit through the door of the DC-3 that would
take it from Manila to Baler, so its handler walked it into the
cabin like a pet dog. Once inside, the tiger decided it would
rather ride on its box than in it. Four Italian wives of the camera
crew got hysterical; the pilot climbed out the window. It might
have been funny if everything else had not been going to hell.

Coppola was increasingly miserable. Often he'd arrive on
the set with no idea of what the dialogue or the camera setups
for the day should be. One night at dinner Storaro mentioned
that he'd been worried about taking a job with an American
production, fearing he couldn't be sufficiently precise and definitive in the American fashion. Coppola confessed in turn,
"Vittorio . . . I am scared every day that you will think I am
an asshole, because I am not definitive enough, that I am trying
to find my way, find the direction for this film."

A small typhoon blew in on May 19 to divert everyone's
attention. Coppola watched with fascination as the floors of his
Dasmariñas house disappeared under six inches of water, the
lawn outside became a blanket of croaking frogs, and dirt from
the flowerbeds streamed into the swimming pool. The wind
was so loud the Coppolas couldn't hear themselves talk. Francis decided to turn on a record of *La Bohème* at full volume to
drown out the storm, but the typhoon cut the power just as he
was starting to feel better. Disgusted, he went to bed. Ellie
woke at four in the morning, in the grip of a surreal, operatic
nightmare, only to realize that the power was back on and
booming out *La Bohème* again.

Five days later the second unit moved to Iba, a coastal village twenty-five minutes by air from Manila, while Coppola and the rest of the crew went to Olongapo, a resort town on Subic Bay, some thirty-five miles southeast of Iba. The shooting schedule called for spending six weeks at both locations, filming a sequence that involved, among other things, a flashy stage show starring a bunch of Playboy Bunnies. But within days another typhoon blew in, and before anyone knew it, the tents full of costumes at Iba had blown away, and a dam had burst, turning the location into an island. When the wind speed continued to rise, three hundred extras returned to Manila by boat and bus.

In the middle of the growing storm Bill Graham, San Francisco's premier rock impresario, arrived in Olongapo to essay the role of the Playboy Bunnies' manager. He had taken charge of bringing the girls and organizing the complicated logistics of the scene, and Coppola rewarded him with a role. Graham was accustomed to staying in the best hotels, spending all his time on the telephone, running his business. But thanks to the storm, he found himself helpless, reduced to sitting in his lousy hotel room, dialing and dialing on the dead phone.

By May 25 the typhoon had turned into Hurricane Olga. Planes were grounded, all the phones were dead, and the road from Iba to the capital was washed out. Most of the Iba crew (including actors Martin Sheen, Frederic Forrest, and Albert Hall) were stranded for three days, reduced to communicating with Coppola via Morse code; Coppola was marooned with Linda Carpenter, Sam Bottoms, Larry Fishburne, Bill Graham, and a rock band at Olongapo, a few miles away. One group of crewmen reportedly found themselves stuck in a house with a Playboy Bunny. When they suggested certain ways of passing the downtime, the young woman locked herself in a bedroom, declaring, "I can do without sex for nine months."

As if it were hell-bent on teaching Coppola a lesson about hubris, Olga split into two parts, each part seemingly aimed right at one of his main sets, Baler and Iba. On the eighth day Olga wrecked the sets at Iba. Coppola made his way to the area and remained behind with the camera crew for a few days, hoping to shoot a storm scene with a medevac helicopter, directing it soaking wet and hip-deep in mud. He told everybody else to go home.

Olga was not impressed with Coppola's grace under pressure. She blew down the medevac set, pushed a boat up the riverbank and into a group of tents, threw another boat onto the helipad, washed away the supplies and props, soaked and ruined the generator, and buried the dolly track under four feet of mud.

Francis and Ellie Coppola, both unrecognizably skinny, checked into a hospital in Manila. They were diagnosed as suffering from malnutrition, dehydration, and salt deprivation. For the next three days they lay in their beds with intravenous feeding tubes stuck into their arms, while Marcos's bodyguard sat staring at them. The production was six weeks behind schedule; Coppola had already spent $7 million (/$13.5 million), $3 million over budget. Returning crew members told tales of a production run amok. Although UA kept a close watch on the situation, Chairman Arthur Krim was surprisingly unflappable. Krim had spent forty years in the movie business and had seen plenty of "productions gone amuck" turn into blockbusters. Most important, he had faith in Francis Ford Coppola.

On June 8 Coppola officially announced that he was closing down the production for six weeks. He'd decided to consolidate and rebuild his sets around Pagsanjan, a resort town merely two hours from Manila by road. Paved road. Coppola (and almost everyone else) went back to the States; only Dean Tavoularis and his crew stayed behind to rebuild the sets.

Ironically, Olga couldn't have arrived at a better time to deliver Coppola from his personal apocalypse. The storm gave him six weeks at home to concentrate on the script. He had realized reluctantly that there was no way of improvising his way to an ending. He needed a whole new approach and a block of time to concentrate on the screenplay.

Eleanor settled down in the Rutherford country house. Coppola, however, was so intensely preoccupied with the work that he preferred to sleep at the Broadway mansion to be close to his filmmaking facilities. At least that's what he told his wife. A year later she discovered other reasons for his absence.

A few weeks after his return Coppola selected two hours of rushes from the ninety hours he'd already shot, and screened them for a group of dinner guests. One of them commented that she found the acting "kind of tentative." Coppola went into a tailspin. He hated what he'd shot. His old feelings of being a fraud returned to haunt him; he began to wonder if he were a good filmmaker or merely a good fund raiser. Shortly thereafter he told John Milius, "I've got to do this picture. I consider it the most important picture I will ever make. If I die making it, you'll take over; if you die, George Lucas will take over."

Plagued by nightmares, he awoke at six every morning to work on the script, but he couldn't concentrate. He had to take time out to haggle for more money to make up his cost over-runs. On July 1 he flew to Los Angeles to negotiate a loan with United Artists. UA agreed to cover the overruns, but if *Apocalypse* earned less than a rock-bottom minimum of $40 million in rentals, Coppola would have to pay it back personally.

On top of everything else, the press vultures, who had been reporting every production mishap in juicy detail, now wanted the inside scoop on his troubles. He'd sworn off interviews, but he made a few exceptions.

"I got problems," Coppola told Susan Braudy, who was profiling him for *Atlantic Monthly.* "I'm too good at adapting other people's scripts. Better than writing my own. I don't want to be known as an adapter of other people's work. . . . I was the first film-school graduate to make movies. I am a very successful amateur. I know more about every aspect of filmmaking, from photography to music—including writing and acting—than any other filmmaker in the world, and that's not a boast. . . . But I'm so dead I want to hire a director to go shoot the movie."

He didn't want to go back to the jungle, he insisted. He wanted instead to do *Tucker,* a film about a hero he understood.

Coppola was not merely playing the suffering artist for the benefit of the press. He *was* suffering. Soon he'd be back in the Philippines, and his script was still a mess. Even Fred Roos, reading the latest version, had trouble following the story. "That's the whole idea," Coppola explained enthusiastically. "The jungle will look psychedelic, fluorescent blues, yellows, and greens. I mean the war is essentially a Los Angeles export, like acid rock." But what about the characters? asked Roos. What did they stand for? "Kurtz has gone savage, but there's this greatness in him," Coppola expounded. "The horror that Kurtz talks about is never resolved. As Willard goes deeper into the jungle, he realizes that the civilization that sent him is more savage in ways than the jungle. I mean, we created that war."

Coppola read a biography of Genghis Khan for inspiration, and then he showed the latest rewrite to his old film school classmate and *Rain People* crewman Dennis Jakob. Jakob, who had developed a reputation as something of a mad genius, helped Coppola reshape the film, tracing the journey up the river in terms that were more coherent both as a story and as a parable of some kind of universal human journey.

Late in July, vacation over, Francis, Ellie, and Sofia Coppola arrived back at Pagsanjan, to settle down in a two-story concrete block house with indoor plumbing (albeit no hot water), ceiling fans, fluorescent lights, air conditioning, and a steady supply of electricity to power it all. (Gio and Roman remained in the United States this time.)

Coppola still had actor problems. Marlon Brando had agreed to play Kurtz, but a few details remained to resolve, such as how much he wanted to be paid. Coppola spent a lot of telephone time in delicate negotiations. Brando finally agreed to a 50 percent cut from his usual fee; for his friend, Francis, he'd do five weeks' work for a lousy $1 million. However, he also insisted on a whopping 11.3 percent of *Apocalypse*'s adjusted gross profits; once the adjusted gross surpassed $8.8 million (to cover his advance), he'd make around 34 cents for each and every $6 ticket sold.

Now Martin Sheen was discontented with his deal. If he was going to spend God knows how many more months in the tropics, he wanted lots of money, too. Coppola and Sheen argued, battled, and reconciled; finally Sheen gave up his demands and reluctantly agreed to settle for the original deal. But he was still worried. He told a friend, "I don't know if I am going to live through this. Those fuckers are crazy, all those helicopters are really blowing things up."

Coppola was equally worried about Sheen. In fact, he was increasingly unhappy with Sheen's performance. Sheen was coming across in the dailies as too bland, and Coppola decided to try to break through the actor's defenses. "I always look for other levels, hidden levels, in the actor's personality and in the personality of the character he plays," he said. "I conceived this all-night drunk; we'd see another side of the guy."

Coppola took a cruel chance. One hot August night he

locked Sheen up, got him drunk, and kept him drunk, prodding him to get deeper and deeper into the role. With Coppola pushing him lower and lower into his worst self, Sheen got so deeply into the part of Willard, in the hotel-room sequence, that he smashed his hand through a mirror. He bled badly, and once the scene was over, he got *really* drunk.

Coppola seemed to think it was all part of the actor's job. "So Marty got drunk" was all he said. "And I found out that sometimes, when he gets drunk, a lot comes out."

An indignant crew member said, "Francis would tell Martin, 'You're evil. I want all the evil, the violence, the hatred in you to come out.' You tell that to a guilt-ridden Irish Catholic and he hasn't a chance. Martin is so pliable. Francis did a dangerous and terrible thing. He assumed the role of a psychiatrist and did a kind of brainwashing on a man who was much too sensitive. He put Martin in a place and didn't bring him back."

Next came the night battle at the Do Lung Bridge. It was filmed at a wonderful set located where a local bridge had stood until the Japanese blew it up during World War II. Hampered by rain, mud, the ever-changing height of the river, eye-watering special effects chemicals, the difficulties of shooting all night every night, the slowness of the multiple camera setups, and the extra rehearsals needed while Coppola fiddled with the script, the sequence took thirteen days and nights to shoot. The film went two more days over schedule, at $50,000 a day.

Tavoularis had reconstructed the temple set, using local labor to place three-hundred-pound stone blocks, mainly by hand. He had never got a chance to go home after the typhoon, and by now he was deeply depressed. He expressed his feelings by spreading blood and skulls and corpses all around, piling up garbage, and collecting old bones from a restaurant in Manila. "It became such a low level in my life," he said, "that somehow putting blood on staircases and rolling heads down steps seemed natural to me."

Even seven thousand miles away United Artists knew that something was going very wrong and dispatched a wise old movie biz pro named Leland Katz to help Coppola reorganize the production. Katz, an ace financial watchdog, stayed about a week. His activities lay mainly in replacing and shifting personnel and duties, altering the shooting schedule, expediting construction, and trimming the dimensions of some of the sets—

in short, behaving like a professional producer. Katz was so good that Coppola's worries about studio interference evaporated.

Meanwhile, Coppola dispatched production assistant Eva Gardos, a former Harlem schoolteacher, to a northern province to recruit a tribe of primitive people, the Ifugaos, to live on the set and be in the film. Reaching them took Gardos fifteen hours of bone-breaking Jeep riding into the remote mountains; talking them into appearing in the film was even harder. She refused to give up, determined to earn their trust no matter how long it took. When no word came from her, Coppola began negotiating to hire extras from the slums of Manila to play the Montagnards. There's no indication of whether he ever worried about Gardos or considered a rescue mission, even though the Ifugaos had given up cannibalism (they said) a mere thirty years earlier.

Then *Newsweek* reporter Maureen Orth appeared on the set, looking for a story to feed the seemingly unquenchable curiosity back home. "The movie company had come to be regarded in the local countryside as a cross between an invading army and Santa Claus," she wrote. Although the local wage was less than $10 a week, for nine months the company had been spending $100,000 a week. Orth quoted the local high school principal, Ricardo Fabella. "Our people have lost their sense of values," he said. "Everything I've taught them is forgotten."

Coppola spent several days shooting scenes at an exquisitely decorated French plantation, where the former colonialists waited out the inevitable as elegantly as possible. (These sequences never appeared in the final cut of the movie.) Coppola was furious to discover that through a communications snafu the set had been filled with genuine antiques and crystal, at unthinkable (and unnecessary) cost. Some of the crew started to complain again about Coppola's temperament.

Storaro and his Italian crew were taxing Coppola severely. They always preferred to do things very, very slowly, whereas Coppola liked to shoot rapidly and intuitively, letting scenes run long and then hacking them down to size in the editing room. (It was the same problem that he'd had with the crew on *You're a Big Boy Now*.) Storaro was a perfectionist about lighting, detail, the composition of every frame—an artist, not a technician. His footage always looked gorgeous, but it took six times as long to get each shot. The American actors, unused to his European methods, often lost their energy in the later takes.

The schedule went to hell. One actress arrived to discover that her scenes wouldn't be shot for at least six weeks. Instead of sending her home, coproducer Gray Frederickson tried to convince her she could enjoy the time shopping and sightseeing. "By that time," the wife of one of the editors recalled, "production was hopelessly behind schedule, and a pall hung over the entire cast and crew. 'Will notify' was the only instruction on the daily call sheet so often that it became a joke." Things got so bad that Coppola declared a press blackout on the set.

Coppola wasn't the only one feeling the pressure. There were long nights of boozing and brawling in the Pit, the recessed restaurant and bar area of the local Rapids Hotel, where the staff was always happy to stay up and pour San Miguels. Larry Fishburne remembered members of the company throwing furniture around, breaking bottles, trading punches, screaming incoherently, and jumping off the roof into the pool. One night an extra got so drunk he beat up the elderly hotel manager in front of guests, journalists, and a pair of high-ranking cops.

The diabolical nature of Coppola's dilemma finally dawned on him. If the film went too far over budget, but did only moderate business, he might lose everything he owned. At times Ellie found herself wishing that *Apocalypse* would bankrupt her husband, so that they could return to a simpler life style and to a relationship of greater equality. Something funny was happening to their relationship, but she couldn't say just what.

In the midst of this endless agony Marlon Brando arrived. He still hadn't read the copy of *Heart of Darkness* that Coppola had given him months earlier, so Coppola handed him another copy and a firm reading assignment. The two of them spent their whole first day together improvising and talking. Coppola must have been persuasive, because for the first time Brando agreed to abandon his naturalistic style and try for a larger-than-life mythic character.

That was the good news. The bad news was that Brando was grossly obese. Coppola decided he could use this to make Kurtz more mythic, by shooting Kurtz's scenes as though the character were six feet five inches tall. For long shots, he would use a giant double. To get a feel for gianthood, Method Marlon put five-inch heel lifts on his shoes and promptly twisted his ankle.

Coppola and Brando fell into a desperate creative dance, trying to come up with an image, a visual metaphor that would provide the key to Kurtz's identity, a key that should have been in the script but wasn't. Coppola thought that Kurtz should be a half-naked Gauguin figure, gone native with mangoes and babies. Brando hated the idea. He saw Kurtz as a Daniel Berrigan type, wearing black Vietcong pajamas and exuding guilt over the war. Coppola, nauseated by the thought, answered, "Hey, Marlon, I may not know everything about this movie, but one thing I know it's not about is *our guilt!*" Finally Brando got an idea: He'd shave his head. It seems like a dubious revelation, but both men were deeply impressed with it.

Coppola's mood had become unbearably intense. Even Brando's double started to feel exhausted by mere proximity to him. "Francis is a brain drainer," he said. "You sit with him for ten minutes and he absorbs everything in your body."

The elusive ending was still not in place. Coppola had gotten into the habit of waking up at 4:00 A.M., hoping to surprise the ending, but it wasn't working. At one point he told his wife that he realized there was no simple solution to the script, just as there was no simple right answer to why we had been in Vietnam.

In September Dennis Hopper showed up to play a part that Coppola hadn't written yet. Hopper wore the same clothes for the whole two months he was on the set, until crew members refused to come within fifteen feet of him and the cameramen prayed for long shots. Coppola had had some vague notion of a character for Hopper, but when he saw him, he changed his mind and decided to cast him as a 1960s version of the Russian in Conrad's story, a friendly, garrulous disciple of Kurtz. This decision was actually quite radical. By introducing a brand-new character, Coppola would have to junk everything he'd roughed in for the entire remainder of his script—the whole Kurtz compound sequence, such as it was. "That day I put on the cameras and we shot the scene where he greets them on the boat," Coppola later recalled, "and from that moment on we were in the twilight zone."

It was just as well that Coppola had somebody new to work with, because Brando was so busy trying to Methodize his character that some days he would hardly work at all. He usually came to the set at 10:00 A.M., several hours late, and left at 1:00 P.M. The rest of the day he and Coppola holed up in Brando's trailer and talked about Kurtz. Whole days disappeared, and hundreds of thousands of dollars went with them.

Then Eva Gardos finally returned from the north, bringing 250 loinclothed Ifugao mountaineers with her. She had promised the recently reformed headhunters a weekly supply of betel nuts and live animals for sacrifices. Brando threw a "welcome to Pagsanjan" party attended by four hundred cast members, crew members, and Ifugaos. He regaled his guests with a catered buffet, nightclub acts from Manila (singers, acrobats, magicians), and fireworks put on by the special effects men.

Coppola was not entertained. In fact, he probably doubted that anything would ever entertain him again. One night he found himself lying on the roof while the rain dripped on him, murmuring, "Let me out of here, let me just quit and go home. I can't do it. I can't see it. I can't see it, I can't do anything. This is like an opening night; the curtain goes up and there is no show."

In the face of the unrelenting pressure, the fragile integration of Coppola's multifaceted creative personality that had given birth to three remarkable films (two *Godfathers* and *The Conversation*) began to come apart. The willingness to make reasonable compromises, the urge for commercial success that he took from Carmine, had deserted him. The flashy salesmanship he based on Preston Tucker was useless; to whom could he sell himself in the jungle? The gift of storytelling that he inherited from Francis the polio kid couldn't help when he didn't know what story to tell. All that was left was artistic Augie, and the desperate hope that if he imitated Augie's intellectual and artistic gifts, everyone would love him.

In desperation, he summoned Dennis Jakob from San Francisco. On September 22 Jakob arrived with his valises overflowing with fruit and vegetables from Napa and fat books from his collection. Jakob was still a fanatic Nietzschean, who believed in the deep power of mythology, especially myths about supermen. He ordered Coppola to read the story in *The Golden Bough* about the corn king who must be sacrificed at the end of the year so that the crops will grow; whoever kills him becomes the new king. Coppola decided that this was the myth that would lend *Apocalypse* the deep resonance he'd been seeking. Kurtz's death wouldn't be an assassination, but a holy sacrifice to the gods of the jungle. He had found his ending at last.

Still, things continued to go horribly. Take, for instance, a scene in which people were playing with severed heads. The heads were actually played by live people sitting in boxes buried in the muddy ground, who emerged only for lunch. The mud was slippery, the cameras could barely move, and gallons of fake blood were shed in vain on takes that went awry, at a cost of $35 a gallon. It was a nightmare, and it took thirty-eight takes.

Coppola was as touchy as a man with second-degree sunburn. One night in October, when some crew members wandered into a screening room while he was looking at rushes, he burst into a screaming rage and threw everybody out. It wasn't just that he couldn't take criticism; it was that anything less than extravagant praise seemed to plunge him into self-doubt and depression. He desperately needed honest feedback on the rushes; but no one dared give it to him, and apparently, he couldn't bear it when anyone did.

Instead of trying to analyze his problems, he gazed rapturously at the beautifully composed still photos Storaro had taken during the shoot, exclaiming, "God! I'd go to see that movie, wouldn't you?"

Decreeing that the shoot would definitely end on Christmas Eve, Coppola left the Philippines for the Halloween weekend. He told his wife he was going away to try to straighten himself out, to learn to accept life as it is, not as it ought to be. Everyone on the set, including Eleanor, was glad to see him go. He'd been angry with everyone and everything for weeks.

Where Coppola went, and what he did, remain a mystery. But not with whom he did it. He'd begun a serious love affair with a talented young screenwriter who was working as an executive assistant on the production.

When Coppola returned to Pagsanjan, he was in dangerously high spirits. He told his wife that he'd had a major insight into his problem. He wanted, he said, to be really talented, but inasmuch as he had always doubted his talent, approval made him miserable because it seemed like a lie. Now, at last, he realized that he *was* talented, but not in the ways he expected. He had turned every disaster into an asset, coming up with solutions that were better than his original concepts, like deciding to turn Kurtz into a giant when Brando arrived hopelessly overweight. He decided that a good director wasn't necessarily someone who came to the set fully prepared and decisive about everything but, rather, "one who could take the situations that happen and utilize them to his advantage."

Coppola told himself he'd entered a whole new mode of being. "Ellie, remember that fat guy who wore those kind of funny-looking corduroy suits and walked around North Beach like a Bohemian?" he asked his wife. "I think he died."

Coppola felt he had experienced a revelation. Years later he told *Rolling Stone*'s Jonathan Cott that he'd seen through a false vision of himself he'd had since childhood. He'd meant to be a writer, not a director, but he didn't think he had enough talent, compared with his father's musical talent and his brother's literary talent. But one day, "right smack dab in the middle of the shooting of *Apocalypse Now*, . . . I knew I had talent."

Coppola seemed to be on a manic emotional upswing, but his wife was too grateful for his good spirits to question the judgment behind them. "On the first of September there was no ending for this film and now there is," she wrote, awestruck. "Where did it come from? Francis didn't write it, it sort of happened, day by day, and it is completely different and better than any of the endings he wrote on for over a year."

When Dennis Hopper's role was completed, he and Coppola said their farewells at a drunken party, and Coppola vowed, "Dennis, pick any place in the world, you'll be the star of a movie I'll make. The deal is, I promise I won't think about what the movie is going to be before we start. We'll just make it, we'll make it real fast, in three weeks, and it will be terrific." As soon as Hopper left, Coppola started complaining about him, but eventually he kept part of his promise and cast Hopper in a major supporting role in *Rumble Fish*.

Time passed, the weather held, filming moved forward, and suddenly it was nearly Thanksgiving. Somebody decided it would be great if the Ifugaos would re-create their ritual sacrifice of a water buffalo. The natives spent two days talking to the buffalo, telling it not to fear death. Then they sacrificed pigs and chickens. Finally they killed the water buffalo by four quick blows to the neck. Coppola watched them and suddenly realized that this ritual would be a perfect parallel for the death of Kurtz inside the temple: Willard would kill Kurtz the same way, clubbing him down with his rifle butt.

He may have forgotten where this inspiring idea had come from, but crew members like Steve Burum, who'd known him at UCLA, hadn't. Coppola and Jakob had just come up with the final detail from *The Host*, Jack Hill's student film (which Burum had shot), in which the mythic corn king was clubbed to death with wood from a sacred tree, while a mysterious native woman watched in stoic silence. (Later, when Hill saw *Apocalypse*, he wrote to Coppola about it, but Coppola never replied.)

The shoot was nearly over now. It was time to break for Christmas. The cast and crew scattered to their homes or to Hong Kong. Eleanor and Sofia returned to Rutherford, where Coppola joined them a few days later.

Over the holidays Coppola made a rough assembly of the footage. It was five hours long, but it was great; he could actually see the finished film emerging. He was thrilled.

Coppola stayed in the Bay Area for more than a month. Eleanor noted his intensely high spirits, his overflowing energy. He wanted to re-redecorate the house and the office; he wanted to cook; he wanted to dance, to play music, to hang out with the kids, to make everything gorgeous. He looked at his footage over and over. It was brilliant. He was brilliant.

Then he returned to the Philippines, with Martin Sheen, to wrap up the shoot. As soon as he left, and Eleanor could see his "high" from a distance, it scared the hell out of her.

He began sending a barrage of telexes. He was directing better than he ever had in his life. He was extending the schedule to add new scenes. He demanded luxury items to make his stay more comfortable. It all felt terribly wrong to his wife. The odor of unreason wafted seven thousand miles over the telex. "I feel as though a certain discrimination is missing, that fine discrimination that draws the line between what is visionary and what is madness," she wrote. "I am terrified."

Then Martin Sheen collapsed. At first it was announced that he had become exhausted from jogging six miles a day in the hundred-degree heat. The true story was much, much worse. Sheen had suffered a serious heart attack. Alone in his room in Pagsanjan when it began, he managed to crawl to the side of the road, where he took a public bus. Then, from the bus window, he spotted a wardrobe van and managed to wave it down. It took him to the production office. Sheen remembers that Dean Tavoularis stuck his head in the van, looked at him, and started to cry. Sheen took last rites from a priest who didn't speak English. He lay in the production office for hours while they tried to decide if a flight to Manila would kill him.

Even as he recovered, he suffered a nervous breakdown. "I completely fell apart," said Sheen. "My spirit was exposed. I cried and cried." His wife called a therapist in New York, and he underwent psychotherapy over the long-distance lines, until he felt he could face the cameras again. He didn't blame Coppola. "No one put a gun to my head and forced me to be there," he reflected. "I was there because I had a big ego and wanted to be in a Coppola film." Nonetheless, his immersion for so many months in a character he had been convinced was evil had scarred him more deeply than he realized. Coppola's merciless encounter group direction hadn't helped. Even after the shoot was over, Sheen couldn't shake the role. He fell back into a deep depression, broke up temporarily with his wife, and continued bouts of heavy drinking and smoking for several years.

The weird telexes from Francis to Eleanor continued to arrive, reporting new triumphs for Coppola's self-proclaimed genius. Finally Eleanor couldn't bear the thought of any more. Late in February she sent Coppola a telex saying that because she loved him, she would tell him what no one else was willing to say; "that he was setting up his own Vietnam with his supply lines of wine and steaks and air conditioners." She told him over the humming telex wires that he really was turning into Kurtz. "I called him an asshole," she noted in her diary. Worse yet, she sent copies to various persons at Zoetrope via an electronic telex distribution list.

Coppola was furious at her disloyalty. Bad enough she was calling him an asshole, but she had sent copies to his colleagues, "over a wire service that anyone could read." By now he was sure the whole world knew what she thought about him. If she had been an employee, he'd have probably fired her on the spot.

Instead, Coppola himself collapsed, both physically and emotionally, and Ellie took pity on him. She flew back to the Philippines to rejoin her husband, and after spending an afternoon with him at Hidden Valley, a lovely resort tucked inside a dead volcano, she decided that he was suffering from a long-term nervous breakdown, which had probably started at least a year earlier.

Coppola couldn't forgive her for the telex. As he recovered, they argued over whether the marriage should recess for a temporary separation or go directly into the divorce court. The agonizing all-day discussions were interrupted by talks with the vice-president of United Artists, the sound editor from London, the composer from Tokyo, and the editor from San Francisco.

Coppola's manic high had long passed, to be replaced by depressive despair. He was surrounded by yes-men. Nobody would tell him the truth. People either kissed his ass or resisted him to prove that his wealth, talent, and success didn't impress them. Nobody would take him as he was. Everyone wanted his film to fail. If *Apocalypse* succeeded, his friends and family would just be more resentful.

He was actually relieved when UA's financial watchdog, Leland Katz, reappeared. Katz remained until the end of the shoot, relieving Coppola of as many production responsibilities as he could. None of Coppola's loyal line producers was comfortable saying no to the boss; Katz had no problem. He was cool, competent, and far too objective to be swayed by anything except efficiency and the real needs of art. It was just what Coppola needed; he was so pleased with Katz's performance he later tried to lure him to Zoetrope.

Martin Sheen recovered quickly and left the hospital, but he was still too weak to work. While awaiting his return, Coppola kept looking at the videocassettes of *Apocalypse,* over and over, and filling in new footage; he even flew Sheen's brother to the Philippines to double for him in several long shots.

Nonetheless, everything continued to go as badly as possible. Typically, Marcos was visiting near Pagsanjan just when Coppola wanted to shoot Monkey Island blowing up. The sequence had to be postponed a full day (another day, another $50,000) in case Marcos might think the explosions represented a rebel attack.

The next day was the 200th day of shooting. This time, when Coppola attempted to blow up Monkey Island, the special effects got out of control and a fake stone wall caught fire and went up in flames, ruining the sequence. But what the hell? That evening an anniversary dinner was held to celebrate the milestone. A half-naked girl jumped out of a big silver box, and a fireworks display spelled out "Apocalypse Now 200th, Good Luck, Francis."

Early in April the special effects crew set off the last, and biggest, explosion of the film. The general consensus was that there had never been anything like it in the world before, except, perhaps, for Hiroshima. Even Tavoularis was impressed. "God," he said enthusiastically, "you couldn't buy a ticket to a show like that anywhere in the world."

Gio and Roman arrived at the Hidden Valley volcano for Easter vacation, only to find their parents' marriage erupting in front of them and everyone else. Even in front of Gina Lollobrigida (who had dropped in to ask Coppola's help in convincing Imelda Marcos to back a film). Finally the Coppolas gave up. Enough! They would get a divorce. But instead of divorcing, they and the children leaped into the warm mineral pool behind the resort and swam nude, all together, for the first time in their lives. Maybe they'd all gone a little crazy with the heat; they would give the marriage another try. Coppola had still not told Ellie about his affair, and she suspected nothing.

Local gossip was that the production might have to close down because of Martin Sheen's condition. Coppola was filling in as best he could, using doubles until Sheen was well enough to continue filming, but he was deeply relieved when the actor returned to work late in April.

Facing the fact that Sheen had nearly died for him, Coppola agreed that the shoot couldn't go on forever. He promised his actor that finished or not, the production would wrap on May 15. Besides, the film's cost was now hovering around $27 million (/$52 million), a whopping $15 million over the original budget.

Although Sheen was deliriously happy to be working again, reenergized by the sheer joy of having survived, Coppola was feeling pressed for time; he actually decided to drop several scenes before he shot them. Later Sheen told a reporter, "I am very fond of him personally, but I don't think he realizes how tough he is to work for."

Just how deeply Coppola had changed, and just how paranoid he'd become, can be seen from a memo he sent, on April 30, to all his employees at Zoetrope and the Coppola Company.

"I realize," he wrote, "that in the last three or four months I have been operating differently than I had in the past and that it must be difficult for the people who have worked with me and are working with me now, during this transition, to understand exactly what I expect of them. Generally speaking, it is my desire to confine my work pretty much to my own personal creative work."

Coppola went on to say that he was consolidating his various companies into one company, American Zoetrope, which would be, purely and simply, *"me and my work."* Zoetrope's equipment and facilities existed not as a service business but for Coppola's own convenience. "Therefore, you are not employees of a company—instead, the staff of an artist." Coppola went on to insist on giving his personal OK to any expenditures over $500 and to warn employees against making personal calls on his phones, losing or damaging equipment, or even sending him nonurgent messages by telex ($6) rather than by pouch (50 cents).

"I know that the amounts of money I deal in seem unreal to most people—they do to me as well," he continued, "but please always remember that I work in these amounts because *I am willing to risk everything for my work* . . . I am cavalier with money, because I have to be, in order not to be terrified every time I make an artistic decision. Don't confuse that technique with the idea that I am infinitely wealthy. Many of you know that is not true. Remember, the major studios and distributors have only one thing that a filmmaker needs: capital. My flamboyant disregard for the rules of capital and business is one of my major strengths when dealing with them. It evens the score, so to speak."

He reminded his staff that he was the boss, not his wife. "Please remember, you are working for me," he added. "Use discretion in the method of communication you use for transmitting information through the office. . . ." (He may have been thinking of Ellie's "disloyal" telex or, perhaps, of his liaison with another woman.)

He wrote to staff members who'd grown long-windedly defensive in their anxiety to please him:

Please trust me. Once I know who the people are who are truly supporting me, not as disconnected employees, but a true staff working in what is probably the most exciting art form of our time, I will not let them go, nor will I leave them unrewarded.

Another matter which is of great importance to me

is that the time has come to end the inner-company politics and gossip. . . . Don't allow yourself to be suckered into or tempted into the notion of being "close" to me, or "close" to someone who has political power in the company. No one has any political power in the company; I will listen to anyone and everyone, and caution everyone that the smart road is just to do your work well. I am tired of inner-company feuds . . . knowing that somehow I am the cause and center of it. . . . As for the "gossip"—that too has gotten out of proportion in the past. It is no one's business to discuss my personal life or speculate on what I am or am not doing; my alleged mistresses, my relationships with other employees; who is being fired; who is being hired—I would like to sever the so-called "grapevine."

In the past, the nature of the company has been referred to as a "family," or as a club or hangout. In the future, I hope it will be none of these. My family consists of my wife and three children. The people working for me and with me are my Staff and Associates. . . . My home, my personal possessions . . . is [*sic*] my property just as your property is yours. Please do not assume the use of these things. I know in the past that I have encouraged this; but simply, I have changed and I no longer see this as a viable way of working.

. . . I expect people to dress and behave as they would for any other company. It is very important for me to dispel the seven-year ambience of a hippy hangout around the old American Zoetrope that attracted a certain group of young people anxious to work in the film business. I do not wish to attract these people.

He warned, "Do not expect to have dinner or lunch at my home unless you are invited." And he added that lack of information was the real source of his financial problems: "The reason my penthouse office is so expensive is because I never really knew or was told what it would cost." He also warned that the open-door policy was over. When he was working in the penthouse, staff members should contact him by phone or

Inane Comedies with Boobs: (from left) Jack Hill, Frank Zuniga (back to camera), and the twenty-two-year-old Francis Coppola during the making of Coppola's second nudie, The Wide Open Spaces. *"It was the only scene I could find that actually gave you a chance to fool around with a camera and cut a film," said Coppola. He later described the nudies as "inane comedies in which you saw a couple of boobs once in a while." 1961. Jack Hill*

Big Boy on the Riviera: Coppola and stars Tony Bill and Elizabeth Hartman leave the festival palace at Cannes; they accompanied Coppola's flashy "youth film," You're a Big Boy Now, *to the film market at the Cannes Film Festival, where they tried to sell it to Europe after it flopped in New York. Nearly thirty years later, Coppola remains close friends with Bill (who became a producer-director and highly successful restaurateur); Hartman suffered from increasingly severe emotional difficulties that culminated in her recent suicide. 1961. AP/Wide World Photos*

Down to One Miniskirted Secretary: Coppola shoots pool at American Zoetrope in San Francisco with longtime colleague editor Richard Marks. By 1974, as Gerald Nachman wrote, "Zoetrope was down to one miniskirted secretary, and instant coffee instead of espresso." Coppola took it hard. "Zoetrope earned a lot of resentment," he said, "and so did I. The look of the company created the illusion of enormous wealth. It was all thought of as my personal toy." 1974. Wayne Miller—Magnum

Thoughts of Chairman Coppola: At his Queen Anne–style mansion in San Francisco's pricey Pacific Heights, under Andy Warhol's portrait of Mao Tse-tung, Coppola marshals his lieutenants for their final assault on the edit of Godfather II. The bearded person at left, tapping his nose with a pencil, is sound technician Mark Berger, later an Oscar winner for the sound of Amadeus. 1974. Wayne Miller—Magnum

Prince of the City: The owner and the chef of the Columbus Cafe, located a few blocks from Coppola's headquarters in San Francisco's North Beach, welcome one of the city's most famous celebrities to their restaurant; Coppola's lunch companions are (from left) Carmine Coppola (back to camera), an obscured woman (probably Eleanor), and art director Dean Tavoularis. Coppola had envisioned San Francisco as a place where he could live out La Bohème, *but his personification of a starving artist left something to be desired; before long, he had bought up $10 million of San Francisco real estate, a magazine, a radio station, an office building, a movie studio, and a theater. 1974. Wayne Miller—Magnum*

The Equipment Is the Aesthetic: Coppola working at a state-of-the-art editing table at Zoetrope. He was convinced that the equipment was the aesthetic. "You go to a Hollywood editor," he declared, "and he'll say, 'Aw, you can't cut film on that.' It's true, you can't cut on [an editing table] the way you cut on a Movieola, but if you adapt yourself you can do it faster. It's like taking a guy who flies a biplane and showing him the controls of a 707." 1974. Wayne Miller—Magnum

Clanking, Shining Oscars: With *Godfather II* sweeping the 1974 Academy Awards, Carmine Coppola accepts an Oscar for Best Score, thanks his son for hiring him, and thanks himself for siring his son. The recipient of Carmine's paternal gratitude brandishes his own trio of statuettes. "He is the most decorated member of our unit," noted filmmaker John Milius. "When Francis walks into a room, you hear and see nothing but clanking, shining Oscars." 1975. Copyright © by Academy of Motion Picture Arts and Sciences.

Airborne Klutzes: Coppola hands a copy of the Apocalypse script to Philippine President Ferdinand E. Marcos. In exchange for an unnamed (but presumably exorbitant) sum, Marcos agreed to rent Coppola the Philippine Air Force. Unfortunately, instead of pilots who could reproduce the tight choreography of the Vietnam aerial aces, Marcos sent Coppola airborne klutzes who made up their own flying minuets. Still, said Dick White, who supervised the air sequences, "There were three or four countries in the world we could have taken easily." 1976. AP/Wide World Photos

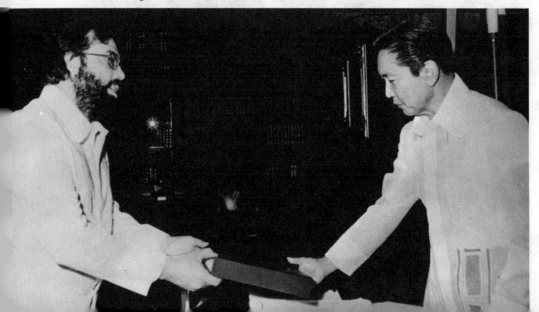

Nowhere to Hide: Prone to worry about the troubled production of The Black Stallion, *Coppola was snoozing under a picnic table when a pesky Canadian reporter awakened him to request an interview. Coppola remained grounded for their chat. As executive producer of Carroll Ballard's first feature, Coppola had taken time out from editing* Apocalypse Now *to fly to the Ontario location where the film was shooting. 1977. AP/Wide World Photos*

Momentary Insanity: Coppola (flanked by Zoetrope stalwart Tom Sternberg and wife Eleanor) reaches for his invitation to the Cannes Film Festival premiere of his still-unfinished Apocalypse Now. *A United Artists executive derided Coppola's decision to screen the work-in-progress, in competition yet, as "momentary insanity born of arrogance." In the end, the Vietnam epic tied for the highest prize. 1979. AP/Wide World Photos*

Giving Her Horns: At Cannes, Francis (still quite thin after his Apocalyptic ordeal) playfully gives Eleanor the "Devil Horns" as they wait for a press conference scheduled to follow the screening of Apocalypse Now. *Eleanor's book on the making of the movie, with painful details of her husband's infidelities, was about to come out. Somehow, the marriage survived both the affair and the book. 1979. AP/Wide World Photos.*

Some Jerk Who Flies Around in the Sky: After the successful Cannes screening of Apocalypse Now *and the epic-scaled press conference that followed, Coppola carries eight-year-old daughter Sofia to the safe haven of a back-street Italian restaurant, with son Roman (age thirteen) and wife Eleanor (front left), son Gio (back left, age fifteen), and (back right) Zoetroper Tom Sternberg. Coppola had defended his saga eloquently while railing at 1,100 journalists about the evils of the press. "Why is it such a crime for me to spend a lot of money about a film which deals with morality," he asked, "when you can spend it on a film about a big gorilla or about a little fairy tale or about some jerk who flies around in the sky?" 1979. AP/Wide World Photos*

Why Don't We Cheer?: Coppola faces hostile reporters after the Radio City Music Hall screening of One from the Heart. *"How do you feel, now that everyone dislikes the picture?" was the reporters' first query. "A lot of people in there looked as though they did like the movie," answered Coppola. And then he added, "I really don't understand . . . why you guys don't seem to like [my taking risks]. Why don't we all cheer the moviemakers on?" 1982. AP/Wide World Photos*

Blowing His Own Horn: With One from the Heart *dying at the box office, Coppola holds forth at his Hollywood home with his faithful tuba standing behind him. "The film will enjoy tremendous financial success," he insisted. ". . . If I'm wrong, it would be the first time in thirteen years." He was wrong. 1982. Copyright © by Raymond Depardon—Magnum*

Take Me Back to Tulsa: Coppola, still fond of corduroy suits, smiles happily during the filming of The Outsiders *in Tulsa. "Rather than go through six months of being whipped for having committed the sin of making a film that I wanted to make," he said, "[after* One from the Heart*] I escaped with a lot of young people to Tulsa and didn't have to deal with the [Hollywood] sophisticates. I like being with kids rather than adults, so it turned into a way for me to soothe my heartache over the terrible rejection." 1982. AP/Wide World Photos*

Turn Them into Trash Cans: (from left) Star Michael Jackson, director Francis Coppola, and producer George Lucas during the filming of Captain Eo. *The seventeen-minute 3-D film turned out to be, minute for minute, the most expensive movie ever made, but for once the astronomical budget wasn't Coppola's fault. The film's best line is delivered by the Supreme Ruler (played by Anjelica Huston): When she sees Eo and his fuzzy crew members, she orders, "Turn them into—trash cans!" 1986. AP/Wide World Photos*

Too Many Cooks: In the kitchen of Paris's world-famous Taillevent restaurant, Coppola and master chef Claude Deligne debate the fine points of sauce making, while restaurant owner Jean-Claude Vrinat stands by with a bottle of wine from Coppola's vineyard. The Niebaum-Coppola Napa Valley "Rubicon" had just been selected as the first California bottling deemed fit for Taillevent's aristocratic wine list. 1988. AP/Wide World Photos

in person by going through his secretary, Nancy Ely.

He begged his staff to be of "great help to me . . . regarding the public and the press. I would very much like to lead a more private life than I have in the past. I really am no longer interested in publicity, magazine covers, stories, documentaries, books, etc. If people approach you inquiring about those things, I would be very appreciative if you would politely discourage them in the beginning. Also, of course, I hope that you will be discreet with them. . . ."

He clarified that he wasn't anxious to help zealous young filmmakers through Zoetrope, he wasn't running some film school.

He also used the memo to announce that he was dropping the Ford in the middle of his name because he agreed with a statement he'd once heard: "Never trust a man who has three names." Moreover, he wanted his building, familiarly known as Columbus Tower, to return to its original name, the Sentinel Building. And the "penthouse" should henceforth be called his "studio." And he warned against duplication of effort, for which he blamed himself: "I am so insecure that people will not act on what I ask of them that I very often give it to three different people, and as a result, I am sitting here with three Minolta 110 cameras."

And he wanted to discuss "requests that seem to you irrelevant or eccentric" and swore "I do not feel the need, nor do I have the time, to explain all of my plans to all of my employees . . . really no one knows the total picture but me. Therefore, please give me the benefit of the doubt and when something comes through that sounds nutsy, just implement it as best as you can."

He concluded, "The era of American Zoetrope being a Haven for young filmmakers or other directors and creative people to find a home is really not in the cards. This will be a one-client studio and the sooner that we are able to gear ourselves to that fact, the better the company will run."

The memo ended with Coppola's playful rewrite of Euripides: "Whom God wishes to destroy, he first makes successful in show business."

The memo reveals, in chilling detail, Coppola's tormented and disintegrating mental condition, his feelings of isolation, paranoia, even worthlessness. Having lost control of his movie, he seemed terrified he might lose control of his empire at home as well. What made it really matter was that this little film he'd meant to knock off in a few months had just swallowed a major portion of his life. If it wasn't a megahit, it could rob him of his home, his vineyard, his office building, his cars, every piece of property he owned. Worse yet, it could wreck his artistic reputation and his status in the eyes of his parents.

Eleanor spent her forty-first birthday alone in Manila. When she got back to Hidden Valley in the evening, Coppola had a surprise birthday present for her. He had flown his parents in from California and had asked his father to compose a tango as a present. A small hired orchestra played the tango as she and Francis danced together in the heart of the dead volcano.

In May 1977, to help defray the cost of his extravagant gesture, as well as the more extravagant cost overruns on *Apocalypse,* Coppola sold all seventy-two thousand shares of his Cinema 7 stock back to the directorate for the same $180,000 he'd paid for it. He'd remain on the board of directors, but by now Donald Rugoff's suit against Cinerama and William Foreman had been dismissed in New York federal court. Rugoff could continue his battle with Foreman without Coppola's investment.

On May 17 George Lucas's *Star Wars* (the space opera that had kept him from making *Apocalypse Now*) premiered. It proceeded to make so much money, so fast, that even *Jaws* (which had surpassed *The Godfather*) was left in the dust. In relatively short order it made Lucas a good deal more wealthy than Coppola—and changed the power relationship between the two men forever. Coppola's protégé had grown up.

A few days later *Apocalypse Now* finally wrapped. It was the 238th day of shooting. "I've never in my life seen so many people so happy to be unemployed," Coppola told the crew at the wrap party.

Back in the United States, the newspaper exposés continued. Many people who cared for Coppola and his body of work wondered if the talented filmmaker had gone stark raving loony. Film critics speculated about his mental health and tried to diagnose his dilemma; reporters swarmed around his cast and crew, trying to get the dirt on the shoot and on Coppola's mental state. Nobody had the slightest idea whether the movie would be a masterpiece, a failure, or something in between.

Chapter Fourteen

Apocalypse at Home
(1977–1979)

THE NIGHTMARE WAS over—except it wasn't. Coppola had already spent nearly $27 million (/$52 million) on the shooting; now he needed to find more money to pay for editors, work prints, a music track, additional music rights, and all the expensive details required to turn raw footage into a completed film. He needed at least $10 million ($20 million would have been better), and rumors began to spread through the media that in order to get it, he had been forced to put up nearly everything he owned. Early in June 1977 *Variety* confirmed it. The headline read COPPOLA HOCKS ASSETS TO UA FOR APOC END MONEY. According to the story, he'd had to put up all his personal assets, including his house, as security for funding to finish his movie.

Coppola did nothing to quash the rumors; in fact, he may have helped start them. It was a brilliant move; announcing that he'd virtually pawned his wedding ring to pay for the film helped counteract the media image of Coppola as a self-indulgent, self-styled genius throwing money around. Instead, it made him seem like a martyr to art, risking everything for his work.

The cleverness of the public relations ploy is especially impressive because in actual fact, the deal wasn't nearly as perilous as advertised. Yes, with UA as guarantor Coppola had borrowed $10 million from Chase Manhattan Bank at 20 percent interest (a normal rate for a movie loan), secured by his personal estate and the future profits from *The Black Stallion*.

However, if he defaulted, United Artists (not Coppola) would have to repay the loan. In exchange, UA would get all the money earned by the film until the loan was paid off. Unless UA foreclosed on him (and it would be unlikely to do so), Coppola's houses, furniture, theater, studio, and offices were safe.

Coppola bought rooms full of state-of-the-art editing hardware. He transferred the footage to videotape, so he could use his brand-new four-screen video editing machine. For the first time his editors would be able to look at three images simultaneously and dissolve them together on the main monitor. The machinery was inspirational. "Pictures can be laid down layer upon layer, the way sound is edited," Coppola said enthusiastically. He also had a new quadraphonic sound mixing facility with a giant console that needed three technicians just to operate it. His wife said it looked like part of a *Star Wars* set.

When he looked at what he'd shot, however, his enthusiasm over the hardware turned abruptly to panic. How had he ever been such a fool as to risk his financial security on this mess? The story line was still unclear, and even 250 hours of footage didn't cover all the plot possibilities that might emerge during the cutting. As he began putting together a rough assembly, he continued shooting, using his Napa vineyard as a location for inserts and pickup shots. He even shot a montage of Kurtz's wife at home (which was never used). In mid-July he admitted he was licked; a Christmas release was out of the question. UA announced that the premiere would now be April 7, 1978, Coppola's thirty-ninth birthday.

Following his old pattern, Coppola found (or manufactured) distractions to pull him away from the cutting room. During the *Apocalypse* shoot, Carroll Ballard had visited the Philippines to show Coppola the latest version of the script for *The Black Stallion,* and Coppola had assigned William Witliffe and then Melissa Mathison (who would later write the screenplay for *E.T.*) to work with Ballard on revisions. Now he looked at the result and decided it was good enough at last. Somewhere he dug up $2.7 million and sent Ballard, *Apocalypse* coproducer Tom Sternberg, and a crew off to Canada to start preproduction.

But now, in midsummer, a mere two days before shooting was to start, Coppola took another look at the script and changed his mind. It still wasn't good enough, especially for a novice feature director. So he hopped into his private jet (with an entourage of twelve or fifteen assorted friends, staffers, and admirers, including a couple of French film buffs and Mathison) and flew to Toronto, which would stand in for small-town America in the last half of the film. The press reported that Coppola spent twenty hours a day in Toronto helping Ballard on his umpteenth rewrite of the screenplay, but Ballard says otherwise.

"It was like Hitler flying into Nuremberg," he recalled. Coppola stayed for a few days, mainly hanging out with his entourage, and then they all flew away again. Coppola never lifted a pencil. "I guess he was on the verge of canceling the whole thing, it seemed to be such a total disaster, but for some reason he didn't."

When Coppola reluctantly returned to editing *Apocalypse*, he found it almost impossible to concentrate. He seemed to leap at any distraction that could keep him from his work, and found a great one in his complicated love affair.

He'd married Eleanor, who was three years older than he, when he was just twenty-three, but he remained curious about the women he had missed. "I've always preferred their company to men's" he admitted years later to a *Paris Match* reporter. "I feel very close to them. Despite my physical appearance, I'm someone very feminine, at the edge of being effeminate." He meant, he explained, "I let myself be totally animated by my emotions." When the reporter asked him why he so rarely shot nude scenes, he explained that he didn't think people with really powerful sex lives could bear to show sex on screen.

He was, as Al Ruddy described him, a man of *enormous* appetites. But Coppola must often have wondered whether the passing parade of up-and-coming models, actresses, wannabe screenwriters, production assistants, and feminist film critics were really interested in him or merely his fame. Then, when he reached his late thirties, an intelligent, exciting young woman who shared his passion for filmmaking had fallen for him. He was flattered; he was enchanted; he was in love.

The deeper Coppola got into the passionate, protracted affair, the harder he found it to edit footage; at times he thought of running away with his mistress or maybe just running away, period. He'd often spoken of how much he valued his family life, but now he couldn't decide whether family or romance counted more. There were times when he must have felt tempted to ask his wife's advice. He was certainly tempted to confront her with the affair so that she'd make the decision.

By late summer the editing crew had completed a rough assembly of the *Apocalypse* footage, and Walter Murch returned from England (where he'd just completed work on *Julia*) to join the team. When he looked at the partial assembly, Murch (always a voice of honesty in the Coppola coterie) expressed severe reservations about it; he thought there was very little chance they could finish in time—even by April. Coppola was devastated and went around muttering that he had only a 20 percent chance to pull the film off at all.

Early in the fall Coppola made a desperate move to resolve at least one of his crises: He told his wife about his lover. Ellie threw a vase of flowers at him. Coppola burst into tears and promised he'd stop seeing his mistress, but such promises are more easily made than kept. Within days he was back in her arms, and now his wife could not be fooled. There were horrible fights. Ellie had been willing to avert her eyes from her husband's playing around, but this time he wasn't playing.

At Halloween a ghost from the past came back to haunt him. A traitor at Zoetrope had given *Esquire* a copy of Coppola's manic memo of April 30, and it had printed the whole thing in its November issue. Coppola had come to view the memo with acute embarrassment as "a memo from a desperate guy trying to hold on to his company from 6000 miles away." By now he'd reversed himself on nearly everything in it except dropping his middle name. It was unbearable to have his private terrors paraded in public. "The press was making me into a fool," he said. "I felt ridiculed and embarrassed."

A few weeks later he told his wife that he'd seen a new doctor and learned that he'd had a real nervous breakdown, but that his condition could be treated. A rumor made the rounds of San Francisco to the effect that Coppola, in a bitterly ironic joke (or, perhaps, in an attempt to keep the situation secret) had arranged for a lithium prescription to be written in the name of Kurtz. His wife hoped that his love affair would be cured along with his mental illness, but this hope proved to be in vain.

His movie was in even worse shape than his marriage. Early

in November United Artists' brass decided to push back the film's opening date to October 1978. He had a year, but he was getting nowhere with his footage. Murch, who was now slugging out the edit alongside Coppola, thought the unusual length of the shoot made it a particularly difficult edit. "If a film is shot in six weeks, you are basically in one state of mind during that six-week period," he said, "and you can get back into that state of mind in the editing room. If a picture takes over a year to shoot, you have been many things during that time."

In November 1977, NBC aired *The Godfather Saga*, the long-awaited seven-hour combination of *The Godfather* and *Godfather II*. Coppola had mapped out the structure and handed the footage over to Barry Malkin, his childhood pal who had edited *The Rain People*. Malkin rearranged the footage from the two movies chronologically, starting with Don Corleone as a little boy in Sicily, and added slightly less than an hour of "lost" footage. It was an amazing work: rich, somber, vivid, and grand in scope, perhaps the grandest *Godfather* of them all.

The telecast was spread over four nights, a total of nine hours, including commercials. The ratings started out low, but each night it got a larger audience; on its final night, 43 percent of the people watching TV were tuned in. If obscure statistics are your thing, you'll want to know that this put segment four in ninety-ninth place among all movies shown on TV since 1961.

Coppola and his wife consoled themselves for their professional and marital woes by screening 8½, Fellini's autobiographical tale of a brilliant but hapless movie director beset by demanding stars, producers, fans, hangers-on, past and future mistresses, and his reproachful, neglected wife. "It was like an autobiography of Francis," Ellie wrote. "Even the fantasies were the same. The dialogue between the husband and wife was word for word things Francis and I have said to each other."

Coppola was still worried about *The Black Stallion*; the shoot had moved to Italy for the desert island scenes, and it was going over schedule. Ballard had followed in his boss's footsteps; he was shooting with a script that no one really liked, and everything was improvised. Afterward Ballard swore he'd never again go into production without a completed screenplay.

By now Coppola's whole life was filled with annoyances. "The circle of people who can make him happy has shrunk to one small mirror image," Ellie reflected. "It's down to Francis being the only one left who can make him happy." Some of his crew started calling him "Ayatollah Coppola" behind his back. Later (when the film was finished), he found the nickname hilarious.

Dennis Jakob (himself subject to unpredictable emotional weather) had taken to sneaking into the editing room at night and recutting the footage. When the editors threatened to quit if he wasn't fired, Coppola told Jakob, in no uncertain terms, to lay off. Jakob was so furious he stole several reels of the work print, burned the film, and sent envelopes full of ashes to Coppola every day for a week. George Lucas told Coppola he should make a movie about *that*.

Coppola was impossible at home, and his wife's suffering was sharpened by the realization that his love affair had become public knowledge; it was, in fact, everybody's favorite gossip topic. The family's Christmas celebration was a travesty. They had a giant, gorgeously decorated Christmas tree they'd cut down themselves, and a grand roast goose dinner, but the atmosphere was unrelentingly tense. Coppola lay on the couch, miserable and angry. He had told his wife the affair was over, and she'd believed him, until she began finding notes and little presents from his girl friend in his pockets.

Nonetheless, as New Year's Day, 1978, came and went, at least *Apocalypse* seemed to be taking shape. Coppola fell in love with his footage again. It was foolish, he decided, to try to maintain a consistent style throughout the film. Instead, he instructed his editors to cut each sequence in the style appropriate to it, without trying to match surrounding sequences. As the audience members accepted each new sequence in turn, they'd be carried along on the trip up the river.

It was a daring decision. "Normally," Murch pointed out, "when a director gets above a certain budgetary level, a certain kind of 'let's play it safe' mentality sets in. With Francis, it happened the other way. Even though it was his own money, and over schedule and over budget, he encouraged daring things, more so as it went on."

Then a new problem surfaced to terrify Coppola. Several years earlier Transamerica, an insurance company with octopus arms in many other fields, had bought United Artists. It had left the UA management staff—some of Hollywood's smartest, most successful producers—in place, but increasingly (and partly in a response to the endless delay on *Apocalypse*) Transamerica was starting to tell the vets how to run their show. The filmmaking bosses at UA found it intolerable. Coppola watched with growing dismay as the situation deteriorated.

Now, in the midst of the traumatic *Apocalypse* edit, Arthur Krim, the longtime chairman of UA (who was often described as the smartest man in the movies), reached the end of his patience. Not only did he walk out, but he took nearly every other high-ranking UA executive with him. They immediately founded Orion Pictures, but that was no help to Coppola, whose film was still locked into an intricate cofunding and distribution deal with UA.

Still, the new lineup of top executives at UA (who came, primarily, from UA's second rank) knew better than to challenge Coppola. They were already on shaky ground with the creative Hollywood community; they didn't need to give any extra credence to their image as Philistines by hassling a man who was widely perceived as an artist. They let him be.

Coppola (who was no fool either) took advantage of the breathing space to cozy up to Jim Harvey, the chairman of Transamerica, the San Francisco conglomerate that owned UA. One day Harvey entered his twenty-fifth-story office in the Transamerica pyramid, overlooking North Beach, to find an expensive telescope, on a tripod, with its lens aimed right at Coppola's Sentinel Building office. A small metal plaque read, "To Jim Harvey, from Francis Coppola, so you can keep an eye on me." Harvey found the gesture irresistible.

The only thing that never changed was the constant need for more money. Within the course of one week Eleanor signed her name thirty-seven times on new loan papers for another $7.5 million. This time the family's personal possessions really did go on the line as security (with no film studio to protect them), but she cheered herself up by redecorating another room of the Napa house with Japanese prints and Chagall and Picasso lithographs. As for Coppola, he cheered himself up by using some of the money to buy back ownership of *The Conversation* from Paramount.

Naturally, the United Artists execs were anxious to see what progress he'd made, so Coppola scheduled a screening of the rough cut for late February 1978, eight months before the scheduled premiere. As the rough cut screening grew closer, he became more frightened. He slept at the Broadway mansion, slaving all day in the editing room, sometimes working alone all night and stopping to sleep only at dawn. New endings would come to him; he'd get excited; he'd abandon them. Coppola and his editors became so obsessed with the material that when they took coffee breaks, they found themselves holding conversations using lines of the dialogue from the film.

The UA screening went relatively well. Although the rough cut still had no ending, the small audience of studio executives, selected Zoetropers, and friends responded positively. Coppola decided to schedule an exhibitors' screening in two months.

One month later Coppola had completed two-thirds of *Apocalypse.* He liked it, but when he showed it to his wife, she thought it was disappointing; it didn't convey the heat, the concussion of the explosions, the excitement of the helicopters. He was deeply annoyed by her lukewarm reaction. They argued in front of the children. One day, when little Sofia yelled "Cut!" Francis had a horrible realization. "Don't you think I wonder if I am just making my next movie right now?" he shouted at Ellie. "Don't you think it scares me that my life is just a movie I'm making?"

Nor did it help when Ellie discovered a birthday card from his mistress reading: "Thanks for letting me participate in your greatness, Love . . ." Eleanor decided to get away for the summer and signed up for an art tour of Japan.

Coppola kept pushing on the rough cut, and when he finally finished, he screened it for his staff. It still wasn't good enough. He decided that maybe a voice-over narration would tie the separate episodes together. It was a desperate decision; voice-over narration had been out of style for twenty years and was generally used only in direst need. Coppola summoned Michael Herr (writer of *Dispatches,* a harrowing, gorgeously written journal of the Vietnam War, and the source of many incidents in Milius's original script) to move into the Napa house and write the narration; Martin Sheen moved into the Broadway mansion and recorded the narration as it came down from Napa, page by page. He was a strange houseguest. One night, still under the effects of his jungle breakdown, he tried to beat up two SF cops, and Coppola had to bail him out of jail. Meanwhile, Coppola shot more inserts and hired a giant sound and music department to start work on the sound track.

Coppola needed to test his film on a real audience. He scheduled the first public screening, an invitational sneak preview, at 9:30 A.M. on Tuesday, April 25, at San Francisco's Northpoint Theater. Just two days before the preview, in a state of sheer panic, he finished the cut. The ending was . . . vague.

After all the horror stories from the Philippines and the continuing media tales of Coppola's financial and editing difficulties, public curiosity about *Apocalypse Now* was intense. When word of the screening got out, every journalist within a thousand miles of San Francisco considered it a professional challenge to borrow an invitation and crash the screening. Coppola stationed security people at every entrance with instructions to bar entry to critics and reporters, but of course, it was impossible to spot them all. Coppola made an appeal before the screening began, begging any critics who had sneaked in to refrain from reviewing what was an unfinished work. He also asked the audience of nine hundred invitees to fill out reaction sheets. When he looked at the questionnaires later, he was horrified to discover that viewers liked the "Ride of the Valkyries" sequence—which he considered merely an action scene, with no philosophical depth—better than anything else in the picture.

If the audience's reaction was mixed, Coppola's was not. Viewing the film with an audience, on the giant Northpoint screen, he loathed it. He'd have to recut it from scratch. Back at his office, he had someone type up forty-eight file cards with a different scene on each one. Then he shuffled and reshuffled the cards, trying to find a satisfactory structure. He now had only one week before the first all-important exhibitors' screening on May 2.

On April 30 the film was still in pieces, scattered all over the editing room. Coppola had come up with a new opening, but he liked it even less than the previous one. "If they don't like the film and don't bid on it," he joked grimly to Walter Murch, "we won't have to come out with it."

The exhibitors were not crazy about the film, but exhibitors seldom are. A second exhibitors' screening was scheduled for May 9, in New York. There was no way Coppola could finish a final edit in time. He showed the exhibitors only a portion of the film, including a different ending from the one he'd screened in San Francisco. This time several exhibitors came out raving about what they'd seen; but Coppola still wasn't happy, and he got UA to push back the opening again until Easter 1979, to buy time to reedit the footage completely.

Eleanor Coppola found a note her husband had written to himself. It said:

> What are my problems?
>
> My greatest fear—I've had for months—The movie is a mess—A mess of continuity, of style—and most important, the ending neither works on an audience or philosophical level. Brando is a disappointment to audiences—the film reaches its highest level during the fucking helicopter battle.
>
> My nerves are shot—My heart is broken—My imagination is dead. I have no self-reliance—but like a child just want someone to rescue me. . . .

The sneak screenings continued. By the end of the month he decided he'd never finish by Easter 1979; he convinced UA to postpone the opening again until August 1979. Now he had fifteen months to complete the film.

The picture was already a year overdue, and the "work in progress" screenings gave the picture the stink of failure. The wisecrack "Apocalypse Never" was starting to circulate around United Artists headquarters, and gossip that the picture was unreleasable spread from Hollywood to New York. Even *The Black Stallion* was a year behind schedule, and UA Chairman Andreas Albeck was growing an ulcer.

Coppola's family broke up, but only for the summer. Gio went off to his first full-time job in Canada, Roman went to France to live with a family there, Sofia went to relatives, and Ellie headed off to Japan to study art. Francis returned to his editing room and his girl friend.

When Eleanor returned, people were only too anxious to fill her in on the details of Coppola's summertime philandering. Of course, he denied everything. "Francis is a master of creating illusion," she wrote bitterly. "He is one of the most skilled professionals in the field around the world. Over and over again he creates the most convincing illusion that he sincerely wants to have a marriage and family life without a triangle."

By October Coppola had at least made some final decisions about the movie. The costly French plantation scene was gone, as were two of Brando's major scenes, including one in which Kurtz shoots a captured North Vietnamese in the head. The first half of the film was locked; the music cues were set, and the looping of actor's voices could begin. The ending was still up in the air, and Coppola wondered if perhaps he should shoot just one more scene, but now that he could see each new cut improving the film, his panic began to subside.

As the new year approached, Coppola was probably beginning to believe that his movie was truly under control at last. With eight months to go before the premiere, he could relax a bit. It was amply clear that United Artists wasn't about to foreclose on his *Apocalypse* debts, no matter how long he dragged out the editing.

Steven Bach, then a top UA executive, explained that "the only way to secure the picture was to keep financing the lengthy post-production. To have closed Coppola down would have been an automatic write-off of the $30 million or so already expended. If the picture failed, UA would be in the uncomfortable position of enforcing the provisions of its loans to Coppola, attaching the assets not only of Zoetrope but of the man himself." Furthermore, Coppola was so superb a media manipulator that he'd have the press totally on his side. "Corporations foreclose on such figures at their peril or at peril to their public images," Bach added. All the UA management could do was bite its nails and hold its breath.

In December Coppola headed for Manhattan to attend the first screening of Michael Cimino's Vietnam movie, *The Deer Hunter*. Observers reported that he looked just as nervous as Cimino. He was inclined to be friendly toward Cimino (a fellow Italian from Queens), but *The Deer Hunter* had already been nicknamed "Apocalypse First," and the amity was becoming slightly strained.

Then, in a *New York Times* interview, Cimino (who was actually just a few months younger than Coppola but pretended to be five years younger so that he, too, could be labeled a boy genius) took a number of gratuitous potshots at Coppola, including one in which he quipped, "Vietnam was not the apocalypse." Cimino sounded like a punk gunfighter bad-mouthing an aging pro. His evident yen to out-Coppola Coppola was to have dire consequences for UA, the movie business in general, and even Coppola himself, but *Heaven's Gate* was an apocalypse still some years away.

Despite Cimino's challenge, when Coppola returned to San Francisco, he'd begun feeling so optimistic about *Apocalypse* that he felt he could afford to turn down work. The first offer he nixed was a sweet deal for $2 million, plus 25 percent of the adjusted gross, to direct a romance called *One from the Heart* for MGM. Coppola loved the script; he just didn't want to make it himself. He offered MGM $500,000 to buy the script, with the idea of having its writer, Armyan Bernstein, direct, but negotiations broke down.

For his fortieth birthday, Coppola threw a giant bash at the Napa vineyard. He also took time off from *Apocalypse* to help his old friend James Caan dub and reedit *Hide in Plain Sight*, Caan's debut as a director. He'd been reading Yukio Mishima's novels and grown increasingly enthusiastic about Japanese culture. Late in April he flew to Washington to eat suckling pig and barbecued bison at a White House dinner with President Jimmy Carter and Japanese Prime Minister Masayoshi Ohira.

To reciprocate for the dinner, Coppola had their mutual media adviser, Gerald Rafshoon, pull a few White House strings to set up a screening of his now nearly completed work in progress for Carter and a few guests. The White House sneak took place on May 3. Reportedly Carter applauded at the end, but other administration officials (like CIA Director Stansfield Turner) sat with their arms folded in silence. Reaction was mixed, with adjectives like "weird" and "gruesome" prominent.

Coppola was eager for reactions and nervous about them as well. As a friend of his told a reporter, "If the film fails, the only thing Francis will have left in San Francisco will be his heart." He followed the White House screening with a public sneak preview in Minneapolis.

By now the main thrust of the ending was clear, but Coppola was still fooling around with the final shot. His uncertainty revolved around Willard's state of mind and the most effective way to convey it visually. Would Willard stay and take

Kurtz's place as king? Would he leave, get into his boat, and call in a bomber attack as he made his getaway down-river? Or would he just stand there, quietly, unable to decide?

Coppola had shot the spectacular bomb sequence, but now he no longer liked it. The ending of the Minneapolis version was fairly ambiguous: Willard stands on the temple steps after killing Kurtz. The natives bow to him. He hesitates, and the shot dissolves to a giant green idol's face, with Brando's voice-over repeating, "The horror, the horror." Slowly Willard's face moves to screen right, until it's superimposed over the green face. The End. Audience reaction to this version was mixed.

Once again Coppola had appealed for a critical blackout, but this time it didn't work. Syndicated columnist Rona Barrett broke the decree of silence on ABC's *A.M. America*, declaring the film a "disappointing failure."

One week later, on May 11, Coppola staged another sneak, this time in Hollywood. It was a benefit for the Pacific Film Archive. He showed a panoramic 70 mm print with a still-unfinished quintaphonic sound track (three tracks in front, two in back), running 139 minutes with no credits. Two thousand people lined up for six hours in advance outside Mann's Bruin Theater in the Westwood section of L.A. to pay $7.50 to attend one of three screenings. Some had arrived at six in the morn-ing. Coppola aides, in T-shirts reading "Trust Me," handed out ice cream and five-page booklets that included a charming "Dear Audience" cover letter from Coppola. "I was and prob-ably still am a theater director," Coppola wrote. "For me, this means I need the opportunity to show my work as close to its final form as I intend it, so I can judge how it affects my audi-ence. . . . In a real sense, it is my invitation to you to help me finalize the film." There were also fifteen questions for audi-ence members to answer: Did they like the film? Which parts? The characters? Was the violence appropriate? How was the ending? And so on.

Just before the doors were opened, Coppola discovered that while the general public had been waiting hours to buy tickets, a large block of seats had been roped off for the press, studio execs, and exhibitors. He burst into a tantrum. "I'm not going to have ropes up for a lot of exhibitors," he shouted. "I'm not a friend of the exhibitors!" He was even angrier to find that rival studios were allowed to buy tickets—in blocks, yet. "Who gave them permission to buy tickets?" he bellowed. "Take down those ropes right now, or I'm taking back my prints!"

As the film concluded, there was a hushed silence. Then a few scattered viewers burst into brief but enthusiastic applause. That was all.

This time it was *Variety* that ignored Coppola's pleas not to review the "work in progress." Its verdict was ambivalent. "*Apocalypse Now* was worth the wait," its critic declared. "An exhilarating action-adventure for two-thirds of its 139 minutes, *Apocalypse* abruptly shifts to surrealistic symbolism for its denouement. Result will be many audiences left in the lurch." The critic felt that the war footage "outclasses any war pic made to date," but that at the ending "*Apocalypse Now* runs aground . . . final third of the picture fails to jell."

In the trades there was speculation that Coppola was still trying to decide among three different endings. He denied it. He said:

> There are no other versions, just things people would like to see me do. This is my version, my ending, my film. I left the decision unclear—whether Willard turns into a Kurtz or whether he goes back [down the river] because I would like my own life to demonstrate what that decision was.
>
> [I'm] trying to say that morality is an issue we have to take as it comes. One day you lie to your wife, another day you don't. And when morality gets up onto its higher levels, so that it's not just a matter of a lie, it comes into that realm of madness where it's life or death. I wanted to push for something almost mythic— recognizing, of course, when you even mention the word "myth," you're considered a total phony.

Morality aside, the studio execs and foreign distributors hated the ending; they urged Coppola to use the spectacular sequence in which Willard calls in an air strike to bomb Kurtz's compound to smithereens. "I just couldn't do it," Coppola said. "Explosions are no substitute for human beings and ideas."

Two days later he took *Apocalypse* to the Cannes Film

Festival. UA executives were horrified at the idea of screening an unfinished film in competition; one of them publicly declared the decision "momentary insanity born of arrogance." But Coppola still owned the film, and he had the power to decide. The sold-out Los Angeles preview made him confident that the Cannes audience would applaud his artistic achievement and provide an invaluable publicity coup to whip up interest for the U.S. opening.

Interest in the film, and in Coppola himself, was immoderate; his staff received no fewer than nine hundred requests for interviews. Coppola entertained a few reporters aboard the yacht *Amazone*, his posh headquarters, but when the demand for interviews became overwhelming, he decided to hold a mass press conference onstage, in the theater, right after the screening of *Apocalypse*. It became the most newsworthy event of the festival.

The screening itself, scheduled for 10:00 A.M., was hyped so heavily that many people expected a mob scene and stayed home. "The most eagerly awaited media event of 1979 ended up playing to a not completely full house," observed critic Andrew Sarris. The press conference, which packed the two-thousand-seat theater, was actually a bigger draw. That should have come as no surprise.

Coppola orated like Moses down from the mountain. Wearing a Panama hat and growling like an angry bear, he expressed his fury over the on-set press coverage, *Esquire*'s publication of his memo, and the "illegal" reviews of his screenings. "American journalism is the most decadent, totally lying kind of profession that I've ever come across," he ranted. "I learned it on this picture. There was never a truthful thing written about *Apocalypse Now* in four years—never one article that ever had the truth in it, about the budget, about what we were doing, or about the film. Journalists would promise that they would come to see an unfinished work, but wouldn't write about it, and then they *would* write about it. So I said, if there are no rules, if there are no ethics, then let me show the film right in Hollywood, right in Cannes so that everyone can see it and get off my back." He went on to order the assembled journalists not to quote him directly on anything. Fat chance.

Coppola declared that *Apocalypse* was "the first $30 million surrealist movie." He noted that he'd found *The Deer Hunter* "politically naive." He pointed out that his film hadn't cost $37 million, as had been falsely reported in the lying press, but only $30.5 million, "not much more than *The Wiz* or a lot of other big films. Why is it such a crime for me to spend a lot of money about a film which deals with morality, when you can spend it on a film about a big gorilla or about a little fairy tale or about some jerk who flies around in the sky?" He continued:

> My film is not a movie; it's not about Vietnam. It *is* Vietnam. It's what it was really like; it was crazy. . . . We were in the jungle, there were too many of us, we had access to too much money, too much equipment; and little by little, we went insane. I think you can see it in the film. . . . You can see the photography going a little crazy, and the director and the actors going a little crazy. After a while, I realized I was a little frightened, because I was getting deeper in debt and no longer recognized the kind of movie I was making. . . . The film was making itself; the jungle was making the film. . . .
>
> I've been in this racket a long time. And one thing I've learned is that whenever you make a film that goes a little here when people are used to it going there, when you don't do it exactly the way people are used to, they're surprised. But two or three years later they come to be interested, and that's the way it's always been. . . . *Apocalypse Now* is a piece of art that I tried to make.

He announced his next film would take about ten years to make and would be "very very long." It would be a love story about love and physics, set between Japan and America, based on Goethe's *Elective Affinities*. "Goethe is my idol," he told a reporter. "He was a great poet, a physicist, a thinker. He was interested in painting . . . and he kept falling in love. He was *always* in love. He had mistresses and mistresses."

The press ate it up. In the end Coppola's decision to bring *Apocalypse* to Cannes was proved 100 percent correct. In addition to the saturation coverage of his press conference, the unfinished film took the top prize, the Golden Palm, sharing it with *The Tin Drum*.

The chairperson of the jury was novelist Françoise Sagan, who claimed at her press conference that she hadn't set foot in a movie theater in more than ten years. Six months later she complained that the vote for *Apocalypse* had been fixed. None of the jurors liked it at first, she explained, but suddenly, a few days later, they all changed their minds. The fix, she said, had to be in. The other jurors responded that Sagan was talking nonsense. She was just angry because the festival wouldn't reimburse her for the $6,000 long-distance phone bill she'd run up during the festival.

In any event Coppola was now the only director in history to have won the Golden Palm twice. Many audience members booed; a Cannes tradition holds that any director who's won this prestigious award should refrain from entering competition again. As for the French critics who reviewed the unfinished film (against Coppola's express wishes), they weren't crazy about it either.

After winning the prize, Coppola and his entourage (wife, kids, staffers) slipped away from the glitzy Croisette area to take over a small Italian restaurant in the working-class section of Cannes. UA's Steven Bach was there. "A Chianti bottle flew from one corner of the little restaurant to another," he remembered, "crashing against a wall. Someone let out a whoop of release, a signal that the frustrations and uncertainties of four years' work were over. Another bottle followed the first, then another, then the glasses. The restaurant floor was a sea of wine and shards of glass, a red sea one expected for a moment Francis might try to part."

Village Voice film critic Andrew Sarris (who had never really liked a Coppola movie yet) was among the first to review the film. He was impressed by the cinematography of *Apocalypse*, but less thrilled by every other aspect of the movie. He summed up his impressions with the phrase "terminal pretentiousness."

Coppola sent a memo to his staff instructing it to ignore Sarris's review. Now he hated journalists more than ever.

Coppola was so delighted with the Golden Palm he immediately initiated two new projects. First, he signed French New Wave master Jean-Luc Godard to direct *Bugsy Siegel*. (It never came off; subsequently Godard was signed to make another film for Zoetrope, *The Story*, which ultimately evolved into a film released as *Passion*.)

His second new project was bigger. Even though he was flat broke, Coppola started negotiations to buy himself a movie studio, Hollywood General, a beautiful old 1930s lot with nine sound stages. He'd passed its gates daily as a child, when his family was living in Los Angeles. If *Apocalypse* made enough money, Coppola thought, he could organize an ongoing, economically self-sustaining group of film personnel that could take chances without risking financial ruin. He envisioned "a family or a large repertory company engaged in making movies"—the very idea he'd rejected in the infamous *Esquire* memo.

Between negotiations, Coppola returned to the editing room, making about fifteen cuts in the picture and changing the sound track drastically. Furthermore, despite his insistence that his artsy multiple-superimposition ending was not open to discussion, he bowed reluctantly to studio pressure and compromised. Willard would leave the temple, taking Lance (now quite mad) back to the boat; however, Willard wouldn't call in the air strike; he would just float away.

The flap over the ending was greatly overblown in the press; there had been similar debates over the endings of both *Godfathers* and *The Conversation*. "It's just that [the debates] were done on the public stage, in full view of the press," said Murch. "Francis played with a masterful hand to publicity. It added an element of suspense about what he'd do."

Coppola now seemed to be in full manic motion, moving full speed ahead toward becoming a one-man studio. For years he'd been saying he wanted movies to return to being special events for audiences. Now, with the enthusiastic support of his old friend Tom Luddy, the director of the Pacific Film Archive in Berkeley, he picked up a German film that emphatically fit that prescription.

Hans-Jürgen Syberberg's *Our Hitler, a Film from Germany* was seven hours long. It had been panned by German critics but elicited raves in England, France, and Israel and from culture maven Susan Sontag in New York. Coppola had seen it at the Filmex Festival in Los Angeles and, filled with excitement, phoned Syberberg. "All films up to now are obsolete!" he declared. "This has to be seen in this country." He immediately offered to buy the U.S. rights.

After the years of editing *Apocalypse*, Coppola must have been delighted to learn that Syberberg had spent four years writing *Our Hitler* and then didn't edit it at all. "Everything that was written we were able to get on celluloid." Syberberg said. "And everything on celluloid we kept."

On July 21, 1979, Coppola premiered *Our Hitler* in San Francisco to a sellout audience of two thousand (paying $10 a ticket, in a benefit for the Pacific Film Archive). The extravaganza actually ran nine hours, including a two-hour dinner-and-discussion break in the middle. The audience discovered, with some distress, that *Our Hitler* was neither a narrative nor a documentary, but a sort of surrealist dream film, using puppets, collages, pastiches of Fascist symbolism, and special effects to accompany a series of monologues, including a full hour of an actor impersonating Hitler's valet, droning on in minute detail about Hitler's preferences in clothing and grooming aids. "I've seen it three times," declared Luddy's future wife, stylist Monique Montgomery, "and it's the best sleep I've gotten in *years!*"

About a third of the audience left before the end; the rest emerged at midnight, looking like haggard survivors of a war. Still, Coppola's involvement (along with the squawking American Nazi party protesters picketing outside) had indeed turned the film into a major media event; subsequent screenings in Manhattan and Washington were sellouts, too.

Francis wasn't the only Coppola in the news. In a wholly unexpected move Eleanor Coppola had sold her personal diary on the making of *Apocalypse* (including every detail of her husband's adultery except his paramour's name) to Simon and Schuster. The book was called *Notes,* and it came out just before *Apocalypse* did. *The New York Times* even ran excerpts from it. It sold well, despite a paucity of reviews and those generally negative.

Coppola never discussed the book with journalists (or even his close friends). He told *Variety,* "It's my business," and complained about his life being "spread out like a sheet of butter." However, he had been the one to suggest that his wife turn her diaries into a book. In any event, its horrifying details of both the shoot and the marital crisis made audiences more eager than ever to see the movie.

Despite (or perhaps because of) Eleanor's public airing of the dirty linen, the rift in the marriage seemed to have healed. "There is no other woman," Coppola declared. "I've been almost asking for a real shakedown. This is a period of strange turning points for me. I used to be sort of a goofy kid: Oh, boy, I have a new sports car; Gee, I'm directing a movie; Wow, that girl likes me. Well, it's not like that after 40. I'd like to build a harmonious relationship between my personal life and my work. I'd like to be happy, to feel good."

Joseph Farrell, head of the National Research Group, was brought into the operation to help shape the marketing policy on *Apocalypse Now*. Coppola was eager to impose a ticket price of $10 (in an era when $4 to $5 was normal) to make the movie seem like something special. Farrell convinced him that audiences would view $10 as a special rip-off. Instead, he and Coppola came up with the idea of focusing the ads on the image of Brando in an elegant campaign that eschewed the use of the reviewers' raves or any mentions of awards. At $9 million, the ad budget was then the highest in movie history.

The invitational premiere of *Apocalypse* took place at the Ziegfeld Theater in New York City; the house was packed. The movie was followed by a few moments of silence, then by scattered applause.

The commercial release began four days later, in New York, Los Angeles, and Toronto, in 70 mm; UA had decided on a twelve-week, hard-ticket (reserved seats) run, like a play. There were no end credits; audiences received printed programs.

Apocalypse Now opens with a chilling montage: Helicopters fly through the jungle, accompanied by the heartbeat thumps of slowed-down heli rotors. As The Doors begin "The End," the heli footage slowly dissolves to Martin Sheen as Willard, lying in a hotel bed. Above him, a ceiling fan revolves like another heli rotor. Willard is a Green Beret and part-time CIA assassin. He's been assigned to go into Cambodia (where no Americans are supposed to be) and terminate Kurtz, a once-promising U.S. officer who's somehow gone amok, ruling over a Montagnard tribe deep in the jungle and refusing to return home. A small Navy boat and its crew are assigned to take Willard up the river.

The boat moves through a series of unconnected, eccentric scenes of war. First, there's Colonel Kilgore (Robert Duvall), a character that only John Milius could have written: a macho, daring, charming ex-surfer whose cavalry outfit has taken to the skies in helicopters. Willard needs his help to get from the ocean into the river, and when Kilgore hears that the waves

at a Vietcong river delta village are good for surfing, he agrees
to help. As the choppers approach the village, Wagner's "Ride
of the Valkyries" blasts over the sound track; Kilgore's helis
carry tape decks and loudspeakers to scare the VCs. After much
good-spirited slaughter, Kilgore's men go surfing in the middle
of the battle.

Farther up the river, one of the boat crew, a New Orleans
saucier named Chef (Frederic Forrest) runs into a tiger, inspiring a fine freak-out ("All I ever wanted to do was cook!" Chef
shouts.) Lance (Sam Bottoms), the Malibu surfer, goes mad and
paints his face green for camouflage; seconds later, during a
routine search of a Vietnamese food boat, the sailors fall into a
homicidal frenzy.

The next major sequence returns to absurd comedy. At a
USO show in the middle of the jungle, underdressed Playboy
Bunnies dance for a giant audience of horny soldiers and flee
back into their choppers when the grunts mob the stage.

The last set piece takes place in deep night, at the eerie
Do Lung Bridge, deep in the jungle, strung with electric lights
like a Christmas tree. Feverish American soldiers defend it,
not knowing who's in charge or what they're supposed to do.
Every day they rebuild the bridge, and every night "Charlie"
destroys it. An enemy, hidden by darkness, shouts taunting ob-
scenities at them in English until a soldier launches a grenade
at him.

Only Willard, Chef, and Lance survive to reach the Kurtz
compound; the other men are killed, one by one, by VC bullets or the spears of Kurtz's savages. At the monumental, bar-
baric compound (it was modeled on Angkor Wat), Willard is
taken prisoner. He passes Kurtz's manhood test by surviving
imprisonment in a bamboo cage, even after Chef's severed head
has been tossed into his lap. The malaria-ridden Kurtz mum-
bles and rambles. It turns out that Kurtz wants Willard to kill
him, and Willard is happy to oblige, dispatching Kurtz by clubbing him with a rifle butt just as the natives are sacrificing a
water buffalo outside the temple. Kurtz's native woman watches
with resignation and kneels to the blood-splashed Willard as
he walks out onto the stairs. Willard returns to the boat with
Lance, his sole surviving companion, refusing the implied offer to take Kurtz's place.

The cinematic set pieces during the film's first ninety minutes are funny, frightening, phantasmagorical; the war is seen

as a mad hallucination, populated by caricatures rather than characters, much like the sketchy, vivid people one meets in dreams. It's closer to *Alice in Wonderland* than to *Heart of Darkness*, but the shots are beautiful to look at, intriguing to consider. It's a superb display of bravado filmmaking, a zippy psychedelic comic book of a film. Then we reach the Kurtz compound, and the fun is over; we're left with an hour-long muddle.

This sequence matches pretentious images with portentous words. Dennis Hopper is amusing as an American photographer, spouting hippie babble about the greatness of Kurtz. His dialogue sounds suspiciously like some of the articles written about Coppola, but is mainly drawn from *Heart of Darkness*. Kurtz himself is inert, filmed like a god incarnate, in deep shadow, showing just the gleam of his bald head or part of his face. His dialogue is bombastically cultured; he reads aloud from T. S. Eliot's "The Hollow Men," a poem that draws its title from Conrad's description of Kurtz as "a hollow man," and he muses about the superior purity of the Vietcong. As Brando intones his lines in a small treble voice, he sounds like a castrato who's been shooting Xylocaine. Perhaps it's meant to convey his malarial fever. Brando and Sheen don't so much converse as exchange pauses.

Coppola has claimed (at Cannes and elsewhere) that the film is politically liberal, but in fact, like *Patton,* it never stakes out a firm position. The Kurtz sequence is full of reactionary elements: slavish natives awed by the white god-man, the appalling polio inoculation story that Kurtz tells, and especially the character of the proto-fascistic Kurtz, a Nietzschean superman facing deeper realities than those of which ordinary men dream.

While Coppola deliberately set out to make a demanding movie, one that would lead to a philosophical conclusion rather than a conventional action climax, the compound sequence fails precisely because the filmmaker doesn't seem to have any philosophical point to express; he merely stumbles into an intellectual swamp that swallows up his ambitions. Coppola's endless difficulties with the ending seem inevitable; he never figured out how to say his piece because he never knew what he wanted to say.

It's interesting to note how much of John Milius's work remains intact, including some of the film's best scenes. While many of the sequences that Coppola wrote (e.g., the Monta-gnards playing with skulls, the French plantation, the montage of Kurtz's wife) ended up on the cutting-room floor, the two most effective episodes—Kilgore's scenes and the Do Lung Bridge—were carried over from the Milius script. The original screenplay even called for using The Doors on the sound track.

"If the film strayed from the first draft, it was not so much away from Milius's conception as it was toward Milius's own source, the Conrad novel," wrote Brooks Riley (a critic who was soon to become a Zoetrope employee) in an exhaustive analysis in *Film Comment*.

When Milius saw the final version, he was delighted. "I love what he's done with it," he declared. "I must admit I liked it better at 3½ hours than I do at 2½ hours, but I do think he's done a great job."

Lucas was not so laudatory. Although Coppola had even-tually given him a couple of profit points in the movie, Lucas still felt he'd invested six years of his life in the project, "only to see his original concept distorted by Coppola's fervid imag-ination." For the next eight years he disassociated himself from Coppola both professionally and personally.

As the reviews began to appear, it became clear that very few critics felt that the film was entirely successful.

Vincent Canby, writing in *The New York Times*, loved the first hour. "*Apocalypse Now* lives up to its grand title," he wrote, "disclosing not only the various faces of war but also the con-tradiction between excitement and boredom, terror and pity, brutality and beauty. Its epiphanies would do credit to Fede-rico Fellini." However, he felt the entire Kurtz mission (and character) were an arbitrary imposition, along with the philos-ophizing. The sound track narration, he noted, "makes one's flesh wet with embarrassment." Brando had no real role to act, and even Vittorio Storaro's extraordinary camera work couldn't save the film from its "profoundly anticlimactic intellectual muddle."

Coppola could take consolation from the rave review in *Newsweek* by Jack Kroll, who found *Apocalypse Now* a "stun-ning and unforgettable film" and even compared it with the stories of Nobel Prize–winning author Jorge Luis Borges.

A few days later *Time* titled its review "The Making of a Quagmire." Its critic, Frank Rich, didn't even like the ride up the river. "What is missing from these panoramas of death," he wrote, "is a human context. There are almost no well-defined characters in *Apocalypse Now*. The biggest nonentity of all, sadly enough, is Willard. It is not Sheen's fault; no one has written him a role."

At the *New Yorker* the luck of the draw had Pauline Kael on leave when the film was released. Veronica Geng reviewed it with increasing displeasure as she went along. Geng thought that the film "earns every second of its display of evil, because it has coherence, truthfulness, and conviction—up to a point. The point is Kurtz." But with Kurtz's arrival, she observed, "The movie begins to parade big ideas, to partake of Kurtz's grandiosity. *Apocalypse Now* falters in conviction, making me feel the way I would if *2001* had ended with some stock green men and Brando, in his Jor-El makeup, as the king of Jupiter." (Some years later Kael said that she would have panned it, too.)

Coppola reacted with anger and hurt. He told one reporter that it wasn't his fault if he was too advanced for the critics. "I feel that I'm a fifth-grader living in a third-grade world," he said with a sneer, "and anxious to get to high school."

On October 1, 1979, *Apocalypse* went into wide release, in 35 mm, with four minutes of end credits that ran over a series of explosions; apparently Coppola had given in on the ending. International distribution was to begin January 1, 1980. And whatever the critics said, audiences did seem eager to see *Apocalypse*. A week after the movie opened, it was packing in the crowds. Even though it was running at only three theaters, it earned grosses of $385,000 (/$620,000) in its first six days, and in Canada it set house records.

Coppola took a print to Russia for screening at the Moscow Film Festival. Black-market tickets went for 100 rubles ($160). When he got home, Coppola told reporters, "The reaction was very much the same as here. I think half the people thought it was a masterpiece, and half the people thought it was a piece of shit." The North Vietnamese who saw it were, he thought, favorably impressed. In fact, he thought the Cubans might like it, too; he even sent Castro a gift copy of the film.

There was one person involved in the making of *Apocalypse* who remained totally uninvolved in the hoopla surrounding the release. When the shoot was completed, Marlon Brando had gone back to his home in Tahiti. A few days after the film opened, writer Tommy Thompson flew to Tahiti, where Brando picked him up at the airport. "I wanted to say something nice to him," Thompson recalled, "so I said, 'Marlon, I saw you in *Apocalypse Now*. You were terrific.' "

Brando's only response was "Is that the one where I was bald?"

Now that *Apocalypse* was finally out, Coppola grew deeply involved in starting a studio with a grandiose new name, Omni Zoetrope. It could be like a little factory, he thought, "making one movie a month in the old style, and at an intelligent price. But I believe we'll be the first all-electronic movie studio in the world. We'll use the full magic of technology. And then there's the possibility of synthesizing images on computers, of having an electronic facsimile of Napoleon playing the life of Napoleon. It's almost do-able right now; it just takes the wisdom and the guts to invest in the future."

More immediately he announced that Zoetrope was already well into preproduction on *Hammett*, which would be directed by Wim Wenders. It would also be producing a feature called *King of White Lady*, directed by Monte (*Ride the Whirlwind*) Hellman.

Coppola seemed confident that he wouldn't have to sell everything he owned to pay for *Apocalypse*, even though he still owed United Artists $27 million. His film needed domestic rentals of more than $40 million just to break even on its release costs (which now included ads, distribution, lab costs, prints, and interest on bank loans). Because he hadn't made the film for a studio, he didn't have his usual deal (a percentage of the gross); he owned the negative, so his cut would come from the net. Television sales, on the other hand, would mainly go to Coppola, and he claimed he'd already rejected one network offer of $12 million (/$19 million). Even so, realistically Coppola thought that it might be five years before *Apocalypse* broke even.

Only one thing was clear: he was sure that he was no longer the man who'd made the *Godfathers*. That man had died in the Philippines. "I think that I'm a more interesting person," he said, "and I'm going to do more interesting films."

A former associate, however, speaking many years later,

observed, "In the jungle, Coppola decided he was a genius, and he never gave up this idea. It ruined him as an artist; it ruined his career."

Another friend of Coppola's (and Luddy's), transplanted British critic David Thomson, saw *Apocalypse* as the source of many of the filmmaker's later woes. Eight years after its release he and Lucy Gray wrote, "*Apocalypse* was Coppola's first disaster, not so much at the box office . . . but for what it did to its still youthful and unduly naive director. The experience brought great damage, for it took his confidence away without providing any replacement. He did not learn."

Chapter Fifteen

Secret Transmissions from Mars
(1979–1980)

AFTER FIVE YEARS of drudgery, madness, terror, and triumph, Coppola just wanted to forget *Apocalypse* and start something else. He certainly didn't want to waste energy worrying about how well it would do. "As long as this picture's not an artistic disgrace, I'm sure I could start all over again," he said. "I'm a well-known film director at a very affluent time."

He still had strong allies in the former United Artists management team that had backed *Apocalypse* and was now at Orion. In fact, Orion's new senior vice-president, Ernst Goldschmidt, was Coppola's foreign distribution executive on *Apocalypse*. By September 5, 1979, Coppola had an open-ended, nonexclusive deal granting Orion first refusal rights for six new pictures, including Monte Hellman's *King of White Lady* and *Tucker*. Coppola wanted Burt Reynolds for the title role in *Tucker*, but first he needed to put *Hammett* into production.

Hammett had been in development for five years, with Fred Roos at the controls. In 1975 Roos had read Joe Gores's fictionalized tale about Dashiell Hammett's early days in San Francisco just after he quit his job as a Pinkerton detective. Roos loved the novel as a straight detective story but also appreciated the notion that it followed Hammett's development as a writer. "It had this aspect of a man changing careers and getting mixed up," he said. "A man who'd been a detective suddenly teaches himself to become an artist, then gets confused between what's fiction and what's fact."

Nicolas Roeg was set to direct and wanted Frederic Forrest in the lead, but according to United Artists (which was then Zoetrope's distributor), Forrest wasn't famous enough to star in an $8 million movie. Zoetrope, UA, and Roeg spent months searching for another actor who'd be acceptable to them all, and finally Roeg pulled out.

While Roos was in Europe overseeing the Sardinian section of *The Black Stallion,* he saw *The American Friend,* a stylish film adaptation of two of Patricia Highsmith's Ripley thrillers by German director Wim Wenders; soon afterward he ran into Wenders himself in Australia. Subsequently Wenders and Coppola met in San Francisco, after which Tom Luddy screened several of Wenders's pictures for Coppola, after which Fred Roos dragged Orion executive Mike Medavoy to see *The American Friend* in Hollywood. Everyone agreed that Wenders would be perfect for the job of director of *Hammett.* He even proved to be a great Dashiell Hammett fan.

Wenders wanted to shoot the film in black and white like an old film noir and tell the story as a flashback with a voice-over narration. It took him and Joe Gores a month just to go through the book. "Wim wanted to know what goes on virtually every minute of every day covered by the story," Gores recalled. "This went on until we had a sort of script—then we started to rip *that* up."

As the script began to depart more and more sharply from the novel, the story line developed holes; as these were plugged, new plot problems developed. "Joe was working in odd territory, trying to please Wim, but he was off his own basic story," said Fred Roos. "It was a hybrid." And since, by now, Gores had pressing commitments to write three other screenplays, it was actually a relief when his contract with Zoetrope expired. A young writer named Tom Pope had submitted an unrelated script revealing a strong flair for period dialogue, and he was hired to take over the screenplay. Pope was a brash, clever intellectual who would get on well with Wenders, thought Roos.

In two months Pope and Wenders produced forty pages of a first draft. "Everyone said 'Great!' when we handed it in," Pope recalled, "except Francis. It was the single best story conference I've ever been in. What he said was brilliant. Francis had seen through to the truth about what was wrong. He was stunning." Pope and Wenders started all over again, and after four months another draft was finished. It was like a San Francisco version of *Chinatown,* heavy on period decor and municipal corruption.

Coppola got the notion to direct the script in the style of an old forties radio drama, tape it, and air it over KMPX-FM, his radio station, with playwright-actor Sam Shepard as Hammett, Gene Hackman as Hammett's partner, and Ronee Blakley (Wenders's new wife and a star of Robert Altman's *Nashville*) as Hammett's girl friend. Wenders wanted to cast Shepard in the film as well. "Sam would have been perfect," he remembered. "Actually, he was the only actor we tested who could type—not only write, but type."

The broadcast was a screenwriter's nightmare. Without pictures to show what was happening, the script made no sense at all. "It was interesting and revealing, but you couldn't follow the story," recalled Fred Roos. Pope bowed out, and Coppola brought in writer Dennis O'Flaherty. By now Wenders had been working on the project for a year and a half.

Just as O'Flaherty was starting on *Hammett, The Black Stallion* was ready to premiere. The film had ended up costing $4.8 million, double its original budget (though still quite cheap), and taken twice as long to shoot and edit as planned. The overtime was due partly to bad weather at the locations in Sardinia and Canada, but mostly to all the rewriting, rethinking, and improvising. Ballard had started with a five-hour rough cut and, with editor Robert Dalva (who'd headed the TV commercial division of Zoetrope from 1971 to 1975), had chiseled it down to two hours.

Although he was paid very little for the lengthy project, Ballard often felt lucky that it was a Coppola production. "In Hollywood they would have burned me alive in three days," he said, adding that as a producer Coppola was the best. "He has terrific artistic judgment, and he's supportive. He knows what it's like to be out there making a movie."

Coppola even went to bat for Ballard against his own father. During the scoring of the picture, several tiny alterations had been made to Carmine's score. Carmine exploded angrily, but Coppola supported Ballard, incurring his family's severest wrath.

In the end Coppola was pleased with the picture, especially the lengthy and beautiful island sequence during which the shipwrecked boy tames the horse. It was this sequence in the book that had given him the idea to hire Ballard in the first place.

Ballard finished editing the horse movie well before Coppola finished his jungle epic. The UA execs flew up to see it, but apparently they had gotten the two films confused—not hard to do considering the giant scale of Coppola's film and the relative lack of publicity on Ballard's. In any case, they expected to see *Apocalypse,* and when *The Black Stallion* came on, Ballard remembered, "they wanted to know why the hell they were looking at this damn horse. They wanted helicopters!"

Perhaps this explains why UA disliked *Stallion* so intensely, but the "bad" screening had an unlooked-for fringe benefit for Ballard. In a side bet attached to the complicated deal through which Coppola and United Artists had traded *Black Stallion* futures for *Apocalypse* completion money, UA had taken ownership of Ballard's contract, under which he was obligated to make two more pictures at the same lousy rates Coppola was paying him. Now, convinced that *Stallion* was a sure money-loser, UA declined to pick up on the low-rent option for the two remaining pictures. As for *Stallion,* the execs doubted the wisdom of releasing it; they would can it and take the loss as a tax write-off. Just as the film was heading for the shelf, Coppola convinced UA that it wouldn't cost anything to screen it at the New York Film Festival. It premiered there on October 12, 1979.

Immediately after its festival debut the film opened commercially in a single New York theater. The reviews were a mixture of pans and raves. The "neigh" sayers included *The New York Times, Time,* and Penelope Gilliatt in the *New Yorker,* but *Newsweek* loved it, as did many small-town papers as the release went wider. Pauline Kael got around to it later and loved it, too.

At the West Coast premiere a few weeks later Ballard and Coppola ran into each other at the theater entrance. Onlookers noticed the chilliness that had developed in their personal relationship. They shook hands formally, and Ballard invited Coppola to go on stage and "do a schtick." Coppola not only refused but had vanished by the end of the show; before leaving, he dutifully told reporters that he thought it was a "wonderful film."

Years later, at the release of his stunning *Never Cry Wolf,*

Ballard was asked if he'd ever work for Coppola again. "Only if I had the power to make decisions," he replied, "if I could do what I wanted to do, call all the shots, do all the casting, have creative control and financial control. All he would have would be the absolute right to say I'm full of shit."

Over the next five years *The Black Stallion* proved to be a slow-motion megahit, grossing no less than $60 million; if Coppola had been able to hang on to the ownership, he later estimated, he would have pocketed straight profits of $3 million during the first two years alone. Even Ballard eventually saw some profits from it, a rare occurrence in the movie business. It proved to be one of the most commercially successful debut feature films ever made and won its graying director the Los Angeles Film Critics' New Generation Award.

Apocalypse was also doing well. By the start of Christmas week 1979 it had grossed $33 million (/$47 million) domestically. Coppola still owed money on it, but he wasn't worried. "I've forgotten about *Apocalypse Now*," he declared happily. "My energy is going into the studio and my next film now." In fact, he was ready to storm Hollywood, like a victorious Caesar crossing the Rubicon. "It's going to be the survival of the fittest," he challenged, "and the long-established studios will be brought down."

He'd already begun negotiations to buy the 8.7-acre Hollywood General Studios lot. Now that he was confident *Apocalypse* wouldn't bankrupt him, he offered a down payment of $1 million. Simultaneously, he opened a business flirtation with Yugoslavian director Dušan Makavejev to do a picture for Omni Zoetrope and began looking for a project for Caleb Deschanel (cinematographer on *The Black Stallion*) to direct as well.

Not everybody was all that anxious to work for Coppola. People remembered his fits of fury during *Apocalypse*, and his reputation for emotional ups and downs was beginning to become bothersome. Furthermore, by early December horror stories about the constant changes in the *Hammett* script were making the rounds. Apparently nobody working on a Coppola production could expect full personal expression of his or her art; Coppola alone had that power. "Whether he's controlling you for good or bad," an ex-Zoetrope writer said, "he's still controlling you. I don't know many writers who are willing to work in that kind of manipulative environment."

By the end of the year Coppola seemed to have succeeded in buying Hollywood General Studios for $5.6 million. Built in 1919 as Jasper Hollywood Studio, it had a glorious history. Harold Lloyd had made *Safety Last* there, and Howard Hughes had shot *Hell's Angels* (with Jean Harlow) on the site in 1927. Renamed General Service Studios in the 1930's, it had been the stomping grounds of Mae West, Bing Crosby, and Gary Cooper. It was even the site of the film Coppola called "my all-time favorite movie," Alexander Korda's *The Thief of Bagdad*. After that it had changed ownership many times, until James and George Nasser bought it in 1947 for $2.5 million (an enormous sum at the time) and changed its name to Hollywood General. It remained in the Nassers' hands until 1976, when an entity called Esquire Holding Company (consisting of Glen Speidel and Ellison Miles) bought it.

As Coppola was closing the deal, with a new loan obtained from a banker friend of sister Talia, Esquire still owed a $2.6 million mortgage on the lot, at a favorable 8 percent interest. Esquire was glad to let him pick up the mortgage, even though the prime rate had now shot up to 12 percent; in exchange, Speidel was promised $1.89 million in cash, or 1,200 shares of Hollywood General stock, plus a new Mercedes Benz 450SL as a bonus. (His partner, Ellison Miles, would get his share in straight cash.) Unfortunately Esquire never told the Nasser brothers that Coppola would be taking over the Esquire mortgage.

Just after New Year's 1980 Coppola planted a palm tree on the studio grounds to celebrate what he thought was his successful acquisition of the lot, which he renamed Omni Zoetrope Studios. It wasn't a giant studio, but it was big enough to have streets, lanes, and squares all around the back lot. Naming those streets was more fun than naming kittens. Coppola decreed Akira Kurosawa Avenue, Sergei Eisenstein Park, Raoul Walsh Alley, and Alexander Korda Boulevard. He would continue to live in Napa Valley, he explained. Northern California would be the think tank, the research and development department, for Zoetrope. But the physical moviemaking would now be done in Hollywood.

Lucas had warned him about moving his operations into the heart of the Hollywood beast. "Being down there, you're just asking for trouble," he said, "because you're trying to change a system that will never change. Here, we don't change a system, because there is no system." Comparing his still-small Lucasfilm with Coppola's ambitious new studio, he observed, "I'll have mine, and it will take a lot longer to get it built, but I don't think it's ever going to collapse out from under me."

Coppola, however, was evidently sure his gambles would all pay off. After all, although *Apocalypse* did not sweep the Golden Globes the way *Godfather II* had, it did pick up three top awards: Best Director, Best Score (Carmine and Francis Coppola), and Best Supporting Actor (Robert Duvall).

The awards may have brightened Coppola's mood, but the bottom-line numbers were less rosy. While *Apocalypse* was doing decent business, its domestic rentals (not grosses) now amounted to only $28 million. Furthermore, its domestic re-lease costs were quite high—at least $41 million, including $31 million in negative costs, $9 million for the domestic ad cam-paign (an all-time high), and an unknown amount (probably $1 million or so) for odds and ends like print costs and interest. The break-even point was still far away.

The financial situation could have been worse. Foreign rentals were still to come, the TV rights were still unsold, and Coppola was sure that people would want to see his film more than once and for years to come. Years later, in a press handout for *Rumble Fish,* Coppola claimed that *Apocalypse* had re-couped its costs within six months of release; it's not impossi-ble, though it seems unlikely. Three and a half years after its release, in an article looking back at the "Big Buck Era" in Hollywood, *Weekly Variety* noted that total domestic rentals of the film were still merely $37.3 million, which just about covered the negative cost, but, of course, neither foreign in-come nor TV sales were included. Yet again, as Mark Twain once noted, there are "lies, damned lies, and statistics." If he'd lived in Hollywood, he might have added a fourth (and higher) level of falsehood: film accounting.

Meanwhile, Dennis O'Flaherty was still slugging it out on the script for *Hammett*. In all, he wrote seven drafts in eight months. Coppola told O'Flaherty that he wanted the script to center on the conflict between appearance and reality, and O'Flaherty decided to deemphasize the crime story, to keep the viewer from getting too involved in the detective movie aspects of the film. "What I did in the first draft was to make it almost expressionistic, and that seemed to do the trick," he recalled.

Orion executives, who had loved Tom Pope's earlier, realist script, were distinctly uncomfortable with the new "expressionist" version. By now, however, they were committed to the project. "They know who they're dealing with," O'Flaherty explained. "Francis. Francis isn't some kind of artsy loony who's going to come in with something that won't play. Francis is the master of film entertainment right now, so they know they're not getting into areas they won't find acceptable." Famous last words.

Nonetheless, O'Flaherty decided to write yet another draft, departing even more radically from a normal crime story into a surrealistic, action-packed tale with an impenetrable conspiracy and an unsolvable mystery. Nobody liked this new version, and by now the film's start date was only three months away.

Dean Tavoularis and his staff had already spent three months scouting locations in Los Angeles and San Francisco, and designing sets to the tune of a $700,000 art budget. Tavoularis wanted to re-create San Francisco's Chinatown, 1928, working from period photographs; Wenders preferred the look of pre-earthquake Chinatown, the tong war period around 1903. Tavoularis decided to synthesize the two and build "a city within the city." He also spent an additional quarter of a million dollars for a set of Hammett's rooming house, including interiors, exteriors, staircases inside and out, two complete apartments, and a panoramic window view of San Francisco in 1928.

The project had taken so long that Sam Shepard had bowed out, but meantime Frederic Forrest had gone from a nonentity to an up-and-coming star. Word of Forrest's skillful handling of his *Apocalypse* role had landed him the sexy male lead opposite Bette Midler in *The Rose,* for which he garnered an Oscar nomination. Finally he was big enough to suit the studio executives. Wenders wholeheartedly agreed, and Zoetrope signed Forrest to play Dashiell Hammett.

O'Flaherty finished another draft just a week before the shoot began, and Orion executive Gabe Sumner was brought in to do a last-minute polish.

The shoot began on February 4, 1980, in San Francisco.

Hollywood General wasn't available yet; besides, the story was set in San Francisco.

In the weeks that followed, it became clear just how far from final the Hollywood General deal really was. The Nasser brothers still held the mortgage and they didn't go for the idea of Coppola's picking it up. In fact, they threatened an open auction on the property unless somebody (they didn't care who) paid off the mortgage on the spot. Two minutes before the court closed on February 15, the California Supreme Court placed a stay on the Nassers' auction. When a reporter asked a Zoetrope spokesman what was going on, he replied, "To be frank, we're in the throes of trying to figure it out."

"Losing the studio is unthinkable," Coppola declared. "It's a worthwhile dream." Days later Coppola finally succeeded in buying the dream by taking a second mortgage and upgrading the original mortgage to 12 percent; he also paid a $500,000 fee to James Nasser. Still, since he expected to use the studio as a rental facility, he expected it would eventually pay for itself.

Coppola declared himself artistic director and signed up Robert Spiotta (who'd played Stanley Kowalski for him at Hofstra, and had been working as an oil executive) to be president and chief executive officer. They would be hiring fifteen hundred people, Coppola said, and in addition to the large down payment he'd already made and the two elephantine mortgage payments that were due immediately, he'd be spending $5 million to modernize the facility.

Coppola signed Dennis O'Flaherty, Dennis Klein, and William Bowers as staff writers. Lucy Fisher, a hotshot from Twentieth Century-Fox, joined as head of production, along with Dean Tavoularis (head of art and design), Fred Roos (commissar of talent), Jennifer Schull (casting head), and Walter Murch (head of the sound department). Rudi Fehr, the veteran editor with whom Coppola had worked on *Finian, Rain People,* and *Apocalypse,* had been forced into retirement by Warner-Seven at age sixty-five; Coppola hired him as editing consultant. In addition, Coppola rewarded Tom Luddy for all those private screenings and public discoveries by making him Zoetrope's head of special projects.

In short order, Coppola was bubbling over with visionary plans. He held a lavish press conference and luncheon for those abominable journalists to announce the official formation of Zoetrope Studios.

Coppola talked about art. The studio would enable him to do special effects far more easily, he explained, and he'd be able to use the sound stages to simulate locations. Hollywood General had six parks to play in, as well as "a complete, fully integrated movie studio with the best features of the studios of the thirties and forties." These included nine sound stages, thirty-four editing rooms, lots of projection rooms and offices, and a special effects shop. Furthermore, Coppola meant to tear out one parking lot to install three more parks. He spoke fervently of running "a studio that is civilized, pro-artistic, makes sense—and also makes money. From the idea through the writing, casting, acting, and post-production, it will be an all-resident motion picture production company, a team, a happy artistic community."

Coppola called the studio his "magical illusion device." It was the best toy he'd ever bought.

Spiotta talked about money. Zoetrope would have resources of $50 million, he said, and would make six to eight movies a year, each budgeted around $7.5 million (/$11 million). The Chase Manhattan Bank would supply half the financing, up to $25 million; the rest would come from distributors, including Orion and the foreign distributors. Orion would also guarantee completion money for all Zoetrope projects that it would distribute. *Apocalypse*, he added, had now earned $69 million in rentals, including Europe (where it was doing quite well). Despite high additional costs for the foreign release (an ad campaign, subtitled prints, more distributor fees), it was now only $26 million away from breaking even.

Coppola was back in negotiations with MGM over a project he'd been eyeing for a year, *One from the Heart*. Other new additions to Zoetrope's upcoming film list included *The Escape Artist* (to be directed by Caleb Deschanel), *Photoplay* (another rock opera, this one starring Sting and Diane Lane, with Martha Coolidge directing), and *The Black Stallion Returns* (which Bob Dalva would direct). All but *Stallion II* would be Orion releases through Warners (which had by now dropped the "Seven Arts" from its name).

Coppola had bought back Carroll Ballard's two-picture contract from United Artists, and now he announced that Bal-

lard would start another children's film, this one based on a
book that Ballard loved: *The Secret Garden*. Ballard had only
one problem with the plan: He suddenly found himself owing
Zoetrope two more pictures, for the same slave wages specified in his old UA contract. He asked for a raise and a bit more
money to do *Secret Garden*. Zoetrope promptly fired him.

At the same time Luddy, head of special projects, was in
the process of acquiring a project that truly was special: French
director Abel Gance's lost silent era masterpiece, *Napoleon*.
Gance had been a seminal director, given to wildly adventur-
ous camera movements and techniques that were decades ahead
of their time. He developed the dolly shot at the same time as
D. W. Griffith, used rapid editing for montage before the early
Soviet filmmakers, and could make claim to having invented
superimpositions, the split screen, the hand-held camera, and
the wide screen as well. For the grand finale of his five-hour
epic, *Napoleon,* in 1927, the curtains had opened out to reveal
a giant screen covered with a triptych of images, shown with a
synchronized triple-projector process called Polyvision that
predated the similar Cinerama process by thirty years.

Unfortunately, like his American contemporary D. W.
Griffith, Gance had gone out of style, which in his case led to
the dismantling of *Napoleon*. In the early 1950s British film
historian Kevin Brownlow (then fourteen) had bought a snip-
pet of the film. "Those two reels changed my life," he said. "I
fell in love with the picture. It seemed to prove that the cinema was capable of anything." He realized that his home-movie
print was merely a fragment of the complete film and decided
that reconstructing the whole movie would be his life's work.
Eventually he devoted almost thirty years to the labor of love.
By 1970 Brownlow had obtained all but twenty minutes of the
original. Two years later he was able to reconstruct the three-
screen climax.

On October 22, 1972, three days before Gance's eighty-
third birthday, a four-hour sound version called *Bonaparte and
the Revolution* was screened during the San Francisco Film
Festival's Homage to Abel Gance. In 1937 Gance had added a
spoken sound track to several sequences (he and Antonin Ar-
taud spoke the words for their original roles of St.-Just and
Marat), and incorporated a musical sound track. In 1972 the
still-vigorous Gance had helped with the restoration process.

The festival audience fell in love with the film, but an even better version was screened, secretly, a few weeks later. With Luddy's help, Geoff Hansen, programmer for the Avenue Theater, a historic old movie house in the outlying Excelsior district of San Francisco, had gotten hold of Brownlow's full-length silent print. Furthermore, he proposed to show it with live accompaniment. A portion of composer Arthur Honegger's original score for the film had been found; Robert Vaughn, the best silent movie organist in town, would play it on the theater's vintage Wurlitzer. Ace projectionist-engineer Chris Reyna (long the head projectionist at the Pacific Film Archive) installed a custom-made three-projector system just to show the finale.

For legal reasons, Hansen couldn't advertise the screening, so he started a round of telephone tag among local film buffs. The strategy worked. The theater was packed with patrons; every seat was filled, and there were fans sitting in the aisles and even standing behind the last row of chairs. With only three days' preparation Bob Vaughn outdid himself at the organ, playing what remained of the wonderful score; for the parts where there was no score, he improvised brilliantly, as he'd learned to do as a professional theater organist back in the silent movie era. When the curtains opened at the start of the final triptych, the entire audience leapt out of their seats, swept away with delight; then they jumped on top of their seats. Surely, few movie audiences had expressed their enthusiasm so emphatically since the silent era itself.

Although Coppola wasn't present at the Avenue Theater screening, Luddy, who was, filled him in about this astonishing movie and its ecstatic reception. Meanwhile, Brownlow continued working on the restoration, and by the time Coppola announced his acquisition of Hollywood General, Brownlow had virtually completed his project. In fact, a version was screened at the 1979 Telluride Film Festival. Since none of the theaters in Telluride was large enough to accommodate the triptych, it was screened outdoors on a near-freezing Colorado night; viewers sat on the grass, huddled under blankets, and adored every minute of it.

At Luddy's urging, Coppola decided that Zoetrope would distribute *Napoleon*. He announced that he'd already commissioned his father to write a new orchestral score for it and to conduct a full orchestra at the special, gala screenings. Carmine promised he'd write only one hour of original music and cop the rest from bits of Beethoven and Bach ("I steal only from the best," he commented), but when word reached San Francisco, not everyone was delighted. Sure, it was good news that *Napoleon* would reach a wide audience, but some people who'd heard the modernist Honegger score thought that Carmine simply wasn't in the same league. (In fact, after hearing Carmine's score, Ken Brownlow maintained a tactful British silence but swiftly commissioned Carl Davis to write a separate score for the European version, which he still controlled.)

Coppola had returned to his role as patron of the arts, and in recognition, California Governor Jerry Brown named him to the California Arts Council for two years, as a compromise candidate to replace Jane Fonda, whose nomination had been rejected by the state legislature on political grounds. It wasn't a hard job; it basically consisted of dispensing grants. Fonda was delighted by Brown's choice, claiming that she had suggested Coppola in the first place.

Coppola was now in a position to hobnob with a governor who considered himself on the political fast track. Brown's 1976 run for the Democratic presidential nomination had nearly derailed Jimmy Carter, who was now running as the incumbent. When Brown decided to run for President again, Francis and Augie agreed to create four television spots for his primary campaign.

A San Francisco filmmaker-cartoonist (and *City* magazine alumnus) named Ernie Fosselius ended up doing a lot of the work on the project. A few years earlier Fosselius had made a short, side-splitting parody of *Star Wars*, called *Hardware Wars*. More recently he'd completed *Pork Lips Now*, centering on a Chinatown butcher and satirizing the media hype that surrounded *Apocalypse*. Coppola had taken it badly, assuming "pork lips" referred to his physical appearance. Still, one evening Fosselius got a phone call at his unlisted home number. To his utter disbelief, Francis Coppola was on the line.

Initially Coppola made no mention of *Pork Lips Now*, although some months later he snapped at Fosselius, "Well, I took mine better than Lucas took his." Instead, he issued a royal summons: Fosselius would report, within an hour, to Coppola's house to work on the Brown campaign.

Fosselius couldn't resist. When he showed up, he found himself surrounded by political heavies, including the governor himself. "Hey, here's Ernie," said Coppola. "He's gonna do the spots for us." It was news to Fosselius, but he decided he'd stick around for a while and see what came next.

First Coppola made everybody sit down and watch *Mr. Smith Goes to Washington* several times. Apparently he was thinking of presenting the Jesuit-educated, Zen-influenced Jerry Brown as Jimmy Stewart, the old-timey, plainspoken midwesterner confronting the corrupt professional pols.

"It was just totally bizarre," Fosselius recalled. "The very next morning I found myself standing on the lawn of the State Capitol in Sacramento." Fosselius set to work on the spots, reediting video footage of speeches Brown had made. "We had to literally edit syllables together to make Jerry Brown sound concise," he said. "I finally realized this was Coppola's form of revenge for *Pork Lips Now*."

Brown's campaign manager loved the spots so much an even larger project was set in motion. Coppola would go to Madison, Wisconsin, along with Brown, on March 28, just before the April primary, to stage a live television show to be titled *The Shape of Things to Come*. "I have no idea what he's going to do," said one Brown staffer. "All I know is that Coppola intends this thing to be one of the collector's items of his career."

Coppola and company spent a scant two weeks planning. Then they moved in on Madison like an invading army—requisitioning offices, commandeering telephones, and altering local scenery. During a nighttime power test of the searchlights, as the camera helicopter flew over, one townsperson was heard to yell, "Holy shit, Francis is going to napalm us!" Elderly residents of a nearby nursing home looked out their windows and were certain the capitol had been seized by Russians or Aliens.

Coppola had never done live TV before, but he arrived a mere sixty hours prior to the telecast with Bill Graham, scientist Dr. Zoltan Tarczy-Harnock, Caleb Deschanel, Dean Tavoularis, son Gio, and assorted staffers in tow. Coppola spent his first day in Madison on the lecture circuit, introducing Brown to local civic groups and the press, who seemed much more interested in the filmmaker than the politician. Coppola waxed eloquent on the subject of the high tech gadgetry he'd brought for the show. He was going to use a new high-resolution video system that Zoetrope's researchers were developing, with five times the clarity of regular television. In addition, the show was to use seven cameras, five searchlights, eight carbon arc spotlights, a $450,000 video projector, twenty-four walkie-talkies, three camera lifts, two video control trucks, and one helicopter, not to mention three steel drums (for fires to keep the crowds warm) and three thousand cups of chicken soup.

Coppola's plan called for Governor Brown to stand alone on a bare stage; behind him, using an electronic chromakey process, Coppola would create a montage of symbolic images to reinforce Brown's speech. It was a technique he'd picked up from *Our Hitler*. The indoor events would be shown to the crowd outside on a twelve-by-twenty-foot Eidophor color television projection screen.

The Brown show would be the first trial run of Coppola's latest technotoys. Rising film and lab costs were propelling many filmmakers toward electronic alternatives to celluloid. Coppola had already experimented with video during the editing of *Apocalypse*. Now, he explained, he was spending 50 percent of Zoetrope's budget on research and development. His immediate plans included feeding all budget information, script changes, and set designs for Zoetrope productions into a central computerized memory bank. "All films will be made electronically in five years," he declared. "I want to make film electronically in a year and a half. Life is not all diodes and semi-conductors, but—"

"But it will be," snapped Dr. Zoltan Tarczy-Harnock.

The next day *The Shape of Things to Come* came, and went, and did nothing positive for either Coppola's reputation or Brown's campaign. "It was as spectacular a failure as any of his awesome film successes," reported *Variety*. "Everything that could go wrong, did."

Airtime was 7:00 P.M. A crowd of three thousand locals showed up; they seemed coolly polite, curious. Bill Graham warmed them up as best he could. Just before airtime Coppola showed up, and Graham introduced him to the crowd. He murmured cryptically about "media piracy" and things "not going as planned." Then Brown came out, and the show began. A better way of putting it, as one reporter did, might be that Coppola's electronic event began collapsing like a house of cards. Brown's microphones wouldn't work; then they did work, but the camera helicopter drowned him out. The chroma-key process went utterly awry, but in any case Coppola's montage of images got so wildly out of sync with Brown's speech that while Brown railed about city slums, the electronic backdrop was showing cows in a meadow. It turned into a hoot, ending with a fractured finale in which Brown recited the Pledge of Allegiance amid a botched triple-image blur of himself live, himself on the giant TV, and the American flag.

Afterward Brown asked one of his staffers how he'd looked on TV. The staffer thought about it for a second, and answered that he'd looked like Claude Rains in *The Invisible Man.*

Coppola was so shell-shocked (or was it future-shocked?) he seemed to have lost his English. "For me, it was a disaster, but I think he got what he wanted," Coppola commented, and then turned around and told Brown, "You got what you needed, but I didn't get what I wanted."

Four days later Jerry Brown received 12 percent of the Wisconsin vote and withdrew his candidacy. On the bright side, he didn't try to fire Coppola from the California Arts Council. Years later Coppola laughed about it. "It was one of the most hilarious spectacles I have ever seen," he recalled. "It looked as if [Brown] were receiving secret transmissions from Mars!"

There was some consolation a few weeks later, when *Apocalypse Now* received two Oscars, one for Vittorio Storaro's cinematography and another for Walter Murch's sound. But it was a far cry from the *Godfather* days.

Meanwhile, things were going very badly for Wim Wenders, who was trying to shoot *Hammett.* Although, theoretically, he had a final script (it was actually number twelve), plus scores of outlines, treatments, and drafts written over the course of four years by Joe Gores, Tom Pope, and Dennis O'Flaherty, rewriting continued nonstop during the ten-week shoot, with addition and subtraction of scenes, locations, and characters. Coppola himself spent two weekends rewriting the ending. Dennis Jakob, who had helped Coppola with the ending for *Apocalypse* (such as it was), spent two weeks on the *Hammett* set, cutting scenes, trying to come up with an ending, and freely dispensing comments and criticism.

Four weeks before the end of the shoot, a brand-new ma-

jor character was written into the script, a femme fatale to be
played by Mrs. Wenders, Ronee Blakley (who'd been introduced to Wenders by Dennis Hopper). The schedule was
lengthened to eleven weeks to provide time for reshoots and
more work on the ending.

At the end of the tenth week, production manager Bob
Huddleston made a surprise announcement: Zoetrope was
pulling the plug. Filming was halted indefinitely. Wenders
himself had been notified only a day earlier. Coppola wanted
him to put together a rough cut from the 90 percent he'd shot.
When they all looked at it, they'd decide what to do next. After
five years of development *Hammett* was about to start postproduction without ever having finished shooting. To those
unfamiliar with Coppola's past, it may have seemed like some
awful "first" in movie history, but Coppola was probably
thinking of how much it had helped when he'd stopped off to
assemble the first rough cut of *The Godfather* before he went
on to finish the shoot in Sicily.

Roos figured that since they'd have to do a lot of second-
unit shooting anyway, they might as well shoot the ending at
the same time, after analyzing the existing footage to discover
what the ending of the story ought to be. Even Wenders told
himself there was logic in the decision. "A lot of things came
late, fell into place only during the shooting," he said. Things
like the plot, he meant.

The mild-mannered Wenders didn't recognize the pattern;
he blamed himself. "Francis has been much more of a colleague than a producer," he continued. "He gave me a lot of
room and a great opportunity. I was relieved to stop. I was so
exhausted at the end of the tenth week I wasn't at my best
any more."

After several weeks of work on the rough cut, Wenders
brought it to San Francisco. Coppola looked at it, and he postponed the continuation of the shoot even further, to mid-August
1980. Now he wanted Wenders to go directly to the fine cut of
the nine-tenths he'd shot.

Coppola had a new project of his own. Instead of starting
work on the script for *Tucker,* he'd signed with David Begelman, president of MGM, to produce and direct *One from the
Heart.* It was the same film he'd turned down a year earlier.
The difference was that this time Coppola would own the project and was going to use the same electronic technology that

had bombed in Madison. He saw that debacle as only a temporary setback; the future of filmmaking was definitely electronic.

"[*One from the Heart*] is not on the scale of *Apocalypse Now*," he commented, "but it will be very strong musically, very funny, and I hope very moving."

Coppola probably assumed that he could work on the *Tucker* screenplay while he was knocking off *Heart*. He planned to shoot it in two weeks, edit it in two weeks, and complete postproduction in just two more. He told his associates that he saw the film as a modest project, "like a student film on a studio scale," that would allow the members of his new filmmaking family to get acquainted and familiarize themselves with the new technology.

Coppola had several other balls in the air. He was eager to turn Gay Talese's study of middle-class marital infidelities, *Thy Neighbor's Wife*, into a film; but UA owned the property, and while UA's management loved the idea of having Coppola film it, they wouldn't even consider selling it to Zoetrope and risking another Apocalyptic cofinancing deal.

One Zoetrope film project that was moving forward swiftly was *The Escape Artist*. Stephen Zito's screenplay had been around since 1969. Coppola bought it and put Melissa Mathison to work rewriting the script for Caleb Deschanel to direct.

Griffin O'Neal, the wild young son of actor Ryan O'Neal, won the lead over a hundred other young actors. And although Coppola wanted Raul Julia to star in his own *One from the Heart*, the *Escape Artist* shoot was expected to run only two months; it wouldn't conflict with Coppola's own film, and he unselfishly suggested Julia for the bad guy. Deschanel needed an old-time small-town look; he discovered just the right locations in Cleveland, Ohio, and shooting began there on July 1.

Despite *The Escape Artist*, Zoetrope's most active function at the moment seemed to be distribution. On July 16 Tom Luddy announced that Coppola was buying U.S. rights to *Sauve Qui Peut la Vie* (*Every Man for Himself*), French filmmaker Jean-Luc Godard's first feature film in eight years. Zoetrope would release it through New Yorker Films, a small East Coast distributor known for handling art films with special care. Coppola's real motivation was his desire to produce Godard's first American film, *The Story*.

In addition, a new Kurosawa film was about to become

another Zoetrope special project. Back when Coppola had been struggling over the *Apocalypse* edit, he and George Lucas had gotten word that the great Japanese filmmaker, seventy-year-old Akira Kurosawa, was having trouble raising $7.5 million he needed to shoot *Kagemusha,* his twenty-seventh film. Even though Kurosawa's *Dersu Uzala* had won the Oscar for Best Foreign Film just a few years earlier, the executives at Toho, his home studio, considered *Kagemusha* impossibly expensive. Its budget was higher than any Japanese film ever made, even though by Hollywood standards it was fairly cheap. In any case, they said, Kurosawa was too old to keep directing. "It was a tragedy," George Lucas said. "It was like telling Michelangelo, 'All right, you're 70 and we're not letting you paint any more.' "

For two months Coppola and George Lucas badgered Alan Ladd, Jr., head of Twentieth Century-Fox, to provide Kurosawa with front money by buying the international distribution rights in advance. The Fox executives finally agreed, but only if Coppola and Lucas would serve as executive producers. This was a coup for everyone involved; *Kagemusha* would be the first Japanese film ever released worldwide by a major American studio.

As executive producer for a director of Kurosawa's exalted stature, Coppola was not even tempted to piss in the pot; his and Lucas's primary function lay in their lending their names to the project and, if necessary, smoothing out any difficulties. But there weren't any difficulties. Unlike his ostensible boss, Kurosawa had done all his homework in the preproduction period, often going so far as to paint and sketch complete storyboards, scenery, and costumes. Editing was a snap; Kurosawa worked on an ancient, tiny, old-fashioned Moviola and finished quickly.

By May 1980 *Kagemusha* was complete; Kurosawa had actually brought it in for $6.5 million (/$9 million), a million less than its estimated budget. When *Kagemusha* opened, it was hailed as a masterpiece, although some critics found it colder than any of Kurosawa's earlier works.*

---

*Later, Coppola and Kurosawa costarred in Japanese television commercials for Suntory whisky. Coppola and Lucas subsequently lent their names and clout to Paul Schrader for his Japanese-location production of *Mishima,* on which they served as executive producers.

Late in July *Hammett* returned to the forefront of Coppola's attention; Wenders screened the latest cut for him, complete with a fully mixed sound track and an elaborate storyboard for a new ending. Coppola didn't like it at all. Partly at the suggestion of editing consultant Rudi Fehr, he postponed the completion of the film yet again, to March 1981, and hired yet another writer, best-selling mystery novelist Ross Thomas, to create a whole new script sandwiched around the nine-tenths of the film that was already finished. Could he have been thinking of *The Terror*?

Wenders was at the end of his rope. His marriage with Blakley had broken up; his work on *Hammett* was obviously at an end. He left the country in despair. Although Zoetrope's official stance was that Wenders would complete the picture when the new script was ready and that he and Coppola were still good friends, everyone knew that Coppola had fired him; one published report claimed that Coppola had decided to direct the film himself.

Reactions to the firing among Zoetrope staffers were mixed; some thought Coppola had to be right, because he was always right. "Francis is erratic, but he's *very* smart," said Stanton Kaye, an independent filmmaker who was at the time writing a script for Coppola. Others were increasingly resentful about Coppola's interference in their own departments and were not surprised that Coppola had refused to let Wim Wenders make a Wim Wenders movie.

"He's more intrusive in the creative process than Zanuck or Thalberg ever dreamed of being," a former employee told *Newsweek*.

Don Guest, who'd been coproducing the film with Fred Roos and old Hofstra buddy Ronald Colby, said, "Wim genuinely tried to give Francis what he wanted, but they're two different visions. One artist shouldn't try to supervise another artist's work."

Frederic Forrest was more critical. "Once Francis had hired someone to do the picture," he said, "he should have let him get on with it. I think he actually wanted to do that, but Francis is like a football player on the bench. He's got to be in it."

Robert Spiotta, head of Zoetrope, saw it Coppola's way: "Wenders didn't stick to the script he was given. I think Francis did feel betrayed by that."

The execs at Orion were the ones who really felt betrayed. They'd bought into a stylish, low-budget mystery movie, and it had turned into an expensive artistic swamp. They'd already put up $10 million ($1 million over the original budget), but instead of giving them a movie, Coppola was now talking about rethinking, rewriting, and reshooting as much as half the material, at a cost of $2.5 million more. They refused to come up with the extra funds, telling Coppola it was his problem now.

Coppola decided to put *Hammett* on the shelf. He was under contract to make *One from the Heart*, a sweet little romance that shouldn't take him much time at all. The shutdown of *Hammett* was actually convenient since it freed Frederic Forrest to play the lead in the romance, and freed sound stages for the *Heart* shoot.

Back in Europe, Wenders explained he'd taken a leave of absence to make two other films: *Lightning over Water* (a documentary portrait of dying filmmaker Nicholas Ray) and *The State of Things* (a fictional film about filmmaking and, perhaps, a sad bit of wordplay on Coppola's *Shape of Things*). *The State of Things* centers on the suffering of a European director who is making a film for a fearful, neurotic American movie mogul, who is, in turn, being pursued by sinister people to whom he owes money. Roger Corman, Coppola's old mentor, plays a small role, and Allen Garfield (a member of Coppola's informal acting company) plays the mogul. Garfield swears he wasn't playing Coppola, and Coppola's name is never mentioned. Nonetheless, this film is still required viewing for anyone looking for the inside line on directors with three names.

Chapter Sixteen

One from the Heart:
Boy Genius Goes Hollywood
(1980–1981)

IT WAS INDIAN summer in San Francisco—warm, sunshiny, fragrant, and soft. Coppola had every reason to be feeling good. *Apocalypse* was still making money. Omni Zoetrope was open for business. He had solved the worst of the *Hammett* problems, if only by putting the film in a closet. He was ready to do something of his own: *One from the Heart*.

To celebrate the kickoff of preproduction, he invited 350 people (the entire Zoetrope staff, plus all the people he'd hired for the picture) to a giant barbecue at his Rutherford vineyard in September 1980. Toasting marshmallows over the fire, surrounded by his friends and associates, Coppola was in heaven. "Something incredibly great," he said, "is about to happen!"

Then he packed his bags and headed for Hollywood, along with Ellie and the kids. "We travel together like a circus family," noted the long-suffering but ever-loyal Eleanor, "with Francis on the tightrope and the rest of us holding the ropes."

Coppola also brought brother Augie with him, to set up and administer a student internship program at Zoetrope through California's Adopt-a-School program. Early in the school year Francis personally led the entire student body of nearby Bancroft Junior High on a tour of the studio—a fat, rumpled Pied Piper, tootling an ebullient account of Zoetrope's wonders with nine hundred kids trailing after him.

When he invited the teenagers to apply for an after-school program, sixty-five of them responded; about half that number passed the auditions. Each intern apprenticed with a Zoetrope employee working in a field that matched the kid's special talent: acting, dancing, writing, sound, or camera. Sometimes the kids would just stand around and watch, but a few lucky ones actually got to help.

For his own apprentice, Coppola chose a tiny, smart-talking twelve-year-old named Michael Cohen, with blond hair, broken wire-rim glasses, and a New York accent. When shooting began on *One from the Heart,* Cohen got to sit with Coppola in the video van. "We watch the tapes," he said, "and he asks me what I think, and I tell him." What was the most important thing he learned? "To be tactful. I learned it's very important not to say the wrong thing." It was Basic Zoetrope Lesson One, as any number of staffers could confirm.

Coppola had great forward-looking plans for *One from the Heart* and great backward-looking ambitions for Zoetrope. He wanted his studio to make old-fashioned movies, he said, like the swashbucklers and fantasies he'd loved as a child. "They're the kind of movies we think people have been yearning to see," agreed production head Lucy Fisher. "People are sick of watching actors walking around New York talking about their personal relationships."

Coppola wanted to do a love story, but not in the usual way. "Like everyone else," he said, "I had had an experience similar to the one in *One from the Heart.* Everyone knows that sort of situation is no laughing matter, and that love can kill." *One from the Heart,* a love story *cum* musical *cum* fantasy, would combine several of the classical genres, but at the same time it would be a radical reinvention of the old forms. How could a Coppola movie be anything less?

Given his everything-old-is-new-again theme, he was particularly overjoyed when veteran hoofer Gene Kelly (who starred in and codirected the great 1952 musical *Singin' in the Rain*) agreed to head Zoetrope's musical division and consult on the dances in *One from the Heart.* Kelly and Coppola had met, briefly, at Twentieth Century-Fox in 1969, when Kelly was directing *Hello, Dolly!* and Coppola was writing *Patton* two doors down the hall. When Coppola invited him out to Zoetrope, Kelly took one look at the operation and signed on instantly. "We're going to use color the way *An American in Paris* did," Kelly said enthusiastically. "We're going to *paint* the picture."

To provide the cinematic brushstrokes, Coppola turned to Vittorio Storaro, who, despite the *Apocalypse* apocalypse, agreed to shoot *One from the Heart*. However, in the face of legal restrictions on foreign film personnel and a protest by the IATSE cameramen's Local 659, Storaro could not be credited officially as director of photography; it was agreed that a local cameraman would receive that honor. Coppola also hired Tom Waits to write nine songs and Crystal Gayle to help sing them.

Then, inspired, perhaps, by Kelly's presence, he announced that Betty Comden and Adolph Green (who wrote *Singin' in the Rain* and *The Band Wagon*) would be coming to work with him on the *Tucker* film, which had now turned into the *Tucker* musical. It would be "a dark kind of piece . . . a sort of Brechtian musical," he said. Leonard Bernstein agreed to write the music, and all four—Comden, Green, Bernstein and Coppola—met for a weeklong planning session at the Rutherford vineyard.

Unfortunately Coppola couldn't decide which of his thousand and one ideas for the project he should pursue. "But, Francis," Bernstein remonstrated in the middle of a memorable Coppola brainstorm, "we can't just work on this in the jungle, like *Apocalypse Now*. You have to decide what it's going to be."

It was the hardest thing Bernstein could have asked of him. Coppola put the film on a back burner until he had an answer; in any case, he had prior commitments to too many other films.

He hired Dennis Klein to direct his own script, *Sex and Violence*, and encouraged Klein to turn it into a musical; he picked up several other scripts by young filmmakers as well. Finally, to top it all off, he summoned seventy-two-year-old veteran British director Michael Powell, who had directed *The Red Shoes*, to establish himself as Zoetrope's senior artist in residence.

It was not a good time to be playing boy genius in Hollywood. Thanks to the inflation of ticket prices, movie grosses were higher than ever, but the number of tickets sold had decreased by three quarters since the golden age of the 1940s. Worse yet, the audience that remained consisted mostly of teenagers with limited tastes in movies. Inflation had driven the production costs of the average film to $10 million (/$14 million) plus another $10 million for promotion and release costs, and just as cable TV and videocassettes were entering into direct competition with movie houses, the government changed the tax rules and shut the doors to the cinematic tax shelter. Within the industry it was generally acknowledged that the movie business was dying.

As if things weren't bad enough, 1980 saw a whole flock of $30 million-plus gobblers, climaxing in *Heaven's Gate,* the turkey that ate a studio. The money people now looked with ever-increasing suspicion at free-spending filmmakers like Coppola. In this climate his shutdown of *Hammett* began to seem like an act of mad defiance to Orion. His high-risk deal with MGM on *One from the Heart* only added to his financial peril.

MGM owned the property. Coppola had refused to make the film as a mere studio employee, with MGM paying all the expenses. But MGM (now headed by David Begelman, who had bounced back nicely from his 1977 fall for check forgery and embezzlement at Columbia) was equally adamant about not selling him the property outright. Instead, a complex deal was crafted. MGM would retain the U.S. and Canadian distribution rights, presumably taking the usual 30 percent of rentals as its distribution fee, plus 20 percent of the adjusted gross. In return, it would give Coppola the property and guarantee an unspecified amount of completion money (for editing, prints, a music track, etc.) once Coppola had finished the shoot. Zoetrope would pay all shooting expenses and would retain artistic control and 80 percent of the adjusted gross. In addition, MGM agreed to pay Coppola $3 million (/$4.2 million) for directing, the highest dollar fee ever paid a director in the history of motion pictures. Hollywood insiders speculated that Coppola had set this price as a clever strategic move. If he ever had to hire himself out to a studio (say, if Zoetrope went bankrupt), the $3 million would set a floor for future salaries.

Even though it had evaded most of the production costs, MGM would still be putting a significant chunk of cash on the line for postproduction, and the executives were not at all sure the no-name cast could carry a $15 million (/$21 million) movie. For the leads, Coppola had signed medium-term, nonexclusive contracts with medium-famous Teri Garr (who had mainly played sexless, nagging wives, as in *Close Encounters*), Frederic Forrest (whose star had risen with *The Rose* and fallen again when *Hammett* failed to appear), Raul Julia (who was big on Broadway, but a movie novice), and twenty-year-old Nastassia Kinski (who had a sexy-looking mouth but spoke German as her first language, barely understood English, and had had only one starring role, in *Tess*). Coppola's old Hofstra buddy Lainie Kazan and veteran character actor Harry Dean Stanton (who wouldn't sign any term contracts, no, sir!) would take on the supporting roles.

But Coppola apparently wasn't worried. He had a plan for *One from the Heart*, a plan that would save *millions*. To start with, at a time when personal computers and word processors were still relatively rare, Coppola decided to word-process his script, saving all the drafts so he could exchange text between various versions. But that was small change compared with the technological breakthrough he had in mind for the actual film-making, a scheme he knew would change the entire industry. Before the first frame of film went through a camera, every scene would be planned, polished, and perfected by use of a three-stage previsualization technique Coppola called the electronic storyboard. It would employ the latest high tech hardware—computers, video recorders, editing consoles—to drag the antiquated filmmaking process into the twenty-first century.

"Science" Coppola was in his glory. He hired Thomas Brown, a skinny, longish-haired, bespectacled technician from Lucas's special effects department to help set up a war room, centered on detailed scale-models of the sets and $800,000 worth of experimental high-definition television equipment, all connected via a computerized mixing board to Sony Betamax video recorders. Coppola's newfound friendship with fellow techno-nut Akio Morita, chairman of Sony, paid off in bargain prices for the state-of-the-art electronics. Morita's vision of the movie business's future involved thousands of small (150-seat) video theaters, with Sony equipment, manned at minimal cost by a single employee who'd sell the tickets and plug in the cassettes. Morita's connection with Coppola provided a public relations coup, plus real-world performance testing of Sony's newest products.

Stage one of Coppola's electronic previsualization process started with a conventional storyboard using sketches and Polaroid photos to represent every shot, camera angle, and set in the script. The electronic part would kick in when Zoetrope's resident (nonunion) technicians animated the sketches by shooting them, scene by scene, on videotape. Simultaneously, Coppola would record the actors reading the script, add music and sound effects, and mix it all together on videotape so the storyboard would seem to come alive. He'd be able to see the entire movie on his monitors before spending money to build sets or hiring an expensive union filmmaking crew. If a scene didn't work, he could fix it before he shot it.

Stage two would gradually replace the sketches and Polaroids with live action, real sets, and real actors. Coppola would start by videotaping the cast during a two-day walk-through in Las Vegas. Video recording would continue through three weeks of technical rehearsals at Zoetrope. Meanwhile, Coppola would be mixing and preediting the video footage to tighten the story and eliminate unnecessary scenes. By the time production started, he would be very close to a finished picture.

Stage three would take place during the actual filming. Coppola had a shiny silver Airstream trailer built for him in San Diego. Its official title was Image Control, but its real name was Silverfish; Coppola filled it with monitors, telephones, control boards, microphones, dials, knobs, buttons, and switches —along with a Jacuzzi and the inevitable espresso machine. Even his studio bungalow (to which he'd affixed a plaque honoring silent comedian Harold Lloyd, its onetime occupant) was filled with monitors. Video cameras would look through Storaro's lenses, sending simultaneous image and sound to the video recorders and screens. Not only would Coppola be able to review instant replays of performances and camera moves, but he could also use his editing equipment to create optical effects, making a preliminary edit while actors, technicians, and lights were still on the set, ready to restage a shot if the video edit indicated a problem. For the first time a movie director would actually see his movie as it was shot.

Although Coppola had given up on the idea of completing the entire film in six weeks, he figured that with the electronic storyboard, he could at least finish principal photography within that period—half the normal time. Reshooting would be minimal, editing would be supersonic, and *One from the Heart* could be in the theaters by July 4, 1981, a mere five months after the shooting began. Interest on production loans would be held to a minimum; his system might cut 25 to 30 percent of *One from the Heart*'s costs.

Then he got another bright idea, but instead of saving money, this one sent *One from the Heart* $8 million over budget before the first rehearsal. Armyan Bernstein's original screenplay had been set in Chicago. Then someone decided it would be better (and cheaper) to shoot closer to Hollywood. On location, say, in Las Vegas. This was the version MGM had gone for, budgeted at $15 million (with $2 million for Zoetrope overhead, a $2.5 million contingency fee for MGM, and Coppola's $3 million directing fee built in). Chase Manhattan agreed to lend Zoetrope $8 million up front and advanced another $7 million against expected purchases of foreign distribution rights. No problem.

Unfortunately, the more he thought about it, the less Coppola liked the idea of shooting on location. After the Philippines he'd sworn never to do another location shoot. Anyway, he didn't need a city; he needed a metaphor. The real Las Vegas wasn't as good as the Las Vegas of the Mind. He wanted magical images that would go right past reality to achieve some kind of superreality, something like a live-action version of a Disney animated film. If he shot in the real Las Vegas, it would be just another relationship movie. Dean Tavoularis could build him a Las Vegas infinitely shinier, brighter, and more artistic than the one in Nevada.

Within weeks Tavoularis had put 200 union construction laborers to work on a series of elaborate sets; by the time the frenzy of set building was over, the crew was up to 350 and construction costs had risen to nearly $4.5 million. Neon lighting, which had been estimated at $300,000, ended up adding a cool million on top of that. "Sets that were meant to be small were huge," remembered one production assistant. "The department store was supposed to be two little three-wall units that actors pop into for a minute or two. It ended up as a two-story structure, Neiman-Marcus reincarnated." Another half million dollars bought a minutely detailed scale model of the entire city of Las Vegas. A one-foot-high version of the Dunes Hotel sign, with sixteen hundred light bulbs, cost $11,000, not counting the electric bill. Other sets included downtown Vegas, McCarran Airport, the midsection of a jet airplane, a surrealist junkyard, and a motel.

Coppola's staff at Zoetrope started getting nervous. Quite a few of them were already uneasy about risking the entire future of the studio on a lightweight puff pastry of a movie; the decision to shoot it on mammoth, costly sets seemed quite mad. Even if the money could be found, it was bound to delay the start of shooting, and Zoetrope desperately needed to get some product out on the screen. "It was difficult for some of us to understand what Francis was thinking," said Mona Skager, by now elevated to associate producer. "His conception was the reverse of everything he's known for. He wanted *One from the Heart* to be full of glamour, makeup, elaborate costumes—everything very theatrical and kitschy."

Not only were the sets expensive to build, but they were expensive to leave up. They filled nine sound stages on the lot—stages that Zoetrope could no longer rent out for extra cash. On the other hand, expensive or not, the sets were absolutely spectacular; visitors who wandered onto Tavoularis's version of downtown Vegas were often so thunderstruck they just stopped and stared, lost in wonder.

Before anyone knew it, *One from the Heart* was $10 million over budget. Coppola claimed he would pick up $2 million of that with the electronic storyboard, but his Chase Manhattan loans still fell $8 million short. He needed to find another source of capital to make up the shortfall, and in a hurry.

MGM refused to put up the extra cash. Not only had it contracted for a $15 million film, but after a string of high-budget failures (including two musicals, *Yes, Giorgio,* and *Pennies from Heaven*), it had set a $15 million ceiling on all its films. Furthermore, its management was not alone in suspecting that a lot of its money was going to buy costly electronic toys for Coppola. "Francis is loading onto the movie a lot more than just the cost of the movie," an anonymous insider told *L.A. Weekly*'s Michael Ventura, "like trying to refurbish a whole studio, and paying himself a $3 million fee, and building the huge sets. The bulk of the costs are not real."

Fortunately, just when things were looking bleakest, Coppola found a group of German tax-shelter investors who were already involved in *Superman II*; they agreed to buy into *One from the Heart* for the missing $8 million. It put off the immediate cash crunch, but the underlying financial crisis ran much deeper.

For years Coppola had spent most of his personal income on real estate. It made him a multimillionaire (only George Lucas was richer, he boasted), but it left him short of ready cash. He repeated this investment strategy with Zoetrope. Zoetrope's staff was now hovering around five hundred paid employees, but most of its $55 million in assets were locked up in real property. There was no cash for the payroll, which was running between $300,000 and $600,000 a week.

Coppola's need for cash was getting desperate. A few months earlier he'd sworn he'd never sell *Apocalypse* to TV, but now he announced that he was thinking of fattening it up with outtakes to make a special six-hour video version. Soon afterward, as the expenses on *One from the Heart* continued to soar, he put out the word that he might consider $10 million for network rights to the original version of *Apocalypse*. He never got it. In November 1980 he sold the cable TV rights for *Apocalypse* to HBO for $2.5 million (/$3.5 million) in its original, non-epicized form. It wasn't a fortune, but it helped.

The Escape Artist returned from Cleveland to complete its final month of shooting at Zoetrope and spend a good chunk of Coppola's change in the process. Coppola had largely ignored the project during preproduction and its initial shoot, but now, despite his preoccupation with *One from the Heart*, he couldn't resist helping Deschanel with the direction. Griffin O'Neal remembered that Coppola would call him, without warning, at eleven-thirty at night. " 'Griff,' he would say, 'come on down.' I was only 15. But I'd drive myself to the studio and we'd work on narration, narration, narration, trying for more richness, until my voice was hoarse."

With Christmas approaching, Coppola tried to shut all the problems out of his mind, and he returned to San Francisco for six weeks of *One from the Heart* rehearsals. The cast read the lines in a recording studio Coppola had set up in the basement of his North Beach office building; he directed by remote control from his penthouse office. The exercise had several goals, one of them private. Along with letting the actors warm up to the material and fixing scenes that fell flat in the reading, Coppola's hidden agenda was to wean the actors from depending on his physical presence; he meant to direct the shoot by remote control, from the Airstream, via electronic storyboard.

Then, right in the middle of rehearsals, came a financial body blow. The German investors changed their minds and

abruptly withdrew their $8 million. Coppola claimed they were
burned out by problems surrounding the completion of *Superman II*, but that didn't change the fact that he was right back
in the same $8 million hole. In light of the financial catastro-
phe, Zoetrope's top executives gave Coppola a thoughtful
Christmas present: They volunteered to take a 15 percent
pay cut.

Meanwhile, business went on as if nothing were wrong;
Jean-Luc Godard arrived in Los Angeles to make a film for
Zoetrope. Sourly doubtful about moviemaking in America, he
did concede that Coppola was "the best producer in Hollywood." Although Godard was accustomed to stingy budgets
(from 1968 to 1980 he'd shot nothing but leftist political tracts,
mainly on videotape and 16 mm), he was surely a bit surprised
to find Zoetrope in such dire financial condition.

Around the same time, avant-garde independent filmmaker
Scott Bartlett arrived from San Francisco to direct another Zoetrope project, a science-fiction love story called *Interface*. The
script, written by Charles Prosser, concerned a severely crippled
pilot whose brain is hooked up to a computer. Jon Davison,
hot from producing *Airplane!*, would hold the production reins.

Like Godard, Bartlett was used to underground budgets,
but *Interface* was budgeted as a mainstream movie, and Coppola had promised him a $75,000 fee for directing. Bartlett re-
membered that when he arrived in Hollywood, Coppola took
him on a guided tour of the lot.

"What's the most money you ever earned?" asked Coppola amiably, putting his arm around Bartlett's shoulder.

"Uh, well, once I got a twenty-thousand-dollar grant,"
Bartlett replied.

Coppola grinned. "I'm going to make you rich beyond your
wildest dreams," he declared. "And I advise you to invest it
in real estate. Believe me, it's the safest investment."

Work on *The Escape Artist* continued as well. It was
scheduled to open in the fall of 1981, only months away, but
when Deschanel finished his director's cut, Coppola took a
look and decided it wasn't finished after all. He put it in a
closet (perhaps the same closet where *Hammett* resided) until
he could get around to fixing it.

Late in January 1981 Gance's *Napoleon*, distributed by
Zoetrope Studios, opened in New York for a triumphant three-
day run at the Radio City Music Hall, sponsored by the Film

Society of Lincoln Center in association with the Museum of Modern Art. With Kevin Brownlow's reluctant approval, Zoetrope had reduced his five-hour-plus reconstruction to a four-hour version that would be easier to watch (and cost less overtime to screen).

The six-thousand-seat Music Hall was sold out for every performance, despite a top ticket price of $25. Gene Kelly introduced the film to a cheering audience, Carmine Coppola conducted the sixty-person American Symphony Orchestra playing his original score, and Chris Reyna supervised the projection (as he had at the Avenue Theatre screening, eight years before). At ninety-one, Gance himself was ailing and was unable to attend, but he sent a message saying that he hoped *Napoleon*'s success would win him funding for a new epic about Christopher Columbus. When the audience burst into a roaring fifteen-minute ovation at the conclusion, a Zoetrope staffer phoned Gance so he could listen to the bravos over the transatlantic wire. The exuberant silent epic grossed $800,000 in just eight screenings.

Although the live orchestra wiped out most of the profits, eventually Zoetrope would issue prints with Carmine's score on a synchronized sound track and the three-projector triptych transferred to a single strip of film. When that happened, *Napoleon* might become a big money maker. Even so, the eight special New York screenings netted Zoetrope $105,000.

The only negative effect of the screening was a sour joke that began to make the rounds at Zoetrope, to the effect that the only films Zoetrope had released were *Napoleon* and *Our Hitler*, both about tyrants who held absolute power.

Napoleon's profits financed only one day of Zoetrope's operations, but nothing else was financing even an hour. In mid-January, Robert Spiotta started selling and mortgaging property, $1 million at a time, to pay off cash debts that now amounted to $17 million. Banks refused to advance more money, and gimlet-eyed bank auditors from New York began to appear on the lot to "review Zoetrope's operation."

Coppola was forced to take out a $1 million personal loan from Security Pacific Bank, at 21 percent interest, putting up his real estate as collateral. He would have to do it again in a week, and again a week after that, week after week, until he'd made up the missing $8 million.

Something had to give. At the beginning of February 1981

Coppola reluctantly cut the budget for new gadgetry and laid off his entire story department. It was the first layoff at Zoetrope; it wouldn't be the last.

On February 2, 1981 (operating, perhaps, on the theory that the best defense is a good offense), Coppola began shooting *One from the Heart*. But first he gathered the crew and made a little speech.

Together, he said, they were about to make cinematic history. "This is a film that will be made through morphosis," he declared, going on to say that it would grow of itself, and within itself, and become itself. Not everybody bought this malarkey. Among the skeptics was Wally Gentleman, who had helped Kubrick plan the special effects for *2001*. Coppola had hired him to be director of special effects on *One from the Heart*, and Gentleman was amazed to hear a professional filmmaker spouting such mystical claptrap.

Two days later Coppola held a press conference at the studio for hundreds of reporters, all of whom he invited to stay for a catered luncheon costing $13,000.

"We're on the eve of something that's going to make the Industrial Revolution look like a small out-of-town tryout," Coppola proclaimed Napoleonically, standing in front of a giant, neon Lady Luck sign. "I can see a communications revolution that's about movies and art and music and digital electronics and satellites, but above all, human talent."

A local TV reporter, unmoved by the hyperbole, asked Coppola if he had really had to hock all his San Francisco holdings to pay for the movie. "I'm *always* in financial trouble," Coppola moaned. Then he turned surly. "I'm trying to tell you what I'm planning to do," he snapped. "You're walking around and making me uncomfortable. Hey, you know what, I get to have the press conference the way *I* want to have it." (He seems to have realized, at some point, that he'd been ungracious; at the end of the press conference he apologized for starting out "grumpy.")

"The only way I can win is by playing my talent for all it is worth," he added. "Once, when I was young and wanted a movie camera desperately, I took $1,000 to Las Vegas and tried to win myself $20,000." He lost it all, he admitted. So how did he feel about Las Vegas now? "It's a perfect place to set a love story," he said. "One minute the city says, 'Come, come and get me,' and the next it looks like Burbank and you're drunk and broke."

Coppola didn't need to travel to Las Vegas to go broke. The next day, February 5, Zoetrope was unable to meet its weekly payroll. Nor could it come up with $600,000 it owed various independent contractors, including the caterer who'd staged the $13,000 press-conference luncheon. The entire San Francisco staff (forty-three employees) was laid off. Spiotta sadly phoned each victim at home, explaining that the layoffs were for "two weeks, a month, or forever."

Then Coppola and Spiotta met with Zoetrope's 155 low-paid "Zoedroids": white-collar staffers, aides, techies, and go-fers who earned about $225 for a fifty-hour week, plus the invaluable privilege of working at Zoetrope. Spiotta begged them to work for half pay; amazingly they agreed.

Next came the scary group, the unionized technicians of *One from the Heart,* including 350 construction workers and a 100-man shooting crew. Coppola expected a mass walkout; union crews in Hollywood don't work unless they get their paychecks on time. With dread, Spiotta announced that Zoe-trope wouldn't be able to pay them until he and Coppola found more money, somewhere.

"Let's get back to work!" called out a voice from the back.

"We're with you!" shouted another.

Coppola was so moved he burst into tears. In the end the five hundred union workers voted to keep working for two weeks on a deferred-salary basis, while Coppola rounded up the cash to pay them.

Back at New World Pictures, the current home of Roger Corman, someone stuck a *Daily Variety* headline on the office bulletin board. It read COPPOLA EMPLOYEES FOREGO PAY. Some wag immediately added a hand-written note at the bottom: "If it's good enough for Zoetrope, it's good enough for New World. (signed), Roger Corman." The wag might even have been Corman.

Coppola's free ride didn't last long. Four days after the unions agreed to work for free, union leaders began pressuring him to come up with at least some cash by the end of the week. "If Coppola doesn't pay, I'll walk off the job Monday," a car-penter muttered.

Rescuers jumped in. Scott Bartlett had been working on a

rough two-hour video draft of *Interface* (with Paul Bartel and Ed Begley, Jr., in cameo roles). One morning, when it was about half done, he picked up the newspaper to read that Paramount had just bought *Interface* back from Coppola for $500,000. It also offered Coppola a personal loan for another $500,000. "Francis is, by any definition, the best in the business," said Paramount Chairman Barry Diller. "His monumental risk-taking, his pushing everything to the wall, is the essence of what any creative enterprise is about. When you go to Zoetrope, you can feel the passion there about making movies."

Bartlett and producer Jon Davison were delighted at the sale, certain it meant that *Interface* would get made. Bartlett continued working on the videotape at Zoetrope, and when it was complete, Davison screened it for several executives at Paramount. They liked what they saw. Paramount's production heads, Michael Eisner and Jeffrey Katzenberg, called a meeting with Davison and Bartlett. Eisner had not seen the tape and turned ashen when he heard that Bartlett meant to shoot the whole thing from the hero's point of view, without ever showing his face. Paramount instantly shelved the project and forgot it had ever heard the name of Bartlett. Davison, who had been on loan from Paramount in the first place, headed for home, where he was reassigned to produce a strange horror film called *White Dog*; eventually he hired the legendary Sam Fuller to direct. "It's a good thing I never cleared out my office," said Davison as he departed Zoetrope. "Now I won't have to schlep everything back again."

Bartlett, who had collected only $10,000 of the money that was supposed to have made him rich beyond his wildest dreams, was left feeling like a wind sock whose wind has died. Fortunately he'd never really believed he'd get rich from his Zoetrope deal. But now he found himself far from home, wondering if he was still supposed to be working for Zoetrope. He hung out at the studio for a few more weeks, expecting to get word from someone about whether or not he'd be reassigned to another project.

"During this period I never saw Francis," he recalled, "and I kept wondering about that. Finally I made him a videotape. I had the videotape guy come into my office, and I stood there pulling down all the storyboards and materials off the wall, and packing my stuff in boxes, and saying, 'I'm not going to hold any grudges, but I'm not going to hang around here. . . . I'd really like it if you'd get in touch with me and tell me what's in your mind.' "

After Bartlett moved out of Zoetrope, he decided to stay in Los Angeles and see what other work Hollywood might offer. It was one full year later when he got a call from Zoetrope. "Francis asked me to call," said Fred Roos, "to say that he didn't think it was a good idea for you to be counting on your association with *Interface* if you're hanging around town for that."

Bartlett wasn't alone. Almost all the exciting projects by young filmmakers were dropped, leaving a residue of resentment as well as disappointment. Franc Roddam, Martha Coolidge, Jonathan Sanger, David Lynch, Michael Bennett, and Paul Schrader found themselves out in the cold, after working for as long as two and a half years on their now-aborted projects. (Roddam, who went on to direct *Lords of Discipline,* later claimed that Coppola owed him $57,000 for the year of his life he wasted developing *The Tourist.*) Only *The Escape Artist, Return of the Black Stallion,* and Godard's *The Story* survived the cut.

Even so, many Zoetrope staff members went around wearing big buttons bearing the credo I BELIEVE IN FRANCIS C. Perhaps it helped, but not enough.

Coppola had now sunk approximately $4 million of his own money into *One from the Heart.* He approached the owners of several Las Vegas hotels, offering them billboards on the Las Vegas set for $5,000 each; only a few accepted. Coppola didn't want to ask Marlon Brando for a loan because he needed more money than Marlon probably had. Nor did he feel right approaching Lucas, although he was overheard bemoaning the twist of fate that had brought Lucas all that *Star Wars* money. "George comes from a conservative northern California family where money is kind of serious business," he later explained. "My attitude toward money is that it is just something to be used."

Coppola may have been desperate, but he refused to sell his dream even when there were eager buyers. Steven Bach (then production head at UA) and Leland Katz went over to Zoetrope to see some of the *One from the Heart* footage. They didn't much like it, but they were sympathetic to Coppola's dilemma. "Instead of offering to buy into *One from the Heart*," Bach said, "we offered to buy the studio from Francis." UA needed the office space at the time; more particularly, Bach wanted to save Coppola from bankruptcy.

"The basic concept was that we would secretly buy the studio from him—I think the price we offered was $22 million—allow him to run Zoetrope exactly as he wished, and we would be allowed to build one or two United Artists office buildings at the farthest end of the lot," Bach continued. "This offer was framed by [UA head] Andy Albeck and communicated to Francis through his attorney Barry Hirsch. It was turned down. Flat."

As publicity on Coppola's dilemma spread, he became something of a cause célèbre. On February 19 an anonymous donor (it was Norman Lear, the man behind *All in the Family*) lent Zoetrope $500,000, unsecured. At USC a student organization held two benefit screenings of *Apocalypse*. Many people who read about Coppola's poverty in *Time, Newsweek, The New York Times, L.A. Weekly,* and their hometown papers sent small contributions. Zoetrope staffers were touched but sent these latter checks back.

Coppola tried to shut the problems out of his mind and concentrate on shooting *One from the Heart*. His son Gio, now age seventeen, had written him a letter, begging to be allowed to drop out of high school to fulfill his own dream of becoming his father's apprentice. Now, with Coppola's permission, he came to work at Zoetrope. Italia and Carmine played small roles in the movie, appearing in a brief scene in an elevator. Eleanor, Roman, and Sofia came to the set daily, and August visited often.

Once filmmaking began, Coppola seemed oblivious of the financial crisis. "We were all concerned," Teri Garr remembered, "but Francis could walk onto the set and turn off the outside world. It's his strength." The only concession Coppola made to the unusual financial situation was a wrap party every Friday night. Wrap parties are usually held when a film finishes shooting, but since Coppola never knew if there would be money to continue shooting on Monday, every Friday *might* have been the last day.

Some older members of Coppola's production crew, like Wally Gentleman and Rudi Fehr, were troubled by the parties, considering them "licentious" and noting the presence of "available young women" who had little or nothing to do with the film.

By the end of February 1981 Coppola was at the end of his rope, at least financially. He needed an old-fashioned theatrical angel who could deal in newfangled cinematic sums of money. Someone from outside the industry probably. Someone who was very, very rich.

Jack Singer was worth at least $500 million. The sixty-two-year-old Canadian financier came from a family of socially prominent Polish Jews and held assets in oil, real estate, and building developments (including the entire town of Poland, Texas, a suburb he had built near Dallas). Singer had invested in only one movie before (a low-budget Canadian film), but when he read about Coppola's financial troubles in the newspapers, he told *Variety* columnist Army Archerd he was prepared to lend the filmmaker as much as $42 million.

He first offered to finance Coppola for three years and to buy a 50 percent interest in the studio. Instead, over the course of several meetings he and Coppola hashed out a less extravagant deal. Singer would lend Coppola $1 million, with $7 million more to follow as soon as Singer himself could borrow it. ("I like using other people's money," Singer explained.) This would complete the funding for *One from the Heart*. Coppola would put up the studio as collateral and grant Singer an undisclosed percentage of the film's gross income. (In the end Singer came through with only $3 million.)

"I'm not in it as a hobby, I'm in it as a business," said Singer. "At least with Francis Coppola, we're starting at the top. He's like a national treasure. If they let a guy like that go down the tubes, it would be a tragedy. I got a look at the technology Francis is using, and I think he already is where the rest of the film industry will be going. He's a modern-day Thomas Edison."

Up to now Coppola had been forced to devote almost all his attention to technical details and financial damage control. Now, with Singer's millions in place, he could turn to shooting *One from the Heart*.

It was, in many ways, a very odd production. Coppola rarely appeared on the set; his disembodied directorial commands issued from loudspeakers which everyone on the set could hear.

He spent almost all his time holed up in his silver Airstream trailer, set a hundred feet outside the sound stage; in addition to the electronics, it had an espresso machine, beds, a kitchen, and a Jacuzzi. The lonely kid who loved remote control was seeing his dreams come true. He was remote, and he was in control.

For all of Coppola's announced commitment to "help the movies develop aesthetically away from television," as Tom Luddy had put it, his methodology was virtually a mirror image of the way TV drama was shot, right down to the seclusion of the director in an offstage control booth, from which he/she directed while watching the monitors. But there were other reasons for Coppola's reclusiveness, reasons he never mentioned.

"If he left the trailer," noted Walter Murch, who had remained in Northern California but visited Zoetrope during the early portion of the shoot, "financial people would have descended upon him, and he would have been eaten alive. The trailer acted as a kind of bathysphere to protect him from the crushing financial pressures that were out there." Although there was nothing to stop the financial vultures from swooping on him when he left the studio each evening, the trailer evidently gave Coppola a sense of psychological sanctuary during working hours.

Cameras had been placed at strategic locations around the set, each of them recording simultaneously on videotape and film. Coppola's plan involved shooting from several different angles at the same time (like a TV show), while he sat in the trailer watching the images on different screens and cutting from one to another. However, he insisted on exceptionally long takes, ten to fifteen minutes each, not only to let the actors explore their characters' emotions but to avoid the kind of restless, brainless quick cutting that he felt marred TV dramas.

Between takes he played Space Invaders on his computerized wristwatch.

Several reporters were allowed on the set to watch parts of the shoot. They all found something disturbing about Coppola's voice booming over the loudspeakers like the voice of God (or the Wizard of Oz). Aaron Latham, writing for *Life*, overheard some technicians whispering unhappily about a scene that didn't seem to be working. Then Coppola's voice came over the speakers. "Don't worry," it said, "we'll get some snappy patter before we're finished." And then it added: "Always remember, I can hear *everything*."

"The amplified power of his voice made him seem omnipotent," wrote Latham, "but not necessarily infallible."

When the articles appeared, Coppola was beside himself that they'd ridiculed him; he seemed totally unaware that his remote-control direction was driving cast and crew crazy. He was having a terrific time, joking and kidding around like a jovial god. When a technician couldn't locate Coppola and began wailing, "Where *is* he? Where *is* he?" Coppola would boom out, "I'm in Palm Springs!" On another occasion, when Frederic Forrest was having trouble reading a line, the loudspeakers explained, "Fred, it's like you're telling your buddy your philosophy. And then you're hit by this contradiction. This movie's about contradictions, right? No, that was the last one."

The actors, too, were increasingly unhappy with their remote-control director. Nastassia Kinski, who was just learning English, couldn't always understand exactly what the Voice wanted from her. "Directors remind me of little boys," she said. "They say, 'I want this or I want that.' It reminds me of a child who says, 'I want a castle built for me,' and they get it. It takes some getting used to, that's for sure."

"It's okay," said Teri Garr. "But we can't talk. Just listen and be seen and take direction. We're little puppets."

Forrest found it particularly difficult to lose himself in his character while threading his way through the complex technical details, not to mention the mass of gadgetry. At times he suspected that Coppola was more interested in the scenery than the characters.

Once, when Garr was doing a nude scene, Coppola's voice came booming over the system: "Let's see more of your boobs, turn this way, more, now turn that way. . . ." Everyone on the set cringed. It may have been the lowest point of the direction-by-remote-control experiment, but not by much.

The problem was that while Coppola was looking at the screen and talking to a microphone, out on the crowded set his voice came booming out of a speaker like Big Brother. Every time he talked to a cast member about a detail of performance, everybody else could hear it; every time he talked to a technician, the actors and actresses would say, "Hey, what does he think is more important here, us or the technical side?"

Cinematographer Storaro didn't complain, but the fact was,

he couldn't understand half of what Coppola was saying over the sound system.

If Coppola had been listening, he might have discovered how uncomfortable he was making his cast and crew, but criticism was the last thing he wanted to hear. "I give other people ulcers so I don't get them myself," he kidded. The gag was uncomfortably close to the truth.

One day, the feisty Allen Garfield showed up on set to take a look. He was amazed to hear Coppola preparing Lainie Kazan for a scene via remote control, giving her no direction beyond a paralyzing, "On this take, I want you to be sexy, honey."

When Coppola saw Garfield on the monitors, he invited him into the trailer, showed him the eight TV screens, and explained the whole process. Finally Coppola asked, "So what do you think? Isn't this a really exciting way to make a movie?"

Garfield said, "I dunno, Francis, is it? You're making the movie. Is it exciting?"

The air temperature in the trailer seemed to drop twenty degrees. "What do you mean?" asked Coppola.

"I remember how we made *The Conversation*," Garfield said. "Very exciting for me, Francis, and, I would venture to say, very exciting for you."

Coppola's eyes grew wary. "You don't think this is exciting?" he asked.

"No," said Garfield, "I think it's sheer death."

"What do you mean?" asked Coppola ominously.

"You are turning your actors to stone," said Garfield. "These performances are becoming entrenched in cement. And worse than that, because everybody loves you as much as I do and everybody is willing to make a leap of faith, nobody is telling you that there is not an ounce of spontaneity, not an ounce of air, people are moving to positions just in order to be placed there, and when you shoot this, you're going to be shooting dead performances."

"What do you think," bellowed Coppola, "that everybody can improvise like you and De Niro? I don't have people like that who can do that all the time. I can't work like that all the time, the way you worked."

"I'm not talking about that," Garfield calmly replied. "These actors are so proud and happy to be in your film they have lost sight of the fact that they *are* actors and not puppets. *You* have lost sight of the fact that they're actors. And I'm here to tell you, in answer to your question: No it's *not* exciting, the way you're doing this movie!"

Garfield strode out of the trailer, followed by underlings. "Are you aware that you'll never work for this man again?" they whispered.

"I guess I'll have to risk that," said Garfield. In fact, Coppola seems to have held no grudge. Garfield was subsequently cast for a major scene in *One from the Heart,* playing Raul Julia's boss, and he had a featured role in *The Cotton Club* as well.

As the shoot went along, the loudspeaker system caused so much tension that Coppola finally gave up and hired a floor manager to wear a headset, take his instructions, and pass them on quietly to the actors. The multiple-camera idea didn't work either; lighting the sets so every camera got enough light produced bland, flat, boring images, just like television.

Many staffers and technicians were losing patience. One of them was Gentleman, whose main complaint had to do with Coppola's lack of professionalism.

"People like George Lucas and Spielberg are aware of the needs of the special effects department," he explained, "and Coppola was very ignorant. You plan for a specific sequence in a specific order, and you know what shots are at the beginning of a take, and where it melds toward a specific action at the end of a take, and you design for that. He wanted more and more takes to make selections from, and I said, 'That isn't how it's done.'"

At one point Gentleman needed to make a linking shot, so he went to the appropriate editor and asked where it was supposed to go.

"Jeez, Wally, I don't know," said the editor.

"What do you mean? You're the editor, are you not? Are you not editing it as we go through?"

"After a fashion," said the editor.

"Well," said Gentleman, "will you *please* enlighten me as to what's going on?"

"All right," said the editor. "The selected takes are put down on videotape, and Francis takes them home and plays with them, and then he comes back and gives me the pieces, and he says, 'Put these together and see how they work.' . . . The following day, I find that some of the cuts that were agreed on have now been changed, and he's using other bits of film, and I honestly don't know from one day to the next what the film looks like!"

On another occasion Coppola wanted a shot of an airplane passing overhead. Gentleman suggested, reasonably enough, that someone drive a camera down to Los Angeles Airport, aim it at the sky, and take a picture of an airplane. Instead, Coppola insisted that they do the shot with a model, via special effects, at four times the cost.

Finally Gentleman went to Fred Roos, to try to get him to take a closer look at where the money was going, and why. "Well," said Roos, "that's how Francis is, and that's what you have to put up with."

In the end, just before shooting the titles, Coppola fired Gentleman—the usual fate of anyone who failed to give Coppola an enthusiastic "Yes!" Gentleman was deeply relieved.

Given this kind of chaos, despite the electronic storyboard and seventy-two days of rehearsals, Coppola did have to reshoot, and plenty. (Only he refused to call it reshooting; everyone was instructed to refer to it as "Phase Two.") The thin story looked even thinner on film. Neither the characters nor the story were very interesting, especially since Coppola had stubbornly refused to compromise his design by shooting any close-ups. Now he found himself frantically revising the script as he reshot—with close-ups. At least it gave him a chance to improvise. The scene where Frederic Forrest meets Nastassia Kinski was shot thirty-five different ways. By the time *One from the Heart* was finished, Coppola had shot twenty feet of film for every foot used, twice as much as most films need.

In addition, there were normal moviemaking disasters— made worse by the rush to finish. At one point, for instance, Storaro decided to try an unusual angle and discovered that the unfinished tops of the sets were in the frame. Hurriedly employees hung expensive black netting over them. Then Dean Tavoularis freaked out. The background was supposed to be *blue,* not black. Hastily the staff painted the netting blue, but the paint made the netting sag. OK, said Storaro, forget the netting, tear it all down, put in hard ceilings. Then Tavoularis insisted that there had to be little stars painted on the ceilings. "We put in those ceilings five times trying to get it right," one Zoetrope employee recalled.

As the six-week picture went on, and on, a curious, baleful weight began to drag the film down. "The longer a film takes," observed Walter Murch, "the more you think that to explain *why* it's taking longer, it has to be *more*. It's like a note that you should write in one day. If you put if off for two days, you say, 'Well, I can't write a note, now I'll have to write a letter.' And if you put the letter off for a week, now it can't be a letter, it has to be an essay. And if you put if off for six months, it has to be the Meaning of Life."

Gene Kelly had hired his young, unknown protégé Kenny Ortega (who made a splash some years later with his choreography for *Dirty Dancing*) to design the dances, a decision some reporters ascribed to Kelly's concern that his reputation might be damaged by a credit on *One from the Heart*. Nonetheless, when *Variety* columnist Army Archerd visited the set, he found Kelly sitting on a tall ladder, directing a dance number.

Kelly and Coppola were having their differences. For one thing, to Coppola's astonishment, Kelly had ordered (not merely suggested) that changes be made in the order of the dance sequences. Furthermore, while Coppola wanted his leading actors center stage at all times, Kelly was underwhelmed by the amateur terpsichorean skills of Forrest et al. and wanted to hide them amid real dancers to cover their deficiencies. Ultimately there was a compromise: Kelly got his dancers, but Coppola added cars, children, and assorted extras to fill the street-scene dance number.

Kelly and Coppola got into several wild on-set arguments. On one occasion Coppola wanted a dance for Kinski and ordered Kelly to figure one out, teach her the moves, and have her ready to film it the next day. Kelly explained that the way he worked it took several weeks to choreograph and rehearse a dance number. Coppola insisted loudly, and Kelly simply walked off the set.

In the end the relationship seems to have foundered. Kelly's name does not appear in the credits or in any subsequent Zoetrope press release, apparently at his own insistence. "In no way does *One from the Heart* represent any of my choreography or direction," Kelly wrote, some years later, in a letter to *American Film*.

MGM was increasingly unhappy with Coppola's cost overruns and delays. Early in March it decided to pull the plug.

MGM attorneys told Zoetrope attorneys that the studio considered the contract broken; it was pulling out of the deal.
Coppola calmly told the reporters he expected another distributor to sign on instantly. In fact, there had already been feelers
from Paramount, home of the *Godfathers*. In many ways, a new
distributor, and a new release schedule, would relieve a lot of
pressure. Coppola had promised MGM that he'd wrap principal photography by mid-March, but realistically the earliest date
he could make was mid-April.

As expected, Paramount was glad to step in and take over
the film from MGM, and it offered a much sweeter deal. Like
MGM, it would deduct the usual 30 percent distribution fee
off the top and provide completion money, but it would give
Coppola 100 percent of the adjusted gross (as opposed to the
80 percent MGM had offered). No mention was made in any
reports of Coppola's $3 million directing fee; it's possible that
Paramount gave him that extra 20 percent in exchange for
dropping the fee. In any case, Paramount would make six
hundred prints and guarantee $4 million in advertising. Fur-
thermore, after ten years distribution rights would revert to
Zoetrope. Zoetrope was still obliged to pay for principal photography, which now had to be completed by mid-April.

The deal was so complicated that apparently no one thought
to address a rather serious problem. One of the critical elements of the MGM deal had been the transfer of the property
from MGM to Zoetrope. That deal had now collapsed. Who
owned the property?

On March 15, with the aid of instant video editing, *One
from the Heart* was deemed complete enough to sneak in
Seattle.

Rudi Fehr tried to talk Coppola out of it. "Remember what
Jack Warner said," he advised. "Never show a picture to anybody until you have it exactly the way you want it."

Coppola wasn't listening. "From now on," he said, "I'm
going to preview it every Saturday night until it's finished."

Fehr persisted. "Francis, you're gonna get hurt. Are you
looking to amateurs to tell you what's wrong with the picture?
If you and I don't know what's wrong with it, then we shouldn't
show it."

"I want to see it just the way the audience will see it. . . ."
Coppola insisted. Besides, this way he'd be able to gauge au-

dience reaction while he still had a month of shooting left. He managed to keep news of the sneak off the front page, but there are a great many film critics in the world, and some of them live in Seattle.

Richard T. Jameson, a *Film Comment* correspondent, reported that viewers saw an incomplete print with rough sound, no opticals, and only a partial song track. Some scenes were just video rehearsals, he wrote, while others were indicated by cards describing the action. Despite the crudity, he enjoyed the film, but he found the title ironic, "for the heart this movie proceeds from is cold." The thin characters and story were "only a pretext for nonstop directorial grandstanding."

The review was to prove highly influential; several national critics came perilously close to plagiarizing it, and Andrew Sarris quoted it at length. Coppola was furious, of course, but the preview audience's reaction convinced him that he really did need four to six more weeks of shooting.

Coppola felt that the funding for the final weeks of reshooting could technically be considered completion money, but Spiotta advised against asking Paramount to come up with the dough. Instead, Coppola signed up for yet another personal bank loan. This left him so broke, he claimed, that within weeks his home phone was disconnected for nonpayment and remained so for over a year.

But money is mysterious stuff. Despite the turned-off phone, Coppola headed a group of American filmmakers (including George Lucas, Steven Spielberg, Martin Scorsese, and Brian De Palma) in an attempt to purchase Pinewood Studios in England. It was the largest and finest studio complex in all of Europe, with the largest single sound stage in the world, the vast "007 Stage" used on the James Bond pictures. The Hollywood whiz kids bid $3 million, escalated to $13 million, and hinted that they might even go as high as $20 million. Pinewood's owner, J. Arthur Rank, insisted he wouldn't consider an offer lower than $30 million. "I must emphasize that we have never suggested the studios were for sale," said Rank spokesman Rodney Rycroft, "and that this bid from Hollywood came as a complete surprise." So much for Pinewood.

With the shooting of *One from the Heart* virtually over, Coppola announced that his musical version of *Tucker* would be shot on videotape, with digital electronics; there would be no film used at all. He was equally eager to produce *Elective Affinities* as a grandiose eleven-hour epic that could be shown in four segments. *One from the Heart* was just a sketch for his great saga, he declared, which would "work on a trillion levels."

In a major interview with *Esquire*'s Gay Talese, Coppola's hatred for journalists seemed more intense than ever. In fact, he explained to Talese, the press was actually responsible for his money troubles. "The issue of money was *never* a big issue," he said. "The *press* created that issue. We had maybe one scary week, but what I did was sit down and say, 'Lookit, I got this movie, and if I can bluff my way through two weeks.' " He seemed to have forgotten that the news reports of his financial difficulties had brought his plight to Jack Singer's attention.

"The press is a millstone around this country's neck," he declared. "It is not a force for honesty, ethics, or truth. It is a bullshit racket."

When Talese reminded him that a free press had been able to expose the crookedness of President Nixon, Coppola responded, "I think that having Nixon in power would be better than a rampant press."

If Coppola had known what the rampant press (and Paramount Studios) were about to do to him, he might have dynamited every city room and statue of Peter Zenger in the country.

Chapter Seventeen

Photographing the Bath Water (1981–1982)

LIKE THE SHOOT, the editing of *One from the Heart* went more slowly than Coppola had anticipated, despite an array of advanced editing equipment that included a portable half-inch video system with two tiny Sony monitors that he carried around with him. Mark Berger, Coppola's sound man (and, later, an Oscar winner for the sound in *Amadeus*), described the process: "He'll try one scene in four different places and then throw it out. This goes on for months and months, and dozens and dozens of cuts. And each time, the film gets farther and farther away from the original conception, more and more bizarre. What's happening is that the threads that hold all the pieces of the story together are being stretched and stretched. Then, when it's just about to break, you start to put it together again."

Titles and last-minute special effects proved much more expensive than anticipated. Coppola had to sell off most of his remaining real estate, including the Broadway mansion in San Francisco. Designer Jessica McClintock bought it, after a feverish last-minute haggle over whether *Godfather* props, like the backyard light stanchions, came with the mansion or not.

The press continued to follow Coppola's financial woes closely. Although some of the stories made fun of his pretensions, most portrayed him positively as an artist with his back to the wall. The saga of *One from the Heart* became a media event, firing the public's curiosity to see it.

In August, Coppola flew to New York, looking for a home for Zoetrope East. As he'd told Gay Talese, he'd had it with Hollywood. He had barely settled down in his luxury apartment at the Sherry Netherland (bought during the *Godfather II* shoot) when he got an interesting letter from a group of teenage students at Lone Star High School in Fresno, and their school librarian, Jo Ellen Misakian. They'd loved *The Black Stallion* and had come up with another book for him to produce as a film: S. E. Hinton's teenage novel *The Outsiders*, about three brothers trying to keep themselves together as a family after their parents have died. "All thirty of them signed it and sent it off," Coppola recalled, "saying that if I read this book I would make this movie."

When Coppola read the book, he was so charmed by the story that he told Roos he'd do it. "I thought it was sweet and youthful and had something in its little, simple theme that was of value, and I wanted to make the picture very much as the book was," he said. *Hammett, The Escape Artist, One from the Heart*, Zoetrope itself were all up in the air. But at least Coppola knew what his next movie would be.

It was a canny decision. Coppola had lost his credibility as a director who could work within normal limits of time and money. The last film he'd completed even roughly on budget and on time was *The Conversation,* eight years earlier, and it hadn't even done much business. The three films he'd completed since had been extravagantly expensive and extravagantly late, and only one of them (*Godfather II*) had been even moderately profitable. Worse yet, thanks to constant press coverage, the whole world knew every appalling detail. He needed to prove that he could still make a movie quickly and on a reasonable budget.

Coppola planned to shoot *The Outsiders* in a naturalistic style, so there would be no multimillion-dollar sets, and with the book's fanatical teenage following he wouldn't need to hire high-priced stars to attract an audience.

Over the next few months Roos secured the film rights to the novel, which Coppola described (with accelerating grandiosity) as a "*Gone With the Wind* for 14-year old girls" and a "*Godfather* for children." S. E. Hinton had written it at the age of sixteen; since then she'd become the wife of a Texas shoe salesman and the author of three more books for teenagers (*Tex, That Was Then, This Is Now,* and *Rumble Fish*—all of which were, as it happens, filmed around the same time).

One thing Hinton hadn't grown into was a financial sophisticate. She only asked for a measly $5,000, but Zoetrope was so broke it couldn't pay even that. Finally it came up with $500, a promise for the remainder, a percentage of future profits, and a part in the movie. "*The Outsiders* was not a major piece of business for Zoetrope," Fred Roos commented. "It had to get developed in the cheapest possible way or not at all." Roos commissioned a young writer named Kathleen Knutsen Rowell to turn the book into a script.

While Coppola continued about his New York business, Paramount stabbed him in the back. Unbeknownst to Coppola, studio execs had decided to screen a rough cut of *One from the Heart* for prospective Bay Area exhibitors. Zoetrope's San Francisco office found out about the screening mere hours before it was scheduled, much too late to stop it. On August 19 Tom Luddy rushed over to the small screening room in San Francisco, stationed himself by the door, and tried to contain the damage by keeping journalists out and by reminding entering exhibitors that this was not the finished version. Despite Coppola's subsequent bellyaching, what the distributors saw was pretty close to a finished film; only some matte work was missing.

First there was a short videotaped intro by Coppola himself, prepared a week earlier, presumably for exhibitor screenings of the finished print. The director stood in front of a set and chatted about the film, making up his lines as he went along. He concluded: "It will enable you to say, at your theater, 'We have a *show!*' " Luddy left as the curtains opened; perhaps he couldn't bear to witness the grim screening. When the lights came up again, the exhibitors looked at each other in wordless gloom. Many of them were friends of Coppola's, but even they couldn't believe what they'd just seen.

Worse yet, Judy Stone, the San Francisco *Chronicle*'s powerful film critic, heard about the screening, too. Smelling a story, she phoned several exhibitors to ask how they'd liked the film. None of them could afford to offend her by keeping mum. "It was probably one of the ten worst movies I've ever seen," one of them told her. Another said, "I almost think the film is unreleasable."

The *Chronicle* ran Stone's story under a headline that read: COPPOLA HAS "HEART" TROUBLE. Stone had even phoned Chase Manhattan Bank to ask if it realized what a turkey it had backed; at least she didn't quote its reactions in the newspaper. The story was picked up by *Variety*, bringing it to industry eyes across the country.

Coppola was utterly outraged with Paramount over the screening. The Paramount execs were equally furious with him for delivering an "almost unreleasable" film. On top of all this, a legal problem surfaced. Paramount's lawyers finally noticed that Coppola might have sold the film to them without first making sure that he (rather than MGM) actually owned it; attorneys from both studios were burning up the phone lines. Paramount began looking for an excuse to pull out.

Editing went on and on. *One from the Heart* was set to open in September. Then in October. Then Christmas . . . no, it wouldn't be Christmas.

Spiotta asked Paramount for $2 million completion funds for *One from the Heart*. It was less than half the actual completion costs; presumably he could have asked for $4 million. But Paramount argued that it wasn't obliged to put up any money because Zoetrope had exceeded the shooting days allowed in the contract. The Coppolas were obliged to take out yet another personal loan from Chase Manhattan, putting up just about everything they owned as collateral, including the Napa Valley vineyard, the art on the walls, the jewelry in Eleanor's jewelry box, and, of course, Zoetrope Studios.

And since he was merely in hock for everything he owned, and since his movie was stuck in the editing room, and since he had laid off most of his staff, and since he might be about to lose Zoetrope to two, if not three, different banks, Coppola decided that this would be the perfect time to revive *Hammett*. The good news was that Ross Thomas had completed a tight, new, action-packed script. The bad news was that 80 percent of the picture would have to be reshot. Frederic Forrest and his wife, Marilu Henner, were still in it, but Peter Boyle would replace Brian Keith in a much expanded role as Hammett's old partner. Numerous other parts (including that of Ronee Blakley) were simply excised.

Somehow, Coppola convinced Wim Wenders to return and complete the shoot on what Forrest called "a nonexistent budget." It took just twenty-three days to film ninety-five pages of script, an incredible high-velocity production; Wenders and his crew shot it like a 1930s B movie, doing up to thirty-five camera setups a day. "We did a lot of masters—three takes and out," recalled Forrest, who was actually delighted with the speed of the shoot and the slimmed-down script. Meantime, sitting in his Airstream trailer and using the sky-spy electronics he'd devised for *One from the Heart,* Coppola could view every shot as it was filmed and often relayed suggestions to Wenders on the set. It's not clear how much Wenders enjoyed having the boss looking over his shoulder.

In November 1981, with *Hammett* in its final days of shooting, Coppola and Tavoularis decided to take five days off for a quick trip to Belize, a newly independent English-speaking republic (formerly British Honduras) on the east coast of Central America. Coppola was scouting locations, but not for a movie. He told reporters he was planning to build "the studio of the future," and although he hadn't made any final decisions yet, Belize was "an extraordinary country. It's a young country that hasn't been touched, there's nothing to be undone." For one thing, there was no broadcast television in Belize, and the population was wild for movies on videocassettes. For another, he was feeling hemmed in by America's legal restrictions, especially in regard to work visas for foreign film personnel like Storaro; Belize might be more accommodating. "My vision is not so much making just movies," he declared, "but building a new city. Plato, in *The Republic,* feels the pursuit of money and power by the merchant class is evil. A society needs to be guided by artists who have devoted themselves to truth and beauty." (Coppola was playing fast and loose with Plato, who actually postulated rule by a *philosopher*-king, not an artist-king, and specified that music, with its capacity to inflame emotions, should be banned from his kingdom of pure reason. It seems likely that Plato would have banned movies as well.)

C.L.B. Rogers, Belize's deputy prime minister, hosted Coppola and Tavoularis throughout their stay and agreed that a resort studio on an offshore island would be a terrific tourist attraction. "Coppola expressed his desire to me that he wished to move his studios to Belize," Rogers reported. "He told us of the future, of advanced technologies, of satellites, of using tape to replace film. As far as any restrictions are concerned, there would be no red tape here."

Meanwhile, as Coppola toured the tropics, the media circus surrounding *One from the Heart* was beginning to back-fire. With no release in sight, and the disastrous distributors' screening to fuel rumors, intimations that Coppola's film might be a loser were spreading fast. Articles in *Life, Saturday Review, Esquire, Vogue,* and *American Film* (whose new editor was compelled to apologize, in his column, for spotlighting a movie whose availability was suddenly up in the air) hinted that Coppola's film might never be finished. One article noted, "The climate of opinion, so much in his favor in the spring, has begun to turn."

In fact, *One from the Heart* was actually very close to completion. It had cost $27 million (/$35 million), nearly twice its original budget, and Zoetrope had paid the worst of the cost. Its staff was decimated by layoffs and defections. Casting chief Jennifer Shull went to Columbia; production head Lucy Fisher fled to Warner Brothers. With the union crews gone, the studio looked like a ghost town, and if *One from the Heart* weren't a giant smash, Zoetrope would never recover. Everything was riding on Coppola's film and its ability to captivate a mass audience.

Coppola was captivated. "I'm very proud," he said, "and I imagine that years from now, just as with my other films, people will see something in it. It's an original work. It's not a copy of anything. It's a lounge operetta, pretty and sweet. I've made too many gangster and soldier movies. I like fantasy and fable."

He decided that since Paramount had sneaked a screening behind his back, he'd sneak one behind its; only his would be at New York's six-thousand-seat Deco palace, Radio City Music Hall. "As soon as things started going bad with Paramount, I decided to open the film," he explained. "It's like being rejected by your lover; it gives you an excuse to call someone else. . . . Besides, I own the picture, not Paramount. It's up to me to make it a success. If it is, we'll be able to make eight to ten pictures a year. If not, the banks get the studio."

It was a first. No one could remember a filmmaker ever going around his distributor to sneak a film himself. "It's a brilliant move," said writer-director-critic Paul Schrader, who'd nearly made a film for Zoetrope himself before the money ran dry. "If it's a hit he can wipe out a year of bad publicity."

One of Coppola's friends, who preferred to keep his name

to himself, wasn't so sure. "Just remember this isn't the story of a little guy against the system," he pointed out. "Francis *is* the system."

In any case Paramount was not pleased. It had planned to open *One from the Heart* nationwide on February 10, 1982, but a week before the Radio City sneak it notified theater chains that the film was being pulled from release until further notice.

On Sunday, January 10, five days before the sneak, Coppola placed a full-page ad in the Sunday *New York Times* to notify the public of the preview of "a new kind of old-fashioned romance." There would be two screenings, one at 7:30 and one at 10:00 P.M.; tickets were $5 for general admission, $10 for reserved mezzanine-level seats.

Now Coppola set to work completing the film, sending last-minute changes to Rome, where technicians incorporated them into the master; the final print arrived by air courier just twenty-nine hours before show time. Coppola spent those final twenty-nine hours working on the sound mix. Special double system projectors, which could synchronize separate reels of sound and film, had to be trucked down from Boston for the screening.

Friday, January 15, was an icy, raw winter day. Coppola finished the sound mix at dawn and headed for Radio City to play with the houselights and take a good look around. He found a long line of people waiting patiently in the freezing cold to buy general admission tickets. The sight was so encouraging that he had $3,000 worth of hot split pea soup delivered to the line standers, free.

Both performances sold out; eleven thousand moviegoers attended, including more than five hundred freebies. Even movie critics were invited. So were Coppola's relatives, friends, friends of friends, and folks from every walk of show biz. Zoetrope employees flew in from California (mostly at their own expense), and film critics arrived from newspapers all across North America. Everyone who got a free ticket was invited to a giant party afterward.

During the screening Coppola paced the lobby, pausing at the aisle doors to listen for audience response. A reporter from *Eyewitness News*, with a portable camera on his shoulder, asked for permission to photograph him as he paced. "I'd rather not," Coppola answered. "I'd rather be free just to hang around the house." Then he slipped inside, sat down on the floor at the back of the center aisle, and watched his movie.

One from the Heart centers on live-in lovers Frannie (Teri Garr) and Hank (Frederic Forrest). Frumpish Frannie works in a travel agency and dreams of going to Tahiti; homely Hank works in a junkyard pointedly called Reality Wrecking. They share a sloppy little house in Las Vegas. And they are tired of each other.

One evening Frannie and Hank are separately invited to dally with more exotic partners. For Frannie, it's suave Ray (Raul Julia), a waiter who claims to be a lounge singer. For Hank, it's Leila (Nastassia Kinski), a gorgeous circus acrobat. After a major spat the pair go off to their assignations and spend the night with their new lovers. Early in the morning Hank discovers he misses Frannie; finding her with Ray, he drags her home naked. She runs off again to go to Tahiti with Ray, but Hank follows her to the airport and begs her to come home. She refuses, and the plane takes off. Then Frannie reappears, unexpectedly, at Hank's side—just like Natalie returning to her husband at the end of *The Rain People*. Frannie and Hank both decide to play it safe, with old loves and old habits.

If visuals were all, *One from the Heart* would be one of the most thrilling experimental films ever made. Unfortunately it also has characters, dialogue, and a plot—all of which are pedestrian and completely dominated by the gorgeous sets, lighting, camera moves, and visual effects. It's the *Apocalypse* problem of too much style for too little content, but magnified a hundred times over. *One from the Heart* keeps its characters at physical and emotional arm's length, with its long shots, long takes, flashy dissolves, and stagey superimpositions.

More important, the characters in *One from the Heart* often seem like an elitist's vision of what "little people" are like: barely capable of a coherent sentence, much less the snappy repartee of the lower-class characters in, say, an old Busby Berkeley musical. Tom Waits's songs are far more articulate than Frannie and Hank. Coppola's characters are dwarfed, not merely by the scenery but by the writing, the direction, and the remote-controlled acting (in which, for instance, Forrest puts on an urban accent so coarse that Hank seems crude as well as stupid). Both Frannie and Hank sell out their dreams, even though, by making the film, Coppola had fulfilled one of his own, and at a recklessly high price. Apparently, grand dreams are a privilege reserved for creative geniuses, not ordinary schmoes. The central, unforgivable failing of *One from the Heart* is that Coppola seems to hold his characters in contempt.

A few people walked out during the screening, but not many. And at the end of the movie the audience applauded politely.

As people filed out, Coppola went backstage to hold a press conference. About seventy-five openly hostile reporters and photographers showed up. They smelled blood. "How do you feel, now that everyone dislikes the picture?" was the very first query.

Coppola seemed stunned by their savagery. "A lot of people in there looked as though they *did* like the movie," he answered.

At the party afterward 647 guests ate shellfish, cabbage soup, several pastas, cold cuts and desserts and drank all they could. The following people told Coppola they thought he'd made a great movie: Norman Mailer, Joseph Papp, Robert Duvall, Thomas Hoving, Andy Warhol, Carly Simon, Richard Gere, Susan Sarandon, Christopher Walken, Robert De Niro, and Martin Scorsese. Then The Dingbats (twelve-year-old Sofia Coppola, and Zoetroper Bernard Gersten's two similar-aged daughters) got up and did a little dance number, several dozen times, as the live orchestra played.

Coppola had spent nearly $90,000 for the Music Hall, the party, *The New York Times* ad, the programs, posters, promotional buttons, and split pea soup. The box-office take had been slightly over $51,000. Not a bad deal, if it would buy his film a better image.

The next morning a New York publicity woman warned Coppola, "It looks as though the press is lining up against the movie."

"From what I saw last night, the audience was interested in this picture," Coppola insisted. "They could see that this picture is different. I think this picture will be like *Apocalypse. One from the Heart* will change the way people look at movies. Just as *Apocalypse* eventually did." (Despite Coppola's frequent pronouncements on this subject, wishing doesn't always make it so. The consensus on *Apocalypse* among film

critics and viewers has not changed greatly in the decade since
its release; it has always had a small core of enthusiasts, but
most people still describe the final hour with such adjectives
as "murky," "pretentious," and "disappointing.")

"I'm tired of making films so that people can come out and
try to shoot them down," snapped Coppola. "I don't know
whether I want people to see this picture. Why can't I just
put the studio up for sale? Liquidate everything? Can't a guy
opt out?"

The Zoetrope executives in the room tried to cool him
down. One of them reminded him of all the great films that
initially flopped. Spiotta assured him he'd find a new distributor inside two weeks. Anyway, he said, Coppola couldn't
shelve the film because he owed too much money on it. Some
comfort.

As always, Coppola had asked that critics not review the
preview of his unfinished film, and as always, they reviewed
it anyway. Hadn't he sent them free tickets?

Rex Reed's critique in the New York *Daily News* was particularly vehement, but not untypical. It was headlined HERE'S
ONE FROM THE HEART: HOGWASH! Janet Maslin in *The New
York Times* was more respectful, but she was far from enthusiastic. David Ansen in *Newsweek* agreed that the visual effects were wonderful but complained that they overwhelmed
the story. *Daily Variety*'s critic loved the film's technique but
was less impressed with its commercial prospects.

Coppola refused to believe the reviews. "We're now certain the public is going to line up at the box office to see it
whenever we show it," he pronounced. "We've demonstrated
that with just a few days prep we could out-gross any movie in
the world." He'd apparently overlooked the fact that the ultra-
hyped Radio City preview had *lost* nearly $40,000.

On January 20 two sneak previews were held in Los Angeles. They sold out as quickly as the East Coast screenings,
and the West Coast audiences reacted with much greater enthusiasm.

Two days later the film received its first (and virtually its
last) mainstream rave, from Sheila Benson in the Los Angeles
Times. "It's so easy to love *One from the Heart*," she wrote.
"You just let yourself relax and float away with it. A work of
constant astonishment, Francis Coppola's new film is so daring

it takes away your breath while staggering you visually." She compared the film to airbrush art, 3-D pop-up greeting cards, neon sculpture. "Musicals have been far emptier than this," she added, "in terms of real emotion, and very few have dared this greatly."

Andrew Sarris's *Village Voice* review was a devastating pan. "What made Coppola think," he asked, "that contemporary audiences were nostalgic more for the sets in the background of old movies than for the sweet sentiments in the foreground? With all his technological huffing and puffing, Coppola has thrown out the baby and photographed the bath water."

The reviews didn't make it any easier for Spiotta to dig up a new distributor; by the last week in January even Avco-Embassy (a studio in deep trouble) had declined, and several other studios had attached impossible conditions to their offers. Columbia was far more interested in Coppola's next project, *The Outsiders,* than in *One from the Heart.* It would consider distributing the film only if it weren't required to put up any front money. Warners wanted *Hammett* and *Escape Artist* but would take *One from the Heart* only if Coppola were willing to sell the distribution rights in perpetuity. Universal offered $6 million but only if it got all the distribution rights, including cable, network TV, videocassette, and sound track record. Coppola nixed 'em all.

Frank Yablans, who many years earlier had gambled on letting a kid named Francis Ford Coppola direct *The Godfather,* looked on in bemusement. "When Francis is Francis, he's worth $60 million," he told writer William Goldman. "When Francis is on an ego trip, he's a disaster."

Finally Spiotta announced that Zoetrope would release *One from the Heart* all by itself. While it couldn't handle wide-release distribution, it could certainly manage a limited art film release in major cities. "Unprecedented excitement justifies our decision to initiate the release of the film ourselves," Spiotta proclaimed. Irwin Yablans, who had served as a consultant for the distribution of *Apocalypse* and produced *Halloween,* set up the bookings, rapidly lining up twenty-five theaters for an eight-city showcase. The film would open on February 11, 1982, in Los Angeles, New York, Las Vegas, Seattle, Toronto, Chicago, Denver, and San Francisco.

The next day Columbia changed its mind; some execs had

looked at the film again and decided that it might be OK after all. "The deal does not involve a great deal of up-front money," admitted Spiotta. "None, in fact. We've decided to go with a lower distribution fee and retain control of all rights."

Meanwhile, Coppola made a few minor changes in *One from the Heart,* if only to justify his attacks on the press for reviewing an "unfinished" film. A few days after the deal was finalized, Coppola saw Columbia's new ad campaign, which promised more lust than romance. He was not amused, but unfortunately there wasn't a thing he could do about it. Zoetrope's whole future now rested on *One from the Heart,* and Coppola needed Columbia much more than it needed him. Only eight years earlier, he had said, "I could make five failures, five pictures nobody liked, and I'd still be the guy who directed *The Godfather.*" It was true, but only in the sense that, presumably, if he had cared to, he could have raised money for a commercial picture of a similar subject. But he didn't care to—and fond memories of *The Godfather* wouldn't save him from his creditors.

As *One from the Heart*'s premier drew closer, Coppola's anxiety mounted. Every filmmaker, even the greatest of them, makes a flop from time to time; it's a given of the movie business and need not wreck a career. Coppola's peril was far worse; his judgment had become subject to question.

Still, maybe a miracle would happen. Maybe the horse would talk again. In a desperate attempt to hype the film to the youth audience, Coppola granted a lengthy interview to *Rolling Stone*'s Jonathan Cott (a close, longtime friend of Luddy's); naturally he took the opportunity to praise the new technology. "Someday in the near future," he said confidently, "it will be possible to put *One from the Heart* directly into your mind." It didn't occur to him that viewers might not want their minds electronically imprinted with *One from the Heart.*

Coppola was still certain that the "little people" would ignore the reviews. Or maybe his old and influential admirer Pauline Kael, who had still not gone into print, would come to his rescue with a paean of praise.

Instead, just before *Heart*'s official release, Kael dealt it the unkindest pan of all:

> When a director announces that the movie he is
> working on is "ahead of its time," you can guess that

he's in deep trouble, because what he's saying is that the public won't know enough to appreciate what he has done. When a director announces that he is becoming a film "composer," you know he's saying that he doesn't have much in the way of a story or characters. . . .

This movie isn't from the heart, or from the head, either; it's from the lab. . . . *One from the Heart* is like a jewelled version of a film student's experimental pastiche—the kind set in a magical junk yard. . . . It's cold and mechanized; it's at a remove from its own action. Everything runs together—the movie is like melted ice cream. . . . Coppola has found a way to shrivel movie magic. . . . The artist has been consumed by the technology.

Investor Jack Singer could read the writing on the wall, if not in the *New Yorker*. Two days after Kael's review came out, it was painfully clear that the movie would never make him any money, and he served Zoetrope with a ninety-day foreclosure notice.

Quietly Bob Spiotta started soliciting bids for the property. He had ninety days to do an end run around Singer. Coppola stewed in silence, deeply hurt by Kael and the other pans. His confidence was shaken. On February 3 he made an unprecedented confession to critic Michael Ventura. There really might, he admitted, be some cinematic factors in *One from the Heart* that put audiences off. He'd done *Heart* as a Kabuki play and realized now that viewers didn't get it. Nor did they like being held at a medium distance when they yearned for the cut to the close-up of conventional love stories. "The lighting was as important as the actors," he conceded, and "a lot of [elements in the film] didn't work the way I intended. You couldn't get into it like you get into it when you're looking into Humphrey Bogart's eyes."

Just before the official premiere of *One from the Heart*, Coppola agreed to an interview with Lee Grant (not the actress, but the reporter) of the Los Angeles *Times*. The critics, he observed, couldn't deal with *One from the Heart* because it was too experimental for them. Then he turned to the betrayer, Pauline Kael.

In 1974, when he'd been riding high on a wave of critical

approval that owed a lot to her thoughtful and passionate *New Yorker* reviews, Coppola had said, "When I make a bad picture, I expect [Pauline Kael] to blast me higher than a kite, and I'll be grateful for that."

Now Coppola said, "I'm insulted she reviewed *One from the Heart*. Everybody knows Pauline has been struggling to maintain her level among the critics. It's also well known that after getting supportive reviews from her in the past, I didn't maintain a personal relationship. I didn't invite her to lunch like Robert Altman did."

"Rex Reed once said I didn't know how to thank them for making me," he said. "Those two and Andrew Sarris are the boring old guard. The New York film critics in particular are like those who run the Golden Globes. All these little people you wouldn't care about if they didn't have their little thing going."

He went on to insist that every film Zoetrope ever made, from 1969 on, had been a hit. He seemed to have conveniently forgotten the dismal financial performances of *The Rain People*, *THX*, and *The Conversation*.

Coppola's shocking outburst caused a sensation. Entertainment reporters who'd enthusiastically covered the ups and downs of Coppola's career began to wonder, in print, whether he was going mad. Even Zoetrope's publicity chief was appalled. "I've had his picture facing the wall for the last two weeks," said Max Bercutt, the tough old newspaperman who headed the shrinking publicity department. "I wish he'd stop giving interviews, all he does is blame everybody else."

On February 11, 1982, *One from the Heart* opened in forty-one theaters in eight cities. Vincent Canby, lead critic for *The New York Times*, hadn't gone to the Radio City preview, and now he claimed to be mystified by the comparative kindness of the reports that came out of those screenings, a kindness he attributed to guests' embarrassed politeness toward a host.

One from the Heart, he thought, was "unfunny, unjoyous, unsexy and unromantic."

In other cities reviews ranged form tepid to frigid. The film opened well in San Francisco, Los Angeles, New York, and Toronto and then abruptly dropped off. Elsewhere it flopped instantly.

In desperation, Columbia did a survey of movie patrons as they left the theater. The results revealed that despite Coppola's determination to blame his problems on bad press, the people who bought tickets did so mainly *because* they'd read about his ongoing struggle to complete the film. However, only half of them liked what they saw.

In a frenzy of market research, Zoetrope hired Pat Caddell (former President Carter's media researcher, who'd been media adviser on *Apocalypse*) to do a more detailed survey, and paid Cambridge Survey Research $20,000 for additional exit polls.

These pollsters confirmed that only half the audience enjoyed *One from the Heart*. Which half? The biggest *Heart* fans, it turned out, were college-educated unmarried males under age thirty-five. The viewers who liked the film least were women of all ages, who expected a warmer, more conventional treatment of sex and romance. "Beware of misleading women!" the researchers concluded.

Instead of opening wider, the usual pattern once a film has premiered, Columbia made a desperate decision to decrease the number of theaters playing *One from the Heart*. It wanted to start all over, hoping to build a gradual public awareness of what the film really was like—a "platform" strategy it used successfully with *Tess* and *Absence of Malice*. It reduced the release to nineteen carefully chosen theaters in affluent neighborhoods.

In the first twenty days of release in these theaters, *One from the Heart* grossed a pathetic $805,000. It became brutally clear that the film had no "legs," legs being the amount of business a picture does after its first week in release. There was not the remotest chance that it would recoup its costs.

Soon afterward Columbia cut the release to just eight theaters in eight cities, hoping for gradual increases in attendance. The hopes were in vain. Coppola looked at the figures and saw his studio disappearing before his eyes.

Desperate to put the failure behind him, Coppola slipped quietly away to Tulsa to start preproduction on *The Outsiders*. The seven-week shoot, budgeted at $15 million, was scheduled to start on March 1. This time electronics would truly keep the costs down since Coppola already owned all the gadgets he needed.

To those who remained behind at Zoetrope, Tulsa seemed a strange choice for a location. Most people (especially Tulsans, who ought to know) regard the city as a hellhole. On the other hand, Susan E. Hinton had been living in Tulsa when she wrote *The Outsiders* at age sixteen; in fact, she had recently moved back from Texas to her hometown. Coppola considered Tulsa the perfect site. Its drab flatland vistas, colorful wrecked-car cemeteries, petroleum-processing plants, and oil-polluted air would serve as an evocative visual backdrop for Hinton's tale. Best of all, it was wholly free from "Hollywood phonies," as he pointedly put it.

The March 1 start date came and went without a foot of film running through a camera. There was no money to shoot and no way for Zoetrope to get a bank loan without a solid commitment from a distributor.

Back at Zoetrope, another twenty employees received pink slips, leaving a staff of only thirty-five, most of whom were working for deferred salaries (i. e., for free) to keep the studio going. Even Coppola could see it was hopeless. Early in March he announced that he was selling the studio. Spiotta had already received bids of $15.5 million and $20 million. Unfortunately, since Singer had already served Zoetrope with a foreclosure notice, he had to approve the bids, and he rejected both of them.

Coppola tried to make it sound like an unforced decision, but behind the scenes the Chase Manhattan Bank was threatening to foreclose, too, unless it got the $31 million still owed on *Heart, Escape Artist,* and *Hammett.* "When a bank loan is in trouble," Coppola told a friend, "the bank turns it over to 'work-out' people, and they are very, very, *very* tough." Coppola turned on his most persuasive manner and convinced Chase and its "work-out" people to let him repay at least part of the debt by going back to work on his new film.

A pair of articles appeared in the Los Angeles *Herald Examiner* under the single headline APOCALYPSE SOON. In the first piece, critic Peter Rainer pointed out: "Coppola [has] misjudged his abilities as an artist. He's cast himself as a visionary—and yet his great work has been solidly grounded in the old-fashioned narrative tradition. Whenever he's tried to move outside that tradition—in *The Rain People, Apocalypse Now, One from the Heart*—he's foundered terribly. He's a great classical director who has disdain for classical forms."

The companion piece by Gregg Kilday (subtitled "Francis the Talking Fool") summed up: "Coppola has yet to display any understanding of the dire situation that faces him. The tragedy is that [his] self-imposed isolation, his self-righteousness, his sense that a serious injustice has been done him, appears to be growing. Francis Coppola is, without question, one of the giants of American cinema, but right now he is talking as if he could become the Jim Jones of the movies."

Zoetrope's departing employees were not shy about assigning blame. "The picture is a big flop," one of them admitted to a reporter. "The studio is broke. And the bubble has finally burst."

Chapter Eighteen

Father Film Among the Teenagers: *The Outsiders* and *Rumble Fish* (1982–1983)

COPPOLA NEEDED CHEERING up, and he turned to two of his favorite remedies for the blues: kids and high tech toys. When he left for Tulsa on March 1, 1982, to start shooting *The Outsiders*, he brought all his electronics with him, as well as the silver Airstream. Coppola also brought a French-style beret, which he wore throughout the shoot; in this, and his corduroys, he looked the very image of a chubby Left Bank existentialist artiste, and not at all like a science nerd.

Coppola's situation was beginning to resemble the heros in a Greek tragedy: the tale of a great man who falls out of favor with the gods through overreaching ambition. Catharsis is achieved when the hero finally achieves godly insight and acknowledges his own responsibility in his fall. But Coppola refused to take the fall. He got mad, and he went back to work.

To fill the leading role of Ponyboy, Coppola found C. Thomas "Tom" Howell. Primarily a rodeo stunt rider, Howell had played a small role in *E. T.* He was to share the spotlight with two teen heartthrobs. Eighteen-year-old Matt Dillon, who had starred in *Over the Edge, Little Darlings, My Bodyguard,* and the just-finished *Tex,* would play Dallas. (To explain his Jersey accent, a line was written into the script referring to him as a graduate of a New York reform school.) And Diane Lane, seventeen, who had top-lined in *A Little Romance* and

Cattle Annie and Little Britches, would play Cherry Valance, a teenage temptress named after the cowboy played by John Ireland in *Red River.*

The plot of *The Outsiders* revolved around two rival teen gangs, the Greasers (from the wrong side of the tracks) and the Socs (well-to-do-kids, who pronounced their gang "SOHshes.") To play the Greasers and Socs, Coppola and Fred Roos cast a group of near unknowns, many drawn from TV family sitcoms. Once again, as in *The Godfather, American Graffiti,* and *The Conversation,* their casting was so good that in retrospect it seems almost clairvoyant; the list reads like an honor roll of today's hottest young actors: Tom Cruise, Emilio Estevez, Rob Lowe, Ralph Macchio, and dancer Patrick Swayze all would go on to starring roles in mainstream movies. Michelle Meyrink (currently a fixture in teen comedies) was a special case; as a junior high school girl she had hung around the *Godfather II* shoot, watching the filming and pestering Fred Roos. When she graduated from high school, she contacted Roos for advice on where to study acting; finally she was signed to make her film debut in *Outsiders.*

There were only two adult roles, and neither was cast to type. Author Susie Hinton was living in Tulsa with her husband, three dogs, a cat, and a horse, and all her movie deals specified that she would get to hang out on the set and play a bit part. Coppola cast her as a nurse. Singer-songwriter Tom Waits essayed another bit part as a bar bouncer.

For his technical crew, Coppola rounded up the usual A team: Dean Tavoularis would be production designer, Fred Roos and Gray Frederickson would produce, and Carmine Coppola would compose the music. Francis, who'd continued thinking of *The Outsiders* as a *Gone With the Wind* for kids, asked his father for "schmaltzy classical music"; Carmine was only too glad to oblige. To shoot the film, Coppola chose cinematographer Steve Burum, his old UCLA pal who'd done second-unit photography for *Apocalypse Now* and *The Black Stallion* and moved up to director of photography on *The Escape Artist.* Gian-Carlo (who was proving an eager and able apprentice in the family business) would serve as associate producer, Roman would work as an assistant, and twelve-year-old Sofia would make her acting debut (under the pseudonym Domino) in a small role as a pesty little girl.

As cast and crew gathered, Coppola tinkered with the script and the electronics. There was still no distributor and thus no way of getting a bank loan to begin shooting. To keep everyone from getting bored (or worried) while the wheeling and dealing continued, Coppola converted an abandoned schoolhouse into a computerized studio and began videotaping rehearsals in what had been the school gym. Luckily the wait wasn't long. Just nine days after Coppola went to Tulsa, Warner Brothers bought into the production. It was already committed to distributing *The Escape Artist* and *Hammett*, which it had picked up from Orion. (The credit on both films read: "An Orion release through Warner Brothers of a Zoetrope Studios production"—Byzantine evidence of armies of Hollywood lawyers at work behind the scenes.)

The Outsiders was scheduled for release on October 18, 1982, seven months away. Warners wasn't putting up much front money, but with a distributor in place Coppola could now raise the modest $10 million he needed from banks and foreign distributors. (*The Outsiders* was set up as a separate company, to keep its finances from getting tangled in the demise of Zoetrope.) Despite his bitter criticisms of Hollywood studios, Coppola was prepared to play the Very Good Boy, at least for the moment. "Cooperation between me and Warner Brothers is the idea all the way, from the concept through the openings," he proclaimed. "There hasn't been such thematic concern for young people since *Rebel Without a Cause*."

Coppola had worked hard on his revisions of Kathleen Knutsen Rowell's screenplay. Her treatment had diverged sharply from Hinton's book, in an attempt to correct some of its adolescent hokiness. Coppola knew he was pitching his movie to the novel's fanatical teenage readers, and he was certain they would resent even the tiniest divergence from their beloved original. He threw away Rowell's script and created a new screenplay, taken, scene by scene and line by line, from the book. He may even have used a marvelous computer gadget he had—a combination of a flatbed scanner, word processor, and optical character recognition software—that could translate novels into screenplay format without human intervention. You fed in book pages, and out came a script.

In any case, now that he was actually in production, he decided that script credit would be nice. Not just cocredit, but sole credit. He may have been thinking about the extra residuals such a credit would pay.

In Hollywood, whenever a production executive, such as a director, requests writing credit, an automatic arbitration process kicks in, administered by the screenwriters' union known as the Writers Guild of America.

Early in the shoot of *The Outsiders*, Coppola informed the Writers Guild that he felt he deserved sole screen credit for the script; then he waited for arbitration to be scheduled.

For once, the shoot went relatively easily. With a video monitor next to the camera, Coppola could see the image as it was shot and check it out with instant videotape replay before moving on. Even cinematographer Burum was delighted with the process. It was much like the drill on *One from the Heart*, with one big exception: Coppola was on the set with the actors, not hiding in his Airstream trailer. Once a scene was in the can, Coppola used his computer to send comments and editing suggestions directly to editor Ann Goursaud, who was back in Hollywood working on the string-out.

It was a happy set. Coppola enjoyed the kids, and they got an equal kick out of him. Matt Dillon affectionately called him Father Film. Coppola paid the teenagers the ultimate compliment: He treated them just like grown-up actors, encouraging their input, allowing them to improvise dialogue, letting them devise details to bring their characters to life. Emilio Estevez dreamed up his own hairdo, a grotesque Vaselined ducktail with a front flip that no professional hairdresser could ever (or would ever want to) get just right. Furthermore, given the unlimited amount of beer they were allowed to guzzle after each day's shoot, the kids didn't even mind the long workdays. "My shortest day on the set was 10 hours," recalled the stoical Tom Howell, "the longest 18."

To underline the tension in the script with real-life emotions, Coppola pulled a wicked trick. He arranged for the Greaser actors to be treated like scum off the set. The company housed them on the third floor of the hotel it was renting, gave them miserly allowances, handed them scripts in Thriftway binders, and instructed the hotel staff to make room service slow and sloppy. Meanwhile the Soc actors were housed on the hotel's top floor, were given allowances big enough to rent cars, were provided with scripts bound in engraved leather binders, and found a hotel staff ready to cater to their every whim. Predictably the cast divided into castes offscreen; Socs visited Tulsa's glitzier discos, while Greasers amused themselves at mud-wrestling matches.

Coppola's passion for realism even extended to offscreen delinquency. On one occasion he encouraged the Greasers to take over a local café and terrorize the staff by throwing food on the ceiling, while he captured the action on videotape for later study. Another time Father Film got Matt Dillon to indulge in some work-related shoplifting, all for the sake of art. "We actually went into this drugstore, and I stole a pack of cigarettes," Dillon recalled. "Francis said, 'Don't worry, man, we'll bail you out.' It was a lot of fun."

Amazingly nothing went seriously wrong. Coppola, who was accustomed to his films being disrupted by acts of God and Banks, didn't know whether to be worried or what. The only difficulties were so picayune they were hardly worth mentioning, like an overenthusiastic rehearsal for the rumble in the rain, when Estevez got a cut lip, Tom Cruise a broken thumb, and Tom Howell a shiner.

The closest thing to a disaster (and it wasn't very close) happened when Coppola insisted on shooting a big scene in a pasture outside Tulsa despite forecasts of thunderstorms and tornadoes. It was the critical scene in which the Greasers rescue some tots from a blazing country church, and it proved the show biz adage about never working with animals or little children. The kindergarten-age extras were maddeningly hard to direct, and a cow kept wandering into the frame and spoiling takes. ("Kill that cow!" Coppola yelled after the third time.) On top of that, the smoke and fire effects were so unimpressive they looked like a backyard barbecue.

"More fire! More fire!" demanded Coppola. The technicians gave him more fire and promptly set the church steeple ablaze. The local fire chief was just getting ready to freak out when, from out of nowhere, the scheduled thunderstorm swept in off the plains and put out the flames.

Coppola eyed the sky with disgust, thinking about the cost of reshoots. Fortunately the twisters that had been forecast to accompany the thunderstorms stayed home that day, leaving the location standing for another try the next day.

One nice thing for Coppola was that the shoot was almost

entirely free of reporters. A few of the noxious pests slipped in, of course, but nothing like the mobs of newshounds that had bedeviled him on *One from the Heart.*

Matt Dillon and Susie Hinton were already pals. They had met on the set of *Tex* (Tim Hunter's film of another Hinton book) and hit it off instantly. The friendship was cemented when Dillon told Hinton that *Rumble Fish,* her least popular novel, was his favorite book. Until then, Hinton noted, every time she got a letter from a kid saying that *Rumble Fish* was his favorite book, the return address would be a reform school.

"We gotta get somebody to make a movie of it so I can play Rusty-James," said Dillon. The only problem with that was that Rusty-James was fourteen, Dillon was already eighteen and it might take awhile to get funding. If Dillon got too old for the part, Hinton asked, would he accept the role of Rusty's big brother? "Yeah," Dillon answered, "and if I'm *really* old, like 27, I'll direct."

With *The Outsiders* proceeding so smoothly, Dillon saw his chance. He rounded up the teenage cast and they all ganged up on Coppola. Hey, Francis, you gotta read *Rumble Fish,* man! Coppola read it, and he liked it. For one thing, it was very short, and he liked short novels. For another, he says, "It was written when Susie Hinton was older—and drunk, I think. It had tremendous, really impressive vision and dialogue and characters and complicated ideas, the kind of ideas you don't totally understand in your head, but you feel that you understand them."

Coppola was ripe for *Rumble Fish* and its "complicated ideas." As so often before, he was growing uneasy with the commercial focus of his current film. Sure, he had to reestablish his credibility with *The Outsiders,* but then he would reestablish his artistic reputation with *Rumble Fish.* "I really started to use *Rumble Fish* as my carrot for what I promised myself when I finished *The Outsiders,*" he noted later.

Although *Rumble Fish,* as written by Hinton, wasn't set in Tulsa, there was no reason Coppola's screen version couldn't be. The means of production were at his fingertips; everything was in place. Coppola decided to make *Rumble Fish* right where he was, back to back with *The Outsiders,* using much of the same technical personnel and starting as soon as *The Outsiders* wrapped. Matt Dillon would play Rusty-James. For his

big brother, the mysterious Motorcycle Boy, Fred Roos nominated Mickey Rourke. Rourke had played a bit part in *Body
Heat* and a featured role in *Diner,* and Roos had pointed him
out to Coppola at one of the auditions for *The Outsiders.* There
had been no part for him in the earlier film, but the *Rumble
Fish* role might have been written with Rourke in mind.

While shooting continued on *The Outsiders,* Coppola and
Hinton went to work on the script for *Rumble Fish.* Ads were
placed in *Variety* to fill out the cast. Getting a distributor was
something else again. A Coppola film was no longer considered a very good risk, and what's more, Hollywood old-tim-
ers sneered at the idea of shooting two films back to back; it
sounded like some old-fashioned B western setup from the era
when a bunch of movie people would go to a location and turn
out two cheap oaters in a row. "No one took me seriously at
all," said Coppola. "Like, you're in trouble and everyone knows
you're in trouble."

Coppola turned to the deal makers at Warners, but they
were unhappy at the thought of Coppola's shooting *Rumble
Fish* just when his full creative energies would be needed for
editing *The Outsiders.* It didn't help when two less-than-fab-
ulous Zoetrope releases opened, and closed, just as Coppola
was pulling Warners' coat.

The first, a refurbished telefilm called *Too Far to Go,* was
a marital melodrama based on several stories by John Updike,
starring Blythe Danner, Michael Moriarty, and Glenn Close. It
had aired just once, in 1979, in a throwaway time slot where
nobody watched it—except Tom Luddy, Zoetrope's head of
special projects. Luddy liked it well enough to suggest that
Zoetrope pick it up for theatrical release. Coppola spent
$250,000 of some bank's money on improved credits, color,
sound, and a new score by Elizabeth Swados.

It opened on April 23, 1982, at one of Don Rugoff's Cinema V (he restored the original name after Coppola had pulled
out) art houses in Manhattan. It closed after six weeks; none
of the national distributors wanted it, and Coppola lost nearly
all of his investment.

Coppola had been far more intimately involved with the
second Zoetrope lemon, Caleb Deschanel's *The Escape Artist,*
on which he'd actively intervened in the rewriting, the shoot,
and the editing. After a series of sneak screenings, the film was

deemed ready for release in April 1982. Receiving mainly pans, it eked out decent but unexciting grosses for a few weeks; then Warners withdrew it.

Back in Hollywood, Zoetrope stood virtually deserted. Coppola had already agreed to put it up for sale; now, on April 15, he sadly named his price. Zoetrope would go on the auction block for a minimum bid of $20 million to cover the $5.6 million purchase price, the cost of renovations, and inflation. On May 4, the day Jack Singer's ninety-day foreclosure notice came due, Spiotta managed to convince Singer to hold off until he and Coppola could have the auction. Spiotta told Singer they were getting lots of nibbles.

As if things weren't bad enough, Marlon Brando bestirred himself from his Tahitian idylls and sued Zoetrope and United Artists for $48 million he said they owed him for *Apocalypse*. In all the time since its release, Brando had received only a piddling $2.7 million for his five week's work. Where was the rest of his 11.3 percent of the adjusted gross? He decided he wanted $8 million, the amount he figured he was contractually owed on a presumed $60 million adjusted gross, plus $40 million in punitive damages. Instantly a press blackout descended over the case; presumably it was settled out of court. (Incidental note: If Brando's calculations were right, *Apocalypse* was still not in profit, especially considering the additional distribution costs for European release.)

The financial disaster facing Coppola was now as complex as the tangle of interlocking loans, liens, and mortgages that had sustained the studio. Coppola owed somewhere between $40 and $50 million. He could declare Chapter 13 bankruptcy and free himself from all the debt, while keeping most of his high tech equipment, but the price would be giving up nearly all his real estate to his creditors: his house in Los Angeles, his apartment in New York, the wonderful old Sentinel Building (his San Francisco HQ, filled with the laughing ghosts of Frisco's earthquake-era scoundrels), and, unbearably, an enormous chunk of the peaceful Napa vineyard he was growing to love, not to mention all the art inside the house, the Scopitone, and his two Tuckers.

Instead, he renegotiated his loans, accepting a more stringent arrangement with the Chase Manhattan Bank in exchange for an extension of his repayment schedule. Under the new terms he could keep his properties, but he had to sign over the rights to most of his films. He'd always been proud of owning so many of his own movies; now Chase Manhattan owned them.

Meanwhile, *The Outsiders* continued smoothly, and on May 15 Coppola completed the principal photography. He had five months until its scheduled release; he could, he thought, edit at night and shoot *Rumble Fish* by day. In fact, the *Rumble Fish* shoot offered a handy fringe benefit. When Coppola looked at the tentative editor's cut of *The Outsiders*, he decided some of the scenes were still not working right (despite his instant video replays). But no problem; since he was filming *Rumble Fish* in Tulsa anyway, it would be easy enough to rebuild a few sets and reshoot the scenes.

More immediately, Coppola had to deal with the Writers Guild arbitration over his demand for sole script credit for *The Outsiders*. Normally, in a WGA arbitration, each claimant submits a lengthy, scene-by-scene analysis of the script in an attempt to prove authorship of more than 50 percent. Coppola, however, merely sent a short, icy letter saying, "I understand the need for automatic arbitration, but this script is totally my writing." Period.

The panel of judges (screenwriters all) were appalled at what they considered the arrogance of Coppola's approach; the guild ruled against him, and awarded sole screenplay credit to Kathleen Rowell. Coppola refused to accept the verdict, and appealed the decision. This time he took the legalistic position that since the arbitration hadn't been concluded "in timely fashion," he should automatically win his claim. The guild remained unimpressed.

In the end, Coppola appealed three times, losing again and again, until (as an associate of Rowell's put it) "he finally ran out of technicalities." Even then, Coppola complained that he only lost because of the guild's "antiquated procedures."

The deal makers at Warners were still uninterested in distributing *Rumble Fish*, and they grew even colder when, on June 6, *Hammett* premiered at the Cannes Film Festival, and they read *Daily Variety*'s review. "Overpolished by too many script rewrites, perhaps emasculated by massive footage scraps and belated reshoots, project emerges a rather suffocating film," it went. "A fast playoff may get *Hammett* some attention, but it does not display holding power in its present form."

The picture was now as smokily atmospheric as any old film noir. The detective story had turned into a murky mishmash having something to do with the corruption of city officials in San Francisco. Its look was as exquisitely artificial as an Art Deco lamp but shed very little light on the convolutions of the plot. Frederic Forrest played Dashiell Hammett in a Humphrey Bogart mode (minus the latter's charisma, unfortunately). Peter Boyle played Hammett's venal partner with more juice.

Warners promptly returned *Hammett* to the shelf. Forrest had even more reason to be upset; between *One from the Heart* and *Hammett*, he'd given his prime acting years to Coppola, years in which he'd had to turn down scores of wonderful offers, and the two failed films effectively put an end to his career as a leading man.

Worse was yet in store for Coppola. Warners had been moderately disappointed by *The Escape Artist* and *Hammett*, but it was *seriously* unhappy with the rough cut of *The Outsiders*. And no, it did not wish to buy any more teenpix from Francis Coppola, thank you.

Coppola focused his energies on reediting *The Outsiders* and finding a distributor for *Rumble Fish*. Once again he gathered his cast and crew and went to work even before the financing was in place. The technical personnel were mainly carryovers from *The Outsiders*, or old *Apocalypse* hands who had been working at Zoetrope.

Matt Dillon and Diane Lane would head the cast again. Vincent Spano (an old buddy of Dillon's, who had played a major role in *The Black Stallion Returns*, which was now completed and awaiting release) was featured as well, along with Larry Fishburne, Christopher Penn, and Mickey Rourke. Coppola was particularly excited about working with Rourke, an Actors' Studio-trained performer who Methodically conceived the adored (and apparently schizophrenic) Motorcycle Boy as being "an actor who no longer finds his work interesting."

Coppola also signed Dennis Hopper (now all cleaned up) to play the boys' alcoholic father (Rourke later said that Hopper had been very helpful) and Diana Scarwid as Motorcycle Boy's dope-addicted ex-girlfriend. Scarwid, who had been Oscar-nominated for a supporting role in *Inside Moves* and starred in *Mommie Dearest*, was quite a catch for so small a role. Tom

Waits would play a pool hall owner, Susie Hinton would play a hooker, and Gio (serving as associate producer again, along with brother, Roman) would appear in front of the camera, too (along with sister "Domino"), as a bit player.

Yet another Coppola entered the family business thanks to *Rumble Fish*. Augie's son Nicolas, who'd studied acting at the American Conservatory Theater in San Francisco, had just graduated from Beverly Hills High School. He went direct from starring in school plays to the featured role of Smokey in *Rumble Fish*, but not under his real name. Risking the utter wrath of his grandmother, he changed his last name to Cage, so as to downplay the family connections.

This time Carmine was not invited to write the score. Francis would compose it himself, using mainly percussion. "The idea is that time is running out on these kids," he explained. "There are clocks all over the place, and you feel it in the beat, too." At one point he even brought an electronic metronome to a rehearsal to set a pace for the actors, driving everybody (including himself) crazy with its infernal ticking.

Carmine's reaction was predictable. "When he heard a little tape," Francis said, "he commented how a section of it sounded just like something he had written. I neglected to tell him that the same section also sounded like something some guy a hundred years ago had written. But my father has never been a very encouraging man."

As Coppola worked on the score, he discovered he needed professional help and signed on Stewart Copeland, the American drummer with the English rock band The Police, to improvise a rhythm track; Coppola soon realized that the drummer was proving a far better composer than he and let him take over. Copeland recorded street sounds of Tulsa—machinery, traffic, sirens—and worked them into the sound track using a new device called a Musync; it recorded the film, frame by frame, on videotape with the image on the top, the dialogue in the middle, and musical staves on the bottom so the composer could match every measure to its visual correspondent.

Another unusual hire was Michael Smuin, choreographer and codirector of the San Francisco Ballet and director of the Broadway production of *Sophisticated Ladies*. Coppola had seen Smuin's ballets of *Romeo and Juliet* and *Medea*, liked the way he choreographed violence, and signed him on to stage the big fight scene in *Rumble Fish*. He asked Smuin to include specific, symbolic visual elements: a steam engine; a motorcycle; broken glass; knives; gushing water and blood. Smuin spent a week writing and designing the sequence and introduced a riderless motorcycle as a weapon. He also staged a wistful little street dance for Diana Scarwid and Mickey Rourke, modeling it after the famous pas de deux by William Holden and Kim Novak in *Picnic*.

There was still no money, but Coppola used two weeks of the downtime for videotaped rehearsals in the former school gym. The day after rehearsals ended, he was able to show the film, shot on video and roughly edited, to the crew. It even had music.

Evenings were equally busy. To familiarize cast, crew, and cinematographer Steve Burum with his visual concept for *Rumble Fish*, Coppola put on a miniature film festival, screening old movies that had the look he wanted. He screened Anatole Litvak's *Decision Before Dawn*, a spy movie shot on location amid the bombed-out ruins of Germany just after World War II. "That was where all the smoke and obscurity in *Rumble Fish* came from," Burum commented. They also looked at *Johnny Belinda* and F. W. Murnau's silent masterpiece *The Last Laugh*—the latter mainly to show Matt Dillon how the great silent actor Emil Jannings used body language to convey emotions. They watched *Viva Zapata*, Orson Welles's savage *Macbeth*, Godard's *Breathless*, and expressionist masterpieces like *The Golem*, Murnau's *Sunrise*, and the ultra-eccentric *Cabinet of Dr. Caligari*. In fact, *Caligari* was Coppola's stylistic prototype. "[*Rumble Fish*] is very Expressionistic," he said. "It's like a fable. It all takes place in a kind of twilight zone."

Another big visual influence was *Koyaanisqatsi*, an eccentric, plotless portrait of the evils of urban life, shot mainly in time-lapse stop motion by Godfrey Reggio, with music by fashionable composer Philip Glass. Luddy had discovered it and was arranging for Zoetrope to distribute it as a special project. Coppola was taken by its surreal stop-motion images of clouds, cars, and people racing across the screen, and borrowed the technique to animate sky effects in *Rumble Fish*.

Because the Motorcycle Boy was totally color-blind, a symptom of psychological alienation as well as brain damage sustained in too many fights, Coppola envisioned the film in black and white, with a few color overlays, such as the shots of the Siamese fighting fish of the title. Shooting in black and

white might have been tricky; a few years earlier Coppola would
have had to send his footage to Europe for processing. Luckily,
Woody Allen's insistence on having Gordon Willis shoot *Manhattan* in black and white had restored the technology in the
United States.

On June 30, after marking time for almost six weeks, Coppola finally nabbed a distributor. Universal Pictures agreed to
take *Rumble Fish* as part of a two-picture deal. The other film
was *Napoleon*, which the studio bought outright for a sum var-
iously reported in the same trade paper as $500,000 and $1
million. It had already grossed more than $3 million for Zoe-
trope. Even so, the studio executives were surely a little worried about the idea of taking on a black-and-white youth movie,
too, but the ever-persuasive Coppola talked them into it.

Shooting began on July 12, 1982, with release scheduled
for late spring 1983, about nine months later. Coppola expressed wild enthusiasm. "*Rumble Fish* will be to *The Outsiders* what *Apocalypse Now* was to *The Godfather*," he
declared. (Could he have thought this was good?) "You could
say it's an art film for kids," he added. "You could say it's kind
of an existential beatnik movie."

Evidently the theme of a boy who worships a nearly mythic
older brother appealed to him deeply. In fact, the credits of
the finished film include a dedication to "August Coppola, my
first and best teacher." The Motorcycle Boy reminded him of
the magical allure that his brother, the teenage existentialist,
had held for him when he was a kid, so he came up with the
idea of making the character look like French existentialist
writer Albert Camus. Mickey Rourke loved the idea and used
the image of Camus, with his trademark cigarette dangling out
of the corner of his mouth, as a visual handle for the role.

In light of the explicit connection he draws between Augie and the Motorcycle Boy, it's fascinating to note that Coppola considered Rusty-James, the unappreciated younger
brother, the better one. "All that beautiful stuff he has is
trapped," Coppola said. "He is living for false idols and needs
to get the fundamental message that it is *he* who will survive,
not the Motorcycle Boy. He has to realize that he, not his
brother, is the one who is blessed." If only Coppola had truly
believed it.

Coppola's zest was obvious to everyone on the location.
Compared with *The Outsiders*, said coproducer Doug Clay-

bourne, "*Rumble Fish* is more akin to Francis' taste. The language is tough, it's hard-edged, it's super-realistic in a sense but goes to a kind of a surrealistic edge. It's very metaphoric and uses a lot of symbolism."

What the language was was foul. Coppola decided not to worry about R ratings and encouraged the teenage cast to improvise dialogue in the casually profane slang they used every day. He preferred to ignore the possibility that because his real teenage actors talked dirty, real teenage moviegoers might be legally barred from buying tickets to the film. "Usually you're faced with cutting it all out," Coppola said of the profanity. "This is a movie for kids, and I want it to make sense to them."

Coppola also wanted to make his two teenpix in such radically different styles that no one could possibly confuse them. The first one would be operatic; the second, expressionistic. "The style of *The Outsiders* was very romantic and passionate because kids think that way," said Steve Burum. "The compositions were classical and pictorial with the camera removed and stoic. *Rumble Fish* was exactly the opposite."

To get the feeling of a wasteland, Coppola shot in deserted areas at the edge of town and had Dean Tavoularis build sets of slightly peculiar proportions. Many scenes were shot with a jiggly hand-held camera, to make the audience feel uneasy. Coppola wanted to confront viewers with images that were physically impossible, so he adapted one of the favorite techniques of the old-time German expressionist filmmakers: He had shadows painted on the walls of the sets to make them look ominous. "We wanted people to feel that there was something wrong, give them that certain feeling of uneasiness, that something is a little bit off with reality," Burum explained.

Curiously, one scene in *Rumble Fish* represented a full circle for Coppola. While Susie Hinton had been writing *Rumble Fish*, she had seen *The Rain People* on television and been struck by the scene in which James Caan opens all the animals' cages. She liked it so much that she wrote a similar scene into her book, in which the Motorcycle Boy breaks into a pet shop and frees the fish. So Coppola ended up filming his own scene twice.

The filming of *Rumble Fish* went just as smoothly as *The Outsiders*, and by mid-September it was in the can, on schedule and on budget. Now Coppola had two films to edit.

When he showed a reedited rough cut of *The Outsiders* to

the executives at Warners, they still hated it and insisted that he cut it even shorter. Worse yet, instead of putting it into distribution in October, as planned, Warners announced it was postponing the release of the picture indefinitely, thus indefinitely postponing any profits Coppola would make from it. The delay was irksome, since Coppola knew the teenage audience was itching to see the movie. Teen magazines were already full of photo spreads on *The Outsiders*; five articles had appeared in five successive issues of *Tiger Beat* alone.

As Coppola worked on shortening *The Outsiders*, he developed very mixed feelings about what was coming out. He'd meant the film to be two hours long: big, expansive, melodramatic, a junior *Godfather*, a teenage *Gone With the Wind*. Instead, it was turning out short, lean, and melodramatic, not the same thing at all.

Halfway through October, Coppola defaulted on his mortgage payments to Security Pacific Bank, which had financed the purchase and upgrade of Hollywood General to the tune of $7 million. The bankers gave him a three-month extension but informed him that if he failed to pay up by January 14, 1983, they would have no choice but to foreclose. Foreclosure would mean that Zoetrope would go up for public auction, not for the $20 million minimum Coppola wanted, but for whatever the highest bidder chose to offer.

Coppola left town. In fact, he left the country. *One from the Heart* was opening all over Europe, and Coppola went with it to help with the ballyhoo. It was just the ego boost he needed. Returning home, he reported that the French reviewers "were really *interested* in what I was trying to do. Business there has been good. In Sweden the movie is doing very *very* good business. In Sweden, they really seem to *like* the movie."

When 1983 rolled in, Coppola did not have any spare millions to give Security Pacific Bank. The officers announced they were foreclosing. Coppola had been warned. Glen Speidel, Ellison Miles, and James Nasser would get their money back after Security Pacific's auction, but junior mortgage holders like Jack Singer and the Chase Manhattan Bank would probably be left holding the bag. If Chase Manhattan wanted its money, it would have to foreclose on Coppola's personal holdings: Good-bye, office building; good-bye, Napa Valley vineyard. Singer's options were fewer; his only hope was to make a move before Security Pacific or Chase Manhattan could make theirs.

Coppola claimed to be on the verge of closing a deal for a bailout loan when *Newsweek* ran an article entitled "Coppola's Cash Crunch." The story noted that unless Zoetrope declared bankruptcy, "not even a blockbuster like *The Godfather* would save Coppola from the loss of his dream factory." According to Coppola, the article spooked his bailout backer and queered the loan. On top of everything else, Los Angeles County informed Zoetrope that it was more than two years behind on its property tax, to the tune of $67,500.

Coppola would have done anything to avoid the grim nightmare that loomed ahead: rounds of foreclosure actions, scheduled auctions, stays of execution stopping the auctions, and constant escalation of the debt from the interest on the loans. In fact, he did do something: He left all the grinding, mind-numbing financial and legal hassles to Zoetrope President Robert Spiotta. For the most part, we propose to follow his example.

Coppola finished another reedit of *The Outsiders* and delivered it to the Warners execs. They still hated it. By now Coppola wasn't so crazy about it himself. Nonetheless, they set up a secret test screening for a largely teenage audience, and to the great surprise of all concerned it went over like *The Godfather.*

Set in Tulsa in 1966, the film centers on the conflict between two teenage gangs. Greaser Pony Boy (C. Thomas Howell) and his friend Johnny (Ralph Macchio) anger the Socs when they strike up a friendship with Soc Cherry Valance (Diane Lane). Five Socs attack the two Greasers, and Johnny kills one of them defending his friend.

Aided by the older, wilder Dallas (Matt Dillon), the two boys hide out in an abandoned church outside town, becoming so bored they actually read books: *Gone With the Wind* and a collection of Robert Frost's poetry. When a bunch of kindergarten kids visit the church and get caught in a fire, the Greasers rescue them. Johnny is critically injured.

The fugitives return to town as heroes. From his hospital bed, Johnny counsels that gang warfare is futile, but nothing can stop the big rumble. Helped by Pony Boy's big brother (Patrick Swayze), the Greasers win, a victory underscored by Carmine Coppola's most exultant musical schmaltz. Back in the hospital, Johnny dies of his burns. Dallas goes nuts, grabs a pistol, and runs through the streets until the cops shoot him down. (He had died the same way in Tim Hunter's dark, obscure, and marvelous teenpic *Over the Edge*.)

Coppola's uneasiness about the ninety-one-minute edit seems justified. In cutting the film down, Coppola seems to have cut most of his identity right out of it. It would be almost impossible to identify *The Outsiders* as a Francis Coppola film if you didn't spot his name in the credits. True, the film has a typically theatrical look: Tulsa looks more like a sound stage than a real location, punched up with garish lighting, red skies, and dramatic silhouettes. Also, it's paced like a musical, starting with a series of quick scenes with a *West Side Story* feel.

The film is briskly paced all right, but it finds time for some oddly bathetic images; for instance, when the fugitive Greasers are reluctantly cutting their hair, Coppola shows us a cute little bunny rabbit (in close-up yet) watching them. Any thematic explanation for this bit of Disneyana seems to have ended up on the cutting-room floor. There are odd failures of dramatic continuity, perhaps as a result of the draconian edit, such as the inexplicable absence of gathering clouds to set up the thunderstorm that drenches the climactic rumble. A homoerotic undertone (with the male camaraderie and leather outfits reminding one of Kenneth Anger's *Scorpio Rising*) adds to the peculiar feeling of the film.

The performances are surprisingly uneven. The entire Soc group (including Diane Lane, sporting an on-again, off-again Okie accent) fares poorly. Among the Greasers, Ralph Macchio is surprisingly good, Tom Howell is appealing, and Matt Dillon is strangely luminous, but Emilio Estevez is the only cast member who remembers to speak all his lines with a southwestern twang.

Despite the successful sneak screening, Warners put the film back on the shelf. Disgusted, Coppola knocked off the *Rumble Fish* edit as best as he could. Then he took a leaf from Voltaire's *Candide* and went home to cultivate his Napa vineyard. It had originally been part of the historic Inglenook estate in the years when Inglenook was California's premier winemaker, and it had every potential to become a first-class winery again. Coppola was still a little awed by his slow-maturing Rubicon Cabernet, but he frequently drank his own Vinoforte ("strong wine"), a high-alcohol jug red made from a mishmash of old vines in a corner of the vineyard. He put a

picture of his grandfather on the label and gave it away to friends
and staffers, who did not always love it as much as he did.

Coppola decided that if he was going to be a winemaker,
he ought to be a great winemaker. Vineyard boss Russ Turner
had departed, to be replaced by Steve Beresini. Now, despite
his $50 million debt, Coppola hired the great oenologist André
Tchelistcheff as winemaking consultant. This is the equivalent
of hiring Stradivarius as a consultant for your fiddle factory.

Voltaire must have been right about the value of tending
one's own garden. Coppola was immensely relieved when, early
in February, Warners announced that it would release *The
Outsiders* on March 23, in 829 theaters nationwide. With all
the extra winemaking expenses, some positive cash flow would
be helpful. If the flow of money was high enough, it might
even save Zoetrope from public auction. Or win postponement
number four. Or was it number five? "It's got to be settled
after this one," exploded James Nasser. "It can't go on any
longer." But, of course, it did.

Just before *The Outsiders* opened, a special preview was
held in Fresno, California, for the students at the Lone Star
School who had started the whole thing. Five of the movie's
stars flew in during the afternoon to meet the kids, and Matt
Dillon joined them for the evening screening. Were the kids
thrilled? Does Francis Coppola have a beard?

The critics who saw the film at its premiere were not
thrilled at all. "Well acted and crafted, but highly conventional," said the reviewer at *Variety*. "Pic feels very much like
a 1950s drama about problem kids such as those directed by
Nicholas Ray and Elia Kazan, but is nowhere as penetrating or
electric. Overall B. O. [box office] may be modest, in line with
pic's achievement."

Vincent Canby hit harder in *The New York Times*. "Think
of a remake of *Rebel Without a Cause* directed by someone
under the delusion he's D. W. Griffith shooting *The Birth of a
Nation*," he wrote. "It's a melodramatic kid-film with the narrative complexity of The Three Bears, and a high body-count."

This time, though, Coppola's "little people" came through
for him in spite of the poor reviews. Teenage audiences loved
The Outsiders. For once, they felt, they were being addressed
as equals in a movie, shown as human beings, not as sex ma-
niacs. There had been no adult publicity, but the marketing

campaign in teen magazines and TV shows paid off, as did a
sound track that included rock and roll by Stevie Wonder and
Van Morrison along with semiclassical clichés from Coppola
père. The film sprinted to the top of the box-office charts, earning $6 million the first week, $5 million the second week; it
was Warner's top-grossing film all that spring and ultimately
made back ten times its cost. *"The Outsiders* threw up just
enough money to help me at a time when I needed some big
bucks," Coppola noted. Subsequently it proved just as hot
throughout Western Europe. And it kept on making money. By
1988 Coppola was claiming that it had earned more money for
him, personally, than even *The Godfather*.

Two days after *The Outsiders* opened, another Zoetrope
youth film premiered: *The Black Stallion Returns*, directed by
Bob Dalva. The horse displayed inferior form in its second race,
and *Variety* justly accorded it a slashing pan, calling it "a contrived, cornball story that most audiences will find to be an
interminable bore." Once again the critics were at least partly
wrong. The movie opened strongly, quickly becoming UA's
second best spring film. All the horsey little boys and girls were
determined to see the sequel to their favorite film. However,
it ran on wobbly legs, quickly sliding off the top-grosser charts.

It was nice and quiet in Napa. Too quiet for Coppola. He
continued to plan new movies, as though Zoetrope were still
viable, but everything had changed. One day he went down to
Hollywood to have lunch with a potential backer. "I was talking about how we were gonna do this and do that, " he recalled "and right when I was in mid-sentence, he said, 'You're
already dead.' God, it was chilling."

After a while he took two months out from watching his
vineyard grow to start work on a project he called *Megalopolis*.
He wrote four hundred pages (half novel, half screenplay, to
be made with the same chromakey process he had used for the
Jerry Brown campaign special) about the evils of modern urban life. He considered it a work of art and merely the beginning of a much longer opus.

Meanwhile, down in Hollywood, an old acquaintance of
Coppola's, Robert Evans, was about to save Francis from *Megalopolis* by dragging him into a blockbuster mass-audience
movie with virtually nothing to do with art. It was, after all, an
Evans specialty.

After producing *Godfather I* and *II*, Evans had separated from Paramount to try his hand as an independent producer. He turned out a few flops like *Black Sunday* but hit his stride with *Chinatown* and *Urban Cowboy*. Now he had a new project, another gangster picture, but with a difference. This would be a *musical* gangster picture, set in a famous Harlem nightclub of the Prohibition era. Evans had optioned Jim Haskins's picture book *The Cotton Club* early in 1981. "Gangsters, music, and pussy," he exulted. "How could I lose?" Ever the huckster, Evans designed a poster for the film before he had a script, a cast, or a cent to spend on it.

Then he came up with a terrific plan. He'd round up private investors and finance *The Cotton Club* himself. "It'll be *me*—and not a studio—who owns the negative!" he bragged. (Where could he have come up with such a strange idea?) Arab arms dealer Adnan Khashoggi (later a major player in the Iran-contra scandal and subsequently indicted for racketeering in the Ferdinand Marcos Manhattan real estate scandal) provided the seed money. The shoot itself would be financed by the Doumani brothers, who owned the El Morocco and the Tropicana in Las Vegas. Evans explained to them that *Cotton Club* was a sure thing, especially at a bargain-basement price of only $20 million (/$23 million). He spent some of his seed money to hire Mario Puzo to write a script. Robert Altman agreed to direct. Evans announced that Al Pacino would star, or maybe Sylvester Stallone, with Richard Pryor costarring.

Then, just as the film was getting into high gear, Evans became seriously distracted. He'd managed to get busted for possession of cocaine the year before, and when his trial concluded, his suspended sentence was predicated on the condition that he produce a couple of spots for an antidrug television campaign. Evans devised a campaign based on the theme "Getting High on Yourself," and got so high on the campaign himself that he spent an entire year doing multiples of the number of spots that were required of him. Somehow, he completely forgot about *Cotton Club*. Altman lost patience and bowed out.

In the summer of 1982, while Coppola was in Tulsa, Evans reactivated the project and personally revised Puzo's script, combining it (for reasons known only to himself) with the story of his marital breakup with Ali MacGraw. It ended up as an awful mishmash of romantic misery, gangsters, dope wars, and jazz, set in Harlem in 1929.

Then Evans got high on the idea of directing this opus himself. When Stallone and Pryor found out, they lost no time in extricating themselves. Gregory Hines virtually insisted on replacing Pryor (it would be his first big starring role), and Richard Gere was delighted to take Stallone's place, especially when Evans offered him an astonishingly sweet deal. Not only would Gere receive a flat $1.5 million fee, plus 10 percent of the adjusted gross, but he'd get an additional $125,000 for every week the film ran over schedule. However, since Gere was signed to do another picture starting in December 1983, it was time for Evans to play or pay.

He booked the historic Astoria Studios in New York and got a union exemption to shoot in the European style, a late-starting eight-hour workday with an all-day buffet rather than a disruptive lunch break. He was sure this would save $10 million. At this point the Paramount executives finally got around to reading Evans's rewrite of Puzo's script and immediately canceled their distribution deal amid a barrage of mutual accusations. Richard Gere hated the script so much he threatened to quit, too; production designer Richard Sylbert was equally horrified. The Doumani brothers read it and promptly withdrew all their money. It was the Script from Hell.

Although Orion agreed to pick up the distribution rights, Evans was not stupid. He took a hard look at his screenplay, saw that it was full of holes, and realized that he wasn't a good enough script doctor to patch them himself.

Then it dawned on him. He and Puzo constituted two-thirds of the surefire *Godfather* team—and the missing third happened to be a great script doctor and also happened to be so broke he'd probably take any work he could get. Even from Robert Evans, who'd nearly fired him from the first *Godfather*, who'd claimed the credit for both *Godfather*s, who'd bad-mouthed him in the gossip columns (and all over town). But hey, you don't get to be a legendary Hollywood producer if you're short on chutzpah.

Thus it was that in March 1983 Robert Evans made a phone call. "Francis," he pleaded. "Francis, my baby is sick and needs a doctor."

Chapter Nineteen

Cotton Club Breakdown (1983–1984)

COPPOLA WAS NOT a big fan of Robert Evans. In fact, if a list of Evans's acquaintances had been compiled in order of their affections for him, Coppola's name would have been quite close to the bottom. But in spite of his better judgment, he was touched by the producer's plea for rescue. "Somehow Bob Evans inspires people to want to take care of him—maybe because he's like a reckless prince or something," said Coppola. "He's gotten in trouble a couple of times, and I've always felt compelled to help him. He called me in desperation with some hokey metaphor about his baby was sick and needed a doctor. I said I'd be happy to help him for a week or so, no charge."

Coppola read Evans's screenplay and was appalled. It was a bizarre combination of soap opera, formula gangster film schtick, and an expensive coffee table picture book, rendered in Evans's signally dreadful prose. After perusing this document, Coppola gave Evans his free advice: The script needed a total rewrite. Evans took it calmly enough; he had come to much the same conclusion himself. Then he offered Coppola half a million dollars if he would do the revision.

Coppola thought about it. He was, at that moment, in more desperate need of cash than he'd ever been in his life. The slow demise of Zoetrope was growing more frightful every day. He was swamped in lien papers and mortgages and ever-deepening debt. His fat line of credit had turned into a long line of creditors.

Realistically Coppola had no choice. Nor did he have any time to waste; he packed his bags and headed for New York to start research on the Harlem Renaissance and the segregated nightclub that was its most contradictory symbol. Evans wasted no time either; he promptly and proudly announced to the press that the *Godfather* team was back in action again. He neglected to mention that Mario Puzo's contribution was now expensive landfill in the dumps of Secaucus, New Jersey.

As Coppola flung himself into the research, he fell in love with the Harlem Renaissance, the bounteous blossoming of African-American literature, music, art, and cultural pride that ripened in New York's black community between the end of World War I and the crash of 1929. It was flush with dramatic possibilities and fascinating real-life characters. There was Zora Hurston, outside the Harlem Opera House on 125th Street, laughing and jiving with passersby so they'd let her measure their skulls with calipers and scientifically disprove the myth about blacks' inferior brain capacity. There were Langston Hughes and W.E.B. Du Bois, deep in joyous argument about literature, communism, and racial uplift in a small side-street restaurant. There was Marcus Garvey, who would sell you tickets back to Africa on his rusty Black Star Liners at high-energy, open-air meetings.

And between 1923 and 1935 there were the greatest black musicians in the world at the Cotton Club, a legendary jazz spot and nightclub located at 142nd Street and Lenox Avenue in the heart of Harlem. But there was a catch. In this club the only way you could hear these black musicians was if you were white.

At the Cotton Club you could see and hear an astoundingly hot series of performers that included Lena Horne, Ethel Waters, Bill "Bojangles" Robinson, and a host of other jazz giants. From 1927 to 1930 Duke Ellington led the house band; when the Duke left, Cab Calloway took over. And while other night spots like the Radium Club and Connie's Inn might pull crowds with entertainers like Louis Armstrong and Fats Waller, the Cotton Club had an unbeatable ace in the hole: a chorus line of beautiful light-skinned dancers ("copper-colored gals"), dressed in scanty costumes, who were known as the Cotton Club Girls. For the white crowds from downtown, the dancers were probably a bigger draw than Ellington; Fats Waller even recorded a song inspired by the brown-skinned sweethearts called "Tall, Tan, and Terrific."

So there was a full deck of dramatic possibilities; the question was how to cut the cards. If black Cotton Club entertainers were Harlem royalty, the nightclub itself was a court (dressed up as a kitschy plantation) where the honkies who controlled Depression-era America—the rich, the powerful, the mob—mingled in the smoky darkness. Even though Coppola was no jazz fan, he saw the Renaissance, and the flowering of jazz, as the film's main focus; Evans was sure audiences would be far more interested in the dope and racketeers. From the very beginning, Evans had intended to lay a snow-white story over the black background, with a white star like Gere in center screen. There was bound to be trouble.

Preproduction was well under way. On the sound stages of Astoria, New York, production designer Richard Sylbert, an old friend of Evans's, was painstakingly re-creating the interior of the Cotton Club, circa 1929. Every detail was accurate, from the tin-can drinking glasses to the whiskey bottles labeled "Chicken Cock" (a Prohibition brand), the miniature frying-pan ashtrays, the menus on the tables, and the wooden drink stirrers in the cocktails. Sylbert had already spent $1 million on the set; by the end of filming, design costs had escalated to $6 million.

By April 5, 1983, Coppola had completed a draft screenplay of which he was quite proud. Instead of exploiting blacks to provide an exotic setting for yet another crummy gangster picture, his story focused on civil rights marches, poetry readings, and the stunning black cultural achievements of the Harlem Renaissance. In the process he neglected to provide much of a part for Gere, but what the hell? Gere was white, and this was going to be a *black* picture if Coppola had anything to do with it.

It was, of course, precisely what Evans and Gere had most dreaded. To them, Coppola's screenplay read like the grant proposal for a PBS documentary; it was a stiff. Where were the "gangsters, music, and pussy" that Evans had promised? Where was the plum role Gere was being paid a fortune to play? Coppola returned to the word processor, but he probably felt as if Evans and Gere were trying to sell him down the river. It was a serious cave-in, but Coppola wasn't the director, just a hired screenwriter—and screenwriters follow orders.

While Coppola stalled, Tom Luddy kept the Zoetrope banner flying by acquiring a series of unusual films: three pre-1950 Chinese classics, Jean-Luc Godard's *Passion*, Hans-Jürgen Syberberg's five-hour *Parsifal*, Kidlat Tahimik's delightful Filipino comedy *Perfumed Nightmare*, and a lyrical Canadian western by Philip Borsos called *The Grey Fox*. Zoetrope didn't expect to make a lot of money on these films, Luddy explained, but as long as they "paid their own way," it was cool.

While Coppola was schmoozing at a Salute to Zoetrope at the Santa Fe Film Festival, Evans took measures to defuse a crisis. The Doumanis were demanding to see the new, high-priced Coppola screenplay, which Evans considered disastrously ill-conceived. Evans couldn't stall any longer, so he sent it along, with a counterfeit note from Coppola (including a forged signature) that started, "Well, after 22 days, here is the blueprint. Now let's get down to writing a script. . . ." The note stressed that this version of the script was just the background; the foreground in the final script would be completely different.

The Doumanis didn't buy it for a second. But Evans had been right about one thing: They hated the script and refused to resume financing. "To me, it wasn't a script," declared Ed Doumani.

Preproduction costs on *Cotton Club* (building sets, buying props, writing and arranging music) were $140,000 a week, and rising. With the Doumanis out of the picture, Evans began a frantic search for new funding; he hit up Hollywood celebrities, Texas oilmen, sports team owners. None of them wanted anything to do with *Cotton Club*; the last black musical, *The Wiz* (a remake of *The Wizard of Oz* starring Diana Ross and Michael Jackson), had come out five years earlier and died like a dog, losing nearly $30 million. The main problem with *The Wiz* was that a lox of any color is still a lox, but its failure convinced investors that black musicals wouldn't fly.

The Doumanis were not exactly pussycats. Evans's spokesman, Bobby Zarem, characterized them tactfully as "Harvard men from Beverly Hills"; others described them as "operators from Vegas." But given their withdrawal, Evans was desperate enough to start playing with *real* tough guys. Perhaps his work on the screenplay had convinced him that gangsters were paper tigers. In any case, Karen DeLayne Greenberger (alias Elaine Jacobs), reputedly the lady friend of a Colombian cocaine concessionaire (who may also have been dealing the stuff herself) introduced Evans to vaudeville revival promoter Roy Radin, age thirty-three, whose main claim to fame was a client named J. Fred Muggs, chimpanzee. Radin swiftly sewed up a $35 million loan from the government of Puerto Rico, and Evans signed a partnership with him to make five movies.

When the shady lady demanded a piece of Radin's share in exchange for making the introduction, Evans vehemently urged his partner to accept, but the promoter refused. The last anyone saw of Radin he was sliding into the backseat of the lady's limousine on the way to do lunch. He might have thought twice about the date if he'd known she suspected him of stealing $1 million worth of cocaine from her home. One month later his remains were found in an isolated canyon. So much for the Puerto Rican deal. When Radin turned up dead, Evans was so terrified he went into hiding for days before resuming his frantic quest for cash. (In 1988 the lady and several associates were indicted for the murder; the associates were simultaneously indicted for killing a prostitute as well. And Evans got a new lawyer, who cited the Fifth Amendment in pretrial depositions.)

Evans was sure that Coppola's PBS screenplay was scaring off investors, so he hired a black actress named Marilyn Matthews to straighten Coppola out. Matthews entered into a long series of political discussions with Coppola. Black actors were desperate for work, she pointed out over and over; Coppola couldn't let them down by allowing the film to fall through.

Coppola insisted that Harlem blacks had been struggling for their cultural birthright and that, if the film was to be anything more than another lying rip-off, it had to show that.

"Nobody wants to pay money to see that," Matthews countered. "You got to have action. You got to have love. You got to have sex."

After several hours of this, Coppola made a pot of espresso, and he and Matthews began reoutlining the script to include more action, more love, more sex, and more white people. Soon Gere, Hines, and Evans joined the ranks of script advisers. Coppola saw where it was leading, bit the bullet, and invited everyone home with him to Napa. "I felt my job was to listen to everybody and try to incorporate their desires into the script," he said.

With the scriptwriting committee hard on his case, Coppola came up with a strange vision of the film. In this musical barely a single musical number would be shown all the way through. Instead, Coppola would intercut the black songs and dances with the white gangster story; the rhythmic percussion of tap-dancing feet would blend with the parallel percussion of machine-gun fire. Even more than Coppola had feared, and with his active collusion, the Cotton Club and its black entertainers had become mere background for a white gangster story.

Evans was delighted with Coppola's cooperative attitude, and the Doumanis even agreed to take a look at the new script when it was done. Coppola's rewrite was extraordinary, Evans told reporters (neglecting to mention that it wasn't written yet). He also told them that he was losing interest in making his directing debut on this high-priced project, especially when a great director like Coppola might step in. "If Francis would like to direct it," he stated in *Variety*, "I would step aside." Secretly Evans was probably pleased at how easily Coppola had caved in on the script; presumably he'd be equally malleable about making a formula hit. "I figured I had Francis at the right time," he said. "He was at bottom, and I figured he would be happy to do something good." Coppola declined. He'd be glad to help out during the shoot, he said, but he wouldn't think of directing.

In fact, Coppola was seriously tempted. Days earlier the Zoetrope lot had been saved from foreclosure number nine with only fifteen minutes to spare; it was clearly just a matter of time.

Worse, Coppola was close to personal bankruptcy. Bankers began coming to the Rutherford house to appraise the art collection, assuming that Coppola would have no choice but to declare Chapter 13 any day. A few months earlier he'd bought Ellie an extravagant diamond bracelet, but within weeks it was repossessed for nonpayment. He had already lost his L. A. house to foreclosure on a mortgage. *The Outsiders* was still the number one grosser in the nation and generating a respectable cash flow, but Coppola had been forced to sign a deal to pay back his $40 million of bank debts at somewhere between $1 million and $2.5 million a year. That money had to come from somewhere. "This picture could put me back into action," he told his intimates.

To increase his frustration, on May 1, 1983, *Apocalypse Now* finally appeared on ABC network TV, but instead of the $10 million Coppola had demanded, United Artists (where not a single *Apocalypse*-era executive remained) had sold the TV rights for only $4 million. Coppola was so furious that three years later, when he sued UA for closure of his *Apocalypse* debt, he included a claim that he could have gotten at least $2 million more if UA had given him time to market it properly. Maybe so, maybe not. The TV showing did very poorly; only a little more than a quarter of the people watching TV in that time slot tuned it in, putting it in forty-fourth place for the year's TV movies (tied with *The Shaggy D.A., Part 2*). Despite Coppola's frequent pronouncements on the subject, America was still not that eager to watch *Apocalypse,* even on TV, for free.

Coppola had never stopped talking about Belize; in fact, he'd scraped up enough money to buy a house there. In mid-May he went to Washington, D. C., to host a private investors' dinner for Belize's Prime Minister George C. Price. He provided three hundred bottles of his classy Rubicon Cabernet and a follow-up dinner the next day. It must have strained his American Express card, but it was worth it to maintain his mutual love affair with Belize. "Ever since I was a little kid," he told *Newsweek,* "I loved the idea of a little country."

With money going out in dribs and drabs, and little coming back, Coppola was finding it hard to resist the notion of directing Evans's movie. "*The Cotton Club* material was so rich that, if I had control, there was no reason why I couldn't make a beautiful film out of it," he said, obviously trying to talk himself into it.

Meanwhile, Evans and Matthews were flattering and cajoling and appealing to Coppola's desperate need for cash. As he neared completion of the "action, love, and sex" rewrite, he found himself becoming infatuated with the idea. "I started to fantasize about what it would be like to direct such a production," he remembered. And then, one June night, sitting at the dinner table with his new extended family (Evans, Matthews, Gere, and Hines, plus Ellie and the kids), Coppola announced that he'd found room in his busy schedule to direct *Cotton Club*. If Evans had $2.5 million, Coppola had the time.

Evans was so delighted he lost even more of his English than usual. "Francis started as a friend," he gushed to the press, "and at a time when he was in trouble. Human relationships are a rare commodity in this industry, and his toward me is something I will long remember." As for Coppola's salary, he added, "Francis is getting too little for what he's worth."

Evans and Richard Gere were equally thrilled with the new script. This time Evans actually seemed to mean it when he crowed to reporters, "Francis has written an extraordinary screenplay. When Richard [Gere] came out of the meeting we held to see the final draft, he was grinning from ear to ear."

The Doumanis were less enthusiastic, and even cooler about Coppola directing; they knew his reputation and feared he might try to turn their commercial gangster movie into a budget-busting art film. "Don't worry," Evans told them, "I can control Francis." It was one of the worst predictions he ever made, but the Doumanis bought it and pulled out their checkbooks once again.

Evans was in producer heaven. He had Gere, he had Coppola, he had a script, and best of all, he owned everything. "It's the first time since Sam Goldwyn did *Guys and Dolls* that a picture has been totally privately financed," he boasted.

If he realized that what he owned was a film in deep financial trouble, he kept it under his hat. Long before a frame of film had been shot, or a director hired, estimated costs had skyrocketed alarmingly. The day Coppola agreed to direct, the production was already $13 million in the hole—$2 million more than it cost to shoot an entire average movie from start to finish. Rumors of featherbedding, personal luxury, and financial intrigue were starting to percolate from the set. The lot in Astoria was crawling with high-paid union technicians who had been working on preproduction for six months, with minimal supervision and no limits on expenses. Over budget? The film *had* no budget, and never, through the entire shoot, did it get one. Evans never got around to finalizing the formal line-item budget that normally precedes even the first step of preproduction.

Back in Vegas, the Doumanis decided that Coppola's latest draft was close enough for them to get serious; they brought in a partner, Denver businessman Victor Sayyah (an in-law, as well as an oil business associate), who added his own share to their investment. Sayyah was dispatched to New York to function as the Doumanis' financial watchdog. And now, with big money on the table at last, the real deal-making commenced.

Evans would get 50 percent of the net profits; the Doumanis would get 25 percent, as would Sayyah. Coppola had already received $500,000 for writing the script. His directing fee would be an additional $3 million as an advance against 10 percent of the adjusted gross, plus expenses to cover moving himself and his family to New York for the duration of the shoot. If he brought the film in on time, he'd get a $1 million bonus.

In addition to the sweet financial deal, Coppola demanded absolute control of the production. He warned Evans that their current lovey-dovey relationship was sure to be affected as the shoot proceeded. "I told Evans that as a writer I would do it any way my director instructed me to," he recalled, "but if I became the director I would need to have total control and final cut. I was very clear on this point, because Bob Evans is a known back-seat driver, a man who tends to fool with other people's work from his office or apartment."

In July *Hammett* finally opened in New York and Los Angeles for short art house engagements. Vincent Canby, writing in *The New York Times*, declared that the film wasn't "quite the mess one might expect, . . . but heaven only knows what it's supposed to be about, or why it was made." Andrew Sarris's postmortem in the *Village Voice* was headlined DARE WE RENDER UNTO WENDERS THAT WHICH IS COPPOLA'S? "I would not want to keep anyone from seeing it," he wrote, "but I cannot describe it as even esoterically successful." Both critics noted the virtual disappearance of Wenders's viewpoint.

Coppola was too busy to take much notice of the *Hammett* reviews; with only six weeks before *Cotton Club* was supposed to start shooting, he found himself increasingly unhappy with the screenplay. The dialogue, in particular, seemed all wrong; it lacked the smell and taste of the 1920s. He decided he needed a collaborator and settled on novelist William (*Ironweed*) Kennedy, an expert on the era who'd written a distinguished trilogy set among the lowlifes of Albany, New York, during Prohibition. One volume of the trilogy was *Legs*, based on the life of gangster Legs Diamond; Mickey Rourke sent Coppola a copy, and when the director read it, he was sold.

Kennedy had never written a screenplay, but he was a great admirer of *The Conversation, Apocalypse,* and the two *Godfathers* and was willing to give it a shot. On July 15 he checked into a hotel on Central Park South and went to work with "this mythic character who earns his myth the hard way."

Kennedy and Coppola settled in to work at Astoria Studios, in a suite so historic the roof leaked. Reputedly, it had been Gloria Swanson's dressing room during the filming of *Manhandled* in 1924; some years later it had housed the Marx Brothers during the shoot of *The Cocoanuts*.

Kennedy and Coppola worked day and night. "Out of an IBM Selectric," Kennedy recalled, "a pile of books on Harlem, gangland, and jazz, out of a phonograph playing Duke Ellington from morning till dawn, there came, in ten days, a raunchy, 82-page, unfinished monster called the Rehearsal Draft, the script the actors worked with for three weeks. It was a peculiar document. Only Coppola and I knew what was really going on with it, and sometimes I wasn't too sure about Coppola. Or me either."

In one month Coppola and Kennedy produced twelve complete scripts, including five done during one memorably sleepless weekend. The big problem, of course, was how to turn the Harlem Renaissance into a vehicle for a white movie star and a hot ticket for white audiences. They decided early that Richard Gere would play a musician; that would get him into Harlem as a soul brother of sorts. But it wouldn't get him into the Cotton Club, which was just as racist about its entertainers as its clientele; if few blacks had gotten into the house, even fewer whites had gotten onto the stage. Like none. (Conceivably Mezz Mezzrow might have sneaked in the back door for an after-hours jam session, but nobody else.)

Evans tried to help, but he caused more trouble than he cured; the producer may have been many things, but a writer wasn't one of them. In mid-August, for example, he sent Coppola a memo about the latest draft, including several suggestions for new scenes of mayhem. His covering note read: "You asked for my comments, my first one is the Cotton Club script of August 8th is on the way to being not good—but great. Spent much, much time—on both the structure & text of the enclosed further comments—Hope they are of some help. At least you know I'm not 'just another pretty face' but rather just trying to do the best I can. Love ya, Evans. Please accept both dialogue & structure as my only *interpretation* for your eyes only—and only to be used as a possible springboard for the 'Coppola' pen. E."

It began to gripe Kennedy that although any fool could see he and Coppola were struggling together, for weeks Evans refused to admit there was any pen at work other than Coppola's. Finally, when Kennedy's script changes made denial impossible, Evans started muttering that Kennedy had gotten Coppola into his power.

It might have been the other way around. Kennedy's account of the collaboration sounds awfully familiar:

A new script, by my definition, is one with major new dynamics, and we had more of those than any writer needs. One of Coppola's methods of rewriting was to lift the climax of reel six, say, and put it in reel two. This does things to reel three that you probably hadn't counted on, and also leaves you with a problematical hole between reels five and seven. At times he would ravage the entire script, insert long-dead sections of old scripts, and offer up an unrecognizable new document. Work would then begin anew to make it make sense. . . .

The continuously unfinished, unfathomable script vexed the production department and created an army of critics and second-guessers who read each new version as if it were the last word. Coppola viewed each version as raw material. Like the actors, he and I were in rehearsal for the final product.

Less than a month before shooting was scheduled to start, Coppola and Kennedy realized they had to deliver something so preproduction could proceed, so they polished their latest version and sent it to the printer. When Sylbert saw it, he was stunned; ten of his expensive sets had been "written out" of the film, as had six of the seven locations he'd locked in.

Meanwhile, as the start of production drew closer, Coppola had Silverfish, his silver Airstream, driven to New York from California; he'd used video assist on his last three films, with increasing success. Once again he meant to shoot the picture simultaneously on film and videotape so he could review each shot before passing it on to editor Barry Malkin. He'd learned the hard way that he could not hide in the trailer, as he'd done on *One from the Heart,* but he still needed it to set up shots, view the tapes, and make espresso.

While the Airstream was crawling across the western prairie, Coppola started thinking about the crew, and these were not happy thoughts. A crew functions as a director's hands and eyes; if the members are not perfect, they can wreck a film as surely as a typhoon. For many years Coppola had picked his own crews, but since *The Cotton Club* had started without him, Evans had stacked the deck with production heads who were personally loyal to him, and they were treating Coppola like the new boy in school. Worse yet, many of them were bigtimers who had insisted on pay-or-play contracts; if they were fired, they would get their full salaries anyway. Coppola had never been shy about firing people, but this time it was going to cost big money. Still, he had no choice, and the slaughter began. "I've never seen anything like it," Richard Gere told Kennedy. "Everybody's afraid they're going to be fired.

The carnage started with music director Jerry Wexler, at the cost of an $87,500 settlement. Wexler was a heavy hitter; he'd been vice-president of Atlantic Records, where, with his partner, Ahmet Ertegun, he'd recorded R&B giants like Ray Charles and Professor Longhair; but Coppola didn't like him. The executive producer, Dyson Lovell, another Bob Evans hiree, immediately rehired Wexler as a consultant, handing him $12,500 to do virtually nothing. Prominent jazz arranger Ralph Burns replaced him briefly, before being banished in turn.

Next, cinematographer John Alonzo bit the dust to the tune of a $160,000 buy-out. Although Alonzo was a champ at both low-budget productions like *Vanishing Point* and lavish ones like *Close Encounters of the Third Kind,* he may have been damned by his association with Evans on *Black Sunday* and *Chinatown.* Coppola wanted Steve Burum, who had shot *Rumble Fish,* but when Evans looked at a print of that film, he nixed the suggestion in a state of terror. Both men finally agreed on Gordon Willis, who'd shot *The Godfather,* but Willis turned them down cold. "I don't know what he thinks he's up to these days," Willis said later, "but I knew it was going to be a shit bath. I don't believe in sitting in trailers and talking to people over loudspeakers." In the end Evans and Coppola compromised on British cinematographer Stephen Goldblatt.

Two production heads who survived the cut were associate producer Melissa Prophet and production designer Richard Sylbert. Prophet was actually an actress; after she'd introduced

Evans to financier Adnan Khashoggi, who provided critical seed money, Evans had given her a job as associate producer. Fortunately she proved a hard worker; in fact, she became the main channel of communication between Evans and Coppola. As for Sylbert, this respected veteran of twenty-five years in the biz (and designer of the stylish *Chinatown*) was simply too deeply involved to be displaced. Anyway, Coppola thought his work was terrific.

Once Evans's officers were cashiered, Coppola refilled the ranks with his own lieutenants, including Gio, who would be second-unit director and montage editor.

Casting was less of a problem.

In the latest version of the script, the leading female character was an older woman, but suddenly Coppola decided that eighteen-year-old Diane Lane, who was currently shooting Walter Hill's avant-garde rock musical *Streets of Fire*, should be Richard Gere's love interest. He'd even let her sing.

For the major role of Owney Madden, owner of the Cotton Club, Coppola hired English character actor Bob Hoskins; it was one of his best moves. Hoskins was not a well-known performer in the United States; he had starred in a high-tension British gangster film, *The Long Good Friday*, but it had mainly played in art houses. Although Hoskins did not get on particularly well with Coppola, his performance (without a trace of his usual cockney accent) would be one of the few things holding the film together.

For Gregory Hines's opposite number, a lovely, light-skinned, Lena Horne type of nightclub singer, Coppola cast Lonette McKee, who'd been in *Sparkle* and, more recently, Richard Lester's *Cuba*. Gregory Hines' real-life brother, Maurice, would play Hines's film brother; Coppola's nephew Nicolas Cage would play Richard Gere's hoodlum kid brother; daughter Sofia (Domino) would be in on the action as a street kid who gets killed; and nephew Marc Coppola (Cage's big brother) had a bit part, too. Tom Waits, who was practically family by now, would play the Cotton Club's tough white stage manager–emcee, Irving Stark.

Evans went along with it gracefully until Coppola decided to sign Fred Gwynne (of the *Munsters* TV show) for a major role as the sweet-natured mobster named Frenchy. Evans hit the roof; no Munster was going to play a mobster in his movie.

It was the first in a series of increasingly cutthroat showdowns between Evans and Coppola, and it followed what would become a familiar pattern: Coppola threatened to quit; Evans sighed, gave in, and moped off to round up more money.

Bit players were no problem. On August 4, responding to an open casting call, nearly five thousand out-of-work singers, dancers, and actors lined up around the block at Astoria Studios to audition for roles. Eventually, fifty-two were hired.

As the first day of shooting approached, Coppola slipped into an old routine. He set rehearsals in a blue-painted room so his video equipment could replace the blue background with images from the Jazz Age, and he watched the actors through a monitor while he recorded their work on videotape. Coppola urged the cast to improvise; late in the evenings he'd incorporate the best new bits of improvised dialogue into the ever-changing script. Most of the cast loved the process; they figured if they came up with enough great stuff, their roles would be expanded.

Richard Gere (who had never worked with No-Script Coppola) didn't go for it at all. He didn't want other people's roles expanded, and he wasn't about to improvise. He was an actor, an artist. He prepared for every scene, carefully, for hours. Furthermore, he had script approval, and improvisation wasn't part of the deal. "We didn't know if Richard was going to stay or not," recalled Lonette McKee. "He wanted it right there written down the way he wanted it. He didn't realize that he had to *make* it the way he wanted it to be."

Shooting was scheduled to begin on August 22, but as of August 21 there was still no final script. The next morning, when everyone arrived at Prospect Hall, in Brooklyn, for the first day of work, Gere was a no-show. None of the secret phone numbers worked; he'd vanished. Maybe it was the script problem, maybe it was nerves, or maybe it was the rumor that Coppola wanted to replace him with Matt Dillon. Gere never said; he simply disappeared.

There were seven hundred people waiting on the set. Coppola, who knew how important starting days were, refused to panic. "I specialize in being the ringmaster of a circus that's inventing itself," he said with a smile, and quickly switched from a wedding scene to the "Tall, Tan, and Terrific" dance sequence. Gregory Hines, who was not expecting to find himself in front of the cameras in a major number on the first day, was shocked. But as Sylbert converted the set, Hines had a hurried consultation with his father, a tap dancer of an earlier era, about how to walk like a Jazz Age hepcat. Finally Hines went on and did his dance—terrifically.

Evans's people were less impressed with Coppola's quick change. To them, his flexibility (which they interpreted as indecisiveness and unpredictability) was a grave fault; later, they sneeringly called it "the Francis factor." They were also scornful that Coppola seemed to have lost the first round to Gere.

Gere remained absent for the whole first week. His main problem, as it turned out, was not the script at all—at least not directly—but certain "financial uncertainties." He was beginning to suspect that with Coppola at the helm, the film might bomb. He wanted his pay, all his pay, up front. Over the weekend Gere, Evans, and a small army of lawyers renegotiated the deal. Evans agreed to buy Gere's 10 percent of the adjusted gross for $1.5 million. With the $1.5 million that Gere already had coming, he was now guaranteed a minimum of $3 million, to be paid immediately. Nor was that all. Evans had originally agreed to pay Gere a $125,000 bonus for every week of shooting beyond October 29; now, it was rumored, Gere would be paid a cool $250,000 for every *day* the shoot ran over. Whatever the numbers, they were sweet enough to send Gere back to work, but Evans never forgave his conduct. Film stars are expected to make their toughest deal, but professionals simply do not miss the first week of shooting to improve their cut, even if they swing enough weight to get away with it. A deal is a deal. "Richard stayed at my house for five months," Evans complained bitterly, "and then he put a gun to my head."

Aside from the desperately improvised dance number, the first five weeks of shooting consisted mainly of gangster scenes, not musical numbers. Coppola and Sylbert were oddly inconsistent about period accuracy. The set was perfect, only non-filtered cigarettes were allowed when the cameras were rolling, but when costume designer Milena Canonero (who had assembled forty-two photo albums of styles from 1920 to 1930) asked Coppola what year the film was supposed to take place, Coppola told her to do it in whatever year and season she thought best. "The script kept getting more and more elusive," said Canonero, "but somehow we managed to wing it."

Coppola was at his best, a rock of calm, confidence, and professionalism amid the confusion of the shoot. On the set he would crack jokes, sing songs, play the musical instruments, even dance. At a hotel rubout scene he amazed a special effects technician when he looked at the fake blood and observed coolly that it needed more green. On another occasion, when the sun came out to ruin a series of shots on a rainy Harlem street, Coppola gazed fervently upward and began to shuffle his feet and pump his arms in a rain dance, whispering to Melissa Prophet that he and God *really* communicated at times like this, and that he was going to *make* it rain. Seconds later everyone was running for cover as a sudden, powerful deluge poured out of the sky.

The fact that they were now in the midst of shooting did nothing to stop the production of new drafts. Even if Coppola had been willing to call it quits (and when had he ever?), Richard Gere had script approval, and he still didn't like the screenplay. Nor did Evans. Nor did the moneymen. Whenever Coppola sent a version of the script to Evans, Evans responded with his own new (but very, very old) plot ideas, trying to prove that he was not just another pretty face. All of Evans's ideas were dispatched to Secaucus, to keep company with Puzo's script in the landfill.

Exasperated beyond measure, Evans began hatching a plot with Victor Sayyah, the Doumanis' watchdog, to fire Coppola (who still hadn't received a written contract) and replace him with a more tractable director. They spent a night drinking, talked it over, and decided to forget it. Then Evans and Sayyah fell out (perhaps the producer was afraid Sayyah might reveal their aborted plot to Coppola), and Sayyah was advised that he was unwelcome on the set. At that, Ed Doumani flew to New York to find out first-hand what was going on with his money.

Doumani walked onto the set and could not believe his eyes. He had flown coach class, as he usually did, was staying in Evans's leased Manhattan town house and taking cabs to and from the studio; he discovered that even the lowliest of Evans's gofers was flying first class, staying in four-star hotels, and riding in rented limousines. The production people were totally out of control, spending (Doumani reported) $1,300 for $700 worth of light bulbs and renting twenty-two period cars when only five were needed. Worse yet, Doumani discovered that Evans had promised several top technicians $50,000 bonuses if they came in under budget but had never bothered to specify just what their budgets were. There was no way this picture would come in for $20 million.

Doumani was equally appalled by Evans's personal habits and the way they affected his judgment. "I lived with Evans in New York," reported Doumani some months later. "He may have indulged in some things on occasion that would not make him function well as a partner."

Doumani was no happier with Coppola. The director, he discovered, had discarded the "European schedule" as impractical. Apparently the only reason Evans had wanted the European schedule in the first place was that he liked to stay up all night and couldn't bear the thought of starting work at 7:00 A.M. When Coppola took over the directorial reins, he had shifted immediately to a 7:00 A.M. to 7:00 P.M. schedule, six days a week, which meant Doumani was paying big overtime. The shoot was now running $1.2 million a week.

Doumani was deeply chagrined; something had to be done. Since he had a business to run back in Vegas, he put down $200,000 to hire Lebanese B-movie producer Sylvio Tabet. Tabet was given the title of coproducer, and the job of hanging out on the set and driving Coppola crazy. "Are we done yet?" he would ask every time Coppola finished a take. "Are we done yet?"

As a result of the Doumanis' clampdown on costs, a love scene Coppola had meant to shoot at a fabulous Art Deco motel Sylbert had found was filmed, instead, on a set. Also, Coppola and Kennedy were forced to rewrite the script yet again, this time to cut its length and trim expensive scenes. On one occasion Kennedy stayed up all night, removing as many adjectives as he could, and changing the line spacing; by morning, the same script looked half an hour shorter. Before the end of the production, the duo wrote somewhere between thirty and forty drafts—they lost track themselves.

Despite the endless permutations, a central (and very personal) theme seemed to persist from one script to the next: All the drafts Coppola and Kennedy wrote were about the bitterness of servitude. Ostensibly the story was about the oppression of black entertainers by the Cotton Club's racist policies and the oppression of white musician Dixie Dwyer by mobster

Dutch Schultz, but as Sylbert noted, "there's something in the central story that seems to be about Francis Coppola himself—the former mogul now reduced to being a wage slave, a director for hire."

If the theme was clear, the plot was not. "Nobody knew what was going on from one minute to the next," said Sylbert. The overall shape of the movie remained a mystery to the cast, the crew, and even the writer-director. At one point, when Sylbert asked Coppola, "Why do you make all this chaos?" Coppola answered, "If nobody knows what's going on, nobody can discuss it with you."

When technicians asked script supervisor Lynn Lewis what scene was up next, which actors to call, where to put the lights, she couldn't answer. When they asked Coppola, his usual response was "Who wants to know? I'm in charge here. When we do the scene, we'll see."

Typically, on any film, there's a lot of waiting around, but since *Cotton Club* was so uncertain, the entire principal cast had to be present all day, every day, in full makeup and costume, just in case Coppola needed them. "I gained 20 pounds waitin' around for something to happen," Bob Hoskins recalled. "You sort of sit around and eat and drink and philosophize, and suddenly you've forgotten what you do for a living." Nicolas Cage got so bored that one day he tore up his trailer in a rage; he was, Uncle Francis explained later, merely getting into character to play his role of Mad Dog Dwyer.

Coppola probably approved. He wanted the perfect dramatic accident, but he could never tell you exactly how to produce it. It drove Bob Hoskins crazy. "He would just toss things out in the air," Hoskins remembered. "I could never figure Francis out at all. I just did what he told me. It's into Aladdin's cave with him."

Typically, for the big love scene between Gregory Hines and Lonette McKee, he plied the pair with wine until they got tipsy, and was delighted when McKee abandoned (forgot?) the script and just blurted out her character's feelings in her own woozy words. ("Oh, Delbert, just make love to me!")

Since nobody knew when the magic would work, Coppola had to shoot scenes over and over until something good happened. "By the sixth take, [Coppola] usually had what he wanted," reported Michael Daly in *New York* magazine. "Seven

is his favorite number, and he sometimes called for a final effort that became known as 'the Francis Take.' "

Sometimes the improvisation worked brilliantly. One of the
most effective moments in the film, in which Fred Gwynne
smashes Hoskins's pocket watch in pretend anger and then
hands over an expensive gold replacement, was devised by
Gwynne during a improvisation rehearsal. But at other times
the acting school exercises could be awkward and unproduc-
tive. "There was no real focus on the set for me," complained
Diane Lane, "because the script was changing so much."

Richard Gere found his preciously bought "script approval" becoming a joke; there was no script to approve. It was
only a matter of time until the tensions between him and Coppola blew up, and the confrontation, when it came, was both
public and spectacular. "Listen to me," Coppola shouted, "you
don't like me, you never liked me at all. But let me tell you
something, I'm not only older than you, I'm richer than you.
Now get out of here."

"It was chaos," remembered Allen Garfield. "You had
someone shouting orders, but you never had somebody really
at the helm. Francis wanted more of everything, but he could
never tell anybody why. Like we'd be in the Cotton Club, and
he'd come in, and he'd say, 'OK, give me 1940s,' and that would
be it. We had a good time helping each other so that we
wouldn't drown, but it became a joke, a serious joke, that we'd
just better fend for ourselves."

Sylbert, the most professional of Evans's hirees, had never
worked with Coppola before, and was amazed at the director's
seesawing moods. Sometimes Coppola would seem to be in
deep despair over his financial situation; moments later he'd
be drifting into happy fantasyland, dreaming of buying a movie
theater he had frequented as a youngster, or setting up an office at the top of the Chrysler Building. Like many observers
before him, Sylbert noted that Coppola seemed to be torn between "his need to make a commercial hit and his desire to
craft a work of art." At one point Coppola told him, "I don't
want to make a gangster picture, and I don't want to make a
musical. I want to make something nobody's ever seen before."

By late September most of the shoot-ups and love scenes
were in the can. It was time to move onto the Astoria sound

stage for the songs and dances. But first there were a few obstacles to resolve. Despite his decimation of Evans's production heads, Coppola was still having major problems with the crew. Even Kennedy noticed that "the naysaying to everything he did or said was endemic." Coppola had complained again and again to Evans but the producer produced no pink slips.

One of Coppola's biggest problems was the executive producer, Dyson Lovell, who had somehow gotten the job of choreographing the dances. Coppola would be chopping the numbers into fragments during the editing, but he still needed good numbers to chop, and when he saw what Lovell had done he hated it. The dances weren't authentic, he said; they were slick and modern, more like the *Ice Follies* than classic black production numbers. There was only one solution.

Sunday, September 25, became known as Black Sunday to the *Cotton Club* film workers. To start with, Coppola fired Lovell as head choreographer and banished him from the set. (He retained his credit as executive producer.) As a replacement, Coppola hired Michael Smuin, with whom he'd worked on *Rumble Fish*. Smuin would take full charge of the musical numbers, with a gang of tap choreographers, assistant choreographers, and special choreographers to assist him.

Lovell wasn't the only Black Sunday casualty. As long as he was at it, Coppola fired seventeen other technicians; many were never replaced. Reportedly their sins included shooing Coppola's daughter, Sofia, out from underfoot and making pointed comments about having children on the set. Once the crew cuts were accomplished, everything went much better, or so Coppola said. Morale sank like a stone.

It was also time to find a new musical coordinator to replace the long-gone Wexler and Burns. Several black musical heavyweights (including jazz great Benny Carter) were suggested, but Coppola vetoed them all. Finally Kennedy recommended a jazzman friend, Bob Wilber. The only problem with Wilber was that he had an unbreakable commitment for a five-day-a-week gig in Bern, Switzerland. But the *Cotton Club* tradition of throwing money at problems worked again; the production simply paid for Wilber to fly from Switzerland to Astoria, and back, every weekend. (The Doumanis must have winced; there went a big chunk of the money Coppola had just saved them.) Wilber wrote remarkably authentic arrangements of Ellington's and Calloway's classic 1920s arrangements and produced the sound track record as well.

Meanwhile, choreographer Smuin was looking at a lot of work and an impossible deadline. Coppola, he said, "locked me in a room with cans and cans of newsreels. He didn't want creation. He wanted re-creation [of the original dance numbers]." Howard "Stretch" Johnson, one of the original Cotton Club hoofers, was on hand as an adviser, but Smuin still had a problem. "At that time, the dancers were shorter and rounder than they are now. Now they're like sleek racehorses. You can't take the authentic steps and just put them on these new creatures."

The script called for forty-eight dance numbers. In the five weeks he worked on the film, Smuin created or supervised twenty-two of the most important ones; his associate choreographers worked up the others. Gregory Hines improvised his own tap solos, as did legendary jazz-tap-dancer Honi Coles, who appears in a single scene, trading steps with Hines at the Hoofers' Club.

Because of the rush and the escalating budget pressure from the Doumanis, Smuin frequently found himself rehearsing dances in the morning and shooting them the same afternoon; on occasion he had to run four rehearsals simultaneously. "The pressure was unbelievable," he remembered, "but at the same time it was very exciting." Even so, Smuin may have winced a bit at the director's methodology. Coppola was so insistent on realism he actually preferred shots in which the dancers missed steps or made other mistakes; the goofs made the numbers look authentic, he thought. (He was wrong; it just showed how little he knew about the history of black dance, especially tap.) Some of the other choreographers were even more disgruntled. They were knocking themselves out to stage fabulous numbers at enormous cost, knowing all the while that their efforts would be reduced to a few brief cutaways to punctuate a gang war or a love scene.

The atmosphere at Astoria went from bad to worse. Coppola's money troubles were driving him into a growing rage. After six weeks of shooting he had yet to receive a penny of his directing fee; his cash-flow problems were so acute that American Express canceled his credit card. In fits of fury he'd stalk off the set, lock himself into his trailer, and cook away the anger, sending garlic fumes wafting over the sound stage. On one occasion, when a lawyer gave him bad news, he slammed his hand on his desk so hard that it was swollen for three days. One morning Gregory Hines arrived at the office to discover a hole in the door where Coppola had kicked it in.

Evans was hiding in his Manhattan town house and losing the tan he'd been cultivating for twenty years. "I look the color of the Green Hornet," he complained. Now and then he'd work on script revisions and send them to Coppola, who forwarded them to Secaucus. He was in an embarrassing position between the difficulties with Coppola, the drain of money, the firings, and the loss of power they demonstrated.

Coppola now seemed permanently angry at Evans. Kennedy recalled that on one occasion, when Evans sent a set of script notes via messenger, Coppola threw them in the wastebasket without even looking at them.

Not satisfied with barring him from the set, Coppola refused to let Evans view the rushes. "He never gave up on the fact that he wasn't directing," Coppola grumbled.

Coppola kept the set strictly closed to the press, but rumors slipped out anyway: whispers about pot smoking and speculation about Coppola's involvement with Diane Lane. Some months later, when *Playboy* asked her which man she'd like to change places with for one day, she named Coppola. "I want to know all his dark secrets," she explained. "He's got such a wide-scope life. . . . He knows how to do everything." On one occasion she even asked Coppola's advice about how to break up with her boyfriend; he told her to set it up so the guy thought he was leaving her.

In fact, Lane was having a hard time on *The Cotton Club,* partly because she had missed the rehearsal period while she finished *Streets of Fire.* "I cut off my hair, and *boom,* I'm on the set, singing live with Richard Gere." Worse yet, the first day she had to sing, she was so nervous she came off in take after take like a tone-deaf zombie. Finally Coppola drew her aside, ushered her into his trailer, and yelled at her at length and profanely. A few days later she got back at him. Having watched *The Godfather* on TV, she went up to Coppola and said loudly, "Hey, Francis, I saw *The Godfather* last night. Not bad." He turned and gave her a frigid stare.

The Coppolas were so broke that Eleanor overcame her

shyness, did an on-set interview with costume designer Milena Canonero, and sold it to *Vogue* magazine for pocket change. Perhaps this was the trigger, perhaps not, but Coppola's smoldering anger about his nonexistent salary and missing contract finally reached flashpoint. He told Evans that if he didn't have a contract, and a check, in his hand by the end of the day, he would be on the Concorde to Paris that very evening. Evans swore he'd deliver both by 5:00 P.M., but of course, neither check nor contract materialized.

The weekend after Coppola demanded his salary, Ed Doumani decided that even though he hadn't yet paid Coppola a penny, he was still paying him too much. The movie was flagrantly over budget; seven weeks' shooting should have cost $18 million, but actual costs were closer to $28 million. Insiders were now predicting a total negative cost in the area of $40 million (/$47 million), which would probably require at least $100 million in grosses just to break even.

Doumani pondered these figures and called a Saturday meeting. If the production went over schedule, he insisted, Coppola should have to pay a penalty. Furthermore, Coppola's cut of the rentals was too high; Doumani wanted to renegotiate his percentage, and since no contract has been signed, there was no way Coppola could stop him. "Who needs this?" Coppola shouted. "It's not my picture. You need me; I don't need you." Coppola gave Evans and the Doumanis all day Sunday to take it all back, but the phone never rang.

When cast and crew arrived at Astoria on Monday morning, Coppola's silver trailer was gone. Its absence made people very nervous, an apprehension that grew even deeper when they realized that Coppola was gone, too. Making good on his promise, he had hopped the Concorde—not to Paris, as he had threatened, but to London. It was rumored that he'd taken the negative with him as hostage. "I've been shooting for seven weeks," he growled to the nearest reporter. "I move my whole family from California to the East Coast, I still have no money and no contract."

Doumani realized Coppola had him over a barrel, and he promptly caved in. On Tuesday he agreed to start paying Coppola's salary immediately, and he dropped the penalty clause. He still thought Coppola should take a smaller share of the rentals, but now he offered to buy it back, in cash.

Coppola was back at the studio on Wednesday, but the payroll wasn't. Doumani and Evans had failed to deliver it, and work stopped dead on union orders. Coppola, who may have felt guilty over the anxiety his power play had caused his cast and crew, leaped into the middle of the stage and swore that he'd pay everybody personally.

Fortunately he didn't have to make good. At 11:00 A.M. an armored car arrived with the checks, and everybody went back to work. For an hour. Then they rushed to the bank on their lunch hours to cash the checks, lest they turn to rubber by 5:00 P.M.

By now Evans was feeling much abused, and he took the opportunity to ventilate his frustrations with Hollywood gossip columnist Frank Swertlow. "Let's set the record straight," he declared. "I am the producer. I hired Mr. Coppola. He did not hire me." Evans insisted that he was not banned from the set and not banned from screening the rushes. "I believe the director is the captain of the ship on the set, not the producer. *And*, I have the best captain in the industry. But I am not checking on every little detail that happens on the set."

Early in October, to boost everybody's morale (including his own), Coppola threw a party on the stage for all four hundred people on the production. It wasn't as much fun as the weekly *One from the Heart* wrap parties since Coppola felt he had to invite Bob Evans. As a special treat for the partygoers, Coppola screened eighty minutes of roughly assembled footage. It was the first time in weeks that Evans had gotten a look at the dailies, and he watched with growing distress. Now he knew why Coppola had kept him away from the screenings; some of the scenes looked like *The Godfather*, all right, but others looked like *Rumble Fish*, a movie Evans detested. "I didn't know which way Coppola was going to go," Evans commented. "I was only hoping he wouldn't esoteric it up."

Evans's unhappiness escalated when *Rumble Fish* premiered at the New York Film Festival on October 7, two days before its commercial premiere. It had raised a fierce controversy among the five-member selection committee; some hated it, but others (specifically critic David Thomson) insisted that it be shown. The festival audience had less trouble making up its mind; *Variety* reported a chorus of boos and hisses as the end credits unspooled.

Rumble Fish is not an easy film to love. It opens as Rusty-James (Matt Dillon), a confused, inarticulate, not too bright teenager, is challenged to a fight by rival Biff. Both boys bring their gangs. Just as Rusty-James is about to win, his older brother, the Motorcycle Boy (Mickey Rourke), shows up. Rusty-James is distracted and gets stabbed; the Motorcycle Boy revs his bike and sends it, riderless, crashing into Biff.

The brothers return home together, where they live with their father (Dennis Hopper), a sad, decent alcoholic who seems to have no interest whatsoever in fatherhood. Seeing his sons covered with blood, all he can say is "Strange lives you two lead."

The Motorcycle Boy, we learn, led a gang back in the "good old days" before heroin. He has been away in California, but the signs of his glory remain all over town; walls and street signs still bear the graffiti "Motorcycle Boy Reigns." Throughout the movie people are constantly telling Rusty-James he's no match for his brilliant older brother; even his best friend, Smokey (Nicolas Cage), justifies stealing his girl friend (Diane Lane) on this ground. Every time the shadow of pain crosses Dillon's face, it's impossible not to think of the comparisons Carmine and Italia made between their brilliant son August, and their other son, Francis. As for the Motorcycle Boy himself, he's charmingly schizophrenic; a younger, more articulate version of Kurtz in *Apocalypse*.

Nor is he any less suicidal. In the film's final episode the Motorcycle Boy breaks into a pet store to free the Siamese fighting fish he loves and identifies with. "They really belong in a river," he says. "I don't think they'd fight if they were in the river." Predictably, a cop shoots him. Rusty-James takes his brother's bike and rides to the sea; the final freeze-frame finds him facing a grainy ocean, free at last of his brother's shadow.

Rumble Fish borders on the pretentious—every element in the film is palpably deliberate—but it boasts a number of strong sequences, notably Michael Smuin's extraordinary fight scene set in a wet alley, a dance of violence in which the gangs form a male corps de ballet, their movements lit by flashes from the windows of a passing train.

Steve Burum's expressionist images assault the eye in hard black and white. The streets are always wet; the heat is almost palpable. And Coppola's focus on the unstoppable passage of

time is worked into the very visual texture of the film, not only
with all the shots of clocks but by using *Koyaanisqatsi*'s step-
frame animation technique. Clouds rush across the sky; the sun
plunges toward the horizon.

Most of the performances are marvelous, especially Matt
Dillon's confused Rusty-James and Dennis Hopper's detached, humorous father. Of all the leads, only Mickey Rourke
is unconvincing; his sadly smiling Motorcycle Boy seems more
mannered than enigmatic. The ensemble work is impeccable.

Coppola's dramatic and technical mastery in *Rumble Fish*
is impressive, but the film's most important achievements go
beyond technique; despite its pretentiousness, it is distinguished by a kind of dangerous self-exposure. Although Coppola later joked that it was his "student film," it is, in fact,
exactly the kind of picture he had been promising (and failing)
to deliver since *Godfather II:* an art film, but genuinely passionate, audacious, and moving.

Very few critics cared for *Rumble Fish*; the press was on
the rebound from its broken love affair with Coppola. *Variety*
called the film "overwrought and overthought." In the Sunday
Times Vincent Canby noted its "unintentional giggles" and
"comically inflated pretensions." He added a kind note, though.
"There is something deserving of attention in its failure," he
wrote. "Mr. Coppola thinks BIG, which is better than not
thinking at all."

Time's Richard Corliss concluded: "*Rumble Fish* is Coppola's professional suicide note to the movie industry, a warning against employing him to find the golden gross. No doubt
this is his most baroque and self-indulgent film. It may also be
his bravest."

The *Rumble Fish* reviews confirmed Evans's worries about
Coppola as artiste. Furthermore, the film was clearly doomed
at the box office; not only was Coppola's "art film for kids" far
too arty for its intended audience, but it had also, as Coppola
feared it might, gotten the dreaded R rating from the Motion
Picture Association of America. Teenagers couldn't get in to
see it unless they brought their mommies, and their mommies
wouldn't go to teenpix. Its brief, profitless run brought in barely
$1 million in domestic grosses by the year's end. (In compari-
son, *The Outsiders* took in more than $12 million in rentals.)
Rumble Fish did much better in sophisticated Paris the follow-

ing year; in fact, it was among the year's top fifty films.

Rumble Fish did little to improve the Doumanis' estimation of Coppola either. By now they'd come to realize that their on-the-set watchdog, Sylvio Tabet, wasn't doing anything except annoying the director; they needed a more effective agent. "I wanted somebody with real street savvy," said Ed Doumani.

His choice was a fellow resident of Vegas named Joey Cusumano. Cusumano was a guy who, as they say, had friends. One of his closest was Anthony Spilotro, whom the FBI suspected as the Mafia boss of Las Vegas, but despite years of tailing and tapping, nobody had ever been able to pin anything on Cusumano himself. (Five years later the feds sent him to jail for labor racketeering.)

Cusumano's mission seemed to be to scare Coppola into hurrying up and finishing, and doing it as cheaply as possible. But Cusumano was not stupid. He had never been on a movie set before and knew next to nothing about filmmaking. So for three weeks he did nothing but stand quietly in the shadows at the edge of the set, fifteen to eighteen hours a day, watching. He hardly said a word to anyone. "Before I open my mouth, I want to know something," he explained later. "Fishes only get caught when they open their mouths." The only substantial conversation he had during this period was with costume designer Milena Canonero. When he heard she had won an Oscar for her *Chariots of Fire* costumes, he grinned and asked her, "How'd you get an award for shorts?"

If the Doumanis expected Cusumano to scare Coppola, they had forgotten one important factor. Coppola was the guy who had made *The Godfather,* a film in which Robert Duvall remembers real mafiosi playing bit parts. Cusumano wasn't the only guy who had friends; Coppola had some friends, too, and knew how to get along with guys like Cusumano. Not only that, but Coppola was impressed by Cusumano's standing there eighteen hours a day, trying to learn something about filmmaking. Moreover, Coppola liked his look. Unlike the Doumanis, Cusumano dressed more like a tweedy college professor than a Vegas operator.

One morning Cusumano arrived on the set to find an empty director's chair right next to Coppola's, with "Joey" written on the back. Coppola waved Cusumano to sit down, and in no time at all they had formed a mutual admiration society. "I like

Francis as a man, and he's not a bad cook either," noted Cusumano after one of Coppola's spaghetti dinners. In fact, Cusumano grew to admire Coppola's working methods so much that he told Ed Doumani to stay away from the set and let Coppola create. "Sometimes you got to aggravate somebody," Cusumano said, "and sometimes you don't. And when you don't have to, don't." Against all expectation, Cusumano turned into a peacemaker; cast and crew members started kidding happily, calling him their "favorite gangster."

Instead of leaning on Coppola, as everyone had expected, Cusumano became one of Coppola's greatest allies in the money wars. Coppola felt that Evans would not allow him to cut the giant staff, but Cusumano felt no such reluctance. As the Doumanis' direct representative, and at Coppola's urging, Cusumano fired sixty unnecessary workers. "They pissed away $10 million," Cusumano said of Evans's crew. "Francis was instrumental in saving money on this film."

Back in Hollywood, the financial maneuvers in the Zoetrope bankruptcy had grown so intricate that it was no longer possible to tell if events were comic, tragic, or merely surreal. For instance, when a squatter, Douglas Lee Carlton, was discovered living rent-free in Howard Hughes's old cottage on the vacant lot, eviction proceedings were initiated. But when the cops came to throw him off the lot, Carlton insisted that he was Jack Singer's representative and a legitimate buyer of the studio on behalf of Newgraphic Pictures, ready to hand over $20 million for the property. The cream of the jest was that no one had any idea how to find out if he was lying or not.

Meanwhile, Zoetrope President Robert Spiotta was about to close a solid deal for $16.5 million with two other businessmen, Jerry Kramer and Robert Sonnenblick; only the sale was in escrow because the studio was under foreclosure, and there was this little problem with the $175,000 down payment, since the buyers didn't want to trust the money to a bankrupt company with a crowd of hungry creditors lined up around the block.

A few days later Spiotta resigned. He had spent two wearisome years doing nothing but hassling over the sale, and he had had it. He stayed on for a while in Hollywood while Zoetrope's operations moved back to San Francisco. Everyone thought that the sale to Kramer and Sonnenblick was a fait accompli, but everyone was wrong. With no down payment, the studio went back on the market again. Any sale would have to be approved by a judge, and the most likely buyer was still Jack Singer.

The death throes of Zoetrope were entering their final stage. Long, jostling lines of creditors, with $16 million in liens, were fighting to elbow one another out of the way. Max Bercutt, still head of Zoetrope publicity, kept up a strong front. "Francis is a born gambler," he said. "He has had a string of bad luck, but for a guy with a record like his, there is usually a croupier who will put a new pair of dice on the table. Coppola could start rolling sevens again."

But he didn't; the dice came up snake eyes. In November 1983, just fifteen minutes before Coppola closed a deal to sell the studio to Security Pacific Bank, Jack Singer did what he'd been threatening to do for months: He filed a Chapter 11 involuntary bankruptcy petition against the studio. That meant that Zoetrope would be able to settle its debts by paying back only a small percentage of the money owed, but it also meant the end of the corporation. The studio would be auctioned off to the highest bidder.

Coppola tried to keep his mind on his work, plugging away at *The Cotton Club,* but he was unhappy enough to have a painted flat with a fairy tale castle placed outside the windows of the trailer so he wouldn't have to look at the set.

Despite Evans's promises that the film would be finished by Thanksgiving, nobody believed him any more. A Christmas wrap seemed possible, though; as a matter of fact, it seemed absolutely essential. If Coppola kept his giant unionized crew working during the Christmas season, the multiple overtime pay would be ruinously expensive.

It was time for Joey Cusumano to earn his money. He whispered a few words in Coppola's ear, and to emphasize the point, he gave T-shirts to the crew with "Dec. 23, 1983" stenciled on the back, to remind Coppola of the date every time a technician turned around. Sylbert remembers Cusumano's gesturing at Coppola's Airstream trailer, saying, "You see this Silverfish? If we go past the twenty-third, this is going in the ocean with the rest of the fish."

Coppola got the message. He stopped revising the script, went into a Roger Corman mode, and began shooting *The Cot-*

ton Club like a B movie (which was probably what Evans and the Doumanis had wanted in the first place). He completed an astonishing forty setups in three days. Then he took cast, crew, and a giant corps of dancers to Grand Central Station for the grand finale, with absolutely no idea of what he'd shoot there.

For nineteen and a half straight hours the cameras rolled. Coppola was so wired and tense that at one point he accused an assistant director of setting his watch ahead so he could call breaks two minutes early. "I've been conspired against by the AD's," he told Lonette McKee; despite her fondness for Coppola, she decided he'd gone off the deep end.

By now the film was so badly over budget that even the Doumanis couldn't keep it afloat; they needed another $15 million to finish shooting.

Evans and the Doumanis went on a frantic hunt for money. They even tried to resell the film to Paramount for $15 million of finishing funds, despite the fact that they already had a contract with Orion. On Friday, December 9, Evans was unable to deliver all the paychecks; in fact, he later admitted that the checks he did deliver would have bounced if everyone had tried to cash them right away. Rumors reached the press that Coppola was prepared to fly back to Paris (or London) on the Concorde for lunch. Just then Ed Doumani got a pledge from Orion to match Paramount's offer of $15 million. The show would go on.

A few days later an article appeared in the *Wall Street Journal,* called "Trouble on the Set of 'Cotton Club,' " in which Evans said of Coppola, "I could kill him and I want to kiss him. I wouldn't want to do it again if I knew what I had to go through making this movie." Evans blamed Coppola's delay in producing a final script for his inability to get a completion bond.

Coppola exploded and sent Evans a telegram, saying, "You have double-crossed me for the last time. . . . If you want a P.R. war or any kind of war, nobody is better at it than me." Evans donned his disposable halo to answer angelically, "I cannot conceive what motivated your malicious thoughts." The men actually discussed the possibility of fighting a duel. No guns, said Evans, just fists. (They could have sold tickets.)

Evans was running short of allies. Even Richard Gere (who now decided that he liked the finished script after all) had switched sides. "Neither Richard nor Coppola will talk to me," Evans complained. "They're in love. Let them be in love. For what this [film] will do for his career, Gere should pay us the $3 million."

Not only was his picture broke, but Evans was personally broke. When his lease on the East Side town house expired, he was forced to move in with friends because he couldn't afford another suitably elegant flat. To keep the film going, he'd taken out a $3 million mortgage on his home in Beverly Hills and even mortgaged his art and antique collections. His moans of misery sounded pathetically similar to those of his movie's director. "I always wanted to own this film myself," he said. "That was my odyssey, that somewhat has become a nightmare."

Although Orion had agreed to come up with $15 million to complete the shoot, this is not a trivial sum; $15 million normally buys a whole big-budget film, lock, stock, and starlets. There were strings attached to Orion's bailout. Ropes even. At the Doumanis' suggestion, Orion insisted that Evans relinquish what control remained to him. "It was like giving up your kid," groaned Evans, "but I had no choice." Coppola was delighted.

It was snowing on December 23, the date on Cusumano's T-shirts, as Coppola returned to Harlem for the final day of principal photography. He finished at 6:00 A.M., after an all-night shoot. He'd made his deadline by a hair. Somebody set out vodka and orange juice for breakfast, but most of the takers were local winos, the disinherited sons and daughters of the Harlem Renaissance; nobody felt like a wrap party. Without any congratulations or good-byes or hoorays for us, everyone dispersed, heading for the airport or the subway, home for the holidays.

Robert Evans took off for a sailing trip in the Caribbean, followed by a vacation in Acapulco to complete the restoration of his urgently missed tan. Meanwhile, American Express canceled *his* credit card; he had to pose for a cosmetics ad to pay his butler. "I learned one thing," he declared. "Being an independent producer is no bed of roses."

Evans still thought the *The Cotton Club* would be "dazzling and singular," that Richard Gere would come off "like a combination De Niro and Gable," and that Orion was a champ.

At least that's what he told the columnists. He'd patched things up with Paramount and had several projects in the studio's pipeline, including *Two Jakes*, a sequel to *Chinatown*, written by Robert Towne and starring Jack Nicholson. (What he didn't tell Paramount was that he was planning to play one of the leads himself. When Paramount found out, it pulled out every cent and shut down the shoot.)

Just before New Year's 1984, Zoetrope Vice-President John Peters announced that the studio would go on the auction block on February 10. A bankruptcy judge had declared a minimum price of only $12.2 million.

Coppola tried to put it all out of his mind. Hell, it was Christmas. He and Ellie remained in New York; not only would he be editing there, but there were still two weeks of reshoots, special effects, and close-ups to complete. Gere had grown long hair and a beard for his next movie, *King David*, so his close-ups had to be postponed for several months. Bob Hoskins had shaved his head to play Mussolini and flatly refused to return to *The Cotton Club*; Joey Cusumano, who was, by now, acting more like a producer than any of the nine official producers, had a few words with him; Hoskins returned to do his reshoots with a wig.

Cusumano was also in charge of managing the cash flow, but there wasn't much cash flow to manage. Only $1.5 million of Orion's money was left, plus a few million in short-term loans, plus (he hoped) an insurance payoff for the day Diane Lane had gotten zits. Cusumano did what he could, talking owners of some locations into granting large discounts, and generally exercising his powers of persuasion to help Coppola finish within the money that was left.

Meanwhile, the Zoetrope saga came to its dreary conclusion. On February 10 the public auction took place as scheduled. This time there were no last-minute reprieves. Pacific National Bank bid $12.2 million, but Jack Singer, who'd forced the studio into Chapter 11 bankruptcy, took it for $12.3 million, just $100,000 over the legal minimum bid.

Coppola had had the studio appraised at the beginning of the year. Its value had been set at $16.8 million, so, theoretically Singer was getting it for about $4 million less than it was worth. In addition, Singer had never delivered the last $5 million of the $8 million he'd promised to lend Coppola. On the other hand, Coppola had never paid back the $3 million Singer had lent him. These matters formed the substance of a $6 million lawsuit brought by Singer, against Coppola, several years later.

A separate auction, scheduled for six weeks later (the press called it "Zoetrope's Garage Sale"), disposed of the technical equipment, props, sets (including the model-size neon casinos from *Heart,* which were bought by an antique store on Los Angeles's trendy Melrose Avenue), costumes, and memorabilia of Coppola's films all the way back to *Apocalypse Now,* plus an assortment of antique furniture and middle-aged motor vehicles. The "garage sale" raised $225,000, all of which went toward debt payback. Security Pacific Bank was out $1.5 million in interest on the original $6.7 million real estate loan, since debt interest can't be collected in a forced commercial bankruptcy.

Fortunately for Coppola, his personal property wasn't affected by the bankruptcy of his studio. He got to keep his Airstream, all the electronics therein, whatever equipment he'd moved to San Francisco, and nearly all the real estate he owned personally. He could continue to pay off his personal loans under the arrangements he'd made previously.

On March 31 the last shot of *The Cotton Club* went into the can. Now all Coppola had to do was edit the mess into a movie that people would be falling all over themselves to see; his 10 percent of the adjusted gross could be his ticket out of debt.

Evans's sick infant had turned into a multimillion-dollar problem child. Costs were hovering around $47 million (/$55.4 million), including $21 million for principal photography, $6.5 million to pay Coppola, Puzo, and Gere, $6 million for sets, $4 million for special effects and miscellaneous items, $2 million for fired production chiefs, $1.7 million for costumes, $1.7 million for extras, $1 million for insurance, $1 million for living and travel expenses, $800,000 for Gio Coppola's second-unit footage, $460,000 for makeup, $450,000 for Richard Gere's overtime, $256,000 for security, $247,000 for the caterer, and $70,000 to pay Kennedy.

The Cotton Club would have to take in at least $100 million in domestic box-office grosses just to break even. This would not be easy. Typically a very big picture will gross about

$75 million in the Unites States (TV and videotape sales are extra); at the time of *The Cotton Club*'s completion, only five films in history (all by Steven Spielberg or George Lucas) had passed the magic $100 million figure: *E.T.*, *Star Wars*, *Return of the Jedi*, *The Empire Strikes Back*, and *Jaws*.

Still, if Evans was panicked, he wasn't letting on. "If the movie is one-tenth as good as the story behind it, it'll be *The Godfather* and *Gone With the Wind* rolled into one," he declared. "And that's what it needs to make any money."

Chapter Twenty

Feuding Filmmakers and Battling Bozos: The Cotton Wars (1984-1985)

DAILY VARIETY CALLED it a comic opera, but it was nothing less than a legal free-for-all. With *The Cotton Club* in post-production, everyone involved in the film commenced suing everybody else.

Had there been a fight card, it might have read:

COTTON CLUB LEGAL SLUGFEST

Main Events

1. Ed "The Vegas Vampire" Doumani v. Poor Bob Evans
2. Poor Bob Evans v. Ed "The Vegas Vampire" Doumani
3. Victor "The Peacemaker" Sayyah v. Everybody
4. Sylvio "Are We Done Yet?" Tabet v. Almost Everybody

Intermission

5. John "The Dark Horse" Rockwell v. Poor Bob Evans
6. John "The Dark Horse" Rockwell v. Orion Pictures
7. Susan "The Little Match Girl" Mechsner v. Francis "The Bearded Meanie" Coppola
8. Orion Pictures v. Syufy Theaters

In the first event, Ed Doumani (with the blessings of
Orion Pictures and Francis Coppola) took up the gloves in a
lawsuit to seize control of the picture from Evans. Supposedly
this all had been spelled out and agreed on in the contract
Evans and Doumani signed with Orion on the occasion of the
$15 million bailout, but Doumani claimed Evans wasn't fight-
ing clean. Doumani's haymaker was the presentation of the
document itself, signed by himself and Evans on December
13, 1983. But the blow fell short; Victor Sayyah, the third partner, had never signed the agreement.

Desperate, Doumani threw a wild punch and connected.
The spectators gasped as he testified that Evans "may have
indulged in some things that would not make him function
well." Now that Doumani had Evans against the ropes, he tried
to hurt him even more by pointing out that he "hasn't a penny
in the picture." Whatever Evans had spent, Doumani insisted,
was just to support himself in the "Hollywood style" to which
he was accustomed. Evans's attorney responded with a volley
of counterpunches, reminding the court that Poor Bob had invested five years of his life and $5 million of his own money.
But Doumani, who'd put up $24 million, had a clear weight
advantage.

Evans rallied with a countersuit in which he claimed
that the Doumanis, Coppola, and Orion were ganging up on
him. He'd agreed to relinquish control, he said, only because
the Doumanis lied to him, claiming that Victor Sayyah was
on their side. But Sayyah clearly wasn't, as evidenced by the
fact that he never signed the agreement. In a touching appeal to the referee Evans further testified that the Doumanis
had thrown a foul blow by making oral threats against his
life.

Naturally Coppola and Orion were in the Doumanis corner, but some ringsiders were still betting on Evans. Robert
Spiotta, of all people, the former president of Zoetrope and an
early consultant on *The Cotton Club*, gave Evans a supporting
written declaration. Then Richard Sylbert came out swinging,
asserting that the Doumanis had let Coppola wrest control of
the film from Evans and escalate the budget beyond all reason
because they were naive about the movie business. "Francis
used the desperate situation to force Bob Evans to give up virtually all controls and approvals that a producer normally has

over a picture," Sylbert averred. "No studio would have agreed to the demands that Francis was making."

Then Victor Sayyah, the Doumanis' coinvestor and some-time partner, threw his hat in the ring with a suit challenging all comers (Evans, the Doumanis, Orion, and the production company) for letting the promised $20 million budget escalate to . . . $58 million! It was the first (and last) time this appall-ing figure (as opposed to a merely monstrous $47 million) was mentioned. Apparently Sayyah had arrived at it by including the interest cost on the Doumanis' investment. But in any case, as far as Sayyah was concerned, they all were guilty of breach of contract for promising him that his $5 million would buy part of a $20 million movie. Furthermore, he claimed, the Doumanis, Evans, and Orion all were conspiring against him, and the whole production company was "a mere sham and shell," an alter ego for Robert Evans.

Now Sylvio Tabet danced into the ring, filing suit against the Doumanis and the production company for coproducer credit and $6 million in damages. Apparently this bout was settled in the changing rooms; after the initial report no further news was published about Tabet's legal debut. He emerged with at least one victory: an on-screen producer credit shared with Fred Roos.

After a brief trip to England, Coppola returned to New York, shortly after his birthday, to resume editing *The Cotton Club*. He was depressed, trapped in the scheme that he him-self had devised to cheapen the Harlem Renaissance and everything in it that he cared about. Once again he had be-trayed himself. Then, as if tensions weren't already high enough, a lengthy report on the making of the film appeared in the May 7, 1984, issue of *New York* magazine. Writer Michael Daly had managed to talk to nearly everyone on the set except Coppola himself; his piece was a highly dramatic tale of intrigue, con-flict, and skulduggery. While Coppola came off fairly well in comparison with Evans, Sayyah, Tabet, and the rest, he couldn't have been pleased to have his dirty laundry in the street again.

Naturally the article was a must-read for nearly everyone in the industry, and it reverberated for months in *New York*'s letters to the editor column. A bit player wrote, "As an actor who worked for six horrendous weeks on *Cotton Club*, I would like to say that my heartfelt sympathies go to Robert

Evans. . . . A pox on Francis 'The Great' Coppola, who spent time and money in a reprehensible manner." Even Sylvio Tabet wrote in to protest "the slur on my character" and to insist that he and Coppola got along just great.

Meanwhile, Coppola and editors Barry Malkin and Robert Lovett (with William Kennedy kibitzing) kept plugging away on the tough first cut of the movie; it was completed late in May 1984, five months after the conclusion of the principal photography. According to Kennedy, it was "stunning but draggy." With Orion urging him on, Coppola reached for the scissors and started chopping major scenes; the sweet sequence in which Dutch Schultz's mama went shopping ended up on the cutting-room floor, along with many family scenes of the Dwyers and Williamses. Coppola nearly chopped Fred Gwynne's improvised watch scene on the grounds that it was "too wacko." Gwynne had to lobby for months to keep it in.

The new cut was only two hours long, and even George Lucas liked it. But according to Kennedy, when Coppola showed it to Orion the moguls decided there was "too much tap dancing; the plot goes too fast and needs some air; needs more love scenes; ending is crazy."

Coppola ducked into the editing room. The next day there was a new cut, two hours and eleven minutes long, and this time Orion loved it. Lloyd Leipzig, senior vice-president for publicity, said it was a "magical, marvelous, cosmic experience." With the cut approved, nothing stood in the way of a Christmas 1984 release. Coppola was ready to start mixing the sound immediately. However, he wanted to work in Northern California, and Bob Evans insisted on using a high tech facility in New York. Back to court they went, so a judge could determine where the mixing would be done.

On June 18 the Doumani-Evans lawsuits came up for trial; the referee was U.S. District Court Judge Irving Hill. As *Variety* put it, the case "exposed a viper's nest of power plays."

Evans started by throwing a volley of verbal blows. The film represented not only his life savings, he insisted, but his career and his pride. He appealed to the ref with a heartfelt pronouncement: "I wanted to have this movie for my family. I ended up without a cent."

Coppola, who was there as a witness for the Doumanis, waded into the donnybrook with a will. He testified that he'd felt great relief when Orion insisted that Evans relinquish control. Evans's return to power "would drive up the budget and delay the picture another month," he told the judge. "It fills me with horror to think that it could go back to the way it was. My only goal is to get out of this job and get on with my life."

Victor Sayyah leaped into the fray from the ringside to explain that he'd always had doubts about the Doumanis' hiring of Joey Cusumano as an on-the-set enforcer. The spectators gasped when he testified that Cusumano had "an unsavory reputation and is reputed to be among organized crime. I'm shocked that Orion sees fit to associate with this individual."

Coppola blocked Sayyah's swing with a muscular "That's baloney." As far as he was concerned, Cusumano and associate producer (and ex-Zoetroper) Barrie Osborne had brought stability to the production.

If Sayyah was miffed at Cusumano, he was even angrier at Evans, swearing it would be "the coldest day in hell" before he would transfer the Doumanis' authority to a producer who allowed shooting to start with neither a completed script nor a written budget.

Judge Hill seemed incredulous at the tales of escalating chaos on *The Cotton Club*, and the foot-high pile of affidavits, which he actually compared with *Rashomon*, in which "every event is reported entirely differently by every person who saw it." Nonetheless, on June 18 he granted Evans a preliminary injunction over the Doumanis. This meant that until the facts could be clearly established, and the suit resolved, Evans had legal control over the film.

For Evans, it was less of a knockout than a knockdown. While he had temporarily won marketing and distribution control of *The Cotton Club*, including cable and TV rights, Hill ruled that since Evans had abandoned postproduction work, reinserting him now would endanger the completion of the film. The judge assigned the right to make all postproduction decisions to Coppola's sparring partner, Barrie Osborne. Now Coppola could go home to Napa and complete postproduction without Evans's kibitzing.

Hill admonished the litigants to stop grousing and get back to work, "ensuring the welfare and good reception of the picture that means so much to you." Furthermore, they had to stop suing each other all the time, at least without asking him first. Finally, since the ultimate judgment was still to be made, Hill ordered Evans to post a $5 million bond against any damages that might be awarded later, and to put it up within three days. Evans was flat broke; there was no way he could come up with that sort of money. Poor Bob had been TKOed by the ref. A few days later Hill agreed to reduce the bond to a paltry $1 million.

As the hearing ended, a new fracas broke out on the way to the changing rooms. Evans's attorney rabbit-punched Coppola, arguing that the director wouldn't let Evans see the film. The Doumanis' lawyer counterpunched with a proposal to show it to Evans within two weeks. Judge Hill ruled that Coppola had to screen the film within two days. When Doumani and Sayyah begged the judge to let them see it, too, the judge said sure. It was around this point that a rumor began to spread that a top Hollywood agent was offering $500,000 for the screen rights to the affidavits.

When reports of the judgment were published in the *Wall Street Journal* the next day, Orion executives called a press conference, *prontissimo*, before their stock went down the drain. Arthur Krim was afraid that another studio-wrecking *Heaven's Gate* might be in the works if Orion didn't counter Sayyah's allegations of $58 million costs, not to mention Evans's control over marketing.

Orion still had the right to act as distributor, Krim's spokesman insisted; its $15 million had bought all rights, including the right to make marketing decisions and sell the film however and to whomever they pleased. What Evans had won was little more than the right to argue with them over whether the film's L.A. opening would be in a theater north of Wilshire Boulevard or south of it. At the same time, since Orion's investment was limited to $15 million, even if the film dropped dead it couldn't be hurt too badly.

Two days later Evans got to see Coppola's cut of *The Cotton Club*. Naturally he hated it and demanded a host of changes. Coppola swore that the only changes he'd make would be in response to comments from the preview audiences. "Evans won't even be told where the preview is," Coppola declared. "And if he finds out, he'll have to pay admission to get in."

Early in August, Evans and the Doumanis kissed and made up. Coppola, for one, was thoroughly repelled at the prospect.

Victor Sayyah had turned peacemaker in hopes of getting some of his money back before the twenty-first century, and arranged a deal under which he and Evans would sell all their interests in the picture to the Doumanis for close to $10 million. Sayyah would receive a $6 million return on his $5 million investment. Evans would pull down nearly $4 million. Except for Orion's portion, the Doumanis now owned 100 percent of *The Cotton Club*. "This has brought the Doumanis and me very close together again," Evans declared, apparently forgetting Ed Doumani's courtroom allegations of dope fiendery. "We are as one."

The Doumanis, in turn, said they'd call on Evans as an adviser on the handling of the film. "We want his expertise," said Ed Doumani. "That's why we got involved with him in the first place." In fact, Evans and the Doumanis told the reporters, they all planned to do another film together. Real soon.

Was the legal slugfest over? Hardly. On August 13 a new contender swaggered into the ring. John Rockwell, the guy who had introduced Bob Evans to the Doumanis in the first place, had long since signed a release accepting a $25,000 finder's fee. Now he was demanding $2.3 million from Evans. A court hearing was scheduled for November 1.

Back in Napa, Coppola continued fooling around with the picture: restoring cuts; moving scenes around; dropping the violins and upping the saxes. The hard work served to distract him from his disgust with the whole project. Early in October sneak previews were held in San Jose, Boston, and Seattle. At each one, audience reaction was progressively better as Coppola cut the film shorter and shorter.

Robert Evans got wind of the sneaks and slipped into the one in San Jose. What he saw was so far from his original vision he immediately wrote a detailed critique (he told the *Wall Street Journal* it was twenty-seven pages long), suggesting changes in everything from the credits to the musical numbers. Then he had his good buddy Ed Doumani drive three and a half hours, each way, to hand-deliver it to Coppola. Barrie Osborne met Doumani at the door and told him he'd pass the critique to Coppola, but Coppola never saw fit to respond. According to Coppola, Evans got revenge by sending copies to several major film critics just before the movie opened. Furthermore, said Coppola, it was only ten pages long.

On October 25, theater owners finally got to see the film, too, as a series of exhibitors' screenings began. Their reactions, it was reported, were "glowing."

It appears to have been a major disappointment for almost everyone else, though. Sylbert seemed less angry with Coppola than sorry for him. "Don't forget," Sylbert pointed out, "he was coming off three flops, pictures that were like parodies of existential college films. On those films I'd say he bit off a lot less than he could chew, whereas on *Cotton Club* he juggled nine balls in the air at one time. . . ."

Still, Sylbert's basic attitude toward Coppola hadn't changed that much. "Francis is emotional, chaotic," he added. "If they hadn't pulled the plug, Francis would still be shooting, looking for a story. You know, there's $10 million worth of film on the cutting room floor, and plenty of scenes, but no more plot."

A few weeks later Sylbert told Jack Kroll of *Newsweek,* "Francis just flails around, hoping he'll pull it out of the air. He desperately wants to be Kurosawa, Fellini, Bergman. He resents being in the commercial narrative, Hollywood movie business. I told Evans not to hire him."

When Coppola read this, he was so sore he fired off a letter to the editor in which he protested, "I have letters from Sylbert saying, 'Please come and work on this film. Evans is crazy.' "

Evans himself had reason to feel annoyed with another magazine story, although he didn't write any letters about it. From the beginning Evans had seen William Kennedy as a major pain in the ass, but Kennedy had won shared screen credit (along with Coppola and Mario Puzo) for Evans's story, as well as a shared screen credit (with Coppola) for the screenplay. Now, adding insult to injury, Kennedy had written a detailed, wryly humorous account of his *Cotton Club* travails, which appeared in the November issue of the brash new magazine *Vanity Fair.* While Coppola was portrayed warmly, Evans came off as a semiliterate motor-mouth who played a minor, even destructive role in the filmmaking. Furthermore, in regard to his writer's credits, Kennedy concluded his article with a short raspberry aimed at Evans. "Dear Bob," it went, "You didn't ask for my comment on this topic, but here you have it anyway: Go poach yourself. Love ya, Kennedy."

On November 1 John Rockwell's demand for a $2.5 million finder's fee from Evans came to court; the decision was inconclusive, so Evans and Orion offered him a compromise settlement just to get him out of their hair. Rockwell turned it down flat.

Coppola tried to relax while he waited for the *Cotton Club* grosses to start rolling in, and for his next hired-hand movie to materialize. He considered directing *Agnes of God,* but his now-standard asking price of $3 million up front (against 10 percent of the adjusted gross) was too steep, equaling nearly the whole budget. Coppola made a few phone calls, trying to peddle a western called *Whore's Gold* with no success. Nor did the studios show any more enthusiasm for a film version of William Kennedy's *Legs* (which Kennedy proposed to script solo) as a vehicle for Mickey Rourke. Evidently Coppola was willing to make at least one more gangster movie.

He spent his free time negotiating to make an old dream come true. He'd been a great enthusiast of the movies of Sergei Eisenstein ever since the screening of *Ten Days That Shook the World* that convinced him to become a movie director. With Tom Luddy's help, he engineered an unusual film exchange with the USSR; in return for good, fresh prints of Coppola's entire *oeuvre,* the Reds would deliver pristine copies of Eisenstein's *Potemkin, Alexander Nevsky,* and *Ivan the Terrible, Part I* and *Part II.* Eventually Coppola might issue them as home video releases, but for the moment it was thrill enough to have them in his library.

Meanwhile, Coppola's next movie was already in trouble, although he didn't know it. That is, he didn't know it was his next movie; like everyone who read the trades, he knew that *Peggy Sue Got Married* was having problems.

Rastar, a production branch of Columbia run by industry heavyweight Ray Stark (for whom the young Coppola had worked at Seven Arts), was prepping a time-travel fantasy-comedy. Debra Winger was set to star as a youthful, forty-three-year-old mother who suddenly finds herself transported back to 1960, age seventeen again. She was perfect for the part, and so bankable that it was hard to imagine anybody else in the role. Then Jonathan Demme (a Corman graduate, whose subsequent directorial career had included a number of highly regarded films such as *Melvin and Howard*) was signed to direct. Within days Winger was threatening to quit; she'd had her heart set on TV director Penny Marshall, best known for the *Laverne and Shirley* sitcoms. Demme knew where the power was; he defected, tactfully claiming "creative differences," and late in October Marshall came in to make her film directing debut. A few days later she quit too, claiming "artistic differences" with the producer, Paul Gurian, and the screenwriters. At this point Debra Winger took a walk. Since she'd never gotten around to signing a contract, there was nothing Rastar could do.

But, said Winger, she would consider reconsidering if a director could be found who was satisfactory to one and all. "I've always wanted to work with Francis Coppola," she murmured as she walked out the door.

In mid-November Rastar executives admitted they were courting Coppola. He was, of course, extremely tempted by the money, although the material was less than thrilling. With the Zoetrope bankruptcy finally resolved, he had arranged to pay back many of his own debts at thirty cents on the dollar, but the arrangement was based on large, regular cash payments, and the *Cotton Club* grosses were still theoretical. *Peggy Sue* would be a godsend. Of course, he'd be a hired hand again, and this time, since the script was already complete, there would be little he could do to make the movie his own. But Rastar seemed ready to meet his asking price, and nobody else was offering him $3 million against 10 percent of the adjusted gross of anything.

He did receive one small-time offer that delighted him greatly. Actress Shelley Duvall had been producing a cable TV series called *Faerie Tale Theater*—video versions of classic fairy tales which bore only a passing resemblance to normal kidvid, and actually charmed quite a few adults. Between Coppola's love of children and his fascination with video, *Faerie Tale Theater* was a natural. He and Shelley Duvall had been discussing it for several years; now, when Duvall asked Coppola if he'd like to do a fifty-minute version of *Rip Van Winkle,* he leapt at the chance. Finally he would get to try some video experiments where the stakes were low and the ante not his own. The pay would be lousy, and the schedule short, but the pleasure would be great. Coppola enlisted *Mishima* production designer Eiko Ishioka to develop a Kabuki-like visual scheme for the story, and started working on the script with writers Mark Curtiss and Rod Ash.

The Cotton Club was scheduled to open on December 10, 1984. Orion started plugging its big Christmas release early, with a barrage of thirty-second TV spots that began on November 7 and increased in frequency throughout the month. In addition, there were trailers in the theaters, lobby displays, an MTV video, and three-page gatefold ads in *Newsweek, People,* and *Rolling Stone.*

On Sunday, December 2, 1984, *The Cotton Club* had its premiere, a gala benefit for local charities at the grand Palace Theater in Albany, New York, William Kennedy's hometown. The New York opening was scheduled one week later, on December 10, but on December 5 John Rockwell demanded a rematch on his finder's fee suit. He filed to enjoin Orion Pictures from distributing the film.

Now he wanted more than money; he wanted an associate producer credit like the one Melissa Prophet got, since, after all, his friend Doumani had put in a lot more money than her friend Khashoggi. Evans testified that Prophet had earned her credit, while Rockwell hadn't been anywhere near the set. Orion's lawyers pointed out, reasonably enough, that if Rockwell won his injunction, Orion would have to withdraw the film right in the middle of the holiday moviegoing season. The judge must have been convinced, for he scheduled the court hearing for December 13, three days after the premiere. When the suit came to trial, it was dismissed out of hand. If Rockwell had worn a cape, he would have flung it over his shoulder and hissed, "You haven't seen the last of me yet!" A year later he sued Orion again, but to this day his name remains absent from the *Cotton Club* credits.

With Rockwell temporarily out of the way, the New York premiere came off on schedule and in style. Several hundred celebrities, including Goldie Hawn, Diana Ross, Michael Douglas, and Norman Mailer, started the evening sipping cocktails with Richard Gere and New York City Mayor Ed Koch at Gracie Mansion. Then chauffeured limos brought them all to the screening at a midtown theater and whisked them to a flashy Park Avenue disco for a champagne buffet supper when the film was over.

What they saw was a fairly conventional gangster thriller with a pleasant jazz score, set in Harlem. The film starts with a superb opening sequence (designed and shot by Colossal Pictures in San Francisco): Art Deco credits, intercut with live footage of a sassy black chorus line, parade across the screen accompanied by a stereo rendition of what sounds like the original 1928 recording of Ellington's "The Mooche." Thanks to Bob Wilber's painstaking re-creation of the original Ellington chart, it sounds, for a few moments, as if the Duke's legendary band had somehow been time-machined into a digital recording studio. The credits leave no doubt: Magic is about to transpire before our eyes.

Then, unfortunately, the story begins. It centers on handsome white cornet player Dixie Dwyer (Richard Gere), who accidentally saves the life of gangster Dutch Schultz (James Remar), falling thereby into Dutch's clutches. For some reason, Dutch (who ought to be grateful) forces Dixie to serve as his errand boy, making him pick up the laundry and escort the mobster's stunning teenage mistress, Vera Cicero (Diane Lane). Dixie and Vera fall into bed. Cotton Club owners Owney Madden and Frenchy Demange (Bob Hoskins and Fred Gwynne) send Dixie to Hollywood to star in a movie (*Mob Boss!*) before the murderous Dutch can find out about Dixie and Vera. When Dixie's little brother, "Mad Dog" Dwyer (Nicolas Cage), gets in dutch with Dutch, Dixie returns to act as a go-between. Mad Dog is beyond help, but now Dixie can resume his illicit relationship with Vera. Happily, before Dutch gets around to killing the lovers, Lucky Luciano (from the up-and-coming Cosa Nostra) has his boys mow down the Dutchman.

A (very) secondary plot involves Cotton Club tap dancer Sandman Williams (Gregory Hines), who falls in love with one of the "copper-colored gals," ambitious singer-dancer Lila (Lonette McKee). Despite Sandman's protestations of affection, she abandons him to become a famous singer, passing for white at Vera Cicero's bland new downtown club. (So much for the "black pride" movement of the Harlem Renaissance.) Then, for no discernible reason, Lila jeopardizes her whole new life by going to a hotel with Sandman. (A sub-subplot involving Sandman's betrayal of his brother and their subsequent reconciliation is worth mentioning only insofar as it reflects Coppola's continuing fascination with fraternal dynamics.)

Finally, just before the end credits roll, all the survivors of the mob wars (except Luciano) reassemble in a surreal, racially integrated dance number *cum* finale set in Grand Central Station. Presumably all are bound away on the express train to happiness.

The acting is uneven. Gere's performance is unobjectionable (except for his cornet playing), but Evans's frequent comparisons of him with Clark Gable seem farfetched. Remar, playing Dutch Schultz in a very broad (and controversial) style, seems not so much directed as unleashed. Hines and McKee have little to do. And while there's something exciting about Coppola and Kennedy's cynical dialogue emerging from Diane Lane's fresh young face, the actress simply isn't up to the role; worse yet, there's no spark between her and Gere. The lovers are no more involving than Frannie and Hank in *One from the Heart*.

The supporting cast is wonderful, though. The film's most exciting moments stem from brilliant performances by Coppola's character actors. Bob Hoskins and Fred Gwynne prove the warmest of the ensemble, there's fine work in small doses by Larry Marshall (in an uncanny re-creation of Cab Calloway), Joe Dallessandro (as a cool, handsome Luciano), Lisa Jane Persky, Gwen Verdon, Larry Fishburne, and Jennifer Grey (who went on to fame in *Dirty Dancing*). Above all, Julian Beck, cofounder of the legendary avant-garde performing troupe The Living Theater, is delicious as Schultz's spectral, vicious sidekick Sol Weinstein, zestfully biting into lines like "I didn't have a mudda. Dey found me in a gahbage pay-ul." It's impossible to guess that Beck was very near death at the time of the shoot.

Stylistically there's little to distinguish the film as an opus de Coppola, and what there is (like a love scene shot through a black lace scrim, with moiré patterns of colored light passing over the lovers' bodies) tends toward the artsy-fartsy *One from the Heart* model. The two exceptions are Dutch Schultz's terrifying death scene, with a bullet-burst water pipe spurting water to match the splashing blood, and the improvised grand finale in Grand Central Station, which finds Coppola at his spontaneous best.

Even with so thin a plot (how in the world could it have taken thirty-seven drafts?) and so little directorial presence, the music Coppola had at his disposal might have saved the film; many musicals have been stupendously entertaining in spite of moronic plots. But Coppola throws away his chance. He had made no secret of his intention to fragment the numbers. "Everything happens during Gregory Hines' dance," he had stated during the shoot. But everything happens during all the dances. Talented black performers do their damnedest to hoof their way into our hearts; jazz classics erupt on the sound track; and every time the film starts to catch fire, Coppola cuts to some white gangster. In fact, halfway through the film, the essential action shifts away from the Cotton Club altogether, to center on Vera Cicero's genteel and boring all-white downtown nightclub.

Coppola's butchery of the dance numbers is shocking. Twenty years earlier, after *Finian's Rainbow*, he blamed money-grubbing studio execs and a last-minute switch in screen ratio for cutting off the dancers at the knees; but in *Cotton Club* he does it again, and he compounds the amputations by chopping nearly all the dances off in the middle. When a rare sequence, like the one in which Honi Coles and Gregory Hines trade steps at the Hoofers' Club, is allowed to run uninterrupted, Coppola ruins it anyway by presenting it as close-ups of separate anatomical pieces: feet; face; torso; a spectator's back.

Variety had already reviewed the film, with muted enthusiasm. *Cotton Club* was less than Coppola's best work, it declared, but not as bad as his worst: "A bit of a letdown, but by no means a disaster, nor is it a film lacking commercial appeal. Nonetheless, it will have a tough go at recouping its money. . . . Generally speaking, *The Cotton Club* serves up more entertainment highs than lows."

There were two significant no-shows at the premiere: Robert Evans and Francis Coppola. Their absence was noted by the press. Julie Salamon of the *Wall Street Journal* managed to get to both Evans and Coppola (who granted her a four-hour interview) and was on the street with the scoop within a week of the premiere.

Evans, back in L.A., admitted to Salamon that *The Cotton Club* was a dazzling movie, but added, "It's Francis's movie, not mine. The picture I wanted is on the cutting-room floor. Francis deceived me. He deceived everybody. Francis is unquestionably the greatest seducer of our time. He makes Elmer Gantry look like Don Knotts."

Coppola, also in L.A., snapped, "I don't want to be involved with those people. They have been my most horrible enemies. What's that word? Calumny. That's the word for it. Evans is a liar, you see. I almost think he would love this picture to be a gigantic flop."

Even if Coppola hadn't been trying to avoid Evans at the premiere, he had good reason to stay in Hollywood: *Rip Van*

Winkle was turning out to be big fun. Harry Dean Stanton (the hero's buddy in *One from the Heart*) was playing the title role, and Coppola had come up with a typically strong supporting cast that included Ed Begley, Jr., Tim Conway, Christopher Penn, and Talia Shire as Rip's nagging wife. Coppola used a new computerized matting technique called Ultimatte to create magical visuals that would bring the classic fantasy to life. "I don't want to be limited by reality any more," he said.

Ultimatte allowed him to combine several moving mattes to create dreamy, ever-changing multiple superimpositions, but not all the fantastic images he used for *Rip* were electronic. Some of the most spectacular effects employed Eiko Ishioka's "human mountain," a standard bit of Kabuki stagecraft consisting of five people crouching under a piece of canvas that changes color and shape to reflect the mood of the scene.

He was working on his shortest shooting schedule and (in effect) his lowest budget since the nudies; he had exactly six days and $650,000 (/$741,000) to shoot the fifty-minute-long film. But in a strange way Coppola enjoyed the stringent limits on time and money. "The bigger the budget, the less freedom you have and the less money you actually have available," he declared.

The critics were deeply divided over *The Cotton Club*. Everybody was impressed by Julian Beck, Bob Hoskins, and Joe Dallessandro, but for the film as a whole there were more pans than plaudits. "It's not a complete disaster," wrote Vincent Canby, "but it's not a whole lot of fun. . . . There is an air of expensive desperation about it. . . . [Even the] potentially fantastic finale seems designed not to tie up loose ends but to pick up lint." *Time*'s Richard Corliss noted that the movie was an indifferent sequel to its prerelease publicity—in fact, a "frigid, juiceless mess."

Several reviews seemed designed more as a critique of Coppola than his film. One such, by David Denby of *New York* magazine, used the film and its "ruinous" dance numbers as a springboard for a scathingly astute personal attack on its director. "Francis Coppola, it turns out, only *thinks* he's an obsessed artist," Denby wrote. "If he were truly a man with a vision, he wouldn't change his mind so often in the middle of his films. Coppola is obsessed with *being* an artist, which is a far-different thing."

There were a couple of raves. Sheila Benson hopped on

board as usual, finding *Cotton Club* "audacious, buoyant, and breathtaking, . . . overflowing with music and dance." And *Newsweek*'s Jack Kroll described the film as "something of a miracle, . . . one of the few original films of the year, a movie of driving pace and swirling style whose major fault is that it should be longer."

The single most devastating mainstream review didn't come out until two weeks later: Pauline Kael called *The Cotton Club* "a movie made by a director who has lost his sense of character." While pointing out, in painful detail, just how badly he "knocks the life" out of the music, she noted, "His expansiveness has become strictly formal. Emotionally, he seems to have shrunk. . . ."

As if that weren't bad enough, two months after that, Stanley Crouch, the *Village Voice*'s perceptive black jazz critic, took on *The Cotton Club* in a lengthy, well-researched, and coldly furious article called "The Rotten Club." Crouch characterized it as "a simplistic gangster tale backdropped by a series of black caricatures, and pegged to a . . . story of the sort a 'socially conscious' teenager might have written 30 years ago." And he hated the music, "played by a band whose timbre and attack identify it as white."

Howard "Stretch" Johnson, who assisted Michael Smuin, was horrified by the finished film. "They had the opportunity to present great black entertainment on a scale never before shown on film. But they lacked the courage and the faith in the public. . . . When Gere saw those black performers performing the way they did, he ran scared and threatened to raise holy hell, threatened to leave the film after they had half the footage."

The Cotton Club opened passably, taking in around $3 million its first weekend. But that same weekend *Beverly Hills Cop* took in more than $11.5 million; even *Dune* (a strange science-fiction film that ultimately flopped, too), *City Heat* (cop high jinks), and *2010* (sequel to *2001*) beat *Cotton Club* at the box office.

On Monday, December 17, when Orion's stockholders read about *The Cotton Club*'s tepid weekend returns, they sold off their shares in a panic; Orion's stock plummeted to its lowest point in a year. In something of a panic themselves, Orion executives called a press conference to reiterate that *The Cotton*

Club was not their problem; the company's investment in the movie was "fixed and limited," a mere $15 million that would be fully recouped, off the top, as soon as the film grossed $20 million. Slowly the stock began to recover.

The next vision of vultures appeared in the San Francisco *Chronicle*. Columnist Herb Caen reported that Coppola might lose his North Beach headquarters, the Sentinel Building, because he couldn't pay $1.7 million he owed on it. "It goes up for grabs at a trustee sale on the steps of City Hall at 1 P.M., Dec 27," wrote Caen. "Unless, of course, the Seventh Cavalry arrives with the cash to save Coppola's Cupola."

Of all the real estate Coppola had owned and lost, and the little he had managed to hang on to, the ornate old Sentinel Building was especially dear to him. Not only was it Zoetrope headquarters, but it was almost eighty years old, and its sale might result in its demolition. In any case, the Sentinel cash crisis seems to have forced Coppola to face the financial facts: He bit the bullet and signed on as director of *Peggy Sue Got Married*. As expected, he was acceptable to everybody. More important, Winger was acceptable to him. Coppola considered her very bright. "Other people have had problems handling her," Coppola said, "so they came to me this time."

His deeper feelings emerged in interviews. He never mentioned *Peggy Sue* directly, but a certain bitterness began bubbling to the surface. "I'm the Red Adair of the movies," he joked, referring to the traveling oil well fire fighter. "It's a wonderful deal—you have a guy who comes in and puts out the fire and it's all his fault. And I do it all for one fee." Worse yet, he added, "as you lose your viability in the minds of the studio heads, then you can't do the projects you want to. So you do the stuff you don't want to do, and you get criticized for it. My problem is that I need to make so much money each year that I have to work."

Coppola, the artist forced to take a straight job to pay alimony to his artistic failures, may have been feeling sorry for himself, but *The Cotton Club* box-office story wasn't over yet. While *Cop* held the lead as top-grossing film in America, by the end of its second week in release *The Cotton Club* had moved up to number two. It was finding an audience.

But at this point, not even money could stop the Evans-Coppola bash-up. "In a way it was my fault," Evans told one reporter. "I was the one who hired Francis Coppola."

A few weeks later, when journalist Dale Pollock tracked Coppola down on the set of "Rip Van Winkle," Coppola seemed strangely serene. He was forty-five, overweight and graying, and if he still sounded defensive at times, he was also occasionally . . . relaxed. He sighed and said:

> I'm not sure I have a career any more. I'm an oddball in the eyes of the public. I'm beginning to be more and more estranged from the movie industry. It's becoming homogenized, and I'm the old standby whipping boy. People have been frightened by what they read about me. I've had a rough time for the past few years. I had my fun, and now I'm paying for it. . . . But why was it so bad that I wanted a little studio to turn out movies? It was good for America for me to have this little stupid studio. . . .
>
> I still love to make movies although I find the system a little trying. On the big films, you don't really get your hands on the money. It gets moved around in lawyers' offices.

As for *The Cotton Club*, Coppola now stated that he felt it was (surprise!) a serious art film, not merely a schlock assignment. "It's my personal movie," he declared, "even though I was the hireling." Its message, he added, was that "talent is the only thing that can break servitude." It sounded like Coppola's message to Coppola. It certainly said nothing to his talented black cast.

By the time Pollock's interview reached print, Coppola was long gone. First he returned to San Francisco, just before Christmas, to give $1.7 million of his *Peggy Sue* money to Security Pacific Bank to save the Sentinel Building, scant hours before the deadline. Then he took off for Europe with the family for the holidays. Partly it was a vacation; he had only a few weeks left before the hard work on *Peggy Sue* would begin. At the same time, *The Cotton Club* was opening in Europe, and he wanted to go to Italy for the premiere. While he was there, he dropped the information that he was about to pass on the filmmaking torch to the next generation. He would be producing two films, to be directed by his sons. Gio, age twenty-one, would direct *The Vector* from his own script; it would be a story about futuristic cars, inspired by his father's tales of the Tucker. Roman, nineteen, would helm a film called *Surprises*.

The night before *The Cotton Club* opened in Europe, a slick ninety-minute $500,000 documentary about the real Cotton Club appeared on TV sets all over France, Italy, and Belgium. Produced by Pierre Kalfon, a friend of Coppola's who happened to head the company distributing *The Cotton Club* in Europe, the documentary was designed to familiarize audiences with the Harlem Renaissance. Diane Lane, Gregory Hines, Lonette McKee, and Cab Calloway appeared in the documentary, along with Yves Montand, Elton John, and Gallic heartthrob Gérard Depardieu.

The strategy worked beautifully. After a month *The Cotton Club* was doing much better business in France than in America, setting attendance records in Paris despite one of the worst winters in memory.

Back in the States, the legal free-for-all refused to quit. Bit player Susan Mechsner announced that she too was about to sue. Coppola had done the tall, blond, twenty-four-year-old actress dirt. During the year and a half before the shoot began, not only had she been paid $100,000 for her "preproduction work," but Robert Evans had given her a point in the movie, and another investor had given her a second point. So what was her problem? Her contract, she insisted, specified that she was to play a "co-starring" role as Gypsy, the Cotton Club's cigarette girl, but in the edited version all she had was two or three lousy lines. Furthermore, her voice and lip movements weren't synced properly, and her name was misspelled in the credits.

Her humiliation started when Coppola took over. The first day she showed up on the set, wearing spike heels and a spangled skintight jump suit with a silver zipper wrapping around the crotch, she and Coppola had a giant fight over Coppola's demand that she cut her waist-length hair to a flapper bob. "With Coppola," she complained, "everything is the film. It took me twelve years to grow my hair."

They compromised on the hair: She would play the role in a flapper wig, with her hair concealed by a filmy scarf. But then, when she saw the final version of the movie, she was appalled. "I've been damaged professionally," she snipped. "I was supposed to have a major role. Evans even offered to list me as co-star. But when I saw what Francis did to me in the final editing, I refused."

Coppola, who was still in Europe, declined to comment. Evans, however, confirmed that the actress had worked only four days and that she really had been paid $100,000, plus two points for it. Mechsner may have had the good grace to be embarrassed by a wry *Variety* headline that read: IN ONLY ONE "COTTON CLUB" SCENE, ACTRESS, WITH POINTS, GETS 100G. In any case, the lawsuit faded away.

Finally, Orion Pictures filed suit against Syufy Theaters, a large San Francisco-based drive-in and multiplex chain, claiming that boss man Raymond Syufy had added a second feature to boost the sagging *Cotton Club* box office, an addition which was not kosher. Syufy claimed that Orion had injured *him* by sticking him with such a bomb. Eventually Syufy won.

When domestic box-office grosses for the holiday season were announced, *Beverly Hills Cop*, which cost $15 million, had made more than $150 million. *The Cotton Club*, which cost $47 million, had taken in less than $30 million. A headline in the Los Angeles *Herald Examiner* read, TWO MORE MEGA-TON BOMBS HIT HOLLYWOOD. (*Dune* was the other one.) And *Film Comment*, which had published many admiring articles about Coppola, now attacked his budget overruns and artistic pretensions with "An 'Assemble-It-Yourself' Francis Coppola Joke Kit," consisting of a drawing of a complicated Rube Goldberg machine, followed by random phrases like "(a) I'm not a mere entertainer," and (b) $30/40/50-million budget."

By the middle of February more than five hundred theaters had dropped *The Cotton Club* and at the three hundred odd that were left, weekend grosses were averaging only $1,000 per screen. Orion had gotten its money back, and since Coppola's 10 percent of the adjusted grosses was calculated on a total that included the strong European rentals, he was beginning to see a trickle of money, too. With a record-breaking $4.7 million video sale already made and TV sales yet to come, he might even see a few dollars more. But the Doumani brothers were out of luck.

Ignoring the reviews, the criticism from the black intelligentsia, and the disappointing American grosses, Coppola insisted that people really liked his movie. "The public appreciates my film because it's generous," he told the European reporters. "It promises and it delivers a lot as spectacle, as entertainment, and as a story."

Richard Gere, looking back on the nightmare a few years later, had a different opinion. "There were levels of madness there," he said, "that will never be surpassed in moviemaking."

Chapter Twenty-one

Nine to Five
(1985–1987)

BY FEBRUARY 1985 *Peggy Sue* was deep in preproduction, moving swiftly toward a shooting date in mid-March; major decisions about locations, sets, crew, and supporting cast needed Coppola's immediate attention. He began work with all the enthusiasm of Bob Cratchit showing up at Scrooge and Marley's on a rainy Monday morning. Then, to make matters worse, Debra Winger suffered a serious back injury; her doctors reported that she'd be out of commission for anywhere from six weeks to six months. She withdrew from the movie, and suddenly everything was back on hold.

Everyone's second choice was Kathleen Turner, star of *Body Heat*, the megahit *Romancing the Stone*, and the upcoming *Prizzi's Honor* (directed by John Huston). Although *Prizzi* had yet to be released, advance word on her performance was extremely high. She was fast emerging as the 1980s' answer to Carole Lombard: a smart, sensual blonde with a comic flair. She looked a good bit older than Debra Winger, but the screenwriters had always envisioned an actress partway between the ages of the young and the older Peggys.

Turner was charmed by the script, met with Coppola, was charmed by *him*, and told the producers that she wished she could jump right into production. Unfortunately she was committed to first doing *Jewel of the Nile*, the sequel to *Romancing the Stone*. It was rumored that she wasn't all that crazy about the rehash, or about the location on the searing sands of

Morocco, but Twentieth Century-Fox made it known that it would sue her if she reneged on her contract. *Peggy*'s producers decided that she was worth a couple of months' wait; once *Prizzi's Honor* and *Jewel of the Nile* had opened, she'd be the hottest actress in Hollywood. *Peggy Sue* went onto the back burner while Turner trudged off to the desert.

Location scouts took advantage of the delay and went on a nationwide search for a good place to shoot *Peggy Sue*. They needed a small midwestern town that looked as if time had stopped in 1960, and they found what they wanted in Petaluma, California. To Coppola's delight (and Ellie's considerable relief) it was less than an hour's drive from the vineyard; for once they wouldn't have to leave home.

His pleasure was doubled by the Showtime screening, in March, of "Rip Van Winkle" and by series producer Shelley Duvall's praise. "He did great," she said. "It was a very complicated show technically and he finished in six days—right on schedule."

Though few would see it, "Rip Van Winkle" was the best film Coppola had made in years: charming, funny, good-spirited, and imaginative, with a fine script by Mark Curtiss and Rod Ash, excellent performances, and powerful visual effects. Once again strict disciplines of time, money, and format had inspired Coppola's best work. Coppola's electronic effects are seamlessly integrated into the narrative. Every frame is strikingly handsome, whether it's tall mountains that grow taller as night falls, an electronically enhanced painted sunset, or the stylized colored lighting that advances the story: lime green for ghostliness; silver-blue for the fall of night; bright red for the rise of dawn.

The nonelectronic Japanese-derived stagecraft works equally well. For instance, when Rip goes off into the mountains, he passes through a pair of mysterious giant doors at the edge of town that are painted with the face of King George; when he returns, twenty years later, the doors bear the likeness of George Washington. The scenes in the mountains, where Rip encounters Henry Hudson and his men, are wonderfully weird, with the ghosts made up in stylized Kabuki face paint. Best of all is the non-optical split screen, which Coppola had tried out on *One from the Heart* and was to use again in *Tucker*. We see Rip and his son in "normal" scale, fishing in a stream;

meanwhile, in the foreground of the same frame a giant fish swims. When Rip casts his line in the background, a giant hook plummets into the foreground—a sudden revelation of the fish's point of view, as powerful and surprising as an offhand epiphany in a haiku.

Ironically, after all the reviews of all the flops and works in progress, most national critics completely ignored "Rip Van Winkle," Coppola's first unqualified artistic success since *Godfather II*. There was a scattering of mixed low-profile write-ups by TV critics in papers like the Milwaukee *Sentinel* and the Cleveland *Plain Dealer,* but not a word in *Newsweek,* the *Village Voice,* or *The New York Times.* Perhaps it's just as well; if there was one thing Coppola didn't need it was more critics.

With *Peggy Sue* suspended, the executives at Tri-Star (the umbrella company under which Stark's Rastar Productions operated) offered Coppola Ronald Bass's screenplay for *Gardens of Stone,* based on a novel by Nicholas Proffitt. It centered on the Old Guard, a regiment that has had the responsibility for carrying out the ceremonial functions of the U.S. Army ever since 1784. Producer Michael Levy, who was already on the picture, described it as "a promilitary, antiwar Vietnam film."

It was definitely a strange project for the writer-director of *Apocalypse Now.* The script for *Gardens of Stone* treated the U.S. military as a grand and glorious institution, staffed by men of great warmth and humanity. Nor was it the sort of avant-garde artistic project calculated to make Coppola's heart beat faster. But there were aspects of the screenplay that appealed to him. He must have liked the warm portrayal of the military as a family, and the paternal relationship between a tough old NCO and a gung ho young volunteer (whose real soldier father had never received proper recognition from the brass). But mainly he needed the money, and he agreed to direct *Gardens* when *Peggy Sue* was finished.

The screenplay was in final form, and there would be little opportunity for Coppola to give it a personal stamp. Worse yet, shooting would require the Army's full cooperation. Levy went off to court the Army, knowing full well how little the military liked Coppola's last Vietnam movie. When he finally arranged a meeting with a high-ranking Army officer, his first words were "Francis is concerned about *Apocalypse Now,* but you know he also wrote *Patton.*"

"That's one of my favorite pictures," the general answered. Then he added, "I like the sound of this movie."

Coppola waited. *Gardens of Stone* couldn't start until *Peggy Sue* was finished, and *Peggy Sue* couldn't start until Kathleen Turner came back from Morocco. He began to work intermittently with Ronald Bass on script revisions for *Gardens of Stone*, but for the moment Coppola actually had some time for a personal life.

He spent one day of it—July 4, 1985—riding down the main street of Calistoga, California, in the backseat of a bright-red Tucker automobile driven by his son Gio. The crowds gasped at the sight of the stunning vintage futurist car, and they cheered when they noticed the passenger. Coppola found himself grinning, waving, and shouting back to the admiring throng. This event takes some explaining.

Ever since his Hofstra days, Coppola had been dreaming about, and talking about, making a film on Preston Tucker. Friends who had heard him talk about it for years had taken to joking, "Francis's *Tucker* is just like Carmine's Tucker. It never arrives."

Son Gio was a car nut, and the similarities between Preston Tucker and his father had not been lost on him. As a little kid Gio used to love going into the editing room and recutting the car chases from *THX 1138*. Gio's own script for his low-budget car movie, *The Vector*, was basically just a version of the Tucker story, moved into the near future: Its hero is an inventor whose technological visions aren't appreciated by his contemporaries.

Gio wanted to see his father make *Tucker*, and he developed a scheme to force the issue. Every July 4 the little town of Calistoga (just a few miles north of Coppola's vineyard) held a parade, in which most of the local winemakers participated. Gio resolved that one of his father's beautiful Tuckers would make its public debut at the parade.

One afternoon in early July he backed the car into the driveway and got Roman and Sofia to help him polish it to a high gleam. When Coppola walked out of the house and saw what his children had done, he knew he was looking at more than a wax job. He was so moved he agreed to their demand. That is how Gio came to be driving the Tucker down Calistoga's main street, with his father riding in the back, on Independence Day 1985.

That night Coppola came to a decision. "You know, this

was a good idea to make the Tucker movie," he told his children. "We ought to ask George [Lucas] if maybe he wants to do it."

Lucas's involvement would be a virtually automatic guarantee of backing and distribution. But despite occasional professional contacts like *Kagemusha, Mishima,* and *Ran,* relations between the two men were still somewhat strained; the rift over *American Graffiti,* aggravated by *Apocalypse,* had never been mended. Worse yet, Lucas had warned Coppola that he was a fool to try to start a studio in Los Angeles, and he was now in an uncomfortable "I-told-you-so" position. Coppola evidently felt sensitive about it. "It took a lot of courage on my part [to ask Lucas]," he recalled several years later. "I wanted to do something with George, but I didn't know if he wanted to do something with me."

Nonetheless, a humbled Coppola approached his old friend, and the answer was a resounding affirmative. Lucas would be thrilled to produce *Tucker.*

The unexpectedly good news put Coppola in such an upbeat mood that he decided it was time, at last, for some of his best bottles to make their gala premier appearance. Down in Los Angeles, his filmmaker pal Tony Bill, who had played a supporting role in *You're a Big Boy Now,* had become a part-time restaurateur. Now Bill was throwing a party to celebrate the opening of his friend Piero Selvaggio's chic new restaurant Primi. Not only would Coppola bring wine, he'd even cook.

Coppola had been growing more serious about his winery, learning to appreciate the slow, natural pace of the vines, the grapes, and the wines themselves as they grew and matured on their own calm schedule. It was a refreshing change from the artificial frenzy of turning out here-today, gone-tomorrow mainstream movies. "I demand of my wine maker that [my wine] be full, rich, and last 100 years," he declared. Like Rip Van Winkle in his video movie, he was coming to feel like the caretaker of a rich land. He'd revitalized the vineyard, and in turn, the vineyard was mellowing him.

Winemaking and filmmaking were carried out in peaceful coexistence in a three-story nineteenth-century carriage house near the mansion. On the top floor Coppola had installed a sophisticated electronic control room for editing sound and projecting movies. The middle floor held a large library of books and films, plus a computerized research facility, all presided over by a full-time librarian. On the ground floor was the winery, where oenologist Steve Beresini made three thousand cases a year of Rubicon, plus a few cases of Chardonnay and Zinfandel for friends and family.

One year, when the vintage was unusually bountiful, Coppola came up with a scheme to sell his excess Cabernet Franc in gallon jugs, for $50 each. Considering that this jug wine would probably remain hard as steel for thirty years, it was an audacious plan, to say the least. Fortunately friends talked him out of it. "I'm sure they were right," he recalled. "No one would have known what the hell we were doing. But I live for that kind of stuff. Every once in a while, you know, it comes off."

Coppola's Rubicon wasn't a standard California Cabernet; the wine was a bold, ambitious blend in the style of a traditional French Bordeaux, mixing Cabernet Sauvignon, Cabernet Franc, and Merlot. He planned to sell it for a hefty $25 a bottle when it was sufficiently aged, but like the aging of the great French vintages, that would take many years. After only six years the 1979 Rubicon (his first vintage in the new style) was still a baby, barely palatable enough for tastings to check on its progress.

Nonetheless, two weeks after he got the *Tucker* go-ahead from Lucas, Coppola headed down to Los Angeles with several cases of the '79. Tony Bill's party was to take place at his own restaurant, 72 Market Street, a fashionable eatery in Venice. The bash was open to the public, if the public had $75 a head, and was announced several days ahead, in the daily papers, as a party thrown by Francis Coppola to celebrate the new restaurant and "sneak preview" his wine.

By now Coppola was a target of convenience, and if there weren't any Coppola movies to review at the moment, well, movie critics weren't the only kinds of critics in the world. And damned if one of them didn't pan Coppola's wine *and* his cooking. Restaurant critic Larry Lipson found the Rubicon "hard-edged, very tannic . . . and extremely difficult to drink. It literally attacked the palate." Lipson panned Coppola's *polenta con porcini e pecorino,* too, describing it as "a sort of bland gruel with a mushroom or two in the center." The review was headlined LATEST COPPOLA PRODUCTION NEEDS TIME.

With a review like that for his cooking, Coppola beat it back to moviemaking as fast as he could. *Peggy Sue* was about to start shooting, and it was time to lock down a cast and crew. This time Coppola had more control over production decisions than in *The Cotton Club*, so naturally, old hands like Dean Tavoularis, Barry Malkin, and Barrie Osborne would be involved. Theadora Van Runkle (who'd done the *Godfather II* costumes) was back, too, trying to come up with dresses that would make the womanly Kathleen Turner look sweet seventeen and back in class again. Doug Claybourne (*Rumble Fish*'s coproducer) came in as first assistant director. Gio came to work, uncredited, shooting the video rehearsals, but this time Roman was absent, off at school in New York.

In an unusual move Coppola signed on Jordan Cronenweth, with whom he hadn't worked before, as director of photography. Coppola had been impressed with his work on *Blade Runner*.

All along, one of the big questions had been who'd play Peggy Sue's philandering husband, car salesman—TV huckster "Crazy Charlie" Bodell. The actor would have to charm the audience into believing that a mature woman would fall in love with a callow youth, knowing for a certainty that he'd stay callow for life.

According to the trades, the two prime contenders initially were Judge Reinhold, who'd tickled several million female fancies as Eddie Murphy's goofy partner in *Beverly Hills Cop*, and *Saturday Night Live* TV comedian Martin Short, who had yet to star in a film but was small, funny, and cute enough to be endearing. Both actors had a certain boyish sweetness and a touch of vulnerability that might make a grown woman want to take care of them.

Instead, as soon as Coppola signed on, producer Paul Gurian fixed on twenty-one-year-old Nicolas Cage. He had the uncle; why not get the nephew? Cage had gone from his supporting role in *The Cotton Club* to a costarring role in *Birdy*, in which he garnered almost universal raves for his ardent performance, but what Gurian particularly loved was his comic impersonation of a punk heartthrob in an earlier film, *Valley Girls*. Coppola must have been delighted. Nonetheless, it was tricky casting: Cage had mainly played proles and punks, so *Peggy Sue*'s middle-class would-be greaser would represent a major change in screen character. Furthermore, he was more than a decade younger than Turner, but Coppola saw this as an advantage. He'd decided that if the "young" husband were played by a man roughly the same age as the actress, it would be hard to make both characters believable at a younger age. "By having that strain in the relationship, my hope was that they would both be forced to reach," he said.

The supporting cast included such veteran actors as Maureen O'Sullivan, Leon Ames, Barbara Harris, John Carradine, and Don Murray, many of whom had signed on mainly for the chance to work with Coppola. Lisa Jane Persky (who'd been Dutch Schultz's wife in *The Cotton Club*) would play a high school bitch. Barry Miller nabbed the role of the class science whiz, and Sofia Coppola would be Peggy Sue's bratty little sister.

A few weeks before *Peggy Sue* was ready to start, a surprisingly similar time-travel comedy opened, and swiftly turned into the year's biggest hit. *Back to the Future*, directed by *Romancing the Stone*'s Robert Zemeckis (for Steven Spielberg), had gone into production after *Peggy Sue*, but all the delays on *Peggy* had allowed *Future* to reach the screen first. Paul Gurian was furious and went around muttering that Spielberg had revived *Back to the Future* (after the project had spent eight years in mothballs) only because he'd read the script of *Peggy Sue*.

Still, it was far too late to back out now. *Peggy Sue* began with two weeks of rehearsals, climaxing with Coppola's usual videotaped run-through. Coppola wanted the major players to develop the easy chemistry of people who'd gone through high school together. "It was like acting school with all the improvisations and trust exercises," said Kathleen Turner. "I was rather impatient, but after a couple of days I realized that people were really getting involved in the process and it was working."

Shooting started in August 1985 and went smoothly. There were the usual minor problems, a few blowups between the director and the supporting cast, but for the most part the shoot was a snap. And this time (unlike *The Cotton Club*) Coppola had his own handpicked crew, and no matter how intense the shooting got, at the end of the day he could go home to the Napa vineyard.

Cronenweth found Coppola easy to work with, a "hands-

off" director who mostly let the cinematographer place the
camera for the most interesting lighting; then Coppola would
stage the action to suit the camera. Coppola's visual scheme
for *Peggy* was based on rich, saturated colors to heighten the
reality; Dean Tavoularis even sprayed the sidewalks yellow to
give them a nostalgic glow. "The basic approach was worked
out between Francis and [Tavoularis] as a contemporary *Wizard of Oz* with broad strokes," Cronenweth remembered.

As usual, Coppola managed to convince himself that the
film was worth making. A few years later, when reporters asked
him about rumors that he disliked *Peggy Sue,* he declared, "I
never took on a film, including *Peggy Sue Got Married,* that I
didn't work up a head of enthusiasm for." The shoot lasted
about eight weeks, and Coppola completed principal photography on schedule and under budget. On October 28 the production company took out a giant ad in the trade papers that
read, "Peggy Sue Got Married! and our baby is now in post
production, *on schedule.* Congratulations and thanks to all, Tri-Star and Rastar."

Coppola and Barry Malkin set to work editing the film in
Napa. But the pressure wasn't so intense that Coppola couldn't
find time to knock off another picture on the side, a musical,
albeit a short one, starring pop superstar Michael Jackson.

Walt Disney Productions had cut a deal with Jackson for a
short, spectacular, 3-D movie to be shown in planetariumlike
theaters at their amusement parks in California and Florida.
Eastman Kodak was cofunding the production so it could show
off a new 70 mm 3-D process it had developed. The film would
be a fantasy (to fit the Disneyland and Disney World ambience) and futuristic (to make the best use of the new process).
Disney's techies planned to enhance the movie even further
by building special effects facilities into the auditoriums themselves; laser beams, smoke puffs, light and sound effects would
explode in the theater, not just on-screen.

Between Eastman's backing and Disney's financial resources, there was virtually no limit on expenses. One is
tempted to take a cheap shot and say that Coppola was an instant choice, but in fact, it was George Lucas who came on first
as executive producer. Disney presented him with three story
concepts from which to choose, and Lucas chose one called
Captain Eo: Jackson would play a spaceman who lands on a

hostile planet ruled by an evil queen. Simultaneously singing, dancing, and fighting, Eo and his crew would barrage the queen and her evil armies with magical multicolored light rays that would turn them all into pussycats and change the gloomy palace into something like Disneyland.

Lucas talked Coppola into directing. Coppola rewrote Rusty Lemorande's draft; then Lucas rewrote Coppola's rewrite. Indeed, the script was much more Lucas's sort of thing than Coppola's, a noisy, effects-laden space opera peopled by creatures out of the *Star Wars* series (fuzzy Aliens, talking robots, armored space knights), all centered on a wicked female ruler who presaged the villainess of Lucas's subsequent *Willow.*

In late autumn Coppola headed south with his son Gio (who would direct the second unit). The minimusical would be shot at Laird Studios in Los Angeles (rather than the small Disney lot in Burbank), with creatures created by Disney's Lance Anderson. Coppola wouldn't have to spend long in Southern California; most of the film (which was mainly special effects, after all) would be created by a giant army of Disney technicians, directed by Harlan Ellenshaw. Coppola's job was to film a few minutes of live action: Anjelica Huston (as the Supreme Ruler) dangling from a flying harness in a fright wig and Spider Woman makeup; Michael Jackson dancing along at the head of a chorus line of shuffling spacers and boogying bogeymen. Coppola brought in Vittorio Storaro to do the cinematography for his portion of the film, with Jeffrey (*Flashdance*) Hornaday contributing the choreography and Walter Murch editing.

As soon as the principal photography was done, Coppola went back to work on *Peggy Sue*, leaving postproduction on *Captain Eo* mainly to Lucas, Murch, and the Disney crew. The seventeen-minute film turned out to be, minute for minute, the most expensive movie ever made; all told, Disney and Kodak dropped $20 million on it, most of it going toward special effects and in-house laser beams. For once the astronomical budget wasn't Coppola's fault.

As expected, just as Coppola and Malkin were finishing the final cut of *Peggy Sue*, Kathleen Turner won a Golden Globe award for her performance in *Prizzi's Honor*. This was not likely to hurt *Peggy Sue*'s commercial chances.

Simultaneously, Coppola (who was still smarting from the

critical attack on his cooking and his wine) got a badly needed ego boost: Nathan Croman, a wine critic for the classy Los Angeles *Times*, tasted two vintages of Rubicon, took account of their need for further aging, and noted, "Both Coppola bottles are exquisite and worthy of cellaring." The headline read COPPOLA GAINING RECOGNITION AS A FIRST CLASS VINTNER. Only a few days later a wine writer for the Santa Rosa paper noted that Coppola's wines were actually a lot like his movies. "They're expensive," he wrote, "take a long time to produce, and sit around for years before being released."

What made the Rubicon rave in the Los Angeles *Times* especially nice was that when Coppola looked at his final cut of *Peggy Sue*, he disliked it intensely; at least his wine was a success. Frantic to shoot on time and on budget, he had filmed the final scene on the last day of scheduled shooting, a Friday, beginning at 1:00 A.M. and finishing at 4:00 A.M. To his eyes, the cast's exhaustion was evident in the rushes, and the direction seemed uninspired. The scene had come out sweet when he wanted it bittersweet, flat when he wanted it touching.

Coppola itched to reshoot the scene, and Tri-Star agreed; it decided that since Coppola had come in under budget, finding the money for reshoots would be no problem. This would push the release date back a few months, but that might actually be a good idea; instead of opening in early May (where it might be lost in the flood of teen-oriented summer releases), an October release would appeal more to the *Big Chill* audience of aging, nostalgic baby boomers, whose movie attendance is highest in autumn.

In March, Coppola, crew, and a few cast members went to work on a new ending. The idea was to make the last shot in the movie match the first one, a symmetry that may have been suggested by Ronald Bass's script for *Gardens of Stone*, which opened and closed with parallel scenes of funerals. In the opening shot of *Peggy Sue*, Kathleen Turner's image is first seen as a reflection in a mirror. Now Coppola and Tavoularis decided that ending the film with a matching mirror shot might provide some of the depth it seemed to lack, indicating to audiences that it could be regarded, metaphorically, as a fantasy of an aging woman looking at a reflection of her life. (Subsequently a story in a film magazine suggested that the reconciliation between Peggy and Charlie was added only during the reshoot, to give Ray Stark the happy ending he demanded. This is untrue; the happy ending had been in the script from the beginning.)

Shooting and editing the new ending took only a few days. Then Coppola moved swiftly into preproduction on *Gardens of Stone*. Once again the crew was filled with Zoetrope veterans like Tavoularis, Roos, Malkin, and a few newer friends. Coppola rehired Jordan Cronenweth as DP; Gio would be captain of the electronic cinema staff, with younger brother, Roman, working under him; Carmine was back as composer.

The cast was equally loaded with old pals. James Caan was playing the lead; it was his first professional reunion with Coppola since *The Godfather* and his official comeback after a five-year hiatus from moviemaking. The press booklet suggests that Caan had taken the time off to care for his son, a fitting notion given *Gardens'* theme of fatherhood. However, Caan later told an interviewer that at least one additional reason for his long absence from filmmaking was a problem with "substance abuse."

Caan found professional help and cured himself, but when he reemerged from his drug-induced space voyage, he found himself *persona non grata* and $200,000 in debt. Despite a vicious profile in *Esquire* that portrayed Caan as a washed-up, ill-tempered cocaine addict, Coppola was eager to give his old college pal a chance.

"Francis really—God bless him—fought very hard for me," Caan recalled after *Gardens'* release. The actor was no longer demanding $2 million a picture; in fact, for *Gardens of Stone,* he took less than a quarter of the money he'd been getting five years earlier. Even so, the producers distrusted him so much they wouldn't pay him at all until the last day of the shoot, "because they thought I was going to drug out or something," he laughed.

Opposite Caan, Coppola cast Anjelica Huston. *Cotton Club* star Lonette McKee nabbed a major supporting role, and for her opposite number Coppola scored a wonderful casting coup: He signed James Earl Jones, one of the finest actors in the country and the voice of Darth Vader in all the *Star Wars* films. Sam Bottoms (of *Apocalypse*) and Larry Fishburne (of *Apocalypse, Rumble Fish,* and *Cotton Club*) would play a pair of young soldiers.

Coppola filled in the cast with newcomers. Mary Stuart Masterson played a young, soon-to-be-widowed bride; her real-life parents (Peter Masterson and Carlin Glynn) were cast as her screen parents. D. B. Sweeney would play opposite her, in his first major screen role, as the male juvenile lead, a gung ho cadet. And Dean Stockwell, fresh from his triumph in *Blue Velvet,* was to play a large supporting role. Stockwell was delighted; years earlier he'd tried out for *The Godfather* and failed to make the cut.

In April the Coppolas packed up the family and headed for Virginia, where *Gardens of Stone* would be filmed at Arlington, Fort Myer, and Fort Belvoir. The picture was budgeted at a moderate $13 million.

Coppola began with two weeks of rehearsals and improvisations, which he videotaped, as usual, and screened for the actors inside Silverfish. The actors had to learn to stand, move, and march like perfect soldiers; there were even drills with rifles and sabers. The older cast members found this hard. Sam Bottoms did better, but only enough to get in trouble. One day when Bottoms, in full costume, was getting a trim in the post barbershop, an Old Guard major laid into him for irregularities in his uniform. Apparently Bottoms had succeeded in learning to impersonate a *slovenly* soldier.

It rained every day. The cast was perfectly happy to rehearse indoors until the rain stopped, but it never did. There was always new dialogue to learn; for Coppola, no screenplay is ever set in stone. James Earl Jones later said that the script changes gave rehearsals "the excitement and spontaneity of a wonderful affair."

For the most part, the Army brass adored the script, which portrayed cultured sergeants quoting Shakespeare, listening to classical music, and cooking gourmet meals. However, just as shooting was about to start, they took a closer look at the final screenplay and demanded a few changes, or cooperation would be withdrawn. One scene that had to go (which the book's author had actually witnessed) had a young widow spitting on her husband's grave at Arlington, shouting, "At least now I know where you're spending your nights." Another showed an angry sergeant punching out an enlisted man who had flunked inspection.

In return for these changes, the Army proved most cooperative. In fact, according to Lieutenant Colonel John Myers, the on-set military coordinator, it hadn't been so cooperative since John Wayne made *The Green Berets* during the Vietnam War. For a reasonable fee it provided Arlington National Cemetery, two forts, the Army Band, helicopters, six hundred extras, uniforms, equipment, military training for the actors, technical advice, and haircuts. There were ample volunteers for the extras' roles, although once the shoot started the cadets were disgusted to discover that moviemaking was even more boring than close-order drill.

This time Coppola asked his cinematographer for a natural look, and the Army brass agreed. In fact, for safety reasons they insisted that the helicopter scenes be shot with natural light, with no exterior lights added. This was a problem: Unlighted choppers against a gray sky are like black cats in a coal bin at midnight. Cronenweth and Coppola solved the problem by shooting the choppers at dusk, when natural side lighting made them easier to see.

Griffin O'Neal, Ryan O'Neal's troubled twenty-one-year-old son, the star of *The Escape Artist* and an old family friend, arrived to help his buddy Gio shoot the videotapes and to play the role of a slobby soldier named Wildman. The character's name was appropriate. O'Neal had recently completed a year of rehabilitation following various drug, driving, and misdemeanor convictions. Still, Coppola had never lost faith in him. "Francis is very fond of O'Neal," said producer Michael Levy. "Francis is like a big father. He's got those big arms. He likes to take care of everyone. He's really cuddly—he loves to cuddle people."

Rehab did not seem to have done O'Neal much good. On May 23, at one-thirty in the morning, an Arlington County police corporal named Garber caught O'Neal speeding through the suburbs in a Lotus Esprit, "like it was running the Indy 500," and busted him for reckless driving, driving without a license, and carrying a concealed weapon—a high tech spring-loaded switchblade knife—in the pocket of his jacket.

O'Neal swore the jacket was borrowed and the knife wasn't his. A few hours later a sleepy production assistant arrived in the predawn hours to hand over the $750 bail. He told the cops that the jacket and the knife did so belong to O'Neal, but the $60,000 car he'd been driving so recklessly was borrowed from Gio Coppola.

Three days later, during a Memorial Day break, O'Neal

and Gio went to a restaurant, where they had two or three glasses of wine with their lunch. Gio had something to celebrate: He'd just been signed for his first real non-Coppola job, as second-unit director on an upcoming Whoopi Goldberg picture, *Jumpin' Jack Flash.*

After lunch the friends picked up a six-pack and rented a small motorboat on the South River, near Annapolis, Maryland. It was great to be out on the water with no work to do. Around 5:15 P.M. O'Neal took the boat on a fast, bouncing course between two larger boats. There was plenty of room to get through, but in the gray, even light he didn't notice that there was a towline connecting the two craft. Without warning, as if in a dream, Gian-Carlo Coppola was snapped off his feet by an invisible blow; his head slammed into the deck. O'Neal didn't even see the rope hit Gio; he only felt the impact. He was just slightly bruised, but he could hear Gio moan; he turned off the engine and leaped to the floor of the boat to cradle his friend's head in his lap. He could see that Gio was dying.

Somehow O'Neal got the boat back to shore. Without knowing how he'd gotten there, he found himself dazedly watching the paramedics lift Gio's unconscious body onto a stretcher and slide it into an ambulance. The last he saw of his friend, the paramedics were hooking Gio up to their life-support equipment; the ambulance went screaming away, heading for Anne Arundel General Hospital.

Left behind on the dock, Griffin O'Neal may have closed his eyes and tried to make himself wake up in his own bed, but this time the old trick didn't work. And when someone asked him how the accident had happened, he heard himself lying. Gio had been driving, he insisted. He refused treatment for his bruises and quietly slipped away.

Francis and Eleanor Coppola rushed to the hospital and paced the hall, while surgeons tried to save their son. At 6:20 P.M. the doctors ran out of options. Gian-Carlo Coppola, age twenty-three, was dead of massive cranial injuries. The autopsy revealed that his blood alcohol level had been well above the legal driving limit. O'Neal's blood alcohol was never tested.

Within the next few days passengers on one of the boats that had been attached to the fatal towline told the police that the driver was a muscular blond man (like O'Neal), not a slim brunet (like Gio). They repeated this testimony under oath at

O'Neal's trial, and O'Neal tearfully admitted he'd lied because he was hysterical.

Back in April 1981, in the midst of the financial crises at Zoetrope, Gay Talese had asked Coppola what frightened him the most, and despite the terrible financial snarls of *One from the Heart,* Coppola had answered, "Losing someone I love." Now the nightmare had come true.

Gio had been nearly a dream son; like the son of Coppola's Rip Van Winkle, he asked no more than to be just like his dad. Since the age of sixteen, when Coppola agreed to let his son drop out of school to become his apprentice, Gio had worked with his father constantly. None of Coppola's professional associates minded; they adored "the Coppola kid" for his exquisite manners and respected him for his earnest professionalism. "He was a very formal, classic gentleman," said Gio's friend Tracy Reiner.

Coppola later made an odd comment. "[Gio] was my best friend and collaborator," he said. "He was perfect, like Pinocchio." What could Coppola have meant by this? Presumably he didn't mean that Gio lied or that he was artificial. Perhaps he meant that Gio seemed so wonderful he could only be his father's construction.

In almost every way, he was Coppola's obvious heir. Tragically he had already conceived his own heir. His fiancée, Jacqueline de la Fontaine, was in her third month of pregnancy when he died.

The schedule called for Coppola to shoot an elaborate scene with hundreds of extras and helicopter support the next morning. A few minutes after Gio died, an assistant director phoned Lieutenant Colonel Myers, who was overseeing the details; he told him about the accident and arranged to cancel the shoot. But two hours later, when Coppola found out, he insisted on making the shots after all.

Coppola moved through the day like an underwater swimmer. He seemed dazed; maybe he hoped that work would keep him from flying to pieces. Gio's colleagues on the set were equally devastated; people found themselves starting to weep in the midst of ordinary technical discussions. The next day, May 28, a memorial service was held in a small chapel at Fort Myer, which was filled with cast, crew, family, and soldiers. Sam Bottoms, Larry Fishburne, and August Coppola delivered eulogies. Outside the chapel the Old Guard, experts in the death of the young, stood sentry.

Filming stopped for five days. Nobody knew whether Coppola would be able to continue with the production. At one point he told Cronenweth that he was sure Gio would have wanted him to continue with the shoot. It was a cliché, but sometimes clichés are all we have to get us through the night.

Finally he went back to work. What else could he do? Without work to occupy his thoughts, he'd probably have been sick with grief. Roman, a low-key, unassuming young man of twenty-one, took over as head of the videotape crew. Coppola petted him constantly, drawing as close to him as he could; Roman's physical presence seemed to give him strength. There were constant reminders of Gio. Coppola cried often, breaking down unexpectedly and then collecting himself. Co-workers were unbearably distressed. Cronenweth's son was on the set, and one day, when they'd been touching, the DP looked up to find Coppola staring helplessly at them, his eyes sick with pain. Nobody knew how he kept going.

For a week Coppola worked calmly but incessantly; then he checked into a hospital for two days. Finally he returned to the set and worked some more. In his sorrow and resignation Coppola told production executive Gary Lucchesi, "The gods gave me Gio and the gods have taken him."

He didn't seem to blame O'Neal; in fact, Fred Roos remembers him saying, "How can we help Griffin?" He even asked O'Neal to stay on and complete his role, but the young man decided to resign from the cast; as Cronenweth remembers it, someone close to Coppola asked him to leave. Returning for sentencing on his earlier speeding and weapons charges, O'Neal pleaded guilty on both counts. He paid a stiff fine for reckless driving but was let off with a withheld sentence for possession of the knife.

Three weeks after Gio's death, Coppola returned to the Fort Myer chapel, site of Gio's funeral, to film the four funeral scenes in the movie. The mood on the set was deeply somber, although James Caan did his best to lighten it. Everybody appreciated his clowning; it seemed the most considerate thing he could do. Once again the sympathetic presence of the Old Guard provided everyone with some sense of consolation.

Coppola drove himself so hard that by mid-July the production was actually ahead of schedule. Bill Graham dropped in (on his way to Europe with a Bob Dylan tour) to play a one-scene role as an obnoxious liberal lawyer whom James Caan punches out at a chic cocktail party; many musicians, rock journalists, and nightclub patrons later considered this scene worth the price of admission by itself.

Toward the end of the month Coppola went into court, briefly, to win back a portion of his financial freedom. Early in 1981 Coppola and UA had set the *Apocalypse Now* debt (which Coppola owed UA) at $7 million; Coppola had agreed to pay it off within a couple of weeks. When he failed to do so, UA declined to take legal action; instead, it simply kept all the profits from *The Black Stallion*. But now it was claiming that Coppola still owed more than $7 million.

In response, Coppola filed a complaint in Los Angeles Superior Court. It was full of accusations about various dastardly aspects of UA's financial dealings, but the main thrust was that he wanted the court to declare the debt settled. As with most civil court cases, there was no immediate decision; Coppola's complaint merely served to start the process of delays, continuances, stays, and pauses that would probably result in an out-of-court settlement.

By now, according to reports in *The New York Times*, *Apocalypse* had earned more than $100 million in worldwide rentals, which seems like it should have paid off the debt in full. However, a big portion of those rentals was foreign and had gone to the foreign distributors who had helped fund the film. UA was entitled only to the domestic rentals, which were still under $38 million, and between the loans to Coppola and the release costs (including that record-setting ad campaign), UA had put up about $39 million, not counting interest. UA's portion of the TV and video sales may have edged its take a million or two into the black, but then, studio accountants practice a black art.

At almost the same moment, in a bitterly ironic twist of fate, Coppola received a multimillion-dollar refund check from one of the banks that had foreclosed on Zoetrope three years earlier, panicking Jack Singer and thus, indirectly, forcing the sale of the studio. At the time, Zoetrope's accountants had vigorously contested the amount claimed by the bank, but to no avail. Even though they lost, they kept going over the books until they finally proved the bank wrong. Now, far too late to save Omni Zoetrope, the bank had returned the money.

On August 5 the last of the principal photography on *Gardens of Stone* went into the can. The shoot had taken only eight weeks and came in a mere 7 percent over budget, well within the industry standard leeway of 10 percent. Before the film company dispersed, the Old Guard adopted Francis Coppola as an honorary member. In a way he couldn't explain, it seemed to help. Immediately afterward he took Ellie, Roman, and Sofia to Paris; perhaps the City of Light would distract them from their grief.

While he was gone, the grand jury of Anne Arundel County indicted Griffin O'Neal on six counts of criminal behavior in Gio's death. Five counts dealt with recklessness and negligence in the operation of a boat; the sixth, more serious, was a charge of manslaughter. A trial date was set for mid-December.

Meanwhile, Walt Disney had finally finished building the seven-hundred-seat Magic Eye Theater for *Captain Eo*. By the time Coppola returned from Europe, the mini-space opera was set for a bang-up premiere at Disneyland, to be followed, within days, by an hourlong Saturday night TV special on NBC about the making of *Captain Eo*.

There were a few snide comments from movie insiders about the trio of "has-beens" who'd do anything to regain the spotlight: Jackson's long-awaited new LP was mysteriously delayed; Lucasfilm's latest releases, *Howard the Duck* and *Labyrinth*, were flops; and Coppola hadn't had a solid hit in eleven years. Nonetheless, you'd have never guessed it from the gala invitational opening. Twenty-two hundred invited guests showed up for a private luncheon, to be followed by screenings of *Captain Eo*. Disney cordoned off the Plaza restaurant, plus all of Tomorrowland; the public stood behind restraining ropes and watched a parade of celebrities riding in antique cars down Disneyland's Main Street to the Plaza. The celebs included Jane Fonda, ex-Mouseketeer Annette Funicello, Jack Nicholson (Anjelica Huston's sweetie), O. J. Simpson, Debra Winger, numerous Jacksons (but not Michael), and Disney's entire executive branch.

Coppola, Lucas, and Huston were on hand for the ceremonial ribbon-cutting ceremony at the entrance to the theater.

The mob of celebs and moguls stood around restlessly, cooling their heels while NBC set up the shot for the TV special. Finally the red ribbon was severed, Coppola, Lucas, and Huston were hastily escorted away, and there was a mad crush toward the entrance of the theater.

Once inside the concrete lobby, the celebs were given pink-rimmed 3-D glasses, which they twirled impatiently while they waited to be seated. Half a dozen television screens issued intermittent warnings to the effect that "some parts of the soundtrack have been recorded at a high volume to emphasize the drama. If you have sensitive ears, please exercise discretion." (Presumably the sensitive could watch the movie with their fingers in their ears.) The warnings were interspersed with video clips of the shoot, featuring glimpses of George Lucas, Michael Jackson, and Anjelica Huston, along with Francis Coppola, in khaki shorts, making eyes at comely members of the corps de ballet. Finally the first seven hundred celebs were seated, the doors closed, and everyone quieted down as the curtains rolled back to reveal a gigantic screen.

"Most of those in attendance seemed dazzled by the show and clapped when it was over," wrote *Variety*'s correspondent, "but at least one disgruntled viewer said he was disappointed that Coppola and Lucas 'didn't break any new ground.' "

Indeed, they didn't. *Captain Eo* is a ride, not a movie, and basically the most expensive, overblown MTV video ever made, disguised as a space operetta. The sets are impressive, looking only slightly smaller than Grand Central Station, and the high-resolution 3-D process is undeniably exciting, although (as always) the stereo illusion is better in the center seats than at the sides. But the dialogue, such as it is, is drowned out by the noisy sound effects, and the dancing is shattered (in typical Coppola fashion) into a distracting collage of high angles, low angles, close shots, and reaction shots guaranteed to destroy any sense of musical momentum. Coupled with the 3-D process, it's all a bit headache-making.

The film was shown repeatedly until everyone got to see it. A Disney spokesman said he expected *Eo* to run "Eo-ns."

There was only one major review, from *Time*'s Richard Corliss. He found it entertaining but concluded that it was "a triumph of the artificial, of high tech wizardry and second-hand emotions," and pointed out that the special effects overkill left no room for the viewer's own imagination to expand.

Meanwhile, *Peggy Sue* was ready to open. For months it had been going through sneak previews. According to the trades, audiences were generally enthusiastic, but Coppola continued to fine-tune the editing. Finally, on Saturday, September 17, the sneaks went wide, showing on forty-five screens in the United States and Canada. According to a story in the *Hollywood Reporter,* many of the theaters were sold out two or three hours before the screenings, audiences were highly enthusiastic, Ebert and Siskel both were planning to give it thumbs-up on national TV, and Tri-Star executives were talking about Oscars.

Critic Andrew Sarris (whose wife, Molly Haskell, was on the New York Film Festival selection committee) had a very different story to tell in the *Village Voice*. He claimed that after "discouraging previews," the studio was ready to dump the film and that only the festival screening had saved it. Nobody else heard that story, though. Jury member Dave Kehr remembered how pleased the jury was to find a good, competently made, upbeat picture that people would probably like. Thus, *Peggy Sue* was chosen as the festival's prestigious closing-night film; the ad copy hailed it as a Capraesque masterpiece.

Peggy was promptly booked to open in New York and Los Angeles on October 8, right after the festival. National release, on eight hundred-odd screens, would follow two days later.

What festival-goers saw was the last thing they expected from Francis Coppola: a light, comical, unpretentious time-travel fantasy with virtually no directorial signature. Of all the films Coppola has made, *Peggy Sue* is probably the least personal.

As it opens, Peggy Sue Bodell is dressing for her twenty-fifth high school reunion. She has just separated from her philandering husband, Crazy Charlie, who she hopes won't show up. Attending the reunion with her teenage daughter (Helen Hunt), Peggy Sue is crowned class queen, and the school nerd, now a millionaire, is elected class king, but at the great moment, seeing Charlie enter the room, Peggy faints dead away.

She awakens to find herself back in 1960, a high school senior. Although she appears unchanged to us, the folks in 1960 perceive her as seventeen. Peggy Sue is thrilled to see her parents looking so young again and is further tickled when Daddy comes home with a brand-new Edsel. Remembering how she was trapped into marrying Charlie by getting pregnant on her eighteenth birthday and how thankless their marriage became, she realizes she has a chance to remake her life.

This time she can make a better match—with the sexy school beatnik (Kevin O'Connor), perhaps, or the brainy science fanatic (Barry Miller). Sure enough, the beatnik makes love to her and the nerd proposes, but Peggy Sue decides that the best prospect of all would be to marry nobody. Furthermore, she wants to go home. At first it seems that a quasi-Masonic ritual (with John Carradine presiding) will send her back to the 1980s, but Crazy Charlie kidnaps her at the climactic moment. At this point, for no discernible reason, Peggy changes her mind about remaking her life. She lets Charlie impregnate her for the sake of the wonderful children they'll have. And then she wakes up in a 1980s hospital room, middle-aged once more, with a repentant Charlie by her side. Her only souvenir of the adventure is an autographed copy of a novel written by the school beatnik, dedicated to her.

If *Peggy Sue* is moderately amusing, it owes its success less to Coppola than to the slick script and Kathleen Turner's warm, thoughtful performance—although it's tough to swallow her as a teenager. And while the supporting cast is appealing, one performance is appalling: No reasonably sane woman could possibly fall for the mumbling, adenoidal lout Nicolas Cage makes of Charlie. Not only does he seem far lower in class, caste, and intelligence than Peggy Sue, but he seems to live in a different movie (or galaxy). Cage went on to successful portrayals of goofy romantic swains in *Raising Arizona* and *Moonstruck*, but here he is monstrously off-key, either misdirected or not directed at all.

The film is not without other problems. The parents are relentlessly bland and sweet, the ambience is smug, and no irony informs the nostalgic glow of the film, unlike *Back to the Future*. Worst of all, the aborted Masonic ritual (with John Carradine hamming it up deliciously in the last substantial role of his life) is a painful dramatic misstep; after the buildup it gets, it really has to work. And yet the movie has charm enough to get by and to make a large audience (and many critics) overlook its improbabilities.

Daily Variety's critic noted it lacked "the director's mark of distinction" but went on to predict (accurately) great com-

mercial success. "It is provocative, well-acted, stylish and uneven," he wrote. "Pic is a marked improvement over anything
else [Coppola has] done lately."

Writing in *The New York Times,* Vincent Canby found it
"a small, amiable, sort of sloppy comedy-fantasy," adding, "In
today's puny Hollywood, Mr. Coppola is both mountain and
Methuselah. . . . Mr. Coppola is a risk-taker who thinks big.
It's not easy to recognize him when he pursues the ordinary
for such inconsequential results."

There were a couple of raves, but among the naysayers
was David Thomson, writing in *California,* who compared
Peggy Sue unfavorably with *One from the Heart* (a film he liked
very much). "Coppola has behaved himself," he concluded,
"and the picture is dull and flat because of it. Francis has been
his own fool and Hollywood's megalomaniac so often in the
past, he has learned too well. . . . For the moment he looks
like an artist crushed by what has happened to him in the
business."

But while art may be long, there's no business like show
business. Audiences promptly went crazy for *Peggy Sue*; it
earned nearly $37 million in domestic grosses in its first nine
weeks. In its tenth week it vanished, all played out; it had
nowhere to go but the tube, for which it seems admirably suited.

Gio's death had drawn the extended Coppola family closer
together, and Francis had been wearily pondering the question of to whom he'd leave the vineyard. After thinking it over,
he told Roman, Sofia, and several of his nephews to start thinking about it carefully; whichever of them would most like to
take over the wine business would inherit the verdant acreage.

In December 1986, just as Jacqueline de la Fontaine gave
birth to Gian-Carlo's daughter (and Coppola's first grandchild),
named Gian Carla Coppola, Griffin O'Neal's trial began. Coppola didn't attend, and the press reported the trial sparsely and
unsensationally. There were no courtroom theatrics and no last-
minute surprises. The judge lectured O'Neal about his waste-
ful life style but acquitted him on the manslaughter charge;
O'Neal was convicted on the five lesser charges of reckless
boat handling, however, and sentenced to 416 hours of community service, 18 months of probation with drug testing, com-
pulsory school or work, and a $200 fine.

In April 1987 O'Neal began serving his community service sentence by manning a toll-free boat-safety line for the Boat Owners Association of the United States. A month later Francis Coppola, as administrator of his son's estate, sued Griffin O'Neal (and seven others—e.g., the boat rental facility) for damages on behalf of his baby granddaughter and her mother. His suit suggested that since O'Neal had left Gio's child fatherless, he ought to take on the financial responsibilities of a substitute father.

Since then O'Neal's legal troubles have reached the front pages twice: In 1987 he was nabbed in Beverly Hills for speeding, probation violation, and possession of a small amount of marijuana, and was sentenced to two more years' probation. In 1988 he was charged with fulfilling fewer than sixty hours of his four hundred hours of community service sentence in the death of Gian-Carlo Coppola.

In February 1987 the Academy Award nominations were announced, and three of *Peggy Sue*'s film workers caught brass rings: Kathleen Turner, Jordan Cronenweth, and costume designer Theadora Van Runkle. But two months later, when the awards were given, all three were left out in the cold. However, soon afterward, the American Society of Cinematographers bestowed its first annual award for outstanding cinematography on Cronenweth for his work on *Peggy Sue*.

Coppola didn't care about any of it. *Peggy Sue* had gone a long way toward buying back his life and restoring his fortune, but the enthusiasm he'd built up for it had burned off in the agony of Gio's death. All *Peggy Sue* was good for now was bringing in money. For once, he never tried to argue that *Peggy Sue* was really a personal art film.

Ironically it became his first undisputed hit since *Godfather II,* but on several occasions he admitted that he considered it far from the best of the bunch. In fact, the popularity of this facile, tossed-off movie seemed to wound him, to shake his increasingly fragile confidence. Audiences had rejected him as an artist, but they loved him as a hack.

But his time of servitude was ending. Thanks to his percentages on *The Outsiders, The Cotton Club,* and *Peggy Sue,* and his salary advance on *Gardens of Stone,* he was back in the black. He'd paid off the last of his Zoetrope debts, he said, with enough left over to buy more real estate, more cars, more equipment. By avoiding personal bankruptcy during the worst of the Zoetrope crisis, he'd retained control of his assets. By now he'd even regained his profit participation in his films, the ones he'd had to sign over to the banks just a few years earlier.

"Movies make more money thank you think," he explained a few months later. "All my projects kept kicking in dough, and the creditors saw it and let me stay out of bankruptcy." Now a multimillionaire once more, he finally could be Francis Ford Coppola again. He could make a movie of his own.

Chapter Twenty-two

The Dream Seller
(1987–1988)

BY CHRISTMAS 1986 Coppola's lifelong dream of making a movie about Preston Tucker was finally about to come true. Shooting would start in fewer than three months. Coppola still needed to finish supervising Barry Malkin's edit of *Gardens of Stone*, but once that was done, he'd be free to turn his attention entirely to *Tucker*. Why, then, did he seem troubled?

Dreams come true are not always a blessing. Dreamers change, dreams fade, and if a man waits too long he may find himself fulfilling not the dream itself but merely the memory of having dreamed it.

Coppola was rich again, wealthier, he said, than ever before. Along with his wine country estate, he owned palatial homes in San Francisco, Los Angeles, New York, Belize, and some less palatial buildings that he rented out. He was worth, he said, $50 million.

But Gio's death had changed all of Coppola's assumptions. When he lost his eldest son, he seemed to have lost his moorings. "I have to be a little less interested in the real world," he said, "because he's not in it any more."

"To that point in his life," mused Carroll Ballard, "there had been many difficulties, but he had always been able to succeed in spite of them. But when Gio died, it was the first time there was *nothing* he could do."

Moreover, while he'd rebuilt his fortune, he had done so by selling out his art for nearly five years, and that time was gone forever. What was worse, even as a sellout (the famous sellout from UCLA again), he was a bust. In his years as a roaming filmmaker-for-hire, only one of his films, *Peggy Sue*, had been a major hit, and that was a film he had neither controlled nor admired, but merely embellished with technique.

He seemed weary to a depth he'd never been before, sick of himself and bored with his work. He withdrew into a shocked quiescence. There seemed no reason not to make *Tucker*, but now, in a strange way, he'd apparently grown to feel oddly detached from it. The film would be a memorial to his son, who had wished so much for it but now would never see it. Only his vineyard offered him solace.

Fittingly Coppola granted his first major interview in more than two years to wine writer (and Napa Valley neighbor) Jim Gordon. Coppola started out in a tone of calm friendliness, but as the afternoon progressed, he returned reflexively to his old showmanly ways, breaking into song as he was being photographed, and shooting rubber bands from a toy gun at a picture of George Bush stuck to the refrigerator.

Yes, he admitted, he'd compromised his movies in order to keep his vineyard, but his fortune was now restored by careful investment of those movies' profits. His wine formed only the tiniest part of his income; his 1986 production of five thousand cases of Rubicon had brought in sales of $500,000—small change compared with his income from movies like *The Outsiders* and *Peggy Sue*. Still, man does not live by bread alone; only months later Coppola must have been deeply gratified to learn that the redoubtable Le Taillevent restaurant in Paris had broken its French-wine-only tradition to place his 1984 Rubicon on its wine list and in its adjacent wineshop.

Although he talked briefly with Gordon about his earlier films, and mentioned two scripts he was working on (*Secret Journal*, evidently a new name for the epic *Megalopolis*; and *Elective Affinities*), he barely mentioned *Tucker*. Perhaps that was because his feelings about the film had become so complicated, or the meaning of the story so equivocal. The sad fact was that artistic control of the film Coppola had been talking about since 1956 was being taken away from him by his friend George Lucas. It was *Apocalypse* in reverse, and Coppola had no choice but to cooperate with the take-over.

Preston Tucker was a go-getting entrepreneur from suburban Ypsilanti, Michigan, with an idea for a new car. He was a gifted hustler, charming, sunny, not quite honest, at once a ladies' man, a con man, and a visionary. He called himself an "imagineer" rather than an engineer, invented a back-rubbing machine and a car-mounted uranium sensor, and prospered during World War II designing armored vehicles. With the end of the war private cars returned to production, and Tucker decided that what America longed for was a brand-new automobile, one that was faster, sleeker, and safer than any car ever made.

As the first step toward creating the car, Tucker made a very modern move: He turned to the media. He sold himself and his ideas in the popular magazines long before he had any product to peddle. Then, with his public profile well established, he hired aircraft designer Alex Tremulis, who came up with the specific plan for the futuristic automobile. It would have a rear engine powered by a 160-horsepower Franklin helicopter motor with tremendous acceleration capability. Other features would include pop-out safety windshields to prevent skull fractures in accidents, a padded dashboard, a special "emergency safety chamber" under the dash to compensate for moving the engine to the rear, a rubberized hydraulic suspension which allowed tight cornering, disk brakes, and a third "Cyclops" headlight in the center of the car that would turn in whatever direction the car was steering. The car would also have fuel injection, a liquid cooling system, and a sexy low-slung exterior that looked like a rocket ship drawn for the cover of *Astounding Science Fiction.*

Tucker leased a former B-29 assembly plant near Chicago from the U.S. government and began to build the first Tucker Torpedo. He planned to sell his cars for an affordable $2,000 each, roughly half a year's middle-income salary and the equivalent of $12,000 in 1989 dollars. (By the time that Francis Coppola and George Lucas bought their Tuckers, the going "collector's" price had risen to an average of $50,000.)

But until Tucker could start manufacturing and selling his cars, the multimillion-dollar tab for parts, labor, the giant plant, and his own high-rolling life-style was higher than even a rich man could afford. To pay his way, Tucker sold stock in his company to small-time investors, ranging from gas station owners to Philharmonic flutists.

Tucker premiered his car at a gala media event in Chicago, a lively affair with a dance number by the skimpily costumed all-girl "Tuckerettes" leading up to Tucker's personal appearance and the car's splashy debut. Unfortunately, when Tucker tried to drive the prototype onstage, the car of the future wouldn't start. As the delay stretched on, and Tucker tinkered with his Torpedo backstage, the audience turned into an angry mob. Finally he got the car running and drove it out to a roar of approval. The audience was entranced by its beauty.

Tucker managed to build fifty cars between 1945 and 1948. There never was an assembly line; the cars were hand-built, one by one. The Car of Tomorrow, Today was exhibited to great acclaim at auto shows around the country, including the one where Carmine took little Francis in 1947.

The Big Three Detroit automakers (General Motors, Ford, and Chrysler) took Tucker very seriously as a threat to their business and urged U.S. Senator Homer Ferguson of Michigan to do something. Ferguson paid back their campaign contributions by pointing out some minor errors Tucker had made in his stock sales to the Securities and Exchange Commission. Tucker was brought to trial for fraud in 1949. The press (especially powerful columnist Drew Pearson) castigated him as though he'd already been found guilty. In the end the jury declared him innocent of all charges, but his company was bankrupt—the reason why Carmine's Tucker never arrived. "He made the car too good," Carmine explained to his little son; in fact, the title of Preston Tucker's final published article, in *Cars* magazine, was "My Car Was Too Good." Coppola never forgot the phrase.

Seven years later Preston Tucker died in obscurity at age fifty-four, ravaged by cancer. At the time of his death he was designing a new car called the Carioca, which he hoped to manufacture in Brazil. *Collier's* magazine ran an obit describing him as "a bewildering combination of P. T. Barnum, Henry Ford, Jimmy Walker, and Baron Munchausen with a talent for telling stories that people believed and a genius for spending money." Most of Tucker's innovations can be found in today's cars.

It was a story that Coppola seemed born to tell; the similarities between the filmmaker and the automaker were striking. The young Francis Coppola had always seen the fast-talking inventor-salesman as a symbol of the best America had to offer. Furthermore, even at the start of his career, Coppola recognized that with the collapse of the studio system, filmmaking would call increasingly for sales savvy as much as for cinematic skill. Movies were going to be based on deals, and deals would be based on promises. The deal maker promised stars to the moneymen, and promised money to the stars, before *anybody* signed anything. Coppola may have been the first director to grasp the fact that ambitious filmmakers would have to resign themselves to being con men as well as craftsmen if they wanted to make their own movies; filmmakers would need to learn to sell dreams, not products.

Also, young Francis Coppola shared much of Tucker's personal charisma; he was as gifted a traveling dream salesman as P. T. Barnum. If making successful films was a con game, he had an edge. Despite his youthful pronouncements about modeling his life after Lenin or Hitler, his real role model was Preston Tucker.

Like his hero, he became a celebrity by using the media to publicize his future accomplishments before he'd accomplished much of anything. Later in his career he even devised an idea for using the latest technology in a new way and was no less cocksure about it than his hero.

Finally, and perhaps most importantly, both Tucker and Coppola were gamblers whose grandest business schemes went broke. Unlike Tucker, Coppola survived physically and fought his way back financially, but his self-esteem was surely deeply shaken.

On a personal level, too, Coppola seemed to be Tucker's spiritual godson: Both men loved luxury and spent lavishly; both were devoted fathers but less than faithful husbands; both were demonically energetic when pursuing their dreams. Both suffered bad press. Even Coppola's description of Tucker's faults sounds like his assessment of his own errors. "He talked too much," Coppola said, "and had too big a mouth. When you tell people your dreams out of enthusiasm, somehow it makes them seem disgruntled."

For thirty years, ever since Hofstra, Coppola had been thinking about how to tell Tucker's tale. As an idealistic young man he wanted to make the film a dark, tragic exposé of the evils of the system, shot in the style of Orson Welles's *Citizen*

Kane. By June 1971, when he told *Variety* that his next film, about the auto industry in the 1940s, would be a "historic dramatic comedy," his conception had obviously undergone a near-total reversal.

In 1977, when he returned from the Philippines, Coppola was thoroughly sick of seriousness, and envisioned an even lighter treatment. Now *Tucker* would be an inspiring comedy, like those that Frank Capra made during the Depression (e.g., *Mr. Smith Goes to Washington*; *Meet John Doe*) to show that an ordinary man could beat the odds. Coppola wanted Burt Reynolds to star and even went so far as to have him taken for a spin in a Tucker.

By the time he plunged into *One from the Heart*, in 1980, Coppola's vision had changed again. As soon as he was done with his Las Vegas fairy tale musical, he said, he would move directly on to *Tucker*, an innovative Kabuki-style light opera, starring Jack Nicholson, with Brechtian lyrics by Betty Comden and Adolph Green, and Kurt Weill-style music by Leonard Bernstein.

Yet, with all these varying visions for the movie (or perhaps because of them), at no stage did Coppola manage to write a usable script for *Tucker*. His exhaustive research material, burgeoning array of concepts, and, perhaps, the growing similarities between himself and his subject served only to confuse him.

Then his studio went belly up. It was, in a way, the ultimate irony, because just as his identification with Preston Tucker became complete (having failed utterly by doing something that was, he thought, *too good*), he was apparently losing his faith in Tucker and the optimistic dream he represented. Tucker was starting to seem like a bad example. Not only couldn't Coppola sell *One from the Heart* to the public with Tuckeresque razzle-dazzle, but the harder he tried the more people were turned off by it. If you showed any kind of open optimism, he decided, people would just hack you down. The world had turned into a lousy place.

In the aftermath of the studio's failure, his enthusiasm for the movie *Tucker* seemed to slip away, too. For one thing, no one would back it. For another, if he hadn't figured out a way to write it when he was on top, how could he do it now? Worse, a story that had once been an exposé was turning into a sort of metaphorical autobiography, which probably made Coppola edgy. It hit too close to home.

By 1985, at the point when Gio had finally convinced him to make the film and he'd turned to Lucas for help, Coppola was at a low ebb. He was all too aware that he had lost his own kingdom, while his protégé ruled a vast and bustling empire. Sure, Coppola owned a vineyard and some buildings, but Lucas owned the entire Lucas Valley in Marin County (the name was coincidental, predating George's arrival), and Lucasfilm's ultramodern filmmaking facilities had overflowed Lucas's Skywalker Ranch to scatter throughout the whole county. Lucas had built his empire by making profitable movies based on simple, old-fashioned yarns, while Coppola had lost his on just one (very expensive) experimental film.

Worst of all, Coppola had evidently lost confidence in his abilities as a commercial filmmaker, and now he saw his one-time protégé as a mentor who could teach him how to make popular movies again. "I guess I began to realize that one of my worst flaws was the fact that I had so many ideas and so much enthusiasm that I tended to make projects so big that I couldn't really pull them off," he admitted. "So I was very anxious to collaborate with George, and have George pull me down to a scope and kind of film that had a chance of being successful, and paying for itself." To those who had followed his career, Coppola's humility was almost as painful as his previous braggadocio.

He still yearned for an avant-garde Kabuki-Brechtian *Tucker*, a dark comedy with a tragic tone, but Lucas was unlikely to let him get away with it. Lucas was encouraging about *Tucker*, but not as an art film; it was *Tucker*'s earthiness that Lucas liked. "Of all your ideas," Lucas had often told Coppola, "that Tucker one is good, 'cause it's the story of the little guy pursuing the dream, and people can identify with that."

When Lucas agreed to back the film, he explicitly rejected anything remotely like *Take Two from the Heart*. He wanted a straightforward, lightweight crowd pleaser, and whenever Coppola started to effervesce about some new technical tangent, Lucas would tell him to stop embellishing like Michelangelo and just concentrate on telling a story. Coppola was in no position to argue. "Francis can get so esoteric it can be hard for an audience to relate to him," Lucas observed later. "He needs someone to hold him back. With *Godfather* it was Mario Puzo; with *Tucker* it was me."

Coppola grew a little dispirited; with his own cooperation, his dream movie was turning into just another job for hire, even if the boss was an old pal. Still, Coppola felt a heavy burden of responsibility to make *Tucker* a hit for his friend George; he would try on a brand-new creative personality and make *Tucker* in the cautious, calculating Lucas manner. He might get a little of what he wanted; perhaps he remembered Carmine's leading the exit music when he couldn't conduct the symphony.

Once again Coppola managed to work up his enthusiasm for a movie that wasn't his own, even though it was based on an idea that had once been his: *Tucker* would be a Capra comedy. Sort of.

The world had changed too much for anyone (especially Coppola) to believe that a Capraesque hero could triumph against the odds. The director's optimistic worldview had soured since Jack Singer and Griffin O'Neal had entered his life. Now *Tucker*'s story would serve as a warning about the perils of modern corporate conservatism (such as that which was strangling the movie industry). "Before World War II," Coppola said, "the United States had a spirit of inventiveness. Our heroes were people who took great ideas and made them into the industries of the future. But after the war came the marketing era, the Harvard Business School philosophy of managing companies, and I believe that the creative person in a very quiet way was suppressed. *Tucker* is this story. America needs people like Tucker if it is to regain the shine it had in the past."

Capra himself hadn't been too crazy about this idea. When Coppola had visited him, some years earlier, to discuss the project, Capra had noted, "You can't make a Capra movie about a guy who fails. Are you saying that the American system is not good?"

It was a dark message, so Coppola would have to sugarcoat it. How could he turn Tucker's defeat into some sort of victory, to keep the tone upbeat? "I came up with an idea of how to solve the problem," Lucas recalled. "In the end, Tucker may not have built the car, but he wasn't defeated as a creative person. They couldn't crush his spirit. You take that theme, and you run it through the movie, and you have an inspiring film."

Lucas insisted on a complete, coherent screenplay *before* the shoot started. Coppola probably planned to write it after he finished shooting *Gardens of Stone,* but he was uneasy. After all, he hadn't managed to write it in all these years, and never once had he written a comedy.

Then Gio died. Writing a comedy was impossible.

At Lucas's insistence, Coppola agreed to hire a screenwriter for the project. It was the ultimate comedown. Coppola, the legendary clutch writer, the greatest script doctor in the world, was reduced to creative impotence. Inexplicably, instead of turning to a big-leaguer like Robert Towne or William Goldman, Coppola, Lucas, and Fred Roos chose Arnold Shulman, who'd written Capra's saccharine 1959 Frank Sinatra comedy *A Hole in the Head;* English-born ex-adman David Seidler (whose work included several lively biographical scripts, including the teleplay for *Malice in Wonderland*) would collaborate with Shulman.

Coppola may have given the script to hired hands, but no one expected him to give up control. Lucas wanted lots of plot, while Coppola demanded character nuances. The screenwriters had their hands full trying to serve two masters; at one point Schulman wrote two separate drafts of the script, one for each of them.

Actually the scriptwriters had a third master to please. Not only was Lucas pushing for *The Tucker Strikes Back,* but Tucker's family (which had final script approval) was lobbying for *Life with Tucker.* The inventor's adult children wanted a sanitized Lucasland version of the story and saw no reason to mention the time Tucker installed his family at Chicago's expensive Drake Hotel using the stockholders' money, or the incident when he sold his $23,000 yacht to his firm for $43,000 and had it write the purchase off as "research expenses." Nor would they allow any mention of his titled mistress. Coppola agreed about that part. "Hey, everybody has a mistress!" he said. "That's not all that interesting." Coppola later told an interviewer that one of the things that most attracted him to making the movie was the idea that he could present a married couple who were still romantically in love, an uncommon element in current films.

Coppola would be left to "futz around with style," as he described it, to his heart's content. However, he dared not do anything that would scare off an audience; he could go backward into cinema history but not forward into the great unknown.

The success of *Peggy Sue* was proving even more of a problem for Coppola than any of his failures. "To be honest," he said, "after *Apocalypse Now,* the only film I made that the public seemed to want from me—although I don't by any means think it was the best of the group—was *Peggy Sue Got Married.* I'd made a lot of films, a lot of experiments, but the only one a lot of people seemed to like was *Peggy Sue Got Married.* So we both agreed to make [*Tucker*] more like *Peggy Sue Got Married.*"

Lucas was having his own problems. Despite his hard line on the script, he had increasing cause to worry about his own sense of popular taste. He had released two failures in a row (*Howard the Duck* and *Labyrinth*); had he lost his Midas touch? Worse yet, his cash flow was seriously depleted; Lucasfilm could ill afford to front *Tucker's* whole $24 million budget itself. In desperation, Coppola turned to his once and often savior, Paramount, where CEO Frank Mancuso was still after him to do *Godfather III*—but Mancuso had no interest in *Tucker.* Neither did any other studio boss; Universal, Disney, and Tri-Star all turned it down. Lucas called Paramount himself, but he was turned down, too. The movie bore no resemblance to last year's hits, he was told, and its price was too high for an easy profit. "No studio in town would touch it," Lucas recalled. "They all wanted $15 million *Three Men and a Baby* movies or *Crocodile Dundee, Part 73* sequels."

Finally Lucas gave up. He would fund the production himself; perhaps it would be easier to score a distributor partway through the shoot, once Coppola had turned out some dazzling footage.

Coppola's staff had rounded up twenty-two of the forty-six surviving Tuckers (along with their intensely possessive owners, most of whom insisted on driving them). Two additional models built in fiberglass were used in scenes that might damage a real car. Coppola's own dark red Tucker, the one that Gio had polished for him, now bore the personalized license plate "GIO 2 28"; it would play Tucker's prototype car.

Coppola gathered as many of his scattered professional

family members as he could, including Dean and Alex Tavoularis and costumer Milena (*Cotton Club*) Canonero. Paula Smuin (wife of Michael) would contribute choreography for the Tuckerettes, and *Faerie Tale Theater*'s Fred Fuchs would join Fred Roos as coproducer. Carmine would write incidental music; the main score was being created by British pop star-songwriter Joe Jackson, who could offer more authentic-sounding period pop. The majority of the crew heads would be either newcomers or Lucasfilm staffers; most of Coppola's A Team was working on other people's films.

Vittorio Storaro would hold down the DP slot. He and Coppola decided to shoot *Tucker* in ultrasaturated colors, just as Cronenweth had done on *Peggy Sue*. The idea was to show a slightly glamorized *Life* magazine version of midwestern upper-middle-class postwar life—not real life, but the life that prosperous people imagined themselves living.

Jeff Bridges nabbed the starring role of Preston Tucker, and his father, Lloyd Bridges, was signed for the villainous Michigan senator. Martin Landau was overjoyed to get the nod to play the complex, sympathetic role of Abe Karatz, Tucker's chief financial officer. Landau was a masterful character actor, but ever since Hitchcock had cast him as the nasty spy who steps on Cary Grant's fingers in *North by Northwest,* he'd been stuck with bad-guy movie roles and dull TV shows (e.g., eighty episodes of *Mission Impossible*). A close friend of James Dean, as well as Steve McQueen's Actors' Studio classmate, he had taught acting to Jack Nicholson, Warren Oates, and Harry Dean Stanton, among others, but even that hadn't bought him a break from the rigid typecasting. "I think Francis Ford Coppola and Fred Roos are the only two guys in the world who would have cast me in this role," he said.

Most of the supporting roles and bit parts were filled by Coppola veterans. Frederic Forrest would portray Tucker's main grease monkey; Dean Stockwell would essay billionaire Howard Hughes; Joan Allen (who had been Peggy Sue's frumpiest friend) would play Tucker's wife.

For the first time in many years the production was tragically short of Coppolas. Gio was dead, and Roman, age twenty-two, was busy with his own movie. Coppola had set up a small filmmaking company for Roman, Commercial Pictures. It had a staff of two (Roman and his secretary) and was supposed to turn out a cheap new movie by an upcoming young director every three months. The movies would be shot on film, but everything else would be done electronically to keep costs down. It sounded like Coppola's answer to Roger Corman.

Roman, who looked more like an art student than a movie mogul, was starting with a film called *Clownhouse*, a horror film about a gang of vicious criminals, dressed as clowns, who terrorize suburban boys. Written and directed by Francis's discovery, a filmmaker named Victor Salva, it was scheduled to be shot simultaneously with *Tucker*.

Early in April 1987, Coppola began working on *Tucker* at a San Rafael sound stage. He started by showing the cast two of the Tucker Corporation's promotional films, along with excerpts from the Tucker family's home movies. Then the usual two weeks of rehearsals began, culminating in a complete, sequential run-through on videotape. Rehearsing for a film remains one of Coppola's innovations that hasn't yet caught on industry-wide, and most of the actors were grateful for the chance to work up their characterizations.

Principal photography began on April 13. All of the locations, from San Francisco's Civic Center to rural Petaluma, were within a reasonable commute from the Napa Valley. Many of the sets were built inside a giant Deco-style onetime Model A Ford factory on the waterfront in Richmond, California. The bottom floor served as Tucker's factory; the upstairs as Tucker's offices. Both sets could be shown simultaneously, allowing Coppola to utilize the non-optical split screens he had tried out in *One from the Heart* and "Rip Van Winkle"; his hands weren't wholly tied.

However, the complex choreography that Coppola needed to make his tricky effects come off required the actors to move with the same precision as the cameras and drove many cast members a little crazy. Many years earlier, on the first *Godfather* shoot, Coppola had fought with cinematographer Gordon Willis because Willis wanted the actors to hit marks, while Coppola wanted them free to express emotions. Now Coppola expected his actors to express emotions *and* hit marks.

Even Jeff Bridges complained how hard it was to emote and stay in frame at the same time. "It's like acting in a Rembrandt painting," he said. "I've never done a film this complicated as far as camera moves and lights. To act in it almost requires a different technique. You have all these marks to hit, and if it goes awry for some reason, it takes another half hour to set it up again." Bridges discovered that the way to handle it was to march calmly through the steps like a robot, right through the first take, and start acting from the second take onward.

The second day of the shoot covered the car's gala near-disastrous premiere. A mob of extras (mainly actor wannabes and retirees) was hired. The women were outfitted in seamed silk stockings, vintage ankle-breaker high heels, and careful replicas of old-fashioned hairpins in their coiffures; the men got short haircuts and hair grease. Performers of both sexes were issued scrupulously timely looking wristwatches and jewelry. After a 6:00 A.M. hairdressing session, the extras were briefed on the approved 1940s slang words ("gal," "dame," "buddy," "pal," "daffy," "gee, that's swell," etc.) they could use in their improvised crowd mutters. Then they were sent onto the set, where they waited and waited and waited, craning their necks to catch sight of the famous director as he and Storaro strode past or squatted together over the video monitors at the far end of the vast room. Coppola looked cozy in a presentable suit and sport shirt, with a scarf instead of a tie. "There is something down to earth about him," one of the extras noted. "He looks more like a drama teacher who has read too many books about directing than a director."

The scene, in which backstage problems delay the emergence of the first Tucker Torpedo, called for the extras to project anticipation, then boredom, and finally impatience. Coppola seduced them into believable performances by reproducing the desired dramatic situation. Early in the morning the crew sat the extras down on cramped, hard seats and kept them waiting for hours, under the heat of 192 light bulbs, while the second unit shot their increasing restlessness. As the crowd perspired and wriggled, the Tucker (which none of them had seen yet) stayed hidden behind the curtain. By the time the antique car was finally unveiled, the extras had become a genuinely angry mob. "It is a matter not of acting, but of real irritation and discomfort," one of them reported. "We became the people they have been nudging us toward all day."

The shoot went fast; having a complete shooting script helped immensely. *Tucker* was slightly ahead of schedule when *Gardens of Stone* was released in May, 1987. There was very little drama surrounding the opening; the film merely started running with minimal fanfare at just sixty theaters across the country. The marketing bosses at Tri-Star wanted to wait and see how the film opened before committing money for prints and expensive ads.

Gardens of Stone begins with a funeral in the rain, followed by a lengthy flashback in which the story is related. Sergeant Clell Hazard (James Caan), a seasoned soldier and combat veteran, is a literate, cultured, and compassionate man. The Army is his family, and despite his cynicism about the then-current Vietnam War, he's loyal to that family. Along with his buddy, Goody Nelson (James Earl Jones), Hazard trains recruits for the Old Guard, the ceremonial unit in charge of funerals at Arlington National Cemetery, but he thinks his battle experience is being wasted. He'd rather train the boys for combat, where his expertise might save some lives.

Hazard is attracted (and attractive) to a reporter (Anjelica Huston), despite her strong antiwar beliefs. He also finds a surrogate son in one of his charges, Lieutenant Willow (D. B. Sweeney), a gung ho recruit who proves to be the son of an old friend who died without ever receiving full recognition from the Army. Intent on bringing honor to his family name, the boy volunteers for Vietnam, where he dies almost instantly, proving Hazard's point that the Army's training course for the jungle war is inadequate. The flashback ends, and the movie returns to Willow's rainy funeral and his young widow (Mary Stuart Masterson) weeping.

The script is surprisingly old-fashioned, larded with familiar war movie clichés like the hazing of a new recruit, the slack-off soldier who turns hero in combat, and the gung ho kid killed in his first battle. Its sentimental portrait of the Army family, and its frequent scenes of roughhouse military comedy, recall classic John Ford "service" pictures like *They Were Expendable, The Wings of Eagles,* and *She Wore a Yellow Ribbon,* complete with a big, tough-talking, tenderhearted sergeant like that played by Victor McLaglen.

Unlike a Ford movie, however, the screenplay is thin and muddled; many of the characters (especially the women) are stick figures, and in an attempt to keep the politics inoffensive, complex issues are reduced to simplistic sloganizing: Army good; brass dumb; war bad. The romantic interest is a peacenik, but so is the most obnoxious character (Bill Graham, as a loudmouth dove). The blandness of the script may have bought the Army's cooperation, but it's exasperating in a film dealing with a war that still makes many Americans wince.

The two male leads are fine. James Caan is both virile and vulnerable, recalling the best moments of his onetime costar John Wayne, and if James Earl Jones is playing Victor McLaglen, he does it with a greater range of wit and unpredictability than McLaglen ever commanded. Unfortunately the leading actresses never overcome their underwritten roles. Mary Stuart Masterson spends most of her scenes streaming tears, and not even Anjelica Huston can make us believe that her activist reporter is anything but a walking plot device. For that matter, the pivotal role of Willow, as played by D. B. Sweeney, seems less a kid than the Kid.

Happily Coppola's direction provides this cut-and-dried story with such surprising warmth that we can't help caring about the characters, even if they are schematic. Like Ford, who used the sky and the weather to underscore the dramatic resonances of his films, Coppola succeeds in making the constant rains of that spring and summer his allies; the film seems bathed in tears. There is no film school flash, only an aching sorrow; the tragedy of the shoot seems to have turned Coppola into an unselfconscious craftsman, and the emotion that invests every frame seems to have have seeped into the film of its own accord. Although *Gardens of Stone* cannot transcend the flaws in its script, it stands nonetheless as Coppola's most passionate and moving film since *Rumble Fish*.

It was not well received. *Daily Variety*'s critic panned it, calling it "a major disappointment" and noting that the film must have gotten its title "from the stiffness of the characters it portrays."

Vincent Canby thought it had "the consistency and the kick of melted vanilla ice cream. . . . The most important missing ingredient is Mr. Coppola." David Ansen at *Newsweek* directed most of his criticism at the inadequate script, while faintly praising Coppola's craftsmanship. *Time* carried only an unsigned, one-paragraph pan, noting that the picture "sleepwalks like a family mourner; it plays taps to its own best intentions." J. Hoberman in the *Village Voice* found the following adjectives appropriate: "inert," "ponderous," "inorganic," "shameless," "ineffectual," "monumentally confused," and "opportunistic." Sheila Benson thought the film "finely-wrought and well-played" but suspenseless. Pauline Kael castigated the script and the jarring alterations between roughhouse comedy and tragedy, but noted, "The picture has some of the best-detailed work he's done in years."

Coppola's public reaction to the reviews was stoical. *Tucker*, which was now halfway through the shoot, was still looking for a distributor, and he clearly cared far less about what some critic thought than about *Stone*'s box-office performance. Unfortunately the public seemed to agree with the critics. *Gardens of Stone* bombed. In its first ten days it grossed only $3.3 million, and then it sank like a stone. It never went into wide release.

Coppola needn't have worried. Behind the scenes at Paramount, old friends were rooting for him. Sidney Ganis, Paramount's president of worldwide marketing, was a Lucasfilm alumnus, and now he threw his weight behind *Tucker*. When Coppola called Paramount for the third time, he was amazed to hear a yes. And within seconds, it seemed, foreign distributors were lining up to grab *Tucker* for Europe, promising full-blown promotional campaigns.

Grateful as they were to have finally scored a distributor, both Lucas and Coppola were uneasy about one part of the deal. Since the film's most marketable elements were its creators, not its stars, the Paramount execs insisted that they'd *both* have to make themselves available to at least a few members of the hated press.

Perhaps that's why Coppola broke his rule and allowed a reporter on the set. Jill Kearney had worked as a reader at Omni Zoetrope from 1980 until its demise and was now a freelance writer covering the shoot for both *American Film* and *Mother Jones* magazines. Kearney reported that despite Lucas's interference, *Tucker* remained very much Coppola's film. "The parallels between Tucker's and Coppola's lives are so apparent to the cast and crew," she noted, "that when they talk about the film they seem at times to think they are shooting Coppola's autobiography." The tendency was especially pronounced among all the old Zoetrope hands on the shoot, but even Jeff Bridges observed how often Coppola would tell stories about Zoetrope, comparing his own venture with Tucker's.

By July 17 principal photography for *Tucker* had wrapped, ahead of schedule, after a quick thirteen-week shoot.

Meanwhile, Coppola and UA had decided to rerelease *Apocalypse,* and now Coppola and Roos hit the phones to hype the picture one more time. It had been several years since Coppola had spoken with any members of the daily press. Perhaps he wanted to get in practice before *Tucker* came out; more likely, he just yearned to sell *Apocalypse* again. In any event, he reassured the journalists that his "little, temporary falling out with the press" was over. Of course, he still blamed the press's hateful on-set reports for ruining the public's reception of the film (and of *One from the Heart*). "But I'm not mad now," he purred. "I was just naive then."

He'd never get to make another film on that epic scale, he reflected. He certainly wasn't going to bash out lousy imitation TV genre films, so there was no room for him in the movie business, no next project. He was leaving the profession altogether, he swore; after *Tucker* he would make movies only as an amateur. (It was about the millionth time he'd sworn such an oath in his twenty-year filmmaking career.) "I just think it would be wonderful to wake up in the morning with an idea for a film, and just to be able to do it, and not make it be this matter of enormous pressure and the possibility of letting so many people down," he said. "If you make a movie and it fails, you feel like you can't walk down the street of your home town without apologizing to everybody."

Coppola moved into postproduction on *Tucker,* and he and Lucas even did the promised interviews. Months passed, and 1987 turned to 1988. Despite his vows to retire as soon as *Tucker*'s postproduction was finished, Coppola was already at work on the screenplay for his next movie. Or, to be precise, his next one-third of a movie. Woody Allen had devised a project, called *New York Stories,* that would consist of three contemporary urban tales, each thirty to forty minutes long, to be shot in a four- or five-week period. Allen would shoot one; the other two would be helmed by Martin Scorsese and Francis Coppola.

Coppola's New York Story, titled *Life Without Zoe,* offered a special fringe benefit: the opportunity to work creatively with his sixteen-year-old daughter, Sofia, and to give her a taste of the apprenticeship her brothers had enjoyed. Sofia would have prime responsibility for designing the costumes, as well as writing the script about a sophisticated eleven-year-old who lives at the Sherry Netherland, has her own credit cards, lunches at the Russian Tea Room, and not only knows how to make strawberry daiquiris, but drinks them. "This is going to be as bad as the horse's head," Coppola predicted.

Coppola could hardly believe he'd agreed to the project. "I have no business doing this film," he told a reporter.* "I just don't want to be doing this any more." Nonetheless, in June 1988 Coppola and his silver trailer headed for Manhattan and *Zoe*.

When he wasn't actually shooting, Coppola talked to reporters about *Tucker*. The ballyhoo, which had begun five months early, was still going strong. The cars were appearing at auto shows all around the country (their resale value escalating daily). In July and August a spate of *Tucker* articles, with Coppola interviews interwoven, appeared in mass magazines, film magazines, and urban newspapers. Most of the interviews sounded like the same tape, run over and over. Coppola, it seemed, didn't really want to talk about *Tucker*, or maybe the reporters didn't. Only a few of the journalists realized that *Tucker* represented a dream deferred, fulfilled, and betrayed.

Instead, in most of the interviews, Coppola would start out boasting of his current wealth and quickly turn the conversation to the collapse of Zoetrope. He also continued to insist on his forthcoming retirement to amateur status. With inexpensive video technology, he explained, he could make $1 million home movies that looked like $50 million epics. But first, he wanted to try his hand at something smaller—namely, the art of sculpture. (At least, he didn't announce that his first work would be a giant head of himself.)

Although he could still rouse himself to put on a show for certain reporters (on one occasion he grabbed his wife and danced with her), he seemed discouraged. And why not? As he hinted in interview after interview, he was basically miserable with how *Tucker* had turned out. He had been forced to make it a comedy, but as he said several times, he still thought it was a tragedy. It was a bit like Galileo turning from his inquisitors to whisper, "It *still* moves."

---

*When the film opened, the majority of critics (and viewers) agreed with Coppola, noting the indifferent direction and jejune script.

When Coppola spoke with reporter Robert Lindsey of *The New York Times*, he conceded that stylistically *Tucker* was little better than *Peggy Sue, Too*. Worse yet, it was largely his own fault; even though he didn't much care for *Peggy Sue*, he repeated, it was the only recent film he had made that audiences seemed to like. "I'd lost some of my confidence," Coppola admitted. "I knew George has a marketing sense of what the people might want. He wanted to candy-apple it up a bit, make it like a Disney film. He was at the height of his success, and I was at the height of my failure, and I was a little insecure. . . . I think it's a good movie—it's eccentric, a little wacky, like the Tucker car—but it's not the movie I would have made at the height of my power."

Apparently Coppola thought better of his candor. The following week, *The New York Times* carried a letter to the editor in which Coppola, playing spin doctor, insisted that he thought *Peggy Sue* wasn't all *that* bad. However, he made no attempt to alter the spin on his comments about *Tucker*.

When George Lucas read the original interview in the *Times*, he leaped into damage-control mode. The article, he told a San Francisco critic, was "slanted considerably. . . . Anyone can bait you, and there are a lot of misquotes—there was no tape recorder, the quotes are not accurate." (Lucas didn't seem to realize that minus only the term "candy-apple," Coppola had said virtually the same things to Jill Kearney and everybody else.) "The truth of it is, Francis and I worked on the movie together, and he made the movie he wanted to make. . . . Who knows what it'd have been if he made the movie on his own? And who knows what it would have been if he'd have made it at the height of his powers, which was five or six years ago?"

On August 4 *Tucker* premiered at a $35-a-head benefit for the Variety Club fund, at George Lucas's pet theater, Marin County's lavish state-of-the-art Corte Madera Cinema. Many of those who had followed Coppola's career over the years hoped that *Tucker* would be a triumph, a creative milestone. Not only had Coppola dreamed about making it all his life, but it marked his closest return to artistic freedom in nearly five years. Furthermore, since Coppola had announced it would be his last movie before retirement, proper dramatic structure called for it to be the capper to his career.

Sadly, as quickly became evident, Coppola had turned this

potentially major career event into a minor footnote. *Tucker* is a slight, stylish, chilly movie, a myth emptied of its meaning, exemplifying the worst tendencies of George Lucas (in his Disneyfication of the universe) and of Francis Coppola (in his fear of self-revelation). Preston Tucker's complex, tragic tale has been reduced to a shallow comic parable about the demise of Zoetrope.

The plot follows a sanitized version of the automaker's life, from his first idea for the Tucker car in 1945 through his vindication in court four years later. It opens much like *Citizen Kane*, with a flashback in the form of an industrial promo film recounting Tucker's (Jeff Bridges's) accomplishments, complete with peppy, sentimental 1940s-style music, a cheerful voice-over narrator, and inserts of family snapshots.

The story begins when Tucker announces to his adoring family (real and professional) his idea for the Car of the Future, Today. Tucker's financial adviser, Abe Karatz (Martin Landau), advises against the whole enterprise. Nonetheless, after dinner, Tucker and his resident mechanics adjourn to the barn to invent a car.

Tucker leases a giant factory from the government, but he has to pledge that he'll produce fifty cars within the next three months. Meanwhile, Karatz hires a villainous (and purely fictional) executive, Bennington (Dean Goodman), to head the company. (Lucas, who believes that all popular movies need a bad guy, may have insisted on this character.) Bennington demands that Tucker compromise his radical design. Tucker refuses.

The first prototype is constructed, and despite some last-minute technical problems, it is exhibited at a car show, where the public loves it. A sympathetic Howard Hughes (Dean Stockwell) gives Tucker a tip about a powerful new engine. Meanwhile, with the collusion of the traitorous Bennington, Senator Ferguson of Michigan (Lloyd Bridges) hauls up Tucker on phony stock fraud charges. (Abe Karatz, explaining why, echoes Carmine: "You make the car too *good.*") Karatz resigns, lest his old bank fraud conviction be held against Tucker.

Tucker is tried before an inattentive judge, but a sympathetic, drab, multiracial jury pronounces him innocent, while fifty new-made Tuckers parade triumphantly around the courthouse. Karatz admits that the Tucker Motor Company is dead, but the indefatigable Tucker drives happily away in his beautiful new automobile, blithely planning to invent a mini-refrigerator.

The movie bears a dedication: "For Gio, who loved cars."

As written, the film is a breezy comedy. Nearly every sequence ends on an upbeat, and there are lots of comic car chases (all accompanied by the relentlessly peppy "Tiger Rag"). While some individual sequences succeed as updated Capra-ana (for instance, Tucker's rousing speech, at his trial, concluding: "If Ben Franklin were alive today, he'd be arrested for flying a kite without a license"), the lighthearted tone quickly grows monotonous. Moreover, it contradicts the story.

This rigid cheerfulness stems from one of the screenplay's trickier turns (and most serious miscalculations): The promo film that starts the picture not only sets the tone but periodically reappears to remind us that we've never really emerged from Tucker's self-advertisement. This means there will be nothing in *Tucker* that Tucker himself wouldn't want said; we see a man wearing his public face, and as in any corporate annual report, failure is reinvented as triumph. Preston Tucker is a grinning advertisement for himself, his façade never falls, and his mania never gives way to doubt or depression. We can't share his emotions when they are so cryptic.

Jeff Bridges's Tucker seems confined (whether by his director or his preoccupation with hitting marks) to the ABC of emotions: Aggressive, Bewildered, and Chipper. As the character goes down to defeat, his unfailing boyish grin begins to seem psychotically inappropriate.

The film does include two superb performances, both in supporting roles. Martin Landau's Karatz is the only main character who seems sufficiently human to move us; the tenderness of his expression and the delicacy of his reading change mawkish moments to emotional ones. And Dean Stockwell's Howard Hughes is a wonderfully weird and lonesome billionaire in disgrace, asking, "Did I change, or the cosmic sense of humor? I used to laugh when *they* did."

The remaining members of the supporting cast don't get much chance to strut their stuff. Shallow writing and perfunctory direction reduce their roles to mere cheerleaders for the boss. Joan Allen (bouncy as June Allyson, but soignée as Bacall) is a better-dressed version of the "spunky little woman" of the postwar movies; Dean Goodman's villain lacks only a mustache to twirl; and comic Don ("Father Guido Sarducci") Novello, as a promo filmmaker, has no part to speak of.

Coppola's clever staging and flashy camerawork (such as when the camera pans past a wall to travel magically from one set to another, or when another set wall is used to split the screen between two sides of a telephone conversation) are quite charming. A few sequences are more than charming. The "roast beef scene" is delicious: Tucker serves a roomful of potential backers a rare roast beef while showing them slides of bloody car crashes to underscore the safety features of his automobile. Naturally, the prospective backers grow queasy and slip out one by one, leaving Tucker dismayed and the audience roaring with laughter. The Howard Hughes episode is equally superb. Shot in a half-dark airplane hangar, with Hughes's ungainly, controversial Spruce Goose airplane looming in the background, it is like a miniature ghost story.

Tucker isn't really about making and selling cars. It's about making and selling movies, and in many ways the most fascinating things in it are the parallels to Coppola's own life. Even though Coppola didn't write the script, internal evidence leaves no doubt that he had immense influence on it; if *Tucker* is of little interest as a film, it is of great interest for the light it throws on Coppola's vision of himself.

Tucker's adoring professional family and its presence at his dinner table are clearly meant to echo the Coppola Court. Abe Karatz is surely the sweetest, most supportive surrogate father and yes-man an artist ever had. Tucker's biological family, too, seems like an idealized version of Coppola's, right down to the son who drops out of school to apprentice at his father's work.

Tucker's verbal challenge, "I'm going to put the Big Three out of business," brings to mind Coppola's "It's going to be the survival of the fittest, and the long-established studios will be brought down." When Tucker's mechanic observes, "No matter how much he makes, he always manages to spend twice as much," it's a clear echo of George Lucas's comments on Omni Zoetrope. Bennington's criticism of Tucker's business skills ("He's not a real businessman.") is a virtual replay of a comment a rival producer made to a *Saturday Review* reporter as Zoetrope was going under. There's pressure on Tucker to get the product (read "film") out prematurely, before the design (read "script") is finished; there's a company executive (read "studio head") demanding a more conventional design; there's a tense, triumphant sneak preview. There's even an ex-filmmaker in disgrace, Howard Hughes, sounding very much like a director who's lost his audience. In fact, there is scarcely a scene in the film that does not carry some plangent reference to Coppola's filmmaking adventures, specifically *One from the Heart* and its aftermath.

There's nothing wrong (in fact, there's plenty right) with Coppola's making *Tucker* as a parable of the demise of Zoetrope, but its glaring artificiality, its shallow sunniness, and its shrill insistence on upbeat entertainment make it smell like the desperate flop-sweat of a stand-up comic whose audience won't laugh.

Because of Coppola's uneasy relationship to the material and, no doubt, the still aching loss of Gio, his creative control seems badly off-balance. *Tucker* represents a fatal failure of Coppola's narrative gifts.

The first review of *Tucker* appeared a week before the film's official premiere, and it was discouraging. John Powers, who had replaced David Thomson at *California* magazine, mixed faint praise with discomfort over the tension between a tragic story and its upbeat treatment. "Chirpy and superficial," he wrote, "*Tucker* feels like a fairy tale by a man who doesn't believe in fairies."

With a week to go before the movie opened, Coppola went on the *Today* show, selling the film the way Tucker sold cars. He radiated the impression that he loved the movie, that *Tucker* was a four-wheeled version of *Rocky*.

Then *Variety* reviewed the film. "Approach leaves little room for depth, emotion, or a rewarding human dimension," wrote the reviewer, "but the upbeat tempo and attitude carry the viewer right along through an irresistibly engaging tale." David Ansen, in *Time*, took much the same tack, praising the technique and the high spirits of the film, while indicating utter disbelief in its "slightly demented" cheerfulness. And in the *New Yorker* (with Pauline Kael absent), Terrence Rafferty compared the film to a big, self-inflating, automotive air bag. "Francis Ford Coppola is a director who no longer allows any incidental pleasures to creep into his movies," he wrote. "There are no real human beings in *Tucker,* no sense of freedom in any of the shots."

The film had its partisans. Janet Maslin raved in *The New York Times* that it was "the best thing Mr. Coppola has done in years," praising its "buoyant yet impassioned tone." *Time* magazine's Richard Schickel reveled in its pep and showmanship and concluded by calling it "a movie of large virtue." Sheila Benson, still reliable, gave it a thumbs-up.

Tucker was released wide, on 720 screens nationwide, in the best summer for movie grosses in several years. In its first weekend in release it was the sixth hottest film in America, grossing nearly $4 million in three days. It did especially well in Los Angeles and in San Francisco, which still looked on Coppola as a hometown boy. But after its strong opening it slid swiftly out of the top ten (and out of many theaters), its grosses plummeting sharply. *Tucker* had no legs.

After twelve weeks, it was selling so few tickets that Paramount stopped tracking it. It had brought in under $9 million in rentals, against a release cost that was probably around $34 million, for a crushing loss of $24 million. No doubt, foreign rentals, cable, network, and video sales would improve the profit picture a bit, but there was little doubt any more: *Tucker* was a flop.

What had happened to Coppola?

Some people would say that *nothing* had happened. The four films Coppola made before the two *Godfather*s were all flops. Maybe he was never more than a moderately talented filmmaker who got lucky with the *Godfather*s, and had been riding on notoriety, chutzpah, and good PR ever since.

We don't think that's true. But if it isn't, then something *did* happen. What was it?

It might have been time. Physically and intellectually, filmmaking is exhausting work. Many of the most promising filmmakers seem to burn out within only five or ten years of making their first good film. Tony Richardson was a washout after five years. John Sturges lasted six years. Buster Keaton, seven (as a director). Preston Sturges hung on for eight. Arthur Penn, nine. Claude Chabrol, ten. François Truffaut, ten.

Coppola's first great film was *The Godfather* (1972). Major works followed in 1974 (*The Conversation* and *Godfather II*), and 1979 (the first half of *Apocalypse Now*). In 1983 he made the flawed but fascinating *Rumble Fish*. But unless you count "Rip Van Winkle," it has now been six years since Coppola made a good film, and ten years since he has made even half of a great one. Still, he had eight good years.

But that's not all.

Coppola had sacrificed his commercial skills on the altar of art, hoping to be blessed with the gift of greatness. He sought to negotiate a purposeful surrender to inner forces he could not control. That this wildly courageous act was also selfish, and a betrayal of his audience, never occurred to him. Even if it had, it's doubtful that he would have cared, or that he could have helped himself.

Worse yet, if Coppola had risked everything for art he seemed to have lost the gamble: While his early commercial films are full of rich emotional and thematic undercurrents (the complexity of family ties, the mutability of responsibility, the inevitability of corruption, the price that must be paid for success), the art films that came later are often cold and shallow. The central purpose of art, in any medium, is to convey a vision of the world, and this requires the exposure of the artist's deepest concerns; the story inevitably mirrors the story teller. Yet, for all the flamboyance of Coppola's public persona, as a maker of art films he seems remarkably reticent, as if terrified of revealing some awful secret about himself. Coppola's fear of personal revelation, and his concomitant inability to laugh at himself, may have cut him off from his deepest sources of creative energy.

Furthermore, in his obsessive hunger for the status of a great artist, Coppola had often seemed blind to the limits of his talents. Unsatisfied with exercising his genius for creating powerful images, and his gift for evoking superb performances, he had insisted on standing as an auteur, a lone genius in a fundamentally collaborative medium. For a time he reserved all the best behind-the-camera roles for himself, including those he was incompetent to play. Coppola had tried to be his own financier, producer, distributor, publicist, and studio boss—playing both Leonardo and the princelings who paid Leonardo's way.

It's possible that three and a half great movies outweigh and justify an infinitude of failures. Maybe that's the mystery of art. The riddle of the artist, however, is the subject of this book.

Coppola was nearly fifty, and he really could retire. But did he genuinely want a life of quietude? And could he bear to go out on a bomb?

With every passing day Coppola's retirement seemed less likely. Three weeks after *Tucker* opened, Francis and Eleanor Coppola went to Italy, where they stayed for more than a month. During that time *Variety* reported that Coppola had signed a deal with Rome's Cinecittà studio to spend five years as its technical adviser and revitalize the moribund studio. He'd make two big-budget films for it, using high-resolution video. The first one would be *Secret Diary*. Nobody was saying what the second one might be. Zoetrope officials didn't even bother to respond publicly, but when questioned, they denied everything.

Simultaneously an intriguing rumor began to make the rounds. According to several members of Coppola's A Team, who had made the mistake of telling their friends, the reason Coppola had gone to Italy was to start work on *Godfather III*, a film he'd sworn never to make unless it was *Abbott and Costello Meet the Godfather*.

Then, just before Christmas 1988, the Los Angeles *Times* printed a story that not only turned the rumor into fact but even provided a convincing motive. Apparently Jack Singer was suing Coppola for $6 million because the filmmaker had never paid back the $3 million Zoetrope bailout loan. (Possibly Singer had read Coppola's boasts about how rich he was and decided that Coppola could now afford to repay him.)

Coppola had countered by pointing out that since Singer had bought Omni Zoetrope Studios for $5 million less than the appraised value, which price difference was considerably greater than Coppola's outstanding debt to him, Coppola owed Singer nothing. A judge had just overruled this argument, meaning that Coppola might actually have to come up with $6 million— the unpaid loan plus interest. Hence, according to the Los Angeles *Times*, Coppola was writing *Godfather III* on the assumption he'd lose the lawsuit and be forced to come up with the penalty payment.

Neither Zoetrope nor Paramount would make any comment. Coppola contacted *People* magazine and confirmed that he was moving to Rome to make "electronic movies." *Godfather III* was not mentioned, but it wasn't denied either.

It sounded, on the face of it, like the old familiar story: Coppola was falling back into debt slavery and would be forced to work on a loathsome project because he needed the money. But on closer examination, there was something else.

If Coppola was worth $50 million, as he claimed, what was to stop him from selling (or mortgaging) some of his investment properties to raise a mere one twelfth that amount? It was possible, of course, that he felt stubborn and simply didn't want to sell off a pennyworth of the things he considered his. But why would he accept another day-job movie merely to indulge this stubbornness?

Unless he *wanted* to make *Godfather III.*

Suppose Coppola were to make *Godfather III*, secure in the knowledge that he had not been hired as an imitation George Lucas, or even an imitation of the guy who shot *Peggy Sue*. Suppose he knew that Paramount wanted *him*, his best self: part success-driven Carmine, part artistic Augie, part hustler Preston Tucker, and part Francis, the best storyteller in the world?

What if Coppola had come to understand that the greatest artists always return to their roots, recycling the things they care the most about? What if he yearned to delve again into the treasure-laden field of the Italian-American family—a field he'd let lie fallow for fifteen years? What if it marked the beginnings of a new phase in his career, that of a mature artist?

What if it finally penetrated that *The Godfather* movies were more than popular? That they were works of the deepest, most profound art? That he might never top them and that he didn't need to? That he had nothing left to prove?

Epilogue

The Godfather's Spaghetti Sauce

SOMETIMES FILMMAKERS reward viewers who sit through all the credits to the bitter end by including a little joke, or reward, just before the curtain comes down.

Here's yours.

For your dining pleasure (or curiosity), we include the Sicilian spaghetti sauce recipe that Clemenza teaches Michael in *The Godfather* (and that Coppola gave to *City* magazine staffers, along with the ingredients, as a Christmas bonus in 1975). We've adapted it a bit to include measurements and timing. By the way, this is a family-sized (not Family-sized) recipe. If you ever have to hit the mattresses, and need to cook for twenty guys (like Clemenza), multiply everything by four or five.

The Godfather's Spaghetti Sauce with Italian Sausages and Sicilian Infierno Wine

---

3	tablespoons olive oil
1	tablespoon minced garlic
1	medium onion, finely chopped
1	cup strong red wine (preferably Sicilian Infierno); reserve remainder of bottle
1	28-ounce can whole Italian tomatoes
1	6-ounce can tomato paste

1 tablespoon dried sweet basil, or ¼ cup minced fresh
  basil

  salt to taste

1 teaspoon sugar, or to taste

1½ pounds mild Italian sausage

In a large pot, heat the olive oil gently over low heat. Add the garlic and onions and cook until translucent. Stir in the red wine. Add the whole tomatoes and tomato paste. Rinse remnants of tomato paste out of the can with water, adding the water to the pot. Add the basil, salt, and sugar, and stir. When the sauce comes to a light boil, add the sausage and simmer over low heat for 3–4 hours, stirring occasionally and adding extra water if sauce gets too thick. During the last hour or so, correct seasonings and partly cover the pot. Serve over spaghetti, and drink the rest of the Infierno. (Author's note: Like many sauces, this will improve immensely if refrigerated overnight. We also find it more flavorful if the sausages are sliced and sauteed with the onions instead of being added whole.)

Bibliography

Much of the library research for this book was performed at the Margaret Herrick Library of the Academy of Motion Picture Arts and Sciences; the material at this library is organized primarily by subject in files of newspaper and magazine clippings. Unfortunately, clipping sources are not always fully identified. As a result, some source information below is incomplete.

Additional information was gathered from interviews, as noted; some interviewees, who provided background data on Coppola's life requested to remain anonymous, and are not listed.

Ablow, Gale. "Coppola's Ultimate Fairy Tale." *Videography*, April 1985 (*Rip Van Winkle* techniques and personnel).

Adam, Christina. "Interning with the Godfather." *Moving Image*, January 1982 (Zoetrope preteen internship program).

Adler, Renata:

"Finian's Rainbow Back from Missitucky." *New York Times*, October 10, 1968 (review, *Finian's Rainbow*).

"The Child-and-the-Warm-Beast Form." *The New Yorker*, November 5, 1979 (review, *The Black Stallion*).

Aigner, Hal, and Michael Goodwin. "The Bearded Immigrant from Tinsel Town." *City*, June 12–25, 1974 (interview with Coppola; *The Conversation*).

Albarino, Richard, *Daily Variety:*

"Coppola's Plans: To Lay Low in Frisco." March 27, 1974 (interview, *Godfather II* shoot, Coppola announces retirement plans).

"Coppola Entering Distribution-Exhibition." August 21, 1974 (Cinema 5, plans for *City*, grosses of *Godfather* and *Graffiti*).

Allan, John H. "Profits of *The Godfather*." *New York Times*, April 16, 1972.

American Film. "Martha Coolidge." December 1988 (excerpted from American Film Institute symposium) (memories of Omni Zoetrope).

American Zoetrope, catalog of services, 1970.

Ames, Katrine, with William J. Cook. "Godfather III." *Newsweek*, July 21, 1975 (plans for *Godfather Saga*).

Anderson, Laurie. "Two from the Heart." *Vogue*, September 1981 (interview; Coppola's attitude toward money).

Anderson, Peter. Letter to the Editor. *American Cinematographer*, March 1987 (*Captain Eo*: who did what).

Andrews, Rena. "Informative Rap Sessions." *Boxoffice*, September 23, 1974 (Coppola on money, as honoree at Telluride festival).

Ansen, David. *Newsweek*:

"Apocalypse Neigh." October 29, 1979 (review, *The Black Stallion*).

"Coppola's Apocalypse Again." with Martin Kasindorf. February 16, 1981 (financial crisis, Omni Zoetrope).

"Coppola's Fairy-Tale World." January 25, 1982 (Radio City preview of *One from the Heart*; review and report).

"Breaking Up." May 10, 1982 (review, *Too Far to Go*).

"Where's the Rabbit?" June 14, 1982 (review, *The Escape Artist*).

"Coppola Courts the Kiddies." April 4, 1983 (review, *The Outsiders*).

October 6, 1986 (review, *Peggy Sue Got Married*).

May 11 1987 (review, *Gardens of Stone*).

"Coppola's Customized Capra-corn." August 22, 1988 (review, *Tucker*).

Archerd, Army. column (various titles). *Daily Variety* except as noted:

Weekly Variety, February 1, 1967 (*You're a Big Boy Now*; Coppola's plans).

June 17, 1969 (Coppola plans *The Conversation* to star Brando).

Weekly Variety, March 11, 1970 (Paramount's plans for *The Godfather*).

April 20, 1979 (*One from the Heart* plans; Coppola's fortieth birthday party).

February 25, 1981 (Norman Lear's loan to Omni Zoetrope).

March 16, 1981 (Coppola talks of *One from the Heart*).

May 10, 1982 (Emilio Estevez pronounces Coppola sane).

June 7, 1983 (Robert Evans on Coppola's *Cotton Club* script).

January 18, 1984 (Evans on *Cotton Club*).

July 28, 1988 (Hollywood benefit premiere, *Tucker*).

Associated Press dispatch (reprinted in various forms under various titles in *New York Times, San Francisco Chronicle, Variety*), October 4, 1988 (arrests made in Roy Radin murder).

Aziza-Ooka, Dian. Conversation, September 1988 (memories of *City* magazine).

Babitz, Eve. "Francis Ford Coppola." *Coast,* April 1975 (on location with *Godfather II*).

Bach, Stephen:
Final Cut. William Morrow: New York, 1985 (United Artists' management reaction to *Apocalypse Now* delays; role played by Leland Katz; Michael Cimino's relationship to Coppola).

Letter to authors, July 13, 1988 (details of above; United Artists' secret offer to buy Omni Zoetrope).

Baker, Dale. *Movie People.* New York: Lancer, 1973 (interview 1970).

Baker, Russell. "Apocalypse Forever." *New York Times Magazine,* August 16, 1979 (satire).

Balandzich-Rimassa, Milena. "Coping with Coppola." *Performer,* August 1982 (Zoetrope staff reactions to Coppola's response to *One from the Heart* failure).

Balcer, Rene. "A Masterwork: Apocalypse Now." *Cinema Canada,* August 1979.

Ballard, Carroll. Interview, November 1988, and follow-up correspondence (accounts of Coppola from UCLA to the present, including *Finian's Rainbow*, American Zoetrope, the making of *The Black Stallion*, and editing period of *Apocalypse Now*; Omni Zoetrope).

Bart, Peter. "As the Censors Move In." *New York Times*, May 17, 1966 (Coppola's nudies; many inaccuracies).

Bartlett, Scott. Interview, October 1988, and follow-up correspondence (memories of American Zoetrope and Omni Zoetrope; *Interface*).

Baseline (on-line film information service): filmographies of Carmine Coppola, Albert J. Locatelli, as of January 1989.

Beck, Marilyn, Syndicated column, *Los Angeles Herald Examiner*:
> January 29, 1983 (release delay, *The Outsiders*).
> "Coppola Rewriting Puzo's Script." May 6, 1983 (Robert Evans claims credit for re-editing both *Godfather* films).

Bell, Arthur, *Village Voice*:
> "Bell Tells" column. August 20, 1979 (Coppola's New York *Apocalypse Now* press conference).
> "One from the Crotch." April 5, 1983 (on set, the making of *The Outsiders*).
> "Tough Harmonies: Singing Along with Robert Duvall." June 14, 1983 (Duvall recalls presence of "the mob" on *Godfather* set).

Benson, Sheila, *Los Angeles Times*:
> January 22, 1982 (review, *One from the Heart*).
> July 1988 (review, *Tucker*).

Beverly Hills Independent, November 12, 1980, title and author not available (Coppola fires Wim Wenders, may direct *Hammett* himself).

Billboard:
> November 19, 1983 (*Rumble Fish* record album ad).
> October 28, 1984 (Coppola's film exchange with USSR).

Biodrowsky, Steve. "Captain Eo." *Cinefantastique*, May and October 1986 (the making of *Captain Eo*).

Bock, Audie. "Zoetrope and Apocalypse Now." *American Film*, September 1979.

Braudy, Susan, *Atlantic Monthly*:
> "Francis Ford Coppola: A Profile." August 1976 (career interview, especially *Apocalypse Now, Tucker, American Graffiti*, American Zoetrope).
> Letter to the Editor response. October 1976 (answer to letter re *American Graffiti*).

Brown, Peter H., and Jim Pinkston. *Oscar Dearest.* New York: Harper & Row, 1987 (Sacheen Littlefeather's Coppola connection).

Brownlow, Kevin. *Napoleon.* New York: Alfred A. Knopf, 1983.

Buck, Joan Juliet. "Godfather II Probes Family's Roots." *Women's Wear Daily,* June 18, 1974.

Bull, Debby. "Taking Off." *Rolling Stone,* March 14, 1985 (interview with Nicolas Cage; *Cotton Club* data).

Burks, John. Interview, November 1988 (*City* magazine recollections).

Byron, Stuart. "Abel Gance: The Last Romantic." *Village Voice,* January 21, 1981 (*Napoleon*).

Caen, Herb, Column, *San Francisco Chronicle*:

July 13, 1975 (*City* magazine).

San Francisco Chronicle, February 1976 (exact date missing) (demise of *City*).

San Francisco Chronicle, December 18, 1984 (possible foreclosure on Sentinel Building).

Campbell, William (Bill). Interview, November 1988 (*The Young Racers, Dementia 13, The Godfather,* Yugoslav location movie).

Canby, Vincent, *The New York Times*:

"Mayor Renews Filming Pledge." May 17, 1966 (*You're a Big Boy Now* location).

"The Great Library Chase Gets Rolling Here." June 21, 1966 (*Big Boy* shoot).

August 28, 1969 (review, *The Rain People*).

"Patton: Salute to Rebel." February 5, 1970 (review).

"Bravo Brando's Godfather." March 12, 1972 (review).

"Godfather, Part II Is Hard to Define." December 13, 1974 (review).

"Faces of War." August 15, 1979 (review, *Apocalypse Now*).

"The Heart of 'Apocalypse' Is Extremely Misty." August 19, 1979 (Sunday review).

February 11, 1982 (Sunday column, *One from the Heart* review).

May 18, 1982 (review, *The Escape Artist*).

March 25, 1983 (review, *The Outsiders*).

April 8, 1983 (review, *The Outsiders*).

July 1, 1983 (review, *Hammett*).

October 7, 1983 (review, *Rumble Fish*).

December 14, 1984 (review, *The Cotton Club*).

October 5, 1986 (review, *Peggy Sue Got Married*).

May 8, 1987 (review, *Gardens of Stone*).

September 25, 1988 (review, *Tucker*).

Canellow, Peter S. "Coppola's 'Gardens' of Sorrow." *Washington Post*, August 2, 1986 (the making of *Gardens of Stone*; death of Gian-Carlo Coppola).

Carroll, Jon. "Coppola: Bringing in the Next Godfather." *New York*, November 13, 1974 (*Godfather II* edit).

Casper, Stan, esq. Conversation, January 1989 (*Clownhouse* lawsuits, countersuits, criminal charges).

Caulfield, Deborah. "Francis Coppola Sews Up 'Cotton' Directing Job." *Los Angeles Times*, June 10, 1983.

Chaillet, Jean-Paul, and Elizabeth Martin. *Francis Ford Coppola*. New York: St. Martin's Press, 1985 (biographical data drawn from film press booklets; filmography).

Champlin, Charles, *Los Angeles Times*:

"Big Boy: Big with Man on Campus." December 12, 1966 (interview on *You're a Big Boy Now*, plans).

"View." August 1, 1975 (interview on *City*, plans for films, *The Conversation* profit).

"Bad Times Behind, Coppola Dances to a Different Tune." *Los Angeles Times*, August 7, 1988 (interview at release of *Tucker*, retirement plans).

Chase, Chris. "Just a Normal Youth Named O'Neal." June 25, 1982 (*Escape Artist* period interview with Griffin O'Neal).

Chiu, Tony. "Apocalypse Is Finally at Hand." *New York Times*, August 12, 1979 (interview with Coppola on the making of *Apocalypse*, plans for Zoetrope).

Clayton News-Daily, c. March 25, 1987 (review of *Rip Van Winkle*).

Cleveland Plain Dealer, c. March 25, 1987 (review of *Rip Van Winkle*).

Cocks, Jay, *Time*:

"The Godsons." April 3, 1972 (*The Godfather*: followup on actors, violence, mob).

"Ready or Not, Here Comes Gatsby." March 18, 1974 (review).

"Sounds of Silence." April 15, 1974 (review, *The Conversation*).

Coppola, Eleanor:

Notes. New York: Simon and Schuster, 1979 (the making of *Apocalypse Now* from start through editing; Coppola's extramarital affair).

"All That Pizzazz." *Vogue,* December 1984 (interview with Milena Canonero, *Cotton Club* costumer).

Coppola, Francis Ford:

Speech, Directors' Guild of America Tribute to Dorothy Arzner, March 1974.

Termination memo to *City* magazine staff, May 1, 1975.

Letter to the Editor. *Wall Street Journal,* December 14, 1984 (Coppola protests Evans's statements re *Cotton Club*).

Letter to the Editor. *New York Times Magazine,* August 7, 1988 (response to article by Robert Lindsey in July 24, 1988, issue).

Corliss, Richard, *Time*:

"I'm Always in Money Trouble." February 23, 1981 (various views of Coppola's financial problems).

"The New Hollywood: Dead or Alive?" March 30, 1981 (big-budget movies, including *Apocalypse Now*).

"Presenting Fearless Francis!" January 18, 1982 (*One from the Heart* Radio City preview).

"Surrendering to the Big Dream." January 25, 1982 (review, *One from the Heart*).

"Time Bomb." October 24, 1983 (review, *Rumble Fish*).

"Once upon a Time in Harlem." December 17, 1984 (review, *The Cotton Club*).

"Let's Go to the Feelies." September 22, 1986 (report and review, *Captain Eo* premiere).

"Just a Dream." October 13, 1986 (review, *Peggy Sue Got Married*).

Cott, Jonathan. "The Rolling Stone Interview: Francis Coppola." *Rolling Stone,* March 18, 1982 (major interview on feelings of persecution by San Francisco; electronic cinema; *One from the Heart*; studio ownership).

Cowan, Lisa. "The Making of 'Tucker.' " *Lucasfilm Fan Club Newsletter,* February 1988.

Croman, Nathan. "Coppola Gaining Recognition as a First-Class Vintner with Two Wines." *Los Angeles Times,* February 13, 1986.

Crouch, Stanley. "The Rotten Club." *Village Voice,* February 5, 1985 (review and interviews: *The Cotton Club*).

Crowther, Bosley. "Is Paris Burning?" *New York Times*, November 11, 1966 (review).

Cutts, John. "The Dangerous Age." *Films and Filming*, May 1969 (interview with Coppola: childhood through founding of American Zoetrope).

Daly, Michael. "The Making of *The Cotton Club*, a True Tale of Hollywood." *New York*, May 7, 1984 (exhaustive article, including background before Coppola's involvement).

Dane, Peter. Letter to the Editor. *New York*, May 21, 1984 (a *Cotton Club* extra's reaction to Coppola).

Denby, David. *New York*, December 17, 1984 (review, *The Cotton Club*; comments on Coppola).

De Palma, Brian. "The Making of *The Conversation*," *Filmmakers Newsletter*, May 1974 (career interview, youth through *The Conversation*).

Desowitz, Bill. "Cronenweth Reflects on Filming." *Hollywood Reporter*, January 14, 1987 (interview, Jordan Cronenweth, re *Peggy Sue*, *Gardens of Stone*).

Dew, Joan. "Coppola and the Calamities He Can't Refuse." *Los Angeles Times*, March 18, 1973 (on location, *The Conversation*; also, *American Graffiti* data).

Dionne, E. J., Jr. "Madison Wisconsin Goes Hollywood." *New York Times*, March 28, 1980 (Jerry Brown campaign show).

Drama-Logue, December 5, 1979 (news brief: *Hide in Plain Sight, Apocalypse Now, Elective Affinities*).

Easton, Nina, Los Angeles Times:
———. "Richard Gere's Complaints." Reprinted from *San Francisco Chronicle*, October 11, 1988 (*Cotton Club*).

"Is Godfather III Next For Coppola, Paramount." December 19, 1988.

Ehrenstein, David. "*Hammett* Nearly Ended His Career." *Los Angeles Herald-Examiner*, May 17, 1983 (Wim Wenders).

Emerson, Gloria. *Esquire*, August 9, 1979 (review of *Notes*).

Esquire:
"Case Histories of Business Management: Hollywood Artistic Division." November 1977 (Coppola's memo from the Philippines to Zoetrope staff).

"Coppola Hoopla." July 1985 (Coppola's artistic status after several failures).

Everson, William K.:

"The Many Lives of Napoleon." *Film Comment*, January 15, 1981.

"Spirit of Zoetrope Infects Santa Fe." *Weekly Variety*, April 20, 1983 (Coppola at Santa Fe Film Festival tribute).

Eyman, Scott. Telephone interview, October 1988 (historical data, eyewitness report of *Napoleon* Radio City premiere).

Farber, Stephen:

"Coppola and *The Godfather*," *Sight and Sound*, Autumn 1972 (career interview: early history through *Godfather*, including founding of Zoetrope).

"Coppola in Hollywood." *Los Angeles Magazine*, September 23, 1972 (interview: *Finian's Rainbow*, *Godfather*, Zoetrope, Director's Company, publicity).

and Marc Green. "Dynasty California Style." *California*, April 1984 (excerpts from *Hollywood Dynasties*).

"Francis Coppola Sallies into TV on a Fairy Tale." *New York Times*, December 27, 1984 (*Rip Van Winkle*).

and Marc Green. *Hollywood Dynasties*. New York: Putnam, 1984 (intimate details of Coppola family relations: Carmine, Italia, August, Francis, and Eleanor Coppola; Nicolas Cage; Talia Shire; Jack Schwartzman; *Godfather II* Oscars sweep).

Fehr, Rudi. Interview, November 1988 (the making of *One from the Heart*; Coppola and Omni Zoetrope).

Film Comment. "1984 And All That." February 1985 (spoof of Coppola's production delays and overbudgets).

Forbes. "I Got a Look at the Technology." July 6, 1981 (Jack Singer, bailing out Omni Zoetrope).

Forbes. "Birds of a Feather." October 14, 1983 (Coppola's relationship with Sony).

Fosselius, Ernie. Interview, June 19, 1988 (Jerry Brown campaign show).

Furniss, Cathy. "Coppola Doing His 'Thing' via Zoetrope." *Film/TV*, February 13, 1970 (founding of American Zoetrope).

Gage, Nicholas. "A Few Family Murders." *New York Times*, March 19, 1972 (making of *The Godfather*).

Galbraith, Jane. "Captain Eo Gets a Big Blastoff at Disneyland." *Daily Variety*, September 15, 1986.

Gardens of Stone, press booklet, Tri-Star Pictures, 1987.

Garfield, Allen. Interview, October 1988 (making of *The Conversation*; sneak preview of *American Graffiti*; failed plans for theater company; renaming of Little Fox Theater; making of *One from the Heart* and *The Cotton Club*).

Gelmis, Joseph:

The Film Director as Superstar. Garden City, New York: Doubleday, 1970 (interview with Coppola, October 1968).

Various titles. *Newsday*, reprinted *San Francisco Chronicle*, October 5, 1986 (*Peggy Sue* background).

Geng, Veronica. "Mistah Kurtz—He Dead." *New Yorker*, September 3, 1979 (review, *Apocalypse Now*).

Gentleman, Wally. Interview, November 1988 (the making of *One from the Heart*).

Gentry, Ric. "Vittorio Storaro, an Interview." *Post Script*, Fall 1984 (*Apocalypse Now*).

Giles, Sarah, *Fred Astaire, His Friends Talk*. New York: Doubleday 1988 (brief mention, *Finian's Rainbow*).

Ginnane, Antony I., and David Stratton. "Francis Ford Coppola." *Cinema Papers*, November–December 1975 (Coppola's early history; *Godfather II*; *Apocalypse Now*).

Godfather II, press booklet, Paramount Pictures, 1975.

Goodwin, Michael:

City, early April 1974 (review, *The Conversation*).

City, December 1974 (review, *Godfather II*).

Gordon, Jim. "Close-up on Coppola." *The Wine Spectator*, February 28, 1987 (interview: wines, *Peggy Sue Got Married*, financial status).

Grant, Lee:

"Francis Coppola Story." *Los Angeles Times*, February 6, 1981 (press conference, *One from the Heart* financial crisis).

"Coppola—Dreamer and Doer." *Los Angeles Times*, February 9, 1982 (interview: *One from the Heart*, financial problems, Pauline Kael, et al).

Green, Abel. "Yablans Builds Directors Co." *Variety*, August 23, 1972.

Green, Judith. "Tapping Feet, Rattling Guns." *San Jose Mercury News*, c. December 1984 (*The Cotton Club*).

Greenberg, James. "Coppola-Cronenweth Union." *Daily Variety*, February 10, 1987 (*Peggy Sue Got Married* cinematographer).

Grove, Martin A., "Hollywood Report" column, *Hollywood Reporter*:

March 6, 1986 (*Peggy Sue Got Married*, delayed release).

October 2, 1986 (*Peggy Sue* preview).

Gussow, Mel. "Parting Shots: Coppola and Dutch." *New York Times*, March 22, 1984 (*Cotton Club* gags).

Guthman, Edward. " 'Tucker' Tells a Director's Kind of Tale." *San Francisco Chronicle Datebook*, August 7, 1988.

Haller, Scott. "Francis Coppola's Biggest Gamble." *Saturday Review*, July 1981 (*One from the Heart* details).

Harmetz, Aljean. *New York Times*:

"Coppola: Will He Break Even?" March 18, 1980 (*Apocalypse Now* debts).

"Coppola Buys Studio for $6.7 Million." March 21, 1980 (follow-up to above).

"Coppola Risks All on $22 Million Movie." February 2, 1981 (*One from the Heart*).

"For 3-Star O'Neals, Films Are Better Than Ever." February 4, 1981 (*Escape Artist* release story).

"Paramount's $1 Million Saves Coppola's Studio and New Film." February 10, 1981 (*One from the Heart* financial problems).

"Puzo Writing Film on Cotton Club." September 17, 1981.

"Making 'The Outsiders,' A Librarian's Dream." March 23, 1983 (background of film).

" 'Apocalypse Now' to Be Re-released." August 20, 1987.

Harrell, Al. "Gardens of Stone." *American Cinematographer*, May 1987 (cinematographic data).

Harwood, James, *Variety*:

"Grape First Cross Fertilization." August 4, 1975 (John

Fante's *Brotherhood of the Grape* published in *City*, optioned as film).

"Coppola Shuns Million-$-a-Week Star." February 11, 1976 (casting, *Apocalypse Now*).

Haskell, Molly, *Village Voice*:

September 25, 1969 (review, *The Rain People*).

"The Corleone Saga Sags." April 19, 1975 (review, *Godfather II*).

Healy, Michael. " 'Apocalypse Now'—Again." *Los Angeles Daily News*, August 30, 1987 (re-release of film).

Herscher, Elaine. "Movie Company Sues Boy Actor from Concord." *San Francisco Chronicle*, March 16, 1988 (*Clownhouse* problems, Roman Coppola, producer).

Higham, Charles,:

"Directors' Guild Winner: Francis Ford Coppola." *Action*, May–June 1973.

"Coppola's Vietnam Movie Is a Battle Royal." *New York Times*, May 15, 1977.

Hill, Jack. Interview, October 1988, and follow-up correspondence (UCLA period, nudies, Corman period, *Apocalypse Now*).

Hoberman, J. *Village Voice*, May 19, 1987 (review, *Gardens of Stone*).

Hofstra Report. "Alumnus Coppola Still Sparks Creative Fires." October 1975.

Hollywood Reporter: newsbriefs, various authors, or no byline:

May 19, 1965 (*Patton* script begun).

January 6, 1966 (*Patton* script finished).

December 2, 1966 (*You're a Big Boy Now* completed).

July 28, 1967 (five-picture deal for Warners, *The Conversation*).

April 11, 1975 (Coppola ballyhoos *Godfather II* as art film).

March 1, 1976 (advertisement notifying principal cast of *Apocalypse Now* of their casting).

January 2, 1980 (bid on Denham Studios, England).

January 4, 1980 (Coppola plants tree at new studio).

March 21, 1980 (Zoetrope staffing and projects).

"Zoetrope Honeymoon Wakes Up to Monday Reality." February 9, 1981 (financial problems).

February 11, 1981 (*Interface*; Zoetrope financial problems).

February 20, 1981 (*Napoleon* profits).

March 31, April 7, April 17, 1981 (bid on Pinewood Studios).

July 9, 1981 (details of Hollywood General purchase).

August 4, 1981 (Coppola's attempt to buy Manhattan annex for Zoetrope).

February 10, 1982 (Coppola addresses National Press Club, scolds journalists).

"Coppola: Another Defeat; WGA Says No 'Outsiders' Credit." June 25, 1982.

February 4, 1983 (details of Zoetrope sale).

December 19, 1984 (Orion investment, *Cotton Club*).

December 21, 1984 (*Peggy Sue* production history).

January 18, 1985 (*Cotton Club* grosses).

October 28, 1985 (*Peggy Sue* completion).

circa March 25, 1987 (review of *Rip Van Winkle*).

May 19, 1987 (*Tucker* distribution deal).

Holzinger, Eric. Interview, December 1988 (background data re August Coppola at San Francisco State University).

Honeycutt, Kirk. "Francis Coppola Drifts Away from His Talent." *Los Angeles Daily News*, April 15, 1983 (career analysis: *Godfather, One from the Heart, The Outsiders*).

Hopkins, Charles A. "Day Two of 'Tucker.'" *San Francisco Chronicle*, July 31, 1988 (an extra's experiences).

Houston Chronicle, c. March 25, 1987 (review of *Rip Van Winkle*).

Hunter, Tim. "The Making of *Hammett*." *New West*, September 22, 1980.

Jameson, Richard T. "One from Coppola." *Film Comment*, May–June 1981 (Seattle preview of unfinished *One from the Heart*).

Johnson, Robert K. *Francis Ford Coppola*. Boston: Twayne, 1977 (high school).

Kael, Pauline. "The Current Cinema." *The New Yorker*, film reviews:

October 19, 1968 (*Finian's Rainbow*).

January 31, 1970 (*Patton*).

March 18, 1972 (*The Godfather*).
April 15, 1974 (*The Conversation*).
December 23, 1974 (*Godfather II*).
February 1, 1982 (*One from the Heart*).
June 14, 1982 (*The Escape Artist*).
January 7, 1985 (*Cotton Club*).
May 18, 1987 (*Gardens of Stone*).

Karman, Mal. "Carroll Ballard Never Cries Wolf." *San Francisco*, January 1984 (interview with Ballard; includes *The Black Stallion*).

Kass, Carole. "Inside Stuff on George C. Scott's Bias Against *Patton* Script." *Weekly Variety*, March 10, 1971.

Katz, Leland. Letter to authors, June 24, 1988 (*Apocalypse Now* visits to set, responsibilities).

Kauffman, Stanley. *New Republic*, January 18, 1975 (review, *Godfather II*).

Kearney, Jill:
    "The Road Warrior." *American Film*, June 1988 (on-set, *Tucker*).
    "Francis Ford Coppola." *Mother Jones*, September 1988 (on-set, *Tucker*; interview; retirement plans).

Kelly, Gene. Letter to the Editor. *American Film*, January 1982 (*One from the Heart*; Kelly clarifies he wasn't choreographer).

Kennedy, William. "William Kennedy's Cotton Club Stomp." *Vanity Fair*, November 1984.

Kilday, Gregg (see also Rainer, Peter). "Those Poor 'Orphan' Films." *Los Angeles Herald-Examiner*, October 15, 1982 (*Hammett*, et al, delayed release).

King, Larry, with Peter Occhiogrosso. *Tell It to the King*, New York: G. P. Putnam's Sons, 1988 (*Apocalypse Now*: Brando's reaction).

Klein, Judy E. "Coppola Makes Rumble Fish—the Coppola Way." *Boxoffice*, November 1983.

Knickerbocker, Paine. "A Crisp, Smart ACT Comedy." *San Francisco Chronicle*, February 24, 1972 (review, *Private Lives*).

Koszarski, Richard. "The Youth of F. F. Coppola." *Films in Review*, November 1968 (based on an interview broadcast on WVHC-FM, the radio station of Hofstra University, in April 1968) (interview, childhood to *The Rain People*).

Kroll, Jack, *Newsweek*:

    "Coppola's War Epic." August 20, 1979 (review, *Apocalypse Now*).

    "Coppola's Teen-Age Inferno." November 7, 1983 (review, *Rumble Fish*).

    "Harlem on My Mind." December 24, 1984 (review, *The Cotton Club*).

Landsen, Pamela. "Take One." *People*, January 9, 1989 (Coppola moving to Italy).

Latham, Aaron. "The Movie Man Who Plays God." *Life*, August 1981 (on-set, *One from the Heart*).

Levin, G. Roy. "Francis Coppola Discusses *Apocalypse Now*." *Millimeter*, October 1979. (full transcription, Cannes press conference after *Apocalypse Now*).

Lichtenstein, Grace. "Godfather Film Won't Mention Mafia." *New York Times*, March 20, 1971.

Life, December 1984 (on-set, *The Cotton Club*, photo feature).

Lindsey, Robert:

    "Coppola Returns to the Vietnam Era, Minus Apocalypse." *New York Times*, May 3, 1987.

    "Promises to Keep." *New York Times Sunday Magazine*, July 24, 1988 (interview: *Peggy Sue*; *Tucker*; *Life with Zoe* segment of *New York Stories*; finances, plans).

    "Martin Landau Rolls Up in a New Vehicle." *New York Times*, August 7, 1988 (*Tucker*).

Lipson, Larry. "Latest Coppola Production Needs Time." *L.A. Life, Los Angeles Daily News*, July 17, 1985 (wine review).

London, Michael, *Los Angeles Times*:

    "Court Says Evans Should Control." June 19, 1984 (*Cotton Club* lawsuits).

    "Judge Puts a Patch on 'Cotton' Suit." June 20, 1984.

Look. November 3, 1970 (American Zoetrope).

Los Angeles Herald-Examiner: news items, various bylines, wire service, or no byline:

    December 15, 1969 (opening, American Zoetrope).

    February 23, 1976 (casting of *Apocalypse Now*).

    April 17, 1978 (San Francisco *Apocalypse* preview).

May 13, 1979 (Los Angeles *Apocalypse* work-in-progress screening).

May 22, 1979 (Cannes *Apocalypse* screening and press conference).

December 19, 1979 (press conference, London, criticizing journalists).

February 18, 1980 (snafu in purchase of Hollywood Studios).

March, 7, March 8, 1980 (Coppola named to California Arts Council).

March 21, 1980 (history of Hollywood General).

January 6, 1981 (defection of German *One from the Heart* investors).

February 3, 1981 (Zoetrope layoffs).

February 7, 1981 (Zoetrope workers work for deferred pay).

February 21, 1981 (Zoetrope payroll crisis).

April 21, 1981 (Coppola and Joseph Papp plan *Pirates of Penzance* film).

"Coppola Unbound." March 16, 1982 (*Outsiders* distribution deal).

May 13, 1982 (*Escape Artist* reshoots).

"Robert Evans Presents: Getting High on Yourself, Part II." December 7, 1982 (*Cotton Club* background).

January 29, 1983 (*Outsiders* production details).

March 29, 1983 (*Outsiders* opens).

"Big Guns Bomb-Out at Lincoln Center." October 10, 1983 (*Rumble Fish* premiere, New York).

"Coppola's First TV Series." November 9, 1983 (*Outsiders* TV plans).

May 31, 1984 (*Cotton Club* lawsuits).

June 4, 1984 (*Cotton* finances).

August 14, 1984 (*Cotton* suits).

October 16, 1984 (*Cotton Club* sneak previews).

Ibid. (Coppola courted to helm *Peggy Sue*).

November 27, 1984 (*Cotton Club* production details).

December 31, 1984 (Sentinel Building foreclosure).

January 10, 1985 (*Cotton Club* actress sues).

February 12, 1985 (casting *Peggy Sue*).

July 10, 1985 (Coppola to host opening of Primi).

February 17, 1986 (*Cotton Club* grosses).

November 21, 1986; March 4, 1987 (Griffin O'Neal charged and sentenced to two years' probation for marijuana possession and reckless driving in Beverly Hills).

December 17, 1986; February 28, 1987 (Griffin O'Neal trial and sentencing in Gian-Carlo Coppola death).

May 28, 1987 (Coppola sues Griffin O'Neal for child support).

October 27, et al, 1988 (several dates, Roy Radin murder arrests and follow-up).

Los Angeles Magazine. December 1984 (*Cotton Club* production).

Los Angeles Reader. March 9, 1984 (Zoetrope prop auction).

Los Angeles Times: news items, various bylines, wire services, or no bylines:

"Coppola to Direct Opera." March 16, 1972.

December 7 and December 21, 1975 (*City* magazine failure).

March 10, 1976 (*Apocalypse* casting).

April 19, 1976 (interview, Harvey Keitel, re *Apocalypse* firing).

January 39, 1979 (*Hammett*).

April 30, 1979 (*Hide in Plain Sight*).

"R.M." May 22, 1979 (*Apocalypse* Cannes press conference).

March 5, 1980 (history of Hollywood General Studios).

March 21, 1980 (press conference, opening of Omni Zoetrope).

April 7, 1980 (Jerry Brown campaign show).

June 30, 1980 (Napa Valley vineyard party).

"Zoetrope Workers Vote to Carry On," February 7, 1981.

February 11, 1981 (Jon Davison returns to Paramount).

"Zoetrope Dream Over," April 9, 1982.

May 7, 1982 (Brando sues for *Apocalypse* payment).

May 12, 1982 (bidders on Omni Zoetrope Studio).

"Coppola, Gere Set to Team Up." June 10, 1983.

October 5, 1983 (*Cotton* production suspended).

October 6, 1983 (production resumes).

March 5, 1984 (*Cotton* reshoots).

" 'Garage Sale' Turns a Profit for Studio." March 11, 1984 (Zoetrope props auction).

June 15, 1984 (*Cotton* lawsuits, production details, rough cut).

October 16, 1984 (*Cotton Club* sneak previews, costs).

December 12, 1984 (*Cotton* sneaks, costs).

December 23, 1984 (Diane Lane on Coppola; additional item, *Cotton Club* budget).

February 13, 1985 (*Peggy Sue* change of casting).

December 19, 1986 (trial of Griffin O'Neal).

February 28, 1987 (Griffin O'Neal's convictions and sentences, several charges).

April 27, 1987 (O'Neal begins serving sentence).

August 5, 1988 (*Tucker*).

October 17, 1988 (follow-up on Roy Radin murder arrests).

Love, Gael, and Andy Warhol. "Diane Lane." *Interview*, November 1984 (*Cotton Club*).

Loynd, Roy. " 'Cotton' Armistice Turns into a Love-Knot of Sorts." *Daily Variety*, August 15, 1984 (conclusion of first-round *Cotton Club* lawsuits for control of the picture).

Madsen, Axel:

"Coppola Breaks the Age Barrier." *Los Angeles Times*, January 2, 1966 (interview: *Dementia 13, Patton*; future plans).

The New Hollywood, New York: Thomas Crowell, 1975 (evaluation and interview, *Dementia 13* through *Godfather II*).

Mann, Roderick. "Lane Rides Out Cotton Club." *Los Angeles Times*, December 23, 1984.

Marcus, Greil. "Journey up the River." *Rolling Stone*, November 1, 1979 (major interview, including Hitler, Roger Corman, Marlon Brando, critics, plans, centering on *Apocalypse Now*).

Maremaa, Thomas. "Celluloid Dreams, Childhood's End." *Penthouse*, May 1974 (interview; details of childhood and early life, *Patton* through *The Conversation*, interview with George Lucas).

Maslin, Janet, *New York Times,* film reviews:
October 13, 1979 (*Black Stallion*).
October 7, 1983 (*Rumble Fish*).
August 12, August 21, 1988 (*Tucker*).
"Cotton Club Ad Blitz." *New York Times,* November 30, 1984.

Mayer, John. Interview, November 1988 (UCLA period; details, *Ayamonn Mourneen*; various later contacts).

Mayo, Michael. "Interface." *Cinefantastique,* December–January, 1983–84.

McBride, Joseph:

"Milius Re-Heats His Apocalypse." *Daily Variety,* September 3, 1975 (interview with John Milius).

"Coppola Inc." *American Film,* November 1975 (interview: *Godfather, Apocalypse,* John Milius, *City* magazine).

Film Makers on Film Making, Vol. 2, Los Angeles: J. P. Tarcher, 1983 (Robert Towne on the *Godfather* script, from American Film Institute symposium).

McCarthy, Todd:

"Coppola's Rescue Spotlights Calgary's Megabuck Clan." *Daily Variety,* March 4, 1981 (Jack Singer).

"Coppola Scouts Belize as Future Site of Electronic Wonder Studio." *Daily Variety,* December 16, 1981 (interview re Belize).

"Actor Forrest Gives Heart to Coppola Films." *Variety,* February 8, 1982 (interview with Forrest).

June 25, 1982 (review, *Tonight for Sure* [nudie compendium], byline "Cart").

McCreadie, Marsha. *American Film.* September 1979 (review, Eleanor Coppola's *Notes*).

McCree, Cree. "The Trials of Griffin O'Neal." *US Magazine,* October 16, 1986 (death of Gian-Carlo Coppola).

McDonough, Tom. "I Am a Camera." *American Film,* May 1986. (interview with Gordon Willis on *Godfather,* with comments on electronic cinema).

McGee, Mark Thomas. *Roger Corman.* New York: McFarland, 1988 (Coppola's Corman period).

McGilligan, Pat. "Coppola on the Beat." *Films and Filming,* December 1981 (electronic cinema; delay in *One from the Heart* completion).

Medjuck, Joe. Interview, December 1988 (movie business details, including "movie money," options, script of *Peggy Sue Got Married*).

Michener, Charles. "Finally, Apocalypse Now." *Newsweek*, May 28, 1979.

Miller, Dick. Interview, October 1988 (the making of *The Terror*).

Milwaukee Sentinel, c. March 25, 1987 (review of *Rip Van Winkle*).

Monaco, James:

    American Film Now. New York: Oxford University Press, 1979 (analysis, Coppola's career through *Apocalypse*).

    Who's Who in American Film Now, New York: New York Zoetrope, 1981 (directory/filmographies).

Monson, Karen. "Coppola Directs American Premiere of 'The Visit' " *Los Angeles Herald-Examiner*, October 31, 1972.

Morgenstern, Joseph. *Newsweek*, film reviews:

    November 21, 1966 (*Is Paris Burning?*).

    "A National Anthem." February 20, 1967 (*You're a Big Boy Now*, plus interview with Coppola covering nudies, Hitler, scripts, plans).

    October 21, 1968 (*Finian's Rainbow*).

    September 8, 1969 (*The Rain People*).

    February 16, 1970 (*Patton*).

Moriarty, Donna. "Apocalypse Then." *San Francisco Bay Guardian*, August 16, 1979 (crew member's wife, on-set in the Philippines).

Mottley, Bob. "Two Godfathers." *New Times*, May 3, 1974 (*Godfather II*, on location, career interview).

Moviegoer, March 1983 (Michael Smuin's work in *Rumble Fish*).

Mulcahy, Susan. "This World." *San Francisco Chronicle*, July 10, 1983 (*Cotton Club* financing).

Murch, Walter. Interview, December 1988, and follow-up correspondence (memories of Coppola from *The Rain People* to the present, especially *THX-1138, The Conversation, The Black Stallion, Apocalypse Now*, and visit to set of *One from the Heart*).

Murray, William. "Playboy Interview: Francis Ford Coppola." *Playboy*, July 1975 (career interview, through start of

Apocalypse Now, at time of *Godfather II* Oscars).

Myles, Lynda. "Zoetrope Saga." *Sight and Sound,* June 1982 (*Hammett, One from the Heart,* Omni Zoetrope financial problems). See also Pye, Michael.

Nachman, Gerald. "Coppola of Zoetrope—Older, Wiser and Poorer." *Los Angeles Times Calendar,* November 7, 1971 (financial failure of American Zoetrope, S.F.).

Naha, Ed. *Roger Corman: Brilliance on a Budget.* New York: Arco, 1982 (Coppola's Corman years).

Natale, Richard. "Jazz Design." *Los Angeles Herald-Examiner,* undated, December 1984/January 1985 (interview with *Cotton Club* production designer Richard Sylbert, including comments on Coppola).

New West, no byline:

August 15, 1977 (Newsbrief, *Black Stallion* production).

March 26, 1979 (Newsbrief, Coppola turns down *One from the Heart* for MGM).

"Citizen Coppola." July 12, 1979 (unnamed Zoetrope source talks of Coppola's "manic state of mind" and "moguling it up").

New York magazine, various authors or no byline:

July 11, 1975 (Warren Hinckle's *City* magazine).

January 26, 1976 (*City* turned over to Eleanor Coppola).

August 30, 1982 (*Outsiders* script arbitration).

New York Times, news items, various authors, wire services, or no byline:

October 28, 1968 (South Africa bans *Finian's Rainbow*).

March 20, 1971 (Al Ruddy agrees not to use the word "Mafia").

March 23, 1971 (editorial criticism of Al Ruddy).

March 26, 1972 (Robert Evans re Gatsby script).

"Profits of *The Godfather.*" April 16, 1972.

"Notes on People." April 26, 1972 (visiting Soviets discuss *The Godfather*).

"Sicily Gets Hollywood Version of the Godfather." October 13, 1972.

July 7, 1974 (Plans for *Apocalypse Now*).
April 23, 1982 (*Too Far to Go* opens).
June 8, 1985 (Background, *Captain Eo*).
Newsweek, news items and reviews, no byline:
"The Sneaking of 'Apocalypse.' " May 21, 1979.
"After Apocalypse." December 24, 1979 (Brief interview: Coppola's plans for Omni Zoetrope; quote from unnamed Zoetrope staffer).
"Coppola's Cash Crunch." January 23, 1983.
May 23, 1983 (Coppola talks of Belize).

Oakland Tribune, c. March 25, 1987 (review of *Rip Van Winkle*).
Oliansky, Joel. Interview, October 1988 (Coppola at Hofstra, Seven Arts, and after).
Oney, Steve. "Coppola's 'Tucker.' " *Premiere*, August 1988 (on-set and background).
Onosko, Tim. "Media Madness." *Village Voice*, April 21, 1980 (Jerry Brown campaign show, in detail).
Ornstein, Bill. "Francis Coppola to Make Only Own Stories in Future." *Hollywood Reporter*, August 12, 1968.
Orth, Maureen, *Newsweek*:
"The New Hollywood"; "Godfather of the Movies." November 25, 1974 (career interview, from childhood to *Apocalypse Now* start, centering on *Godfather II*).
"Watching the 'Apocalypse.' " June 13, 1977 (on-set report).
Osborne, David. "Two Who Made a Revolution." *San Francisco*, March 1982 (Coppola and George Lucas career and personality analysis; interviews with associates).
Outsiders, The, press booklet, Warner Brothers, 1983.

Paris Match. "Francis Coppola." January 18, 1985 Trans. Naomi Wise. (a French magazine staffer asks Coppola his thoughts on sex and romance).
Pearce, Christopher. "San Francisco's Own American Zoetrope." *American Cinematographer*, October 1971.
Peer, Elizabeth, with William J. Cook. "City Slickers." *Newsweek*, September 1, 1975 (*City* magazine under M. Parrish).

Peggy Sue Got Married, press booklet, Tri-Star Pictures, 1987.

People:

November 12, 1979 (*Apocalypse* costs; Coppola criticizes journalists).

August 11, 1986. (death of Gian-Carlo Coppola).

Pileggi, Nicolas. "The Making of *The Godfather*." *Readers Digest,* February 1972 (details on deal with "the mob").

Playboy:

August 1982 (on-set, *The Escape Artist,* brief report).

"20 Questions: Diane Lane." January 1985 (post–*Cotton Club* interview).

Pollock, Dale:

"Has Coppola Won Battle for Studio?" *Los Angeles Times,* March 5, 1980 (purchase of Hollywood General).

Skywalking, the Life and Films of George Lucas, New York: Harmony Books, 1983 (Lucas's relations with Coppola over the years).

"When George and Francis Were Friends." *Esquire,* May 1983 (Lucas and Coppola relations).

"Trouble at the Cotton Club." *Los Angeles Times,* December 4, 1983.

"Cotton Club Rift Mended." *Los Angeles Times,* August 15, 1984.

"Coppola The Artist: 'I Think I'm a Threat." *Los Angeles Times,* December 23, 1984.

Powers, John. "One from the Hearth," *California,* August 1988 (review, *Tucker*).

Prial, Frank. Wine column. *New York Times,* December 14, 1988 (prestige of Coppola's winery).

Pye, Michael, and Lynda Myles. *The Movie Brats.* New York: Holt, Rinehart and Winston, 1979, chapter on Francis Ford Coppola (brief biography, through production of *Apocalypse Now*).

Quincy Patriot-Ledger, c. March 25, 1987 (review of *Rip Van Winkle*).

Rafferty, Terrence. *The New Yorker,* August 22, 1988 (review, *Tucker*).

Rainer, Peter, and Gregg Kilday. "Apocalypse Soon." *Los Angeles Herald-Examiner*, March 7, 1982 (discussions of Coppola's behavior at *One from the Heart*'s failure).

Rawlins, Lisa. "The Runaway Production That Never Left Home." *Hollywood Reporter*, December 16, 1986 (*Peggy Sue Got Married* location choices).

Reed, Rex. "Offering the Moon to a Guy in Jeans." *New York Times*, August 8, 1966 (early interview).

Reveaux, Anthony. "Stephen H. Burum, ASC, and 'Rumble Fish.' " *American Cinematographer*, May 1984.

Rich, Frank, *Time*:

"The Making of a Quagmire." August 27, 1979 (review, *Apocalypse Now*).

"A Ride on a Dream Horse." *Time*, December 10, 1979 (review, *The Black Stallion*).

Riley, Brooks, *Film Comment*:

"Heart Transplant." September 1979 (comparison of Milius and Coppola scripts, *Apocalypse Now*).

"Film into Video." May–June 1982 (Coppola re electronic cinema, high-definition television).

Robb, David, for *Daily Variety* (except as noted):

"Coppola's Zoetrope Studios Facing Foreclosure and Possible Public Auction." January 6, 1983.

Follow-up stories on same subject by same author: January 18, January 20, March 3, March 10, March 15, March 18, April 18, April 19, April 29, May 23, June 16, August 31, September 20, September 29, October 7, October 12, October 26, October 27, December 29, 1983.

"Zoetrope Presents." *Weekly Variety*, March 23, 1983 (Zoetrope distribution of *Grey Fox*, *Koyaanisqatsi*, *Passion*, *Perfumed Nightmare*, three Chinese classics).

"Zoetrope Prez Resigns, HQ Moves to SF." October 20, 1983.

"Singer Buys Zoetrope Lot for $12.3M." February 13, 1984.

Follow-up story March 7, 1984.

Rockwell, John. "My Own Little City, My Own Little Opera." *The Saturday Review*, December 2, 1972. (interview, Coppola as opera director; *The Godfather*; Retirement plans).

Rolling Stone. September 16, 1982 (production details, *The Outsiders*).

Rosen, Marjorie. "Francis Ford Coppola." *Film Comment*, July 1974 (career interview: nudies, *Rain People, Gatsby, Conversation, Godfather II*).

Ross, Daniel, Mary A. Nelson, and Paul Jacobs. "Cotton Club." *US* magazine, February 13, 1984.

Ross, Lillian. "Some Figures on a Fantasy." *The New Yorker*, November 8, 1982 (detailed report, *One from the Heart* financial debacle).

Ruddy, Al. Interview, October 1988 (*The Godfather*, deals and production).

Rumble Fish press booklet, Universal Pictures, 1983.

St. Petersburg Times, c. March 25, 1987 (review of *Rip Van Winkle*).

Salamon, Julie. "Budget Busters: 'The Cotton Club's' Battle of the Bulge." *Wall Street Journal*, December 13, 1984.

Salmans, Sandra. "Cotton Club Is Neither a Smash nor a Disaster." *New York Times*, December 20, 1984 (brief interviews, Coppola and Robert Evans; box office for first weekend).

San Francisco Chronicle, news items—no byline, or wire service:

Television listing. *Dementia 13*, August 10, 1975.

"Newest Chapter in Zoetrope Saga." March 3, 1985 (auction of studio postponed).

July 23, 1988 (Benefit premiere, *Tucker*).

"Four Charged with Murder." Associated Press, October 4, 1988 (Roy Radin murder).

"Ryan O'Neal's Son Accused of Violating His Probation." November 30, 1988 (UPI dispatch).

"Griffin O'Neal Gets 18-Day Jail Term for Violating Probation." January 21, 1989 (UPI dispatch).

Santa Fe Film Festival Brochure. "Spirit of Zoetrope," April 8, 1983.

Sarris, Andrew. "Films in Focus." *The Village Voice*, film reviews:

November 7, 1968 (*Finian's Rainbow*).

February 26, 1970 (*Patton*).

March 16, March 23, 1972 (*The Godfather*).

"Postscript from Cannes." June 6, June 13, June 20, 1974 (*The Conversation*).

"First Assault on Apocalypse." May 28, 1979 (*Apocalypse Now*, including press conference, Cannes).

"Riding on Coppola's Rollercoaster." January 27, 1982 (*One from the Heart*).

"Dare We Render unto Wenders That Which Is Coppola's?" July 12, 1983 (*Hammett*).

"Teenage Teorema and Flash-Dance Football." October 15, 1983 (*Rumble Fish*).

October 21, 1986 (*Peggy Sue Got Married*).

Sayre, Nora. "A Grim 'Conversation.' " *New York Times*, April 8, 1974 (review).

Schickel, Richard:

"Growing Up Frantic in Cloud Cuckooland." *Life*, March 24, 1967 (review, *You're A Big Boy Now*).

Time, August 15, 1988 (review, *Tucker*).

Schloss, Hank. Interview, November 1988 (UCLA film school faculty recalls Coppola as student).

School Daze press booklet, Columbia Pictures, 1988 (Larry Fishburne remembers *Apocalypse* shoot).

Schreger, Charles. "Coppola and Kelly Singin' in the Sun." *Los Angeles Times*, October 8, 1980.

Scott, Jay, *American Film*:

"Father Francis in Boys' Town." April 1983 (making of *The Outsiders*).

"He Who Treads on the Tiger's Tail." March 1985 (making of *Mishima*; Coppola as star of Japanese TV ads).

Screen International. September 26, 1981 (*Cotton Club* production details).

Seale, Jim. "Growing Up Tough." *Marquee*, September–October 1982 (*Outsiders* shoot).

Searles, Jack. "Two More Megaton Bombs Hit Hollywood." *Los Angeles Herald-Examiner*, February 17, 1985 (*Cotton Club* box office).

Sharpe, Mal. Conversation, November 1988 (personal observations of Coppola in action).

Short, Martin. "The Mob and the Movies," *Stills*, March 1986 (touches on *Godfather* films and *Cotton Club*).

Simons, Dan:

" 'Rain People' by the Rule Breaker." *Los Angeles*

Times, September 7, 1969 (interview with young Coppola).

"Cinema San Francisco Style." *Entertainment World*, March 27, 1970 (American Zoetrope).

Skow, John. "Going for the Cheeky Gamble." *Time*, January 15, 1982 (*One from the Heart* Radio City preview).

Smith, Liz:

"Yet More Rumbling on the 'Cotton Club' Front." Syndicated column. *San Francisco Chronicle*, October 7, 1983.

Syndicated column. *New York Daily News*, November 14, 1983 (*Cotton* concatenations).

Smith, R. Sue. "Rumble Fish." *Movie Magazine*, Summer 1983.

Sragow, Michael:

"The Case of the Parboiled Private Eye." *Rolling Stone*, October 14, 1982 (first national review, *Hammett*).

"George Lucas' Car Wars." *San Francisco Examiner*, July 31, 1988 (interview with Lucas, release of *Tucker*).

Stack, Peter. "Sexy Film Star with Four Wheels." *San Francisco Chronicle*, July 13, 1987 (feature on *Tucker*).

Stone, Judy. "Coppola Has 'Heart' Trouble." *San Francisco Chronicle*, August 21, 1981 (exhibitors' screening, *One from the Heart*).

Suid, Lawrence. "Hollywood and Vietnam." *Film Comment*, September 1979 (U.S. military reaction to *Apocalypse Now* script).

Swertlow, Frank. "Mr. Cotton Club." *Los Angeles Herald Examiner*, "Page 2," October 14, 1983 (Robert Evans talks of *Cotton Club*).

Tabet, Sylvio. Letter to the Editor. *New York* magazine, July 23, 1984 (*Cotton Club* shoot).

Talese, Gay. "The Conversation." *Esquire*, July 1981 (Coppola criticizes journalists, defends *One from the Heart*).

Taylor, Clarke. "Production Suspended on Cotton Club." *Los Angeles Times*, October 5, 1983.

Thomas, Bob. "Coppola to Get Another Roll of the Dice." *Los Angeles Herald-Examiner*, June 17, 1983 (Zoetrope foreclosure postponement; interview with Coppola).

Thompson, David and Lucy Gray. "Idols of the King." *Film*

Comment, October 1983 (career interview during *Cotton Club* shoot; data on *Outsiders, Rumble Fish,* plans to place Zoetrope atop Chrysler Building; criticism of journalism; retirement plans).

Thomson, David:

"The Man Has Legs." *Film Comment,* March–April 1985 (interview with William Kennedy; *Cotton Club* details).

California, November 1986 (review, *Peggy Sue Got Married*).

California, June 1987 (review, *Gardens of Stone,* with reference to *Apocalypse Now*).

Thompson, Howard. "Growing Pains." *New York Times,* March 21, 1967 (review, *You're a Big Boy Now*).

Time, no byline given:

"Bang-I-Gotcha." November 25, 1966 (review, *Is Paris Burning?*).

"Growing Up Absurd." February 3, 1967 (review, *You're a Big Boy Now*).

"Instant Old Age." October 25, 1968 (review, *Finian's Rainbow*).

"Old Blood and Guts." February 9, 1970 (review, *Patton*).

"Citizen Coppola." June 30, 1975 (*City* magazine).

May 17, 1982 (brief review, *Too Far to Go*).

June 15, 1987 (brief review, *Gardens of Stone*).

Tuchman, Mitch, and Anne Thompson. "I'm the Boss." *Film Comment,* July–August 1981 (interview, George Lucas, with comments on Coppola).

Tucker, press booklet, Paramount Pictures, 1988.

Turnquist, Kristin. "Grape Expectations." *Newsweek,* November 1985 (Coppola's wines).

TV Guide, March 2, 1985 (Shelley Duvall on *Rip Van Winkle*).

U.S. News and World Report, "A Conversation with Francis Coppola." April 5, 1982 (Coppola proposes government by artists).

Vallely, Jean. "Martin Sheen, Heart of Darkness, Heart of Gold." *Rolling Stone*, November 1, 1979 (post–*Apocalypse Now* interview with Sheen; comments from crew members).

Variety, Daily: (See also: Albarino, Richard; Archerd, Army; Harwood, Jim; Loynd, Ray; McBride, Joseph; McCarthy, Todd; Robb, David, et al.) News articles by various authors, wire services, or no byline:

March 17, 1967 (Coppola receives M.F.A. degree; *Big Boy* is thesis film).

September 24, 1969 (union concessions to American Zoetrope).

February 3, 1971 (Brando cast as Don Corleone).

February 24, 1971 (*Godfather* preproduction problems).

"Coppola Directs Private Lives." January 26, 1972.

August 8, 1973 (DeNiro set for *Godfather II*; Brando refuses role; *American Graffiti* opens; *Gatsby* completed).

October 1, 1973 (*Godfather II* starts shooting).

January 16, 1974 (*Graffiti* grosses).

January 26, 1974 (Golden Globes).

February 6, 1974 (Pacino with pneumonia, *Godfather II*).

March 27, 1974 (*Gatsby* opens, New York City).

May 29, 1974 (*Conversation* awards).

"God II Completes 8 Months of Photography." June 19, 1974.

"An NBC-TV Offer Par Couldn't Refuse," July 31, 1974 (*Godfather* TV saga).

December 18, 1974 (*Godfather II* personnel payments; grosses).

December 20, 1974 (*Conversation* awards).

January 1, 1975 (*Conversation* and *Godfather II* awards, grosses).

January 8, 1975 (1974 rentals).

January 23, January 29, 1975 (Cinema V deal).

February 26, 1975 (*Godfather II* Oscar nominations).

March 19, 1975 (*Godfather II* Directors' Guild award).

April 16, 1975 (Oscars awarded).

May 29, 1975 (Cinema 7 projects).

June 6, 1975 (UCLA honors Coppola).

October 25, 1975 (Coppola visits Fidel Castro).

January 7, 1976 (yearly and all-time rentals).

"Hopes for City Come a Cropper as Mag Folds." February 12, 1976.

February 18, 1976 (*City* demise).

March 1, 1976 (advertisement notifying principal cast of *Apocalypse Now* of their casting).

March 9 and 10, 1976 (casting of *Apocalypse Now*; long-term acting contracts; plans).

April 19, 1976 (firing of Harvey Keitel, *Apocalypse*).

May 5, 1976 (Martin Sheen replaces Keitel).

May 12, 1976 (*Conversation* bombs in Paris).

July 7, 1976 (Pentagon uncooperative with *Apocalypse*).

"Coppola Hocks Assets to U.A. for Apocalypse." June 6, 1977.

May 7, 1979 (Coppola at White House barbecue).

May 14, 1979 (*Apocalypse* work-in-progress premiere).

May 15, 1979 (review, *Apocalypse Now*).

May 16, 1979 (Hollywood General negotiations).

May 29, 1979 (*Variety* justifies reviewing *Apocalypse* "work in progress" screening).

August 13, August 15, 1979 (two endings for *Apocalypse*).

August 29, 1979 (*Apocalypse* plays Moscow).

September 5, 1979 (Coppola's plans: *Hammett, Tucker*).

December 11, 1979 (*Our Hitler* screens, New York).

February 1, 1980 (*Apocalypse* awards, ad campaign).

March 5, 1980 (Hollywood General purchase).

March 20, March 26, March 27, April 2, 1980 (Jerry Brown campaign show).

May 12, June 4, 1980 (Coppola to direct *One from the Heart*).

May 21, July 30, 1980 (*Kagemusha*, Coppola-Lucas executive producers).

July 16, 1980 (Coppola-Godard plans).

November 21, 1980 (*Apocalypse* TV sale plans).

January 12, 1981 (Godard arrives in LA).

"High-Roller Coppola Gambles Studio on Future of Electronic Cinema." February 5, 1981.

February 11, 1981 (Zoetrope finances and layoffs; *Interface*).

February 20, 1981 (*Napoleon* profits; Jack Singer loan).

August 24, 1981 (SF exhibitors' screening, *One from the Heart*, and press coverage).

September 26, 1981 (Coppola buys "Sweat Shop" rights for TV series).

December 4, 1981 (Coppola plans to film Joseph Papp musical).

December 11, 1981 (Coppola visits Belize).

"RCMH Previews Offend Par," January 7, 1982 (*Heart* preview).

January 18, 1982 (Coppola breaks with Paramount on *Heart*).

January 19, 1982 (More *Heart* sneaks).

January 26, 28, 29, 1982 (*Heart* distribution problems).

March 1, 1982 (*Outsiders* start delayed).

March 10, 1982 (Warners to pick up *Outsiders*).

"Zoetrope Goes on Block." April 16, 1982 (see Robb, David, for subsequent developments in auction of studio).

June 30, 1982 (*Outsiders* script arbitration).

September 22, 1982 (Coppola's *Mishima* involvement).

November 23, December 9, 1982 (Coppola to direct *Pope of Greenwich Village*).

March 23, 1983 (review *The Outsiders*).

April 22, 1983 (*Cotton Club* script).

May 4, 1983 (new analysis of all-time top grossers, including *The Godfather*, adjusted for inflation of ticket prices).

June 9, 1983 (*Interface*: Coppola to direct).

October 7, 12, 14, 1983 (*Cotton Club* shoot suspension).

" 'Cotton Club' Court Showdown." June 19, 1984; Additional articles June 20, June 22, June 26, August 5, August 8; see also Loynd, Ray.

December 10, 1984 (review, *Cotton Club*).

December 12, 1984 (*Cotton* homevid rights sold).

January 2, 1985 (Sentinel Building saved from foreclosure).

January 23, 1985 (*Cotton* grosses).

March 4, 1985 (*Peggy Sue Got Married* casting).

May 1, 1985 (*Cotton* followup: Robert Evans, *Two Jakes* suspension).

May 6, May 9, 1986 (*Gardens of Stone* casting).

"Coppola's Son Dies in Mishap." May 28, 1986.

July 21, July 23, 1986 (*Gardens of Stone* production details).

"Zoetrope and Coppola Seek to Close File on UA Debt." July 30, 1986 (*Apocalypse* money).

August 6, 1986 (completion, *Gardens of Stone*).

September 15, 1986 (*Captain Eo* premiere).

September 22, 1986 (review, *Peggy Sue Got Married*).

April 14, 1987 (*Tucker* shoot begins).

April 30, 1987 (review *Gardens of Stone*).

August 19, 1987 (*Apocalypse Now* re-release; debts).

August 1, 1988 (review *Tucker*).

August 5, 1988 (possible *Godfather III*).

"Coppola Set to Sign with Italian Studio." September 8, 1988.

"Coppola to Lens High-Definition Pic." September 16, 1988.

August 16–November 1, 1988 (weekly grosses, *Tucker*).

"Woman Booked in Radin Murder." January 10, 1989.

Ventura, Michael. "Coppola." *L.A. Weekly*, February 19–25, 1982 (Coppola discusses problems with *One from the Heart*: his intentions and how audience received results).

Waggoner, Dianna. "Homage to the Master." *People*, October 27, 1980 (history of *Kagemusha*, including Coppola's part in it).

Wall Street Journal, August 22, 1979 (*Apocalypse Now* early grosses).

Washington Post:

February 10, 1982 (Coppola scolds journalists and Pauline Kael, National Press Club).

Interview with Dean Stockwell, August 24, 1986 (*Gardens of Stone*).

Wax, Steve. Interview, December 1988 (American Zoetrope; *Santa Rita* film project; labor unions).

Weekly Variety, news items, various authors, wire services, or no byline:

"Left, Right Hail War Pic." February 11, 1970 (*Patton* response).

"Coppola-Par Tie." September 30, 1970 (*Godfather* contract).

"Coppola Fighting Ruddy Re Gotham." October 14, 1970 (*Godfather* location choice).

January 6, 1971 (all-time and 1970 film rentals).

"That Unknown Face: It's Marlon Brando." February 3, 1971.

"Make-Believe Mafia Picket Paramount." February 17, 1971 (Italian actors picket *Godfather* studio for casting non-Italians).

"Hollywood Sound Track." February 24, 1971 (Robert Evans on protection for *Godfather* shoot).

"Inside Stuff on George C. Scott's Bias Against 'Patton' Script." March 10, 1971.

April 7, 1971 (protests of *Godfather*; Frank Yablans replaces Stanley Jaffe as Paramount head).

"Godfather in Final Stages of Production." June 9, 1971.

"Godfather Not on Christmas Tree." July 21, 1971.

December 15, 1971 (news brief on publication of Mario Puzo's *The Godfather Papers;* Puzo's payment for script).

"Await Marlon Brando at Godfather Preem." February 16, 1972.

"Loews, National Share Godfather on LA Start." February 16, 1972 (distribution specifics).

"Par Conservative on Outlays." February 23, 1972 (*Godfather* sequel planned).

"Par's Godfather Date Scuttled by London Daily." March 1, 1972 (London rave review and its effect).

"Brando's Mute Test Copped Role." March 8, 1972.

"A Novelist Is Nil in Hollywood." March 15, 1972 (Puzo complains).

"It's Everybody's Godfather." March 22, 1972 (public reaction).

"Par Uses Coppola; Ruddy Separated." May 10, 1972 (*Godfather II* plans).

"Trade Sees Brando's Godfather Share Maybe $1.5 Million." May 10, 1972.

August 2, 1972 (*Godfather II* premiere date set).

"Oscar in Godfather's Future." September 6, 1972.

"Brando Makes Demands, Can Paramount Refuse?" November 29, 1972 (*Godfather II* casting problem).

January 2, 1974 (film rentals, 1973).

"Yablans 'Apologizes' for Gatsby." June 19, 1974.

November 27, 1974 (*Godfather* TV screening rating).

May 26, 1976 (Pinochet government censors *Godfather II*).

August 15, 1976 (Coppola hires Tom Luddy).

December 19, 1979 (Françoise Sagan claims "fix" at Cannes Film Festival for *Apocalypse* award).

September 2, 1981 (*Escape Artist* reshoots).

"Big Buck Era Screened." January 12, 1983 (*Apocalypse* costs and grosses).

March 30 and April 6, 1983 (box office returns, *Outsiders, Black Stallion Returns*).

October 12, 1983 (*Rumble Fish* premiere in New York).

January 1984 (several issues) (film rentals, 1983).

April 8, 1984 (Coppola and Lucas visit Walter Murch at Elstree).

September 12, 1984 (*Cotton Club* completion).

December 5, December 19, 1984 (John Rockwell's injunctions on *Cotton Club* production).

"Coppola, in Rome for 'Club' Bow, Blasts Uniformity of Yank Pics." December 26, 1984 (Coppola also announces sons will direct films).

January 2, 1985 (French television special heralds *Cotton Club*).

January 9, 1985 (Bit-part actress sues *Cotton Club*).

May 1, 1985 (*Cotton Club* boffo biz in Paris).

November 13, 1985 (John Rockwell sues again).

August 19, 1987 (Joey Cusumano, *Cotton Club* associate producer, sentenced to jail for labor racketeering).

August 26, 1987 (*Apocalypse* re-release and remaining debt).

Weiler, A. H. *New York Times*, May 7, 1972 (interview with Coppola on *The Conversation*).

Wells, Jeffrey, *Film Journal*:

"Francis Ford Coppola." September 21, 1981 (interview: *One from the Heart*, Zoetrope plans, electronic cinema; Coppola criticizes journalists).

"Zoetrope Goes with TV Pic." May 3, 1982 (*Too Far to Go* pickup).

Whiting, Sam. " '40s Car Set to Be an '80s Hit." *San Francisco Chronicle,* August 5, 1988 (*Tucker,* car-buff viewpoint).

Williams, Christian. "$40 Million in Debt and still Forging Ahead." *Washington Post,* reprinted in *San Francisco Chronicle,* September 26, 1982 (*One from the Heart* debts).

Willman, Chris. "Coppola's 'Rumble Fish': Not Just Another Teenage Wasteland." *BAM* [Bay Area Music], November 18, 1983 (Copeland's score).

Wilmington, Michael. "Pro and Caan." *L.A. Style,* October 1988 (interview with James Caan; *Gardens of Stone*).

Wilson, Jane. "The Strange Career of Shirley Knight." *Los Angeles Times, West,* November 23, 1969 (Knight's reaction to *The Rain People* shoot).

Wise, Naomi. "Summertime for Hitler in San Francisco." *Washington Post,* July 23, 1979 (U.S. premiere, *Our Hitler*).

Wolf, William. *Wall Street Journal,* "Trouble on the Set of 'Cotton Club." December 12, 1983.

Woodman, Sue. "The Fall and Rise of *Napoleon.*" *Village Voice,* January 21, 1981.

Zimmerman, Paul D., *Newsweek:*
"The Godfather: Triumph for Brando." March 13, 1972 (review, *The Godfather*).
"The Bug People." May 13, 1974 (review, *The Conversation*).
"Godfathers and Sons." December 23, 1974 (review, *Godfather II*).

Zuckerman, Ira. *The Godfather Journal.* New York: Manor Books, 1972.

Zuniga, Frank. Interview, January 1989 (Coppola at UCLA and as "nudie" filmmaker).

Index